WALLS COME TUMBLING DOWN

Daniel Rachel wrote his first song when he was sixteen and was the lead singer in Rachels Basement. He was first eligible to vote in the 1992 general election and now lives in North London with his partner and three children. Daniel is the author of *Isle of Noises: Conversations With Great British Songwriters*, a *Guardian* and *NME* book of the year, also published by Picador, and a regular guest contributor on BBC Radio 5.

Also by Daniel Rachel

ISLE OF NOISES

Daniel Rachel

WALLS COME TUMBLING DOWN

The music and politics of

Rock Against Racism, 2 Tone and Red Wedge

1976–1992

PICADOR

First published 2016 by Picador
an imprint of Pan Macmillan
20 New Wharf Road, London N1 9RR
Associated companies throughout the world
www.panmacmillan.com

ISBN 978-1-4472-7268-7

1 3 5 7 9 8 6 4 2

A CIP catalogue record for this book is available from the British Library.

Printed and bound by CPI Group (UK) Ltd, Croydon, CR0 4YY

Dedicated to Allan Bowen,

tutor at Solihull VI Form College,

who validated the link between music,

politics and the ideological struggle.

And it shall come to pass, that when they make a long blast with the ram's horn, and when ye hear the sound of the trumpet, all the people shall shout with a great shout; and the wall of the city shall fall down flat, and the people shall ascend up every man straight before him.

Joshua 6:5

Are you gonna try to make this work
Or spend your days down in the dirt –
You see things CAN change –
YES an' walls can come tumbling down!

Paul Weller

Contents

3. FREE NELSON MANDELA

HATS OFF TO JERRY DAMMERS!
Artists Against Apartheid. 1992. Political pop 517

List of Illustrations

BOOK ONE: ROCK AGAINST RACISM

BOOK THREE: RED WEDGE

INNER PRINTING

Introduction:
Poison In The Machine

On 5 August 1976, on stage at the Birmingham Odeon, a drunk Eric Clapton harangued an audience of 2,000 rock fans. He called for 'fucking wogs' and 'Pakis' not just to 'leave the hall', but to 'leave the country', before speaking in favour of the Conservative MP Enoch Powell, who eight years earlier had made his inflammatory 'Rivers of Blood' speech, predicting, 'In fifteen or twenty years' time the black man will have the whip hand over the white man'. Perhaps it was a coincidence that Powell's address had been made in the Midland Hotel across the street from the Odeon but Clapton had no hesitation in echoing the former cabinet minister's language, warning fans that the country was in danger of becoming a 'black colony within ten years'. Clapton's seven-piece band included the mixed-race Honolulu-born backing vocalist Yvonne Elliman and the percussionist Sergio Pastora Rodriguez, who were joined onstage by the evening's special guest Van Morrison to perform Little Willie Littlefield's R&B classic 'Kansas City'. Birmingham was a multiracial city and, understandably, there was shock amongst the crowd. Clapton was not only an internationally renowned rock star, but, more astonishingly, one who had forged his musical identity through the blues: the music of the black man. His outburst, when reported, provoked indignation and was to become the starting point of a sixteen-year period in which music and politics would combine with unprecedented force and energy. A letter of response, written by Red Saunders – a cultural activist and freelance photographer for the *Sunday Times* – during a rehearsal with his left-wing agitprop theatre group, Kartoon Klowns, was published in all the national music papers. It called for 'a rank and file movement against the racist poison in rock music', and signed off with a PO Box address. The response was immediate. More than 200 letters of support were received within a week and Rock Against Racism was born.

Over the next five years, Rock Against Racism developed into a national campaign, later spawning groups across Europe and as far away as the

United States of America. Its inaugural gig at the Princess Alice pub in the East End of London in October 1976, headlined by the blues singer Carol Grimes, took place less than five miles from where Oswald Mosley and the British Union of Fascists had marched and been confronted by anti-fascist demonstrators in the Battle of Cable Street forty years earlier. History was central to the ethos of Rock Against Racism and its resolve to fight prejudice in music, especially as it had identified an increase in right-wing political sympathizers in the younger generation. Support for the National Front strengthened alarmingly throughout the seventies, and, with candidates pledging to 'Keep Britain White', they polled progressively higher at both local and national elections. The music world responded. Johnny Rotten of the Sex Pistols sang of the *poison in the machine*, the Clash cried 'White Riot', and the Cimarons and Steel Pulse, and China Street, black and white reggae bands respectively, recorded tracks called 'Rock Against Racism'.

In an atmosphere of mounting racial tension, the Anti-Nazi League was established in 1977, immediately forming an association with Rock Against Racism. Combining the Anti-Nazi League's political focus – to defeat the National Front electorally – with Rock Against Racism's drive to crush fascism through music and culture, this alliance had a pronounced influence on young people, culminating in the great Victoria Park Carnival of 30 April 1978. An estimated 80,000 people marched the seven miles from Trafalgar Square to Hackney to make a stand against racism and to be entertained by an array of bands including X-Ray Spex, the Clash, and Steel Pulse. The event showed that an unconventional grass-roots organization, in little over eighteen months, had attained nationwide recognition, generating front-page headlines and lead coverage in the national news. Yet behind the scenes, Rock Against Racism was made up of a relatively small circle of people, many of them coming from backgrounds shaped by the counterculture movements of the fifties and sixties. Their varied influences and experiences were crucial to Rock Against Racism's thinking and informed the content of RAR's propaganda periodical, *Temporary Hoarding*. The magazine, designed with a mixture of eye-catching graphics influenced by the punk Do It Yourself cut-and-paste style and pre-war montage techniques, addressed not only the threat of the National Front but also broader issues such as British troops in Northern Ireland and international concerns in Zimbabwe and South Africa.

The emergence of punk rock and British reggae in the mid-to-late seventies was vitally important to the success of Rock Against Racism.

Through music, and through a general sense of disenfranchisement, both first-generation black British and disaffected white youth – often educated in integrated schools and socializing in the same pubs and clubs – began to recognize common grievances. It could be heard in Culture's prophetic 'Two Sevens Clash', Bob Marley's 'Punky Reggae Party' and the Clash's '(White Man) In Hammersmith Palais'. And gradually, despite the very different rhythms of punk and reggae, there emerged a mutual platform of tolerance and acceptance shaped by issues of class, race and, to a lesser degree, gender and sexual identity struggles, exemplified by the Tom Robinson Band anthem '(Sing If You're) Glad To Be Gay'.

Under Rock Against Racism's banner of 'Black and White Unite and Fight' and the Anti-Nazi League slogan 'Stamp on a Nazi', there followed a period of mass demonstrations, riots, concerts and anti-fascist carnivals in protest against increasingly frequent and violent attacks on black and Asian communities. *Walls Come Tumbling Down* documents these battles and argues that politics was at the heart of pop music for the first time in British musical history. The phenomenon culminated at the end of the eighties in a global television audience of 600,000,000 across sixty-seven countries watching a spectacular eleven-hour concert at Wembley Stadium demanding the release from prison of Nelson Mandela. In response, the final chapter of *Walls Come Tumbling Down* deals with the formation of Artists Against Apartheid and the events that led to that monumental concert. In doing so, it provides an uplifting conclusion to the cultural fight against racism that was first triggered by Eric Clapton's deplorable comments a decade earlier.

Inspired, in part, by Rock Against Racism and by the philosophy of punk and reggae bands sharing the same stage, a Coventry musician, Jerry Dammers, founded a mixed-race band and a socialist record label as a way of making both a racial and an ethical statement. Dammers' involvement in social politics at this juncture would be hugely influential in not only challenging bigoted music fans, but making anti-racism 'hip' by the late eighties. Red Saunders described Dammers' band, the Specials, as being 'like a dream come true', and, by late 1979, the music of 2 Tone had swept the nation, replacing punk rock as a significant anti-establishment movement. And, although formed under a Labour government, 2 Tone bands – the Specials, the Selecter, Madness, the Beat, and the Bodysnatchers – would all come to prominence during Margaret Thatcher's first term in office as prime minister, four years after she was elected leader of the Conservative Party.

The groups on the 2 Tone label were largely multicultural. This was the practical realization of the anti-discriminatory ambitions of Rock Against Racism: black and white musicians not just sharing a stage, but playing in the same bands. And, although it was not without precedent, never before had ethnically mixed groups made national news and dominated the British charts. 2 Tone records, including the Specials' first two releases, 'Gangsters' and 'A Message To You Rudy' and the Beat's debut, 'Tears Of A Clown', sold in the hundreds of thousands and the label's first ten singles all made the top twenty national chart. What's more, the music came with a message. Songs addressed the political issues of the day: racism, sexism, violence, unemployment, youth culture and, in the Bodysnatchers' 'Easy Life' and 'The Boiler', gender equality and sexual violence, respectively. Yet, with an irony not lost on the artists, the bands involved also attracted the attention of right-wing activists. 2 Tone concerts were often infiltrated by National Front or British Movement sympathizers. Whereas previously, punk fashion had flirted with Nazi imagery, now 2 Tone bands were confronted by neo-fascists using their gigs to recruit impressionable youth and to cause maximum disruption. Madness, in particular, the only all-white band on the label, were singled out. Their first single, in 1979, was 'The Prince', named after and dedicated to the Jamaican singer, Prince Buster, but this was still not enough to deflect controversy. Madness initially kept their counsel, preferring to allow the fusion of reggae and Motown rhythms in their sound to speak for itself. Criticism mounted, not least with the easy comparison to be made with Eric Clapton's apparent refusal to see any irony in his success with Bob Marley's 'I Shot The Sheriff' whilst arguing for an 'England for white people'. Madness listened to the criticism and, although they had been slow to speak out, categorically denied any racist philosophy; Clapton, on the other hand, continued to back Enoch Powell's inflammatory views. Yet across 2 Tone – by definition an anti-racist movement – bands were forced to deal with the bizarre contradiction of black and white musicians who embraced the music and fashions of Jamaica playing to audiences which often included overtly racist elements. Similarly, the groups themselves – in some cases conceived as political statements – had to tackle their own prejudices towards each other. 2 Tone highlighted the question of whether black and white musicians could mix harmoniously; it called attention to the challenges of mixing different class and educational backgrounds, and to the role of women in music; it questioned the notion of a collectivist record label; and it demonstrated how the integrity of political ideals could be affected by the influence of money and success. While they may not have been conscious considerations, the realities of working and living as a 2 Tone band brought these issues to the fore, and they determined the behaviour and lifespan of many of the groups involved. In many ways, 2 Tone was an experiment that was fated to self-destruct. By the summer of 1981, whilst mainland Britain witnessed rioting across many cities, and with the Specials at the top of the charts with the prescient 'Ghost Town', 2 Tone imploded.

Challenging racism was the stated aim for both Rock Against Racism and 2 Tone, but as Margaret Thatcher's ideological agenda began to shape British politics, working-class youth in particular was hit by the economic effects of her policies. These magnified the divide between the forces of capitalism and socialism, between the middle class and the working class, between the supporters of the peace movement and those of nuclear re-armament. The Campaign for Nuclear Disarmament (CND), backed by most 2 Tone bands, reached the apex of its support in the early eighties. As an active pressure group, CND appealed to and brought together liberal-minded musicians, as it had previously done in the late fifties and sixties, and in doing so resurrected the popularity of political protest for a younger generation. In 1982 the Conservative Party took the decision to send a Task Force to defend British sovereignty over the Falkland Islands in response to an Argentinian invasion. As a move towards political awakening amongst young people saw increasing support for pacifism, the gulf between government militarism and opposition appeasement widened. It can be heard in Heaven 17's breakthrough hit '(We Don't Need This) Fascist Groove Thang' or Clive Langer and Elvis Costello's sublime 'Shipbuilding'.

Nonetheless, Margaret Thatcher sailed to a second term of office in 1983 and celebrated by intensifying her assiduous assault on socialism. The trade union movement was specifically targeted by Thatcherite policy and when the National Union of Mineworkers went out on strike in March 1984, the left-wing musical community was galvanized in support of the miners, whose cause they viewed as a class war. Many musicians came together for benefits and rallies against the government, and in doing so shared ideas and defined their aspirations for a different and fairer Britain. A leading figure was former Jam frontman Paul Weller, and the second Style Council album, *Our Favourite Shop,* brims with rage and despair at the political landscape. Likewise, Billy Bragg, a relative new-comer to the world of pop success, sharpened his political conscience during the Miners' Strike, resulting in the chart-bound *Between The Wars*

EP. Weller and Bragg, committed socialists and declared opponents of the incumbent government, joined forces. And in the summer of 1985 Red Wedge was conceived. It was a loose collective of independent artists with a simple remit: to oust Margaret Thatcher from office, and by default to return the Labour Party to power, under the leadership of Neil Kinnock. Performers, musicians, actors, filmmakers and designers united and, with the catchphrase 'Don't Get Mad. Get Organized', demanded influence on party policy. In return they offered national tours and, backed by a political unit, attempted to connect with marginalized youth and encourage first-time voters to register. Red Wedge debunked the myth of rock 'n' rollers as outsiders and was a bold endeavour bringing pop stars of the day, including the Blow Monkeys, the Communards, Junior, Madness, and Tracey Thorn, into the mainstream of political campaigning. Never before had pop music directly aligned itself with a major political party, and Red Wedge carried the argument to the heart of parliamentary power and, symbolically, to the halls of the Palace of Westminster. And unlike Rock Against Racism and 2 Tone, both of which operated outside establishment parameters, Red Wedge embraced its historic opportunity to change society from within.

Red Wedge centred its energies on the 1987 general election, with a succession of tours of marginal constituencies headlined respectively by musicians, by comedians, and finally by an all-women bill including poets, raconteurs and songwriters. All the evening gigs were accompanied by groundbreaking Day Events pioneered by Red Wedge's political leader, Annajoy David. In youth centres and town halls up and down the country, local and national politicians debated alongside musicians, and engaged audiences. Red Wedge was teaching the Labour Party how to listen and creating for the participants a new form of social and political encounter. However, in the wake of Margaret Thatcher's victory in the general election which gave the Conservative Party a third successive term in office, Red Wedge was forced to redirect its ambitions. A little-remembered chapter of the Red Wedge story is its post-election activity and its attempt to secure political advancement. As a new decade loomed, the Labour Party's freshly appointed director of communications, Peter Mandelson, pragmatically redefined the image of the Party whilst entertaining, albeit ambivalently, Red Wedge's ambition to accomplish its founding objectives and to embed policy into the Party manifesto. The final years of Red Wedge's existence would lay the cultural foundation for the New Labour victory of 1997 and the Tony Blair years.

With Red Wedge committed to working alongside the Labour Party, many artists remained sceptical about the union between music and party politics. But with the Prime Minister labelling the African National Congress, of which Nelson Mandela was Deputy President, a 'typical terrorist organization' and apparently endorsing white minority rule in South Africa, the cultural left united behind the establishment of Artists Against Apartheid. Often working alongside Red Wedge musicians, Jerry Dammers launched an initiative to make the British public aware of the plight of the banned ANC. Following the largest ever anti-apartheid protest in 1986, mounted on Clapham Common, the concert at Wembley Stadium, two years later, demonstrated how pop music could awaken the conscience of a generation.

The period from 1976 to 1992 was not only the last time cultural engagement would play a defining role in British politics but it would also coincide with three momentous world events: the fall of the Berlin Wall in 1989; the release of Nelson Mandela after twenty-seven years in prison; and, in November 1990, Margaret Thatcher's resignation. Even though Tony Blair's 1997 general election triumph would become associated with politicians' courting of Britpop artists like Damon Albarn and Noel Gallagher, the political engagement was now merely cosmetic.

Walls Come Tumbling Down charts the battle for the musical and political terrain of Great Britain: when youth culture demanded a voice; when counterculture became national news; when politicians campaigned alongside contemporary pop stars; and when the political persuasion of musicians was as important as the songs they sang. The sixteen-year period between 1976 and 1992 was characterized by badge-wearing, flag-waving, rioting, marching and partisan alliances. Political activism brought a young electorate to an understanding of the ideological struggle; it brought them to protesting on the streets, to free festivals, to concert halls, to rallies, to comedy gigs across the country, and finally it brought those ideas to Parliament. The revolutionary spirit was that of People Unity: *Governments crack and systems fall . . . lights go out – walls come tumbling down!*

•

Walls Come Tumbling Down is an oral history told by the key protagonists in Rock Against Racism, 2 Tone and Red Wedge. The text brings together a unique cross-section of contributors, ranging from parliamentarians and political activists to musicians and cultural campaigners, and embracing a broad spectrum of race, gender and class. The process of preparing the text involved interviewing over 100 people and as a result the manuscript offers an exclusive, if not exhaustive, history of the period. That said, a handful of the contributions are not as a result of direct conversations. Paul Weller, for example, declined my invitation to revisit the past. Having given his blessing to the use of his song title for this book, Paul also granted permission to use anything he had previously said on this subject, believing it would give a more accurate historical perspective. David Widgery, a key architect of Rock Against Racism, died in 1992, but it was essential that his voice should be present, so *Walls Come Tumbling Down* draws heavily on his own account of the period, *Beating Time*, written in 1986. Two important cultural and political events of the period, albeit covered by the text, are largely absent. Whilst the staging of Live Aid was obviously of enormous humanitarian significance, the event is recorded more thoroughly elsewhere by books dedicated solely to the subject. Likewise, the history of CND and the political consequence of the Falklands crisis are alluded to rather than examined in detail.

Collating an oral history poses many challenges, not least the reliability of memory. Time plays havoc with the sequence and exact detail of the past. I have researched and cross-checked facts from the period but remain frustrated by a number of small, inconclusive details. For example, there is confusion as to which bands played on the back of the flatbed trucks at either of the two London Rock Against Racism Carnivals, or whether a particular disturbance at a 2 Tone or Red Wedge night happened in Bradford or Liverpool. I trust these inconsistencies will not hamper readers' enjoyment of the book and that they will make allowance for any errors in detail that may subsequently come to light.

Lastly, a project of the magnitude of *Walls Come Tumbling Down* calls for a great deal of cooperation and help. I would like to take the opportunity to acknowledge my gratitude to all the people I have spoken to and who contributed to the work. Many of them have offered support and friendship way beyond my expectation. My special thanks to Richard Boon, Billy Bragg, Jerry Dammers, Annajoy David, Tiny Fennimore, Lucy Hooberman, Mushi Jenner, Steve Rapport, Neil Spencer, Karen Walter, Kate Webb, Bernie Wilcox and Juliet de Valero Wills.

Many more people behind the scenes have helped with the progress of the project, and I am incredibly grateful to Steve Blackwell, Judy Paskell, Emma Burns, Sebastian Cody, Don Coutts, Lizzie Evans, John O'Farrell, Katrina Fallon, Linda Jenks, Chip Hamer, Zoë Hood, Richard Howe, Rod Ireland, Jonathan Kyte, Roland Link, Juliet Matthews, Claire Moon, Conrad

Murray, Victoria Schofield, Jamie Spencer, Christine Staple, Darren Treadwell and Jo Wiser.

Walls Come Tumbling Down features over one hundred images and I would like to extend my immense gratitude to all the photographers who have helped to make this such a visually exciting book. They are: Adrian Boot, David Corio, Kevin Cummins, Chalkie Davies, Hunt Emerson, Jill Furmanovsky, Robert Golden, Tony Mottram, Bob Perry, Steve Rapport, Tom Sheehan, Syd Shelton, Pennie Smith, Ray Stevenson and Virginia Turbett.

In the publishing world, Paul Baggaley, who commissioned *Walls Come Tumbling Down*, has been a positive and integral force from the outset, guiding and honing the finished piece. My gratitude extends to Dusty Miller for offering key introductions, Rachel Wright for copy-editing the book and her incredible eye for detail, Stuart Wilson for his cover artwork, Wilf Dickie for the inside layout and Nuzha Nuseibeh for coordinating the final stages. I would also like to express special thanks to the author Travis Elborough, who creatively helped to shape and structure the second draft of the book. My agent, Carrie Kania, who also read and recommended important changes to the first draft and has continued to offer precious support and friendship.

Lastly, when I remember that love and life are more than just music and politics, I have the cast-iron support of Susie, who has patiently and lovingly shared my passion. Lily, Eleanor and Lottie – I hope you are inspired.

Biographical notes

Dotun Adebayo Music journalist

Ashtar Alkhirsan Red Wedge video and film workshop coordinator

John Baine Poet, also known as 'Attila the Stockbroker'

Colin Barker Secretary of Manchester Anti-Nazi League

Angela Barton Backing vocalist with Junior Giscombe

Pauline Black Lead singer of the Selecter

Chris Bolton Co-manager of Misty In Roots

Richard Boon Manager of the Buzzcocks and New Hormones record label

Dennis Bovell Founding member of Matumbi, multi-instrumentalist, record producer

Paul Bower Red Wedge political coordinator

Billy Bragg Musician and co-founder of Red Wedge

Geoff Brown Manchester Anti-Nazi League organizer

Jimmy Brown Drummer with UB40

Colin Byrne Labour Party Press Officer

Jake Burns Lead singer of Stiff Little Fingers

Lloyd Cole Lead singer of Lloyd Cole and the Commotions

Richard Coles Keyboard player with the Communards

Sue Cooper Temporary bass player with Poison Girls. Assisted Richard Boon at New Hormones

David Corio Photographer

Elvis Costello Musician

Jona Cox Entertainments officer at Newcastle University

Hilary Cross Editor of *Well Red* 1987–9

Rhoda Dakar Member of the Bodysnatchers and the Special AKA

Alex Dallas Member of Sensible Footwear

Jerry Dammers Founding member of the Specials and the Special AKA. Founded British Artists Against Apartheid

Annajoy David Vice President of Youth CND and Red Wedge co-founder and political coordinator

Chalkie Davies Photographer

Neol Davies Guitar player with the Selecter

Joolz Denby Poet

John Dennis Central RAR committee

Angela Eagle Labour MP

Robert Elms Journalist for *The Face*

Tiny Fennimore Press officer for Go! Discs, the Labour Party and Billy Bragg

Brinsley Forde Lead singer with Aswad

Paul Furness Co-ran Leeds RAR before joining central RAR

Sheryl Garratt Member of Birmingham RAR

Lorna Gayle Also known as 'Lorna Gee', MC

Bill Gilby Executive officer of National Union of Public Employees

Andy Gill Guitarist with Gang of Four

Norman 'Junior' Giscombe Musician

Lynval Golding Guitar player with the Specials and Fun Boy Three

Johnny Green The Clash road manager

Ruth Gregory Graphic designer for *Temporary Hoarding* and central RAR committee member

Carol Grimes Musician

Peter Hain Founding member of the Anti-Nazi League and Labour MP. Now Baron Hain of Neath

Keith Harris Worked at Motown Records before managing Junior and Stevie Wonder

Anna Healy Labour Party press officer. Now Baroness Healy of Primrose Hill

Paul Heaton Lead singer with the Housemartins

David Hinds Lead singer with Steel Pulse

Mike Hobart Saxophone player with Limousine. Anti-Nazi League North London coordinator

Paul Holborow Founding member of the Anti-Nazi League

Lucy Hooberman Film producer

Robert Howard Better known as Dr Robert, lead singer with the Blow Monkeys

Roger Huddle SWP member and central RAR committee member

Bob Humm Worked in the SWP print shop

Peter Jenner Manager of Pink Floyd, the Clash and Billy Bragg

John Jennings Also known as 'Segs', bass player with the Ruts

Karen Johnson Cooperative member of Newcastle Riverside

Linton Kwesi Johnson Poet

Phill Jupitus Also known as the stand-up poet 'Porky the Poet'

Neil Kinnock Steering-committee member of the Anti-Nazi League and former leader of the Labour Party 1983–92. Now Lord Kinnock

John Lydon Also known as Johnny Rotten. Lead singer of the Sex Pistols and Public Image Limited (PiL)

Andy McSmith Labour Party press officer. Journalist for the *Independent*

Gered Mankowitz Photographer

Tony Manwaring Political assistant to the general secretary of the Labour Party

June Miles-Kingston Drummer with the Mo-dettes, Fun Boy Three, Everything But The Girl and the Communards

Wayne Minter Central RAR committee member

Doug Morris Comedy promoter for Red Wedge in Scotland

Sarah Jane Morris Vocalist with Republic, Happy End and the Communards

Jane Munro Bass player with the Au Pairs

Frank Murray Former manager of Thin Lizzy and the Pogues. Tour manager on the first 2 Tone tour

John Newbegin Special advisor to Neil Kinnock

Gordon Ogilvie Journalist and lyricist for Stiff Little Fingers

Horace Panter Bass player with the Specials

Miranda Pitcher Non-performing member of Sensible Footwear

Mykaell Riley Founding member of Steel Pulse

Penny Rimbaud Drummer with Crass

Tom Robinson Lead singer with the Tom Robinson Band

Ranking Roger Singer in the Beat

Rick Rogers Founded Trigger Publicity. Manager of the Specials and Fun Boy Three

Dave Ruffy Drummer with the Ruts

David Saunders Also known as 'Red'. Founding member of RAR

Tom Sawyer Deputy general secretary of the National Union of Public Employees and a member of the Labour Party National Executive Committee

Syd Shelton Photographer and graphic designer for *Temporary Hoarding* and Central RAR committee member

Clare Short MP for Ladywood 1983–2010

William Simon Also known as 'Smokes', poet with Misty In Roots

Paul Simonon Bass player with the Clash

Frances Sokolov Also known as 'Vi Subversa', lead singer with Poison Girls

Jimmy Somerville Lead singer of Bronski Beat and the Communards

Cathal Smyth Also known as 'Carl' or 'Chas', singer and trumpet player with Madness

Neil Spencer Editor of *NME* 1978–85, Red Wedge spokesperson and policy former

Neville Staple Lead singer with the Specials and Fun Boy Three

Joe Strummer Lead singer with the Clash

Nicky Summers Bass player with the Bodysnatchers

Richard Swales Guitarist with Poison Girls

Tracey Thorn Lead singer with Everything But The Girl

Dave Wakeling Lead singer of the Beat

Karen Walter Assistant to the editor of *NME*

Tom Watson Librarian at Walworth Road and MP for West Bromwich.
    Now Deputy Leader of the Labour Party

Kate Webb Central RAR committee member

Paul Weller Lead singer with the Jam and the Style Council and
    co-founder of Red Wedge

Tim Wells Poet and former member of Red Action

Steve White Percussionist with the Style Council

Lucy Whitman Journalist for *Temporary Hoarding, Spare Rib* and
    fanzine *Jolt*. Founding member of Rock Against Sexism

Larry Whitty General secretary of the Labour Party

David Widgery Writer for *OZ* magazine and RAR central committee
    member

Bernie Wilcox SWP member and Manchester RAR

Juliet De Valero Wills Trigger Publicity partner and manager of the
    Selecter. Director of Go! Discs

Lesley Woods Lead singer of the Au Pairs

BOOK ONE

ROCK AGAINST RACISM

1. WHO SHOT THE SHERIFF?

MAKE WAY FOR THE HOMO SUPERIOR

Eric Clapton. Black Britain. David Bowie

DAVID 'RED' SAUNDERS Everything begins with the letter. It was 1976. There were one and a half million on the dole, belts tightened, cuts biting, prices soaring, wages frozen, the government looking for someone to blame and the loony fascists cashing in by stirring up hate. Three Asians killed in London. Notting Hill Carnival attacked by the police. The right-wing activist Robert Relf doing his house for sale – 'to an English family only' – bit. Enoch Powell ranting about 'alien wedges' in our culture and predicting a racial war in Britain. It was in this climate that I read a review in *Sounds* about an Eric Clapton gig in Birmingham on 5 August:

> . . . he shambled on stage and began warning us all about 'foreigners' and the need to vote for Enoch Powell whom Eric described as 'a prophet' and the danger of the country 'being a colony within ten years' and of how Eric was thinking of retiring to become an MP . . .

DAVE WAKELING I was at the gig. Here's this bloke singing Bob Marley songs telling everybody to get the 'wogs out'. It seemed like he had had a few, so some of the speech was more gargling than pontificating but the thrust of it was 'Enoch was right' and that 'we should all vote for him' and that 'England was a white country' and then a lot of saying 'wogs' and 'get 'em out.'

DAVID CORIO I was fifteen or sixteen at the time and I remember him coming on stage and being obviously drunk and saying something about how there were so many Pakis in Birmingham. He sounded like some bad, old racist stand-up comedian.

DAVE WAKELING And then there was a bit about Arabs annoying him in Harrods and that's what piqued our interest: 'Oh, hang on a minute. He's just an aggrieved toff. He doesn't give a sod about Birmingham.' It was like, 'Come on. We gave you the steam engine. Isn't that enough?' It didn't seem to us that he had any particular knowledge of our city other than that he knew the Enoch Powell 'Birmingham speech', as we called it, had been made over the road. I don't remember it all happening in one go. There were two or three episodes of it and he had a bit of a recap towards the end. But from the first rant there was a conversation going on in our area, down on the floor, and all you could hear was, 'What a bleeding nerve'. And that carried on as we came out in the foyer.

RED SAUNDERS This was when David Bowie was prattling on about Hitler being 'the first superstar' and Rod Stewart decided Britain was too over-crowded for him. It just made me sick with disappointment, but then fucking pissed off. I was an activist on the left and I'd been involved in Vietnam solidarity and street demonstrations but I wasn't a great believer in writing letters. So it was a letter of anger. It wasn't difficult to write. I whacked it off quite quickly. I was in a theatre rehearsal and we all signed it because I wanted it to be a group of people. The next day I phoned round friends and said, 'I've written this thing.'

ROGER HUDDLE Red phoned me up and said, 'I've composed a letter about Eric Clapton to send to all the music papers.' He read it to me over the phone and said, 'Would you sign it?'

> When I read about Eric Clapton's Birmingham concert when he urged support for Enoch Powell, we nearly puked.
>
> What's going on, Eric? You've got a touch of brain damage. So you're going to stand for MP and you think we're being colonized by black people. Come on . . . you've been taking too much of that *Daily Express* stuff, you know you can't handle it.
>
> Own up, half your music is black. You're rock music's biggest colonist. You're a good musician but where would you be without the blues and R&B?
>
> You've got to fight the racist poison, otherwise you degenerate into the sewer with the rats and all the money men who ripped off rock culture with their chequebooks and plastic crap.
>
> Rock was and still can be a real progressive culture, not a package mail-order stick-on nightmare of mediocre garbage.
>
> We want to organize a rank-and-file movement against the racist poison in rock music – we urge support – all those interested please write to: ROCK AGAINST RACISM, Box M, 8 Cotton Gardens, London E2 8DN
>
> PS. 'Who shot the sheriff', Eric? It sure as hell wasn't you!
>
> Signed: Peter Bruno, Angela Follett, Red Saunders, Jo Wreford, Dave Courts, Roger Huddle, Mike Stadler, etc.

RED SAUNDERS I was a fan of Clapton. I had his albums and had seen Cream. I had a part-time job in the evenings at the Marquee Club in Oxford Street. I was a mod. I had to clear up the ashtrays and Coke bottles. This was the early sixties. I was seeing the Who when they were the High Numbers and Cyril Davies – who looked like a bald middle-aged school-teacher – and the All-Stars. He got Mick Jagger up on stage. That was the first time I saw the Rolling Stones and the first time that I'd got consciously into the root of serious music. I'd gone beyond pop. Every now and again they'd have black American blues artists down there. I remember buying a pint for Sonny Boy Williamson in the pub up the road. All of us gathered round him in awe and he was giving us small renditions of mouth-organ music. The root of all this music was the blues and rhythm and blues and slave music, and then to hear Clapton, that's what provoked not just massive disappointment but anger.

RUTH GREGORY 'Who shot the sheriff, Eric? It sure as hell wasn't you!' That is so Red! You could have written a letter like that at any point in history and it wouldn't have had the same effect. I was a fan of Clapton. Who wasn't? If he had been a musician that nobody liked then nobody would have given a shit. He was one of the greatest guitarists of all time.

DENNIS BOVELL It's very hard to believe that someone who was supposed to be an intelligent man and an accomplished musician would utter such dross.

KATE WEBB That a man who had made his living playing the blues could think like that was extraordinary. It was the inherent contradiction. And astonishing for who Clapton was and where his heart had been. He clearly understood the blues.

PAULINE BLACK If you're a creative of any kind you assume that people maybe have looked at the world with a bit of a leftish understanding. And suddenly some idiot, who may well be the king of playing the guitar, turns round and reckons that Enoch Powell – a former Conservative cabinet minister – is a prophet. It just seemed incredible.

DAVID HINDS Clapton was hailed as a god because of the Yardbirds and then Cream, but I thought 'I Shot The Sheriff' was utter rubbish. It was nowhere on a par to Marley's version: *Sheriff John Brown always hated me . . . every time I plant a seed he said, 'Kill it before it grow.'* You could hear the suffering and frustration in Marley's voice, but he did an interview saying all kinds of positive things about Clapton's version. I was saying, 'Is Bob crazy? What's he talking about?' Then it dawned on me: 'Why wouldn't he? He's raking in the money for it.' Reggae had different ways of being born to the public and if it took Clapton for other people to start listening to reggae, so be it.

MYKAELL RILEY Bob Marley was being marketed as a rock act. Rock bands were looking at reggae and looking how they could get some of that focus, and that's where Clapton comes in because – after 'Layla' two years earlier, his career hadn't been doing that well – he took on 'I Shot The Sheriff' and it went to number one in America and top ten here. So for a while we were going, 'Yeah, reggae's on the up,' and being recognized by international rock stars. And what was good for reggae was good for us.

DAVID HINDS My parents came over to England from Jamaica in the fifties and had very thick Jamaican accents. They were already in their thirties and were very set in their ways. They came trying to survive in a country that promised them that the streets would be paved with milk and honey. So there I am raised as Jamaican, speaking as Jamaican, eating Jamaican food, and then all of a sudden I'm thrown into school and exposed to racism: 'Get back on the banana boat.' 'Wog's the matter?' 'You're browned off.' 'Nigger mind.' 'You all white?' My parents were very strict: 'We want you to be a lawyer or a doctor,' but then in school I'm being kicked in the rear and clapped around the ear. And they would be coming home and moaning about how they'd been treated by the hierarchies in the workplace.

DENNIS BOVELL Linton Kwesi Johnson wrote *Inglan is a bitch / Dere's no escaping it*. It described how hard it was for our parents' generation to survive and to hold their dignity while being subjected to all kinds of abuse. They had families to feed and they couldn't just down tools and walk off the job. They had to bite their lips and swallow unscrupulous behaviour: *Yu haffi know how fi survive in it*.

MYKAELL RILEY I'm part of the first-generation British-born Caribbean community, but the issue is we're not aware we have a dual identity. We assume we're Jamaicans because we're brought up in a Jamaican community. Handsworth in Birmingham was as close to Jamaica as you could get whilst living in England, but there was still very much a focus of 'Everything we're doing here is to purchase a property back in the Caribbean and to move back home.'

ANGELA BARTON I remember having serious conversations in school when we moved to Putney with people making out, 'You should go back to the jungle.' I'd say, 'There's no jungle in Birmingham where I was born. Where do you want me to go?' I was challenging conversations with people and saying things like, 'I've got probably got more lineage to the Queen than you have, mate, because you're blond and probably came from Sweden.'

WILLIAM SIMON I knew people with great brains who were academics in the Caribbean but here they worked in the post office or on the buses because their teaching qualification meant nothing in England.

LYNVAL GOLDING I didn't realize how painful it was for my mother when I had to leave her in Jamaica to come and live with my father and step-mother. There was an outside toilet and I locked myself in it and cried. I was eleven years of age. It was the same year that Jamaica got independence: 1962. It was incredible – *ska, ska, ska, Jamaica ska*. At school they gave you little cups and flags. I brought all that sort of vibe with me to England when I went to school in Gloucester. Then I became aware of racism when this guy spit in my face and called me 'golliwog'. I got mad and smashed his face in. I was one of about ten black kids. I couldn't understand why this teacher was picking on me all the time.

NICKY SUMMERS There were a few black girls at school but the groups separated outside, so socially black people hung around black people. There would be black music and black people would follow that and there would be white music and white people followed that. It was rare for cultures to mix.

MYKAELL RILEY At school there was a constant stream of new kids with proper Jamaican accents and real Jamaican history. You gravitated towards these individuals because they had authenticity. They made you more Jamaican. You polished up your accent and you polished up your sense of history and relationship to this place that you'd never visited. Then immigration policies made it more and more difficult for Caribbeans to come and then almost impossible: suddenly your grandmother had to be born in the UK. It was very calculated; it was how local politicians were appealing to the white community; the notion that the black community was taking away white jobs. It was political hype. The black and Asian communities were actually quite closely knit but we felt as though we were being oppressed and targeted. You would be stopped by the police on the way to school. Your parents would say, 'Don't go out alone . . . where are you going . . .' for the simple reason some of the kids didn't come back. It was not uncommon for a group of us to say, 'We'll meet you at eight o'clock at the club,' and for a member of that group not to turn up. The first place we'd go was the local police station to check if they'd been arrested.

LINTON KWESI JOHNSON There was quite a significant amount of socializing between black and white kids. As bad as things were in this country, we didn't grow up in an apartheid state. We went to the same schools, grew up in the same neighbourhoods, played football and rugby and cricket together and all the rest of it. It wasn't as though we were alien to each other.

KEITH HARRIS My mum was a founder nurse in the NHS and my dad was a doctor, so yes, my parents were immigrants but they had contributed to British society. And I was born in Newcastle. I have black skin but everything else about me is British: my accent; my education; my upbringing; my friends. When we moved to the appropriately named Whitehaven in Cumberland we were the only black family in the town, and years later I went back to my infant school. I was looking over the wall and this old woman came up and politely said, 'What brings you up here, then?' I said, 'I used to go to school here back in the fifties.' She said, 'I was your dinner lady. You must be one of Dr Harris's children.'

NORMAN 'JUNIOR' GISCOMBE There were six black people in the whole of my primary school. It was common to be called 'sunshine' or 'golliwog'. 'Can I touch your hair?'

BERNIE WILCOX When you lived on the council estates, words like 'wog', 'Paki' and 'nigger' were used day in, day out at pubs and bus stops. Manchester was as racist as anywhere else.

LYNVAL GOLDING Some of the TV sitcoms that were around then couldn't be broadcast today. They'd have people calling a black person 'coon'.

DAVE RUFFY When the sitcom *Till Death Us Do Part* was on telly, some viewers, my nan included, who was a nice old lady, thought Alf Garnett was speaking for people. But they weren't really racist. You've got to remember that people went through the war and they were promised a better life and they didn't really get a lot.

JOHN JENNINGS There was a thin line between Alf Garnett and Enoch Powell. People were ignorant. It was very easy to say, 'Look at all these people coming over here. They've got all that and you haven't got any-thing. You fought for this country?' And everyone was, 'Yeah, you're bloody right.'

SYD SHELTON I firmly believe you have to learn to be racist. It was cranked in you by papers like the *Daily Mail* and the *Daily Express* and the *Sun* and all those racist jokes on TV and *The Black and White Minstrel Show*; all that history that we were taught about. You never saw a black policeman. You didn't see any black politicians. There were no black judges. There were no black TV presenters.

TIM WELLS Older generations did have different attitudes about race and a lot of the time the children didn't share that. When I was a young kid you could sit in a pub and tell a racist joke and most people would be, 'Yeah, whatever.' That's why music is important. If the culture is, this is acceptable and it's OK to strut around Sieg-Heiling and putting shit through letter boxes, then it's, 'Oh, that's what we'll do.' But if it's, 'Nah, mate, that's wrong,' then they'll stand against it.

BRINSLEY FORDE Scenario: one-thirty in the morning. You have got to go down this dark alley and on one side you can see a lot of black guys with hoods playing reggae music and on the other side there's white guys. Which side of the street do you choose to walk on? You walk where you think you're going to be safer. Racism is a security measure. All you need is someone to trigger it to start that fear. That's what Hitler did. It was an economic situation so they used it. I remember when Aswad played in Liverpool. After, Tony and I went to this club with a couple of girls. It was like a massive house with all these different rooms and we were probably the only black guys in there. We could make out these boys who were checking us out. Suddenly, the group got bigger and bigger. I said, 'Tony, we're going to get a kicking. Let's go to the bar, get a drink and get some-thing to defend ourselves.' It seemed like the longest time and my heart was beating really fast. Suddenly I saw one of them. I said, 'Here they come.' The guy walks up to us and says, 'Are you guys in Aswad?' I said, 'Yeah.' He said to his mates, 'I told you.' We might have struck out at those people just out of fear.

LESLEY WOODS Enoch Powell had made his 'Rivers of Blood' speech: 'Thirty additional immigrant children are arriving from overseas in Wolverhampton alone every week.' Black people who wanted to get hous-ing were discriminated against. And at school we were learning about the

Berlin Wall and apartheid. I was saying, 'How can people put a wall up between people? How can you stop a white person sitting with a black person on a bus? That can't be right. Mum, you just can't do that.'

DAVE WAKELING My dad could recite the Enoch Powell speech. He was his hero. That's when the trouble started. It was bad enough watching Alf Garnett on TV, without your dad doing impressions of it. It was against everything you'd ever been taught at primary school about share and play nice. I knew from being on the swimming team at school that you won by everybody working together.

LYNVAL GOLDING Powell's speech was aimed at us. He said, 'In fifteen or twenty years' time the black man will have the whip hand over the white man,' and then the famous line, 'Like the Roman, I seem to see "the River Tiber foaming with much blood".' We understood the hatred that he was drumming up was directed towards blacks and Asians and Indians. Jamaicans had been invited by Sir Winston Churchill to come and rebuild the mother country. That's why my father came. It's not like they could go back home every year for a holiday. It might take five years before they could afford to go back, because of the cheap labour.

CLARE SHORT People say when the American soldiers were here in the Second World War white and black soldiers were segregated and British people were shocked at how badly they treated their black soldiers. Birmingham had been a city of inward migration since the thirties because there were jobs. And then from the Powell days when people came to work from the Caribbean and the Indian subcontinent we saw racism increase.

DOTUN ADEBAYO I remember saying to my best friend at school, 'I don't know how long I'm going to be here.' I thought I was going to be asked to leave the country and go to Nigeria.

BRINSLEY FORDE Enoch Powell initiated the influx of people from the West Indies to work on the transport and then suddenly he was saying, 'I made a right fuck-up.' But I much prefer a person to be outspoken about what they believe. A lot of the rock artists were not really working class so their ideology came out when they were in a position to say what they really and truthfully felt. To progress they had to appeal to the working class.

GERED MANKOWITZ Clapton did everybody a favour by bringing to the fore what was being said backstage by musicians.

KATE WEBB A month after the Birmingham gig Clapton wrote a hand-written apology of sorts to *Sounds*.

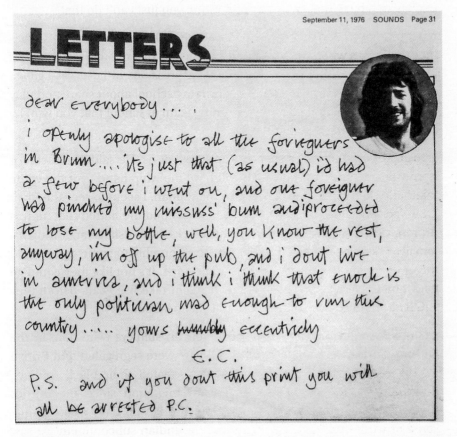

September 11, 1976   SOUNDS   Page 31

LETTERS

dear everybody... ,
i openly apologise to all the foreiguers
in Brum .... its just that (as usual) id had
a few before i went on, and one foreiguer
had pinched my missuss' bum and proceeded
to lose my bottle, well, you know the rest,
anyway, im off up the pub, and i dont live
in america, and i think i think that enoch is
the only politician mad enough to run this
country ..... yours humbly eccentricly
                                        E.C.
P.S. and if you dont this print you will
all be arrested P.C.

RED SAUNDERS Clapton has never really ever apologized. His interview with *Melody Maker* two years after the Birmingham rant was equally shocking:

> I think Enoch is a prophet. He's not a racist – I don't think he cares about colour of any kind. I think his whole idea is for us to stop being unfair to immigrants, because it's getting out of hand. The government is being incredibly unfair to people abroad to lure them to the Promised Land where there is actually no work. The racist business starts when white guys see immigrants getting jobs and they're not. The whole thing about me talking about Enoch was that it occurred to me that he was the only bloke telling the truth, for the good of the country. I believe Enoch is a very religious man. And you can't be religious and racist at the same time. The two things are incompatible.

PAUL FURNESS I've never trusted Clapton since. If that had happened to me, I'd be grovelling to explain it.

•

RED SAUNDERS The phrase 'rock against racism' just came straight out of my head. No one was using music to fight racism so a group of rock fans and musicians thought it was high time we stood up to be counted. What a simple fantastic idea. I had a studio. I was a functioning photographer. I had all the accoutrements – an electric typewriter – so we could write out several letters. Jackie, who used to work with me, did all that, and the letter appeared in everything we sent it to.

JOHN DENNIS 'Rock against racism' was an important slogan because it was 'against' racism. To be 'against' something is a political expression.

JOHN JENNINGS A lot of people said, 'You can't mix music with politics.' I'm sorry, but Clapton just had. He laid the gauntlet down.

ROGER HUDDLE At the end of Red's letter it said, 'All those interested please write to . . .' but we had no way of doing anything, so before sending it out me and Red went and saw a man called Chris Harman who was the editor of the *Socialist Worker*. We said, 'Can we use your PO Box?' Within two weeks there were 500 letters. It gave us real hope.

TOM ROBINSON I read *NME* religiously, and *Melody Maker* and *Sounds*. It was a way to keep track of the music scene and what was happening. That's why I saw the letter. It was under the heading, 'Enoch Clapton?' I wrote to Rock Against Racism [RAR] and said, 'I'm in this band and we'd like to be part of it. How can we join?'

DAVID WIDGERY Clapton was not the only musician coming out with this garbage. David Bowie told a *Playboy* interviewer of his sympathy with fascism, which he rightly defined as 'a very extreme form of nationalism', and staged a Nazi-style return to Victoria Station with Mercedes limousine, outriders and salutes which chillingly mixed rock-star megalomania with Third Reich references.[1]

SYD SHELTON Clapton's outburst was a great trigger for Red to write the letter but I think it's wrong to have demonized him. I don't think Clapton was a racist; same with David Bowie, who said in *Playboy*, 'Adolf Hitler was one of the first rock stars.' The journalist said, 'How so?' And Bowie riffed off:

Think about it. Look at some of his films and see how he moved. I think he was quite as good as Jagger. It's astounding. And boy, when he hit that stage, he worked an audience. Good God! He was no politician. He was a media artist. He used politics and theatrics and created this thing that governed and controlled the show for twelve years. The world will never see his like again. People aren't very bright, you know? They say they want freedom, but when they get the chance, they pass up Nietzsche and choose Hitler because he would march into a room to speak and music and lights would come on at strategic moments. It was rather like a rock 'n roll concert. The kids would get very excited – girls got hot and sweaty and guys wished it was them up there. That, for me, is the rock 'n roll experience.[2]

And then in 1977 Bowie did that wave in Victoria Station and the still photograph made it look like a Nazi salute.

<u>CHALKIE DAVIES</u> That photograph caused an awful lot of trouble. Bowie had been absent from Britain for three years and to herald his triumphant

David Bowie at Victoria Station, London, *NME*, 2 May 1976.

return to these shores an elaborate arrival at Victoria Station was planned. He stepped off the train and into a waiting open-topped Mercedes limousine near to where screaming hordes of fans were gathered. He stood up and waved to his adoring admirers; the whole thing lasted about thirty seconds. I managed to grab two frames, but, sadly, when I saw the negatives I realized my image was a little blurry and Bowie's hand had been reduced to a mere sliver. The *NME* needed the picture first thing Monday morning but after I'd sent it the retouchers attempted to draw a hand onto his arm. When the image appeared in that week's edition he appeared to be giving a Nazi Salute. Given the headline said 'Heil and Farewell' and the copy used a quote about fascism it inflamed the situation. And then the whole thing was blown out of all proportion.

SYD SHELTON *Melody Maker* asked him about it and he panicked:

> That didn't happen. THAT DID NOT HAPPEN. I waved. I just WAVED. Believe me. On the life of my child, I waved. And the bastard caught me. In MID WAVE, man. And, God, did that photo get some coverage . . . As if I'd be foolish enough to pull a stunt like that. I died when I saw the photo. And even the people who were with me said, 'David! How could you?' The bastards. I didn't . . .³

JOHN BAINE Clapton was an old hippy whose music was shit but Bowie was someone I really admired: *you gotta make way for the Homo Superior*. I was confused and smashed up his albums.

KATE WEBB Bowie unequivocally apologized. He said, 'I have made my two or three glib, theatrical observations on English society and the only thing I can now counter with is to state that I am NOT a fascist. I'm apolitical.' The point is, Red's letter was really important, but without it Rock Against Racism would have happened anyway. It wasn't just that Clapton was saying those things and Bowie and Rod Stewart – who had told *International Times* in 1970, 'I think Enoch is the man. I'm all for him. This country is overcrowded. The immigrants should be sent home.' There was the National Front [NF] – there was a climate.

WHATCHA GONNA DO ABOUT IT?

Princess Alice. Sex Pistols. Punk

CAROL GRIMES One day, Red came knocking on my door. He was quite a big man and my place was like a doll's house. He asked a lot of questions and then said would I do a gig because they wanted to set up as Rock Against Racism. I had had my own falling-out with Eric Clapton about something else before then. I did a tour in Scandinavia supporting him when he was in Blind Faith with Stevie Winwood and Ginger Baker. I knew, as everybody in the music business knew, that he was a mess from drugs and drink. We've all been guilty of coming out with things that perhaps aren't deeply held and at first I thought, 'What a silly man,' then I was very angry.

RED SAUNDERS Carol was wonderful. I knew her through the benefit scene. She was the classic left feminist; a real Notting Hill bohemian girl. The beginning of RAR was totally organic. The response to the letter was a complete shock. And then it was, 'You better get your fucking act together. We better do a gig.'

ROGER HUDDLE The first gig was at the Princess Alice in Forest Gate in the East End in October 1976 as a one-off. It was quite funny because one of Carol's band made an Irish joke and when it was pointed out to her she sacked him at the end of the gig.

RED SAUNDERS We were doing the soundcheck and Carol's sax player comes on and goes, 'One, two. Did you hear the one about the Englishman, the Irishman . . .' and does a soft, idiot joke. We were like, 'What? Hold on, mate . . .'

CAROL GRIMES The Princess Alice was like any other scruffy pub that had live music. I remember thinking, 'Blimey, talk about going into the lion's den.' The East End had quite strong support for the National Front from old displaced indigenous white communities that had suffered. Their lives had been turned upside down post-war: bomb sites; the docks dying. It was very easy for the National Front to influence people who were less able to speak up for themselves. It was a very good place to start. There were a couple of people there who said to me, 'I'm not here for the politics. I'm here because I like you.' But this wasn't like a normal gig. We had banners and it was very clear what we were doing.

MIKE HOBART It was in the air to use music with politics; but nobody knew how Rock Against Racism was going to work. The question was how the hell do you build it? But enough people came to give everybody hope.

DAVID WIDGERY Security had to be reliable, and the Royal Group of Docks Shop Stewards Committee were recruited to provide it. They arrived on the night with a bulky Adidas bag, saying, 'Not to worry, the tools are here.' There was one racist in the audience who happened to like Carol Grimes. There he was, enjoying himself, but there was a big banner up saying 'Black and White Unite' and stickers and leaflets asking 'What are we going to do about the NF?'[4]

•

RED SAUNDERS *NME* called me up. I used to know Miles, the great hippy writer, and he said he was doing this story. 'There are these people called "punks". Have you heard about them? I'm doing this interview with this band. Would you come and take some photographs?' So I go, and the Clash are doing their sixth gig ever at the Institute of Contemporary Art. It bowled me over: the fucking energy! Our chance to do this was because of the punk explosion. It was a cultural awakening. Without punk the intervention of Rock Against Racism would have been tiny. Reaching a white punk audience and involving a British black reggae audience was vital because that was the principle of what we were doing: you're showing a better future; this is how we can be; we can work together; if we can work together we can live together; if we can live together we can work together. We don't have to love each other. We just have to have a realistic situation where we get on.

DENNIS BOVELL I met Red in a pub in New Cross and he had this idea for black and white bands to play on the same stage. So over a few pints I went, 'Yeah, Matumbi will do it.' Then he called up and said, 'Are you ready to do it, NOW?'

JOHN DENNIS The first official Rock Against Racism gig was at the Royal College of Art with Carol Grimes, Matumbi and Limousine on 10 December 1977.

Poster for RAR gig at the Royal College of Art, 10 December 1976.

MIKE HOBART There were banners all round and we tossed up who would go on first. I was knocked out by Matumbi. They were very deep, musically. Limousine went middle, and we went down a storm. We were a mixed band: black bass player, three white horn players, white drummer, and a black guitarist and vocalist. We were sharp and focused and on a mission. Funk had a fantastic energy live. We could see the power of the music pulling people in. Then afterwards, we all got up and jammed.

WAYNE MINTER The audience was mostly students. It was a good gig, maybe a couple of hundred people, not that big.

JOHN DENNIS I was a student there and saw the poster and thought it was deeply uncool. Carol, bless her heart, represented old school R&B; pub rock and reggae did not fit. I was into jazz and the uniform of the day was OshKosh dungarees, Hawaiian shirts and Kickers. We were hipsters. So I didn't go. Until punk was welded with British reggae, RAR was not the phenomenon it became.

RUTH GREGORY People said, 'All this white rock music is getting very boring.'

BOB HUMM It was beyond ordinary people. It was getting so grand and pompous.

NICKY SUMMERS I remember being so tremendously bored. *Top of the Pops* had gone stale. It was either novelty bands, or long-haired relics from the Sixties playing prog rock, or the Brotherhood of Man. I didn't relate to any of it. A whole generation was waiting for something. There was absolutely nothing to do. There were only two or three channels on TV. No technology. No jobs around. It was electricity blackouts and garbage strikes. Something had to happen; something had to give.

TOM ROBINSON We got rumbles of punk quite early with what was coming over from New York – Television and Richard Hell – people who were ripping their clothes and wearing razor blades round their necks. We were playing the Scarborough Penthouse and at the end of the evening the DJ came on and said, 'OK, ladies and gentlemen, that were Café Society and next week we've got this band coming up from London. I don't know anything about them except they're meant to be the worst band in Britain and they're called the Sex Pistols.' You knew the place was going to be rammed just on that sell.

RICHARD BOON It was Neil Spencer's review in the *NME*, 'Don't look over your shoulder but the Sex Pistols are coming.' He was obviously intrigued enough to go backstage and get the quote from Steve Jones, 'We're not into music. We're into chaos.' It was brilliant.

NEIL SPENCER The Sex Pistols was deliberate moronic-ness. It was like the Ramones: *Now I wanna sniff some glue / Now I wanna have somethin' to do*. And the Pistols were, *We're so vacant and we don't care*. It was liberating after Pink Floyd moaning away on *The Dark Side Of The Moon*.

TOM ROBINSON I went to see them at the 100 Club. They were being supported by a prog rock band called Krakatoa so most of the audience were dressed in denim flares and had long hair. The Pistols were late turning up. They didn't bother to tune up and then they ambled onto the stage in a completely unprofessional way. The first thing Johnny Rotten said was, 'Who's going to buy me a drink, then?' Part of me was completely appalled by the sloppiness of it. It was loud and out of tune and aggressive. They did a Small Faces tune and changed the lyrics: *I want you to know that I* hate *you baby / I want you to know I* don't *care / I'm glad when you're* not *there*, and then the refrain challenging the audience, *whatcha gonna do about it?* They converted it into a Dadaist statement. I hated it and left after about fifteen minutes. But I couldn't forget it.

PAUL WELLER You hadn't seen a band with that sort of attitude. My generation's wake-up call, I thought. Seeing the Pistols, and the Clash as well, who were writing about unemployment, writing about society, teenagers being bored; just things you could relate to.[5] I was really influenced by a lot of the things that Joe Strummer said. It was so different, no group had ever fucking said it before.[6]

SUE COOPER There was this sense of the Sex Pistols and the Clash being something different. It was really fast and intense and very loud. They were brilliantly anti-establishment. I thought here was a resurgence of the energy that was there in the Sixties. I pulled down a poster when we were walking out but then somebody asked me for it and I gave it away.

RICHARD BOON I persuaded the student union in Reading to put the Sex Pistols on in a bare white-painted studio with no lights and a tiny PA. There were about thirty people. The opening act was Harry Kipper from the performance artists the Kipper Kids, who sat on stage rambling, kind of like Peter Cook and Dudley Moore, drinking whisky and punching each other in the face. Then the Pistols rocked up. 'We've seen your paintings,' says Johnny (Lydon aka 'Johnny Rotten'), 'that's a waste of taxpayers' money.' He'd just whine a lot and moan and go off at tangents. He had such presence; a fallen angel and utterly compelling to watch. And doing 'No Fun'; how many Stooges fans were there in the country? 'THEY'RE DOING "NO FUN!"' And all these mod songs like 'Substitute' and Dave Berry's 'No Lip'. It was speed, clothes, rapid songs, in your face but with a funny thing John brought to the stage; very Brechtian and breaking the fourth wall. Janey, from my painting studio, ran up to the manager at the end and said, 'MORE! TELL THEM TO PLAY MORE!'

PAUL FURNESS I remember walking along the Headway in front of Leeds Town Hall and seeing this woman called Audrey who was a lot older than me and she said, 'You can sniff this rebellion that's in the air.' You could. Something was happening but nobody knew what it was. There was a sense of change.

NICKY SUMMERS Then the Sex Pistols were interviewed by Bill Grundy on Thames TV's *Today* programme, and swore, and the next day there was the *Daily Mirror* headline 'The Filth and the Fury' and everyone was talking about it. And coming home from school and walking to the Tube station, people in the street were calling me 'punk' because I had reworked my school uniform. I decided to check out some of the bands, thinking the whole scene might be something I might be into. The Damned, Buzzcocks, Subway Sect, John Cooper Clarke, X-Ray Spex, Penetration, the Jam, XTC, the Slits – and the Clash, who were glamorous – but the Pistols were really like a knife-edge. I saw them at Brunel University. You could go out every single night and for £2 you could get in anywhere.

DOTUN ADEBAYO We had just started doing our A levels and a friend of mine said to me he had this great record called 'Anarchy In The UK'. I remember going to several record stores saying, 'Can I hear the new record by the Sex Pistols?' 'We don't stock that record.' Then the next place, 'We stock it but we don't play it.' Then after about the third place I said, 'Just give me the record.' I was immediately hooked. My friend said, 'These guys that love the Sex Pistols; they're called punks.' I said, 'What do you mean, "punk"?' I was thinking of some kind of American terminology that James Cagney would have used: 'You dirty punk.'

DAVE WAKELING It seemed to me that punk came from an artistic intelligentsia that had access to New York art. Even the word 'punk' was American.

NEIL SPENCER A lot of the most significant artistic and cultural movements are created by a tiny cadre of people: surrealism, Dadaism. The Sex Pistols were once described by Barbara Harwood as a homeopathic remedy for the nation. She said you take a tiny amount of ultra-diluted toxic material and you administer it into the cultural body politic, which then goes into spasm and all the poisons come to the surface. It is exactly what happened. Within a matter of months you'd got all those Welsh Calvinist nutters threatening to burn down the church hall and these four slightly dodgy London teenagers being denounced as the Antichrist. All kinds of bigots and idiots were denouncing this threat to society.

RICHARD SWALES The Pistols were brilliant self-publicists and by bringing out a single called 'Anarchy In The UK' and then 'God Save The Queen', bloody hell! They completely got under the skin of the establishment. They were like something else. You can't imagine what sort of effect they had on the general public. They thought it was the end of the world and the whole of civilization was going to crumble.

RED SAUNDERS Jamie Reid's artwork was fantastic; sticking a safety pin through the Queen's nose. And the lyrics were outrageous. No wonder they banned them. And then it was number one.

BRINSLEY FORDE 'God Save The Queen' really shook the whole music industry establishment. We were having problems with Island Records and Chris Blackwell said, 'Punk's happening. Why don't you use it?' We said, 'Chris, come on. If we do it we're convicted.' Can you imagine if the Sex Pistols were four black guys?

TOM WATSON The first disco I ever went to was a Labour Party Young Socialist one at the Market Tavern in Kidderminster. I was only eleven or twelve and my mum cut holes in an old jumper and sewed some zips in because I wanted to be a punk rocker. 'God Save The Queen' was played and we pretended to like it. But the truth is, the Sex Pistols were incredibly inaccessible for a provincial kid like me. Punk seemed like middle-class London rebels, and 'bollocks' was a rude word.

PAUL BOWER Punk was about getting off your arse and making your own future. You didn't have to spend three years in a rehearsal studio practising your guitar solos before you could go out and play, but in Sheffield we thought a lot of the London scene was posturing: £40 for a pair of rubber trousers in Vivienne Westwood's shop; over two weeks' wages. We went down to the Roxy Club in Soho and thought it was hilarious: a lot of people sucking their cheeks in and trying to look cool.

NICKY SUMMERS The Roxy was hostile. I expected people to be discussing ideas and getting things going and people were just posturing and sneering. I didn't feel at ease in that environment so I didn't bother to go back.

SYD SHELTON Punk could very easily have been a nihilistic bunch of people who were against everything and stood for nothing. The way in which people like Siouxsie Sioux took to the swastika as a symbol of opposition to their parents and normality; it was something that you could get up people's noses with instead of being about empowerment.

LUCY WHITMAN I saw Siouxsie Sioux at the Screen on the Green. I don't know if she was performing or just posing. She was wearing a black cupless bra, fishnet stockings and a swastika armband. Punk's flirtation with Nazi imagery was very dangerous and needed to be challenged. People were making films and writing plays to warn each other about what could happen if we let a fascist party get a grip on our national life. I was at UCL doing English and I started a fanzine called *Jolt*. I did three issues from my bedroom and in the first edition I wrote:

> I know just 'cause punks wear swastikas doesn't mean they really like the idea of fascism; it's just supposed to shock our parents etc. who sacrificed so much in the war etc. . . . chances are that while we're putting our energies into playing the guitar or pogo dancing we won't feel the need to join the NF. The only trouble is we won't feel the urgent need to bring about real anarchy in the UK either. Punk isn't going to change the world but punks might – one day.

NEIL SPENCER People don't realize how finely poised things were in punk rock. It could have gone another way quite easily. A lot of those early punks were really racist. This goes back to the irresponsibility of Malcolm McLaren and the whole conundrum of the Jewish rag trade shopkeeper flogging swastikas on the King's Road. The worst of it was the Cambridge rapist T-shirts. It was fucking nonsense. But then people get seduced by it and buy into the bullshit. Malcolm filled up a lot of people's heads.

NICKY SUMMERS Even if punk was orchestrated by Malcolm McLaren, it was bang on the moment and gave a sense of empowerment to a young generation initially through music and subsequently art, fashion and film. Punk opened the doors for the future and the next decade. It kicked out the stale dead stuff.

FRANCES SOKOLOV I hated the sight of the swastika. My family were refugees from the war. My father's family disappeared and he arrived here as a baby. Once or twice we went to a gig and found a bloody great swastika banner hanging up behind where we were playing. We took them down and burnt them.

PENNY RIMBAUD Sieg-Heiling, for fuck's sake; kids arse about. To say to some Glaswegian kid who lives in pretty dire poverty, who's been given virtually no education, who lives in some shitty unbelievable place which they're told is a home which they have to pay rent for and they can't even get a fucking job; to say these guys have got Nazi ideologies. They wouldn't even know what *Mein Kampf* was. When the economic system is collapsing the right always appears. People start becoming threatened and the middle classes' inability to understand working-class anger is because they haven't experienced that sort of insult in life, the insult of un-allowance. Any idea of neighbourly love goes out the window for self-protection; it's people really fearing for their lives.

ROBERT ELMS The same people that wore swastikas also wore a shirt with Karl Marx on it. It was shock tactics and winding up the establishment. I was an eighteen-year-old from a council estate. I'd got Vivienne Westwood bondage trousers on and a leather biker jacket and walked into the London School of Economics looking for like-minded souls. There was a big poster for a meeting with the proposal 'Punk rock is fascist.' This was a riven, driven, angry, violent England.

DOTUN ADEBAYO At the 100 Club you would see a group of guys going *Sieg Heil, Sieg Heil, Sieg Heil*. I didn't know whether punks were racist or not, and with tunes like the Clash's 'White Riot' it wasn't altogether clear: *Black man gotta lot of problems / But they don't mind throwing a brick*. It was the kind of thing the National Front would say.

JOE STRUMMER There was a time when that wasn't clear. But when the West Indian community realized punk rockers weren't NFers they were much more open to it. They could see that it was a rebel thing.[7]

TOM ROBINSON I reviewed 'White Riot' in *NME* and said, 'It's the first meaningful event this year,' and they put the headline, 'The answer is a

Brick . . .' because I'd quoted the lyric . . . *but they don't mind throwing a brick.*

DAVE RUFFY Joe Strummer took himself very seriously. The kids he was speaking to were a few years younger than I was but if I'd been fourteen or fifteen and heard 'White Riot' I would have gone, 'Fuckin' hell.' I always wanted to do music for a living and it was the punk movement that made me take the leap to say, 'This is what I wanna do.' It was liberating. I stopped wearing flares and had my hair cut short. Music was a way out of the ghetto. I couldn't do football. I'm not a boxer. Ghetto music, rock 'n' roll, roots music, reggae, it's the voice of the poor people; the only voice they've got. We did Rock Against Racism because we had black friends and we were working class. It wasn't that we were ever particularly politically minded. That and of course the fucking Eric Clapton fucking speech. Music is music. And the whole thing about music is, it liberates one above the common muddy ground of stupidity. It's not about being a bleeding-heart liberal. There is no argument for racism.

RED SAUNDERS The swastika didn't become a big part of punk because of Rock Against Racism and because of Joe Strummer as well. He was extremely clear in interviews about his anti-fascism and that the National Front were Nazis. He clearly articulated that as part of the argument against his contemporaries like Siouxsie Sioux or Soo Catwoman or all those hangers-on from the Sex Pistols.

KATE WEBB History was so important in Rock Against Racism and trying to get people to think about things historically, which is an odd thing to do if you're talking about being at the front of pop. RAR had a didactic educational function. It wasn't, 'Don't do this.' It was asking bands to think reflectively about what they were up to; getting kids who are growing up in a multiracial Britain to think about was there a connection between contemporary racism against their mates at school and the Holocaust. And to see how easily these things can just arise out of ignorance and blindness.

LESLEY WOODS Suddenly it was like all these things that I'd been feeling as a child were being articulated and given a voice and a language in music and what was being discussed politically. And punk gave me the freedom to express that. That's what it was about. Not dyeing my hair and putting swastikas on and dressing up in uncomfortable clothes. It was about getting up on stage and wearing what you liked. I had feelings inside me but I didn't have a language or a way of articulating those things; suddenly you could write songs about things that you felt passionate about that didn't conform to what would normally be perceived as a good song.

PAUL WELLER Just singing about anarchy [wasn't] going to achieve everything; then what are you going to do? You still have to have leaders and so it starts all over again.[8] We [were] all standing around saying how bored we [were] and all of this shit, right? But why [didn't] we go and start an action group up, help the community? How many people can you see getting up off their arses – not fucking many![9]

PENNY RIMBAUD We regarded the Pistols and the Clash as very good rock 'n' roll bands that had very little genuine political motivation. They were signing up to big labels and becoming part of the music industry. They were slightly revolutionary, slightly edgy, but always in a rather cosmetic way. If Lydon said, 'Make your own band,' then we made our own band. And if he said, 'Anarchy In The UK,' he also said, 'No Future.' We were deadly serious. We said, 'Anarchy in the UK with a future.' We were going to take it literally.

FRANCES SOKOLOV The music business were doing very well out of punk. The contradictions were so blatant. The Sex Pistols' anarchy didn't mean anything to me. What were they about, philosophically? John Lydon was a naughty boy and he did it very well. The young needed to hear something like the Sex Pistols. I liked the disrespect for authority. The anarchism I had grown up with in the fifties was a fairly intellectual analytical discussion around the history of the Soviet Union and Trotsky. There were people there who were organic gardeners and farmers and had ideas about education and schools. And that appealed to me. I was a social anarchist. I wanted a better way of life without so much violence and bullying.

TINY FENNIMORE Punk was important in that it was anti-establishment but I couldn't see where we were heading with it politically.

RICHARD BOON Johnny Rotten said, 'I wish there were more bands like us.' He meant bands with similar attitude but it became hundreds of bands that slavishly sounded like the Pistols. It wasn't the point. We didn't really use the word 'punk' except later when you said, 'Oh, it's another fucking punk band sounding like all the other fucking punk bands.'

DOTUN ADEBAYO I disappeared to Nigeria for the first time in November '77 and on the flight back in January we were given a free copy of the papers and to my dismay it said the Sex Pistols had split up after a gig in San Francisco. I knew I was coming back to a post-punk London.

RICHARD SWALES John Lydon said on stage at the Sex Pistols' very last gig, 'Do you ever get the feeling you've been cheated?' You got the impression he knew exactly what he meant.

BEAT THE WHITES WITH THE RED WEDGE

Socialist Workers Party. *Temporary Hoarding.* **Roundhouse**

RED SAUNDERS Why did Rock Against Racism take off? There had been so many campaigns. There are lots of different reasons: the times are so important; the historical and cultural moment of what was happening in society is absolutely crucial. And then you've got the participants who all had experience of left-wing campaigning. I knew David Widgery and Roger Huddle and later through them I met Ruth Gregory and Syd Shelton at the *Socialist Worker* print shop. At the beginning, the core was around a fantastic group of culture headbangers and I would joke, 'Comrades. We're setting up an ad hoc committee.' It was only later RAR became rub-a-dub, 'Right on, yeah man.'

RUTH GREGORY The first Rock Against Racism meetings were at Red's studio – that he shared with Gered Mankowitz – on the top floor of 41 Great Windmill Street in Soho where he rehearsed with his theatre group.

SYD SHELTON It was a former boxing ring on the top floor. Gered was Britain's premier rock 'n' roll photographer, who had taken photos of Jimi Hendrix. And his first-ever job had been on the first American tour with the Rolling Stones. He photographed everybody. There was always rock 'n' roll hierarchy in and around the studio. It gave us a lot of contacts. Gered was never part of RAR but he was a supporter of it and helped us quietly in the background.

GERED MANKOWITZ In the corner of the studio there was a sitting area which had a ridiculous multi-unit-shaped red plywood sofa with awful brown-coloured fur cushions. And there was a coffee table made out of an old drum from a Kodak rotary print dryer. Everything was props that got put to use. There were gatherings at the end of the day with people piling in and I remember crowds of people talking enthusiastically, scribbling on large pieces of paper, and out of that RAR emerged as a force and an identity. Red was a huge driving energy.

SYD SHELTON There was a core of people – David Widgery, Roger Huddle,

Ruth Gregory, Kate Webb, Clarence from Misty In Roots, Aswad or their manager Michael, Lucy Whitman, but she was a bit later – who were there almost for the whole five years of RAR's existence. It was an anarchic mixture of artists, fashion designers, photographers. There were quite strong differences amongst us. We weren't a unified group, in a sense. We were a bit chaotic. But what we all had in common was we loved music and hated racism. We'd organize a meeting and the word went out. I didn't have a telephone in those days but you'd find out because you'd see so-and-so out and about. It was whoever turned up.

KATE WEBB I'd come straight from work, at Debenham's on Oxford Street, and I was dressed quite formally. I had this skirt and a jumper on and they were all there in their punky clothes. They must have thought, 'We've got a mainstream target person here'. I was very enthusiastic and would later become RAR's first full-time worker. They were overwhelmed with letters and things that were coming in. You might have had 100 people writing in to say, 'What can I do?'

ROGER HUDDLE The meetings were run like a Socialist Workers Party [SWP] or a union meeting. They were very structured and we got a lot of work done. We took it very seriously and then we'd cross over the road to the pub and chat. Being in the heart of Soho, RAR meetings were the only time I got propositioned for business by prostitutes each week.

KATE WEBB I'd go up every morning about eight or nine and all the men would be rolling out of the sex shops, having been in all night. That was odd. There was a sense that everybody had been doing things all night. It was like an upside-down world. Gered did a lot of the stuff for the *Sunday Times* and album cover shoots. I remember seeing Kate Bush with a wind machine and her hair blowing out everywhere.

GERED MANKOWITZ It's not difficult to create a romantic and exciting vision of what life was like in the studio. I'm tickled by the idea that there was an RAR meeting going on one side of the big blinds that separated the sitting area while Kate and I were taking photos; and you might imagine 'Wuthering Heights' playing on the turntable over the big speakers.

KATE WEBB It was so central you could meet people, interview people, talk to people. When you're seventeen things are just what they are but I always knew from the beginning that it was an extraordinary group of people and what we were doing was an extraordinary thing. The others were about a decade older than me. That's a big period at that age and had a lot to do with the dynamics, but very quickly I felt very comfortable with what they were trying to do. It was kind of like a gang: Red was the energy and the prime mover of RAR. He was a big, physical, towering force. He corralled everybody and got everybody in line because everybody was slightly nuts. He was one of those people who had thrown down seeds a lot of his life and some of them had taken up a bit and others hadn't. But it was RAR that caught light.

SYD SHELTON Kate was very young and came from a fairly posh background. Her dad was a journalist on *The Times*. She never fell out with anybody. She got to know people all over the country because she was always on the phone to them. She was doing all the admin stuff and looked after the money and the bank account.

JOHN DENNIS There are so many different versions of RAR because we all have a very personal investment in it. There were big personalities involved. It was the dynamic at the beginning: a bunch of creatives all sitting round with great ideas and lots of energy. It was fucking amazing.

TOM ROBINSON The early meetings were passionate. They were revolutionary socialists who had some experience with the SWP and saw the great evil of the fascist right rising in the UK. Although I wasn't a revolutionary socialist I had broad sympathy with a more just and fair society, but if the Young Conservatives had been organizing a sensible, credible anti-campaign I would probably have supported that as well because the point was, racism had to be combated.

SYD SHELTON The relationship between the Socialist Workers Party and RAR was very complicated. They saw RAR as a swimming pool which created this massive number of youth where they could go fishing with their little fishing line and try and recruit people. We were a totally autonomous organization and we wouldn't have been exploited. The SWP did supply troops on the ground: people to put out leaflets; put up posters; sell badges and our fanzine. We were really grateful for their contribution but it was very important that we had no party politics. We were not trying to effect a revolution. We were trying to change people's attitudes about racism, sexism and Northern Ireland. We were also trying to defeat racism in the police and the National Front. As Widgery put it, 'your regular four-pint family fascist'.

DAVID WIDGERY It is intriguing that the first initiative to form a quite new sort of anti-fascist organization came from an off-the-wall bunch of left-wing arties outside the leadership of any of the established organizations.[10]

KATE WEBB The difficulty was of getting know-how in a culture where there was massive cultural gatekeeping. There wasn't access to knowledge in the way there is now. RAR was people trying to consciously break down those barriers and enable people to make their own culture and say their own thing, to speak for themselves and to celebrate what they wanted to celebrate. The separations between politics and culture and between mainstream and the outside were enormous. Although there were people involved in the SWP, RAR was a resistance against authoritarian politics and dogmatic leftism. It was about the history of writers and thinkers and artists who have been involved in the left, which is an anarchic and wild and uncontainable legacy. The prime movers in Prague in '68 were writers and artists and bands. That's the kind of strain RAR came out of.

RUTH GREGORY The SWP was all about Marxism and reading the texts. There wasn't much cultural understanding of the history of art or music. That was all considered to be something you did in your spare time, if you did it at all. Dave Widgery got away with it because he was so famous from being involved in the underground movement and writing for *OZ* maga-zine. He just told them to bugger off. They didn't try and mould him into getting up at six o'clock in the morning selling *Socialist Worker.* People like Alex Callinicos and Tony Cliff who ran the Party in those days listened to classical music. They weren't really interested in popular culture. RAR wasn't on their radar, which is astonishing, with what was going on. The SWP were integral to RAR but you had to have an extra interest in cultural politics. People in the leadership of the SWP wouldn't have even noticed RAR. Syd and I decided it was too much of a conflict to be in both so we left the SWP. Anti-racism in music was our prime driving force. It was having a good time while being political.

BOB HUMM RAR could be anything to anybody really, so long as you liked music and you hated racism. The *Socialist Worker* went through a punk phase when Paul Foot was editing and there was a group of people in the SWP saying, 'We've got to get back to the serious matter of the Party.'

BERNIE WILCOX RAR was a front for the SWP in a lot of cases. In Manches-ter we looked upon it as a way to politicize people. And then once they were newly politicized and active it was easier to move them over to the SWP. That's how we thought. It was just a natural process.

PAUL FURNESS I joined the SWP in Leeds as a teenager. All of my mates were involved in left-wing groups. There were loads of us. Prior to that it was a middle-class, ex-student organization so all of a sudden they got about thirty or forty working-class kids from the estates and had their work cut out. But you couldn't do anything without the music.

RED SAUNDERS A hell of a lot of the early members of RAR were SWP members – it would not have taken off without that base – but I wasn't. People called me 'a fellow traveller'. I'm not a Leninist. That's a big thing. I don't fit in their thing totally but I'll work with them. There were a lot of anti-RAR people. They'd say, 'That red star is like the bloody Red Army,' and you'd go, 'We've got fucking pink stars and green stars and blue stars. We have different stars all the time, mate.' They didn't see any libertarian side of the SWP; they just thought they were hard-line Trotskyists. I once formed a band called the Humourless Trots.

ROGER HUDDLE RAR was completely and utterly led by Red and his imagination but also his dictatorialism or his ability to do things behind people's backs.

KATE WEBB Red was a charismatic presence and he was a fixer, but he didn't do day-to-day stuff.

SYD SHELTON Red was absolutely crucial to Rock Against Racism but he didn't have all the baggage of the party line. He was an independent freethinker. He was great to work with. I was from a working-class background. I'd come to London from Yorkshire. Red was from a middle-class background and a completely different life background.

RED SAUNDERS It was a perfect vehicle for me because I'm no good at inter-minable meetings. It's all very well to say you want to do this, that and the other, but actually the thing is to manifest it and do it. And we did. The first thing I did was to get an RAR badge organized: something to rally round. And then, very soon after, we set up our fanzine.

LUCY WHITMAN The *Temporary Hoarding* collective was not the same as RAR Central, which was an elected working committee of six people. It was all very ramshackle. The fanzine was a powerful vehicle for spreading progressive ideas. I was encouraged to write all these cultural pieces and it gave me a platform to write about feminist ideas to an audience who were

David Widgery circa 1978.

probably not familiar with them. Punk had an enormous influence on the graphic design and everything had to be presented in a very lively and eye-catching way: collage; mixing typefaces; the juxtaposition of images. The point was, people would come along to gigs because they wanted to hear the Buzzcocks or the Ruts or whoever. They weren't necessarily committed anti-racists. That was why we had to do the paper, because we wanted to give them something to take home and read and think about. *Temporary Hoarding* reflected the energy of the gigs. It was educational agitprop.

RED SAUNDERS If there's such a thing, I'd call Lucy a feminist punk intel-lectual. And Widgery joined after about a year and became one of the main people in the RAR collective. I'd known him since the Vietnam soli-darity days and from the theatre. He was a GP in the East End and a brilliant writer.

SYD SHELTON Widgery was a complicated character. He was the chronicler of RAR. He didn't use to go to demonstrations much because he'd had polio. He limped quite badly and couldn't run. We used to try to persuade him not to come on things because he was a bit of a liability. When the Clash played the Rainbow everybody ripped out the seats and Joe Strum-mer was saying, 'Pass 'em up here.' We just got carried away with the excitement. David was trying to undo his seat with a little spanner so he got pounced on by security and thrown out and missed the gig. That was hilarious. David died in 1992 from the classic rock 'n' roll death. He used to make himself all these weird cocktails of drugs. He injected it and then drank a bottle of vodka and choked on his own vomit. He didn't fit the SWP mould at all.

ROGER HUDDLE Dave Widgery wrote the key text on the front of the first *Temporary Hoarding*: 'We want rebel music, street music. Music that breaks down people's fear of one another. Crisis music. Now music. Music that knows who the real enemy is. Rock Against Racism. LOVE MUSIC HATE RACISM.' I was working at the *Sunday Times* colour supplement taking pictures as a freelancer and I knew a brilliant designer called David King. I said to him, 'We need a logo,' and he came up with the RAR star. It was taken from the five-cornered star which was designed by El Lissitsky for the Bolshevik Party. There are five stars because of the five continents. It's the star of the Internationale. Red and I were Marxists and were influenced by the art of the Russian Revolution.

RUTH GREGORY The RAR star has a slight curve. If it was straight it would look really sharp and pointy but because it's slightly curved your eye sees it as straight; it's got a softer and slightly cuddly look to it. We were all frustrated as graphic designers working for the SWP because they had very little understanding or interest in culture. I remember being told by one of them once that a poster has to be able to be read from the top of a bus. That was the criteria. You weren't allowed any freedom to do what you wanted. So starting a fanzine was a real chance to educate and agitate.

DAVID WIDGERY We took the idea of the underground press with its cheap mass production and extensive use of visuals but purged the hippyism, replaced the conceptual squiggles with the harder edge of the punk fanzines and added our dubbed version of Marxism.[11]

TOM ROBINSON The visuals of RAR were amazing. They completely got how important graphics were to putting across an idea. They had this torn, DIY, semi-punk visual style, cutting up photographs and

RAR roundel.

printing slogans and breaking up lots of text. It made it much more appealing as an idea. The British left was so dry and non-visual and didn't understand branding.

RUTH GREGORY Red coined the name *Temporary Hoarding*. It was from the Chinese wall posters when there was a bout of putting political anti-government writings on the wall and nobody knew where they'd come from. It was the whole idea of walls and graffiti. Write your own fanzines. Make your own clothes. Young people were disillusioned. All that ripped and torn stuff and the *Temporary Hoarding* logo itself, the lettering. Punk definitely affected the way we did graphic design. The print world had been through several revolutions and part of the reason punk happened was because suddenly there were all these possibilities. You didn't have to have everything made in metal to print it.

SYD SHELTON Robert Rauschenberg really inspired us and I'd always liked the way *Rolling Stone* folded into a small newspaper and then opened out. That's where we got the idea of *Temporary Hoarding* opening out to a poster for people to stick on their walls. When I was a child I loved the Rupert Bear books because I was mostly a visual person and slow to read: they had a one-liner at the top so that was level two after the picture; then they had another level where there was a caption underneath each picture; then a third level with five or six columns of text at the bottom. They all told the same story but depending on your level of literacy you could still read the book. I've always liked to approach design in that way so it's accessible to every level of engagement. It always starts with the visual argument.

RUTH GREGORY Sometimes an image conveys more than words. A lot of the time we'd do a visual illustration of a song that we liked. We'd do a montage and have the words of the song or sometimes dub them out, but do it in a graphic way, and that'd be the only thing that we'd present. We all saw *Temporary Hoarding* as the political front of RAR and a way of putting out ideas. RAR wouldn't have run without it. It was dealing with areas that young people cared about: South Africa; apartheid; Zimbabwe; Northern Ireland; sex; fascism; the roots of Nazi thinking; even football and the way that Franco used Real Madrid. It was quite broad. The left was stuck back in the days of the Russian Revolution and everything was subservient to the party line. [The SWP newspaper] *Womens Voice* had been disbanded. The black organization Flame was disbanded. Punk was like a breath of fresh air and suddenly there was this organization that was relating to all these people who had been isolated and thought they were the only ones. *Temporary Hoarding* was a way of us getting out there to people who felt disenfranchised all over the country.

KATE WEBB The ethos of RAR was the ethos of punk: the DIY ethos. It was absolutely essential. When people wrote to us and said, 'How can I be involved?' we would send them back information about who they could connect up with or what to do to set up things themselves. They sent in their loose change and stamped addressed envelopes in return for badges and Day-Glo stickers. It was like social networking before the media provided it. It was crucial putting people in touch with each other to find like-minded people that they could join up with and become empowered – people who felt isolated or the odd kid in school where somebody had made a racist remark in class and they had got bullied for opposing it. It was the world before the Net. You started to think about the different groups in society: who beat up on who either on the street or in the Houses of Parliament. You started to think about power and how it connected.

RED SAUNDERS I called Ruth 'the tranquil force', which is the phrase they used in the French elections about Mitterrand, but I liked the phrase. She was quiet and got on with it but she had very strong opinions.

ROGER HUDDLE Ruth was one of the great graphic designers. She understood the punk sensibility. Her fastidiousness and patience, to cut little dots out of a Letraset sheet and build up layers without technology; it was all hand cut. Me, Syd, Ruth would spend maybe two days dominating the SWP print shop and then send things down to Bob in the basement. Bob Humm is the unsung hero of all this. He made the bromides and took photographs and turned them into halftones which were then pasted into *Temporary Hoarding*. It had to be visual. It had to be exciting. It had to be slogans that were not tired.

BOB HUMM I was working in the camera room. I used to go in on Sundays and help put things together when people were turning a blind eye. Without *Temporary Hoarding* it would have been far more difficult to spread the word around. I used to go out fly-posting and there was a lot of anticipation for a new issue.

RUTH GREGORY There were all these people who did stuff for nothing like Bob. We only paid for 1,000 copies and we got 6,000. One time we produced *Temporary Hoarding* on this lovely paper called French White which is really expensive. Kate went bananas because it cost so much money. She was always saying, 'We can't afford another *Temporary Hoarding*,' and we were saying, 'Yes, but we have to put one out.' We'd do a copy of *Temporary Hoarding* when we had the money in the bank. We'd save up like kids: 'Right, we've got enough now. Do another copy.'

KATE WEBB They were explaining to me the different papers and I was so proud of myself learning 'French White'. I would point it out to my friends, 'Oh, that's on French White.' It was pedagogy with passion: a sharing network machine.

SYD SHELTON We did a centre-spread interview with Peter Tosh and we literally had to cut the words and the images out with a scalpel and a ruler on a big drawing board. Then you'd put in this bit and one down there and then it made that look wrong so you'd have to change that. We were back and forth into the darkroom until we got it exactly how we wanted it. It was an all-nighter, that piece.

RUTH GREGORY You had to spend hours calculating how much space it was going to take up to then decide what type size you needed to use. It involved a lot of work and sleepless nights. You could do that in no time now on a computer. And Red was a fantastic motivator. He's one of these people who can just galvanize people to do things even when they're almost dropping on their feet.

SYD SHELTON Red would turn up at three in the morning and he always had this big Bellingham camera bag. He'd pull it out and there'd be a couple of bottles of beer and a sandwich and he'd go, 'THIS IS WONDER-FUL . . . got to go now . . . Nina and the kids . . .' Red was extraordinary. I called him the MC: the Master of Ceremonies. He could enthuse anybody: 'THIS IS FANTASTIC, SYD. I love this word THEATRE here . . . why don't we just blow that up MASSIVE, thirty foot across. Let's have that in the background.' And we'd all go, 'Yeah, yeah, brilliant.' He was like a great football manager. He could motivate people to do things who maybe wouldn't have done it without him.

RUTH GREGORY Syd and I had been lovers but we got on better as friends. We were called Hot Pink Heart / Red Wedge Graphics. It was from the El Lissitzky painting *Beat the Whites with the Red Wedge*. We loved Russian constructivist work. But it was always a big struggle and the letters and articles would build up. *Temporary Hoarding* was printed by the *Socialist Worker* and the two chief machine-minders, Mike and Drew, would just let the printing press run. We'd have vans waiting outside to load them up in bundles as they came off the press and then get away before the management came.

ROGER HUDDLE The SWP didn't charge anything. They might have given us an invoice but they never expected to get paid for it. The print shop manager, Mel Norris, would turn a blind eye.

JOHN DENNIS *Temporary Hoarding* was way more influential than it was distributed. The music press loved it. A lot of energy went into the process of making it, and by the time it came off the press there was no energy left. It was always overprinted. It hit the SWP paper-seller syndrome: 'Who's going to sell it?' That problem was never dealt with.

WAYNE MINTER It was mainly rank-and-file *Socialist Worker* supporters. That's why RAR spread so fast, because there was a network of organizers throughout the country who were really great in facilitating us on every level.

KATE WEBB The SWP had relationships with newsagents who were taking their papers, so *Temporary Hoarding* could go out on that distribution network – small bookshops, polys and unis, RAR groups. It meant we didn't have to establish the relationships.

Temporary Hoarding came out three or four times a year so leaflets were also part of the ongoing constant communication. You just needed a Gestetner which was like a round machine and you pushed paper around and it inked it and pages and pages flew off.

SUE COOPER Rock Against Racism was using music to help people think differently about racism. Culture is an integral part of political activism. Emma Goldman said, 'If I can't dance, I don't want to be part of your revolution.' The arts can get you to think differently about something; and that's political.

DAVID WIDGERY A new political agenda of feminism, workers' control, rock and roll and republicanism was being pursued by workers in the hospital wards, offices, shipyards and car factories, from Aberdeen to Derry, imaginatively advocated by a socialist and underground press which had, in total, a readership of hundreds and thousands.[12]

SYD SHELTON We were lucky to have good writers. We used pseudonyms for a lot of the work we did because there was a lot of firebombing and razor blades through the post.

RED SAUNDERS Column 88 burnt down the whole fucking SWP headquarters in Cotton Gardens which we used as our original mailing address.

WAYNE MINTER And then the office at 2 Cable Street got firebombed, which is ironic because it was the site of the old battle against Mosley's fascists in the East End in the thirties.

KATE WEBB Firebomb is an explosive word. We had some sort of device through the letter box and bricks through the shop front window a couple of times. We got death threats all the time.

RUTH GREGORY We were all terrified of being firebombed. My pseudonym punk name was Ruth Shaked. Syd was Syd Tune. Nigel Fountain was Grizzly Peach. David Widgery was Andy Xerox or Zerox: he couldn't spell, which was an issue. Bob Humm was just Bob Humm because nobody could possibly think that was his real name.

KATE WEBB I was Irate Kate because I was angry about everything that was going on in the world. It was a stupid name.

LUCY WHITMAN You had to have a silly name. Lucy Toothpaste came to me in a dream.

SYD SHELTON Red was really David. It was because of the colour of his hair. He was quite a good writer when you could keep him away from his sloganeering.

DAVID WIDGERY The music provided the creative energy and the focus in what became a battle for the soul of young working-class England. But the direct confrontations and the hard-headed political organizations which underpinned them were decisive.[13] On our letterhead it said, 'RAR was formed to fight back against the creeping power of racist ideas in popular culture,' but at the gigs, giant Fablon banners flickered out 'Reggae, Soul, Rock 'n' Roll, Jazz, Funk, Punk – OUR MUSIC.' By May Day '77 we had filled the Roundhouse.[14]

CAROL GRIMES I was booked for the Roundhouse before RAR became just about punk and reggae. Whenever I got a gig I would ring up my mates and say, 'Who's available . . . who's in town?' Mitch Mitchell from the Jimi

Carol Grimes at the Roundhouse, London 1 May 1977.

Hendrix Experience said, 'I want to do it.' I said, 'But I've already got Glen LeFleur on drums . . . I'll call him.' Glen said, 'We'll have double drums.'

SYD SHELTON Carol put together this brilliant band. And then Red got Aswad.

RED SAUNDERS Brinsley was very articulate. He was straightforward and clear. 'We have to support this.' And Mikey, their manager, who was a big Rasta guy, was fantastic and facilitated everything. They would never say no to RAR. There were plenty of white middle-class people but we were white middle-class anti-racists trying to fight racism amongst white kids. If you're a Rasta nationalist you're not going to work with honky fucking middle-class people, but Mikey went, 'No, these are good crew.' Many's the time we'd get spliffed up backstage and talk Isaiah chapter 1, verse 2. The room would be acrid with smoke and one of the crew would be reading, getting everybody nicely into it, 'I and I' and Revelations and 'Daniel said to Josiah'. That would be part of the pre-gig ritual.

JOHN DENNIS Red tells a story about being approached by black entrepreneurs going, 'You've got a good thing going here. We could really make this work commercially, promoting black reggae artists.' Red was going, 'This isn't what it's about.'

BRINSLEY FORDE Red was boisterous: 'Listen. We've got to do this.' He was a big character; larger than life. At the Roundhouse he performed with his agitprop theatre group Kartoon Klowns. He had a ladder and was leaning over and talking from the top.

RED SAUNDERS It was a great gig. I'd organized all the banners to be made up and hung them from the balconies, and Gered lit the stage and pulled out all the theatrical and emotional stops. It was packed out.

GERED MANKOWITZ I was in the lighting booth looking down on the stage. And we bathed the stage in the Jamaican colours. But Aswad came with a heavy presence and felt insular and quite intimidating; but their set was absolutely fantastic.

RED SAUNDERS There were fucking loads of people there. Then towards the end of the show, Ari and Tessa from the Slits raided the stage and shouted down the microphones. Aswad were like, 'Who are these mad white women?'

BRINSLEY FORDE Ari was from the Grove. They were rebels like us. It wouldn't have been an intrusion, more of a laugh.

MIKE HOBART Some kids started spitting at us during our set and Lee James, the singer, suddenly dropped down his arm. Dead silence. He said, 'No white man spits on this black man.' Then he put his arm around me and said, 'Mike came out of the oven earlier than me and that's the only difference.' Those things had to be fought for. It was great.

CAROL GRIMES I was a single mum with a small boy, trying to earn a living. Sam was with friends in the audience and I felt this tug at my jeans. I looked down: 'I need to go to the toilet, Mummy.' I had to call somebody from the audience: 'Would you please come and take my son to the toilet?'

ROGER HUDDLE Then Noel Redding and Mitch Mitchell from the Jimi Hendrix Experience, and Paul Jones from Manfred Mann, playing harp, came on for an amazing jam session with members of the pub rock band Kokomo.

CAROL GRIMES Mitch was wild and in good shape. We did a couple of blues numbers which lurched into reggae. I bashed a tambourine and did some vocals. It was a really good night of music and feeling. I was drinking Guinness in those days and I was three sheets to the wind by the end of the night.

RED SAUNDERS What those early gigs did was to give you cultural confidence and the building blocks to say, 'Hey, this may be actually possible. This isn't just some mad idea. We're doing it. There are all these other people out there who agree with Rock Against Racism.' We'd stuck the cultural flag in the ground. And people were saying, 'Yes! And hold on: there are black and white musicians on stage together,' because before it had just been jazz musicians working together in the underground twilight world. Without action nothing moves forward. It was a stunning thing.

NAZIS ARE NO FUN

Royal College of Art. Hackney Town Hall. Sham 69

JOHN DENNIS My first formal involvement with Rock Against Racism was the Nazis Are No Fun gig at the Royal College of Art in September '77. That was 999, Misty In Roots, the Members and John Cooper Clarke. Punk was really taking off, and all these snotty little shits used to hang around a lot, people like Sid Vicious. We were like, 'Fuck, man, what are you doing here?' I'd never seen John Cooper Clarke before and he was getting heckled by the punks. He said, 'I can't understand what you're saying, mate. Your mouth's full of shit.' It was such a great put-down and they loved it. Musically, punk wasn't speaking to me, but I saw the way the kids reacted to it and that was fucking amazing. I was like, 'I love this. I really want to do this.' The dynamism of the 'fuck you' attitude was seductive in its rebellious veneer and some people bought into that as being pure RAR.

999 at the Royal College of Art, September 1977.

WAYNE MINTER We'd woken up to punk because it was happening down the road with Malcolm McLaren and Vivienne Westwood's shop and the Sex Pistols. We advertised the Nazis Are No Fun gig in all the pubs in Chelsea so the college was full of punks. We had four or five photographers taking pictures on little black-and-white film cameras as the audience came through the door in all their finery and then we were taking the strip film, developing them on the spot in portable tanks, making them into slides and projecting them up on the stage. It sounds archaic now because you could do it in five minutes, but in those days it was quite remarkable. So somebody would walk in and then half an hour later they'd see a picture of themselves on the stage and think it was fantastic.

JOHN DENNIS Coincidentally, the firefighters were on strike down the road at Kensington Fire Station. We went down and said, 'We're doing this gig and we'll do a collection if you come and talk.' So these firemen came along with crew cuts and fair hair and military-style tops with yellow fluorescent plastic trousers and axes on their belts. They looked like punks and one of them went on stage and said, 'I'm a firefighter,' and the audience all went fucking mad. That's all he had to say!

BOB HUMM Nazis Are No Fun was a strong idea: that if the Nazis did get in you wouldn't have any fun; you'd be marching around in a military fashion. It became a key slogan of Rock Against Racism.

JOHN DENNIS I designed the badge. We made a thousand of them and gave them away at the gigs.

RUTH GREGORY Most of the fundraising money for Rock Against Racism came from badges. They cost 10p or something. We sold millions of them. People walked round covered in badges.

SYD SHELTON You'd pick up a newspaper and there was Patti Smith with an RAR badge on.

WAYNE MINTER The wonderful Universal Button Company down in Bethnal Green let us run up massive bills. We'd send badges and stickers out all over the country.

BOB HUMM The stickers were quite political: 'Love Music. Hate Racism.' 'Troops *Out* of Ireland: would you want one in your garden?' 'Coming Soon: Zimbabwe.'

RUTH GREGORY We did one sticker with just 'N . . .' and 'F . . .' and people could fill in what they wanted: 'Nasty Fuckers'. There were loads of stickers.

'Nobble the Nazis.' 'They said wanking would turn you blind. Now they say punk is dead.' 'Apathy is Out. Action is In', which was on a black-and-white Union Jack. 'Right on, Sister! Bondage Up Yours!' 'Soul Satisfaction Society.' 'All Power to the Imagination', that came from the surrealist days. We were a visually orientated organization. John Heartfield's montage

Rock Against Racism set of 12 stickers, 1977.

started it all. He was an influence on us graphic designers and the writers as well.

JOHN DENNIS We would project visuals to bring the political content to the gigs. There was always this danger of the motives of the band. A lot of the 999 fans wore swastikas.

WAYNE MINTER John and I made the *Nazis Are No Fun* film, which was designed to whip up people's feelings between the bands. It was black and white, made with stuff we had shot at the Grunwick photo-processing factory strike and the Notting Hill Carnival and the Wood Green anti-National Front demonstration. We also projected slides and political collages: 'Rock Against Shit Jobs', 'Homes Not Profits', 'Rock Against Shit Housing'. They were all banged up in quick succession on the wall. The idea was to whack it down in any way as punk graphics and use your John Bull printing outfit.

NEIL SPENCER I went to a very early Rock Against Racism gig at Hackney Town Hall in August 1977 with Generation X snarling their way through 'Wild Youth' and the Cimarons chanting down 'Babylon'. My jaw was on the floor. I thought, 'Wow, I've never seen anything quite like this.' There was this juxtaposition of the municipal surroundings and photographs of these Victorian councillors looking down on us, and the ultra-modern and something that had never been seen before.

RED SAUNDERS That was a motherfucker of a gig. Generation X with such sixteen-year-old energy. They were unbelievable. The town hall couldn't believe it. They'd made a terrible mistake. The whole place was seething with punks and people pissed and stoned, and they turned the music off. But the jam at the end was fantastic.

ROGER HUDDLE When the bands did the 'Black and White Unite' at the end of the gig, Generation X's guitar player could only play a Chuck Berry riff, so they did 'Sweet Little Sixteen'. Billy Idol said it was 'one of the greatest days of my life'.

KATE WEBB RAR was reggae, soul, rock 'n' roll, jazz, funk and punk. But the majority of bands were punk and reggae and that tended to be white and black, and that was why there was always an End of Concert Jam.

RUTH GREGORY The idea of putting black and white bands on together came as soon as we realized that reggae and punk were coming from the same place. The Clash wrote 'White Riot' and then later '(White Man) In Hammersmith Palais' because they saw the connection.

SYD SHELTON The theatrical statement of multiculturalism from the stage was our biggest message and that message was self-perpetuating. We were arguing with white people. They were the ones we had to convince to change their ideas. Putting together UK reggae and UK punk was in itself a political statement. We weren't going on stage to preach to people. The theatre of the stage was a political act. That was absolutely central to Rock Against Racism.

NEIL SPENCER I got in a lot of trouble for putting black people on the cover of *NME*. The first cover I did as editor was Joseph Hill and Culture. The phrase that was used by members of the staff and people in IPC International Publishing Corporation was, 'There's too much ink on the cover this week, Neil.'

TRACEY THORN I'd got a lot of my political education through the *NME*. It was a starting point. I wouldn't like to think that all someone knew about politics was what they got from songs, because that's going to be a piece-meal approach, but it was a trigger. Like anything else, you'd hope that music has an inspirational quality for people and starts things off rather than being the end point.

NICKY SUMMERS *NME* was a way of communicating and finding out about who was playing or what was happening.

SHERYL GARRATT I was a mad *NME* fan. Our local newsagent only had six copies, so you had to get up really early to go to school so that you got a copy. It came out on Wednesday in London so one of the most thrilling things in the world was to be in London on a Wednesday and get it a day early. It was like the word of God from heaven.

ROBERT HOWARD Some of the writers were better than a lot of the bands. People like Nick Kent and Tony Parsons and Julie Burchill and Charles Shaar Murray, even Paul Morley. It was an education. They made all sorts of connections to political ideology and I would search those things out. Music politicized me and made me realize how my heart lay. It wasn't just about pop music anymore. It had a social connection.

SYD SHELTON *NME* was the Bible. You had to have it. It was required thinking. That's where you found out what was going on in the world. There were many unsung heroes like Caroline Coon and Vivien Goldman and to some extent Garry Bushell. They took on the idea of multiculturalism. It was part of putting forward that argument. Also Neil Spencer, who was a friend of David Widgery, would always make sure that he'd slip in, 'There's an RAR gig going on in Aberystwyth on Saturday night. Be there.' Support came from all over the music industry, from journalists to musicians to photographers to fashion designers.

KATE WEBB The big RAR interview was with the *NME*. There was a photograph of all of us in the office looking completely bonkers, pointing at things. It was done by Angus MacKinnon and Charles Shaar Murray, who came down in his full hippy gear (see p.179). They asked us questions about our position on sexism and Rastafarianism and things like that. It was a double-page spread. Julie Burchill said to us, 'You've got no Asian bands. That proves you're racist.' *NME* attacked us in the same breath for being too political and not political enough. Putting black bands and white bands together was political. The fact of doing that in a public space and bringing people together; it was a conscious act to break down the spread of fear and alienation and let people get to know each other through a shared love of music.

SYD SHELTON There was a Sham 69 gig at Central London Poly where a group of right-wing skinheads, who had adopted the band, tried to trash it, and a posse from Southall who came with the reggae band, Misty In Roots, protected the stage.

RED SAUNDERS The 'Smash Race Hate' gig in February 1978 was one of the real down moments. Once again, saving the day were the Royal Group of Docks shop stewards, who did the security. They arrived with old-fashioned leather tool bags and said, 'We're ready, Red. We're tooled.' It was like, 'Fuck me.' There was a club hammer with a hole drilled through the end of it with a big leather strap round it. I said [to one of them], 'What's that for?' He said, 'If you're street fighting you need a strap round it because in the heat of the moment if you let go of your hammer your tool's gone.' This was a world where I was a complete innocent. It was like mortal combat. These were hard trade unionists who were quite prepared to stand their ground.

WILLIAM 'SMOKES' SIMON Not all skinheads necessarily came for a racist fight. You don't have to go to a stage tooled up; there was always a mic stand.

RED SAUNDERS The British Movement [BM] turned up in force because of Sham's fan base, which was majority working-class skinheads and West Ham supporters. That was in the days when people had glasses from the bar and I was terrified there was going to be mass glassing. It kicked off in a couple of spurts.

CHRIS BOLTON I saw one hand go up to Sieg-Heil but Smokes got to the guy first from the stage. I grabbed one of the punks and said, 'They're fucking up your show. Are you gonna let them do that?' So all the punks turned

Poster for RAR gig at the Central London Poly.

on them and chased them out. Obviously the talk was that Jimmy Pursey had this attachment [of fascists] to him which he'd encouraged through his songs like 'Hersham Boys' and 'Borstal Breakout', so we'd brought a lot of people with us from Southall: a good contingent of Asian lads, Sikh boys. I thought we did Pursey a great favour because he was pretending the skinheads were nothing to do with him.

RUTH GREGORY There was a big fight that started in the audience and some NFers with shaved heads got in through the stage door and got onto the stage. They were there to see Sham and they didn't want to see this black reggae band. They were picking up chairs and hurling them, until Misty saw them off. It was really scary. It was quite an important gig in the history of RAR because it made us realize you have to keep control of the stage.

SYD SHELTON That was one of our dogmas: you never lose control of the stage. The stage was sacrosanct.

RED SAUNDERS What I would always say as an organizer was, 'If there's fascists in the audience let's make sure people don't get backstage. Then if you lose that it's like a military retreat, then whatever you do, protect the stage. Then if we lose the stage turn off the fucking power so they can't use the mic to go "*Sieg Heil*".' Those were the three steps. But some of Sham's roadies were clearly National Front supporters, so what was frightening was, backstage you had these NF-sympathizing road crew mixing with Misty, the full-on Rastas, with their road crew and their heavy boys.

JOHN DENNIS Pursey got out of his depth. He was at fault for not making a distinction between the kids that were his mates and those that were British Movement and, consequently, politically motivated; if they couldn't have him, then no one else was going to have him. I remember going down to Reading and blagging my way backstage to talk to him. We couldn't find him and I was almost attacked by a roadie, who was a Nazi sympathizer: 'Where do you come from?' I said, 'I grew up in Dover.' 'There's no blacks down there, are there?' Sham's audience was our target audience.

RED SAUNDERS The atmosphere was extraordinary. There I am on stage doing a bit of compèring, for lack of a better word, just shouting at the audience who were Sieg-Heiling. People were going, 'Why have we let them in?' I was going, 'This is what we're about. This is the fucking real world, mate. This is Rock Against Racism. Here's the white working class and here's a reggae band and we've brought them all together.' The visual fact of seeing that was a fantastic political act.

ROGER HUDDLE The pull towards the right in the punk movement amongst the working class was definitely Sham. We had heavy duty on the door but then about thirty or forty young NF-following skins turned up with the uniform: Doc Martens, jeans, astrakhan mod jackets. They were only about sixteen or seventeen. But also a lot of skins were ska fans and RAR supporters. It was a tense night. The dockers were over the top, very scary, actually, and one of them went backstage and said, 'Jimmy, these bloody lefties are stopping us from doing this and that.' Luckily, he said, 'Don't get me involved.' They tried to get on the stage once and we stopped them. But whatever happened during the gig, Pursey had to join Misty on stage to end the night and show unity.

RUTH GREGORY It ended up with them jamming doing 'Israelites' and Jimmy Pursey and the lead singer of Misty holding hands in the air.

ROGER HUDDLE A few weeks later, Sham made their debut on *Top of the Pops* performing 'Angels With Dirty Faces' and Jimmy shouted, 'Look at this!' and he had a pink and black RAR badge on the strap of his braces.

JOHN BAINE Violence was an endemic and everyday part of gigs; at my third gig someone threw a dart at me. But Jimmy started off thinking he was going to lead an army and that they'd listen to him. His message was 'we're all the same' but he underestimated the contradictions in the social backgrounds of the people that came to see him: a lot of young working-class blokes with the baggage of racism. Sham supported the Clash at the Rainbow, and the Sham Army ripped off the seats.

LUCY WHITMAN The question of violence at many gigs was on a knife-edge. But I used to go on my own so I obviously felt perfectly safe. A lot of that aggro was a joke; it was put on.

RANKING ROGER The gigs were rough, big holes all through the audience and likkle fights breaking out. Jimmy said, 'We tried to do bits of reggae influence in our tunes, so how could we be racist?'

LESLEY WOODS When the Au Pairs played with Sham 69, Jimmy Pursey came backstage to talk to me. He said, 'Somebody's just thrown a beer can at me.' He was almost in tears. He was suffering from being the target of a lot of senseless violence from strangers. Having to stand up and have all that coming at him. It would get to anyone. It wasn't a good place to be. Can you imagine being a lead singer in a band and all of a sudden you're getting very popular and then you find that 75 per cent of your popularity is because NF skinheads think you're the greatest thing since sliced bread? But then it's like, what came first: the chicken or the egg? What kind of audience were you trying to attract? I mean, we played hard. We played thrashy. We played loud. But we didn't get an NF following. The fact that Jimmy was going out with a classical ballet dancer kind of said it all. Ian Dury had the right sort of appeal to attract a right-wing audience, but he didn't because he deflected it. What I'm trying to say is, would you get an NF following unless you were actually welcoming it?

KATE WEBB Those kids were people that reflected Jimmy. You can feel with him that great passion for the Sham Army. There was a massive loyalty. They were like a tribe. He then realized the problem about fascism amongst them. These situations are very complex and people's politics develop and change over time. I went with Red and some of the guys from Misty to see Jimmy's mum in Hersham. She made us tea. It was part of the attempt to woo Jimmy to RAR. It was important to get him because he was the person with the most connection to the NF-supporting skinheads. We wanted the kids being pulled towards the right to come over to us.

RED SAUNDERS Poor old Jimmy Pursey. He was absolutely articulate but nobody took any fucking notice of him. I did a whole series of photographs of him and his rabbits and his mum and dad in his back garden in front of the 69 bus. He was a lovely guy with his heart in the right place.

ROBERT ELMS Jimmy wasn't a Nazi but Sham toyed too close to the edge of that. At Acklam Hall it all kicked off when suddenly all these Sieg-Heiling cropped-haired boys came from one side of the stage. We were in Ladbroke Grove, for fuck's sake, the middle of the West Indian community, and there were just pitched battles and black kids from outside coming in to fight them. It was going off everywhere. But as much as I despised them I can sort of understand, with distance, some of those young working-class white kids feeling very disenfranchised, very scared, and trying to blame the wrong people and searching for some lost halcyon world.

TIM WELLS At the gigs you knew there'd be a fight. It was something to look forward to when you were young. But you had to be careful what you wore because it was going to get ripped, so it was Doc Martens and Harringtons.

PAUL HEATON My best friend Joe was black and he wouldn't come to gigs because it was dangerous. People were scared of going out to enjoy the music. We're talking the middle of football violence and it was safer going to a match. People were getting attacked at gigs and there was always far-right literature about. Jimmy Pursey was fighting a losing battle trying to be a man of the people. Every time you saw him there were skinheads crawling all over the stage and Sieg-Heiling. It was the same in Croydon when we went to see Siouxsie and the Banshees. Sham's first single had a song called 'Red London' on the B-side: *London's streets are turning red / There's no democracy*, which is why they had the bonehead following.

GORDON OGILVIE I was there the night Sham 69's Last Stand gig was broken up by skinheads at the Rainbow. They came on and there was obviously going to be trouble. There were organized blocks of people who were clearly intending to stop the gig. Sham managed to play three or four numbers and then fights broke out. Jimmy committed the cardinal and got down off the stage and went into the crowd. He gave up the advantage. There was a stage invasion and the whole thing had to be called off.

ROGER HUDDLE It was so necessary to win Sham. And we did. We showed we weren't out to meet violence with violence. It was about mobilizing numbers. Marx said this wonderful quote: 'Men make their own history, but they do not make it as they please; they do not make it under self-selected circumstances, but under circumstances existing already, given and transmitted from the past.'

KATE WEBB It was an absolutely fertile movement. The rise of this nasty, aggressive, neo-fascist National Front, and there was not a lot else around. It was obvious what needed to be done: somebody was going to speak up in anger and fury. It came out of music.

2. INGLAN IS A BITCH

PUNKY REGGAE PARTY

Aswad. Steel Pulse. Clash. Bob Marley

LINTON KWESI JOHNSON Reggae was the music of the black youth of Britain. It provided us with the means of an independent identity in a racialized environment and culture. It provided us with a nexus of resistance against police brutality and against institutionalized racism. We rejected political parties. We were of the left. Our basic philosophy was people's power; whether you were a group of workers in a factory or some students in a college or a community under siege or whatever your situation was, you organized yourself to bring about change. We didn't see the Labour Party or any of the other left organizations as being the vehicles through which we could wage our struggle. We believed in autonomy.

MYKAELL RILEY Reggae and punk were oil and water. We were busy learning our instruments to be as proficient as possible and they were going, 'Just pick it up and play.' Punk was going in the absolute opposite direction that we were going in. We were practising harmonizing and delivering a performance. Punk was a revolution that we couldn't engage with the mindset at all. Culturally, it just jarred at first. We were rebelling in a different way by talking about politics and by the way we dressed and by having politicized lyrics. Punk was just saying, 'Fuck off.'

LINTON KWESI JOHNSON The oppression was coming from the state and arms of the state and the organs of the state and the institutions of the state: the courts, the police, the educational system, and far-right groups like the National Front. I started recording around the same time that Rock Against Racism emerged. And music was a suitable vehicle for bringing my verse to a wider audience because more people would be interested in music listening to a record than picking up a book of poems. It was a cultural dimension of that struggle and part of the fightback against what we were experiencing. We organized ourselves politically. We agitated. We demonstrated. We had riots. We wrote poems. We made records. We put on plays. It was all part and parcel of the same struggle. It was inevitable our experiences would be articulated through reggae music.

MYKAELL RILEY Traditionally, promoters didn't promote a mixed gig: you had a black gig; you had a white gig: rock or reggae. You were targeting a different audience. Steel Pulse was the first black band in the UK to be playing white clubs outside of London on the same bill as punks. That was the interesting synergy because punks understood and identified with what we were doing.

DAVID HINDS We did tours with the Buzzcocks, the Adverts, Ian Dury, the Police, and we had a lot of spitting. We were at a rock concert at Reading and we'd been on stage for no more than forty-five seconds and there was bottles thrown left and right. I pulled my lead out and just walked off. They were like, 'We've come to watch rock music. We don't want your bloody reggae.' It was the quickest salary I've ever earned.

MYKAELL RILEY Audiences didn't know how to react or how to dance to the music or whether to be racist or not. The irony was, we might get out the van and we would be harassed but once you entered the premises it was, 'Can I buy you a pint?' 'Hold on a second, weren't you just giving me grief outside?' 'Yeah, that's outside, mate. It's different. It's a gig now.' Then during the gig you'd be dodging beer glasses or phlegm because if they liked you it was popular to throw beer and spit at you. We'd go, 'We're not a punk band. Don't spit at us.' Then they'd end up on stage starting a fight. We were famous for fighting them. If you came on our stage you'd get punched. I'd say, 'We don't do violence. That's it. You listen. You stand there. You clap.' We were telling them how to behave.

DAVID HINDS The Sex Pistols were saying *Never Mind the Bollocks*. It was anti-establishment. I related to their ideas more than the music. But generally, the white audiences were totally supportive of us. The idea was to play to who respected our philosophy.

BRINSLEY FORDE We were exposed to the punks on the Eddie and the Hot Rods tour. They came piling in slamming beer on the front of the stage. Jesus Christ! We'd never seen this before. 'Shit, what's going to happen now?' We were like, 'We've got to play.' Ten minutes into the show they were jumping. Then we played with the Stranglers at the first punk festival and they were throwing bottles and spitting and I said, 'I'm not taking this,' and we walked off.

MYKAELL RILEY Aswad walked off the tour so we got the call, 'Do you want to do a punk gig in Leicester?' Thirty seconds into the first number the same thing happens to us: some guy at the front flobs; it caught the lights and you saw this big snot float across the stage and land on the bass player's hand. Ronnie stopped playing and slowly the whole band stopped and we're all looking at him. The silence is broken by the Stranglers' bass player Jean-Jacques Burnel walking to the front of the stage and saying, 'You bunch of wankers. We invited this group. They're our guests. And if we like them you fucking love 'em.' There was a whole roar from the crowd. And he goes, 'Now, fucking play.' We had a fantastic gig and did an encore. The Stranglers came on after us and, to script, someone flobbed on Jean-Jacques, who is fifth dan karate. He slowly takes his bass guitar off, puts it down, goes up to the edge of the stage and kicks this bloke out cold. Then he picks his instrument up and says, 'All right, play.'

DAVID HINDS The Stranglers used to host a lot of parties and bring strippers down. I'd never seen anything like that; women putting their tits in your beer and then blokes drinking it, and all kinds of sexual activity happening on the carpet in front of you. After a while we said to ourselves, 'Race, colour, creed, it doesn't matter to us, we just want to play to people who are about improving justice and liberation and racial harmony throughout the world.' But obviously when we went to places like Ghana and the Ivory Coast and it's an all-African audience, you felt as if the music had come home, because it was those people that we had in our hearts in the first place writing the music. Being associated with the punks was almost like black acts being related to by white people and that became the catalyst for us being involved in Rock Against Racism.

LINTON KWESI JOHNSON Rock Against Racism was the white man saying, 'Racism is our problem. We have to deal with this and address white people.'

KEITH HARRIS I was impressed that people got themselves organized very quickly. And it was young white people who saw the danger. It made me feel good and that we were not alone in this. Once when friends of mine were walking home with a white girlfriend the police got out their car to spit in the girl's face. For someone outside of that society they wouldn't believe that this was going on, but RAR was great because people were prepared to stand up and speak against it.

WAYNE MINTER Some of the more pointed arguments against RAR were, 'Why aren't there more black people involved in it?' RAR was predominantly a white organization preaching to white people with a massively effective contribution from black artists. It was a white problem. It wasn't my job to make people live in racial harmony. It was to fight racism and fascism in white working-class Britain. It wasn't important to have black people in the audience but it was important to have black and white people on the stage playing together.

LUCY WHITMAN All people of goodwill should challenge oppression and reactionary attitudes wherever they find them. So if you hear a racist joke it shouldn't be the one black person in the room who has to complain about it. White people have a duty to challenge racism. Rock Against Racism was about celebrating music. And we came from a genuine love of music. And particularly as white fans of black music we were incensed by musicians expressing racist views. Of course bands like Steel Pulse, Aswad and Misty were singing about liberation and slavery and Babylon, any group has the right to self-determination whether it's lesbians or black people, but it was really important that we united to face a common threat.

JOHN DENNIS We weren't targeting black kids. We needed to get to white kids. They were the potential National Front members.

RED SAUNDERS When you met NF you always waited to hear what they said. If they were full Nazis, forget it, but if they were just naive then you could talk, argue, maybe put something in their head that changed things.

ROGER HUDDLE There might be a bloody lot of racists within the British working class but they're soft, by and large. If you argue against it, it falls away. It's the complete opposite of Eric Clapton's racism, which is a hard racism. It's an important distinction.

PAULINE BLACK 'Soft' and 'hard' racism is a white construct. It's just bullshit. It's racism. How do you make bullshit smell better? Damn it. I examine myself for racist attitudes towards white people. If I have to do it then every person should do it. We didn't need anybody to tell us what racism was; white bands telling you how bad racism was. Racism is a white person's problem to deal with.

RHODA DAKAR I didn't really think Rock Against Racism was going to change the world but I thought, 'Yeah, carry on. You see if it does. I don't really need to do this. You do.'

MYKAELL RILEY RAR was the first movement to embrace community and politicize music in the UK but it was also a paid gig and, for us, access to a larger audience.

KATE WEBB The specific reason why punk and British reggae were the primary focus of RAR gigs was because they were the most political; both of them shared a politics with us and understood the project.

COLIN BYRNE Punks were angry and the reggae bands were angry, so there was that connection. It brought black music to a lot of white kids for the first time. And punk bands suddenly thought it was very cool to tour with reggae bands. We all pretended we were Rastafarians.

RANKING ROGER Johnny Rotten said more punks should listen to reggae music because what they were saying was exactly the same. That statement alone made a lot of punk people get into reggae and accept it. The head of punk made reggae cool.

DOTUN ADEBAYO There was a battle for the heart and soul of punk. It was only when Johnny Rotten came out saying he was anti-racist and didn't give a toss about the National Front that the agenda was reclaimed by the kids. He did an interview in *Temporary Hoarding* and said:

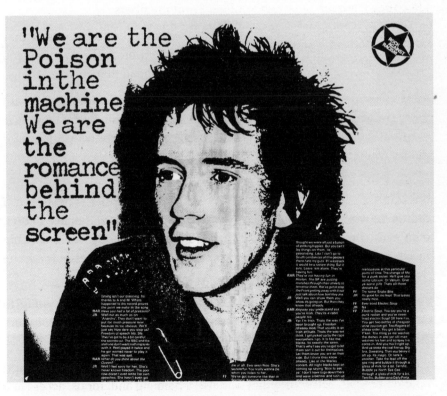

John Lydon interview in *Temporary Hoarding* No. 2, 1977.

I despise them. No one should have the right to tell *anyone* they can't live here because of the colour of their skin or their religion or whatever, the size of their nose. How could anyone vote for something so ridiculously inhumane? Like all this rubbish about Teddy boys beating up punks. I went to several Teddy boy concerts. No trouble. They knew who I was. They come up and said, 'What you doing here?' I said, 'I like music. Full stop.'

DENNIS BOVELL Lydon was a huge fan of reggae. He liked things like Prince Far I and Keith Hudson and Dr Alimantado. We had heard stories of people being deliberately booed off where the audience was largely non-black. Linton Kwesi Johnson opened one Christmas at the Rainbow and he came out to read his poetry without his band and the first thing he said was, 'I am no wise man from the East. I bring you no glad tidings of joy and peace,' and then went into 'Sonny's Lettah'. The audience went, 'Off, off, off.' John Lydon came out and said, 'Oi, hold it down. He's my mate,' and they all hushed. Linton recited his poetry to a still audience. Then when he'd finished they went, 'Waaaaayyyy.'

LINTON KWESI JOHNSON I became good friends with John Lydon. I could identify with punk because it was anti-establishment and an expression of disenfranchised youth rebellion and dissatisfaction with the prevailing state of things. This was a period of high unemployment amongst both working-class white youth and black youth. There were grounds for solidarity and that's basically what happened. A lot of the places, the audience was overwhelming white youth, but they were into what we were doing, and into our culture, and into our ideas of rebellion. It was a shared experience and it was wonderful. A lot of the gigs I did were with groups like Siouxsie and the Banshees and Public Image Limited.

TRACEY THORN Reggae was like punk's sister music. I remember vividly going out to see X-Ray Spex and being bombarded with really loud dub reggae before they came on and thinking that was completely normal.

ROBERT ELMS For kids growing up in villages and towns where there weren't many black people we were winning that battle culturally and RAR were part of the tide. Rock Against Racism had a message whose time had come.

JERRY DAMMERS One of the first RAR gigs I went to was at the Butts College in Coventry with Misty In Roots, and maybe the Ruts, and my friend Stan crammed himself into the dumb waiter to get in. Punk and reggae had a certain common cause. And for me it was the reggae and DJs playing it between the bands that made the gigs bearable.

MYKAELL RILEY We knew punks were into reggae because they were turning up to the gigs, but for punk to embrace reggae it was taking a risk and going against what traditional pop musicians did. Then the Clash did 'Police And Thieves' and that confirmed there was an audience; before that they were just another punk band. But it was a duality: where on one hand we were saying 'great', some were saying, 'They killed the fucking song.' But it brought attention back to Junior Murvin and confirmed that reggae had value. And then the Clash did '(White Man) In Hammersmith Palais', which was their way of saying, 'Here's what it looks like from the other side.'

BERNIE WILCOX The Clash were great for introducing us to reggae. We hadn't heard songs like 'Police And Thieves' and 'Pressure Drop' before. It introduced us to the original reggae artists.

JOHN JENNINGS I loved Junior Murvin's original of 'Police And Thieves' and because of the subject matter it worked with the Clash. They'd just done 'Complete Control' with Lee Perry, who had been Bob Marley's producer, and that had an effect on me too because we were reggae fans.

TOM ROBINSON Mick Jones played me '(White Man) In Hammersmith Palais' before it even came out. We had a quote from it on the sleeve of our first album: *You think that's funny . . . turning rebellion into money.* People said, 'How on earth did you know about the song?'

DENNIS BOVELL The Clash weren't afraid to turn up the bass or to make the drums sound reggae-ish and get a good rimshot sound. Reggae brought to punk the realization that tunes didn't have to be full of meandering chords.

DAVID HINDS Bands like the Clash, we saw them emulating reggae, not coming with the real thing. My mind couldn't get past the fact they were a white act but we did appreciate the fact they were respecting us as a people. We felt you can't take the originality from us when it comes to chopping the rhythm guitar and the drums with the right accent. You've got to feel that shit.

PAUL SIMONON We weren't trying to do a slavish copy of 'Police And Thieves'. We were trying to give our interpretation of ingredients to our music. It wasn't meant to be like reggae. We were a punk group. Lee Perry said when we finally met him, 'What do you think of our version?' He said, 'You ruined it,' which made us laugh.[15]

DOTUN ADEBAYO I was living in Sweden writing for *Schlager* and the Clash were playing in Gothenburg. I knew them from London and they used to let kids come backstage after the gig and there'd be all this food and booze. There were some journalists trying to get an interview and picking from the food, and Kosmo Vinyl, their publicist, said, 'Get your fuckin' hands off. That food's for the kids.' Joe Strummer was sitting with this Swedish girl on his lap dressed in a skimpy white outfit showing her white stockings and suspenders. I sidled up to him and said, 'Joe, it's a shame that Mickey Dread's not with you at the moment but I do know the best toaster in Sweden.' He said, 'Yeah? If you can get him to the gig tomorrow he can play support for us.' I said, 'Joe, I'm talking about myself, of course.' He said, 'All right, you can do it.' The gig was in Stockholm in an ice hockey stadium and I took a train there. I was doing Kung Fu at the time so I wore my whole outfit. Peter Tosh was my mentor and he'd taught me to do some kicks. I went on the stage maybe half an hour before the Clash, and the lights were on in the auditorium because people were still finding their seats. I gave the DJ a selection of my dubs, which included Augustus Pablo and Lone Ranger's 'Love Bump', and some of my friends were down on the front row: 'Dotun, what are you doing up there? Get down before anybody sees you.' It was really funny. Joe was watching from the wings and, after, he said, 'That was wicked.' The headline was, '*Schlager*'s Dotun was king for a day.'

RANKING ROGER When the Clash toured in England they'd say, 'Hey, Roger, come with us on stage and do some toasting.' The Clash did so much. They set the trend for others to come through. Anarchy was to destroy the old but you've got to make sure you build a good new thing. Their records were like the anarchist rebuilding. Before I knew them I always used to hear '(White Man) In Hammersmith Palais': 'Sounds like a racist tune, man.' Then I really got into it. 'Hang on, he's mentioning reggae stars.' *Dillinger and Leroy Smart / Delroy Wilson your cool operator.* Mick Jones told me in the mixing room Lee Perry sat laughing his head off. It was like, 'You guys are terrible. You'll go far.' He wasn't used to hearing the guitar 'played with an iron fist'. Perry knew it was ground music and reggae music is earth music. The Beat got their name from the Clash; to beat two things together. That was Wakeling. It was very clever.

DAVE WAKELING I looked up 'music' in my *Roget's Thesaurus* and found the word 'discordant' and then 'clash'. I thought, 'This is fertile ground.' Then I saw the word 'flam' and I read it too quick and thought it said 'sham' – whoa! Two great band names! So I looked in the antonyms and under 'harmony' it said 'beat' – why had nobody called themselves the Beat? I presumed it was because of the Beatles and everybody had shied away from it. But I thought the Clash were a little idealistic.

RHODA DAKAR My biggest problem was, Joe Strummer talked in slogans. I never believed him. It was a stance. But everybody thought he was the hero of our time. Mick Jones was always who he said he was. He didn't pretend to be a great revolutionary but he lived his life a bit like that. He walked the walk rather than talked the talk.

RICHARD BOON Pete Shelley and I were in the audience when the Clash played the Manchester Apollo and he turned to me and said, 'I'm so glad I don't have to do this,' meaning all that sloganeering. It was pure propaganda. It was largely their manager, Bernie Rhodes, saying, 'This is what you should be writing about.'

GORDON OGILVIE When you saw Strummer on stage there was honesty and sincerity. And a great force about them. Their music was clearly urban. It was youth angst and had a lot of anger in it. There was a famous occasion when the Clash came to Belfast and didn't get to play. There was a lot of anti-feeling because they used the day before they left for a photo opportunity against barricades and they were all dressed in militaristic gear. If they'd lived in Belfast they would have been put against a wall and searched by the army just as a matter of course. That wasn't happening in Shepherd's Bush. Let's face it, you can disagree with your dad in leafy suburbs of plenty of English cities and have family ructions but if somebody says to you with a gun in his hand, 'You're either with us or against us,' that's a pretty tricky choice. It was a lot easier in punk rock to write things about what you were against rather than what you were for.

JUNE MILES-KINGSTON Strummer was electric. He was like an automaton; and so passionate. It was mesmerizing. He had that edge about him but you'd never want to stand in front of him because he used to spit when he sang. There's never a definite way of doing it, is there? There can't be because the world's not like that. It's not, 'This is right. This is wrong.' You just do what you can and try and make a mark on a few people.

ROBERT ELMS You just knew that the first Clash album came from your world. You're living in squats; they're living in squats: I'd grown up with reggae and they had all of that stuff. It reminded me of the skinhead thing in that it was proud and hard and shining and vividly urban and songs about the Westway. The Clash were the first band that did that. It wasn't peace and love. It was 'Hate And War'. It was social politics.

JOHN JENNINGS When Bob Marley did 'Punky Reggae Party' it was like he said, 'Punk's all right,' by name-checking the Damned, the Jam and the Clash in the lyrics.

CHRIS BOLTON It was Bob's tribute to the scene. He realized that the popularity of his music outside of Jamaica gave him a platform as a messenger. He was giving thanks and praise to what this had brought.

BRINSLEY FORDE: I had a job at the Co-op greengrocer's in Neasden and found out the Wailers were staying two minutes around the corner and a friend who knew Bob took me round to the studio when they were laying 'Punky Reggae Party' down. 'Wow! Bob's singing a song about punks and reggae.' Suddenly the door opened and we heard this music. I said, 'That

**Bob Marley holding a
Ruts album, Miami Lakes,
Miami, 13 September 1980.**

sounds like "I A Rebel Soul". That sounds like us, man.' Bob was stood there: 'What's up?' We ended up playing table football. It was me and Bob against George and Drummie. Bob saw us as the young lions.

DENNIS BOVELL I had a Friday night residency a few streets away so we would occasionally acquire dubplates from the studio and say, 'Guess what Bob Marley's been up to?' and put it on. He and Family Man would be in there sometimes drinking Guinness and checking the way people were grooving to it and how it sounded on the system, but we weren't allowed to say he was in the room.

LINTON KWESI JOHNSON The influence of Bob Marley and the traditional expression of African consciousness, which has been a hallmark of reggae music, naturally filtered down to groups like Aswad.

NEIL SPENCER Reggae music belonged to Jamaica and Jamaicans. It didn't belong to the British, and then all of a sudden Aswad and Steel Pulse came along.

DAVID HINDS Aswad were one of Steel Pulse's major contemporary influences: 'I A Rebel Soul', 'Can't Stand The Pressure', 'Natural Progression', 'Back To Africa', 'Concrete Slaveship'. We were down in the trenches with Aswad; the difference being we were in Birmingham and they were in London and more cosmopolitan and ahead of the game as far as the industry was concerned. We looked up to them for a long time because of that. They showed us that reggae could be born in England.

BRINSLEY FORDE Aswad was the first British reggae band to sign to a major record company. Island didn't know what to do with us. We were about Rasta: 'I'm not a product.' It took a long time to come to the understanding that you have to be in it to change it. It's a rat race. I have to get in amongst those rats, come out the other end, and not become a rat myself. The Western idea of music is very much melody and harmony. Africa brought rhythm. We had the rhythm. We had the whole thing in one.

JULIET DE VALERO WILLS Because the punk movement had embraced reggae music, that made people start to look at how the black community was being treated.

DAVID HINDS I said that 'The only black man a white respects is an entertainer, a musician; white man's sympathy stops at Rock Against Racism; there's never going to be peace between black and white.' I was seeing guys owning yachts, and they're white and corporate and they're talking to me, and I was saying to myself, 'If I was Joe Blow who was wiping down the windows in a hotel, you wouldn't have any time for me.'

BRINSLEY FORDE Ordinary working-class people heard for the first time that there was another melody playing. We were writing and singing about our experiences and hoping that people related to or identified with it: *not satisfied with the life we're living*. People were going, 'Yeah man, I understand what you're saying. I don't have to be black to identify with that.'

MYKAELL RILEY On the first Steel Pulse record, *Handsworth Revolution*, we were saying, 'This is our concrete jungle. This is our realities.' And our look reflected the language that was used, which was a combination of Jamaican-isms and Britishness

BRINSLEY FORDE Suddenly a black person wasn't this alien, and it was music that started to break the barriers down. That's what reggae did for punk and what punk did for reggae. You'd done punk gigs. You'd been accepted by the punks and viewed them as people so there wasn't this divide. Music had brought everybody together. That was the most dramatic thing about it. People going, 'But I love this music so these people can't be that bad.' That is what Rock Against Racism really did. It's no good preaching to people who know. You have to get into the lion's den to make that change happen.

MYKAELL RILEY There were two ways of presenting a band back then. If you were a black band you generally got dressed in a suit. However, all the rock and pop bands just wore T-shirts and jeans. So we said, 'There must be a middle ground? Why don't we reflect the songs in terms of characters and dress in that way?' My mum was a seamstress so I bought our early clothes from what we called the 'dead man shop', which is a second-hand shop. I made a red, gold and green cape-type thing for Basil, silver tails for David. Alphonso was dressed like an eighteenth-century pageboy with a fluffy, frilly shirt. Ronnie was a squire with suit and tails and a Derby. Selwyn dressed as a soldier. And I was a priest. And we all had bowler hats. There was a narrative that linked the songs and ran through the performance and you lived out the character on stage.

DAVID HINDS I was seeing the parallels between what was happening in the black community in England versus what was happening in the black communities in the United States: the Black Panthers rising up, Huey

P. Newton, Eldridge Cleaver, Elaine Brown, Stokely Carmichael, Angela Davis, George Jackson. I'm saying, 'Damn, similar shit is going on.' Then I heard that David Duke, who was the head of the Ku Klux Klan, was coming over to Britain to influence John Tyndall, the chairman of the National Front. That's why 'Ku Klux Klan' was written. In the opening verse I'm saying, imagine, *I'm walking along*; every kid in England played football, so *I'm walking along kicking stones.* You kick a Pepsi-Cola can walking to school, *minding my own business*; all of a sudden these guys come out in fucking white pointed hoods to terrorize you. I was saying, 'Let's imagine that.'

MYKAELL RILEY Then I said, 'We're all going to put on Ku Klux Klan hoods,' and the band were saying, 'No.' I said, 'Come on, let's just do it for a laugh.' I got these pillowcases and cut slits in them. Three or four songs into the set we all turned around, donned the hoods and stood up. Dead silence. 'What the fuck do we do now?' We couldn't see to play. It was ridiculous. So the rest of the band took off the hoods and the three of us at the front kept them on and that became the performance. It was very powerful. But what became clear was, the audience didn't understand the symbolism of the hoods because we'd taken an image from somewhere in the back southern states of America. For them it was just theatrical, but odd, but soon as 'Ku Klux Klan' became a single and it was in the press it became political.

DAVID HINDS We took it to another level of theatrics to preach our philosophies. I had a prison uniform because all the guys I admired throughout history had served time in prison: Kwame Nkrumah, Martin Luther King, Malcom X, Marcus Garvey, Nelson Mandela. During 'Ku Klux Klan', Phonso would disappear offstage and get his gear on and then jump on stage with the hood on and I would defend myself using my guitar to ward him off. One time we did it in Wales and they started booing. But what we didn't know was they weren't booing for racial reasons. They were saying, 'We're not about that shit so why bring that here?' Then when we went to the States we wore the hoods in Birmingham, Alabama; north and south didn't mean shit to us. We were on tour with Walter Savage and he said, 'David, I'm afraid for you guys.' When we left we saw on TV a nineteen-year-old kid had been hanged the day after.

MYKAELL RILEY The hoods were a metaphor for how we were being treated by the state: by the police; by the system. We used to call it 'the shitstem'.

And the other word was 'Babylon': an all-inclusive term for the system that was against us. So it was referring to how we felt we fitted into society, and our relationship with society. The police were killing people and getting away with it, so they were the face of the Ku Klux Klan.

RHODA DAKAR Steel Pulse were doing reggae better than some of the people in Jamaica and dressing up made them more British. In this country we value our eccentrics.

DOTUN ADEBAYO Steel Pulse understood that a performance was also a theatrical piece. David Hinds would say, 'There are some people who think that black people don't have any right to be in this country. Well, this is what we say to them.' And they'd pull on the hoods and then sing, *A Ku, a Ku, a Ku Klux Klan.*

PAULINE BLACK I was gobsmacked the first time I saw them all wearing pillowcases with the eyes cut out. It said, 'Fuck it. You can stick it to them and get away with it.' End of.

RANKING ROGER The first time they did it on television it created an outrage. It catapulted them right to the top of the media; everyone was talking about it.

MYKAELL RILEY We were about to chart with 'Ku Klux Klan' but the BBC banned it so it just missed making the top forty. We were really hacked off because that would have cemented our existence in history.

BRINSLEY FORDE We needed our records played on the radio. Our music was inspired by Elvis Presley and the Beatles and all the stuff we had heard on the radio. We'd been to the same schools alongside these people that we were talking to so we said, 'Why aren't we being given the same opportunity?'

DOTUN ADEBAYO Reggae was definitely underground. It was seen as anti-establishment, marginal and ethnic. John Peel played it on his late-night Radio 1 programme mixed in with punk, and of course Don Letts had already broken down a lot of the barriers by DJ-ing dub records between the New York Dolls and Richard Hell and the Voidoids at the Roxy.

WILLIAM SIMON It would be a very big thing for a white man to play reggae on the mainstream radio back in those days.

DAVID HINDS Reggae was simply not accepted within the industry. There was resentment in the reggae world because it seemed as if the only way reggae was going to get airplay and get into the charts was if it was white people fronting the music. In the eighties, Madness made more money than all the reggae bands put together. I thank John Peel who played Steel Pulse. He overrode the BBC controlling how much reggae could be played by having bands make live recordings. It gave us a foot in the door.

CHRIS BOLTON Peel was of principal importance to all of independent music. He was the catalyst for punk and reggae, and the BBC gave him carte blanche to do what he wanted. He was the best person that ever promoted bands like Misty In Roots. It was like, 'We're in the door'; breaking into somebody's palace; a thief in the Crown Jewels room.

RED SAUNDERS On Sunday when we were cooking dinner we'd listen to David Rodigan on the radio, and everywhere round Hackney you'd hear it coming out of the kitchens. I took a picture of him outside Capital Radio for *Temporary Hoarding*. The headline was 'White Man in Capitalist Radio.'

WAR AMONGST THE REBELS

Linton Kwesi Johnson. Dennis Bovell. Rastafari

MYKAELL RILEY Linton Kwesi Johnson is really important in the narrative because black poetry was not on the map. Linton introduced this crossover where it was Jamaican dialect and spoken word. You could make out the meaning even if you didn't understand every word. It was groundbreaking. The audience didn't know if they should sit down or stand. Also it uncompromisingly targeted British black subject matter with really smart, informed lyrical content. The media didn't know how to handle it.

RANKING ROGER When Linton first came along, a lot of white people felt threatened because they heard this black guy talking Jamaican over reggae music: *All wi doin is defendin soh set yu ready fi war*. It was like, 'Whoa!' It was tribal, almost. It was on the edge because he was the only black voice talking for black people in England. He was asking questions and really homing in on politicians and saying, 'What are you going to do about it?' Linton was a knife straight to the heart of the English system. He was a warrior.

LINTON KWESI JOHNSON It was poetry rooted in orality of the Caribbean and in the music of Jamaica. Since I was talking about the Caribbean experience it seemed to me to make perfect sense to do so, not in the rarefied language of English classical poetry, but in the language that the Caribbean people understood. One of the basic criteria of poetry is authenticity of voice. Just like how Robbie Burns wrote his verse in the Scottish vernacular I thought it perfectly natural to do so in my own national spoken language, Jamaican.

LYNVAL GOLDING Linton was talking to us: *Mi don't have noh acamadaeshan / Mi haffi sign awn at di stayshan / At six in di evenin*.

TIM WELLS I had white mates at school that could reel out Linton Kwesi Johnson poems in his accent. We had more in common with a working-class black man than with a middle-class white man. I became aware of that from a very early age.

<u>**WILLIAM SIMON**</u> Linton was one of the strongest political figures. Linton is a thinker so he may look deeper than another man.

<u>**RHODA DAKAR**</u> He was the most miserable man but he was a great artist. His work was groundbreaking and a precursor for rap and toasting; rhythmic poetry. You felt the pain of what was trying to be said. He performed in patois but in an intelligent way; using it as a rhythmic language and showing its richness. He elevated the language and gave it an artistic legitimacy.

<u>**LINTON KWESI JOHNSON**</u> It was a political act because it was about identity. It was about challenging the domination of the English canon and we were waging a political struggle; and culture and creativity was an important aspect of that struggle. It's the difference between a poetry reading and a pop concert. People go to a poetry reading to listen to poetry; the imagery;

Linton Kwesi Johnson outside *Race Today* office, Railton Road, Brixton, 1979.

the voice – the cadence leaves an impression on the listener. Music, it's song and it's melody; it's rhythm; it's for dancing; it's for joy and for having a good time; and sometimes that experience is amplified by the fact you like the words as well.

DENNIS BOVELL I've spent forty years producing and listening to Linton working in the studio. He's never recorded an album that I haven't been on. I saw him as custodian of the journal of our existence in Britain, documenting mostly injustice and realizing the importance of social stance; realizing the involvement of other people in our struggle.

WILLIAM SIMON Dennis [Bovell] was a powerful force in music. The British sound had to be different from Jamaica and that comes down to influence and the music they listened to: the music of Marvin Gaye, the British pop scene, what came from the British charts. It was a natural process.

MYKAELL RILEY Dennis's band, Matumbi, would be promoted as, 'Just in from Jamaica,' but they were a mixture of people who essentially grew up in the UK. Dennis cloned himself as a Jamaican but every so often he'd break into a broad Bajan accent which is hilarious because you'd go, 'Who is this person?'

Matumbi's Bevin Fagin (centre), Dennis Bovell (left, with beard), Clapham, 1980.

CHRIS BOLTON Dennis was the first through the door, getting hit by people saying, 'It doesn't sound right.' 'It's not authentic reggae.' That was the shadow that was cast over what we were all doing. He ended up putting out his own white labels and said they were from Jamaica.

DENNIS BOVELL In the beginning people were always saying, 'You're never gonna get a good reggae sound unless you go to Jamaica or unless you're Jamaican.' I was like, 'I've never seen a Jamaican tape recorder; you just to have to know where the beat is.' So we thought, 'No, we can play reggae.' Then I hit on the idea of making these dub albums where I didn't tell people where it was made or who played on it. I made up a group called the 4th Street Orchestra and put it out on white labels and it started to sell really well. Then a writer called Snoopy who wrote for *Black Echoes* put out a spread: '4th Street Orchestra are not from Jamaica. It's Matumbi in disguise.' 'Fucking hell! How did he know that?' Our singer, Bevin, came to me and said, 'You couldn't keep your mouth shut, could ya? Had to brag about it, didn't ya?' So I went to Snoopy and said, 'Tell me, how did you know?' He pulled out 'Right Then' and said, 'Isn't that Bevin Fagan singing on that track?' Fuck!

BRINSLEY FORDE In the early days the black community were saying, 'It's not authentic music. Reggae doesn't sound like that.' We made so many trips to Jamaica to try and make that music and when it came to the mixing it just wasn't up to what we had here. We thought, 'Hold on. We could make this music anywhere.'

CHRIS BOLTON The advantage of reggae that came in from this country was you had other influences: Misty came from different parts of the Caribbean so they brought with them their own music and traditions.

TIM WELLS Good music is good music; good people are good people. It's not a big jump to go from black to poor. When someone is singing *me a sufferer* you know what he's singing about.

WILLIAM SIMON Reggae is reggae. I wouldn't put it in a country. No matter where you live. Reggae is like a language: from Birmingham to Liverpool, the language varies from town to town; it's based on the streets that you're from. So what is authentic? We went to British schools so your conversation will be different; your talk will be different; your song will be different. Jamaican musicians don't listen to one music. Reggae has many influences. Kids were listening to Michael Jackson and the Osmonds so their reggae was a different reggae. It's one music with everything in it. Asian kids and white kids and black kids all went to school together and formed alliances. There was a bond. We met in the local caffs, played pinball and ended up in the clubs together. Every man is influenced by what he's taught. No one teaches themselves. The fact that people, regardless of race or different class, could sit down together and talk in itself was very significant. Rock Against Racism was for those people who didn't know how to mix.

DOTUN ADEBAYO Sound systems were deciding what tunes the black youth were listening to, and until Lovers Rock they were only playing Jamaican. You were not going to hear Steel Pulse or Aswad on a sound system.

MYKAELL RILEY There was a sound system culture where the live band had to be as good as the records that came from Jamaica. That was the challenge. You went on stage at your peril. A bottle in the head was the indication that they didn't like you.

BRINSLEY FORDE The sound system was being played and suddenly it was the turn of the band. They were like, 'Enough of the band, man.' So next time we came with our own sound system. That was one of the things that changed music for reggae artists. People heard bass and they heard it heavy.

CHRIS BOLTON I played in shebeens with my Red Star sound system. A shebeen was an unlicensed drinking establishment. Mary Seacole ran a shebeen in the Crimea. The word comes from Ireland, síbín; a place where you drink and have a dance. Music's got to be a part of it and when you couldn't get live music you'd have a sound system. We all went to them. That's what you did on a Friday or Saturday night and heard the latest music.

LESLEY WOODS The shebeens or 'blues parties', as we called them, were amazing. You'd go to someone's house and the room would be completely dark and there'd be all these Rastas smoking big reefers. And there'd be huge speakers in the room and a fridge full of Red Stripe.

JANE MUNRO They very often took place in Handsworth, which was the big centre of where Jamaicans and Afro-Caribbeans lived in Birmingham. There was a lot of dope-smoking and Monkey rum. Sometimes they'd go on for several days. It wasn't unusual to have white faces but we would have been the minority.

LINTON KWESI JOHNSON The significant breakthrough came with Lovers

Rock, which was more or less romantic reggae which mostly featured female singers. Once that British style of reggae emerged it gave people the confidence to begin to articulate how they felt about their experiences in this country through reggae.

DENNIS BOVELL I was intent on changing reggae to suit my taste, which is why I invented Lovers Rock, which was the first British-made reggae that made it onto the sound systems. Reggae seemed to be a bit macho. If it was a sound system the audience would certainly be 80 per cent men and if it was just a blues dance or a reggae show girls would be there. So I spotted a space in the reggae sphere where there was a shortage of female vocalists taking the lead.

DOTUN ADEBAYO Lovers Rock broke that stranglehold and was the first unique artistic expression of the second generation of black Britain in this country.

CATHAL SMYTH Matumbi and Lovers Rock was the pop end of Dennis Bovell. I much preferred his involvement with Linton Kwesi Johnson: *War amongst the rebels / Madness / Madness / War*. It felt like a rallying cry.

LINTON KWESI JOHNSON Initially, we, that is, the alliance of the *Race Today* Collective, the Black Parents Movement and the Black Youth Movement, were a little bit suspicious about Rock Against Racism because it was an initiative of the Socialist Workers Party, who we knew were Trotskyites. And we didn't subscribe to their position on blacks and Asians, who they saw as victims. Victims are people who don't fight back. We were engaged in the business of fighting back, not only against racism, but for social justice to transform the society we live in. That was soon dispelled when one saw the effectiveness of what they were doing.

WAYNE MINTER Linton was the militant voice of Brixton and although he and Steel Pulse did early gigs for RAR, it was like, 'We've been struggling away down in Brixton for the last twenty years and suddenly whiteys have discovered black music and they want us all to dance.' I understood that.

*

MYKAELL RILEY The whole notion of black was negative from the media. Everything that was said about your community was negative. Your history in school was that it starts with slavery. That was it: you were a slave; you've got no history before then; there is nothing constructive or positive;

we gave you everything; within the community you were bottom. So, aspirationally, you were challenged at every point to go beyond what they had designated you could do. By the time *Roots* came on television in 1977 – 'The Story of the African', Kunta Kente sold to the white man – everyone was so fired up that the next day black kids just attacked white kids; it made people so angry and they wanted to align themselves with the blacks who were rebellious and fought the slave masters.

DAVID HINDS *Roots* was a phenomenon. Up until then a lot of black people never really digested deeply what it was like for our ancestors to be in chains: 'What? We were treated like that 400 years ago?' We went apeshit.

MYKAELL RILEY *Roots* gave you a visual representation and underscored what was coming across from Burning Spear and Bob Marley albums: slavery, the system, Babylon. The music gave us the history.

DAVID HINDS The second Steel Pulse album *Tribute to the Martyrs* was my knowledge of history and we tried to make the artwork have meaning with certain parts of the Bible attached to it. I said to the art department, 'Imagine it to be Mount Rushmore. And instead of having Abraham Lincoln, Teddy Roosevelt, George Washington and Thomas Jefferson have Marcus Garvey, Haile Selassie, Malcolm X, Steve Biko, Martin Luther King, Paul Bogle and George Johnson'. What I noticed about a lot of reggae acts, and Marley in particular, was that he never uttered who the enemy who was. It was always *we* and *them*. I said, to hell with that. I'm going to start naming these people. So in 'Jah Pickney' I wrote, *I've come to the conclusion that we're gonna hunt the National Front / Cause they believe in apartheid / For that we gonna whop their hides*, whereas Marley would say, *We're going to chase those crazy bump heads*.

MYKAELL RILEY 'Jah Pickney', which was subtitled 'Rock Against Racism', had this stance which was *rock* against racism: 'rock music' or 'rock' in terms of dancing? I took 'rock' as a stone, a fight against racism. But I don't think Steel Pulse embraced that. It's not, 'Let's embrace everyone.' It was, 'Let's take a step away from the white audience and do our own thing.' From a Midlands perspective the RAR thing was a London project; we saw them as cashing in on what we were already doing: 'What difference does it make to us?' It's not to say Rock Against Racism wasn't relevant but we had a different version of what took place before that came about.

BRINSLEY FORDE I was beginning to take an interest in Rastafari. It was there you found answers to what you were searching for. It was Babylon;

society is the struggle. It's establishment. We have a prophet that gives us understanding. They have a profit that's all about the pound. I remember arriving for Christmas dinner late one year and my sisters and parents being annoyed and then I proceeded to come out with my books and say, 'Look at this. It's all about this.' I remember my father getting really angry and going, 'Are you trying to tell me that all my life I've been fool?' We were Rasta seeing ourselves in a political environment. Our view of politics was food, clothes, shelter and medical help. That's what politics is. It's one person speaking for the livelihood of his constituency.

LORNA GAYLE I went through a phase where I was following the Rasta movement. They seemed really solid to me and words of wisdom. The problem was my parents. It would be like your parents not wanting you to be a punk rocker with pins in your nose. They didn't want you to have dreads and they were under the opinion that all Rastas did was sit down and smoke weed.

WILLIAM SIMON Rasta stands for defiance. It gave people a sense of certified identify. Hearing 'Christopher Columbus' by Burning Spear encouraged a lot of black kids to turn to their books and study their history: *What about the Arawak Indians . . . and the few black man who were round here before him?* If I want to be defiant I would say Rasta is anti-religion because the history you've got is not your own. Although there may have been many biblical overtones, that was not the fundamentals of Misty music. It was the other punchlines in between that's significant. Say, for example, the introduction to the band I would make at each show: *The music of our art is roots music / Music which recalls history / Because without the knowledge of your history you cannot determine your destiny.*

CHRIS BOLTON That was like a manifesto. The song explains itself in the lyrics: *Sodom and Gomorrah was destroyed by brimstone and fire* and this society is going this way.

RANKING ROGER What Rastafarians were singing about in reggae music had a profound effect on the way I turned out. I put 'Haile Selassie is God' to one side, but the 'oppression' and 'Babylon must fall' and 'We must all unite no matter what colour we are,' all those things coming from the working man's heart I would bring into the Beat.

DAVID HINDS We'd been hearing about Rasta for a long time. My brothers came over with that culture. The talk of the town was, the only job they could get in Jamaica was working in a field as a scarecrow because they were that scary. People said they were evil because their hearts were black. We did a tour with Bob Marley and saw how the whole Rasta philosophy worked for him. It was then I decided, 'This is for me, man.' We were ready to go out there and say, 'Jah, Rastafari.' I said, 'I'm cutting and combing my hair no more.'

MYKAELL RILEY One of the things that happened as part of the Marley tour was, the focus of Steel Pulse changed. It was like getting too close to the sun, almost. The majority of the band came back growing dreadlocks. Suddenly it was them and us; England is Babylon. On the bus it was, 'I don't care what that music paper's written; it's all Babylon. We're not talking to Babylon anymore.'

DAVID HINDS We were doing punk rock venues but the lyrics were developing and becoming Afro-centric. We were slowly and systematically heading towards the direction of Rasta whereas Mykaell was seeing the business side of it but was not recognizing why we were doing the music in the first place.

MYKAELL RILEY I had been doing the vast majority of the press but now the band didn't want to engage with the system, so increasingly what I was saying was not what they wanted to say. It was difficult. I was not prepared to go down that road: 'Are you growing dreadlocks?' 'No.' 'Are you going to become a Rasta?' 'No. I don't see why I have to conform to that stereotype.' So I accused the band of being racist. I was being provocative. I thought it was a phase. And then one day I arrived late for this particular rehearsal. I walk on stage and everybody walks off. The manager comes up and says, 'I don't think they want to be on stage with you, Mike.' No one ever got in touch again.

DAVID HINDS Our publicist, Claudine, had someone from the *Daily Mirror* come down to Handsworth into the black community for a couple of days. We took this journalist around to the snooker halls and all the hideouts and cafe bars and places where black people were accumulating. She got a first-hand view. Apart from the police, white people generally couldn't walk into the black community. As far as they're concerned he's working for the police, and before you know it there are six of us down in the station getting our fingers printed. I said, 'If you really want to know about us, this is the deal.' But the feature never happened. She said the paper couldn't print it because there was so much shit going on and it would have really rattled Britain.

NOTHING TO BE GUILTY OF

**Rock Against Sexism. Slits. Mo-dettes. Poly Styrene.
Poison Girls. Au Pairs**

SYD SHELTON As you talk to people you'll get very different views about what Rock Against Racism was. It took a while to get going and for people to understand what we were doing. And attempting to bring together black and white people also meant addressing major cultural differences and attitudes amongst the bands and their audiences.

KATE WEBB As we put on more gigs and RAR groups began to establish around the country there were a lot of accusations against a lot of reggae groups for misogyny and particularly language about women and their periods and lack of cleanliness; the use of the word 'bloodclaat'. The importance of Rasta as a heritage and culture to those black musicians and what it meant was not fully understood then, so those clashes happened all the time.

BRINSLEY FORDE I can write a song and the amount of times journalists have come back and said, this song is about this and is about that and I've gone, 'No.' I can understand where all that misconception came about. I may not believe that being gay is the correct order of things but I am not going to discriminate that person for his belief. It's the same situation I've been fighting for: 'Look, I'm black. I can do this. I can do that. Why don't you give me an equal opportunity?'

LUCY WHITMAN At the RAR 'Dub' Conference in Birmingham, David Widgery asked me to facilitate a discussion about sexism and music which didn't go well at all. I was twenty-two and completely out of my depth. Poco and Clarence from Misty In Roots and Michael and Brinsley from Aswad tried to defend sexism within Rastafarianism by saying, 'It's our culture.' I was stumped and I wasn't able to articulate any sensible argument even though I didn't agree.

BRINSLEY FORDE I don't know the exact text but I imagine they said, 'No, man. Man is the head. Women listen to man.' I subscribe to this point of view but it's not that this woman must be subservient to me. It doesn't mean that. It's the relation of how life is. There's a place in everything in life just like there are certain foods I won't eat; just like in a natural state the hog is there to clean the earth. If you have an aquarium a catfish will eat a dead goldfish but a goldfish won't eat a dead catfish. It's just the order of things. I believe that the guidelines have been set in the Bible.

PAULINE BLACK I admired that Aswad existed but I'm afraid I didn't go too much for the English variety of it. We had a bit of a run-in much later on the television programme I hosted, *Black on Black*, about women and the Rasta religion. That didn't go down real well. Rastas were outsiders from Jamaican life so they were to be admired for that but if you start breaking down how they felt about women then that wasn't too good. But you could say that about men in this country who probably felt equally bad about women and they weren't Rastas.

WILLIAM SIMON Who's equal to who? I don't think woman is equal. I think she's superior because she can do things that I can't do. She's the mother of my children. I could never be that.

SYD SHELTON Misty were out of their heads most of the time but they were totally passionate about changing people's minds. They understood the argument. They were always first on the line but it was riddled with con- tradiction: they'd sing, *Do you remember Judas Iscariot*, all this religious crap which I'd argue about with them for hours and everybody would go, 'Rastafari' and 'Jah' – but they were good to dance to.

WAYNE MINTER Misty had strict rules about women and what they were allowed to do, particularly if a woman had a period – then she was unclean and she wasn't allowed anywhere near anything. There were a lot of debates going on about that.

RED SAUNDERS We had to deal with ultra-lefties and ultra-feminists and the Rasta debate. My line was always, 'You can't choose your friends to your perfection fucking level on your bloody temperature gauge. This guy is prepared to stand with you now. He is 23 per cent on your gauge of what you want someone to be. Do you want him with you as the fascists come running in the door with fucking broken glass or not?' I had that simplistic argument: 'It's an emergency. Asian greengrocers are being stabbed to death in Brick Lane, right now. Altab Ali is dead.' People were being attacked and murdered. The National Front were kicking, punching and knifing their way into the headlines with great success. They were terrifying the ethnic and immigrant community.

DAVID HINDS I didn't hold the Rasta view that women are not equal to men. We weren't about that. We were not against women expressing themselves. I'm a believer that if you've got a smart woman why not utilize her mindset. If she's capable of doing something, give her the right to do it. Just because she's wearing a skirt she shouldn't remain behind the kitchen sink. But there were Rasta: 'You can't wear trousers. You got to wear a skirt. Girl, keep your head wrapped.' I never stooped to that. We recognized Rasta was a new philosophy to us and anything new also meant there was room for development and change. Religion is all about rules and environment and people making up rules according to their financial circumstances: 'Who wants to wear shoes anyway? I'm a Rasta man.' But as soon as fame and fortune came there you find them with a pair of Clarks. I said, 'To hell with that.'

RANKING ROGER There's lots of conflict as far as Rastas and women go but you have to realize that Rastafarianism is a way of life. It's not a religion. So that means there's always room for improvement and change. The twenty-first-century Rastafarian is a lot more aware of gay people and lesbians and women.

LESLEY WOODS I remember once talking to this Rastafarian who said that he'd seen a woman coming up the street in a tight skirt and he thought she deserved to get raped. I said, 'Well, if you walked up the road in a tight skirt you'd deserve to get raped.' There was that Peter Tosh interview in *Melody Maker* with Vivien Goldman, when he said, 'Sometimes many wives deserve battering. Seen? You have some women if you don't clap them twice a month they're not alright.' It was quite shocking. Historically, women in left-wing politics, their role was if somebody was going out to do something like bomb a railroad she would be expected to fuck him the night before so that he felt virile and strong and manly. Look at people like Angela Davis: she had a pretty hard time of it confronting endemic sexism. There's that saying, 'They're your brother in the street but a fascist in the bedroom.'

RUTH GREGORY It was always an issue with the Rastafarian bands, but the same could be said of most of the white bands. Just like white people understanding that racism is a white issue in the same way sexism is a male issue. Unless men are ready to take on the battle and want to equalize things then we're not going to get all that far. It's a bit like anti-slavery groups coming from the slaves themselves; you can't just do it on your own. Quite often men will be in a group of men and they will say things they wouldn't say in front of women, but those men don't speak up. It's like racist jokes that get told. People feel embarrassed but don't really want to stand up against it. Like the Special AKA said, *If you have a racist friend now is the time for your friendship to end*. Those discussions have got to be had. But sexism wasn't on the agenda. Even though punk presented a blindingly obvious opportunity, the world wasn't ready for it. And with Margaret Thatcher as the leader of the Conservative Party the whole situation was rife for Rock Against Racism to go into Rock Against Sexism.

LUCY WHITMAN There was one band called Rape. And I remember a very articulate letter from a group of seven women who had been to a Fabulous Poodles gig at Brighton Poly, saying, 'If you're against racism you should also be against sexism.' And how upsetting it was for them to go to a Rock Against Racism gig and then feel threatened as women. After that we had a protocol so RAR groups had to check out bands in advance. But a lot of women said, 'We need to have a Rock Against Sexism to promote women musicians and challenge sexism in the music industry.' Our motto was 'LOVE SEX HATE SEXISM!!' We started issuing a bulletin called *Drastic Measures* and I wrote:

This is me posing

Lucy 'Toothpaste'
Whitman, 1977.

If women musicians don't play up to typical expectations of beauty / sexiness, insults are hurled at them from all sides – Patti Smith is 'as ugly as hell', Poly Styrene 'has a somewhat prolonged puppy-fat problem' (*NME*), etc., etc. You can't win. And indignant male rock journalists have been known to write spiteful reviews of concerts to pay performers back for refusing to go to bed with them. Women journalists who sleep with some of the musicians they meet are of course denounced as slags and groupies, but men who sleep around are studs to be admired.

Women in music were under constant pressure from the record companies to flaunt their bodies in order to sell more records. I remember booking this pub on the Tottenham Court Road to have our meeting and I said, 'It's for Rock Against Sexism.' 'What's sexism? Are you against sex?'

That was not unusual. We had to argue what we meant by it. Another piece I wrote was written after we got a short slot on the radio:

> When Capital Radio interviewed me about Rock Against Sexism last night they asked me what I objected to in the Stranglers. I said, 'How sadistic some of the songs were,' and they obligingly faded an extract from 'Sometimes': *Someday I'm going to smack your face / Somebody's going to treat you rough / Beat till you drop*, and then the interviewer rounded off by saying, 'Well, I still think sexuality is a vital ingredient in rock 'n' roll and I don't think rock singers can be too sexy but if you disagree you can contact RAS.

That's what we were up against!

CAROL GRIMES If they signed a woman in the sixties it was a woman up front being sexy and packaged. I was hauled into the office to see Robert Stigwood and told, 'You're not playing the game.' I was supposed to hang out in the right clubs where they all went. I was supposed to be seen, be photographed and screw the right people; have a nice juicy affair with a big rock star. In radio interviews I had hands up my skirt and fingers groping my tits. And if you said anything, 'Oh, it's just a bit of harmless fun.' That was the culture in the music business. It happened in studios, bars, at gigs. Women were treated really poorly. Anything that flagged strong women saying, 'Hang on a minute, we're not putting up with this anymore,' was a positive thing.

SUE COOPER In the early seventies, through the Women's Movement, there was a band called the Northern Women's Liberation Rock Band and they did a series of weekends in Liverpool to encourage women to play music. I had a go on a drum kit and the bass. It was using music as a way of empowering women. What had been presented to me as a teenager growing up was that music was mainly men. If you saw women on stage they would sing, and that was about it. Punk was very much overthrowing the status quo and doing alternatives, and that meshed for me with a feminist perspective which was also about challenging the balance around gender roles.

LUCY WHITMAN It was very hard to get any of the women artists to say they were feminists. Punks didn't want to be associated with an organized movement, whether it was political or feminism, because they found that to be too constraining. Feminist music was very much wavering-voiced American folk music because that was the antithesis of cock rock.

JUNE MILES-KINGSTON In the Mo-dettes, we were always very anti-industry because of what it does to women musicians. We were all pretty strong feminists but without saying the word. Punk was: anyone can do it. Feminism was: you're the underdog. It labels you as someone fighting for something and stops you growing. We were already there. We weren't fighting for our place. We had a place. All we were doing was proving it. We didn't do, 'We're women and we're strong.' Fuck that. If you've got to explain it, it's not going to happen. We wanted to prove that we could do it but we didn't have to preach it. We could still be sexual. We could still wear feminine clothes. Ramona loved to wear short skirts and little heels and she looked beautiful. Jane had a great mean look with cropped blonde hair and mean eyebrows. Kate had a white stripe in her hair and that New York swagger. She was absolutely brilliant. We said things like, 'Feminists are just bored housewives.'

LESLEY WOODS We didn't shirk away from being labelled as a feminist band. If I was asked if I was a lesbian I would say yes, because I didn't give a fucking shit what they thought. I would steer clear of personification in songs. If I was writing a love song I wouldn't use *he* and *she* because love songs are always written about men and women. They fail to acknowledge that these feelings are things that gay people or transgender people go through. I love that Barbra Streisand song: *we've got nothing to be guilty of.* It doesn't ever let you know that it's a man and a woman saying it to each other. It could be anybody.

LUCY WHITMAN I spent many hours trying to persuade musicians to say they were feminists. But it didn't matter, because what they were doing in their music was challenging to conventional ideas of femaleness – the Slits were singing about 'Typical Girls' and not looking like typical girls and Poly 'I-den-tit-y'. They were saying, 'I'm not going to be your plaything.' I'm not going to be bound or confined by expectations of being a housewife or a dutiful girlfriend. That's why in *Temporary Hoarding* I spent a lot of time quoting people's lyrics, because they were challenging. Punk as a whole was very anti-romance and most songs were not about boys meet girls. It was 'White Riot' or 'God Save The Queen'.

JUNE MILES-KINGSTON We didn't feel Rock Against Sexism was the way to present the band. We had four different views on everything. We didn't all stand behind the singer who represented us. It wasn't like the Slits, where they were all competing.

SUE COOPER The Slits supported the Clash on the White Riot tour. It's really hard to explain how unimaginable it was to have women on stage playing musical instruments. You just didn't see it. There was a contradiction because punk was quite macho but the Pistols and the Clash were so anti-establishment.

NICKY SUMMERS There was nothing to refer to, growing up. There weren't girl bands. There were just Sixties girl singers who were manipulated. Then the Slits came along. They were quite rakish musically and they had wild personalities; very inspiring and groundbreaking, but challenging. It was such an exciting period. The whole thing was exploding and we were at the beginning of it.

RICHARD BOON The Slits empowered women with their attitude: *Silence is a rhythm too*, but touring with them was hard work because they were really brattish, particularly Ari. She was terribly young: fourteen, fifteen. You'd have thought they might have needed some help but there was no one to give them any guidance or boundary. People were like, 'Yeah, it's really fun. It's the Slits.' That wasn't applauded by me, in men or women, but they were also fun to be around; and possibly for the same reason.

MYKAELL RILEY We played with the Slits reluctantly. You look at their style and it's not very Rasta. Steel Pulse was redefining itself and that was not in the image of the Slits.

DAVID HINDS They were a law unto themselves. They were outrageous. Prior to going on stage they asked me to tune their guitar and when I did they said, 'I don't like that,' and grabbed the guitar and started detuning each string and said, 'That's better.'

RANKING ROGER It didn't matter if they could play their instruments or not. I could hear all the mistakes but also I could hear a groove. They were really brave. We were like, 'Give 'em a go.' We used to call them the Sluts.

DENNIS BOVELL The Slits' take on rhythm was quite feminine. I was like, 'Listen. It's a hybrid. It's a new style. It's called Fem-punk!' Ari had this fascination with marrying reggae rhythms with rock drums; she would mouth the beat and Budgie would play it. Tess would then have a very heavy bassline. Then Viv would come with guitar parts and get the lyrics together for Ari to sing. I was fascinated by such a young girl who had all these big ideas. But I wasn't surprised, because she was German and classically taught. One of her party pieces was to put a coin on both the backs of her hands and then do piano scales without the coins falling off: 'This was something I learnt when I was a child!'

TRACEY THORN I'm a bit uncomfortable with the idea of female rhythm. Rhythm's rhythm, isn't it? I can appreciate the idea of just being women in a band and making up your own rules – that's what we did in the Marine Girls – but if you're going to make a strong case that you've defined some essentially female version of rhythm then it doesn't help if both your producer and drummer are men. I was never comfortable with versions of feminism that used female essentialism as being part of its defining thing. That's dangerous. You end up on shaky ground saying 'women are this' and 'men are that'.

FRANCES SOKOLOV In my own sense of rhythm, three-four time is more female than male. It has associations with waltzes: *1*, 2, 3; it's not driving. It's spinning. It's going round in circles whereas the male march, 1, 2, 3, 4, is driven.

JUNE MILES-KINGSTON The cover of *Cut* was fabulous and it got everybody talking about the Slits. I used to secretly wish I'd played in them when I was in the Mo-dettes. It was the tribal beats. And then I played with them just before Ari died. She was fucking amazing; a complete and pure natural.

DENNIS BOVELL When people saw the Slits cover they were like, 'Bovell, come on, what's the story behind you with these three naked girls?' I'd be like, 'They weren't dressed like that in the studio!' When they were taking their clothes off and hosing each other down I was in the swimming pool and somebody said to the girls, 'Why don't you jump in the pool?' I said, 'NO! NO! NO!' Suddenly all three of them jumped in the pool and somebody whipped out a camera and went snap. I went, 'If that fucking appears anywhere I'm going to kill you.' They were very brave. They weren't page three. They were page one.

PAULINE BLACK The *Cut* cover came in for a lot of flak at the time from feminists: 'It's sexist.' 'Why get your tits out?' That wasn't getting your tits out. That's how they looked. It was pretty damn primal.

TRACEY THORN I was seventeen when the album came out and just discovering feminism, so suddenly having your tits out on your record cover, albeit covered in mud and obviously not meant to be sexual, I really wasn't quite sure what to make of it at all. There was something slightly hippy about it; and ideas of liberating the body. It was very challenging and defiant. I think men were probably frightened by them, which was no bad thing. And the looks they're giving are very 'fuck you'.

LESLEY WOODS Apparently, bus drivers crashed when the cover was put out on billboards. *Cut* was very important to me. It was all women. *Typical girls get upset too quickly* – I could relate to that. It was very brave of them.

JULIET DE VALERO WILLS You were buying into something. They were women that didn't care that they didn't have perfect bodies. They were totally in control. They were taking rock 'n' roll back for the girls. It was, 'We're not going to pander to any of your ideals of who we should be or how we should look.' It was girls doing it and still managing to be incredibly feminine. On top of that, the record sounded brilliant. They didn't try to be technically brilliant. They didn't try and be girls playing boys' rock 'n' roll. They just did their own thing. It became my Saturday afternoon tidying-the-flat album.

LUCY WHITMAN The whole thing about punk is, it is very jokey. It's very visual. It's all about dressing up and it's a bit of a pantomime. The way Ari used her voice was unusual. The statement was: I'm not going to be Cilla Black. I'm going to be something that will surprise you.

Slits advert in *NME*, September 1979.

NICKY SUMMERS Punk was a different take on female style: you could wear a bin bag or spiked hair. You were not dressing for men. It was about creativity and expression, and the guys at the time supported you in that.

RHODA DAKAR I'd wanted to be in a band for a long time but it was all about boys that had been playing in their garages for about 100 years. Punk made it seem possible. And then I heard about the Mo-dettes being put together and they were looking for a singer. I thought, 'Should I? Nah, I won't.' Then I went to see them at Acklam Hall and thought, 'Oh, I really wish I had now.' The Mo-dettes made more sense. I liked the punk-pop kitsch Sixties influence. It was more like who I was.

JUNE MILES-KINGSTON I loved the way that people of my age at last were taking control of everything. I was a huge fan of Tamla Motown and Stax, all that American pop soul stuff, and all those women were put up front with their hairdos and their dresses. The Mo-dettes was a reaction against all of those groups. We felt like punk gave us the opportunity to get away from that to say, 'We're all women. We're all in a band. We all play instruments. We're not just pretty faces. And we're also taking the piss.'

SUE COOPER We had a women's big band called Contraband. Musically it was a shambles, but it was amazingly empowering for the women who were in it: just the image of twenty-odd women playing Glenn Miller or an arrangement of 'I Will Survive'.

JUNE MILES-KINGSTON Being female is not a disadvantage in any way whatsoever. Yes, of course, it is if you're married to a bloke that's going to beat you up or you work for a horrible boss that keeps you down. But then you fight to change it. I felt privileged being a woman.

NEIL SPENCER I remember going to a meeting with CBS Records and I said to them, 'The future of popular music is with British black people, and women have to be accommodated.' I got a lot of stick for doing the 'Women in Rock' cover on the *NME* but it brought the issue to the fore. And what did CBS say? 'Where are your black lesbian writers, Neil?' I always tried to recruit female writers onto the *NME*.

JULIET DE VALERO WILLS The music industry had managed to lag behind spectacularly in women's equality like no other industry. I had a strong work ethic. That's how I dealt with being a girl.

PAULINE BLACK Everybody knows that sex sells music. If you've got a pretty woman up front, the more flesh that she shows the more records you'll sell. You only had to look at Debbie Harry.

LUCY WHITMAN Blondie's first album was promoted with a picture of Debbie Harry and the slogan, 'Wouldn't you like to rip her to shreds?' A lot of the imagery of women in early punk was very sexist because the whole industry was really sexist. It's very hard for women to try to subvert sexist imagery, and given the history of the representation of women in our culture I don't think there's anything radical about baring your breasts. You might say you're doing it satirically or ironically but it doesn't make any difference because men still get off on it. I used to wear a little black plastic jacket covered in badges and I used to cut my hair with a razor so it would stick up in odd peaks. I didn't want to conform to other people's expectations of what a young woman should look like. What I found subversive was the sort of clothes Poly Styrene used to wear.

RUTH GREGORY I think Poly Styrene got more optimistic through Rock Against Racism. We gave her a voice into a different audience, different possibilities.

KATE WEBB Poly Styrene was the greatest product of punk ever. She was part Somali, part Scottish-Irish and was like the advance party for the new self that was going to remake Britain. I think she captured the spirit of the time like no one else and brought that fantastic aesthetic style. She was so unprecedented and completely her own thing and of the moment. So many great songs like 'Germfree Adolescent' and 'Oh Bondage! Up Yours!' *Bind me tie me / Chain me to the wall / I want to be a slave / To you all*; it's one of the greatest feminist anthems ever.

NICKY SUMMERS Poly's message was different and important. It was about being female and not dressing or looking or behaving how you're expected to. Punk had a different aesthetic of female beauty. It was beyond liberating.

RICHARD BOON Poly was a remarkable woman. She was talking to teenage girls about not being objectified.

DAVE RUFFY Being mixed-race with a brace on her teeth; and not being beautiful traditionally but being beautiful because she was young and exciting.

PAULINE BLACK Poly Styrene probably influenced me more than anyone.

It wasn't what she did or what she said, it was more that she had freedom to express what she was. No holds barred. The backdrop to these women was the Nolan Sisters or Chic or Donna Summer or whatever the fuck Diana Ross was doing. To come up with those ideas was extraordinary.

SARAH JANE MORRIS I wasn't a punk but I loved the statement of wearing a very badly hand-knitted baby-pink dress and a brace; a pop singer wearing something that was always considered ugly. It was such a statement.

FRANCES SOKOLOV Males are very defensive when you try to speak to them about these things. It's a male world and one is afraid of what's going to come back at you. You want to speak your truth but there's a risk involved. I don't know whether that risk is real or imagined or part of the air that we all breathe in or whether every bloke has got the potential to hurt us.

PAUL FURNESS Frances was known as Vi Subversa. Her voice was a great rasping razor blade. She was in her forties but her age was seen as wonderful and she was up there with all these other young people doing what she was doing and couldn't give two fucks about it.

FRANCES SOKOLOV I liked the excitement of rock music. I learnt to play the guitar because I wanted to join in the delivery of sound of large electric music. But I was forced to sing over this noise with not very good equipment. I'd end up with sore throats and headaches. I found the whole gigging thing quite unpleasant: too loud, and too noisy. But I had my message and I wanted to be up there doing it. If you've got something to say then bloody well say it.

RICHARD SWALES Frances is a really important person in popular music. There is nobody who has done anything like what she did: she was an evacuee during the war; with the anarchists in Soho in the fifties; a dropout in the sixties; ended up in Brighton in the seventies with two kids fathered by one of the editors of *Black Flag*; and then suddenly decided she could sing. It's quite an extraordinary life experience that got channelled into rock music. There's no other rock singer, male or female, who talked about the issues that she talked about. At forty you were well past it, and to stand up in front of 500 kids in leather jackets gobbing, singing songs about being a single mother and the anger and angst of all that, is something quite extraordinary.

FRANCES SOKOLOV I never dressed or called myself a punk. I was too old. People often thought I was the manager or somebody's girlfriend until I got on stage. That was an expectation and certainly true of the early years. On stage I would get things like, 'Get 'em off.' It's hurtful if you're not taken seriously. In the end I stopped wanting to be taken seriously.

LUCY WHITMAN Frances was the most amazing poet. The *NME* mocked her as 'a bulky middle-aged woman forced into a red satin skirt, which gives [the Poison Girls] a visual incongruity.'

SHERYL GARRATT I remember thinking Vi Subversa was so old and how magnificent it was an old codger like that was doing gigs.

RICHARD SWALES Anarchism was making the personal political and making the political personal, twinned with feminism and twinned with pacifism and anti-racism.

FRANCES SOKOLOV My obligation to myself and women is to try and say the truth as it is; our truth. My children didn't like having their mum open to abuse. They didn't know why I was talking about atom bombs and fear and poison. I feel very sad about what I put not only myself through, but also put them through. It was painful and I wanted to run away and hide many times, mostly just before a gig. I didn't like the violence in the music. I was fed up to the bloody back teeth with violence in any form whatsoever. I just wanted to play music. I didn't have a particular political agenda. I was a feminist by then more than anything else and that seemed to me as much as I could handle. I was too sensitive for the whole rock world, really.

SUE COOPER Poison Girls was a statement and a challenge to a cultural stereotype which is not only can women not play bass guitar or electric guitar but you don't have to be young and pretty to do those things.

FRANCES SOKOLOV We had two men in Poison Girls and they would call themselves feminists and they would come in for quite a bit of flak about that. Radical feminists were saying, 'Why are you playing with men?' Working in all-women situations wasn't what my life was like. It wasn't who I was. Poison Girls' lyrics were full of feminism. I knew there were other women making songs and speaking out and I wanted to be another woman; of that chorus of women's voices which were coming up from under.

•

JANE MUNRO The Au Pairs didn't want to sound like a rock band. We wanted to be more challenging but not to go down the totally punky route of being a complete cacophony. So Rock Against Sexism chimed with what we were doing. We happily said to the press we were a feminist band. Feminism had bad press with the bra-burning stuff and quite a lot of women didn't want to be associated with that, but that's not the only way of being feminist. We could hardly deny it with our lyrics. I remember John Taylor of Duran Duran saying Lesley and I 'would be better going off and working in a factory'. It was par for the course.

LESLEY WOODS One time, Jane came to me and said she'd overhead one of this all-male band saying about us, 'It's all right. It's only a couple of birdies and two guys.' That was like a red flag to a bull. It just made you more determined: 'I'll show him,' kind of thing. The Au Pairs wanted to show that men and women could work together as equals. 'Au pair' means in French with equality: on a par; an equal member of the family. We were saying the personal is political: if a man and a woman in a personal setting have a properly functioning healthy relationship where it's built on equality, but with the recognition of your differences, that can be a model for how society deals with the structures within it.

SHERYL GARRATT God, Lesley sounded like she meant it. A lot of her songs were about sex from a woman's point of view and I'd never heard that kind of stuff. The Au Pairs were very subtle musically and doing things influenced by dub and space but also with an abrasive funk influence.

JANE MUNRO We recorded 'Come Again' for the TV programme *Something Else* and then were told it was unsuitable and too rude for the BBC. The song was about men's cack-handedness and lack of skill at giving women orgasms; and the fact that a woman might want more than one, which isn't unreasonable. It was the sort of territory that people didn't go into. John Peel said it was the flip to 'Je t'aime'.

LESLEY WOODS 'Come Again' is all about encouraging a woman to have an orgasm. *I can feel you hesitating. Is your finger aching?* I felt embarrassed about it for a long time. It was semi-humorous. I used to get young men come up to me at the end of a gig and say, 'I really do want to give my girlfriend an orgasm. She won't come.' I was trying to highlight there's an issue here that everybody's shying away from articulating. [Our guitarist] Paul's mum was really quite horrified and said, 'That's between a man and woman in the bedroom.' I was trying to put the female orgasm on the sexual agenda. I don't think it had ever been shouted out about in a song before.

JOOLZ DENBY I toured with the Au Pairs. Lesley was as thin as a rail and used to do press-ups like a man. I was terribly envious of her because I'm the big muscular type. They were a little bit older than me and very intense. They were polite but they were a sealed unit on a mission with an agenda to pursue for social justice. I remember the song, *we're equal but different.* I thought she put that nicely.

LESLEY WOODS 'It's Obvious' just about says it all really, doesn't it? That definitely had a gay influence. That song crosses all those things: race, sexism, men–women, black–white; recognizing at the end of the day that we're all individuals: *we're equal but different.*

As a band, we were quite shy and withdrew from being in the spotlight. It's one thing going down in the cellar, getting off your head and having a great time bashing your guitar and writing these lyrics, but it's completely different from suddenly having to deal with the media. I had this golden moment to be on the front page of the *NME* and what do I do? I wear clothes from a second-hand clothes shop. I thought, 'I don't give a fuck. I'm not dressing up for the *NME.*' You felt that you were beyond them; that you didn't need their favour or need to be in their good books to be what you were. Female politics was quite topical in women's groups and they used to have men's consciousness-raising groups as well. Paul, our guitarist, went to one and said there was a guy in the meeting who said, 'My girlfriend likes me to call her names and I'm not sure how to reconcile that to being a non-sexist man.' I thought it was really sweet they were talking about things like this.

DEDICATED FOLLOWER OF FASCISM

National Front. Lewisham

LINTON KWESI JOHNSON As time went on, one saw that Rock Against Racism was a very important initiative and was an important aspect of the response to the rise in racism and fascism, especially in combating groups like the National Front. I was sold on the idea of music being a great leveller to bring people together to challenge forces of oppression. What persuaded me to discard my cynicism about their motives was the Lewisham Riot in August 1977; that made me sit up and pay attention to what they were doing. So with the benefit of hindsight, Rock Against Racism was a great initiative. It isolated the fascists and helped to bring a significant number of black and white youth together with a shared vision of change. It was using music to bring people together to challenge right-wing forces.

DAVID WIDGERY The National Front had been formed in February 1967 by a merger of traditional anti-Semitic, fascist and nationalist sects. They ran only ten candidates in the 1970 general election and all did very badly. Their breakthrough came in May 1973 in the aftermath of the Ugandan Asian crisis when Martin Webster won 4,789 votes in the West Bromwich by-election and saved his deposit. At an estimate, the NF's total paid-up membership in this period was 17,000 (some 7,000 larger than the highest total recorded by the British Union of Fascists) and it was producing five or six million items of printed propaganda a year.[16]

PETER HAIN The National Front caught the moment to a worrying degree. They had pushed the Liberals into fourth place in the Greater London Council [GLC] elections and were doing very well in by-elections. It was on the back of all sorts of wage freezes and wage constraints; the pound had been devalued and the economy was not in a good shape. In those circumstances the far right is able to prosper by appealing to discontented working-class citizens.

GEOFF BROWN Inflation in the mid-seventies hit 25 per cent. And then under Callaghan's government working-class living standards in an eighteen-month period fell 10 per cent, in the context of a huge amount of strike action which led to the so-called 'Winter of Discontent' of 1978–9. There was an explosion of anger that this was a Labour government suppressing living standards. It created a huge demoralization and disorientation which gave Thatcher her opportunity. It was meant to be a two-sided deal, but most workers couldn't see what they were getting out of it and the National Front was ready to exploit that.

JOHN JENNINGS I remember seeing 'NF' sprayed on some flats and thinking, 'What's that?' That was the beginning. We were just doing music but at the same time there was an ominous feeling and it started to take a foothold, but everyone went, 'We've seen it all before with Enoch Powell.'

RANKING ROGER We'd get leaflets through the letter box, 'Vote National Front.' They marched past my house in Stechford and straight up Bordesley Green East: 'Go home, you black bastard.' I'd shout back, 'I was born here, mate.' You'd walk through the parks and hear, 'A black bastard.' Man, talk about Bolt: faster than him!

RED SAUNDERS There was this NF patriarch called Derek Day who lived on a big estate in Tower Hamlets. There's an amazing bit of film where there's a small anti-racist march and he actually climbs out of his ground-floor window seething with rage and he's shouting and screaming at the demonstration, 'I don't want blacks . . . I am a racist. I don't like these people,' and they're all shouting, 'Fuck off.' And then down the road come two very nice, very neat black girls with their shopping and they politely circumnavigate him. He stops for a moment and then goes, 'That's why I don't like 'em.' It was a momentary little thing that encapsulates that time.

TOM ROBINSON Instead of three manifestos – Conservative, Labour and Liberal – coming through the letter box, a fourth manifesto came through for the National Front. That was what really made me think, 'We've got to do something.' Society was in flux and anything could have happened. It really felt to us like end times. Hitler's right wing had come to power in Germany in the thirties as a minority government and then through sheer brutality held their own. We had a feeble, discredited Labour government and industrial unrest; the three-day week; Thatcher in the wings; and actual certifiable fascists marching though areas like Lewisham and Wood Green actively trying to stir up unrest and at the same time achieve credibility as a political party. It was the dual track of having thugs firebombing and beating up people whilst simultaneously wearing suits and putting manifestos through people's doors. It was exactly parallel to how the fascists had come to power in the thirties.

RUTH GREGORY When the Labour Party is in power the left grows in strength because people get disillusioned with whoever's in government, and the same happens when the Tories are in power; the right wing grows very easily. The Labour Party didn't have a great track record in government. It was a very scary time. The number of Asian people who got killed was huge; more than even during the Mosleyite period. And just general things like having shit put through your letter box and not being able to go out.

RED SAUNDERS We'd just had our child and we got death threats. We had to put sand on the floor and screw up our letter box. You don't realize how strong the fear was. I tried to get our phone number changed because it was terrifying my wife. It was always, 'You fucking nigger lover', 'Red cunt'. So we got a system whereby people had to give two rings, put the phone down, two rings, put the phone down and the third time I'd pick it up. But your heart is hurt by these things. You just don't want to hear it. I started having bizarre theories because when you're anti-fascist you read so much stuff about its roots and all this Nordic mystical stuff. The next time somebody phoned I thought, I know, I'll pretend to be the fucking devil to frighten them, so I went, 'Beelzebub is going to fucking burn you. Cunt.' And put the phone down.

ROGER HUDDLE I had a copy of *NF News* pushed through my letter box one night, which was a bit scary because I'd just had a baby. I expected for ages it would be a petrol bomb next. The National Front tried to control the streets in old-time fascist fashion but also went for the ballot box.

WAYNE MINTER The National Front would humiliate and attack mixed communities and the police would at best condone and at worst be complicit. John Dennis and I organized youth from the Socialist Workers Party, quite a lot of whom were Irish, to go and attack the NF on King Street in Hammersmith. If the coppers were around we'd try to hit them before they set up – we'd run at them, give 'em a whack and then clear off and bin the papers. Joe Pearce was the local National Front youth organizer. He was a good speaker and charismatic. We saw him as somebody who had to be dealt with.

LESLEY WOODS The racism amongst young people was a part of disaffected youth wanting to belong to something. They hadn't really thought it through. Fifteen-year-old kids who came from working-class backgrounds went out Paki-bashing because they were bored. When I was about nine this little black girl came up to me in the playground and pointed to this boy and said, 'That boy over there has just told me that my skin is the colour of shit.' I was really stunned. I was like, 'Your skin's a really beautiful colour.'

CLARE SHORT The National Front had a demonstration in an Asian area and we called a counterdemonstration in the middle of Birmingham, but everybody wanted to go over there and stop them. And of course that was right because their candidate would go on to poll almost 3,000 votes in Stechford, ironically the same constituency where Enoch Powell was born. Their vote peaked at around 15 to 17 per cent broadly across the country, which is very high in local elections.

DAVE WAKELING There was a big march in Handsworth when the National Front had a candidate running. A lot of us were working on building sites and pretty good with bricks, and people were throwing Molotov cocktails so policemen's ankles set on fire where the street was full of petrol. But then, walking home, I didn't feel so clever about it. Somehow the National Front had managed to get us lot to act just as animalistic as they were and in some ways they'd won by that, in the same way as Margaret Thatcher by being so bitter and divisive could force us to become bitter and divisive. At home, I was looking at the *I Ching* and in it was why violence didn't work and why you had to go to such an extent to have your opinion prevail. It was saying, all the fight has done is sharpen both swords, and the image in the book was two swords, which became a song on the first Beat record: *Two swords slashing at each other / Only sharpen one another / And in the long run even he's your brudda / Even though the cunt's a Nazi.*

RANKING ROGER At these demonstrations there'd be about 200 National Front and 3,000 of us. You'd go, 'Where are all the black people, man?' But I saw it as the way the country was on a bigger scale; the majority of people are actually against this.

ROGER HUDDLE Trotsky said, 'Fascism is the politics of despair and communism is the politics of hope.' As the seventies unrolled despair became the dominant factor.

TIM WELLS A lot of the middle-class left failed because it had nothing to offer working-class people. Fascism acts against an organized working class and is against unions. It acts in favour of bosses. I don't see fascism as a black and white problem. You can be fervently fascist without having an issue with race. The political problem is to convince the white working class they're being used. That is the difference between anti-racism and anti-fascism. And there was fascism and racism at gigs. Bands were targeted. And that needed to be confronted directly, physically and politically – a lot of the mobs were bullies and weren't that active politically but because a couple of active fascists would put themselves about a bit, young impressionable people would follow them. If the ringleaders were confronted and the bloke has gone down it's, 'Fuck that. I'm not following him anymore.' If that stopped them actively on the streets, if it stopped them putting shit through people's letter boxes, if it stopped them firebombing shops, that was a good thing. You've neutralized them even if you haven't converted them to your way of thinking.

DAVE RUFFY You used to get NF contingents at gigs. There was a lot more violence at gigs per se. If you thought about it too much you'd fucking shit it. Our manager, Andy, was fearless. He wouldn't have it. There'd be one or two troublemakers and he would go straight for the toughest one and then say, 'And I'll do you, you and you. Who wants it?' He was really strong. He'd just front it when most people would fucking run.

JOHN JENNINGS Andy would usually come out with a skinhead under each arm. At Essex University they were all Sieg-Heiling and it kicked off; the bouncers all disappeared so [our singer] Malcolm dived into the audience. Andy saw his boy going in and these skinheads jumped on him and were just kicking him. He came out on all fours, clapped his hands together, and went back in and grabbed two of them and went bang into the wall with two of their heads. He wasn't that violent. He was just taking care of business. He could handle himself and wouldn't stand for injustice. I'd like to think that Rock Against Racism and the Anti-Nazi League [ANL] and the things that we were doing quashed it. It gave the youth a chance to have something to belong to.

CHRIS BOLTON One night we played an RAR gig and someone came in and said, 'The National Front are meeting downstairs.' My greatest weapon is my ability to use my tongue with my brain in charge, so about eight of us went down and they sent out their biggest guy to intimidate us. I said, 'Terry, what are you fucking doing in there with that lot?' He had been in my brother's class at school and I had taught him boxing. He did a 'cherry' [went red-faced] and went home. We barricaded the others in and said, 'Leave them in there,' and then went and finished the gig.

JAKE BURNS I saw the Ruts at the Nashville where there was a huge fight. It was absolutely packed and this young skinhead girl couldn't get to the bar and my girlfriend said, 'Here, have some of mine.' The girl said, 'Thanks. And since you've been nice to me I'll warn you there's going to be a huge fight about to start right here.' So we knew it was orchestrated.

And then Stiff Little Fingers started to attract a right-wing following and people would Sieg-Heil at a few shows. It was worrying and it was difficult to work out how to deal with it. Jim would throw drumsticks at them and a couple of times it descended into punch-ups. It was a difficult balance because you were trying to stop people getting hurt and at the same time you were trying to put people down for doing it. It didn't matter what you were trying to say or what your background was; any band that was perceived as punk was fair game. There was a review of us which finished with, 'The Sham trap is right ahead of you. Put your foot right here.'

FRANCES SOKOLOV There was an incident where we were playing and the stewards wanted to ban some kids coming in because they were associated with the right wing. That set up a very negative vibe between us and Rock Against Racism because we had an open-door policy. We thought it was healthier to talk through these things rather than get into polarizing with banning people. People were being used by the right who were manipulating groups of young lads who needed the gang culture. I don't think a lot of them knew what they were talking about. Sometimes the nastiest-looking lads would come up to us after a gig and would say, 'I really liked the gentle songs you did, Vi.' As far as I was concerned they were other people's children.

RICHARD SWALES I am sure that most of the 'right-wing' kids of the late seventies had no more idea of the politics of the National Front than I had of Maoism when I was sixteen and trying desperately to appear cool. We thought it was better to talk to them than to not talk to them. I have a diary of all the gigs we did at that time and just about every one of them says, 'Trouble', 'Tense atmosphere'. We knew what the signs were when a fight was about to start. There would be a group of maybe ten skinheads and they would move very quickly across the room and attack somebody. Our idea was to put some people in between them and that actually nearly always defused the situation. If there was fighting we would stop playing.

Generally, it was just a really bad atmosphere, but we did get attacked on stage. At the Theatre Royal in Stratford I got knocked out by a beer can, the guitar player got hit by an umbrella and the sound guy got beaten up.

KATE WEBB There was massive anxiety about the Front coming into those halls, but there was no one at the centre of RAR who validated what should or could happen. So if somebody experienced something going wrong and went, 'Oh, that's RAR'; Who's RAR? Anybody could stand up and say, 'I'm RAR.'

DOTUN ADEBAYO With all of these things there is a beginning, middle and an end; and the National Front was the end of punk for me. The punk message had been compromised. An element was coming in that was being usurped by the extreme right. Of course, we fought the National Front if they marched down our street saying 'niggers out', but a lot of the anger at places like the Notting Hill Carnival riots was fighting institutional racism and police oppression or your lot as a black man; not being able to find suitable accommodation. People talk about 'No Dogs, No Wogs, No Irish' from the fifties but that was still going on in 1977. The whole frustration of young black Britons at that point was not about the National Front. It was almost insignificant. I'm talking about from a street level, not from an intellectual level, because you can talk to people who were active politically in the black community and they'd say the fight against the National Front was fundamental.

PAULINE BLACK The police used to collude; they would not actively restrain those tendencies and it was in their interest for things to kick off. It was reprehensible what used to go on around Notting Hill and at the Carnival. I used to go down every now and then and the more conscious young white people that were around punk, albeit through smoking weed, found some common cause with black people and reggae.

JULIET DE VALERO WILLS There was a smell around Notting Hill that came off the pavements. You had an absolute sense that you were in the middle of something happening. The Carnival was a rare expression of confident black identity in Britain and could often get violent, triggered by a deep mistrust between black youths and the police. You'd have a lot of white onlookers but few taking part. There was no language or real understanding between them.

CAROL GRIMES I was living in All Saints Road in Westbourne Grove, loosely known by its residents as the Grove. My bedroom window overlooked a cafe called the Mangrove which was run by a wonderful man called Frank Crichlow. He was pretty much daddy for the African Caribbean community in the area. There was a lot of harassment and restrictions being put on by the local police which the local community leaders didn't like. Then the community suddenly exploded at the Carnival. It had been a peaceful, enjoyable event that the locals really looked forward to but a lot of kids would go round using it as an excuse to tea-leaf; wallets in pockets and whatever. These things can start off very small and before you know it, it's like the domino effect; it only takes one small incident. It happened on the last night and I was horror-struck. I have a memory of piling loads of kids up in my flat. It was chaos. The Boogie Band had a gig that night at the Hope and Anchor in Islington. I rang up the venue and said, 'We're stuck.' 'Yeah, yeah, you're just having a good time at the Carnival. I know you lot. You're probably pissed.' I said, 'Turn on the telly.'

ROBERT ELMS I have a very distinct memory of walking in Notting Hill dressed as a punk and there was a line of riot police stopping people, and I said, 'Can we get through, please?' and a copper said, 'Why do you want to go in there; it's just full of niggers?' I thought, 'Fuck you.' So when it kicked off I knew exactly what side I was on. Those black kids were righteous. They had every reason to be as angry as they were and to show that they were just not going to put up with it.

Notting Hill Gate Carnival, 30 August 1976.

BRINSLEY FORDE We were driving to rehearsal in a friend of mine's white Hillman Hunter and the police were following us. I remember banging and doing percussion and hitting the car and that's how 'Three Babylon' started. My great memory was, after we'd recorded it we had these bright yellow T-shirts printed with the original lion on them for the Carnival. We played on the corner of Basing Street and Lancaster Road on this little stage and said, 'This is our new single: *Three Babylon try to make I and I run / They come to have fun with their long truncheons'*. When we finished we started to pack the gear in the van and someone shouted, 'Babylon a-come,' and that was the start of the riots. They came tearing around the Portobello Road. During all of it we were out there looking for our family to try and get them back to a place that was safe: 'I've got Mum. Where's my sister?' It was like a war zone. That night after it all quietened down we were playing at the club in Ladbroke Grove and all the police were outside. I didn't think we were coming out of there. I thought, 'That's it. The police are going to charge in,' but we did the gig and came out.

SYD SHELTON Aswad had forged their teeth at the Carnival. The police had a ritualistic 'putting people back in their place' every year at Notting Hill. The jump squads would go in and arrest people and it would end up with a pitched battle on the streets; every year, year after year. It was about being 'under heavy manners' – a phrase used by Jamaicans in 1976 to describe the state of emergency and state oppression – and if the police could convince the community and the politicians that there was an epidemic of mugging and the people that were doing it were black male youth, they could increase the sus laws without problem.

•

DAVID WIDGERY The National Front's first big demonstration of 1977 was planned for April, through a multicultured inner-city suburb where long-standing Jewish and Irish citizens had been joined by post-war migrants from the Caribbean, Cyprus, India and Pakistan. A loose alliance of political and ethnic groups including the local Labour and Communist parties united to oppose the Wood Green march.[17]

DOTUN ADEBAYO You could walk on Wood Green High Street and there'd be white guys selling copies of the National Front magazine *Bulldog* outside Marks & Spencer's. And this was a heavily black area.

WAYNE MINTER Wood Green was the first time I'd gone on a demonstration, and there were 3,000 people on the streets opposing the National Front. As soon as they came round the corner, red smoke canisters came over. BOOM! The whole street was full of smoke. Everybody just piled in. I thought, 'God. This is not Britain anymore.'

BOB HUMM People linked arms. I looked down afterwards and I had a woman's handbag on my arm.

DOTUN ADEBAYO I remember running up to the stage that the Front had erected and shouting, 'The National Front *is* an affront,' which I thought was hilarious. And then I got trapped in a backstreet when it all kicked off. I was suddenly surrounded by police and NF. The cops looked at me and said, 'You can go towards them or come towards us.'

SYD SHELTON There was a Freeman Hardy Willis right next to us and when they started marching we all just grabbed the shoes and started throwing them at the NF. I got arrested and was put in a cell.

MIKE HOBART We were chucking bricks and baiting them about their sexuality, mainly about being up the bosses' arse. You could see someone getting red in the face and losing their temper and then they'd try and break through.

RUTH GREGORY The police marched the Front through the demonstrators while people were throwing smoke bombs and all sorts of stuff at the police, but we didn't manage to stop them. I got arrested for throwing a brick but I actually threw a pebble. A couple of police started running towards me so I ducked into the crowd and they followed me and dragged me out. When I came to court the arresting police officer looked like a very young Michael York. He was absolutely gorgeous-looking with his blond hair and blue eyes and I just trusted him. But he got up and said he'd seen me throw a brick, so I got a fine and spent a night in jail.

RED SAUNDERS The papers were saying, 'It's warfare on the streets. What's happening to the country?'

COLIN BARKER And then between Wood Green and Lewisham at the end of the summer there was the Grunwick strike, which was a really important shift.

ROBERT ELMS There was a big dispute at Grunwick in North London near Cricklewood of a load of Asian women who worked in a photo-processing factory. They were on crap money and conditions and they went on strike for about a year. There was a big picket every week.

WAYNE MINTER It was fucking grim at Grunwick's. We'd been there the whole winter. It was bloody cold and numbers were getting fewer and fewer. The police had been basically letting the buses in with the scabs and battering back anybody who was demonstrating outside. Every morning the strike committee would come out and stand outside the gates with all these huge coppers around them and this little lady at the centre of the dispute, Jayaben Desai. The police were dragging the pickets behind the privet hedges and giving them a good kicking, and we'd film them. There was this rumour that the miners were going to come down and 'see off the police', and eventually they did turn up.

ROBERT ELMS Arthur Scargill from the Yorkshire National Union of Mineworkers brought the miners down, and the steelworkers from Sheffield. I was just in awe of these guys. I remember thinking, 'This is my class's big battalions.'

WAYNE MINTER It was incredible. We were standing there and you just saw the tops of the banners coming up the hill and you could hear the brass band playing behind them. Two hundred miners pushed straight through all the police and set up in front of the gates. It was absolutely incredible. Everyone went bonkers. You'd go off for a cup of tea and there'd be Yorkshire miners, who are probably not the most politically sophisticated people, sat in cafes with Asian women in saris talking politics. The next day the police were bashing everybody to pieces again but it was an incredibly uplifting moment.

JOHN DENNIS When the miners came down we surrounded the factory and stopped the buses of scabs coming in. The police had to turn round and go away. Standing in that crowd, that mass picket, it was like being at a huge gig when you love the artist and the hairs on the back of your neck stand up and you think, 'Oh my God.' RAR was the opportunity to recreate that experience.

LUCY WHITMAN There were a lot of susceptible young people who wanted some excitement in their life. RAR came on the scene and articulated the issues.

PAUL HOLBOROW Shortly after the strike, the National Front announced an 'anti-mugging' march in Lewisham, and the Socialist Workers Party initiated a crucial counterdemonstration in conjunction with other local organizations. We mobilized about 8,000–10,000 people, largely made up of young black kids and the local community. Lewisham had been deliberately chosen by the NF as an area of high Afro-Caribbean population where the police had been operating a policy known as PNH: Police Nigger Hunt.

SYD SHELTON In early June the police raided houses in Lewisham and New Cross, literally smashing down front doors at five o'clock in the morning. I had done two or three rolls of film on this black family called the Fosters who were typical of that 1950s Afro-Caribbean *Windrush* generation: very law-abiding, kid brought up to go to church every Sunday and polish his shoes, more the archetypal British family than any British family that I knew of – and they dragged out young people like Christopher Foster, who was sixteen, in his underpants. They threw him into jail and accused him of mugging. They had no evidence. His father, David Foster, started the Campaign for Justice for the Lewisham 21, and his house became the de facto headquarters. The police did all kinds of tricks where they tried to pretend to be friends of the campaign, having arrested lads as young as fourteen, and a couple of girls as well. The National Front picked up on this and it turned into a massive demonstration.

JOHN BAINE Lewisham was a defining moment in modern British anti-fascist history. The Front came boasting that they would control the streets of London.

BERNIE WILCOX We had coaches coming down from St Peter's Square in Manchester. This guy walked along with two sacks. I thought, 'What's he got there?' He started handing out these chair legs. He must have bought a job lot or summat. He said, 'The Front are up at the Grand Hotel on Aytoun Street. Let's go up there.' So we all went up there, smashed the fuck out of their coaches and then went back down to our coach and we were away to London.

DAVID WIDGERY The *official* protest march, including the Catholics, the councillors and the Communists, made indignant speeches about fascism in Lewisham and carefully avoided going within two miles of the fascists, who were assembling behind the British Rail station at New Cross, where the atmosphere was less forgiving. As a group of NFers left New Cross station, I saw a young East London comrade just pick up a brick and lob it at them very coldly.[18]

RED SAUNDERS There'd been a lot of waiting, with people not quite know-ing what was happening. There was a fish and chip shop and launderette on one side and on the other side three-storey terraced houses, and there was some communication going on between an old Caribbean lady on the first floor and some youth. She gets the window open and very purpose-fully takes her geranium pot plants off the windowsill and puts her hi-fi speakers there. BANG! Bob Marley's 'Get Up, Stand Up' comes bellowing out of her speakers and everyone went, 'Yeah!' I went, 'Fuck. This is going to be some day.'

DAVID WIDGERY Almost directly opposite her a Cypriot woman replied with a clenched-fist salute from the first floor of her boarded-up kebab and chips shop. Two minutes later an officer with a megaphone read an order to disperse. No one did; seconds later the police cavalry cantered into sight and sheared through the front row of protestors.[19]

SYD SHELTON At first there was a little bit of a party atmosphere, until the fighting started. There was no way the National Front could have marched through that crowd, it was so dense from one side of the street to the other, so the police cleared a path by charging with horses and swinging batons. People were throwing bits of burning wood and smoke bombs and bricks. I've got a picture and it's just debris, and another picture of these three young kids with bits of braid from the honour guard's Union Jack. They'd dived in and got the lead flag and ripped it to shreds.

BERNIE WILCOX The Front had this triangle of the honour guard. You wouldn't want to mess with these guys. Then they had the flag carriers with Union Jacks. Behind them were John Tyndall and Martin Webster and people like this and behind them was the regular dross. The SWP had this guy who had been in the SPG [Special Patrol Group] and he taught us the 'wedge tactic', which was a police thing where they get into a human wedge: you let twelve rows of the regular dross go through. Then, POW! Split them in two.

RED SAUNDERS These were Cypriot kids not marching quietly into the gas chambers, but burning the Union Jack. They were the same kids I'd seen at Wood Green, who had come down to join the blacks in Lewisham to fight the enemy and kick the shit out of them. They threw flour and eggs and shit all over them. Your enemy's enemy is your friend.

BERNIE WILCOX Because Lewisham had lots of demolished buildings, somebody had quite thoughtfully put all these half-bricks into little piles. We were picking them up and lobbing them in. The NF were in disarray. The police then came back and attacked us on Deptford High Street. There was some old woman that happened to get caught up in it. She was a bit bewildered so I grabbed her and pulled her into this shop doorway. This copper came along and he smashed the window above our heads and all this glass came crashing down. I had to turn my back so it came onto me instead of her.

DAVID WIDGERY At one point, a detachment of twenty-four policemen, shields at the ready, emerged from the police station and met head-on a fusillade of bricks and bottles.[20]

SYD SHELTON There was no doubt whose side the police were on in those days. We knew a lot of NFers who were policemen and they had buses waiting for the Front at the other end of Lewisham High Street and bussed them out. That's when they brought the riot shields out. Red said they were like plastic cupboard doors – it was the first time they'd been used in main-land Britain. And then it became a battle between us and the police – 110 injuries were reported, of which 50 were police, and 214 arrests. It went on till way after dark. I remember getting home feeling absolutely exhausted

Lewisham demonstration, 13 August 1977.

because I'd been running, fighting, taking photos, trying to get into good vantage points from one end of Lewisham to the other, since about eight, nine o'clock in the morning.

WAYNE MINTER An hour before the Front was due to pass in the morning I was at the crossroad at the top of New Cross Road in an empty property at the top of this block above a disused shop, ready to film it all. And we had a load of youth in there too who were making Anti-Nazi League lollipops and Rock Against Racism banners. We had this old video camera, which was a two-person job, so I had a thing round my neck with two huge Sony U-matic reels on and John had the camera itself, with a cord connecting us. We were going to film the marchers who came past out of the window. About half an hour before the march went past, the SPG started bashing the door down underneath us. John was filming it. A guy, Danny Philips, leaned out of the window and said, 'Hang on. You don't have to break the door down. I've got the key here.' They completely ignored him and smashed their way in, burst into the room, pinned us against the wall and then arrested us.

RED SAUNDERS John got arrested before he could even film anything. I think he was charged with being the main organizer. He was just a student. The Met were going, 'You're the number one conspirator, making Molotov cocktails.'

WAYNE MINTER During this I'd got the video tape and put it in my sock and put another tape back in the camera. They took all the kit off us and exposed the film out of the cameras: 'Oh dear, your film has been exposed.' After they'd taken us away, a group of marchers came down and protested outside Ladywell police station and set a police motorbike alight whilst we were in there.

JOHN DENNIS I'd never been in jail before. It was horrific. We were bundled in a two-person cell with about twelve other people. I got kicked out about four in the morning but they gave me back all the video stuff.

WAYNE MINTER We were released later on and charged with conduct likely to cause a breach of the peace. When we came out, which was five hours after everything had finished, it was incredible. We were walking through the debris in the streets and there was this incredible feeling that the Front had been stopped. There had been a massive attempt to stop the march legally. All of the arguments were brought out. You can't allow the fascists to march through a large area of population and intimidate people. They completely ignored that. It was a complete victory. They were absolutely annihilated. I knew people in the Front who admitted that: 'We just got done. We got a damn good hiding. The bloody hippies fought back.' But hundreds of people got arrested and were sent to the magistrates' court in Camberwell. They were being processed for months afterwards. The Front turned up and were attacking people going in. We had to organize protection. We had a great lawyer, Danny Philips, who had also been arrested, who said to the magistrate, 'We can save you and everybody else an awful lot of time if you'll just admit that our clients weren't causing any disturbance at all; some of them were making placards; they didn't resist entry to the police.' But the police wouldn't accept this. So we showed the film.

JOHN DENNIS It was hilarious because someone puts their head out the window, 'Hang on a minute, we'll let you in. Don't break down the door.' It was so clear it was a bullshit charge. People didn't like the SWP, they didn't like the riot or want the violence, but they certainly didn't want the National Front.

WAYNE MINTER We got away with it because they didn't know you can't expose U-matic video tape. It was beautiful. It ends with me and John being pulled down the stairs. We all got off apart from two sixteen-year-old kids who admitted to stapling ANL lollipops onto a stick, because a stick can be construed as a weapon.

SYD SHELTON The youth who had grown up in multiracial, multicultural inner cities were not racist. The truth of the inner city was quite a different place from what both the police and the National Front tried to exploit.

WAYNE MINTER Lewisham was the real tipping point. After, there was such a burgeoning sense of power and liberation in the anti-racist and anti-fascist movement. It's horrible to talk about the glorification of violence as actually achieving anything, but the fact was that people had actually gone out there and defied the Front and the police and the establishment, and said, 'We're not having it.' The soundtrack to Lewisham was Rock Against Racism.

SYD SHELTON Tony Parsons and Julie Burchill wrote a piece in the *NME* which concluded, 'Perhaps you think this wasn't your battle. Tell it to the blacks. Tell it the SWP. Tell it to Rock Against Racism. Over to you.' We were elated and it helped to swell our numbers. The Front hadn't marched unopposed and the local community had joined with loony lefties like us in opposing them. It was a day of fantastic unity. It had broken down barriers between people. We wrote a reply that said, 'It's too late for love and peace; we need some heavy unity and the courage to fight back. The black youth know it already; it's time we caught up with them. ROCK AGAINST RACISM.'

BERNIE WILCOX When the *NME* wrote about Lewisham, that was it. The headline was 'DEDICATED FOLLOWERS OF FASCISM'. It was the first time that politics entered the music press and from that day on it became cool to be an anti-racist.

NEIL SPENCER The *NME* thought Lewisham was really fucking important. The National Front marching through black South London: What the fuck? No way. You don't know what happened in the 1930s in Germany? The police were heavily recruited by the National Front. You've got to stand up.

TOM ROBINSON At Lewisham, at Wood Green, the appearance was that the police were on the side of the fascists because they were protecting them and holding us back. They would have said, 'We're keeping the peace,' but from where we stood it looked like there wasn't much between them. The Met was pretty much out of control and it didn't seem out of the question that at some point, if the chaos got worse, they could make a serious bid for power.

RED SAUNDERS In Lewisham we pulled back the Union Jack to reveal the swastika underneath. Something cultural was happening in Britain that had never happened before, in terms of black and white youth working together in a progressive way to try to stop the rise of fascism in Britain. You cannot believe the terror that the NF were striking into us all. They were street gangs. They weren't people discussing things. This was a gang who would come up and smash your fucking face in, who'd smash your pub up, who'd smash your bookshop, your stalls. This was fascism. This was like brownshirts in Germany and Italy smashing in their opposition. Hitler's great quote was, 'Only one thing could have stopped our movement – if our adversaries had understood its principle and from the first day had smashed with the utmost brutality the nucleus of our new movement.'

RUTH GREGORY And then they firebombed Acklam Hall and the Albany Empire. Both incidents came three weeks after Martin Webster told *The*

Times, 'It will be very interesting to see how these people like a taste of their own medicine . . . they are going to reap the whirlwind.'

BOB HUMM We had regular RAR gigs at the Albany and the fire was attributed to the right because it was seen as a political, left-wing place. The next day a note was pushed through the door which read, 'GOT YOU'. And there was also the Moonshot Club, which was a black club and advice centre, and that got burnt down too.

RED SAUNDERS Why would you petrol-bomb the Albany – the Albany, which was multiracial, black, Asian and white in South London? – because niggers play drums there. That's why. The Albany was culture. Nazis don't like culture. They were coming from both sides so you got the street fascist: 'Fucking burn niggers,' and then you'd got the suit-and-tie Nazi: 'Hold on, we're standing a candidate here.'

PETER HAIN Lewisham was very important. From the SWP's point of view they had confronted the National Front, but it had got out of hand and discredited the cause. It had been seen as a battle against the police rather than a battle against the National Front. The publicity around it was very negative. That made the more thoughtful SWP people, like Paul Holborow, think, 'We've got to do this in a different way.' I didn't condone violence. It's one thing to say, 'We're not going to be moved,' but I didn't ever approve of attacking them. I've been quite honest about conceding that if you are campaigning on the basis of confrontation there's a danger of violence happening. The alternative was to do nothing and let them swagger through, intimidating local people: synagogues being attacked, evangelical churches being attacked, people being physically assaulted and frightened out of their lives. I thought, 'Better to take the risk whilst marshalling it as carefully as possible.'

NEIL KINNOCK This dilemma exists which is: do you attack them and inevitably get them more attention or do you stay silent and deny them attention? But the National Front know they are likely to provoke: the reason they dress like they do, the reason they talk like they do, the reason they always move in groups, the reason that they have incendiary demonstrations in particular places, is in order to manifest aggression.

ONE DOWN, A MILLION TO GO

Anti-Nazi League

PAUL HOLBOROW Lewisham was a decisive moment in the fight against the Nazis but the Socialist Workers Party suffered a barrage of press abuse. The Paymaster General, Shirley Williams, was prominent in denouncing us, and Michael Foot, who was the employment secretary, said, 'You don't stop the Nazis by throwing bottles or bashing the police. The most ineffective way of fighting the fascists is to behave like them.' We were branded the 'Red fascists'. But the message from all quarters was basically, 'We don't agree with the Socialist Workers Party but we do agree the Nazis have to be stopped.' And so Jim Nichol, National Secretary, myself and the founder of the SWP, Tony Cliff, decided to set up the Anti-Nazi League, which was to be a single-issue united front focused on stopping the rise of the Nazis.

RED SAUNDERS The Socialist Workers Party and some of their leading intellectuals, knowing their history – 'They Shall Not Pass' in Cable Street, and the Anti-Nazi League in Hollywood in the thirties in which Dorothy Parker was a founder member – decided to form a broad-based organization. People said the Anti-Nazi League was a front organization of the SWP. It couldn't have been. It had to be broad-based. SWP activists were strong, committed anti-fascists so you had to have that central core. Once they started to roll it was a real juggernaut.

PAUL HOLBOROW There was a tradition in British Labour history of 'anti-leagues' and we wanted to make it straightforward and use the pejorative title 'Nazi' in order to pin the description on them from the beginning. The Anti-Nazi League arose out of a period from 1970 through to 1977 whereby there had been the growth of the National Front under Martin Webster and John Tyndall. Martin Webster in particular was a very effective organizer and dragged the National Front from their openly Nazi origins to making a serious electoral challenge. That reached its high point on two occasions: in the West Bromwich by-election in May 1973 when Webster got 16 per cent of the vote; and secondly, in the GLC elections of 1977 when the

National Front got 119,000 votes and knocked the Liberal Party into fourth place in about thirty-one of the ninety-two constituencies.

COLIN BARKER Some people said it was too stark but actually it was its selling point. We said, 'That's what they are. They're Nazis.'

PAUL HOLBOROW Within their ranks they had people who denied the Holocaust; John Tyndall said, '*Mein Kampf* is my doctrine,' Martin Webster said, 'We are busy building a well-oiled Nazi machine in this country.' The essential point is that there was an umbilical connection between their leaders and their forebearing Nazi predecessors.

PETER HAIN The National Front was an overtly Nazi organization. We had photos of some of their leaders wearing Nazi regalia. I put my reputation on the line. I'd only just joined the Labour Party and there was suspicion about the Anti-Nazi League's SWP connection on the back of Lewisham. You can have your disagreements about the parliamentary or the revolutionary socialist road but what mattered was unity in action against the threat of the National Front. There are a lot of people on the left who are all-or-nothing people and I'd always been an all-or-something person; that in going for 100 per cent you constantly fail to succeed. I'd rather aim

Anti-Nazi League poster.

at a more practical lower level and achieve something. I tried to build bridges and we pulled people round when they realized that this was an organization that was more than just opposed to anti-Semitism. And that it was the best way of exposing, attacking and getting into what the NF was about. It was a very simple message and it just caught on. Suddenly this popular movement developed.

PAUL HOLBOROW I was organizing secretary, and the key person I drew into the project was Peter Hain, who had a good reputation running press campaigns, particularly in opposition to the earlier South African rugby and cricket tours. Through Peter, Neil Kinnock joined the steering committee. So we had the hard left represented by the SWP, Peter Hain who represented both the young Liberal and Labour Party element, and the third key component was Ernie Roberts, who was the assistant general secretary of the Engineering Union and represented the trade unions which were heavily influenced by the Communist Party. And then we got the Indian Workers' Association aboard and several other key Labour MPs.

PETER HAIN Neil Kinnock was quite important in stabilizing the Labour Party.

NEIL KINNOCK I was a young backbench Labour MP and the Anti-Nazi League was pretty unpopular in some quarters. People said, 'We're not in the 1930s. What is this bloody nonsense?' But eventually we got people from trade unions and the Communist Party and then the Labour Party.

COLIN BARKER It made electoral sense for Labour to have a big anti-fascist operation to undermine the National Front. They were mindful of the forthcoming election. After Neil Kinnock, two dozen Labour MPs signed up.

PAUL HOLBOROW We had a very successful launch at the House of Commons followed by a number of press stunts. Manfred Roeder, a former SS officer, came to launch his book in London and I burst into the press conference with an ANL poster, which made the news. Also there had been the murder of Gurdip Singh Chaggar, which had prompted John Kingsley Read, who was the former chairman of the National Front and a councillor in Blackburn, to say, 'One down, a million to go.' Read was charged with racial incitement. And at the Old Bailey, Judge McKinnon acquitted him. I stood up in the public gallery and shouted, 'Your remarks have led to the acquittal of a Nazi . . . it's an affront to black people in this country.' I was grabbed by seven policemen and marched out of the building. So that also attracted huge publicity and made the front page of the *Evening Standard*.

As a result of Neil Kinnock, the Labour Party had a party political broadcast in 1977 devoted exclusively to the dangers posed by the National Front. Neil was much more radical than he subsequently turned out to be and therefore we had very good information about the internal discussions inside the Labour Party. They were worried they were going to lose votes to the National Front. Always, the backbone of fascist movements is the lower middle classes: small businessmen, shopkeepers, people who are the first to feel the cold winds of economic depression and recession; people not buying in their shops, savings being eaten away, not being able to maintain their respectable slot above the working class.

COLIN BARKER I was charged with setting up a Manchester branch and he wanted me to get academics on board. I phoned up this guy called Valdo Pons who was a white South African and a lecturer in sociology at Hull University. He said, 'My parents recently died in South Africa and up to now I've never signed anything because I didn't want to compromise their situation, but now I can. Furthermore, I'll give you a list of all the academics who I think will sign as well.' I wrote to them all, and all but one of them said yes. Then we heard that Glenda Jackson had signed. Oh wow! All those professors were suddenly terribly pleased: a famous Royal Shakespeare Company actress. Then we got Michael Parkinson but he later withdrew his support, as did Melvyn Bragg and the footballer Jack Charlton, because an edition of the youth paper of the Anti-Nazi League used the word 'fuck' in a poem.

PAUL HOLBOROW It was alleged Michael Parkinson objected to the expletive. And Jack Charlton was quoted saying, 'It seems the League has set itself up as an organization that intends to meet force with force, and I'm not going along with that kind of thing.' We also had a stiff argument with Arthur Scargill, but the row was very quickly abatted.

PETER HAIN There was initially hostility from the Jewish community. I went to see the Board of Deputies who were hostile to the Socialist Workers Party because of its quite aggressive anti-Zionist stance. *Searchlight* was initially hostile for the same reasons. They both came on board, but there was a certain reserve amongst others, which was fine.

PAUL HOLBOROW Miriam Karlin was important because the Jewish community was split on how to deal with the Nazis. Miriam was a very

prominent Jewish actress and an active Zionist. It was an incredibly deli-
cate issue because the Board of Deputies was also obviously pro-Israel. I
was very honest with her and said, 'I'm an anti-Zionist, but what unites us
is opposition to the Nazis in this country.'

PETER HAIN People look back at the Anti-Nazi League and think it was a
fantastic success but at the time it was quite hard launching and establishing it. We were strongly opposed by a lot of the established anti-racist
groups because they saw it as ideologically unsound under the anti-Nazi
banner. They thought you weren't dealing with institutional racism, which
I didn't dissent from, but my view was, 'What is the most effective strategy
at this particular moment?' It was an organic growth from below which is
what excited me. There was a central committee but it wasn't dictating or
controlling. If you were living in Melton Mowbray or Bognor Regis and you
wanted to set up an ANL, you did it.

NEIL KINNOCK Within months we had School Kids Against the Nazis
[SKAN], Teachers Against the Nazis. Skateboarders Against the Nazis.

WAYNE MINTER We had a Skateboarders Against the Nazis sticker in red
and green with chevrons; the perfect size to stick underneath your skate-
board so when you did a rampart you'd see these colours go WHOOSH!

ROGER HUDDLE We had Firework Night Against the Nazis, Bus Workers
Against the Nazis, Postmen Against the Nazis, Women Against the Nazis.
And they all had hundreds of different badges that they wore to work: in
the factory, in the office. It was more and more difficult for the Nazis to
open their mouth. We got a lot of SKAN kids from an all-girls school in
Walthamstow, where the NF was really strong and selling their paper on
the street. They occupied the school hall so they couldn't have their meeting. Tony Cliff always used to say, 'The reason you get a Nazi is because the
person that hurts the worker is in government and you can't get hold of
them, you're powerless, so you turn on your neighbour.'

PAUL HOLBOROW We had near forty occupational subgroups: Vegetarians
Against the Nazis, Students Against the Nazis, Civil Servants Against the
Nazis, Miners Against the Nazis who in Yorkshire went to work with ANL
stickers on their helmets. And Teachers Against the Nazis, where the ILEA
[Inner London Education Authority] and the NUT [National Union of
Teachers] issued teacher packs about the dangers of the Nazis and the
Holocaust. You could become a member of the Anti-Nazi League and
people would send you ten shillings or £500; some people gave us £5,000.

We never had a problem with donations. There was one paper merchant in Stratford who gave us all the newsprint we required, and their lorries would drive up outside the print shop with huge rolls for us to print leaflets on. It was a huge operation. I was absolutely focused on using every method possible to broaden us out and to get activists involved. I've calculated we produced ten million leaflets with many different colours and templates and we had up to forty different leaflets to match. We had the slogan 'Let a hundred flowers bloom.'

COLIN BARKER The National Front was going to march in Hyde but the incredibly reactionary Chief Constable of Manchester, James Anderton, banned it. Instead, Martin Webster had to walk solo and was protected by 2,500 police. A young Asian woman, Ramila Patel, from the Bolton Asian Youth Movement, walked in front of Webster as he was having his 'right of free speech demonstration', holding a placard that said, 'This man is a Nazi.' It was beautiful. We had a demonstration outside where the National Front was having a public meeting and this box of badges arrived: bright yellow with a red arrow. They sold like hot cakes.

GEOFF BROWN I was the guy who always made sure there were enough leaflets and badges. Within a few months you couldn't walk through Manchester without seeing people wearing badges. If you were anybody in Manchester and you were on the left I reckon we got you. We tried to have a very light touch. This was not an organization which had endless meetings. There was lots of activity. We had paint-outs where we'd knock on doors and say, 'There's racist graffiti in the park: can we get together and clear it up?'

COLIN BARKER I gave out leaflets to children at the local secondary school and the headmaster came out and berated me. I argued back and the kids were really enjoying the confrontation. On the Sunday afternoon of the paint-out several dozen people came, and the cleaning materials were provided by *Granada Reports*. Their presenter, Bob Greaves, asked Violet Carson, who played Ena Sharples in *Coronation Street*, to sign up and she said, 'How dare you ask me such a question.' She was a Tory through and through. Jim Allen, who was a Trotskyite, was writing the scripts for *Coronation Street* and in one episode when Ken Barlow returned from an evening class his wife said, 'What did you learn?' 'We read about Trotsky.' 'And what did you make of it?' 'I think he was right.' That was the extent of what Jim could politically smuggle in.

GEOFF BROWN There was a Youth Against the Nazis conference and they decided to make 21 March 1978 a national day for leafleting outside football grounds. Peter Hain said, 'We must take our banners onto the football terraces to oppose their Nazi banners and their racist chants.' I remember us going to Old Trafford to leaflet there. We had a special badge made: 'Reds Against the Nazis.'

PAUL HOLBOROW The National Front was interested in football fans because they thought they were into street fighting. Racist chanting in the seventies was common at football grounds when there were very few black players, so it took some courage to leaflet those places.

WAYNE MINTER It started at Nottingham Forest where the NF had a big following. Brian Clough, the team manager, was completely non-racist and was fantastic, not least because of the club's initials, NF. He introduced Viv Anderson as captain and he became the first black player to get into the England team. Anderson used to get barracked with banana chants. Clough walked out onto the pitch and addressed the fans: 'I will not have racism in my club. I'm not standing for it.' He became one of the first sponsors of the Anti-Nazi League. And then Tottenham, who obviously had a problem with fascists because of their huge Jewish following, formed Spurs Against the Nazis.

COLIN BARKER When Clough put his name to the statement it was front-page news in the *Daily Mirror*. And the same day Jackie Charlton signed. It was a real breakthrough. All of a sudden we were real news, and we hadn't done anything yet.

GEOFF BROWN Clough said, 'When you tread in something on the street you don't talk to it, you scrape it off your shoe. Nazism is just as much a disease as cholera, leprosy and smallpox and it must be must treated to stop it spreading. I believe the Front must be removed from the life of this country and I will play my part in whatever way I can.'

COLIN BARKER When you joined the Anti-Nazi League you got the famous statement by Pastor Niemöller on the membership card.

ROGER HUDDLE Paul Holborow said, 'We need a logo for the Anti-Nazi League,' and David King came up with the red arrow and the slogan 'Never Again', which was taken from the anti-Nazi movement in Germany in the 1920s when they would stencil a red arrow over the posters in the street.

First they came for the Jews
and I did not speak out —
because I was not a Jew
Then they came for the communists
and I did not speak out —
because I was not a communist
Next they came for the trade unionists
and I did not speak out —
because I was not a trade unionist
Then they came for me
and there was no one left
to speak out for me
Pastor Niemoeller
Victim of the Nazis of Germany

member's card £1

Anti-Nazi League membership card.

PAUL HOLBOROW David was highly influenced by Weimar Republic iconography and he did a number of key posters for us. He was a nightmare to work with because he was such a perfectionist.

NEIL KINNOCK The ANL was very deliberately and quite aggressively using artwork and evocative photographs. We had one poster that gave the result of a local government by-election in Stepney and Poplar, where the National Front had got 19 per cent of the vote, with a big picture of Auschwitz. Then we used a photograph of Waffen-SS in helmets and jackboots. We unmercifully and relentlessly went after the National Front and their connection with the history of fascism. But we never stood for organizing or attempting physical assault.

PAUL HOLBOROW The National Front was a legitimate political party in the eyes of the state, which gave them protection. But the National Socialist Party in Germany was a legitimate political party, so our argument was simple: if the National Front were allowed to march then we meet them and mobilize the maximum number of people to block their way, just as we had done at Cable Street in 1936. We didn't want to draw a line between people who wanted to physically confront the Nazis and people who wanted to propagandize against them. The formulation in our founding statement had been very carefully worded: '. . . wherever the Nazis attempt to organize, they must be countered.'

COLIN BARKER The purpose of the Anti-Nazi League was to bring the largest number of people out into an open declaration against the Nazis and build a counterforce against them in elections.

GEOFF BROWN Matching violence with violence was a question of, when was it appropriate? Most people who got involved in the Anti-Nazi League never saw any violence at all. We didn't break the National Front physically.

PETER HAIN We had a policy of confronting in the Anti-Nazi League which was very controversial: if you're going to march we're going to be there; we're not out to cause violence; we're not out to attack the police; but we're not going to let you march. Similarly controversial was the policy 'No Platform for Nazis'. In other words, town halls or student unions shouldn't agree to allow them to book their halls to preach their message. I remember a story in the *Sunday Times*, saying 'Peter Hain and the forces of darkness'. This was about a year after the ANL had been launched. If that article had come at the beginning it could have been very difficult for us. We ran the 'Pull the plugs on Nazi thugs' campaign because the National Front were entitled to a party political broadcast. It turned into an issue of free speech. I was arguing that 'You can't defend free speech to preach hatred and violence and racism. That is not free speech. It is a method of attacking.'

COLIN BARKER Margaret Thatcher was running on a very right-wing ticket and came out with that famous quote on *World in Action* in January 1978, '. . . people are really rather afraid that this country might be rather swamped by people with a different culture and, you know, the British character has done so much for democracy, for law, and done so much throughout the world, that if there is any fear that it might be swamped people are going to react and be rather hostile to those coming in.' That was racism. She was talking about a minority; 95 per cent of the population being swamped. Thatcher was bidding for the right-wing vote. This was polite racism.

NEIL KINNOCK I would be the first to acknowledge for all the wrong reasons, by giving a strong appearance, that Mrs Thatcher fully comprehended the anxieties of the British domestic population and by using that word 'swamped' she mitigated the impact of the National Front.

GEOFF BROWN The National Front responded: why vote for the copy when you can get the real thing? We had a very clear distinction between right-wing politics and fascist politics. Fascism is a movement aiming to physically smash the left and trade unions, and the National Front were using physical violence to break up meetings. It was a constant issue.

CLARE SHORT Thatcher further said, 'If you want good race relations, you have got to allay people's fears on numbers . . . what Willie Whitelaw said at the Conservative Party Conference in Brighton, where he said we must hold out the clear prospect of an end to immigration because at the moment it is about between 45,000 and 50,000 people coming in a year. Now, I was brought up in a small town, 25,000. That would be two new towns a year and that is quite a lot. So, we do have to hold out the prospect of an end to immigration.' It was clearly racist. She went for the Union Jack and a lot of that disgruntled working-class, lower middle-class racist vote went to her.

COLIN BARKER You had to physically protect a meeting. You never had to do that against a Tory, however racist they were. I was in a meeting in

Red Saunders at an Anti-Nazi League conference, London, 8 July 1978.

Bolton where everybody was in fear of their lives because there were fascists banging on the windows trying to break into the building.

PAUL HOLBOROW We weren't interested in Tory support. And indeed Malcolm Rifkind, the Conservative MP, on several occasions tried to join the ANL and we evaded his solicitations. We were a Labour movement and a student community-based organization and the hatred of the Tories was deep-seated and emblematic.

•

GEOFF BROWN Rock Against Racism had been set up earlier but the question was, 'How are they actually going to get the masses out onto the streets?'

RED SAUNDERS You've got to link RAR and the ANL together. One wouldn't have had the mass impact without the other. The reality was we were going to get our hands dirty. We were not going to be purists. I believe that society is about class. That's why we were so radically opposed to the National Front, because theirs is a nationalistic race analysis whereas we believed in internationalism. We believed there's class in society and that we're not all in this together. It's different if you're from this class or that class. It was inevitable that as it went on and it grew there was more and more of an element in the supporters of RAR who didn't like the revolutionary socialist element. Some band members would be, 'What is all this fucking left-wing shit?' Some of them hated politics. They weren't sophisticated enough so they'd think all left wing was communism or Stalinism. They had no idea we were libertarian and into sex and drugs and rock 'n' roll.

ROGER HUDDLE The Anti-Nazi League was the mother and Rock Against Racism was the child; not that the ANL gave birth to RAR, but ANL was by far the more important organization because it wasn't a meeting of youth culture. ANL was for all workers. Its agitation and its propaganda was much broader. How would RAR get nurses from the hospital? The Anti-Nazi League went to the hospital. But the people giving out the leaflets were the SWP. So there was an organic link. The SWP understood to fight Nazis you had to have hope. And the hope is in numbers where people don't feel isolated and atomized and alienated but they feel strong, together and united. But Rock Against Racism gave the Anti-Nazi League its core street feel and its imagery, which came from people like me, Red and Syd, who had come from cultural backgrounds. Unofficially, RAR was the cultural wing of the ANL.

PAUL HOLBOROW Rock Against Racism had a great flair and a huge energy and was outside the traditional way the left had previously organized. They were rallying the young punks mainly to an anti-racist position which in itself was quite a challenge, because there were bands who undoubtedly flirted with Nazi ideas. I was aware of punk and pop culture and I was interested in any avenue that would get through to the kids and stop white kids being pulled towards the Nazis. Music was extremely important but RAR was a much smaller organization. The Anti-Nazi League had branches in every town and city across Britain. I would go and do meetings three or four times a week around the country where two or three hundred people would turn up.

PETER HAIN Rock Against Racism wanted to do bigger-scale concerts and we wanted to do anti-Nazi politics. We were sisters and brothers together and we went on our parallel tracts, distinctly, but joined together, and music provided a basis for that dialogue. RAR knew they couldn't deliver without us and we knew that RAR was absolutely indispensable to us because otherwise we were a conventional political campaign. We didn't have that ability to break through to the world that wasn't interested in politics. There was an important role to be played by making a stand in a public place together but I was always more interested in outcomes rather than striking a pose. People were saying, 'What can rock musicians do?' I was interested in what was going to have a practical result. The ANL was reaching the people that would actually do the organizing for these events: the political backbone; the organizational backbone; getting the leaflets printed; the penetration out into the community.

KATE WEBB The ANL was not RAR. The Anti-Nazi League was a political mobilizing organization: a mainstream anti-fascist organization. It had none of the cultural, aesthetic stuff. We were much more anarchic and we needed their structures and organizing capabilities. They had much stronger roots and connections up and down the country, so in smaller places if you were in the ANL group you might also be in the RAR group.

RUTH GREGORY The ANL didn't really get the cultural side of things but they did stand aside and say, 'You know what you're doing,' so you've got to give them that. RAR was totally autonomous. We had a sticker saying, *I and I against the British way of life*; the Anti-Nazi League wouldn't have understood that. We saw it as a direct lineage from the days of Empire and colonialism. You get the message across because you have all your banners and badges. You have a whole array of ways of doing it and you try and do it through music. Tom Robinson used to say something on stage but most of the bands just came on and did their set. It was the whole atmosphere.

WAYNE MINTER We wouldn't have direct political speeches on stage. There was always a stall at every gig, and the politics was in *Temporary Hoarding*. We'd be selling that and we'd give out any that were left to people who didn't have any money. We were disseminating anti-racist information. Red, who'd introduce the bands, might make the odd comment but he certainly wouldn't preach to people from the stage. We were much too sussed for that. You don't educate young people politically by debate necessarily. You educate them by example and by feeling; if they're in a situation where what they've been told or what they might have thought before is contradicted, then that is the best sort of education. I think people are naturally good. The best thing about humans is they help and get on with each other; you set up situations where that's reinforced and celebrated. That's what RAR gigs were. They were very loud, rebellious fun. That's a pretty strong political statement. Most political parties and particularly fascist parties are all about control. It's about telling people what to do and how they should live their lives. Obviously society needs agreement and some sort of order to function so that everybody gets a fair whack, but there's a point where you've got to oppose that. I think we had the right balance.

JOHN DENNIS There were always stresses and strains between Rock Against Racism and the Anti-Nazi League. They had a political agenda. It was not a cultural organization. We wanted a cultural movement that had a political relevance. The ANL had one mission, which was to stop the National Front being elected, and quite rightly focused on that: 'You may be a racist but you're not a Nazi. Don't vote National Front.'

3. OH BONDAGE! UP YOURS!

THIS AIN'T NO FUCKING WOODSTOCK

Carnival Against the Nazis

DAVID WIDGERY What really announced the Anti-Nazi League as a mass movement – a movement which genuinely brought culture and politics into each other's arms and set them dancing – was the alliance with Rock Against Racism in the great outdoor carnival of April 1978.[21] We agreed on the format: a juxtaposition of a meeting in Trafalgar Square and an open-air concert in Victoria Park would make the politics more fun and the music more political. But RAR's unannounced ambition was to turn the event into the biggest piece of revolutionary street theatre London had ever seen, a tenth-anniversary tribute to the Paris events of May 1968.[22]

PAUL HOLBOROW We thought it would be a few thousand people in Victoria Park on a tiny little platform provided by Tower Hamlets council and a couple of stacks of speakers. Until then there hadn't been a demonstration in London of notable scale.

RED SAUNDERS The original idea for a carnival came from Jim Nichol, who was a civil rights lawyer and a member of the Socialist Workers Party. But he wasn't cultural.

RUTH GREGORY The ANL wanted to have the bands on the back of a truck and we said, 'No, no, that won't work.'

SYD SHELTON We said, 'That's Mickey Mouse. We want to do a Rock Against Racism Woodstock. We want it to be on the main evening news; not off-the-back-of-a-lorry stuff.' We used to give out RAR stickers and sell *Temporary Hoarding* at the Notting Hill Carnival – it was a great example of how multiculturalism worked – that's why we borrowed the word 'Carnival'. And the Anti-Nazi League dictated the date.

RUTH GREGORY It was the day before the May Day elections: 30 April 1978, in Victoria Park in Hackney.

KATE WEBB Victoria Park was a statement. The East End was the place of the forgotten.

ROGER HUDDLE I was in meetings with the park authorities and I kept telling them we didn't need Portakabins because we only expected five or six hundred people. Me and Jerry Fitzpatrick went and met a couple of blokes in a pub in Covent Garden and gave them £4,000 cash for the sound system. Jerry was a revolutionary who would always take a chance. Then Red got a stage via contacts of his and Gered's and we got a sound system, but it was a rock 'n' roll system and couldn't deal with bass at all.

KATE WEBB Pink Floyd offered us their PA because some of the old hippies understood what we were doing, but there wasn't a crew to rig it up. It was done in this great well of enthusiasm.

SYD SHELTON In the end the Who's recording studio provided the PA for nothing and Star Hire built us a stage.

ROGER HUDDLE The stage was overseen for a week before the actual gig – it was attacked three times by the National Front – so Tower Hamlets SWP and people from the ANL slept on it and protected it.

RED SAUNDERS I was busy worrying about if the NF were going to burn down the stage and the thousand others things we all had to do. All these people had been round our house a couple of nights before and we had a bathtub full up with cheese rolls to sell at 20p each. And our daughter was only a few days old, so the build-up was just extraordinary because I had all these emotions.

SYD SHELTON We originally had the Tom Robinson Band, Steel Pulse, Patrik Fitzgerald the punk poet and X-Ray Spex to do the opening. The posters went up – we used this man in Hendon called Terry the Pill who was the main mafia for fly-posting in London. It was a semi-illegal set-up – and the Clash apparently saw them. Their manager, Bernie Rhodes, rang up and said, 'My boys want to be involved in this.' We said, 'All right, bring 'em round. Let's have a talk.' A few days later the whole of the Clash turned up with Bernie. They sat on these old sofas in the studio and they were really friendly but Bernie was completely 'out to lunch'. We talked to them for about an hour saying they couldn't be the headline act. It wasn't fair because Tom had worked so hard for Rock Against Racism.

RUTH GREGORY Bernie was trying to negotiate and he said, 'If you buy a tank for the freedom fighters in Zimbabwe then my boys will do it.' We just laughed and said, 'We haven't got any money. What are you talking about?' And Joe Strummer turned round and said, 'Fuck off, Bernie. Get it into your head there ain't any money.'

KATE WEBB The question of getting the Clash was a big thing. But the question about the running order was also important because of the egos of the bands involved. And for us there was also the question of how the Carnival would be rounded off. Everybody was aware of the Clash's massive, dynamic ferocity and energy and how great that was going to be, but was that where you wanted to end the thing? Roger and I argued that it should be the Tom Robinson Band [TRB]. The others said, 'Fine. You go and tell the Clash why they can't go on at the end.' So we went to see them at Rehearsal Rehearsals in Camden. It was a completely lunatic meeting. They had a painting on the wall in black paint and an effigy of Bernie Rhodes with candles on either side of it and they kept on trying to do things to freak us out. The lights went out and they all did this, 'Heil, Bernie.'

PAUL SIMONON I painted this mural on the wall of Bernie naked and another one on the ceiling of him with pigeons on his head. The naked one was over the fireplace and I hung a piece of silk material over it, and lit candles so it looked like an altar. Mick and Joe were laughing their heads off when Bernie came in with these guys from Rock Against Racism and we were singing, 'Praise Him, Praise Him,' and they must have thought they'd come into some weird sect or something.[23]

KATE WEBB Mick and Joe were worried and wanted to know exactly how many members of the NF were going to be there. Questions like that that we couldn't possibly answer. And they asked us about our allegiance to different political groups and our feelings about the Red Army Faction and Baader-Meinhof. It took various negotiations with various people over a period of time. It wasn't straightforward.

TOM ROBINSON In all the smaller gigs up to Victoria Park, RAR always made a point the black band did the last slot. It was only at the Carnival that they changed the game from local unknown to biggest names possible. Bernie Rhodes was saying, 'The Clash are a much more important band.' And the guys from Rock Against Racism were saying, 'That's as maybe, but TRB have been with us from the start.' So there was all this, 'Will they, won't they,' because the Clash wouldn't confirm whether they would turn up or not.

ROGER HUDDLE We had long discussions because the key bands for RAR up until then had been Matumbi, Misty In Roots, and Limousine. We didn't get them on the stage list so they were really pissed off. We had a big row with Widgery that Tom Robinson should be top of the bill, then the second one must be Steel Pulse and third the Clash. It seemed totally logical because Tom was really buzzing on the airwaves and '2-4-6-8 Motorway' had been top five.

RED SAUNDERS There was a crucial moment when the Clash weren't going to do it because their manager was so fucking annoying and had no real understanding of what RAR was about. In a sense the Tom Robinson Band were even more political than the Clash, and they were having a run of hits in the charts and doing 'Winter Of '79' and 'Glad To Be Gay'. Then somebody said, 'The Clash are rehearsing at Jacksons Lane Community Centre up in Highgate and they'd be happy to see you again.' Me and Nina went with the baby and there were all these leather-jacketed punks throwing flick knives at the wall and we came in with a pushchair. They were all absolutely charming and Strummer went, 'Oh, hello, little 'un.' It was really nice and we talked and they said, 'Look, we'll do it, mate. Don't worry about what Bernie said.' In the *Melody Maker* the week before there's a quote from me saying, 'We've finally got the Clash and thank God we got their energy and passion.'

SYD SHELTON I was so thrilled that they agreed to do it. But there was no real publicity because it was too late to change the posters, except for the music papers who picked it up: 'The Clash join the Rock Against Racism Carnival.'

COLIN BARKER Paul Holborow phoned me up in Manchester and said, 'We've got this idea of having a carnival with Rock Against Racism and we can get some acts. How many people do you think we can get there?' We talked about it and Paul said, 'Let's say we've got 5,000 in the SWP and everyone brought one person on average. We'd have 10,000.' So when he negotiated with the police they agreed to send enough for a demonstration of that size. I booked a coach and it filled up so I booked a second coach. I thought, 'Ooh, I'm doing really well here.' Then I got a call from the National University Students' Union and they said, 'We're thinking of booking coaches to go to this Carnival. Is it all right if we do it ourselves?' I said, 'Yes, of course. How many?' He thought about twelve. All of a sudden we realized that something much bigger than we had expected was going to happen.

Poster for Victoria Park Carnival.

GEOFF BROWN I booked the last coach to go down to London the night before at about eleven o'clock. It was coach number forty-nine. We sent 2,500 people just from Manchester. I was organizing, organizing, organizing. Coaches were leaving from Bolton, Rochdale, Stockport, Salford, and all across Greater Manchester.

COLIN BARKER The Albert in Rusholme was the first pub in Britain against the Nazis – Albert Against the Nazis – where the local SWP branch used to meet. They all went down wearing black bin bags and badges saying, 'Albert Against the Nazis'. There was about thirty of them. We were overwhelmed by the people that wanted to come.

PAUL HOLBOROW It was deliberate to start the event at Trafalgar Square – with speeches and then a march – because that was the apex of public political protest. I was anxious to marry that tradition of protest with the new tradition of protest music. I can remember arriving there on the Sunday morning and it was drizzling and I thought, 'This is going to be a complete failure.' It had poured with rain for three days before and it poured with rain the three days after.

RUTH GREGORY I was squatting in Charing Cross Road. There was a whole bunch of us living there and we could hear all these people going down the road in the middle of night but we really didn't think much of it because we thought most people would just go straight to the park.

SYD SHELTON The ANL said to us, 'They'll only come for the music. They'll all go straight to Victoria Park.' I remember hearing people throughout the night from my third-floor room on Charing Cross Road singing Clash songs. I couldn't sleep any longer, so about half six, seven in the morning I went down to see what was happening. When I got there, there was 10,000 people singing and dancing, mostly Scots. They'd come so early. It was like the show was already on the road. Coaches and trains started coming from all over the country.

RED SAUNDERS We had no idea if anybody was going to turn up. I went up to Soho to get a bacon butty and a cup of tea and by the time I got to the Square all these coaches were arriving. Two arrived from Liverpool, the doors opened and it was like a smog, and out tumbled a bunch of punks. By ten o'clock dozens more coaches had arrived from Sheffield and Middlesbrough and Newcastle and Aberystwyth and Bristol and Norwich and Oxford: everywhere. By elevenish the square was packed and we just knew it was going to be fantastic.

NME Carnival issue,
Trafalgar Square,
6 May 1978

PAUL FURNESS We left from Leeds in the middle of the night. We had tons of coaches from all over the place all going down the M1 with ANL posters in the windows. When we got to Trafalgar Square me and some friends climbed onto the steps of the National Gallery and it was just a sea of colour and yellow Anti-Nazi League lollipops. It was unbelievable.

PETER HAIN I'd been to anti-apartheid rallies and anti-Vietnam War protests there for years but I had never experienced anything like this. There were thousands and thousands of kids. Tom Robinson spoke and said, 'The message of this Carnival, not only to the loonies of the National Front but all bigots everywhere, is hands off our people: black, white, together, tonight, forever.' I spoke briefly, adding, 'We're building a people's movement to defeat the Nazis.'

PAUL HOLBOROW I spoke after Peter and then led the pivot of the march from Trafalgar Square to Hackney. People laughed at us when we said we expected youngsters to march seven miles. And there had been some tension with RAR whether we would march or not. They wanted just the Carnival, which would have diluted the politics.

SYD SHELTON We all had different jobs. I was in charge of Trafalgar Square because it was easy to get there early. Roger was in charge of the stage and the park, and Red was in charge of the procession and getting the trucks with the bands on and the PA running at the right intervals. There was some sort of veterans' event going on at the same time in Whitehall, so the *Telegraph* reporter saw the marchers leaving Trafalgar Square hour after hour: 'This is the most despicable ragbag group of miscreants from every lowest dregs of society that you've ever seen.' It was wonderful in its condemnation.

PAUL FURNESS And then we just marched this endless march and there were floats with bands on like the Ruts and Misty.

TOM ROBINSON The march was amazing. We were tens of thousands strong; this incredible feeling of solidarity and strength. I was blown away by the sheer fucking numbers.

COLIN BARKER The deputy chief constable told Paul Holborow, 'Thank God everybody wanted to march off in a hurry because we couldn't have contained the situation.' They were outnumbered but it was not a crowd that was in the mood for a confrontation.

RED SAUNDERS The most extraordinary thing was, it was a seven-mile march and all the coppers were going, 'No, no, they're never going to go all the way. No, mate . . .' Roger Law was an old friend of mine from the *Sunday Times* and I said to him, 'Why don't you make some models for us?' So they made giant papier mâché heads of John Tyndall, Martin Webster and Adolf Hitler, and they were on a float.

RUTH GREGORY I made a compilation tape of reggae and punk for a lorry and that was blaring out on a little sound system. I remember I put 'Police And Thieves' by Junior Murvin and 'Police And Thieves' by the Clash next to each other, and when it came on I was really thrilled because I thought people who liked the Clash wouldn't know there was another version. How silly is that!

WAYNE MINTER I drove one of the flatbed trucks from Trafalgar Square with the Gang of Four and the Mekons on the back. We'd never seen anything like it. It was just an incredible turnout. There was so much going on everywhere.

TRACEY THORN I had to wheedle around my parents to be allowed to go because I was only fifteen and just a little suburban schoolgirl from near Hatfield who'd got madly into punk. We were huge fans of TRB and we'd been writing fan letters to them and actually got replies from the guitar player, Danny Kustow. So we were fired up because they were playing and we actually bumped into him on the march and were a bit screamy-schoolgirl. 'This is like . . . somebody from a real band . . . AAARGGH . . . !'

RED SAUNDERS A couple of weeks before, Tom Robinson had said to me, 'I'm meeting the head of EMI. What can I do? I can't ask him for money?' It popped into my head. 'Get him to give us 10,000 whistles.' He said, 'What?' I said, 'Whistles. If we get fucking hundreds of whistles it will be brilliant.' And he did. So the noise was just deafening.

SYD SHELTON It was joyous; people marching and singing. We had stilt men and clowns and all sorts of entertainers on the way, with the Ruts and the Mekons and the Piranhas and Misty all playing on floats. And we were throwing out plastic whistles and everybody was blowing them and making a huge noise. It was a rowdy, mad affair. In those days I would buy my cigarettes from this wonderful Jewish lady, Mrs Grier. She had fought against Mosley in the thirties. She stood outside her shop on Cambridge Heath Road and clapped for three hours. I saw her the next day and she said it made her incredibly proud.

NEIL SPENCER That was the first time I ever saw loads of Asian people on a march all mixed up with black and white people.

JANE MUNRO I went with friends. It was amazing. I'd never seen anything like it. You were carried along by the whole atmosphere.

TRACEY THORN I was young and naive and excited and a bit out of my element and the whole march was overwhelming because I hadn't had much experience, even of being up in London, and people were chanting, *The National Front is a Nazi Front. Smash the National Front.* There'd been lots of publicity beforehand questioning if was there going to be violence, so I was looking out of the corner of my eye all the time, thinking, 'This is great. Beat the Nazis. Aaaarrrgghh skinheads!'

RUTH GREGORY In Bethnal Green Road we marched past the NF pub and they were all out to heckle us.

RED SAUNDERS The Blade Bone was a well-known National Front pub. Inside the fascists were all getting tanked up and then coming outside with sixteen holes in their boots and shouting, '*Sieg Heil, Sieg Heil*, red scum.' They're doing this and the march is coming along with the police in front of them, and the march is coming and the march is coming and the march is coming, and it's ten minutes and it's twenty minutes: 'Si-eg H-eil,' and it's thirty minutes and they're really weary: 'S-i-eg H-e-il . . . ,' and it's forty minutes and the march is still coming. And then finally there's this group from Gay Liberation holding up a placard: 'QUEER JEW-BOY SOCIALIST SEEKS A BETTER WORLD' and waving it at the fascists, and they went, 'Fucking cunts . . . oh, fuck off,' and went back in the pub, overwhelmed.

PAUL HOLBOROW We filled the whole of the Bethnal Green Road and as we walked past they were dejected and silent. We knew by then that this was a stunning success.

BILLY BRAGG I saw this little old guy with a pint of beer and a fag on doing a Nazi salute and we were jeering at him. I remember thinking, 'That's him. He's the last of Mosley's Blackshirts.'

LUCY WHITMAN We were all taken aback by the numbers. We walked or danced or ran all the way to Victoria Park. There was a fantastic number of people, mainly young, but not all, and it really was a carnival atmosphere of incredible joy and excitement. There was a thrill of feeling that you were part of this massive thing with people of goodwill. Even though we were going right through the heartland of the National Front there was such incredible strength of numbers we didn't feel frightened. We were just incredibly excited to see that it wasn't just us but that there were thousands of people who were on the right side.

COLIN BARKER The march was the fastest march I've ever been on, because everybody wanted to get there before the music started. It pounded through the streets.

SYD SHELTON We'd hired some sort of radio telephone but it didn't work so nobody knew what was going on in the park.

KATE WEBB I remember standing on the back of the stage at about twelve and a few people dribbling into the park and thinking, 'Oh, fuck. Nobody's coming.' I don't think anybody had looked at the mileage.

ROGER HUDDLE I had got to Victoria Park about six o'clock in the morning. It had been raining all week and the park was sodden. The chief of the park keepers turned up and we gave him a bottle of Johnnie Walker Black Label and the last time I saw him he was sitting with the Steel Pulse cooks with great bells of bloody smoke. We had to start at half past one dead or otherwise it wouldn't have worked. The bloody rain stopped about half past twelve and round about one o'clock the clouds opened and the sun came out. There were only a few hundred people in the park and I had to say, 'And now, X-Ray Spex.'

COLIN BARKER We got there just as Poly Styrene shouted into the mic, 'Some people think little girls should be seen and not heard but I say, "Oh Bondage! Up Yours!"' That was the opening of the Carnival. It was absolutely fantastic.

ROGER HUDDLE They finished the first number and just started the second and the demonstration came in. They saw Poly and ran. I was standing on the stage with nothing. And then, WHOOMPH! They got to the front and

Poly Styrene at the Victoria Park Carnival, 30 April 1978.

all started pogoing and our security fence collapsed and people started fainting. They were bringing them backstage – and then they were out again – young women, young blokes, punks, completely gone! We laid them on the wall around the back of the old swimming pool. There was this old guy, must have been about sixty or seventy with grey hair, St John Ambulance, with his little hat and his blue top and his little white bag with a red cross on it: 'Do you need any help, here?' He took a look and said, 'It's all right. It's just heat exhaustion. Let them lie here for a few minutes.' He stayed for the whole gig looking after anybody that got injured.

PETER HAIN The whole park just filled up as if people appeared from nowhere. I went on the stage to have a look. You looked down on it and it was huge and you saw all these different banners coming in. It was something very different culturally and politically to anything I'd experienced. It astounded me. It astounded everybody. Nobody expected it to be that big. And nobody expected it to be that broad in terms of working-class kids and just music lovers coming to see their bands; the message got imbibed somehow. They were wearing ANL badges and they were taking leaflets. There were buckets all over and we collected thousands and thousands of pounds in donations. It was a first in every sense and it had an incredible aura about it.

BILLY BRAGG When we got to Victoria Park there were 100,000 people just like me. I remember getting hold of a megaphone and chanting, *The National Front is a fascist front. Smash the National Front.*

COLIN BARKER I remember seeing friends going round with this huge crowd of predominantly under-twenties wearing safety pins in their ears and looking amazing. I thought, 'Thank God they're on our side.' Above all it was a youth demonstration. But there was a great toilet shortage because the women took over the seated accommodation in the gents.

TRACEY THORN You fondly imagine that everyone was a cool punk but it was a real mixture of people, some scruffy and wearing second-hand clothes, and still a few wearing flares and long hair.

RICHARD SWALES The most memorable thing was when Poly Styrene took her turban off and she'd shaved her head. She was taken off to a mental hospital after the gig. The band didn't know she'd done it.

FRANCES SOKOLOV She did this strange thing with cutting her hair off. I think she suffered. It was the pressure, the feelings, knowing the heavy weight of what we were taking on.

DOTUN ADEBAYO It was a beautiful day and there were thousands of people that just kept on coming and coming. We were trying to chirp girls. I remember most clearly that there was a bunch of skinheads who wanted to disrupt it. I knew it was going to get rowdy. Patrik Fitzgerald came up and they bottled him off the stage. I thought, 'Phew, it's going to be tough for the Clash.'

ROGER HUDDLE Patrik Fitzgerald came out and all the punks started booing him because he was playing acoustic: *Got a safety pin stuck in my heart.* Red went out on the stage and was brilliant.

RED SAUNDERS There were bottles coming at him and I ran out: 'Whoa! Stop all this; this geezer's playing for us.' I went into this rant, 'There ain't no police here.' Then of course they all started going, 'Fuck the police.' I remember orchestrating that. Then I said something like, 'If anybody throws any more bottles I'm going to come out there and fucking get you.' And it stopped. Patrik was upset, and I said, 'That's life, mate.'

BOB HUMM I was in the mixing tent playing records between the bands. I remember Prince Jazzbo was there and he gave me a record to put on. Halfway through I thought, 'This is going on a bit,' and I took it off and he told me to put it back on. I remember reading in the *NME* that John Cooper Clarke played. He didn't. It was a record I played.

JOHN JENNINGS We had set up to play on the back of a truck at the beginning of the march and our driver went the wrong way up a one-way and ended up going across the central reservation because we had to get out. Tom Robinson was running along behind us. When we got to the park we kept on playing.

DAVE RUFFY In the park we got called fascists because we were playing when the other bands were playing – the rabble didn't get on the main stage.

CHRIS BOLTON We made dual bands with Misty and the Ruts with our own PA and this big crowd that had followed us there then stayed with us in the park. Someone tried to tell us to turn off but people just demanded we keep playing. I said, 'The wind's going this way so our music's not even reaching them.' People were being drawn off the main stage because they saw a whole fucking big party going on.

COLIN BARKER Red was on stage prancing about doing an absolute wonderful job as a compère. He's a big man and was wearing a big top hat and red tails.

RED SAUNDERS I did this great screaming shout, 'THIS AIN'T NO FUCK-ING WOODSTOCK. THIS IS THE CARNIVAL AGAINST THE FUCKING NAZIS.' And the whole crowd went, 'AARRGGHH!' It just lifted me for the rest of the day.

SYD SHELTON It said in our publicity we wanted to see 20,000 people in the park. We had no idea it would be as big as it was. Red came backstage saying, 'Syd, how many people do you reckon are here?' I said, 'Maybe 100,000?' He said, 'Let's say 80,000,' and went straight out to the front: 'WE'VE JUST HAD THE OFFICIAL COUNT THAT THERE ARE 80,000 PEOPLE HERE.' Red had that confidence. He knew what had to be done. The next day the press and the *Ten O'Clock News* quoted, '80,000 people . . . the largest anti-racist demonstration since the 1930s.'

JOHNNY GREEN Fuck me, there were a lot of people . . . it was very egalitarian but you're always going to fight for your fucking band. And here we are supporting Tom Robinson, well, nah, it ain't supporting because we're all in this together. But you know road crews are sneaky people. And they've got a guy up there pulling strokes on me and I'm pulling strokes on him and then suddenly, BOOF! The Clash are up there running.[24]

KATE WEBB When they came on it was heaving, massively exciting and exhilarating, and the energy was amazing. But there were a lot of skins towards the front because they knew Jimmy Pursey was going to be there and some NF kids were throwing bottles. It was threatening and I felt the stage was going to break and fall down underneath us.

RED SAUNDERS All the people from the *Socialist Worker* print shop were standing at the front of the stage holding the scaffolding because of the weight of the crowd and the enthusiasm.

TOM ROBINSON There was a curfew at six o'clock and the Clash deliberately carried on playing. They were starting their third song over their time, ignoring all gestures from the side of the stage. I was at my wits' end. It was my favourite band stealing my set.

JOHNNY GREEN There's these people going, 'You're overrunning. Come on, off.' We were going, 'Fuck off. Look. People are loving it.' It was getting argy-bargy.

ROGER HUDDLE Red said, 'They've got to get off the fucking stage. NOW. Pull the plug.' I said, 'We can't.' He said, 'Pull it. It's *our* fucking plug.' They finished the song and I went 'pff' and that was it. Johnny Green called us long-haired hippies.

JOHNNY GREEN I ran onstage to Strummer saying, 'They've pulled the plug.' I dived down and got through the guys' legs and whacked the mains plug back in and back comes the backline and on they go.

KATE WEBB The Clash were making a film called *Rude Boy* and their film-makers had a different agenda. And then Jimmy Pursey ran on stage and joined them singing 'White Riot'.

JOHNNY GREEN Then it came to blows. And then, dare we say, not I, somebody pushes Ray Gange out and says, 'You love the Clash. Don't you think they all love the Clash? Go and ask them.'

RED SAUNDERS There was shit from the film crew and their actor was fucking around, running onstage and shouting down the mic, 'More Clash. More Clash.' One of our guys went, 'Get the fuck off.'

TOM ROBINSON So we got painted the bad guys. They were saying all these people had come to see the Clash and we got jealous. I don't think Joe Strummer ever liked me. Perhaps it was because he saw me as a phoney or perhaps he had left his middle-class roots behind and simply concealed his a lot more successfully than I had.

JOHN DENNIS I read Paul Simonon saying 'I'm glad we did the anti-Nazi rally because it was important, but it was a bit off-putting with all these hippies wandering about because we wanted to make the left-wing seem more glamorous'. But that was the biggest gig the Clash had ever done.

ROGER HUDDLE The Clash all left after their set except for Mick Jones, who stayed to the end.

HILARY CROSS After the Clash they got new equipment or something because the sound had been terrible. There was a break of about twenty minutes and speeches were made and then next were Steel Pulse.

DAVID HINDS Victoria Park was the biggest audience we'd been exposed to. I was being patted on the shoulder for being such a strong representation for reggae music.

RUTH GREGORY Steel Pulse came on in their Ku Klux Klan outfits. I don't

Steel Pulse's David Hinds (left), Mykaell Riley (centre), at the Victoria Park Carnival.

know what the sound is for shock but somehow there was shock in the crowd.

KATE WEBB 'Ku Klux Klan' moved me to tears.

SYD SHELTON You could have heard a pin drop. Nobody knew they were going to come out in these big pointed white hoods. That was one of the great moments. That and when the Clash did 'White Riot' and the whole place was pogoing. There was so much energy in that crowd. It was like alive.

TOM ROBINSON It was all done on a shoestring. Nowadays you think of mass gigs having backstage hospitality, a press area, being covered by the news: this was our SWP friends ransacking the war chest. You came down these wooden planks and there was a concrete bit of ground open to the sky; nowhere to sit down, nowhere to change, no glamour whatsoever. There were these dodgy old generators to supply the power for these feeble lamps and a wobbling PA. It was barely adequate for 20,000 people and we had 80,000 and the generators weren't supplying the full 250 volts, so when we went on, the Hammond organ, which finds its pitch from the voltage, went out of tune. It sounded awful. If you think how much PA you need to

Tom Robinson at the Victoria Park Carnival.

fill Wembley Stadium and then if you look at the photographs of how much PA we had. The faders were all pushed up to the very top so the sound was distorting.

HILARY CROSS Tom Robinson was totally amazing. He had everyone hanging onto every word. I kept a diary. He said, 'You don't have to be black to like reggae, don't have to be a woman to like Joni Mitchell and don't have to be gay to sing this – but it helps.' Then I wrote: 'Everyone in the whole crowd – hippies to punks to Teds to little kids, gay or not – joined in with "Glad to be Gay" and it was amazingly moving.' I felt something had really been achieved and felt proud of having been there.

BILLY BRAGG We were standing under a banner that said 'Gays Against the Nazis' and when Tom sang *Sing if you're glad to be gay*, all these blokes around us started kissing each other on the lips. I'd never seen an out gay man before. My immediate thought was, 'What are they doing here? This is about black people.' And literally in the course of that afternoon I came to realize that actually the fascists were against anybody who was in any way different and just liking black music and being a punk rocker was sufficiently different for the National Front to be the enemy. I realized this was how my generation were going to define themselves, in opposition to

(L–R) Danny Kustow, member of 90° Inclusive, Tom Robinson and Jimmy Pursey.

discrimination of all kinds. This was our Vietnam; our Ban the Bomb. It had a very powerful catalytic effect on me.

KATE WEBB There's that great photograph of Tom from behind where he's sort of embracing the crowd.

COLIN BARKER It was a fantastic moment. Questions of gay rights had not surfaced that much. This was a real jump into the unknown and Tom just took the crowd with him. The whole crowd were singing *Sing if you're glad to be gay* with their fists in the air.

DAVID WIDGERY The concert ended with a jam round a white reggae riff which had Mick Jones and Danny Kustow from TRB dropping power chords into a chant by Steel Pulse, 90° Inclusive, and Jimmy Pursey.[25]

TOM ROBINSON We were all chanting, *black and white together* over a reggae rhythm.

SYD SHELTON The jam was absolutely magical. They performed 'We Have Got To Get It Together', which Tom had especially written.

COLIN BARKER At the end, Jimmy Pursey grabbed the microphone and said, 'All the newspapers thought we were going to go like that but we went like this,' and clutched his hands together. It was an amazing end to an astonishing event. It made the first item on the *Ten o'Clock News* that night and they had footage from the stage of everybody pogoing. Tariq Ali wrote an editorial with the headline, 'Hats off to the SWP'. It raised our prestige enormously.

TRACEY THORN I'd pushed down the front when the Clash were on because I was mad about Joe Strummer and I got separated from all my friends. I remember mooching about feeling really lost and thinking, 'I don't know what to do,' and I realized I didn't even know where I was. I'd just been swept along like on a river and been washed up in this park so I just started walking, thinking, 'I'll find a Tube.' I was walking down Mile End Road and then it hit my little head, 'My God, they said there's going to be violence and I've got all my punk badges on and maybe there's going to be racist skinheads.' I was the only white person: 'God, what do I look like to all these people? Is it clear I've just been on an Anti-Nazi League march and so that's good; or do I look like a nasty punk?' But of course no one paid me any attention at all and I made my way back to a Tube and found my friends in Islington.

ROGER HUDDLE The Carnival changed the course of British history. It became a rallying point.

KATE WEBB Did the Carnival change people? It's like the Clash's question, 'How many fascists will there be?' It's very hard to quantify how many people you've converted but you can see a process over time. It made the Front unacceptable and it made people think about who they were. There hadn't been anything like that since the Isle of Wight Festival so it was a massive generational marker between the hippy movement and their creative revolt and our creative revolt. We were ecstatic. A fucking amazing thing had happened: one of those things when people say, 'I was there,' or, 'It changed the way I thought.' We felt massive exaltation like we'd arrived and what we were saying mattered. And that passion had been expressed in all these different ways. We pulled it off and the thing hadn't descended into riot.

There were two massive yellow dustbins full of pennies and money and somehow these ended up over at my mum and dad's house. The money was on the floor and there was about twelve people counting it up. There was the odd note but it was nearly all pennies and a tiny bit of silver.

BILLY BRAGG I was working in an office in the East End where people made sexist and racist remarks or homophobic comments behind people's backs. I had never said anything because I was the office junior and these guys were all ten, fifteen years older than me. When I went back to work on Monday morning I knew I was not alone. I knew I was different from those arseholes. Being in that audience and singing those songs together and that sense of belonging gave me the courage of my convictions to go back to work and stand up for what I believed in. It wasn't the Clash – but they did a really important thing. They got me there.

PAUL FURNESS To be at the Carnival was confirmation that what we were doing was right, with the sheer amount of people that were there. My parents bought the *News of the World* religiously, and ironically they really helped because they had full-page headlines against the National Front.

COLIN BYRNE Rock Against Racism was my first involvement in politics and Victoria Park was the first political march I ever went on, where music, fashion, style and politics all converged for the first time. It was our political Woodstock. It was the first time that you felt that you were part of a mass populist movement. It wasn't full of depressing-looking lefties and donkey jackets. It was fun and there were kids running around. Rock Against Racism was reaching out to people who didn't see themselves as political. They were young and concerned but they didn't have a party membership card. It got politics into the *NME* and it made it legitimate and cool to be involved in politics. If you were a student politician you were one of those miserable gits in a raincoat who went to weird meetings or would be flogging *Socialist Worker* in market squares; now suddenly there was a platform to talk about serious issues but in a cool way.

ROGER HUDDLE The row after the Carnival was between Dave Widgery and me because he said, 'We don't need the ANL anymore. We can go on without them.' That would have been a disaster. What was above the stage? 'ANL / Rock Against Racism Carnival'. Who booked the buses, the tickets, who were the organizers? Not RAR people, because they couldn't organize a piss-up in a brewery.

RED SAUNDERS Here was a huge group of enthusiastic amateurs putting on what is now regarded as one of the top ten festivals of all time. The *Socialist Worker* said, 'God had joined the ANL.' I just knew it had taken it to another level and then RAR really took off around the country.

PAUL HOLBOROW It was an unprecedented departure from previous types of demonstrations, combining both the youth and the music in the park and the politics in Trafalgar Square. And the message going back from the Carnival was, 'Build your own branches.'

GEOFF BROWN After the Carnival, me and Bernie Wilcox had a conversation and we decided wouldn't it be a good idea if Manchester had a carnival.

BERNIE WILCOX There was a train going back and I was sat with Geoff. He said, 'God, that was fantastic. We'll have to do one.' I said, 'Yeah, we'll do that.' We got together two weeks later and said, 'Right, when can we do it?'

COLIN BARKER Two weeks after the Carnival the SWP had a meeting in Birmingham. Everybody across the country was, 'Yeah, look what we've achieved.' One of our more enthusiastic members, Geoff Brown, stands up and says, 'After Victoria Park, we can do anything,' expressing what most of us felt. There were two people who disagreed. One was Jim Nichol, the man who had come up with the idea in the first place, and the other was Tony Cliff, who says, 'So, Geoff Brown, how many factory branches of the Anti-Nazi League do you have in Manchester? Life is not a carnival. Come back down to earth.' It was a brilliant intervention and they deflated us.

SYD SHELTON RAR were the rowdy neighbours of the Anti-Nazi League. They didn't understand us at all. They were much more political and electioneering. We were this rabble of uncontrollable anarchic loonies to them. And we were. But we were also passionate about art, photography, fashion, clothes, music. And they weren't.

JOHN DENNIS The Carnival was the point at which Rock Against Racism became a national campaign. The central committee collectively went, 'Oh, my fucking God.'

POWER IN THE DARKNESS

Tom Robinson Band. Stiff Little Fingers

TOM ROBINSON I had been politicized by the gay struggle so coming out as gay was a crucial part of my political development. Once you've written a song called '(Sing If You're) Glad To Be Gay' there's no going back in the closet. The basic tenet of the Tom Robinson Band was you either live in a free and fair society or you don't. You can't ask for freedom and fairness for just homosexuals on the one hand but not people of a different skin colour or for women or for workers versus bosses. You didn't just fight in isolation.

RICHARD COLES I saw the Tom Robinson Band on *Top of the Pops* doing '2-4-6-8 Motorway' and I liked the look of them so I got their album. Then I got the *Rising Free* EP with 'Don't Take No For An Answer', 'Glad To Be Gay', 'Martin' and 'Right On Sister', which was putting into words and music what a lot of us were living. I played it to my mother about three times in a row and she said, 'Darling, are you trying to tell me something?' I said, 'Yes.' She said, 'Do you think you might be gay?' I said, 'I *know* I am.' And that was that.

SHERYL GARRATT The only image of a gay person I'd ever seen on TV was *The Naked Civil Servant* about Quentin Crisp which my parents had watched with me in this awkward silence.

TRACEY THORN I loved 'Right On Sister' but TRB did get the piss taken out of them. They weren't cool. But I was very fired up by their politics. The gay feminism stuff made it stretch a little bit broader than the Clash's rioting in the streets kind of approach, which was very cool and glamorous but a little bit exclusive if you were a suburban schoolgirl.

'Glad To Be Gay' was my first real opening my eyes to the idea of Gay Pride. I'm sure I hadn't given the matter any thought before then. At gigs everybody was singing along. It was a proper anthemic song. The verses are very detailed and involving; they tell you stories and then you get the chorus that's a slogan. It's a good way of writing political songs.

TOM ROBINSON 'Glad To Be Gay' was originally a privately made record that was pressed up by the Campaign for Homosexual Equality. It was a totally different song and my first attempt at writing a gay anthem. The new 'Glad To Be Gay' was written for Gay Pride about eighteen months later when I realized that a key element of punk was being real. It was bitter and savage and angry at gay people who would turn up at gay discos wearing 'Glad to be Gay' badges and then take them off when they went home. So it was realizing that it was an 'unnatural fact' saying *it's good to be gay* and the song was a catalogue of what society was doing to us at that time. People would say, 'You make it all right to be gay because you look so normal.'

GEOFF BROWN We'd been discussing gay politics at meetings since the early seventies and had a number of comrades who were active, but Tom Robinson was the first high-profile public figure that was gay and doing something that we were involved in.

PAUL FURNESS I remember Tony Cliff saying if he had organized a big Carnival he'd have put on a symphony orchestra with Beethoven and they would have got about sixty-odd people but if you get Tom Robinson to sing 'Glad To Be Gay' it's 70,000 people. He said, 'I'm gay from now on.'

DAVID HINDS It wasn't fashionable for anybody to come and say they were gay, and unheard of if you were black. It was definitely taboo, hell no, and against Rasta philosophy. When I look back on it I think, 'Fucking hell! That kid I used to go to school with used to act in that kind of way.' Many years later we heard he died of AIDS. Homosexuality was everywhere, as we know, but Tom was one of the first to bring it out of the closet. Even Elton John wasn't admitting he was gay then.

TOM ROBINSON At the height of our fame we played the Hammersmith Odeon and the whole audience sang along from the first chorus and I thought, 'It's only a year since we were doing this in pubs and risking getting bottled off the stage. The world hasn't changed that much.' So I stopped the song and went over and kissed the keyboard player full on the lips and this shock wave of revulsion went through the audience. A friend of mine was at the back of the stalls and he described these 'two beer boys' in front of him singing along and they froze and one of them turned to the other and said, "'Ere, you know what, I reckon these geezers are bent.'

KATE WEBB In the middle of the song Tom would often stop and ask the audience how many of them were singing along because it was a nice tune and how many of them actually knew what he was talking about? Tom made it clear that homophobia, racism and sexism were all part of the same problem. He was hugely charismatic but understood how to express and channel anger.

I was in this group of girls called the Robinson's Rats and when RAR moved from Red's studio to 27 Clerkenwell Close I used to corral a lot of these people to come and help me. We'd have these all-night sessions, just gangs of TRB fans, answering mail and putting badges in.

ROBERT ELMS I was proudly singing *Sing if you're glad to be gay* because I had plenty of gay mates. I'm from a council estate where ten years previously it probably would have got you beaten up. It was enriching and enlightening. You'd walk into a club like Billy's and see Boy George dressed as a woman and yet he was this tough Irish working-class kid from South London. All these things made a difference. They were all part of your personal education and learning that music was a potent weapon.

LESLEY WOODS We toured with Tom Robinson. 'Glad To Be Gay' was drawing out all those things that had been simmering under the surface and finally laying it out there: telling people to stop trying to hide it and pretending to be something you're not.

DAVE RUFFY It's probably the biggest gay anthem ever after 'YMCA'. It was fucking common sense: all fighting for the underdog. The Damned used to do a comedy version of it: '(Sing If You're) Glad To Be A Poof'.

RICHARD COLES I joined RAR because it said on the back of the *Power In The Darkness* album sleeve, 'Rock Against Racism is a campaign supported by rock fans and musicians alike, including TRB . . . for more information send stamped addressed envelope to . . .' It was my first connection to the radical politics of the punk movement. I saw RAR as an allied thing; a sense that the world was changing and that minorities were no longer so acquiescent in negative stereotypes. And what was good news for black people was probably also good news for gay people, was probably also good news for women, at a time when the traditional structure in society was beginning to shift.

ROGER HUDDLE I designed the Tom Robinson Band logo with an old tin-plate stencil we had in the SWP print shop, which the band used as a backdrop and on the front cover of their first album, *Power In The Darkness*.

TOM ROBINSON I said to Roger, 'I want you to nick the Gay Liberation fist' – which in itself may have been taken from the Black Power movement – then at EMI the art department said, 'We could make a great stencil out of your logo and put it in the record sleeve.' When we went to Belfast, Catholic kids took us on a guided tour of the Falls Road. And there was the fist on the ends of buildings.

RICHARD COLES You realized there were other people doing things that you could be part of. It was really important and a big motivation for me and Jimmy Somerville in the Communards six, seven years later. We were very conscious that there were people in places who perhaps might not have any contact with a world that would be kinder to them other than through records

PAUL FURNESS There was a pub in Leeds called the Ford Green which was really rough – it's now a big Asian supermarket – and Tom's band was playing there. Somebody said, 'Go and book him for a gig at the RAR club.' I went over and there were three blokes wearing gay badges and he said summat like, 'Course I'll do it, but I just want to talk to these people here.' I said, 'Some of us don't wear badges.' That was the first time I'd said it out loud. There were three of my female friends standing there and they all burst out laughing – they're all lesbians now, oddly enough.

RICHARD COLES RAR was a template. It gave a feeling of common purpose and common experience – *Bliss was it in that dawn to be alive, / But to be young was very heaven!* – it was halfway between the British trade union movement and political Motown songs. The dance floor became not just a place of entertainment but a place of self-actualization and of protest.

TOM ROBINSON A record was a perfect place to stick a little bit of connection and information details. 'Glad To Be Gay' got into the charts with both the Gay Switchboard twenty-four-hour advice number on the sleeve and the World Health Organization International Classification of Diseases code for homosexuality, 302.0.

PAUL FURNESS I used to work in the medical records department at Leeds General Infirmary and their phone number was the contact number for Leeds RAR. Somebody told me that people thought I worked for a record company, Medical Records. Part of my job was to classify a patient's illness once they'd been diagnosed by a doctor. There were two massive books, really thick like Bibles, called the *International Classification of Diseases*, which were put out by the World Health Organization and you had to take the diagnosis and look down to get a code. There was one patient file that came through. It was a fairly young bloke and the doctors couldn't figure out what was wrong within him. He died of a psychosomatic illness – the one that involves the mind tricking the body – and they put down he was homosexual. It was horrendous because he'd got all these weird symptoms and they reckoned it was because he couldn't accept himself. So I had to look 'homosexual' up in the diseases and there it was: 302.0. I couldn't believe it. So I made two badges and gave one to Tom, which he used to wear on his shirt. He was on tour in Hamburg and somebody had made a whole load of T-shirts with 302.0 printed on them and thrown them on the stage. Tom sent me a postcard that said, 'What have you started, Paul?' A massive campaign started and 302.0 got removed from the World Health Organization directory.

TOM ROBINSON To follow up the album we were booked to play our first major tour of big venues and we invited Rock Against Racism to bring a stall and Stiff Little Fingers to support us, who I'd heard about through John Peel and the *NME*. They were much more punk than we were but the audiences loved it and went ape-crazy night after night. They had this extended version of Bob Marley's 'Johnny Was' which was a real highlight of the set.

JAKE BURNS As a connection to the main line of Rock Against Racism we couldn't have got a better source than Tom Robinson. He took a stand and spoke intelligently and it impressed us. At least in England it was nominally legal to be homosexual after the age of twenty-one; in Belfast you were still put in prison.

GORDON OGILVIE It was a fantastic tour to be on. We got a copy of the TRB fanzine in which they'd had a poll and Stiff Little Fingers walked away with best support band of all time.

JAKE BURNS We were received incredibly well. It was one of our biggest breaks. Rock Against Racism was always something I hoped we could get involved in. I had read Red's letter in the *NME* on the back of the Eric Clapton concert. It was a real shock given the background to the music he played, and I was always aware that Enoch Powell was this menacing figure. Having grown up in Northern Ireland and seen the divisions that sectarianism brought about, racism was that bit more obvious. In Belfast there was very little racism because basically there weren't other races as such. I was eleven years old when I first encountered a black person. We had a small influx of boat people, refugees from the Vietnam conflict, just as all the civil unrest started. I was thinking, 'Jesus! Poor bastards.'

SYD SHELTON RAR always put forward the argument about anti-Irish racism. Those famous notices in Notting Hill: 'No Blacks. No Dogs. No Irish.' It was always there. Anti-Irish jokes were as prevalent as anti-black jokes and because of the horrors of the IRA bombs it could so easily be turned into a really vicious anti-Irish sentiment. The other thing is that Unionist organizations like the Ulster Defence Force had links with the National Front and they had very many similarities, like their marching styles with the Union Jacks. We were keen to exploit and explain and argue without supporting the IRA's violent campaign.

SHERYL GARRATT Stiff Little Fingers had this fresh Irish view. You hadn't heard people talking about what it was like in Belfast before.

GORDON OGILVIE Belfast was a mess. It was divided into tribes. The whole of the city centre was ghettoized. We had a big map on the *Daily Express* office wall where I worked as a journalist, which was coloured according to the predominant religious grouping that was living there. The Protestants were marked in orange and the Republican areas in green and anything in between was yellow. There wasn't enough yellow on the map to make a case of jaundice. Everybody knew somebody who had been shot. You were constantly stopped and searched. The first evening I was in Belfast a 300lb bomb went off in the city centre.

CLARE SHORT We had the monstrous Birmingham pub bombings in 1974 which killed twenty-one people. My dad's Irish. And it was pretty clear they'd got the wrong people but if you said that everything came down on you like a ton of bricks; the *Sun* attacked you as a mad IRA supporter.

RANKING ROGER When the Birmingham bombings happened every Irishman was suspected of being in the IRA; for the first time the Irish realized how I would feel about racism. Black people got the blame for everything. We were the scapegoats. It was dangerous walking round town but you walked with pride. I realized that blacks and Irish were both oppressed by the English.

CATHAL SMYTH I lived in Northern Ireland in '71 when the political process was hijacked by violence and vested interest. I was aware how the Irish ethnic community had suffered from being perceived as associated with terrorism. So I had an Irish passport and one got stopped and kept back by Special Branch at the airport all the time. I like to think of myself as London Irish, growing up with songs like 'McAlpine's Fusiliers'. My uncles worked as navvies and I saw the truck in Camden Town in the mornings to get them to work. It was the days when people worked under names like Mickey Mouse and Donald Duck. I worked on the concrete with my uncle Brendan on the M20 extension. When you see a man agitating the concrete to get it settled in the pouring rain at 8 a.m. you think, 'Fuck that for a game of soldiers.' The limestone on the concrete never really left my hands.

SYD SHELTON I went to Northern Ireland on three, maybe four occasions. One evening I'll never forget. It was a Republican club in the Falls Road area. Suddenly the doors came open and maybe thirty British army came in with blacked-up faces and loaded guns. They went round and then pointed this gun straight at me. Everybody started slow handclapping. It was terrifying. You thought, 'Are they going to kill us all?' They wanted to know who was drinking with who. They clocked every person in the club and then left. RAR managed to forge some quite interesting links with people around the IRA. We got a letter once written on Rizla paper from an Irish Republican prisoner held at H-Block 4, Long Kesh, called Felim O'Hagan. It was addressed, 'THE SECRETARY, ROCK AGAINST RACISM . . . EXCUSE THE UNORTHODOX WRITING PAPER BUT I'M SURE YOU'LL APPRECIATE THAT THE LIKES OF THIS LETTER HAVE LITTLE CHANCE OF PASSING THE CENSOR.'

RUTH GREGORY The letter was written on two cigarette papers stuck together, in block capitals. You needed a magnifying glass to read it. It wasn't one of the hunger strikers but it was someone that was there at the same time. He ends up saying, 'THE STARK REALITY IS THAT UNLESS JUSTICE PREVAILS [Bobby Sands and Frank Hughes] WILL BE DEAD WITHIN A FEW SHORT WEEKS. PLEASE DON'T LET THEM DIE.'

JOHN DENNIS We did a Rock Against Repression tour in Belfast and later 'Rock The Block' marking the ninth anniversary of the introduction of internment without trial. Jerry Fitzpatrick was a Sinn Féin activist so he had very good links – we would never have pulled off the gigs without them – and wanted to support the kids growing up in that political environment and to support the prisoners and hunger strikers in the H-Blocks. We ended up persuading Star Hire, because they were the only ones mad enough to do anything, to take their rig to Ireland. At the top of the Falls Road there was a community centre and out the back there was a field where we put the gig on. I arrived the day before with just a name for somebody. I went into this bar where it was like, 'Who the fuck are you, Johnny Brit?' The army were everywhere looking down the sights of their rifles; helicopters up all the time. There were kids glue-sniffing and being dragged off round the corner and beaten up. That night we were in the local bar and this bloke got hold of me; he'd really been fucked up and been in prison, and kept saying, 'What do people in England think about us?' The next day there was a fucking huge riot. There was a gathering in one of the estates and suddenly these guys appeared from the crowd with masks on and little Browning revolvers firing shots in the air. Suddenly the army is everywhere and armoured cars driving up the street; bricks being thrown at the soldiers. I was with the Au Pairs manager and his girlfriend. We were cowering, trying to avoid being beaten up by these fucking troops. It was horrendous. The kids who had been involved were from the house where we were staying so the army were searching through it. Then the mums were out on the streets cleaning up all the mess. It was just like a normal bloody day. It was so far removed from London. There was a Belfast RAR group but it was all a bit cagey and nervous about being identified with one side or another. We went down to Andersonstown for some fish and chips and all the little kids were saying, 'Do you want to come round the corner and have my sister?' It was disgusting. And the chips; you couldn't possibly eat that shit.

WAYNE MINTER The aim of the tours was to campaign against the British military presence in Northern Ireland and to focus attention on the harassment and cultural isolation and deprivation of youth sections of the Irish community. The gigs were declared as non-sectarian and 'open to all', but in practice they were almost exclusively in IRA areas. It was very frightening. We took over two London bands – Charge, and Oxy and the Morons – and there were four Belfast bands.

LESLEY WOODS I was shocked about what was going on in Northern Ireland. Our manager, Martin, was getting these political pamphlets and little booklets smuggled out. There was a lot of stuff about these women in prison who were on hunger strike. The authorities didn't want anybody else to know what was really going on. That triggered me writing 'Armagh': *Alleged crimes withheld information / She gets no sanitation / Dries her shit on her cell wall / Feeling cold and sick / She gets a couple of Valium / Now* *she's relaxed for the next interrogation / Naked spreadeagled on her back / It's a better position for an internal examination / It's a better position for giving information.* It was all plagiarized, if I'm perfectly honest, from these little booklets. I was lifting phrases and then putting them together so that they rhymed.

GORDON OGILVIE I had the perspective of being a slightly older, avuncular figure but I thought, 'If the Clash think they've got it bad under the Westway, what about kids in Belfast.' I was friendly with a guy called Colin McClelland who was a columnist at a local Belfast paper and he said to me, 'I've been getting letters from this kid called Jake Burns who says Stiff Little Fingers are the greatest thing to come out of Northern Ireland since Van Morrison.' This was just after they'd started up. So Colin and I went to see the band and they were doing what by then were pretty much punk standards: the Jam, the Damned, the Clash. I spoke briefly to Jake at the end of the evening and said, 'I'd really like to talk to you about this. It's really exciting.' That night I had this idea for a song. I'd never written a song before in my life. The phrase 'suspect device' was everywhere on the news: such-and-such a street is closed because the army are investigating a suspect device; and that set me off, *you've got to sus out their suspect device.* It was a pacifist song expressed in the most violent terms.

The *Express* photographer in the office had been to a press conference where the police proudly displayed what they'd seized from the IRA and there was a black-and-white photo of the IRA's suspect device of choice, which was a firebomb. I cut and folded the photo so that it fitted into a cassette case and went to see Jake. '

JAKE BURNS Meeting Gordon was a defining moment in my life. We'd written 'State Of Emergency' and felt we'd dealt with the situation in Northern Ireland. But then Gordon was saying, 'Have you written anything about the Troubles?' I said, 'We think that would be unfairly exploiting people's unhappiness.'

GORDON OGILVIE I said, 'You're wrong. If you're gonna write songs they have to be about your life. Could you write a song called "Suspect Device?"'

JAKE BURNS I said, 'Yeah, I suppose so. Why?' then he said, 'Something like this,' and he pulled the cassette box out of his pocket and handed me the lyric to 'Suspect Device' and said, 'Because we could market it like that.' Suddenly, the rest of the room just disappeared from me and all I could see was this piece of paper. I was thinking, 'Jesus! What I can't do with this.' It triggered Stiff Little Fingers as you know it. And it was obvious I couldn't let this guy out of my sight. This is the guy I can write songs with. It was like somebody flicked a light switch on.

GORDON OGILVIE About ten days later I went to see them rehearsing in a church hall on a Saturday afternoon. I walked through the door and Jake said, 'This is "Suspect Device".' And then he said, 'And this is a song I call "Wasted Life".' It was at that point hairs on the back of my neck started pricking up. If I'd had any ideas in the back of my head that all I was doing was having a bit of fun and being a Svengali figure manipulating this poor teenager, that all had to go out of the window. I said, 'I've done something here. This kid really means this.' I lit the blue touchpaper and stepped back.

LUCY WHITMAN Stiff Little Fingers were more writing about being a teen-ager and feeling constrained by society than explicitly writing about the situation in Northern Ireland. There was a lot of negative feeling towards Irish people in general but most English people didn't have any idea of the background to the struggle. There was a Troops Out movement but if you allied with that you were seen as some kind of apologist for IRA bombs.

NEIL SPENCER Stiff Little Fingers articulated a suppressed aspect of British society which is that we were meant to be the United Kingdom and yet Ulster was run as an Orange fiefdom. The reality of life in Ulster was never really articulated before them.

GORDON OGILVIE Jake and I often had to go out of our way to explain we were not a pro-IRA band. We were anti-violence. I felt that no cause justi-fied putting a bomb under somebody's car and blowing them up. I covered a story where a thirteen-year-old girl was shot for answering the door. Nothing's worth that. Before I moved to Belfast, I said, 'What's it like over there?' I was told, 'It's like Glasgow with a war on.' The poverty was appall-ing. People were being told, 'You haven't got much but you're better off than the nigger down the road.' The IRA claimed that innocent people were being taken in off the streets and brutally tortured by the army and white noise was used. I wrote 'White Noise' about people being racist about the Irish. *Turn up the white noise* was the pay-off line and then the record went into actual white noise.

JAKE BURNS We got banned from playing in Newcastle by a Councillor Williams because of 'White Noise'. He was Pakistani and had heard his daughter playing the record at home. She was protesting, 'No, they're Irish. You need to hear it all.' The whole point of the song was to set it up at the beginning: *Rastus is a nigger . . . Ahmed is a Paki*, and then knock it down at the end with *Paddy is a moron* and *green wogs*. The final irony was, the only picture that the *Newcastle Chronicle* could find of us was us playing a gig with a large Rock Against Racism banner behind us. Sometimes I thought we were perhaps too clever for our own good.

CARRYING PICTURES OF CHAIRMAN MAO

Northern Carnival

RICHARD BOON Manchester has a very proud tradition. There have been black people there for hundreds of years, as there have across most of the northern cities. There is a statue of Abraham Lincoln in the middle of the town with around the base a transcript of a letter he wrote to the workers of Manchester thanking them for their support during the American Civil War. The first line reads, 'I know and deeply deplore the sufferings which the working people of Manchester and in all Europe are called to endure in this crisis.' On a Friday night you always ended up at the Afro-Caribbean Cultural Centre dancing to ska. Punks would go and old hippies and some blacks, who would dress up because that was their Friday night. There was never any bother because everybody just wanted to drink Red Stripe and listen to bluebeat.

BERNIE WILCOX I was twenty-one and had a full-time job as a structural design engineer for Shell. I had a council flat on the overspill Partington Estate and I had two accents because I'd got some support from the Buttle Trust who sent me to a posh boarding school, so I used to be able to switch instantly between the two. There were very few working-class people on the far left in the Socialist Workers Party in general. Rock Against Racism connected because that was through music. It's like Lennon said in 'Revolution': *If you go carrying pictures of Chairman Mao you ain't going to make it with anyone anyhow*. RAR and the Anti-Nazi League got over that middle-class barrier and got through to the working-class kids.

I went on this local TV programme called *Granada Reports*. Tony Wilson was a reporter on it and after that a guy called Dick Witts approached me who ran the Manchester Musicians Collective.

RICHARD BOON The Manchester Musicians Collective is really quite interesting in terms of local musicians making a platform for themselves because there was hardly anywhere to play. There was a very small village of people who met like-minded people.

BERNIE WILCOX Dick knew loads of up-and-coming bands so with his contacts and my drive we got together to put on nights. We'd rent community or leisure centres and take it to council estates to reach out to the kids there. We said, 'We need to go where the kids who are racist live.' We'd put on bands like the Fall, Joy Division and John Cooper Clarke. The Frantic Elevators did quite a lot of gigs for us with Mick Hucknall years before he formed Simply Red. And we always had a stall and sold *Temporary Hoarding*. A lot of these places it was the only time there'd ever been a gig on, but we kept getting hassle from the local council so I had this idea that there must be some dirty club in the centre of Manchester that does nothing on a Thursday night and would like a hundred punters in there. A mate introduced me to this guy, who was definitely part of the underworld, and he said, 'I can do that.' I said, 'I need a stage.' 'No problem.' Turned up on the Thursday: no stage. Joy Division turn up, and the manager says, 'There isn't a stage.' Peter Hook, the bass player, says, 'We'll get one.' So he went with the drummer, brought back a collapsible stage, and erected it. I thought, 'Fuckin' hell!'

John Cooper Clarke at Stretford Civic Theatre, 23 December 1977.

GEOFF BROWN The joke was always that I would only see Bernie when we changed shifts. I would be going to bed as Bernie was getting going. He went into these very seedy clubs where he organized local bands in various rotten cellars on Tuesday nights. And then after the success of the Victoria Park Carnival we pressed ahead with our plan to do one in Manchester.

BERNIE WILCOX People think we planned the Northern Rock Against Racism Carnival for 13 July 1978 to coincide with the Moss Side by-election, but we didn't know that was on at that point.

GEOFF BROWN The Moss Side by-election was very significant. The National Front put up this candidate, Herbert Andrew, and we used the opportunity to build the Anti-Nazi League. It was a clear challenge to us in the lead-up to the Manchester Carnival.

BERNIE WILCOX We had to get permission from the town hall and all I had was a white suit. Geoff said, 'Fucking hell, Bernie. How are we going to get permission to do this if you're in a white suit?' Geoff knew somebody who was very influential in those circles and he smoothed our way.

GEOFF BROWN Colin Barnett, who was a Methodist lay preacher and the secretary of the North-West Trade Union Centre and quite an ego, caused all kinds of difficulties because things could only be done his way.

COLIN BARKER Colin Barnett was very cross that the Anti-Nazi League had been started without his permission and involvement. We got summoned to his office and had to bargain to get the site for the Carnival. Initially, me and Roger Huddle went up to Heaton Park, which is right out of town, but when we got to Alexandra Park, Roger saw a bunch of black and white kids all kicking a football and said, 'This is it.' It cost £3,000 to put the stage up with all its gear, which was a lot of money.

GEOFF BROWN On the same Saturday as the Carnival was set, Bob Dylan was doing a concert in the huge Blackbushe Aerodrome in Camberly, Surrey, and Graham Parker and the Rumour were to be his support. They'd never done an outside concert before and they heard we were setting ours up. Parker's management got in contact and said, 'If we come on the Thursday and do a little warm-up for an hour or so we'll bung you a bit of money.' The agreement was no publicity.

BERNIE WILCOX Tosh Ryan was a music entrepreneur who had taken control of the fly-posting scene and was a kind of socialist gangster. When we started putting up the Graham Parker posters – despite the 'no publicity' agreement – over his, he got annoyed. I went to see him and he said, 'Let's come to some arrangement, here. You give me the posters and we'll put them up.' And then he said, 'Who's doing your stage management at the Carnival?' I said, 'What the fuck's stage management?'

COLIN BARKER Putting up the posters provoked a huge row. Paul Holborow had to come up from London in a hurry on the Wednesday because the official councillor said, 'You've gone beyond the agreement. I'm cancelling the whole event.' Paul had to hang around in the antechambers of the town hall because at first they refused to meet him. Eventually he got seen and Paul gave it the 'there'll be a riot if you call this off' warning and refused to leave until he got something. Finally, a Mr Bee consented to 'an open rehearsal' on the Thursday on the condition he came to judge whether it was a 'rehearsal' or actually a 'fake Graham Parker concert'. It was a beautiful summer evening. Two or three thousand people came. I saw Mr Bee sitting in a pair of grey flannel trousers and a white shirt like Buddha on the grass, and between every number Ernie Dalton, who was on the stage in full dress, would say, 'DON'T-CLAP-TOO-HARD-THIS-IS-JUST-A-REHEARSAL. IT'S-JUST-A-REHEARSAL.' Mr Bee smiled and reported back to the council, 'Saturday can go ahead.' At the end, some teenagers from Moss Side had gathered at the far end of the field. There were up to a hundred of them with really thick bamboo poles, and when the crowd dispersed they stayed. The stage crew were tidying up and all of a sudden the kids banged their sticks together and ran at the stage, split around it, and then ran off. They never said a word. It was a protest against an all-white line-up. That was our reading of it. And then later that evening we heard a group of young people smashed all the windows in the Tory Party offices in town during the by-election count.

BERNIE WILCOX Glen Matlock had started the Rich Kids with Midge Ure after Glen had been kicked out of the Sex Pistols – which Malcolm McLaren claimed was because, 'he liked the Beatles' – and they were on tour and said they wanted to get in on the Saturday gig. We said, 'We're full up, but you can do UMIST [University of Manchester Institute of Science and Technology] on the Friday.' The Fall supported, but Mark E. Smith was pissed off. He was saying, 'We've done all these RAR gigs, why haven't you put us on the big stage tomorrow?' After we all slept over in tents in the park to protect the stage for Saturday's gig, Trevor Hyatt from Granada TV came along with this guy called Bob Williamson who was a folk singer who told jokes. Somebody else brought loads of 'Bob Hope' and we had this fantastic sort of campfire-type impromptu concert, getting stoned. If the National Front had turned up they could have turned us over easily. We were all on cloud nine.

RICHARD BOON There was a press conference at the Piccadilly Hotel which was not very well managed. That was when Pete Shelley and I saw that that they lacked some organizational sense. There was a funny mix of professionals and amateurs trying to deliver a fun afternoon with a message.

PAUL HOLBOROW There was a creative tension between making a cultural impact and making a political impact. Jerry Fitzpatrick was central to all of this. He was my right-hand man and a brilliant negotiator and fixer. We would meet with Red and Roger and say, this is what we've got to do, and then Jerry would smooth any ruffled feathers that emerged out of those meetings.

BERNIE WILCOX Jerry was the workhorse. He was from the centre in London. He was the guy who would do the nitty-gritty organization of things like sorting out Steel Pulse to come and play. But I really struggled with Richard Boon and booking the Buzzcocks. I collared him a few times leading up to the Carnival and he was very dismissive of the whole thing. Richard was more sussed than anybody else. He said, 'This thing's an SWP front so I'm having nothing to do with it.' I was walking down Oxford Road, and out of this second-hand instrument shop comes Pete Shelley. I said, 'Pete, too good an opportunity to miss, this' – Mark E. Smith had already said he'd had a word with him but I didn't know if he had. I said, 'Look, we've got this gig. There's going to be 50,000 people there. You'd be mad not to do it. Come on. Just do it. Tell Richard to do it.' Richard phoned up a couple of days later and said, 'Right, we'll do it.'

LUCY WHITMAN Pete Shelley wrote incredibly witty and challenging lyrics: *Ever fallen in love, in love with someone / You shouldn't have fallen in love with.* Buzzcocks had previously done a Rock Against Racism gig in Barking and afterwards I met Pete and gave him a questionnaire and he sent me a typed reply:

> I'm against ignorance. I try to educate people and be educated by them. Racism can only be solved by education. People must be informed and it is up to YOU as much as it is up to me to show and tell others that racism does not bring about a better society, only hatred.

Northern Carnival poster, Manchester, July 1978.

RICHARD BOON Buzzcocks were approached to take part in the Northern Carnival and of course we said yes. I don't remember any deliberation. There might have been a thing about logistics and how the event was being put together and delivered, but there wasn't any hesitation.

GEOFF BROWN I had an argument in the West Indian Community Centre in Moss Side with Gus John, who would later become a national figure. He made the point they weren't going to encourage people to join our demonstration on the day of the Carnival because the concern was, when the police come to attack demonstrations, they go for the black kids first. On the day, we gathered outside Strangeways Prison at noon. Strangeways is a fabulously forbidding Victorian structure and has a large open space in front of it where you could get tens of thousands to line up, but Alexandra Park was a good four-mile walk so the speakers were under pressure to cut it short. The chief police officer said, 'Could you just hold that lot,' and he pointed to several thousand who were on the side road. I said, 'You and I can agree that they should wait but I can tell you, looking at them, they ain't going to.' They were itching to get off.

PAUL FURNESS All the prisoners were banging cans outside the windows in solidarity. The atmosphere was totally anarchic; everybody was just running round being drunk and swearing and telling everybody to fuck off. I had a bucket of badges saying 'Gays Against the Nazis' and there were tons of coppers and one of them tapped me on the shoulder and said, 'Give me one of them,' and put it in his pocket.

GEOFF BROWN We had half a dozen flatbed trucks and we had local bands like the Mekons and the Gang of Four playing on them, with hundreds of people dancing around each truck. There was a huge snake of people all the way through the middle of Manchester and then into Hulme and Moss Side. It was quite an event; an incredible atmosphere. There was a sea of lollipops. My calculation was about 15,000 people marched and there were about 25,000 more at the concert itself. During the march, Paul Holborow turned to me and said, 'We've just thrown away 1,000 quid; if we'd just had a row of people with buckets across the entrance of the park . . .'

COLIN BARKER We marched from the centre of town to Alexandra Park and Tony Wilson was waving to his fans. I thought, 'You bastard,' because it was the only time we'd ever seen him. People were going, 'Ooh, look, there's Tony Wilson!'

PAUL HOLBOROW The march was huge and more overtly working-class than London. I can remember a group of white cleaners saying how they worked with Afro-Caribbean workers. And Fluck and Law phoned up and said they could make a papier mâché cast of John Tyndall with an axe going through his head, and also one of the local Nazi candidate.

SUE COOPER It was our local park because we were living in Whalley Range. It had bloody rained all summer. I'd never lived in Manchester before and it rained every day for week after week after week. It was really depressing. But that day it didn't rain.

RICHARD BOON There was a moment where the head of the march was just about to hit the park. We were just finishing soundchecking and someone said, 'Why don't you start playing when they come in?' I said, 'No, that's not what's supposed to be happening. We're supposed to play when we're supposed to play.'

BERNIE WILCOX Buzzcocks wanted to go on when the maximum of people were in the park. Richard was annoyed because we couldn't tell him when this was going to happen because it was a fucking march. He's going, 'This is a shambles.' It wasn't a shambles at all.

RED SAUNDERS Richard Boon was screaming, 'You couldn't organize a piss-up in a fucking brewery. The organization is a shambles.' And the SWP were going, 'You're a fucking shit.' It was all little arguments.

RICHARD BOON I said, 'They know a lot about propaganda but nothing about rock 'n' roll. If the people who are organizing this are the revolution, then I'm emigrating.'

COLIN BARKER It was fair comment. We didn't know anything about rock 'n' roll.

ROGER HUDDLE We produced a fantastic Northern Carnival edition of *Temporary Hoarding* and Red found them in a tent at the back of the park in bundles, unopened. The last thing you wanted to say to some punk kids was, 'Can you distribute these papers?'

RED SAUNDERS We worked really hard on a special edition for the Carnival and sent 10,000 of them up on the early British Rail. At the gig I saw a big ANL tent so I went in to say hi and saw them all sitting in the corner in bundles. That's where the organization didn't work.

GEOFF BROWN Red's ability to shout and have a real argument is crucial. The fact that he could say, 'You bunch of tossers; you can't organize anything.' You can't build something without that ability to really let rip.

BERNIE WILCOX I was backstage making sure everything was working. People were coming to the gate and saying, 'Can I get in here?' 'No, you can't.' When the Buzzers came on, then it was different. Pete Shelley said, 'This wasn't politics, it was fun. But the best kind of fun is with people, and being with people is politics.' His mum turned up with a Tupperware container and some sandwiches for him. He was quite embarrassed.

RICHARD BOON During the song 'Sixteen', which has the refrain *I hate modern music / Disco boogie and pop*, Pete changed the lyrics to, *I hate modern music and the National Front / They go on an' on an' on an' on an' on / How I wish they would stop.*

PAUL FURNESS China Street did their single 'Rock Against Racism' and Steel Pulse were a joy to listen to. The hood over the head was a really strong image. There's a mutation from Billie Holiday singing 'Strange Fruit' to 'Ku Klux Klan'.

Pete Shelley of Buzzcocks at the Northern Carnival, Manchester, 15 July 1978.

BERNIE WILCOX China Street were a white reggae band from Lancaster and Martin Pilkington, their leader, persuaded me to put them on. But like Exodus, they were great in small clubs but on stage in front of 40,000 people they didn't cut it. Steel Pulse finished it and they were absolutely fantastic. Diggle, the Buzzcocks guitar player, came on at the end to jam with them: *Black and white unite and fight.*

RICHARD BOON Diggle fell off the back of the stage. He gets very excitable and runs around a lot and didn't judge the distance properly and just fell off.

COLIN BARKER The black youth of Moss Side looked extremely happy; everybody looked happy. There were two black bands and there was a reggae sound tent. It was like imagining what socialism would be like; nobody gave a damn about what colour anybody was. It was an amazing atmosphere. You have to understand what a difference it made. Manchester was horrible in the 1970s. There was racial tension and graffiti on the walls.

RICHARD BOON Rock Against Racism was an attempt to focus these young kids out there who were almost a lost generation. There hadn't been anything like it. There was an enthused atmosphere. You saw a big sea change where it was cool to be an anti-racist whereas before it was cool to be racist.

BERNIE WILCOX Manchester had such a buzz. You couldn't walk down Market Street after without seeing loads and loads of young kids, sort of twelve, thirteen, fourteen, right up to twenty-odd, absolutely full with anti-Nazi badges. I think me and Geoff should be very proud of that because a lot of those people have got their own kids now and they brought them up as anti-racist.

GEOFF BROWN The Northern Carnival was a political event. Everybody was carrying these 'No Front' lollipops. It had a really sharp edge to it. It was the strength and ability to combine the politics and the music. And we were focused on our political objective which was to build a movement to overwhelm the National Front and break them as a political organization. They came fourth in the by-election, 229 votes ahead of the actress Vanessa Redgrave who stood for the Workers Revolutionary Party. The following Monday, every corner of Manchester had got kids who had been there. They'd bought their badges and their lollipops and they'd say to the local racist kids, 'Where were you on Saturday?' Manchester didn't have a problem with Nazis after that.

KNOCK HARD. LIFE IS DEAF

Carnival 2. Militant Entertainment tour

GEOFF BROWN It was very carefully thought out whether there should be a second Carnival in London, but after the Northern Carnival in July the tide was turning our way. We felt supremely confident. So Brockwell Park was booked for 24 September '78 and timed carefully to fit the possibility of an October general election, because Labour was ahead in the polls and I remember sitting in a pub two weeks before and somebody comes into the room and says, 'Haven't you heard, Callaghan has just announced on television he's going to leave it until next year.' It was a disastrous decision.

PAUL HOLBOROW Callaghan ducked it. But even so, where it had been an anxious time leading up to the first Carnival in April, second time round we knew Brockwell Park was going to be massive. The only risk was, it was getting cold and wet and we were on tenterhooks as to whether we'd called it too late. But it was massive. We claimed 150,000. I remember walking into Hyde Park for the beginning of the march and people were streaming in. The atmosphere was fantastic. Tony Benn was a key speaker, which was unprecedented for a cabinet minister to talk to a demonstration and clearly outside of the traditional parameters of British politics. Then we marched down to Brockwell Park and there were a lot of motorized floats with bands playing. It was joyous. I had a team of runners who kept me informed about what was happening on the march and in the park. Ted Knight, the left-wing leader of Lambeth Council, provided us with lots of facilities and built the stage at the council's expense.

SYD SHELTON We saw the second Carnival as a celebration: a victory parade. We had a better PA. The weather was great. We knew what we were doing. We organized a lot more food and toilets. At Victoria Park, we'd prepared for 20,000 people and got 80,000; this time we expected 100,000 and we got 150,000. It was huge.

PAUL FURNESS We went up Railton Road which had a big gay commune and they had a huge banner across the street that said, 'BRIXTON GAYS

WELCOME ALL ANTI-FASCISTS'. When you saw things like that you knew you were getting somewhere. Brockwell Park was on a slope and when we got there you could see all these people in trees and on the roofs of the flats and on the lido wall.

PETER HAIN Brixton was carefully chosen because it had its own solidarity message where the black community was very strong and had its own history of trouble.

RHODA DAKAR That many white people in the park didn't feel normal. I saw my mates march down Brixton Road and waved to them: 'I'll see you up there for Elvis Costello.'

JOHN DENNIS There were presentational issues about the banners on the stage. At Victoria Park, the Rock Against Racism banner was at the back and the Anti-Nazi League banner was at the front of the stage. Brockwell Park was a victory because we got the RAR star so big on the poster and on the stage we got a bigger billing. That reflects the kind of antagonism that was developing.

PETER HAIN Paul Holborow was keen that I tried getting Paul McCartney. I was in touch with his people and he was interested. That would have been into a whole different league.

RED SAUNDERS 'Fuckin' Paul McCartney, no!' He was too much of a good boy. I remember saying to *NME*, 'There's no point us putting on Queen or Judas Priest when they strut around the stage with their bollocks hanging out and all dressed up in leather, giving the whole sexist thing.' We were strictly roots! We used to say the ultimatum RAR concert would be John Lennon and Bob Marley. Funny enough, a couple of years later I went to Marley's studio in Jamaica to do a series of photographic portraits of his wife, Rita, for the *Sunday Times* and on the wall was the letter I'd written to *Melody Maker* about Eric Clapton.

PETER HAIN RAR were right. It was more grass roots: challenging and alternative; more street bands and therefore you could appeal to precisely those groups who were vulnerable. For punks and skinheads, their bands were rebellions against the established rock and pop order.

RUTH GREGORY Stiff Little Fingers got in touch and said, 'We want to play,' and people were arguing because nobody had really heard of them. This was before their first album. But because they came from Ulster and they

CARNIVAL 2

ASWAD
SHAM69 MISTY
ELVIS COSTELLO
& THE ATTRACTIONS
11am·Sept 24 th ·
Hyde Park·
March to Brixton

Anti Nazi League

ROCK AGAINST RACISM

RAR Carnival 2 poster, September 1978.

had a song called 'Alternative Ulster' we thought they'd probably be good, so we put them on first. They should have headlined it, man. They absolutely blew the audience away. They had that raw energy that the Ruts had. Relentless. You can hear it in their records: *An alternative Ulster / Grab it and change it, it's yours . . . ignore the bores and their laws.* I loved that. Everybody was like, 'Who's this?' It was like when Jerry Dammers put on the huge anti-apartheid Nelson Mandela birthday celebration at Wembley Stadium in 1988 and nobody had heard of Tracy Chapman. She just came on and blew the whole audience away.

SYD SHELTON Stiff Little Fingers slept on the living-room floor in my council flat in Stamford Hill because they didn't have two halfpennies to rub together. I got on really well with Jake, who was vehemently anti-racist.

JAKE BURNS Brockwell Park was a chance to show willing and we just grabbed it. We were first on and borrowed amplifiers because we were supporting the Tom Robinson Band that night in Cardiff. Straight after our set we raced to Paddington Station carrying our own guitars, hot and sweaty from the gig, with a journalist in tow from *Sounds*. And we got on the wrong fucking train. We ended up in Slough. Eventually we made it to Cardiff with half an hour to spare.

DAVE WIDGERY When Jake Burns took off his specs and donned his leathers he transmogrified himself into one of the most stinging vocalists and fiery guitarists punk ever possessed. The Stiffs' incendiary songs brought in the Irish dimension so important to any movement against racism in Britain, even though Burns denounced Troops Out. But better, they did punk homage to Bob Marley's classic 'Johnny Was'.

GORDON OGILVIE I suggested to Jake that they do 'Johnny Was'. I said, 'It's about a kid in Jamaica being shot down and that's happening in Belfast.' In Marley's original it was about three minutes flat; in Stiff Little Fingers' set it grew and grew until it became one of the centrepieces of the show.

JAKE BURNS 'Johnny Was' was a mournful ballad for the loss of a young man's life. Gordon loaned me the record and I was listening, thinking, 'This is beautiful, but how the hell are we going to play that?' Also we were a punk rock band and I thought our audience would kill us if we did it. Gordon said, 'Live with it.' I took the Clash's version of 'Police And Thieves' as a template, making the bassline the guitar part, and that toughened it up. And when Brian put the military drums on the front it all clicked into place and I threw in some Belfast references: *A single shot rings out in a Belfast night.*

RUTH GREGORY We had got Stiff Little Fingers in at the last minute to replace Sham 69 who had pulled out because Jimmy Pursey got death threats from their own fans. Jimmy was incredibly brave to turn up there and speak to the audience like he did. There's that brilliant photo of Syd's where Jimmy's just turning away.

SYD SHELTON They said they would kill Jimmy Pursey if he played the Carnival so we said, 'You can't do it.' We knew it would ruin it and there would be a punch-up. Up to that stage Jimmy had never openly come out and said he opposed the National Front. Misty had just finished their set and I was on the stage reloading film in the camera. I saw Jimmy come through these massive gates and he charged straight to the front of the stage and made this fantastically impassioned speech: 'I decided in bed last night that I wasn't gonna come today. But this morning I met this kid who said, "You ain't doing it 'cos all your fans are National Front." And I thought, "That's just what everyone'll think if I don't turn up." WELL, I'M

Jimmy Pursey at the Brockwell Park Carnival, London, 24 September 1978.

HERE! I'm here because I support Rock Against Racism.' It was a seminal moment.

KATE WEBB Becoming involved with an organization like RAR some bands would have seen as a betrayal of who they were and their fans. So there was a big rumour about the National Front coming to attack the Carnival.

RED SAUNDERS The NF did a clever thing and organized a march in Brick Lane. We were fucking stuck between two horses and it wasn't handled well. At the last minute we organized some coaches to counterdemonstrate against them but we also got attacked by other anti-racists; a purely sectarian attack because they didn't like us and didn't take into consideration what was going on.

RUTH GREGORY It nearly split the Carnival because people were being encouraged to go and join the march in Brick Lane. They would have loved that if we had called it off.

SYD SHELTON It was a very clever trick because all the militant anti-racists were going to be at Brockwell Park. Jim Nichol managed to organize at short notice some Empress Coaches and we asked for heavyweight volunteers to go down and see off the Front.

DAVID WIDGERY The counterplan was to divert a sizeable section of the march to tackle the Front, but as Paul Holborow put it, 'We collectively bungled it.' The transport logistics were not worked out and the anti-fascists who did attempt to block off the Front were demoralized and easily pushed about by the belligerent police pressure.[26]

JOHN DENNIS When you organize these events you don't enjoy them too much on the day. You're stressed out. We were paranoid about security and who was going to turn up and whether they were going to attack us. We weren't tooled up but we were ready and there were some fairly heavy characters on our side: 'OK, let's get prepared for this. Let's not ignore what Jimmy's saying. They'll know he's coming.'

ROGER HUDDLE I couldn't go to the park because we were instructed to stay and protect the SWP print shop, because the National Front had threatened to burn it down. There was all us lot sitting on the roof with baseball bats and binoculars to see if there's any Nazis coming: complete Toytown stuff. So I missed Brinsley from Aswad holding his newly born baby up in the air. He did that African thing and held the child up to the sun.

BRINSLEY FORDE We got to the park late. We were driving round trying to find how to get in. It was a massive gig. We were playing to an audience that probably for the first time was hearing a live reggae band in the way it should be heard, because normally the PAs were not that fantastic in smaller venues. That was important because it opened up the views of lots of people going, 'Oh, wow! I like this. Let me find out a little bit more about it.'

RUTH GREGORY Aswad were almost like classical musicians in their professionalism. They were like gods on the musical scene and we were all a bit in awe of them. They made the hairs stand up on the back of your neck. Brinsley said to the crowd during 'Natural Progression', 'This is ire, ire that's there's so many people here today.'

BOB HUMM Aswad were the best of all the British reggae bands. They were classy. You had confidence in them you'd be entertained and see something special. You know how you can rely on some people: like watching ice-skating on the television and you know they're not going to fall over. But I missed it because I was told not to go by the print shop in case I got arrested. I got on the bus and the conductor came along and saw my RAR badge and said, 'That's a free pass.'

DAVID WIDGERY Misty were joyous that day, lilting and weaving into the rhythms so evocatively that for a half hour Brockwell Park was transferred to the Jamaican mountains by their open, rural, spiritual magic.

PAUL HOLBOROW On the stage, I was trying to get something done and I brushed past somebody and he said, 'Hey, what are you doing?' I apologized and said, 'I've got to get on.' It was Elvis Costello. I didn't recognize him.

JOHN DENNIS I ended up being in charge of security because nobody else would do it, and his manager Jake Riviera was like, 'You can't have any photographers there,' and 'Elvis doesn't want this or that.'

DAVID WIDGERY Elvis Costello and the Attractions bounced on stage saying, 'Welcome to the Black and White Minstrel Show, 'ow about jumping up and down against racism?'[27]

BERNIE WILCOX I lost all my mates and Kate Webb was on this stall and I saw this backstage pass. I thought, somebody's gonna nick that if I don't

Elvis Costello and the
Attractions at the Brockwell
Park Carnival, London,
24 September 1978.

first. So I walked in and Jerry Fitzpatrick said, 'How the fuck did you get in?' I said, 'Ah, well.' Elvis was on and I was watching it from the side and he did '(What's So Funny 'Bout) Peace, Love And Understanding'. Nick Lowe, his producer, was just to my left with tears in his eyes.

KATE WEBB Elvis Costello had written quite a lot of anti-fascist songs. He was an obvious person to be asked and he was part of the punk movement. There was a fight backstage and some sort of racial epithet was thrown at some point. The tension was combustible. You have the bands but then all the different people around them: the managers and roadies with their own ideas and ways of doing things.

•

DAVID WIDGERY By the end of the summer, a quarter of a million people had rocked against racism. The fascists didn't know what had hit them. In London their local elections vote plummeted and in their so-called West Midlands strongholds their vote fell: in Leicester from 70 per cent to 5 per cent, and in Wolverhampton from 11 per cent to 3 per cent.[28]

RUTH GREGORY By 1979, Rock Against Racism had done 200 gigs and thirteen regional carnivals in places like Edinburgh, Cardiff and Southampton. We didn't want RAR to be London-centric. By then there were more than sixty local groups around the country. So we came up with the Militant Entertainment tour which went all over the country. Just the fact that something was happening in their local area was enough, but something that was political and giving an anti-racist message was quite incredible really.

ROGER HUDDLE One of the reasons for doing the Militant Entertainment tour was the general election. We finished on the last day of April 1979 and the election was three days later.

JOHN DENNIS We announced the tour just as Eric Clapton came out with another load of crap in *Melody Maker*: 'Enoch was the only bloke telling the truth, for the good of the country.' I responded, 'The only difference between Powell and the Nazis is that Powell would ask the blacks to go back, and the National Front would tell them.' It ended up on the front page. Big news!

KATE WEBB The Militant tour was the logical and obvious thing to do next. It was to do with helping and reinforcing and getting to know local groups

RAR office, Finsbury Park, London, 24 March 1979: (counting L–R) John Dennis (1), Red Saunders (3), Kate Webb (4), Syd Shelton (7).

better. There was so much work involved and we were just a few people in the office.

JOHN DENNIS Three of us organized the tour: Kate, me and Wayne. This was the strategy: if we were going to build an organization that was coherent as a national campaign we had to have a vehicle to pull together all the local RAR groups. Kate had developed this very useful network base of contacts so she became the conduit from the centre, communicating with people by phone or letter. I persuaded Wayne to come in full time and he had the job of going round the country and liaising with all the groups. That gave us the confidence to just throw ourselves into it.

RED SAUNDERS There was a Canadian surrealist called Mimi Parent who did a rhino and underneath it said, 'Knock hard. Life is deaf.' I thought, 'That's brilliant.' By then Gered and I shared the Old Chapel Studios in Hampstead. It was a big old church hall and I got John and Wayne and a whole load of students from the Royal College of Art and said, 'I want a fucking massive backdrop of a pink rhinoceros.' We got a canvas and projected it up and we painted it in the studio. It was fantastic.

SYD SHELTON The rhinoceros was a huge unstoppable beast and we painted this big backdrop red and blue. 'Militant' was a bogey word and we wanted to turn it on its head. The idea was, 'You've come to see us, now we're coming to see you; the circus has come to town.' RAR was our life. I was like, 'I'm going. I'll drive one of the vans, help put the PA up, take some pictures, whatever.'

DAVID WIDGERY The point of bringing the cultural circus into town was to have the political argument and take the anti-racist message to the parts the other political organizations didn't reach.[29]

WAYNE MINTER I hired a little green Mini and travelled round the country sleeping on floors and meeting people for three weeks, charged with finding RAR groups and letting them know about the tour. It kicked off with a big list of bands wanting to do gigs, from Steel Pulse and the Clash right down to the Leyton Buzzards and XS Discharge in Glasgow.

PAUL FURNESS Wayne came up to Leeds for a recce. Whenever we knew that somebody from national RAR was coming it was a bit like, 'The landlord's coming round; put your best face on.' The club was run on a shoestring but we broke even and sold loads of badges. We used to get ratty letters from central RAR demanding money, so we'd bung them a tenner every now and then.

WAYNE MINTER The point was to destroy the support for the National Front before the general election and have a really good time. We ended up with 22 gigs, 33 bands, 100,000 leaflets, 30,000 posters, 20,000 tour badges, 20,000 stickers, 15,000 copies of *Temporary Hoarding* and 4½ tons of PA and lighting to take around the UK. Each gig had two headliners and then we took on local support bands in each town. The first leg was Cambridge, Leicester and West Runton and we took the Ruts and Misty. The biggest trouble we had was booking everybody into hotels. We'd contact a Trusthouse Forte with a reservation for fifteen people, but two or three of them found out in advance we had Misty and they wouldn't accept a black band. They'd say, 'Rather strange names, sir . . .'

RED SAUNDERS In one town we'd called ahead to say, 'We've got a band with us and they have special dietary requirements,' and the hotel had gone, 'Yeah, all right.' We were cooking for twenty-eight people and there was Sinbar, Misty's cook. He was a magnificent Rastafarian with a big stave and massive locks and full fucking gear. He was like the Angel Gabriel. We

Militant Entertainment tour poster.

were trying to organize the food and there were all these fucking blokes in Seventies' suits and moustaches and of course the office hadn't told the kitchen and, as we were explaining, all of this the doors flew open and Sinbar walks in and says, 'I, Sinbar. I tell chef.' The guy went, 'Fucking what? You're not coming in my fucking kitchen.'

SYD SHELTON Sinbar was six foot eight. He came out of the kitchen with dozens of pots and pans and dreadlocks flowing and he just stood there. All the people turned round and went, 'What!' We were killing ourselves laughing. They didn't know what had hit them; all these dreads from Southall turning up.

RED SAUNDERS One of the best gigs was West Runton Pavilion, right out on the Norfolk coast, miles away from anywhere. I met this guy who was a bus driver and a Transport and General Workers' Trade Unionist. He goes, 'I'll get transport organized for you.' I don't know how he did it but he turned up with a double-decker bus and at two in the morning drove all these drunken punks home twenty miles along the coast back to Norwich.

JOHN JENNINGS There was no one there and then suddenly loads of coaches full of punks arrived. It was heaving. We did it with the Gang of Four and Misty and it broke down a lot of barriers. It's very easy to say, 'Let's do it,' but if more fans are there to see one band than the other . . . but it was very much a thing of unity.

WAYNE MINTER The Ruts were unstoppable. Segs played four numbers lying on his back. It was just dynamite. And then you'd see them sitting at the side of the stage watching Misty's drummer who'd sit really low behind their kits and play up to the cymbals. The next week Ruffy had adjusted his kit and would be playing reggae paradigms and that hi-hat stuff.

SYD SHELTON West Runton was a long drive but we decided we would do it there and back in a day. There were about five of us and I had Red's old Commer. On the way we stopped to take a photograph of a sign that said 'Welcome to Rutland', and then the Ruts turned up and then suddenly half of Misty, and I took photos of them all. After the gig we ran out of petrol at four in the morning and nobody had any money. It was seven o'clock in the morning when we got home.

JOHN DENNIS Punk was transforming, and all those second-wave punk bands like the Gang of Four, the Au Pairs, Delta 5, and the Mekons were very political: very active, and very supportive.

Red Saunders (wearing shades) on the Militant Entertainment tour,
West Runton Pavilion, Cromer, Norfolk, 17 March 1979.

ANDY GILL Often with these gigs there isn't that much to report. We would not typically speak out from the stage, but the political content is there because it's underneath a banner, and people come because they are sympathetic to the cause or they just want to see the band. I remember trying to get the attention of somebody from Misty once and I touched his foot with mine and he went off on one: 'Touch me with your hand. Don't touch me with your foot.'

SYD SHELTON I had to share a room with Vince and Smell, the Ruts roadies. I didn't get a wink of sleep. They'd have farting competitions. It was just ridiculous. And they set off fire extinguishers on stage. They were a bit wild. Red did the MC job and wore a dirty old man's raincoat with his mutton-chop sideboards and Ray-Bans. When we went to Coventry he'd had a few beers and he'd got a takeaway and then came on stage drunk and was dropping curry down his front. It was hilarious.

RED SAUNDERS These kids started diving off the stage into the audience. I started throwing them: 'Go on, get off,' and they loved it. All night long, I was throwing punks off the stage.

Jake Burns (left) and Ali McMordie of Stiff Little Fingers, on the Militant Entertainment tour, March 1979.

JOHN DENNIS We had some kids glue-sniffing and had to physically kick them out. And then at Leicester Polytechnic, Wayne got beaten up by fascists. That was really upsetting.

WAYNE MINTER A load of Front turned up outside and I said, 'Four or five of us won't be threatening,' so we went out and I got smashed in the head and spent the rest of the gig in A & E and had to have stitches.

JOHN DENNIS The big one was when we got to Edinburgh with Stiff Little Fingers. *Inflammable Material* had gone top twenty so the demand was massive. They were so bloody hot. We could have done five nights.

JAKE BURNS We did the Scottish leg with the Mekons and this massive pink rhinoceros behind us.

RED SAUNDERS Carol Grimes was meant to be on the bill but I had to break it to her that we couldn't afford to get her and her band up to Scotland.

JAKE BURNS There was a huge fucking blizzard so we couldn't get to Stirling and ended up doing a second night at Clouds in Edinburgh. Aberdeen was a disaster because the venue was made out of granite, so the acoustics were a nightmare.

WAYNE MINTER Aberdeen was incredible partly because we had to drive a day to get up there and had a puncture. It was a burgeoning oil town, so money was beginning to flow in and the local group had hired us a club that was frequented by American oil men. We didn't get many people there but it was a storming gig. But the Stiffs got aggro: 'Fuck off, Paddies.'

BERNIE WILCOX In Manchester we had the Cimarons playing with the Sunsets, who were Shakin' Stevens' backing band. There was a sort of Teds-versus-punks thing and we wanted to address that so it was old rock 'n' roll Fifties-style playing with a reggae band. It went down really well.

KATE WEBB The Angelic Upstarts played Manchester and Liverpool and had a tough following but Aswad kept them in line.

PAUL FURNESS The Angelic Upstarts had this song 'The Murder Of Liddle Towers' about a building worker who was killed by the police and when they sang it they kicked a pig's head into the audience. This punk girl caught it and took it home. I asked her what happened to it and she said the dog got it. After, we had to account for ourselves with the venue owner. He was this West Indian fellow called Lee and he had a cane with a crown on the top of it and a gold tooth and an amazing accent. He was always threatening to boot us out and right at the end he said, '. . . and no more pigs' heads.'

RED SAUNDERS In Wales we arranged to meet the organizers for the last leg of the tour at a motorway station. They said, 'These are the lads doing the security.' I was talking to them and suddenly realized one of them had a swastika amongst his badges. 'Oh shit!' I thought, 'I've got to confront this. But this guy's here for Rock Against Racism. He's obviously not a Nazi.' I said, 'Mate, why have you got that badge on?' He said, 'It don't mean nothing. It's just a biker badge.' 'Is there any way you could take it off for me?' 'That's no problem.'

WAYNE MINTER Llanelli was incredible. It's a little town right out past Cardiff in West Wales. They had this beautiful venue, the Glen Ballroom, with fountains and palm trees. We had Shakin' Stevens and the Sunsets but they had a lot of support from racists. About an hour before the gig all these motorbikes roared into town from the valleys. They got off and said, 'We're here to stop the fascists.' They all went in and rocked away to Shakin' Stevens, who made anti-racist comments on stage. It was a storming gig.

KATE WEBB There were miners in the audience. I was brought to tears by the jam at the end; bringing all these people together. It seemed an incredible thing that we'd come there and done that.

WAYNE MINTER After, the local Socialist Workers Party person arranged for an Indian to stay open because his brother made naan bread for the restaurant. We all went down there and got pissed till three o'clock in the morning. It was a stunning tour but we'd just about had it by then and we ran out of steam a little. We did Exeter and Plymouth with John Cooper Clarke and the UK Subs and then we got back and started organizing for the finale at Alexandra Palace.

RUTH GREGORY Alexandra Palace is a massive place and it was completely full. I'd never been there before and it just seemed incredible perched on top of this hill in North London. And the fact that's where the first BBC TV went out. The atmosphere was just electric. I remember Alex Harvey – of the Sensational Alex Harvey Band – doing 'Small Axe', which is one of my favourite Bob Marley songs: *If you are a big tree we are a small axe sharpened to cut you down.*

JAKE BURNS We had the idea to put together a version of the Tom Robinson Band. Tony James from Generation X played bass and I played second guitar and sang on a few songs. We were sharing a dressing room with Aswad and suddenly Alex Harvey appeared: one of my all-time heroes. Alex was saying he wanted to play and did we know 'Small Axe'. We'd been rehearsing for a week and nobody knew it. I said, 'I know it. It's dead easy. Three chords.' So we ran through it. Tom said, 'OK, I've got it.' Then Alex said, 'All right, I need a guitar.' As an act of generosity, I said, 'Take mine.' He looked at me and said, 'You're the one that taught us the song, son.'

So I missed my chance to play with him, but later I went on and we did 'Johnny Was' and just before the solo I hit the guitar and managed to break three strings in one go so I had to bum it on one string.

RUTH GREGORY We had our own staff to man the gig and we had to search people for weapons when they came in the doors.

WAYNE MINTER In the early days, we just made sure we had enough people there to keep them out. Then we started thinking, 'Nobody's been seriously hurt. We'll let them in and handle them in the gig. They'll see how much bloody fun it is and feel excluded and go away and resign from the Front.'

RED SAUNDERS As RAR grew it attracted different elements, so you'd have people who were street fighters and who would know the enemy. The Anti-Fascist League would go, 'That crew there, Red. The tall one. He's East London NF. He's a bit of a geezer. We'll have to deal with him.' I wouldn't have a fucking clue who they were, but generally most people would get in.

CHRIS BOLTON They had a wonderful security system there by which as people came in they were taken one way, searched properly, and then interrogated. They vetted the Nazis. It was like having Simon Wiesenthal there in a fucking office, saying, 'Come in.'

WAYNE MINTER There were three or four bands that attracted the NF because of the nature of their music and they'd interpreted the lyrics in ways that might be racist. Our job was to counter that with all the propaganda in *Temporary Hoarding*. Also the bands had a responsibility and we'd tell them that. We wouldn't accept bands who wouldn't actually take that responsibility on stage. But at Alexandra Palace we were worried about security and the Front turning up because the event was publicized all over London. I don't think they came in the end. But what a line-up: Aswad, John Cooper Clarke, the Ruts, Alex Harvey, the Leyton Buzzards; whenever we couldn't get another band within fifty miles of London we'd say, 'Ring the Buzzards', and they'd pile off and do it so we put them on as a thank you.

JOHN JENNINGS Malcolm went on with muslin round his head. He just found it and was mucking about doing some sort of burka thing.

JOHN DENNIS The Ruts were great but the venue was such a nightmare. We had all these conversations about acoustics. In the end it was like, 'Fucking turn it up: beat the echo with volume.' It didn't work. It was just a fucking row.

BRINSLEY FORDE The Palace was so big, so when we were trying to use our echoes and stuff it was crazy and all over the place. I heard John Cooper Clarke for the first time that day, 'Oh! He's a poet.'

KATE WEBB Spoken word was part of the scene. It wasn't unusual to mix up music with other forms.

JOHN BAINE When I saw Joe Strummer I knew what I wanted to do for the rest of my life. Then when I saw John Cooper Clarke I realized that the best

The Ruts: (L–R) John 'Segs' Jennings, Malcolm Owen, Paul Fox,
at Alexander Palace, London, 14 April 1979. Red Saunders can be seen
in shadow standing by the guitar amp.

way to do it was with poetry. He was bleakly political rather than directly
confrontational but there was definitely the perspective of a working-class
bloke from Salford talking about his life: *Keith Joseph smiles and a baby
dies in Beasley Street*. That was brilliant.

BERNIE WILCOX I was going to this folk club in Manchester and Clarkey
would get up and read poems, y'know, *Never seen a nipple in the Daily
Express*, with blond hair tied back in a ponytail, like a hippy. I next saw him
at a punk gig and he'd got this *Blonde on Blonde* Dylan-type hair.

WAYNE MINTER John Cooper Clarke had a broken arm in a sling. We had a
lot of trouble finding him. He was wandering round the back somewhere,
out of it. I thought, 'We'll never get him on stage.' He was sort of wheeled
out and this woman who was looking after him propped him up on stage and
he went CLICK! *I was in a shithouse in Salford*, straight into it. He
didn't stop for half an hour and the punks loved him: just the look of him.
He was so thin and he had a great sharp suit and winkle-pickers and the
black shades and the hair.

LUCY WHITMAN There was this big banner across the whole stage, 'Hello, it's all yer Alien Kulture.' It was just after Thatcher had made her speech about people feeling 'swamped by an alien culture'. And there were stalls around the outside and a lot of misogynist stuff against Thatcher, like an image of her being hanged. It was a good example of where people who thought themselves to be progressive didn't have any qualms about portraying her as a witch. I wrote a piece about it in *Temporary Hoarding*: 'We must challenge her not because she's a woman but because of her policies.' The concert was a little bit like the Carnivals: you weren't concentrating on the music, you were drinking in the atmosphere.

RED SAUNDERS We didn't do too much sloganizing on stage. I said, 'Let's just do our politics projecting slides round the room.' We put linen up on the walls and projected the Queen with 'sponger' written across her face, or Martin Webster with shit on him. I had these overalls that I wore that we stencilled with all our slogans: 'Love Music Hate Racism.'

ROGER HUDDLE The left before RAR was so amateurish. I used to do a DJ for the Trades Council where there was only strip lighting because it was in council premises. And Red did a gig where they had to put money into the meter to feed the PA. It was so Mickey Mouse. Our attitude was, we had to use sound and lighting and colour properly. You look at the Italian Communist Party in the sixties on their demonstrations: the flags; the whole cultural colour manifestation.

WAYNE MINTER We had some ambitious audio-visual there and hung sheets down from the ceiling and projected all this stuff. And we projected our *Nazis Are No Fun* film. But I have a suspicion we still owe Haringey Council for the hire of the venue!

KATE WEBB After everybody was gone the floor was strewn with stuff. The DIY ethos was fun but there was also the cleaning up. And we were in big debt from the tour.

JOHN DENNIS The coverage we got was huge. Everybody sat up and said, 'Fuck. They've pulled this off.'

KATE WEBB That week the Labour Party put a full-page advert in *Sounds* and *NME*: 'Don't just rock against racism . . . Vote against it. Vote Labour.' Red was furious and wrote to *NME*:

Rock Hard – Politicians are Deaf

Rock Against Racism is a little miffed that the Labour Party should suddenly leap on its already strained back with full-page adverts in the music press . . . 'Don't just rock against racism . . .' Don't just what? We've just rhinoed around the country, arguing, and playing our unmistakable anti-racist message and it's left us knackered. And seven grand in debt. We weren't voted in. We grew up because we were necessary. Necessary because of growing racism and fascism under a Labour government which was looking the other way so fast that its neck is still stiff. You don't fight against racism or control your own lives by putting a cross on a piece of paper – that's copping out. You stand up, speak out, and Rock Against it. OK, it seems like most of us will be putting our shaky little crosses in Labour's box on May 4th. Rock Against Thatcher – we mean it! But no illusions. We're looking forward to seeing Labour start to really Rock Against Racism – ending the racist immigration laws, abolishing Sus etc. Are you listening?

NEIL SPENCER Red led an invasion of our office and they made a lot of fucking noise and shouted and paraded around and pissed everybody off and stopped us doing our work and had to be kicked out.

RED SAUNDERS We were cross the music papers had printed it and people were saying, 'We've got to do something,' so I said, 'All right, I'll meet you all in Carnaby Street,' and then we stormed the *NME* office and kicked up a fuss. I think we ended up in the pub arguing.

REGGAE FI PEACH

Southall Kids Are Innocent Benefit

PAUL HOLBOROW A week before the '79 general election the Nazis booked Southall Town Hall and planned to march. The Home Secretary, Mervin Reece, had allowed the National Front to hold election meetings in town halls across England. It was a gross provocation in an Asian area so we called for a massive demonstration. And it was huge. But the police, in defending the status quo, behaved in an utterly disproportionate way and they attacked the demonstration to clear the way for the Nazis. And in trying to disperse the crowd a teacher, Blair Peach, got a fatal blow in the side of his head.

KATE WEBB Five years earlier Idi Amin had ordered the expulsion of his country's Asian minority and the United Kingdom accepted 27,200 refugees. Southall already had an Asian population numbering almost 18,000 who had come to work in the area during the fifties and sixties. The Borough of Ealing informed the Home Office that an influx of any more Asians would cause serious difficulties, but these were families with British passports who naturally would want to be in their own communities.

JUNIOR GISCOMBE We were hearing that Idi Amin would cut people's heads off and eat it. All this stupidness, but being beloved Britain it was, 'We don't want them. They've come to take our jobs.' Ted Heath's government was saying, 'Put your money into our country and you can bring your families over.' So here's all these people coming over and everybody's going, 'What the hell's going on?'

RUTH GREGORY The Asian population was targeted. But where black people would fight back, the Asian community was set apart because they hadn't been here that long. I went to an all-girls' grammar school and all the black kids went to the secondary modern down the road. I was really friendly with this one girl who was Asian. It was at the time that they all got thrown out of Kenya. But I didn't know any of that then. We just thought she was a bit weird because she oiled her hair. We had this discussion about the riots in Notting Hill and a friend started talking about black people and how they should all go home. I was so angry with her. She wasn't my friend after that.

JOHN JENNINGS You go either way when you're young. For a young white kid it only takes a couple of West Indian people to become friends with you and your whole outlook changes: 'Oh, this is cool.' But in the first skinhead days when I was fourteen, fifteen, listening to Prince Buster, I couldn't quite understand when the skinheads went out Paki-bashing. They didn't even know where the kids were from. That was an insult in itself.

DAVE RUFFY I heard the term 'Paki-bashing' when I was about fourteen from the West Indian immigrants. I know it's true because I've spoken to some of my spars from back in the day and they've said, 'Yeah, there were some boys who did that.' They saw shopkeepers maybe doing a bit better than some of them, and then of course the skinheads go, 'Yeah, fuck . . . let's do it.' It was the same as it ever was because young men are full of testosterone and easy to manipulate. Ignorance is ignorance and it ain't exclusive to any race. It's about people uniting together for a common cause against stupidity. We played with black groups and we had black people in our firm. But also there'd be black people in the NF groups of skinheads: 'Oh, he's all right because he's with us.' I met a grown-up, a successful chap, who said, 'I came down from Scotland and I was a little Paki-hater. I met you guys and I saw that you had people around you and it completely changed my life because I didn't know fuck all.' You can only make judgements on what you experience. Another guy, he was an adopted black kid from Sunderland who suffered from depression, he said, 'I heard "In A Rut" on John Peel. I was just about to give up and that record saved my bacon.'

JOHN JENNINGS I remember him. He said, 'I really wanted to meet you because for a white band to be on label called People Unite: a black people's label . . .' He said, 'I started to meet people that had similar think-ing to myself and we thought, "Fuck, we're going to fight back," instead of being kicked down and abused.'

ROGER HUDDLE We were never able to build the bridges between Rock Against Racism and the Asian community. There wasn't Asian youth music in the same way as reggae came out of black youth, because it was much more difficult for them to break from their community leaders.

RUTH GREGORY: It has been asserted that RAR was racist towards Asian people. It's a bit silly when you look at the history of it. 'Black', to us, meant 'not-white'. A lot of Asian people came to the gigs. Alien Kulture did lots of gigs. They were like an Asian punk band.

JOHN BAINE Alien Kulture were a punk band from Paddington. They had songs like 'Asian Youth' and 'Culture Crossover', which had the chorus, *first generation, illegal immigrants / Second generation juvenile delinquents*, and then ended, *I want to play my records . . . I want to read my N-M-E*. They weren't technically very good but they were the only band from that scene. There was a Pakistani punk who had 'Zaki the Paki' on the back of his leather jacket.

DAVE RUFFY A lot of the girls would have to sneak out to come to the gigs because they came from very strict families and they weren't meant to be out in male company. This was Rock Against Racism in action, for me, because it was youth from different cultures going out. It was a natural part of the punk ethic. It was about liberation and freedom to do what you really want to do.

JOHN JENNINGS The headline in *NME* was 'Pogoing Pakistanis'. They weren't from Pakistan at all but it was amazing for us to see these Asian girls who used to come to the gigs. We used to look after them and make sure they got home. It was the closest you get to community within music.

DAVE RUFFY The girls said they felt safe because there was a little community of fans and they'd look out for each other: 'Hello, come in . . .'

CHRIS BOLTON No one noticed where people were coming from. That was the beautiful thing. You didn't think, 'Oh, there's an Asian punk.' It wasn't seen that way. People were people. Everyone was on the same level. You left all those prejudices behind for that moment. Imagine the spiritual uplifting that would give to people. That's why RAR was a very important part of musical history.

•

KATE WEBB Tensions in Southall had been growing since Gurdip Singh Chaggar had been stabbed to death in June 1976 by a white gang of alleged racists. Galvanized by police and community leaders' apathy, the Southall Youth Movement was formed 'to give a voice to the aspirations and concerns of young people in Southall' and 'to fight and challenge racial discrimination, racism, and demand justice and equality'. On St George's Day in April 1979, 3,000 protesters gathered outside Southall Town Hall, where the National Front had been bussed in to hold their meeting. The planned protest was to be peaceful but with the presence of over 2,500 police it soon became violent and more than forty people, including twenty-one police officers, were injured, and 300 people were arrested.

CHRIS BOLTON We knew the Southall Riot was going to happen because in the preceding weeks there'd been conflicts with the National Front marching in South London and Leicester, so we had decided to make the People Unite a medical hub in the forlorn hope that the police would respect the Red Cross. We were out of the country and we came back two days before the march. We'd left local community people running the project and there were faces I didn't know in the house. I checked down in the basement and I saw this crate of Molotov cocktails. I said, 'What the fuck is that doing there?' 'Oh, we made them with these guys last night.' 'Where are these guys now?' 'Upstairs.' I emptied all the petrol out, smashed all the bottles, put them in a bag and then went upstairs to the main room and said, 'I'm having a preventions check of everyone in this room. I want to know who you are and where you're coming from.' I put someone on the door and said, 'Watch anyone who comes out.' You could see these two guys starting to sort of back away. I thought, 'There they are.' They went downstairs and I followed them and they ran round to the police station: straight through the main door.

DAVE RUFFY Southall was multicultural. There wasn't any trouble but it was always seen as a threat by the authorities. It was a whitewash. The police did exactly what they wanted.

CHRIS BOLTON On the day of the march there were thousands of police surrounding the place, all parked up in coaches. You couldn't get into Southall because they had one outside barrier and another internal one around the town hall from the park up to the station. On that day murder was committed, not by the Metropolitan Police but by some anonymous force: a blacks ops thing of soldiers who didn't wear any numbers. If you understand you're in a trap, sometimes there's not a lot you can do. We had ensured in publicity that this was to be a peaceful protest. Misty's manager, Clarence, could be seen with a megaphone: 'No violence. This is peaceful.' There were women and children there. You don't go in for a pitched battle with kids on the street. We knew this was a provocation because we'd seen exactly the same thing in Lewisham two years before. The National Front were ferried in and started taunting people.

WILLIAM SIMON Southall was locked down. People trying to go home from work ended up in police stations. I ran into the house and there's some footage with a flare coming over. Everyone at the time thought it came from the house at Park View. It did not. It came from the back: near to the police station. It was at that point that they stormed the house.

CHRIS BOLTON We had made all these false phone calls saying we were going to assemble at Southall Park and suddenly we saw all these police vans pull up there so we knew they were listening to us. Then our phones were cut. I tried to get back to People Unite to warn them that they were coming but they had a whole snatch squad after me. I managed to drag them into the middle of the road and then they beat me up and dragged me around and I ended up in an SPG van. I could have well have been with the people that killed Blair Peach because they were just driving round, pulling up, jumping out, whack, whack, whack. And they were all armed with coshes. No numbers. I think it was because I was white and I was bleeding a lot, they said, 'He's had enough,' and threw me to the floor. I was well fucked up. I was pissing blood for about three days and had kidney trouble after. That day they fractured so many skulls.

SYD SHELTON The police turned everybody out of People Unite and as they came out the door they ran a gauntlet of batons and the police beat the shit out of them. They smashed Clarence's skull. He had a blood clot on the brain and was in intensive care for a week. We were told it was touch and go. That photograph of John Sturrock's on the front of *Temporary Hoarding*, with the police – and the bolts in the head, which we added – throwing the man into the gutter, tells you a whole story about Southall irrespective of reading a single word.

CHRIS BOLTON The police were looking for payback for the Notting Hill Carnival riot. They were shouting, 'You're the bastards from Ladbroke Grove.' A lot of us got beaten badly and Clarence was repeatedly hit round the head. We ended up in Vauxhall police station and they brought Clarence out to take him for interrogation and put him on the seat and he flopped out. He was unconscious. I thought, 'They're gonna fuck me as well,' so I made out to be more dead than I was. They took me in there and I saw this mixed-race fat copper there and another one. I saw them as Gestapo and I ran at the first one and squashed him with a table. He nearly popped. It was so nice. They didn't ask me any questions and they beat me again. Clarence was in a bad way and was bleeding. They left him in the cell with me. Then they let me out and took him somewhere else. I was in a very bloody, torn state. I didn't have any money. I walked to Vauxhall Tube station and told the guard I'd been in Southall and he let me on the Tube. My family thought I was dead.

DAVE RUFFY Vernon, Misty's keyboard player, went down for two years on a trumped-up charge of rioting and assault and never came back to music. They really fucked him up.

CHRIS BOLTON Clarence suffered a subdural haematoma and ended up in Central Middlesex neurological unit. He was in a coma for ten days or so. And that's when the people at Rough Trade were wonderful and got in a very good neurologist. People Unite was completely fucked. The SPG ruthlessly and needlessly damaged and destroyed £20,000 worth of sound and medical equipment. They wantonly destroyed records and other property, all of which was vital to the functioning of the Musicians' Co-op, including Misty In Roots. Not only did they destroy our premises and our studio – they'd methodically poured battery acid over the mixing desk mixers – they destroyed our people; some people never played music after that.

TIM WELLS I saw the police as a part of the problem. Anti-fascism was approached as a policing problem. How many people were being killed in police stations? Who killed Blair Peach? What side was the law on?

COLIN BARKER My nephew, who was seven, was in primary school in Bristol and they had an officer come to explain to them how policemen are your friends. Young Garrick puts his hand up and says, 'But I don't understand. Why did you kill Blair Peach?'

JOHN JENNINGS The SPG thought they could do anything. Thirty-six barristers wrote a letter saying there'd been a miscarriage of justice in Southall. It was a complete travesty.

JOHN DENNIS Being down there every day was very immersive: sitting in court, and Blair Peach's wife was there. There was a big deal around the coroner's report and whether it was murder. We were all going, 'This is very serious shit.' A comrade had been killed; Clarence was nearly killed; People Unite had been trashed; Thatcher got elected with the largest electoral swing from Labour to the Conservative Party since the war; and the

NF had been smashed, losing the deposit on all of their 303 candidates. We'd won the battle but lost the war. We were in collective shock.

RED SAUNDERS How did the Met get away with that murder? The downright lies. It was so utterly depressing.

DENNIS BOVELL When Linton recorded 'Reggae Fi Peach' I remember saying to him, 'What's Blair Peach got to do with this?' He said, 'Well, he was from New Zealand. He was a schoolteacher. It should be documented that that man lost his life in a struggle that he could well have not bothered himself. We should never forget that.' When I heard the lyrics I said, 'Linton, they're going to lock you up.' I really feared for him because he was accusing the paramilitary arm of the British police force of murder.

LINTON KWESI JOHNSON The police killed Blair Peach. I'm not accusing them of nothing. They did. It's not, 'Linton Kwesi Johnson says the police killed Blair Peach.' The police *killed* Blair Peach. 'Reggae Fi Peach' was basically expressing the fact that a lot of people in the black and Asian communities were moved by the killing. It was an expression of solidarity with the family and comrades of Blair Peach because he was an important activist in the struggle against racism and fascism. Yes, he was a Trotskyite but ideology wasn't a consideration. Blair Peach could easily have been a black or Asian man.

JOHN JENNINGS Whereas Linton recorded *They killed Blair Peach the teacher*, we wrote 'Jah War' about Clarence Baker: *He got whacked over the head with a truncheon*. And Malcolm wrote those brilliant lyrics. But most of the reviews were god-awful. They couldn't deal with white blokes trying to be black. There was one from Julie Burchill: 'Obviously, they've never been near this genre of music except listening to "(White Man) In Hammersmith Palais".'

DAVE RUFFY I thought, 'You've no fucking idea.' They accused us of being like Black and White Minstrels for doing reggae; it was a story about our friend who got fucking brain damage. We used to jam with Misty so we learnt how to do a lot of the roots. It wasn't like, 'We know how to play reggae.' It's really hard. When we jammed I was like, 'Don't take it for granted. Try and keep it fresh. Stay on top of it.' We just did it the best we could, with enormous respect.

CHRIS BOLTON Malcolm was married to Rocky, who was originally from Antigua and one of the only black people in Hayes. She was his childhood

**Misty in Roots' William Simon (centre) at the Counter Eurovision, Belgium,
31 March 1979.**

sweetheart. It must have been one of the most influential driving forces in his life to experience racism first hand with someone he loved. Rocky sings on 'Jah War' with Poko and Bertie from Misty. I was married to a girl from Dominica and we had mixed-race children. My wife was taking my son, who was nine months old at the time, to the doctor's, and on the way a car pulled over and attacked them with baseball bats. It nearly broke her heart. When you're in a relationship like that you get hit by traffic going both ways because there's also black people saying, 'What are you doing with my sister?' Southall was a hotspot of people coming in and attacking people.

DAVE RUFFY We had two black roadies, Mannah and Stacey. They were being pulled over all the time. We weren't getting pulled because we were white and we had short hair and dressed sharp. The cops only pulled you over if you had long hair. They could pull you over for no reason except suspicion.

CHRIS BOLTON During this period, the Ruts had their first major hit with 'Babylon's Burning'. Malcolm was trying to explain the tremendous anxiety of the collapse of this system: this Babylon, this Roman Empire, this terrible system of oppression which is destroying the world as we see it right before our very eyes. *You'll burn in the street / You'll burn in your houses with anxiety*. It was a very revolutionary song, and referring to 'Babylon' put it to the reggae core.

GEOFF BROWN The same day as the Southall Riot, the National Front also called a demonstration in Leamington Spa. But then they arranged with the police to move the demonstration, so we spent the day trying to find them. We found them near Nuneaton. The police stopped us as we got to the outskirts of the town so we headed off on foot with no real idea of where we were going. We got to an inner ring road and suddenly there comes a coach full of Nazis and they see us. They were bragging and laughing at us through the windows. At which point, out of the pockets of about twenty people came rocks and half-bricks and whatever. The coach and the coach that followed it got all the left-side windows smashed. It was a wonderful moment. The Nazis were all cowering. But then we came home and heard of the death of Blair Peach.

PAUL HOLBOROW After the autopsy Blair lay in state at the Dominion Cinema overnight with a guard from the Asian youth. Ten thousand people turned out to accompany his coffin, which went very slowly through Southall and then on to Phoenix School in East London where he taught and where there was another 10,000 people. I spoke at the cemetery, as did Neil Kinnock; Ken Gill, the president of the TUC; and Tony Cliff for the SWP.

JOHN DENNIS Pete Townshend had been mentoring Misty and supporting them through this period and said he wanted to do a benefit. And then I got a call from Joe Strummer out of the blue. He was slightly drunk and was saying, 'The punks are all falling apart. I want to put a gig together with all the big names in punk and record it for an LP to sell to support RAR. Can you book Hyde Park?' That's how the Southall Kids Are Innocent benefit gig came together, and later the idea for an *RAR's Greatest Hits* record.

SYD SHELTON We hired the Rainbow in Finsbury Park for two nights and booked the Pop Group, the Ruts, the Clash, Misty, Aswad, Bongo Danny and the Enchanters, and the Members to raise money for all the legal fees for all those arrested in Southall and to buy new gear for People Unite. We approached Pete [Townshend] for the PA. He said, 'I'll play as long as there's a bottle of Rémy Martin in the dressing room.'

**Pete Townshend at Southall Kids are Innocent, Rainbow Theatre,
London, 13 July 1979.**

JOHN DENNIS I was such a stingy man, I thought, 'What! Rémy Martin, £20 a bottle! You can't be serious.' The real idiot came out in me so I don't think he got it. To get the Clash we went to see them somewhere south of the river and somebody suggested we had a game of football. It was in the middle of the summer so everybody was wearing light shoes, but Strummer was wearing fucking motorcycle boots and kicking the shit out of us. We still beat them 4–0. They were going through that period with Bernie Rhodes and maybe not having a manager, so sometime after I went to see them again in a pub in Soho. I was chatting with Mick Jones and about two hours later Strummer turned up, totally pissed off: 'Who the fuck are you?' Mick was going, 'No, Joe. He's fine.' Then Simonon turned up. He was such a cool-looking guy but he was bored. He had this little penknife which he started throwing at the door and it wouldn't stick. It was such a naff thing to do.

RED SAUNDERS There was talk that Townshend was going to bring Clapton. I was, 'Fuck me! How on earth are we going to deal with this?' I was going to be a right old hack and go, 'Unless we have a clear written apology you ain't coming, mate,' but it never happened.

**Brinsley Forde (front) of Aswad, Southall Kids are Innocent,
Rainbow Theatre, London, 14 July 1979.**

<u>WAYNE MINTER</u> The Rainbow was a beautiful art nouveau cinema – it's now a Pentecostal church, which is ironic – and Pete paid £2,750 for us to take all the seats out. That was the first time that had been done. We expected trouble so we had the Southall Youth Movement, who were highly trained in martial arts, patrolling the outside of the building, and women in RAR T-shirts policing inside.

<u>BRINSLEY FORDE</u> I had seen Bob Marley perform at the Rainbow. We couldn't get in and so a lot of people pushed through the door. It was a great memory because it was the gig they filmed for *Bob Marley Live at the Rainbow*, so having the opportunity to perform there was like, 'Wow! I'm at the Rainbow.'

<u>WILLIAM SIMON</u> It was a brilliant gig. They came to see Pete and they were handing him roses at the stage door. Music is like a smile and everyone knows what a smile means. No matter what language you speak, everyone can relate to a musical smile. If people are smiling they're not going to be firing guns. It brought people together.

<u>CHRIS BOLTON</u> I was still trying to formulate what to do, what's got to be

The Clash at Southall Kids are Innocent, Rainbow Theatre, London, 13 July 1979.

done; thinking of people who were in prison like Vernon, and Clarence who was still not well. But it was wonderful that people came forward to support us. It was a monumental gig and helped us keep going.

JOHN DENNIS The Enchanters were a bit of a pain because they were part of the People Unite Musicians' Cooperative and thought they should headline the gig. There was a big argument about that. 'This is about us. We should headline the gig.' One of Misty said, 'Fuck off. You're not head-lining this.' And they shut up.

WAYNE MINTER It went like a dream. I was in the projection box. The Pop Group were quite unusual, quite strange: arty, powerful jazz sound, very radical. And Pete Townshend played solo with an acoustic guitar doing blues, with Peter Hope-Evans playing some great harmonica, John 'Rabbit' Bundrick behind the keyboards, Tony Butler on bass and Kenney Jones on drums.

LUCY WHITMAN It was important to have bands that were cool, which didn't necessarily mean bands in the charts.

KATE WEBB This was all part of the move into whether or not we were becoming more mainstream. We could have put on bigger bands earlier on but that wasn't what RAR was about. It was like the Clash sang: *No Elvis, Beatles or the Rolling Stones in 1977*. It was cultural cleansing: rejecting the past to say, 'We are about now.'

JOHN DENNIS The Clash were fantastic but punk was moving on – tellingly, their expenses for the night were £230 compared to Aswad and the Ruts, who got £60 – and the audience was the blue-jean jacket brigade. It wasn't the RAR audience that we knew. That began the conversation that we were having internally about the genre thing.

RED SAUNDERS The solidarity, the enthusiasm, the buzz: it was of those young people. It was their music, their three-chord stuff, their lyrics. These were extraordinary times. Members of the Clash and Steel Pulse had demonstrated outside the NF headquarters in South London with placards. You weren't going to get Paul McCartney on the fucking picket line at Southall, d'you know what I mean? RAR was about the culture and energy of that moment. We were dedicated to the spirit of the time. It was a short window of punk and reggae. It was our policy to have black bands playing with white bands because we had black cultural friends, musicians, actors. It was so important not to use superstars – it would have diluted it – because we were so rolled up in punk and the whole working-class piss-take of punk and the beauty of *God bless her fascist regime* and all that stuff.

RENOUNCE ALL SIN AND VICE

Leeds. Birmingham

WAYNE MINTER Since the Militant Entertainment tour our role was to try and make RAR grow locally: maintaining a register of hundreds of bands, seriously distributing *Temporary Hoarding*, ordering badges, booking venues, giving advice, developing the DIY ethic. The best thing about Rock Against Racism was its localism, in every sense: local bands, local production, local organization. Look at all the people involved in it: we had weekly RAR clubs in Liverpool, Manchester, Paisley, Leeds, Birmingham and across various London boroughs; events were going on in Glasgow, Aberdeen, Belfast, Sheffield, Hull, Southampton, Cardiff, Luton, Edinburgh, Bath. The Pop Group in Bristol, the Beat and the Specials in the Midlands, the Mekons and Delta 5 and Scritti Politti in Leeds, the Piranhas down in Brighton. And there were some great local EPs recorded for RAR. Glasgow had a habit of turning out unlistenable punk records full of extremely bad language, like XS Discharge: *Ha! Ha! Funny Polis*. It was the small groups that fired me up: the people in Upper Heyford in Oxfordshire hiring their village hall to put on a local band. That was the heart of RAR and what made us unique historically. It was why RAR grew so fast. And it was those people that got on the buses and came down to the Carnivals. I don't think that alliance of localism in DIY, political awareness and music had happened before.

RED SAUNDERS RAR had tuppence ha'penny and it was put together with a couple of elastic bands, but it was that driving passion and energy and your solidarity with the culture and the bands. Somebody would write to me from Aberystwyth and say, 'We read your letter in the *Melody Maker* and we think it's fantastic. We're a bunch of fifteen-year-old schoolkids and our teacher's a fascist. How can we get involved?' And I'd write back saying, 'Great. *You* are Rock Against Racism Aberystwyth. Get on with it.'

ROGER HUDDLE If an SWP member in Swansea phoned me up: 'What should I do?' I'd send them our gig guide, which gave step-by-step advice on how to put on your own events, or say, 'We've got one or two RAR contacts, why don't you go and talk to them?' And they did, in their thousands, all over the country.

JOHN BAINE A group of us at Kent University set up a Rock Against Racism society with a £50 grant from the Student Union. We produced leaflets and posters and we put on gigs: the Jam in '76, 999's first gig, the Stranglers, the Damned supported by the Adverts, Misty, and the Enchanters. It was a really exciting time and we covered the room in home-made slogans sprayed on bits of paper: 'Black and white unite and fight!' 'Smash the National Front!' 'Punks and Teds and Natty Dreads, smash the Front and join the Reds!' We didn't have a direct link with central RAR. We just sent off for badges and stickers and *Temporary Hoarding*.

KATE WEBB What was extraordinary was how much we were able to do without contracts. How much looser everything was. We just opened an account at the Co-op and did stuff. You made some money from a gig and then you had enough for the next thing. And we set up a supporters' scheme: a quid for life!

John Baine (left) aka Attila the Stockbroker, with Steven Wells,
Central London Polytechnic, 24 February 1982.

Andy Gill (left) and Jon King of the Gang of Four, at West Runton Pavilion, Cromer, Norfolk, 17 March 1979.

PAUL FURNESS In Leeds, we put on the second-ever RAR gig, after the one with Carol Grimes at the Princess Alice. It was in a prefab, some sort of social club used by trade unions, that backed onto Leeds Poly. It was with my friends who were in a band called Foxy Maiden. I used to buy all the music papers religiously. There was this hard core of us – myself, Linda, Barry, Dave and a few others from the SWP – who set up the Leeds RAR Club. And we would gear the nights towards anything that was coming round, like International Women's Week or Irish things, South Africa, Chile or gay stuff. And we always had a stall selling left-wing books and *Socialist Worker* and *Temporary Hoarding* and badges. We deliberately made the gigs feel political. We ran the club for eighteen months. Sometimes we'd have bugger-all people and sometimes it was absolutely packed out. We put two or three bands on at each gig and then twice a week for six months at the end. The bands didn't get paid much. I'd be surprised if we paid the Gang of Four more than a fiver.

KATE WEBB I remember being at a party with some of the Gang of Four. They were talking about 'How do we get these kids to turn away from fascism?' which was a massive question. They were very bright guys and very interested in sexual politics and aggression from the stage and how you portray that. They were pretty articulate. They were asking, 'Is music enough?'

ANDY GILL At its crux Gang of Four was most defined by the issues involved in Rock Against Racism but we were never promoting a party political point of view. It was about trying to describe the reality around us in a truthful way. It was never straightforward sloganeering like the Clash, who almost had a stance by association. Gang of Four was more cerebral about it. I wanted to construct songs in a certain way that wasn't the old formula: something that was minimal and rhythmically interesting. It was almost like saying, 'I haven't got a musical language which is working for me so I'm going to try and construct something.' And then lyrically saying, 'Let's describe our lives and how we think it works and what we think impinges on us and influences the decisions we make every day.' It was realism, and people hadn't really done that. It was a totally new set of subjects and a totally new way of talking about it.

LESLEY WOODS I loved the Gang of Four. We managed to get a gig supporting them and they offered us a support on an American tour. They were very supportive of us. Paul was very influenced by Andy's guitar playing, which he played almost like it was a machine gun. He'd go to the front and look very stern and play this real gashy riff, really strong. It was like, 'Wow!' I'd never seen anybody play a guitar like that before. I was staying at their flat and I found a piece of paper with two lines on it: *He works the car / She the sink*, and I stole it for the Au Pairs song 'Diet'.

ANDY GILL It was seeing the personal as political. We were interested by the idea that what people often explained as the 'natural order' of things are actually man-made constructs. For example, women should have kids and look after the home. When you say something is 'natural' then it's a catch-all and it's hard to argue with. We were challenging man-made ideological constructs within different power relationships, whether it was the church or the monarchy or the ruling class or male over female. The song 'Natural's Not In It' is about that. The lyrics give you image after image and things from the Bible: *renounce all sin and vice*. But some women felt we'd got a nerve taking a feminist stance because it can look like you're setting yourself up as if you're not guilty as well. I was profoundly guilty. There's a massive difference between trying to say you're righteous and just making observations about how society works. We profoundly disagreed with many aspects of male rock culture and found it quite unpleasant, but you can imagine the dialectic going on with four males in the band; sometimes the conversation got distinctly sexist.

JOHN DENNIS Gang of Four had the track 'At Home He's A Tourist', with the lyric about *a rubber in his pocket*. *Top of the Pops* wanted them to take out the *rubber* reference. They refused so didn't do the show. They should regret it, because that commercial breakthrough was the only thing missing: huge integrity, huge creativity, really intelligent lyrics, musically really influential.

SHERYL GARRATT There was a ready-made circuit for bands like the Au Pairs and the Gang of Four to play on, with a PA and resources to share. The Gang of Four and the Mekons would come and play Birmingham, and the Beat and the Au Pairs would go and play Leeds. Before that there was no real reason to have interaction between those cities. Rock Against Racism gave a voice to this huge burst of creativity and the gigs gave everybody a platform and a confidence. You could meet people all around the country that felt the same way. It connected dots. You can't imagine how isolated it was. The only reason a working-class kid from Birmingham would travel to Leeds would be to watch a football match and fight.

PAUL FURNESS Leeds was a very big industrial city then. It was very monochrome, and the buildings were really black with over 100 years of pollution and lots of the streets were derelict. The whole place looked like a building site. There was this real sense of fear. The National Front were vicious and running riot. They used to put razor blades under their stickers so people would get their fingers serrated pulling them down. There was 'NF' graffiti all over, daubed massively on walls. One time we came out of a gig and an Asian brother and sister were with us. We got into their car and we were suddenly surrounded by National Front. They got onto the roof and the bonnet and were hammering on the windows. It was awful. They were absolutely brutal. People would have their windows put through. I went to Sheffield for a week and came home and there was a KKK sign painted on the pavement outside saying, 'We know where you live.' We'd be selling *Socialist Worker* on a Saturday and they would come down and be selling their paper as well. It ended up in fights all the time. There was a pub called the Fenton where a lot of the bands from the left, like the Gang of Four and the Mekons, used to go, and the NF led an attack and the place was wrecked.

ANDY GILL It was shocking when the National Front smashed up the

Fenton. Friends of ours were there: lots of chairs flying, glass smashing, people getting hit. They targeted art students and bohemian types and gays. There was also a series of nights when right-wingers came onto Leeds University campus looking for people. A friend went out to confront them and got knocked down and his head was smashed in with a metal traffic cone. Violence was almost like a hit of cheap speed. There was this one guy in particular who was brandishing a knife at one of our gigs. I could see it from the stage and we stopped playing and I said, 'We're not going to be the soundtrack to your violence.'

PAUL FURNESS The Leeds RAR club moved to Chapeltown in a building that had been a synagogue and then a West Indian club. I was there one night and the next day I found out that Peter Sutcliffe, the 'Yorkshire Ripper', had killed a woman at the back of it. There was a bar underneath where all the prostitutes and their pimps used to go when it was their tea break. I remember Crisis coming down, who had this aura of tough South London street punks. I said, 'I'll come up after work; meet me in the bar downstairs.' I went in and they were literally cowering in a corner. They said, 'Why didn't you tell us about this place?' I said, 'What do you mean?' The tough Londoners were terrified.

Another time, we put Joy Division on and their manager wanted us to take the RAR banners down. He was just arguing, but we stuck to our guns so they played under the banner. Ian Curtis ended up at ours and Sheryl took him upstairs. There was a bakery that we called the 'second-hand food shop' because you could get 100 pasties for 50p and that's what we gave him for his breakfast. He had this two-tone suit and shirt on in this dump that I lived in. I thought he was a bit miserable and withdrawn and he just moaned about the manager all morning.

•

SHERYL GARRATT I was about sixteen when I joined Birmingham RAR; just a suburban kid. One month there was a news story in *Broadside*, this little left-wing magazine, saying Birmingham Rock Against Racism is forming. There was a meeting in this pub in Digbeth on Sunday lunchtime. Me and my friend Kim went, both absolutely terrified and excited and we met all these people with exotic lifestyles. And Pete, Paul and Lesley from the Au Pairs came with their manager, Martin Culverwell. It was a small close-knit social thing more than anything. We ran a weekly club on a Friday night in Digbeth Civic Hall, called Room at the Top. Every week we would religiously book a white band and a black band, naively thinking that you could solve racism by putting punk with reggae. Soundchecks were about five minutes. The whole thing was so amateurish.

LESLEY WOODS The Au Pairs were very active in Rock Against Racism. It gave a voice and an articulation to the fact that racism that already existed. I had come to Birmingham when I was eighteen and I remember Clapton being discussed at the meetings and being shocked: 'Oh my God! A musician said that?' Music is a means of a communication. It's almost like a musician's duty to be at the forefront of righting the wrongs in society and being conscious of injustices. If you're a true poet you see things as they are, not as a product of your class or your race or your gender. You transcend that.

PAUL FURNESS We all became big friends with the Au Pairs. They were quite visceral and raw. We put them on loads of times. They used to stay in our house. Lesley was great. She had a voice like a razor blade when she talked to you. She could be a bit scary. Everyone was in love with her and she was in love with everybody. The bands were putting what I was reading into music. It was a compliment to my political activity.

SHERYL GARRATT One night we got a minibus and went to an Angelic Upstarts gig somewhere outside of town and just argued with all the National Front skinheads there. We were pretty fearless. 'Liquidator' came on; they were chanting *British Movement* and I steamed onto the dance floor and said, 'Do you know how fucking absurd this is? Do you know what colour these people are?' And then at the end of the night we gave a bunch of them a lift home and argued with them all the way back to Birmingham. They were National Front in the same way as I was left-wing. It was like a vague unease that things weren't right and life wasn't fair and the future was mapped out for you as a working-class kid. And their unease was, 'We blame the Pakis.' They were just young lads looking for something to do.

LESLEY WOODS The Angelic Upstarts were meant to play a gig with UB40 at the RAR club but they didn't turn up. The whole hall was full of skinheads so they asked if we would play.

SHERYL GARRATT I was on the door and there were skinheads demanding their money back and I wouldn't give it because we had to pay for the hall. They were going, 'This is shit.'

JANE MUNRO We'd gone along in the afternoon to help with setting up and the PA didn't turn up because it was with the Upstarts. There was some great scramble to get a van and we had to get our PA, which was not entirely suitable for Digbeth Civic Hall, but it was that or nothing. UB40 went on and did their set and went down all right-ish. We were still praying the Upstarts would turn up but they didn't, so we had to go on instead and the skinheads were throwing everything that wasn't nailed down at the stage. I was on stage ducking missiles. Our manager, Martin, had to jump offstage to help a girl down the front. The skinheads were being really obnoxious because they were so pissed off that their heroes hadn't turned up and they were getting this rubbish feminist band.

LESLEY WOODS We arranged between us that UB40 would go on first because we thought they might not get such a hammering. Then we came on and got gobbed at and bins thrown at us. It was just mad. They really went crazy but we just stood our ground. You had to stand up to them: 'You missed.' At the end I got talking to a few of them about why they were in the National Front and managed to turn them, and they joined the Anti-Nazi League. That's probably the best thing I've ever done in my life. I was very young and had the energy and the motivation to talk to them. I'd probably just shout at them now, but nobody had ever bothered to take the time to talk to them before.

KATE WEBB At its best, Rock Against Racism was about the regional groups; people who had been inspired by the DIY ethic and organized themselves locally. Bands like the Au Pairs and Gang of Four who helped to carry the anti-racist, anti-sexist agenda beyond just punk and reggae and addressed those issues in their songwriting. By the summer of 1979 we had achieved great things, but also Margaret Thatcher had been elected. There was a new Conservative government and the mood of the country was changing, both politically and culturally.

RINSE OUT THE BLUE SCUM

RAR's Greatest Hits. **Northern Carnival Against Racism. Legacy**

JOHN DENNIS RAR got bigger than anyone ever expected, with a level of responsibility for making it work and moving on. Red had put a lot of time and energy into the first Carnival and he was knackered. Roger was knackered. After a few meetings I got really pissed off – I was working as a play leader. I'd done a master's degree – I said, 'Enough of this. I'll come in and work full-time.' A deal was done with the Anti-Nazi League to pay me £30 a week to work on the second Carnival with Jerry Fitzpatrick.

RED SAUNDERS There was too much shit piling up and we were all part-timers. John was a brilliant organizer, very patient guy, but quite opposite to a lot of us. He came into the office with Wayne and joined Kate. And that was phase two of RAR with a new group of younger people. I was like, 'Hallelujah.'

KATE WEBB We hired a small office at 265a Seven Sisters Road in Finsbury Park, above the Socialist Workers Bookshop. It was cold and had a horrible stinky gas heater. We didn't have a lot of money and the room was chaotic. It was kind of like a half-slum but underneath the mess there was quite a lot of organization. There were badges, leaflets, T-shirts, and all these things had to be organized, designed, made, ordered, brought in, shipped out. Then there was all the stuff about organizing any gig: book the hall, persuade people that you were credible. People were constantly coming in and out and dumping their stuff.

WAYNE MINTER We would sit in there pumping out all this stuff, being paid a meagre amount a week but enough to be off the dole. It was nearly all phone calls and postcards and people saying, 'We want to put on a gig.' It was basically, 'Just go and do it yourself: hire a local hall, sort out a music licence, find bands . . . blah, blah, blah.' We had a huge list of bands, some absolute troupers, who would go and play anywhere for Rock Against Racism.

KATE WEBB Increasingly people just took the name of Rock Against

Racism. Brent Council was run by Harriet Harman's husband Jack Dromey and they just thought, 'Let's put on a Carnival. They've done it in Victoria Park. The kids come along. It makes a nice anti-racist atmosphere and it brings the community together.' There was a band, I think it was Ultravox or maybe Another Pretty Face, and I realized they were pumping applause through the PA system. It said a lot about where pop music was heading, and was the antithesis of what RAR was about. There were small carnivals like that all over the place. It then became a question: how do we control what people are doing in RAR's name?

DAVE RUFFY We all got a little bit tired of the slogans at every gig: 'Anti-vegans', 'Anti-hunting', 'Battered Wives Against the Nazis'. There were so many people hanging onto your show: 'Can we put this up? Can we put that up?' 'Yeah, but we're trying to do a show for the people here.'

JOHN JENNINGS If you've got a bill: the Ruts, Misty In Roots, and the Rasta drummers, it's pretty obvious it's black and white. In the end we said, 'D'you know what? Let's just do some gigs.' There was equal billing and then we'd jam at the end but the essence of Rock Against Racism was still there. You didn't need a banner. Like everything, RAR had its time.

SYD SHELTON Thatcher getting in, in May, had been an absolute disaster. That was the beginning of the end of Rock Against Racism. Red wrote, 'Suddenly there was a frightening new set of cherries come up on the great fruit machine of life . . . now the real gangsters have come . . .'

RED SAUNDERS Then you're taking on the Tory Party and the government. I mean, fucking hell. It was a different question. It was another campaign. And Thatcher represented everything that we were against. I wrote, 'Get out your dancing shoes, get your glad rags on, turn that volume right up loud, tell them RAR's coming; we're gonna blow this fucking lot right out of town. Rinse out the Blue Scum.'

TOM ROBINSON The National Front had been trounced at the general election and destroyed as a political force, but we couldn't have carried on as we were. If Callaghan had got another term I don't think the world would have become a better place as a result.

ROGER HUDDLE Thatcher won, not because people supported her but because they were disillusioned with Labour. Remember the poster campaign 'Labour Isn't Working' with a long queue of unemployed people outside the dole office.

RED SAUNDERS There's a long discussion about Rock Against Racism and the Anti-Nazi League and Thatcher and the National Front decline. You can see the National Front were already well on the decline before Thatcher had started her 'alien culture' speech. She was clever. And Norman Tebbit's cricket analysis: which team would you back if you were black – the West Indies or England?

DAVID WIDGERY Margaret Thatcher caught the mood perfectly by accosting a black mother in the streets of South London and inquiring querulously, 'Now, which part of Africa do you come from?' 'Tooting,' she was told.[30]

JOHN DENNIS The racists didn't vote for the National Front, they voted for Thatcher. They weren't going to be Nazi but they were going to be Tory. How right-wing Thatcher was going to be nobody really knew.

PETER HAIN You could feel the National Front receding as we dominated the scene. They were becoming demoralized and you could feel their confidence draining away. They weren't able to march. They weren't able to organize. And that disillusioned group of working-class youngsters found another identity under RAR and the ANL. I later sued Martin Webster for libel and he admitted in the court case that the Anti-Nazi League had been responsible for shutting down the National Front. He said, 'Wherever we were the ANL was. Whatever numbers we had, they had more, and that destroyed us, both in physical opposition and through propaganda.'

RED SAUNDERS Webster said, 'Whenever we did anything these red thugs were there. They disrupted us, they messed us up, they broke our cars, they smashed our vans, we'd try to have a peaceful British march and they'd be there demonstrating.' The reason that we took off was that most of what you would call the RAR crew in the early days were people who were all like me: products of the Sixties. So they'd been through counterculture, the underground, political activity; they'd had some experience in all these areas, so they weren't completely naive about the daunting task of maybe trying to change the world in a tiny way by stopping the rise of fascism amongst youth with the power of music. Our job was to strip the Union Jack to reveal the swastika, and the NF was defeated.

KATE WEBB After the Tory victory we did a leaflet which quoted the Clash lyric, *What are we gonna do now?* and asked local groups for their opinions, which we discussed at the national conference in Birmingham. Two things that came out of that were the Dance And Defend tour and Rock Against Thatcher.

JOHN DENNIS Dance and Defend was a pet project of Wayne's in September '79 after the Southall Kids Are Innocent benefit gig.

WAYNE MINTER As a response to the police riots, not only in Southall, but also in Leicester and West Bromwich, twenty-plus small-scale gigs took place with bands like Scritti Politti, Delta 5, the Mekons, Misty, Gang of Four and the Au Pairs to draw attention and raise money for the defence campaigns where eighty-seven people had been charged and four jailed. And then Kate organized Rock Against Thatcher.

KATE WEBB Rock Against Thatcher was a fresh initiative trying to get local groups to do gigs under a new regional framework. We strung a few gigs together and called it a tour. The Jam did one and I did UB40 at the Ritzy in Brixton. It was setting out the new mood abroad in the country. And asking what kind of figure Thatcher was: that she was something new, a grocer's daughter, and not like the old patrician Tories. It was about RAR shifting gears and moving into the new decade.

The Jam at Central London Polytechnic, 24 February 1982.
Note: the year on the banner has been altered from 1981 to 1982.

RED SAUNDERS All through this I was still working as a freelance photographer, and the *Sunday Times* commissioned me to do a photo story about Richard Branson. I spent several days with him doing 'Richard Branson learning to fly', 'Richard Branson cooking in the Manor House', 'Richard Branson's houseboat'. We became quite friendly but Richard would say, 'You're really exaggerating about racism, Red.' So I gave him books and I'd talk for a long time about racist attacks in Tower Hamlets. To cut a long story short, he got sympathetic and said, 'I'll do an RAR album on Virgin.'

SYD SHELTON We went to see Simon Draper at Virgin who ran the office in Notting Hill Gate: Branson's number two. We were talking about the RAR record and how we wanted it to be celebratory. He was pointing out snags and problems with distribution and suddenly said, 'The nigger in the woodpile on this one is . . .' I said, 'What? What did you just say?' He said, 'What did I say? What are you talking about?' I said, 'Are we just going to walk out of here or are we going to sort it out?' He didn't have a clue what I was talking about. He was going, 'What? . . . what? . . . what have you got upset about? . . . Oh, it's just an expression.' I said, 'We're doing a Rock Against *Racism* album!'

WAYNE MINTER I never supported the album project, considering it at best a dangerous diversion of energy and resources from grass-roots activism and spreading the RAR anti-racist ethos, and at worst a gift to the growing number of anti-RAR pundits claiming commercial and political sell-out. The idea of an album with centrally selected bands and 'greatest hits' seemed contradictory to the spirit of RAR and an insult to all the stalwart bands not included. They were arguing and negotiating its release for over a year to do with rights and choosing tracks. It seemed to be moving further and further away from the do-it-yourself street-punk ethos. Elvis's manager, Jake Riviera, got heavily involved. I suggested naming all the local groups and bands that had ever played an RAR gig on the inner sleeve. It didn't happen.

KATE WEBB The album was mostly John's thing. He compiled it with Red. I didn't like the music much.

JOHN DENNIS There was Carol Grimes, Stiff Little Fingers, Gang of Four, the Piranhas, Barry Ford Band, X-Ray Spex, Matumbi, Steel Pulse, Aswad, TRB doing a live version of 'Winter of '79', 'Goon Squad' from Elvis Costello, the Mekons, the Cimarons, the Members, and I had three different versions of the Clash's '(White Man) In Hammersmith Palais' to choose from.

RAR Greatest Hits poster, September 1980.

CAROL GRIMES 'You Won't Let Me Down' was on it. That was during a period of time where I couldn't record. That track was already done and I just said, 'Have it.' It was written by Penny Wood, who was the sister of the comedienne Victoria Wood.

JOHN DENNIS It was a compilation of the best supporters from RAR so Carol's track was Red saying, 'We've got to pay dues.' The Gang of Four track 'Why Theory?' was recorded specifically for the album. I spent a day in the studio with them. They wanted a shaker going through the whole track and Hugo the drummer could only do that for about thirty seconds and keep it in time. Half a day was spent on this fucking thing. Andy Gill was amazing. He just knocked it out. The real surprise was Jon King doing his vocal. He couldn't get the sound. I got impatient and said, 'Sing it like Andy.' 'Fucking shut up, man.' We were there to the early hours of the morning and they kicked us out because it was in a house and they wanted to get to sleep. The advertisement was of a copper with a brick coming over and knocking his hat off. I got a call from Jake Riviera: 'How the fuck did you do that, man? The posters are everywhere.'

RED SAUNDERS By that time the organization was starting to break into factions. It's that old thing, 'When the enemy's gone the united front starts to fall apart.' There were lots of different opinions and there was a split in the RAR camp.

RUTH GREGORY *RAR's Greatest Hits* was due to be released in September 1980 and out of that came John Dennis's idea that we could make masses of money. We went, 'This isn't what we signed up for.' The end was all quite bitter really. In the beginning it was a whole assortment of people who were interested and would turn up at the meetings to plan what we were going to do next and how logistically we were going to raise funds for the next *Temporary Hoarding*. They were very informal but minutes were taken and we voted on some things. There was a lot of just general chit-chat but further down the line it was all about business and what the next intervention ought to be.

KATE WEBB The difference between me and a bunch of Tom Robinson fans sitting up all night sending handwritten letters to people in Paisley or wherever, to the point where you've got up to 100 groups in the UK and active RAR groups across Canada, USA, Sweden, Norway, West Germany as it was, Belgium and Holland, and you're doing big gigs and tours, all happened within a couple of years. It moved very quickly. People came and went. There was never really a single static centre other than the office. We were continually improvising. That's why in the end it's not surprising it fell apart. It wasn't a rigid structure.

RUTH GREGORY In any organization you get personality conflicts. John Dennis went into the RAR office and proceeded to take it over from Kate by not telling anybody what he was doing, and Kate kept complaining that it was no longer a democratic situation. He wanted to make RAR into a limited company and go down that corporate route. There were big ructions over that. We didn't see the point. It would have destroyed it.

KATE WEBB There was a clash of politics over where RAR should go, and involved in all that was the combustible emotion of individual relationships. People had their own jobs and their own lives, as well as all this stuff. I was the age of the bands. They were the age of the managers. John did not communicate in the same way and I don't think he trusted me politically. He was different to us all. I felt that from the beginning. He was a more guarded person. The biggest problem was the secrecy. Things didn't get talked about enough. We didn't have cool discussions about what was happening to RAR and where we wanted to go. What kind of organization were we? Was the money leading us or us leading the money? Having a cultural organization with a political slant – which is what John wanted it to be – is a perfectly valid idea but it wasn't what RAR was. The lead towards becoming a limited company broke RAR but I can't see how that could have happened without Red's approval.

JOHN DENNIS Kate was a teenager with no experience. She was swamped but she kept the office going. It was as good as she could make it but it wasn't a campaign. My inclination is always to look at the organization. Strategically: 'What are the issue involved here?' 'Where do we go from here?' The disagreement focused on a misunderstanding about bureaucratic detail around RAR Ltd, but RAR was not a commercial company. I think people misunderstood that. There were other issues, personal things. And there was a genuine debate to be had about what kind of organization RAR was and could become. Frankly, there were no other ideas put forward. They were arguing against something that nobody was arguing for. Everybody was well pissed off. I'm not going to blame anyone. I disagreed with them. The misunderstandings were there to be resolved. There was a lot of tiredness in the organization, just genuine, 'Fuck, this is getting really exhausting.' The position I took was, 'Look, we're not selling

RAR badges at the volume that we were. We were not getting rid of as many *Temporary Hoarding*s as we did. The music scene is fragmenting.'

WAYNE MINTER John is good at playing his cards quite close to his chest. It's a bit of a cliché but we were a victim of our own success. After the Front was completely blown out in the May '79 elections there wasn't that impetus anymore. I didn't want to be a record company executive. I didn't want to be even a gig promoter. I was a campaigner who loved music. I was disillusioned. I recall being suspicious of the idea that RAR Ltd could allow us to run the campaign with a defined membership without stopping the growth of grass-roots activity. I was bored. We debated everything at length until the early hours of the morning.

JOHN DENNIS We had a collective failure of imagination. The challenge was huge. And after Thatcher being elected, as far as I was concerned – and I don't think this was wholly shared – the thing was that RAR was anti-racist and that battle wasn't finished. It would go on. We had 'brand recognition'. We had loyalty. We had this influence. It meant that the campaign would have longevity by consolidating what we had. We could have a record label. That's what we used the album for, to launch the idea; *Temporary Hoarding* could have become a viable magazine. That was my position and that's what I argued for.

PAUL FURNESS I'd been coaxed down to London by David Widgery to work nationally and I was in the office with Wayne and John and writing a lot for *Temporary Hoarding*. John always wore a suit, never a tie, and sat at a desk. The criticism of him at the time was that he was a careerist, and if you wanted to make RAR last longer then it had to be something else completely. I felt like an intruder. I had arrived pretty unaware of all these machinations going on so I entered into this cesspit which I couldn't make head nor tail of. There were silences in the office.

RED SAUNDERS I was sympathetic to John. He worked so fucking hard. Widgery and Ruth put forward a little manifesto that RAR was going in the wrong direction. And that was aimed against John. I was in the middle, as I often found myself, trying to go, 'Look, hold on.' I was so disappointed.

SYD SHELTON We had this national conference to elect a committee. It was farcical because everybody knew who was doing the work. John and Red wanted to put the money that we had in the bank on one side so if we didn't get elected we could still carry on, which would have left the prospective company unaccountable to RAR members. I thought that was totally undemocratic. Me, Ruth, and Widgery all resigned from the central committee on the spot. RAR was disintegrating by then anyway. We were all exhausted.

WAYNE MINTER Ruth and Syd and Dave walked out several times and nearly always walked back in at some point.

RUTH GREGORY RAR had run its course. We had done the things we'd set out to do. We were all burnt out. At the conference we issued a statement which said, 'We have no confidence in John Dennis's ability as the dominant figure in RAR's day-to-day doings to bring together the cultural electricity we are going to need to generate to get Margaret to Stand Down. RAR is in danger of changing from a roots, anti-racist culture campaign into another hip capitalist company . . .' It ended, 'RAR means all power to the imagination, not all power to the pocket calculator.'

KATE WEBB The response of the committee to Ruth, Syd and Widgery's resignation was a three-page document which ended with the line, '. . . We will use any weapon in the fight against racism, pocket calculators included.' I refused to sign it. So that left the whole question of who or what the RAR central committee was by that point. It was John, Wayne and Red, which was not enough people for it to be a committee. When the biggest fights happened it felt like it was the men, and the women being ignored. RAR was a male-dominated organization.

RED SAUNDERS RAR was an ad hoc group of people but there was a move to tighten up and get more organized and that led to faction fighting. I tended to be more central. I was trying to hold everybody together. But the disagreements very quickly erupted and RAR fell apart. It's a reality of political campaigning. Within the rainbow of the coalition, can you imagine all the different opinions? You'd have hippy-dippy people in purple loon pants and fucking green hair going, 'Yeah, man, this is great – let's get stoned, man,' next to hard-line fucking street-fighting organizers. It was such an extraordinary alliance. That's why these things don't last that long. They burn like a meteorite. Five years and it was all over. The alliance couldn't hold together once the enemy was defeated.

•

DAVID WIDGERY RAR had taken off because ordinary unfamous people had worn badges, won arguments, volunteered, raved, hustled and fly-posted. Most of all, musicians – of all waves – had come good.[31] It was about how black and white people, outside conventional politics, inspired by a mixture of socialism, punk rock and common humanity, got together and organized to change things. It was temporary. We didn't stop racial attacks, far less racism. Indeed, the gloomy political predictions made by RAR about the social consequences of Mrs Thatcher's self-serving political philosophy, Britain's deeply embedded involvement with the regime in South Africa and the remorseless militarization of our police force proved only too accurate. But the simple, electrifying idea that pop music can be about more than entertainment has endured and deepened.[32] For a while we managed to create, in our noisy, messy, unconventional way, an emotional alternative to nationalism and patriotism, a celebration of a different kind of pride and solidarity.[33]

JOHN DENNIS Rock Against Racism had created a confidence in a community and a sense of belonging which wasn't one of the boxes to tick on the campaign mission but was a consequence of it. Racism became identified with the state, institutional racism in the police, not racism person to person. Elections are quantitative, you can see the results, but the qualitative effect: I think we did achieve more than perhaps we thought. There were people around who were like, 'What the fuck is RAR on about?' 'What are you trying to do?' and misunderstanding who our audience was. We were not nice people. We were not anti-racist because we loved everybody. We were anti-racist because we hated fascists and we didn't want those bastards in. It was not a moral thing. It was about class. It was about, whose side are you on?

KATE WEBB We were political from the beginning, trying to change hearts and minds. I had an argument with Melvyn Bragg, trying to get him to do a *South Bank Show* on Rock Against Racism. They wouldn't do it. Can you imagine that today? An arts programme not reacting to something as big and powerful and political and cultural as RAR. We were so far off the radar. The incredible ambition and how much work we did: *Temporary Hoarding*, the Carnivals, the hundreds and hundreds of gigs, local groups across the country and around the world, the Militant Entertainment tour, the record, Rock Against Thatcher. There was always more stuff. It was the reach of people that RAR got and that we were able to speak to quite a wide variety of people without becoming anaemic and meaningless. It was an incredibly energetic, innovative group.

LUCY WHITMAN Popular music has an emotional power, whether it's Beethoven or the Sex Pistols. Art of any kind can be inspiring and Rock

Against Racism captured people's imagination and excited them. You didn't feel you had to go to a meeting and be bored to death while people went through the agenda. You could have fun but also be changing the world at the same time. Obviously a cultural movement is never going to change things completely, but it did have an influence, and actually most of the things which activists were arguing for have now come to pass, like equal rights for gay people or talking to the IRA as a way of moving things on in Ireland. The point is, there was an intellectual ferment going on from the late seventies into the eighties. It changed what was thought of as acceptable discourse. You only have to look at the so-called comedy shows of the 1970s to know that certain things then wouldn't be allowed to be on TV now.

SYD SHELTON The story of RAR is fantastic because it's an anomaly. It wasn't part of a great plan. We couldn't invent the Clash or the Au Pairs. We didn't know when RAR started that we'd have bands like that appear. There were times when it was scary and there were times it was dangerous. And we had arguments. Red and I had times where we didn't speak to each other for months but the great thing is that we thought we were unstoppable. I don't mean that we were arrogant but we really believed that we could do what we wanted. But we can also say there was a great deal of luck involved in terms of UK reggae coming to prominence; before Bob Marley it was an obscure thing. It all came together at the right time: before Thatcher, before the real clampdown. It's like in chemistry: sometimes you put all the ingredients together and you get putty and other times you end up with a fantastic firework display. We got the firework display.

BOB HUMM A lot of people wanted something where they could express their feelings against racism. They were at home seeing these horrible things on television and reading about them but then they could go to an RAR gig and feel like they were doing something different and being positive with other people who felt the same way as them. RAR was about those people. It couldn't carry on forever.

COLIN BARKER RAR gave a dimension that no political campaign had ever had before. It offered cultural identification. It talked about freedom and liberation grounded in ordinary kids' experience. There was a politicized generation that hated racism and was delighted to be able to say so. In the eighties you get the Live Aid concert. It borrowed the idea of a political music event from the Carnivals. We didn't have a Saint Bob – and what

Richard Boon said is true in one sense, that the rock scene couldn't have organized it by itself – it had to be political people who were really boring to make it happen. It's like a really successful manager of a rock band is not necessarily any good at music but he is good at wheeling and dealing. If there weren't rock managers there wouldn't be rock 'n' roll either. The Anti-Nazi League didn't create the fan base for Rock Against Racism but we did create the machinery for it to create itself. I'm quite happy to be seen as boring in all of this but we came with certain skills and a certain openness to be ready to deal with worlds we didn't know anything about. It was a political activity as well as a cultural one. Music gave anti-racism a radical edge of a quite different character than 100 demonstrations could ever have done.

GEOFF BROWN I meet people for whom the Anti-Nazi League and Rock Against Racism was their first political experience. It wasn't just music. It was people talking politics in relation to that music. You were into black music and you were white and you were aware of the National Front as a threat. And then something comes along and gives you a good time and fits with what you believe in. It was an incredibly powerful mix and nobody had done anything like it before.

PETER HAIN I remember meeting punks and skinheads who were becoming openly political and saying, 'I was on the point of joining the National Front and then RAR and the ANL came along. I went along to see my band and I suddenly started thinking, "What am I doing? Do I hate black people? Why do I hate black people? No, I don't, actually."' It was quite moving. The Clash and Stiff Little Fingers and others getting involved and supporting us brought the audience into contact with the political message. They performed on platforms under Anti-Nazi League banners and suddenly skinheads and punks were on our marches and joining up. And it was really important to have reggae bands like Steel Pulse and Aswad involved too, but we were most effective at mobilizing white working-class youth who were dangerously vulnerable to being brought under the arms of the National Front. That could never have been done without Rock Against Racism. If you called it an Anti-Nazi League concert you wouldn't have got anybody there except the activists. Once you called it Rock Against Racism it was different.

PAUL HOLBOROW Darcus Howe, who was the editor of *Race Today* and was on the ANL steering committee, at David Widgery's funeral told a brilliant story. He has four children. He said the first three grew up in racist Britain through the sixties and early seventies but his fourth child grew up in a totally different atmosphere and that was down to the Anti-Nazi League and Rock Against Racism.

ROGER HUDDLE Darcus said we had created a world that his children could live in because we stood up and we stood firm and we were a white organization by and large, and it showed that not everybody was racist. We understood that the alienation and the anger amongst black and white youth that expressed itself in reggae and punk was an important social manifestation of the deeper underlying anger and frustration within the system itself. It was not just an accident. Punk was not just an accident, even though people say it was just Malcolm McLaren or Bernie Rhodes. Not true. When we said 'NF No Future' we really meant it. If we hadn't existed, the pessimism of punk would have taken the whole thing in a different direction. RAR was set up against the Nazis and when they were defeated RAR was no longer necessary.

DOTUN ADEBAYO Rock Against Racism caught the imagination: right place at the right time. It didn't end racism – you would have been naive if you expected that as the outcome – but it certainly opened the way for young black men and, to a lesser extent, women, to be brought into the white musical firmament.

KATE WEBB It was the question of how long RAR could have gone on. Once punk waned RAR had to become a very different organization. We were always at the front of the wave and often put on small bands before they'd done much else and became well known. New Romantics were never going to be a natural fit with RAR. Their whole aspirational Thatcherite style was a completely different thing to the political energy and anger and ferocity that there was in the music before. It was the difference between Duran Duran singing 'Rio' on a boat off the island of Antigua and the Clash playing in front of backdrops of World War II fighter planes. Once punk waned, RAR would have had to become a very different organization.

DENNIS BOVELL Seeing the Stranglers with Steel Pulse, Steel Pulse with the Police, Matumbi with Ian Dury and the Blockheads. People got to see bands that had different ethnic mixtures and they were then exposed to other beats. It was a tremendous bridge to have built. Rock Against Racism saw Linton Kwesi Johnson doing poetry with John Cooper Clarke and Roger McGough, going into different poetic spheres. It was a tremendous act of unifying England. It was a tremendous attempt at healing and fusing together people from all different walks of life and racial backgrounds. It was hugely successful. It came to the fact that – 'Hallo!' – England is now full of many different races. It's like Noah's Ark floating in the town; it's got all the different species there. It led to integration and after that it felt that people were true reggae fans, irrespective of their racial background.

NEIL KINNOCK The fundamental significance of Rock Against Racism, like all cultural engagements in politics, was to do with three things: one, to manifest the freedom that you're seeking to uphold and expand, and nothing does that better than music; secondly, to secure the interest and attendance of an audience that otherwise would almost automatically say they were not interested in politics; and thirdly, having done that, to convey to them you've got to be interested in politics because politics will otherwise control you.

•

PAUL FURNESS Leeds put on the second RAR gig ever and Leeds is where RAR finished. We'd been arguing for a Carnival for years. I'd come down to London and there was an obituary in *Sounds* that said, 'The Club is dead, long live the Club.' But Linda and Barry were determined to go out with a bang. In 1967, a bloke called Arthur France started the Leeds West Indian Carnival, and Potternewton Park is where it traditionally ends up: right in the heart of the black community. So that's where it was held on 4 July 1981 with the Specials, Misty In Roots, Joolz the Poet and the Au Pairs.

KATE WEBB By this point 2 Tone music had swept the nation and the black and white ethos of bands like the Beat and the Specials culminated with Rock Against Racism's final triumph: the Leeds Carnival.

CHRIS BOLTON It was all new people: a new generation and a new music. You come in at ground level and you go out on a high. What could be better? I felt like a respected elder. The whole thing had moved on and it felt like, job done. RAR had changed the face of music. It was a party and a great place to stop. You have to finish a book some time. It's best not to finish the book '. . . and it petered out and died.' RAR went out with a bang.

TOM ROBINSON Up to 2 Tone we were singing about Rock Against Racism and having black and white bands on the same stage but the Specials were black and white musicians together. Things had moved on. It needed a spring up from the grass roots of society. They were obviously the right people to headline the farewell Carnival.

RUTH GREGORY 2 Tone was like a dream. Suddenly there was energetic music that was neither black nor white. It was a mix. It came out of British reggae and punk. It was a fusion and that's what we wanted. That's what two-tone Britain was: people just getting on and creating, regardless of colour or sex or background or sexual orientation. The Fifties generation set up this comfortable world where everything was determined. It came from the war. And ever since then we'd been trying to break out of that. People are very scared of disruption in their lives. They think, 'If only we could go back to having no foreigners here then life would be safe and I'd have a job and everything would be fine.' But it's not true. There's always someone that's the scapegoat.

SYD SHELTON RAR was so successful because it empowered people who felt powerless. 2 Tone had taken it over. The baton had been passed.

KATE WEBB We didn't give birth to 2 Tone. Those kids were coming into their influences long before RAR. 2 Tone was more what we wanted to happen. This was the Britain we were talking about.

RED SAUNDERS When you saw 2 Tone you went, job done. The Farewell Carnival in Potternewton Park had a natural bowl. The stage was at the top and I looked down and went, 'That's it! This is what we dreamt of in 1976.' 2 Tone music and their spirit and their story and everything Jerry Dammers went on to do for Nelson Mandela. It trumped the whole fucking lot of us.

BOOK TWO
2 TONE

BLACK SKIN BLUE EYED BOYS

Bluebeat. Skinhead. Coventry

NEIL SPENCER Like Aswad and Steel Pulse before, the 2 Tone movement stood for a new generation of black Britons, one whose identity was first and foremost British and secondly West Indian. A black and a white person being in a band together was not without precedent – the Equals' 'Black Skin Blue Eyed Boys' was an early outrider – but 2 Tone was a first in modern popular music. The Specials and the Beat and the Selecter articulated a roar from the Midlands, as did UB40. It was almost like saying to London, 'You invented punk rock but we've got this.' You could never get music as uptempo as 2 Tone out of Jamaica. It was too hot.

CLARE SHORT After the first people came from the Caribbean you've got the next generation that had been to school together and were wearing similar clothes. 2 Tone was very important politically because it was an answer to the National Front.

NICKY SUMMERS Punk was dead. The Clash went to America. It became a no man's land again. I was bored and looking to do my own thing. I needed direction and pointers. 2 Tone filled that gap.

JERRY DAMMERS I thought of the name '2 Tone', which originally referred to the shimmery tonic material that skinheads used to wear, but I didn't see it as a racial thing at first, but when people read that into it I had no problem. It may have been exaggerated or a media stereotype but the kids who dressed in the so-called skinhead style in the early seventies that were interviewed on the telly definitely were racists. History seems to have romanticized the idea that the original so-called skinheads were some kind of united working-class movement; if there was bashing of Asians or hippies there was just as much bashing of other skinheads, either at football or just of the gang three streets away.

ROBERT ELMS The original skinheads were the best-dressed people I had ever seen. It was sartorial brutalism but it was beautiful in the way that great brutalist architecture is beautiful. It was the Mies van der Rohe of style. It was Crombies with red hankies. It was really shined brogues or boots. It was Levi's Sta-Prest. It was jeans with a precise half-inch turn-up, worn up. It's one of the greatest looks ever invented by a bunch of fifteen-year-old herberts from council estates, and it was the first incarnation of multiculturalism in Britain because these are the first kids who had grown up with West Indian kids as their neighbours, where you're gonna hear ska and reggae music coming from next door's flat. Where you're gonna see boys with pork-pie hats with trousers worn very high, with that sauntering style and skanking dance. And there were always black skinheads. I'm not saying it wasn't racist. If it was racist it was against the Asian community, which was unforgivable, but it certainly wasn't anti-black. If anything it was young white kids who were in awe of black kids. A decade later it was the bastard offspring. It was Oi! It was ugly. It was tattoos. I was very angry with that version of skinhead. It was an abomination. It was lumpenprole-tarian. It got hijacked very early on by the far right.

CHRIS BOLTON You have to understand in the discos the popular music from the early seventies had been reggae and ska so songs like Bob and Marcia's 'Young, Gifted And Black' got to number one; the theme song from Chelsea Football Club was 'Liquidator'. Soul influenced a lot of the early reggae. Original skinheads loved reggae.

DENNIS BOVELL From the time when Derrick Morgan had a hit with 'Skin-head Moon Hop' in 1969, I used to go to a club called the 'A' Train in Battersea Town Hall on a Wednesday and Sunday night. Sir Coxsone was the resident sound and there used to be hundreds of white kids in there. Those kids must have got older and had kids who they told, 'This is the music we used to listen to.' And then you get 2 Tone.

ROBERT HOWARD 2 Tone was one of the first things that looked back. It was a revival movement, a bit like the mod thing.

RED SAUNDERS London mods were the very beginnings of multiracialism. Down the clubs you were meeting black boys and girls. It was the begin-ning of it. And the rockers were all white and their traditions were the Teddy boys, who were of course the people who attacked the Caribbean community in Notting Hill Gate.

ROGER HUDDLE I was a young mod: mohair suits, very New York. I didn't realize that until I saw Martin Scorsese's *Mean Streets*. I thought, 'Shit, that's what I looked like.' I was just copying Italian youth style. I was a working-class bloke working in a factory, going to clubs and weekends at Margate, and really getting into Georgie Fame and the Blue Flames and Zoot Money's Big Roll Band. It was rhythm and blues, black American music, ska, Prince Buster, and then house parties in the estates where the black population lived within my community.

DAVID WIDGERY Black music was our catechism, not just something we listened to in our spare time. It was the culture which woke us up, had shaped us and kept us up all night, blocked in Wardour Street mod clubs. It was how we worked out our geography, learnt our sexuality, and taught ourselves history. And if white musicians were as good and as exciting we worshipped them too. Our experiences had taught us a golden political rule: how people find their pleasure, entertainment and celebration is also how they find their sexual identity, their political courage and their strength to change.[34]

CAROL GRIMES When I first started singing with bands it was all very organic. Some of the musicians were African, some mixed-race, some English, some Irish. I didn't think twice about it. Mixed races have been in this country since the *Windrush*. But most of the bands were four white men.

DAVE RUFFY There was the Jimi Hendrix Experience with Noel Redding and Mitch Mitchell. But to me, Jimi was neither black nor white. He was like a god who played this mad music. Then you had the soul thing which was huge. You'd go to parties and everyone had *Tighten Up Volume 1* and *2* and *This Is Soul*. The Motown tours came over and they were amazing, and then the Stax Volt tour with Booker T and the MGs: two black and two white. And the Equals. They were called the fucking Equals.

DENNIS BOVELL The first racially mixed group in this country was the Equals: three black guys – Eddy Grant and Derv and Lincoln Gordon – and two white guys. Britain was the melting pot of everything: the Beatles singing Isley Brothers songs and going off to do their Indian stuff and playing with Billy Preston; the Small Faces singing 'Sha-La-La-La-Lee' written by Kenny Lynch, a black comedian.

FRANK MURRAY In 1969, John Lennon put on a show at the Lyceum with the Plastic Ono Band and the opening acts were all reggae: the Young Rascals, Desmond Dekker and the Aces, Jimmy Cliff, the Hot Chocolate Band.

TINY FENNIMORE I used to go to the California Ballroom in Dunstable, where there were quite a lot of black people. It was a bit like the Wigan Casino and they played loads of northern soul. They had black American bands coming over every week to play: James Brown, Curtis Mayfield, Diana Ross, Detroit Spinners. It was a great place to cut your teeth. Music was evolving. Calypso and ska was coming together with white skinheads and white street culture and white youth: just ordinary people who didn't like the National Front.

DOTUN ADEBAYO At Alexandra Palace there was the biggest youth roller disco ever; there were thousands of kids and they had DJs who were in tune with the underground stuff. That's where we heard our ska tunes but also things like 'Everything I Own' by Ken Boothe way before it got into the charts.

NICKY SUMMERS We used to go to a disco around Highbury, and towards the end they would play Prince Buster. I was about twelve. There was one black kid in the whole hall and he did this form of dancing and somebody said to me, 'That's northern soul.' When I was ten I was invited by a friend who was Jamaican to this house and they had a Dansette record player. They played Freda Payne's 'Band of Gold.' It was like, 'What!' I'd heard 'My Boy Lollipop' but black music hadn't registered. I stared at this record. That was it. That was a change. That was one of those moments where you start to go on a path in life.

CHRIS BOLTON It would be impossible to live in Ladbroke Grove without coming under the influence of reggae, as it would be in Brixton or Shepherd's Bush or any area where there was a large reggae community.

TIM WELLS We were all into reggae. Jamaica and England have always been in conversation. There's a great story about King Tubby: he never left Jamaica but he could give directions around Dalston. Jamaica knows London.

NEVILLE STAPLE Our parents grew up with music from Jamaica: Desmond Dekker, the Skatalites, Derrick Harriott, Millie Small. My cousin used to have a sound system and play all of that stuff.

PAUL HEATON I was going to Beanos in Croydon nicking loads of bluebeat and ska records. And at the Greyhound they'd be playing people like Dillinger and Steel Pulse. John Peel was playing *Handsworth Revolution* and I-Roy and U-Roy. My first band, Tools Down: every song had an offbeat.

DAVE WAKELING My first listen to ska was on the football terraces; at Wolves and West Brom they'd play 'Liquidator'. It always struck me as deeply ironic that the skinheads were dancing to ska but the football grounds were also the place where the right worked really hard at recruiting.

PAULINE BLACK Black had been assimilated into the workplace because of the motor industry. You'd got Peugeot and Triumph and people had settled in from the Caribbean by way of Gloucester or Oxford or Luton. After Coventry was bombed in the war they built the ring road around the city and stuck everyone outside it so there wasn't so much a city centre. And people got mixed up: in the workplace; schools weren't ghettoized; there was more freedom of exchange. You listened to each other's records. There were places that were black areas, like Hillfields, but it was so tiny.

HORACE PANTER Coventry was a multicultural city before the phrase was invented. In the street where Neol Davies – who would later form the Selecter – grew up, there were Greeks, Poles, Italians, Irish and Jamaicans who all went to school together. I'd been brought up in Kettering in Northamptonshire, which is a little sleepy market town, so Coventry was the big city as far as I was concerned. It was quite multicultural musically as well. You got the gig not because you were black but because you were a good guitar player. I was at Lanchester Poly, which is where I met Jerry Dammers, and the chap in charge of the halls said, 'Be careful when you go out at night. People get murdered.'

LYNVAL GOLDING Coventry was voted one of the most violent cities in England. I've got the scars on my neck to prove it. When I was about eighteen, nineteen, I was walking in Foleshill Park and these two guys got their little brother to beat this Indian kid up. He was crying and I said, 'Leave him alone.' These two guys said, 'That's my brother you're talking to.' I said, 'You should be ashamed of yourself.' It was blood everywhere. Another time there was about nine of us blacks in the Forty Thieves nightclub dancing with all these girls and these white guys at the bar got jealous and a big fight broke out: hitting with bottles and all sorts of things. A friend of ours was glassed right across the face and ended up in hospital. I was chased down the road. There were two fences. I jumped over the first fence and a white taxi driver saw what was about to happen and swung open the door and said, 'Jump in. Where do you want to go?' I said, 'Anywhere.'

NEVILLE STAPLE I got attacked on Holyhead Road where the Specials used to rehearse. I was walking up the road and I was jumped by four National Front guys. I grabbed the leader and held him by his throat and walked him about 200 yards up to the youth club. His mates were following him and I was squeezing harder and harder. Once I got to the door I let go and bolted inside shouting, 'Any of your friends come looking for me, I'll kill 'em.'

WAYNE MINTER I was doing Fine Art at Lanchester and Jerry Dammers was the year below me. He was a very good illustrator. He was in the design studio making animated videos of Rocky Marciano boxing fights. Horace Panter was in my year and used to paint removal vans. He was doing things like Steely Dan covers in the college band Breaker; they were bloody good. Coventry was a strange place: half of it had the heart bombed out of it. It was a hard town but there was a really good music scene.

JERRY DAMMERS Coventry was quite a violent and divided city with a lot of racism against black and Asian. And the sectarian tensions with the Irish and Scottish didn't help either. I don't actually remember a huge amount of white musicians playing with black musicians; Neol Davies was one of the few. I played with him and Sixties soul singer Ray King, doing Three Degrees and Hot Chocolate covers with a little bit of commercial Bob Marley thrown in, in a band called Nite Trane. Ray did a lot for the community and encouraging young black musicians, and a lot of his protégés ended up in the 2 Tone bands. Neol and I tried to persuade him to be a bit less cabaret and more funky, but it was hopeless and Ray walked out. It was as much frustration with the Coventry music scene that drove me to form the Specials. I made a conscious effort to form a multiracial punk reggae band and make an anti-racist statement. I loved reggae music and to combine that with rock music, it seemed obvious.

PAULINE BLACK Music wasn't worth doing if you weren't dissenting about something. You didn't waste your time doing loads of love songs and crap like that. If you were going to write a song you made it about something.

NEOL DAVIES Jerry and I had a very close friendship. He'd come round to my flat and we recorded a couple of his tracks on my four-track. We'd talk a lot about clothes and music and I was in the original bunch of musicians that he was rehearsing to form the Specials. One day there was a rehearsal which I wasn't told about but I went along anyway and found Lynval Golding there instead: 'I understand, see ya.'

JERRY DAMMERS The first line-up of the Specials I put together was Horace Panter on bass, Neol Davies on guitar, a black drummer called Silverton Hutchinson and a singer called Tim Strickland. I soon replaced Neol, one of my best friends at the time, with Lynval Golding. I felt horrible but the music came first. I liked Lynval's authentic trebly reggae Telecaster and I wanted a more multiracial band. Lynval promptly left the band! I had to beg him to come back. Then I brought in Terry Hall on vocals and Roddy Byers on guitar as the punk elements.

HORACE PANTER The first black person I met in my life was Lynval Golding. Most of us in the Specials were in our mid-twenties – so we all knew how to play soul or funk or some kind of live dance music – and a generation older than the punks.

JERRY DAMMERS I told Terry the Clash and the Sex Pistols were about my age, actually, and that pogoing and wearing a leather jacket didn't make him a real punk. I said, 'We should try and do something truly original like they had; that would be real punk spirit. It's about creating fashion, not following it.'

NEVILLE STAPLE I used to hear this reggaeish sound coming from the next room in the Holyhead Youth Club where I had the Jah Baddis sound system. I was intrigued. I popped my head round and said to Jerry, after a few times, 'Can I come along? I'll tidy up the wires for you.' So I used to travel around in the back of the transit van on top of the speakers. This was when we were going out as the Coventry Automatics. They were doing a soundcheck at a gig in Leeds and I was on the talkback mic at the mixing desk, DJ'ing over them, playing the Toots and the Maytals classic 'Monkey Man'. They didn't know where it was coming from until the lights came round so Jerry called me onstage.

JERRY DAMMERS My original idea was for Neville to mix us. I built a little mixer with switches and I wanted the whole band to go through it and Neville to switch instruments in and out while we played, to get live dub effects. And then we got a tour supporting the Clash and Bernie Rhodes persuaded him to jump on stage and get on with it.

HORACE PANTER We wanted to fuse the energy of punk and the sinewy rhythms of reggae and come back to ska combining white and black music. Later, I remember Dave Wakeling saying that some journalist came up to him and said, '2 Tone is a fantastic socio-political stand you're making here with black and white musicians.' And Dave was like, 'We got Everett [who was black] because he was a good drummer.'

JERRY DAMMERS The idea of 2 Tone was to try and promote anti-racism hand in hand with and as an integral part of working-class unity in general. I did drawings of how I hoped it might all look and what I might be able to persuade people to wear. Lynval and Horace especially were a bit older and started off looking very old-wave. I knew it was really important that we were identified with punk and the new wave and I had to persuade them to dress differently. And part of the plan was that we should keep changing and adapting, staying creative and ahead of the times.

NEOL DAVIES Jerry had a specific idea of taming what he saw as potential fights between National-Front-leaning people and black people. It was social insight more than political. He was a passionate believer and I bought into the 2 Tone idea completely. It was a real simple statement of, 'Whatever difficulties different people have, you've got to work it out, and why not with music?'

HORACE PANTER I remember going round to Jerry's flat in Albany Road with notepads: 'OK, what are we going to call our record label?' '2 Tone' was a cool name for a label. It came with its Sixties thing. We wanted to do what Stax or Tamla Motown did in America for British music. You would hear the first drum roll and you'd know that it was a Tamla tune.

JERRY DAMMERS I had decided I was going to have a band when I saw the Who on *Top of the Pops* singing 'My Generation'. I was ten and a 'mini' mod, so the 2 Tone logo was generally a Sixties pop art thing. The black-and-white-check idea came from the sticky tape I used to decorate my bike with back then.

DAVE WAKELING I liked the way 2 Tone used the black-and-white chequer-board and stole it back from the police. It was taking icons back from the opposition.

LINTON KWESI JOHNSON The Specials were British white kids being influenced by Jamaican culture and music: a coming together of the youth through music . . . the power of music, full stop, to bring people of different races and cultures together. It was part of the cultural melting pot that was taking place.

LYNVAL GOLDING Me and Neville come from rural Jamaica where we'd only wear shoes on Sundays when we went to church; we didn't have TVs

Rock Against Racism poster, March 1980.

or radios or running water or a fridge or anything like that. Roddy, the guitar player, came from a coal-mining village. Terry and Brad were born in Coventry. Jerry was born in India. Early on people didn't understand what we were trying to do because we tried to merge a different culture and rhythm together. It's like that song: *What we need is a great big melting pot.*

TRACEY THORN It's interesting because the Specials were after punk and they were different to punk but it seemed what they did couldn't have been done without punk. And there was something about them being so mixed that looked right; they seemed representative of young people. And Terry Hall was this wonderfully gloomy frontman who was a brilliant foil for it all with a slightly sour take on Britain. In their best songs there was always that slightly queasy contrast between the party atmosphere and a stark awareness of what was going on.

JERRY DAMMERS The French surrealist André Breton said, 'Revolutionary art has to be revolutionary in its form.' There's a lot of truth in that and finding new ways of doing something to excite people and get them interested. Hopefully music can bring people together and put a message across and inspire the way people think. Punk rock and white rock music in general was always limited in what it could achieve politically because it wasn't that inclusive. It alienated as many people as it involved. I wanted to create a more mixed atmosphere.

PAULINE BLACK 2 Tone was never sold as an idea. It was demonstrated. 'Here we are, black people and white people in the same bands – isn't that amazing? – getting along and fusing rock with reggae and ska.' Young white people were intrigued because reggae was very different. And they were not that far removed from our beginnings; we were just placing their lives in some kind of perspective and setting it to music, so they could relate to it.

RHODA DAKAR I read 2 Tone as everyone in it together: a community of like-minded spirits. It was mostly anti-racism and a bit of anti-sexism. It was fun and edgy and a bit aggressive.

NEOL DAVIES People could see with 2 Tone there was a chance of something really British but intrinsically black being created. At that point I thought reggae had lost its way and lost its sense of invention and humour and sexiness. I didn't want to hear about Rastafari any more than I wanted to hear about God or Jesus.

JERRY DAMMERS Rasta, if only as a feeling, had a huge amount in common with 2 Tone. Politically, it had always been a revolutionary call for justice and equality, and not to, at least, respect that would make no sense to me. 2 Tone wanted to celebrate Caribbean culture and values and I was made up when black kids got into it.

JULIET DE VALERO WILLS It was like for the first time the black and the white youth had found a language they could talk to each other in. And to see young black and white guys on the stage together was like a little microcosm of what was starting to happen in society. Punk had been very white. And even though the punks latterly started getting into reggae and embracing black music, there was still 'punk bands' and 'reggae bands'. 2 Tone was trying to make a statement about literally mixing black and white cultures and making music out of the two. And if you do that, can you therefore break through deeply rooted cultural racism? And can you also empower a generation who had no future? It sounds quite grand but in Jerry's mind I think that's what he wanted. All the bands totally believed in that. It was about them thinking, 'If we do this we're helping ourselves, too.'

THE KINGSTON AFFAIR

Specials out on parole. Gangsters vs the Selecter

LYNVAL GOLDING If it wasn't for Joe Strummer and Mick Jones the Specials probably wouldn't have broken. They gave us a break on the Clash Out On Parole tour in May 1978.

JERRY DAMMERS I couldn't believe I managed to blag our way onto the Clash tour. Some pub rock bands had done reggae but when the Clash did their punk version, although it was less like reggae, it seemed much more raw and credible because it took on board the political message of reggae. That was a musical inspiration when I formed the Specials but I wanted black people involved. The Clash had done the Rock Against Racism Carnival in Victoria Park a month earlier but I don't remember being aware of that. I lived in Coventry and never really read the rock press so I didn't particularly associate the Clash with Rock Against Racism any more than the other bands.

HORACE PANTER The Clash tour was incredible. Those three weeks really formed us. The Clash set the benchmark for a Specials performance. They were just full on. The reaction they got from the crowd scared the shit out of me. We started the tour as civilians but ended as a combat unit. It was our rock 'n' roll boot camp. We played this infamous gig at Crawley Sports Centre where there were loads of skinheads with Nazi badges and tattoos. The atmosphere was horrible. You could palpably sense this kind of malevolence brewing. That was a wake-up call to us. We weren't just going to be a pop group.

JERRY DAMMERS Skinheads took over the stage at the Crawley gig and attacked Alan Vega from the other support band, Suicide. It was the night the 2 Tone concept was really born. It was obvious there was going to be a skinhead revival and I wanted us to become part of the scene and change it, so it didn't become affiliated to the far right.

LYNVAL GOLDING In Leeds, we had pretty bad racism and things thrown at me and Neville. That's why we started doing all that crazy mad dancing.

And we were heavily influenced by the way the Clash moved around on the stage and the energy they had.

JOE STRUMMER They were rough but I really enjoyed their energy. You could tell they had something going. A lot of the bands were doing the punk–reggae thing at the time, us included, but they were taking it all very seriously, very rootsy. [The Specials], though, had a really different approach, which was down to a lot of things, but mainly, I think, Terry's voice. He didn't have a reggae voice. He sounded so English, and that was the difference.[35]

NICKY SUMMERS At the end of the tour, the Clash played at the Camden Music Machine and I went to all four nights. On the Tuesday and Wednesday they were supported by a band called the Special AKA. I thought they were interesting but nothing more, a bit art school. They didn't sound like how they became. And then I saw them again about eight or nine months later at a Rock Against Racism gig at the Hope and Anchor with some friends. We checked them out, thinking, 'Is this the same band?' They'd totally transformed and came on in tonic suits. We were down in the basement. It was very small and hot and sweaty and we just danced for an hour. They were fantastic. I was taken by the fusion of the music and the energy. Shortly after that the Clash's manager, Bernie Rhodes, looked after them for nine months.

JERRY DAMMERS When the Clash tour ended we went back to Coventry and adopted ska and the Rude Boy look in order to get through to those kids and try to make the skinhead revival anti-racist in contrast to the first time around. One thing that Bernie said that had stuck in my mind was, 'Don't ever think the audience dress like you; you dress like the audience.' I then stuck musical quotations onto the songs I'd already written, like Prince Buster's 'Al Capone' into 'Gangsters'; and 'Birth Control' by Lloydie and the Lowbites into 'Too Much Too Young'.

RANKING ROGER It was going backwards with a forward message. The Specials brought Lloydie and the Lowbites' 'Birth Control' forward with topical things going on like the *population boom* and the *welfare state*; added punk to it so that it was a new type of music.

JERRY DAMMERS No one had really mixed ska and punk before. It was a political message in itself. We also wanted to have fun and be pop stars. That was a big driving force like any band. But to me the music and the politics and the visual side were all part and parcel of something people could relate to, and with it a general left-wing socialist message.

DAVID HINDS 2 Tone came with a style of music that said, 'We've been there, done that and worn the T-shirt.' God, man, my brothers came with ska music in 1962. Why bring it back? We saw it as a revival and a lot of old musicians who were probably done out of their royalties. We didn't see the musicians as that talented because of the chords they were jumping to. We were going onto minor and major seventh and eleventh and thirteenth chords; those chords were unheard of in the kind of music they were playing. We didn't think they played it that well and thought the singing was off-key and the energy was too fast. It was like it was punk wired up to the point where everybody's gone off their rocker, especially coming from people like Madness with all their gimmicks.

HORACE PANTER We played with Steel Pulse at the Top Rank and all of Handsworth turned up to see the revolutionaries. We were five white guys and two blacks trying to play reggae and the crowd cut us dead. Arms crossed. It was really scary but we toughed it out. Then we decided to play ska – our punk songs slowed down and our reggae songs sped up – which unified all of the songs; and everything was a lot more danceable. At first, Lynval said, 'It's old-man music. Music must move forward.' 2 Tone looked back to go forward.

BRINSLEY FORDE That music was old now. We were making new music. We'd moved from ska. Then suddenly you were hearing tracks you knew from before. It took bands like the Specials and the Selecter and Madness to bring it back but they were marketed to a different audience. If a black band did it they probably wouldn't have a hit with it. But then you have to stop and go, 'Wow! It means that people are accepting and listening.' It was all about understanding and tolerance and accepting it may not be how I want to do it. It was the music that they loved and the music that I loved; why shouldn't they get the opportunity?

DENNIS BOVELL Lynval said to me when he heard the Matumbi lyric, *What happened to rock steady . . . won't somebody tell me where is bluebeat and ska?* 'I'll tell you what happened to it. It's living in Coventry and here's a new band called the Specials playing it.'

JERRY DAMMERS Matumbi's question, *Where is bluebeat and ska?*, was definitely an influence on my idea to take up ska. Also 'Smoking My Ganja' by Capital Letters, which was a roots track but had a ska beat. And the Leyton Buzzards song 'Saturday Night Beneath The Plastic Palm Trees', with the line *Dancing to the rhythm of the Guns of Navarone*. 'Guns of Navarone' and 'Al Capone' were continually played in nightclubs all through the seventies.

NEVILLE STAPLE It was always about enjoying yourself. We were mixing the rebellish punk music with the Jamaican ska. Jamaican music was against violence.

JERRY DAMMERS Growing up through the sixties and seventies, I had come to the conclusion that all the different tribes and youth cults were just dividing people up, really, and by the end of the seventies they were all there at the same time, thinking they were rebels, but to some extent fighting each other, whilst the people keeping everyone down just stayed in power. I wrote the opening to 'Do The Dog' – *All you punks and all you Teds, National Front and natty dreads, mods, rockers, hippies and skinheads keep on fighting till you're dead* – as a general call for unity against the powers that be.

NICKY SUMMERS There were a lot of different youth factions and 2 Tone was about bringing the black and white youth and people from different cultural backgrounds together to enjoy music.

•

NEOL DAVIES The Specials were playing a lot of gigs up and down the country, building up an audience, and people were dressing like the band. It was beginning to shape up before they recorded anything.

JULIET DE VALERO WILLS They were wearing these smart suits, really sharp silhouettes, short hair, clean-shaven, very angular and clean. For Jamaicans it was as much about looking the part and being able to dance really well. It was a package.

NEVILLE STAPLE The fashion of the Specials was how the original Rude Boys in Jamaica used to dress: pork-pie hat, nice and smart, slim pencil tie. I used to buy my suits from second-hand shops. Jamaicans wouldn't do that, but we did because we were young and we were brought up in England.

HORACE PANTER My suit cost me seven quid, and another £2.50 to get it altered. Lynval was like, 'Me not wear dead man's clothes.'

LYNVAL GOLDING I wouldn't buy second-hand suits at first because my auntie who brought me up always said, 'If you haven't got it, you get it. You go in a shop and buy it. You don't share it. It's yours.' We used to get our suits made at Burton's and then Jerry got me into buying second-hand clothes. I grew up wearing all those clothes. The visual was a political statement. And then suddenly the high-street shops were full of 2 Tone stuff. It was amazing how fast it happened.

JERRY DAMMERS The skinhead revival was coming anyway when the Specials adopted that moddy, skinheady, Rude Boy look. The idea was to try and influence the revival, not to be racist and violent like the first time, and I think, amazingly, to a large extent it worked.

SHERYL GARRATT You had kids like me, who didn't know that bands like the Beat and the Selecter were taking a 1950s Jamaican style. It wasn't until later I realized where the look had come from. The Specials just looked fantastic. And it felt very British. Although 2 Tone audiences were overwhelmingly white you didn't see a lot of black kids dressed like their grandparents in the audience, but for white kids it was certainly a way into that heritage and that history.

BRINSLEY FORDE The clothes that the skinheads wore were about black and white coming together. It was a real two-tone time: the boots, the Harringtons. I used to wear all that stuff. It was a conflicting story.

LYNVAL GOLDING A lot of people misunderstand the image. It wasn't about glorifying being like a Jamaican Rude Boy; it was about why you shouldn't be a Rude Boy. I would say, 'Go and listen to Prince Buster sentencing the hooligans to *four hundred years in prison*.' That's why you had all those original songs: the Wailers' 'Simmer Down' telling Rude Boys to calm down; Desmond Dekker singing *Dem a loot, dem a shoot, dem a wail – a shanty town*. Being a Rude Boy was not something to be proud of. It was a criminal lifestyle. We'd play 'A Message To You Rudy' and I'd say to the audience, 'Listen to this carefully: *Stop your messing around / Better think of your future / Time to straighten right out / Creating problems in town.*'

•

HORACE PANTER The Specials had had no luck trying to convince record companies to sign us so we said, 'Let's do it ourselves like everybody else does.' The great thing was you could go to a local studio and in three hours you could come out with a record: Rough Trade could distribute it, you could get it reviewed in *Sounds* or *NME*, and John Peel would play it. You didn't need major record labels like CBS or EMI. So we borrowed £700 and recorded three songs, 'Nite Klub', 'Too Much Too Young' and 'Gangsters'. Jerry had written 'Gangsters' leaning on the back of Joe Strummer's guitar when we used to rehearse at the Clash's space in Camden. One of the original verses had the line *On the back of Joe Strummer's guitar*.

LYNVAL GOLDING We ended up having the track 'The Selecter' on the B-side because we ran out of money. It had been recorded a couple of years before by Neol Davies and John Bradbury, before he joined the Specials and replaced Silverton on drums. I don't think anyone had ever had two bands on one record before.

JERRY DAMMERS 'The Selecter' was this great track, like a disco dub sort of thing. I told Neol if he was willing to add a ska beat, which would give it a bit more energy and fit in with my idea for the label, we'd love to put it on the other side of the record.

NEOL DAVIES 'The Selecter' was originally called 'The Kingston Affair', credited to Davies/Bradbury. I credited Brad because he instigated the whole process by saying, 'Let's make a record.' It took us about three months to make the whole track, during which I thought of the name 'the Selecter'. I hadn't heard of the Jamaican 'selector' at that time – I got it off my hi-fi amp switch which said 'Selector'. I said, 'How about the Selectors?' Brad said, 'Yeah, that's great.' So I said, 'Let's mess with the spelling. Let's have three "e"s, it'll look good like that.' So I made up a record sleeve on black card and I used white ink to write 'The Selecters' in the bottom corner. We took the master tapes and pressed a one-off acetate and mocked up a single. We took it to all the clubs around Coventry and people danced to it.

HORACE PANTER I had first heard the record in Mr George's in Coventry. We used to play there on a Monday night and they brought the test pressing down. We thought, 'Wow! This is good.' Neol and Brad were standing at the back of the room, grinning. On old reggae singles there was often a 'version' or something by a different artist on the other side so that's what we did. It was Jerry's idea to have 'THE SPECIAL AKA Gangsters' and 'VS. THE SELECTER' rubber-stamped onto the plain record sleeve. Me and Terry did them in my front room because he was the only one who came round. We did 1,500 of them on our knees and my hand hurt.

The Specials 'Gangsters' sleeve bag, March 1979.

NEVILLE STAPLE Then Neol had to get an actual band together.

LYNVAL GOLDING I knew most of the people that ended up being in the Selecter. Neol lived just across the road and one day I suggested to Pauline Black she should meet up with some of these people because they needed a singer.

PAULINE BLACK We all met at Charley Anderson's house, which was a one-up, one-down terrace. I was introduced to Neol and he played 'The Selecter' on a red Dansette player. It was the first time I had heard a record where I knew the person who had made it: 'Whoa! That's amazing.' The song was eerie and weird. It wasn't like any ska I'd heard before. It was quite other-worldly. And everyone who was in the room that night would go on to become the Selecter.

JULIET DE VALERO WILLS I was working at Trigger Publicity. I knew that a friend of a friend of Rick Rogers was sending somebody in to see him with some music who he thought was promising. Rick had been the Damned's manager and he had got himself a little office above Holt's shoe shop just behind Camden High Street where we worked. There were these old rickety stairs and halfway up was a disgusting little bathroom. I was in the loo and I could hear this incredible ska beat coming up from downstairs. I got excited because I was born in Trinidad and I'd grown up with ska. I launched myself down the last couple of stairs and cracked my head on the top of the door frame and landed in the office. That was my introduction to Jerry Dammers, who had come down with Neol to play 'Gangsters'.

RICK ROGERS Somebody at Rough Trade had said to Jerry, 'You shouldn't be thinking about pressing 1,000 copies of "Gangsters". You should do 5,000. But you need to get some PR and I know the person for you. Go and see Rick.' There was also the parallel story with Alan Harrison who did occasional work at the art college in Coventry and we had bedsits in the same house in Crouch End, and he had mentioned this band from Coventry: 'You've got to go and see them.' So Jerry heard my name from two different sources. He came in with a cassette of 'Gangsters' and played it. I thought it was amazing and said, 'I'd be very interested in working with you but I want to see you live.' So that weekend I went up to Lanchester Poly in Coventry and they were just amazing; far and away the best band I'd ever seen live, even at that early stage. People talk about the melding of ska and punk and that's exactly what it was. It had the entire attitude and the energy of punk but playing a music that just moved you both physically and mentally. It was everything that was good in one package. They had such an aura and an incredible stage performance.

NEOL DAVIES 'Gangsters' and 'The Selecter' came out in the spring of 1979 so we didn't have a lot of time to get ourselves sorted. And then John Peel played it on his late-night Radio 1 show. It was fantastic. You're in your sitting room and all of a sudden you're on the radio: 'He's playing the record!' Then he said, 'That's "The Selecter" by the Specials.' 'NO!' I immediately got on the phone and they put me through to him in between records and I told him the whole story. And then he played both sides and said, 'I've just been speaking to Neol Davies from the Selecter . . .' That gave it the kick and by the summer it was number six in the national charts.

JERRY DAMMERS The first time I saw the newly formed Selecter was when they all turned up in the same gear as the Specials wore and were playing ska. At first I thought, 'Blimey! They ripped us off,' but then, almost immediately, I thought, 'No . . . brilliant! There's strength in numbers,' plus I still felt bad about kicking Neol out of my band, so it was like a happy ending. 2 Tone was about working together, not competition.

RHODA DAKAR I remember hearing 'Gangsters' and thinking, 'Whoa! What's that?' It stopped me in my tracks.

RICK ROGERS I started looking after the Specials and I put together two weeks of gigs in London to introduce them to the right people: three dates in one week, two in the other. I knew if I had the maximum number of journalists in the first week, in the second the reviews would be in the music papers, which meant they went from playing to thirty people at the Hope and Anchor to selling out the Nashville by the end of the fortnight. That was my plot and plan.

JULIET DE VALERO WILLS The Specials played the Moonlight two or three times in that run-up, which was a tiny club in West Hampstead on the road where I lived. The first gig was not full and then the next one there was a queue outside. It was completely rammed, with everybody dancing like crazy. There was an immediate sense that something was happening and an incredible excitement about them. And they looked amazing.

WAYNE MINTER I took a load of mates who'd come down from Coventry to the Moonlight. I said, 'You've got to see this band. You won't have seen anything like it.' They were blown away by it. Visually they were an example of multiculturalism and anti-racism in practice and it was blatantly obvious how they fitted in with what Rock Against Racism stood for. It was black and white people in the band together, which was relatively unusual then, and in the audience as well. Ska and bluebeat for a period had been the province of British skinheads.

LYNVAL GOLDING The second Moonlight gig was fantastic. Terry started the set by saying, 'It's the eve of the election, and "It's Up To You."' The timing couldn't have been better. And then the thing just took off and went.

HORACE PANTER It was the day before the general election when Margaret Thatcher would get elected and the next night we played in Dingwalls so I don't think anybody voted.

Rick Rogers in the 2 Tone office, Camden, London, circa 1979.

JERRY DAMMERS We supported John Cooper Clarke at Dingwalls. Afterwards he came in the dressing room and said one word: 'Belting!'

RICK ROGERS I was tasked to find a way that they could have a label within another label and to build a movement around the label that would be guided by the ideology of equality and fairness. There were many, many conversations with Jerry in the early days about what 2 Tone meant and how it should run. And my interpretation of that dream and vision was incredibly political in terms of socialist and anti-racist agendas. There was enormous pressure in a very short period of time of people wanting to sign the band. The conversation would always start with explaining that you wouldn't just be signing the Specials, you would be signing a label. And we wanted to put out singles by other bands that would be A&R'd by 2 Tone and they would not be held to any kind of contract. So after one single a band was free to go. That in itself was a completely unheard of and mad, to most people.

HORACE PAINTER Rick was our music business conduit. He had been the press officer at Stiff Records so he knew people and got us an initial deal with Rough Trade. He was lovely and became part of the gang. I remember him at the Fulham Greyhound when Mick Jagger came along to see us with a bodyguard. Arista, Polydor, CBS were all at the bar and Rick came backstage rubbing his hands together, going, 'Yeah, great.'

RICK ROGERS The Rolling Stones wanted to sign the Specials to their label but when it was politely explained to them that it had to be 2 Tone Records they quickly went away. The only label that turned us down flat was Muff Winwood at CBS, who didn't see it at all. The only person who we felt understood the concept and the sociology and politics of it all was Roy Eldridge at Chrysalis. We ended up with a deal that gave us the ability to record and put out ten singles a year. Then, literally two days before we were going to sign, I got a phone call from another label who said, 'I know exactly what you're getting paid. I'll double it. Come and sign to us.' I was like, 'It's not about the money.' It got to the point where I was offered a very large personal bribe if the Specials would sign. At which point it was just, 'Fuck off,' and I put the phone down.

LYNVAL GOLDING We signed to Chrysalis and two big cars came and whisked us off to their office by Bond Street. Being chauffeur-driven, from my background: that's film stars. That night we played at the Nashville with Madness. What a night! People were outside and the place was packed.

NOBODY IS SPECIAL

First 2 Tone tour. Madness

SHERYL GARRATT 2 Tone went from being a small underground idea of Jerry Dammers and the Specials playing at the Birmingham Rock Against Racism Club to exploding in the national consciousness in a matter of weeks. 'Gangsters' and 'The Selecter' charted in the top ten and within weeks Madness were also rapidly climbing the charts. And then suddenly all three of the 2 Tone bands appeared on the same edition of *Top of the Pops*.

JERRY DAMMERS I first met Madness when we played at the Hope and Anchor in Islington at an RAR gig around the time of the '79 election. Some of them and their mates were dressed a bit like us and after the gig they told me they had a band too and they did a bit of ska. I went to see them and they were really basic, just like a school band; they did a bit of Prince Buster and rock 'n' roll, mainly covers, but some of their own songs. Suggs, their singer, gave me a cassette and that was extremely basic as well. For the first year Lee Thompson played everything a semitone wrong because he'd stuck the mouthpiece on his sax on too far. I seriously don't think anyone would have signed them at that stage, but there was 'My Girl' and I could see they could write a real song, so I offered them a chance to put something out on 2 Tone. They recorded 'The Prince' and a cover of 'Madness'. It was amazing how quickly they improved; they had no choice really, they'd been thrown in at the deep end.

RICK ROGERS The 2 Tone tour in October '79 was the beginning of what the 2 Tone movement was meant to be. It was like, 'Let's go on tour together – Madness, Selecter, the Specials – like a Motown Revue.' There was nothing more natural. This was more than just going to see your favourite band. It was the idea of celebration and doing something that was worthwhile.

JULIET DE VALERO WILLS Organizing the 2 Tone tour was crazy. There was going to be forty-odd people out on the road. I had drafted in my sister Sarah to help out and we stayed up until 2 a.m. stapling and assembling tour itineraries by hand. There were stacks of paper and we had to use the copying shop down the road. This was the night before because the arrangements had been changing constantly and the bands weren't exactly organized or easy to pin down. So as we were launching off up the motorway I was completely exhausted, and then seeing everybody not giving a shit about the itineraries and tearing off the bottoms to make roaches with, I was like, 'Great. Thanks. Cheers.' But for them it was like a load of kids going out on a school outing, all really excited. There was a lot of laughing and joking and a lot of energy. They'd all come from nowhere not long before: shitty jobs, living in shitty bedsits, no money, trying to get things off the ground. There was a fabulous sense of unity and starting an adventure. The whole 2 Tone ideal was about to be lived and borne out in these dance halls across the country. I had just a flash of that moment before I went back to being tired and worried.

NEOL DAVIES It was a really old-fashioned fifty-five-seater coach, cheap as chips. It didn't have headrests, just really basic. It was the first proper tour that any of us had done: three seven-piece bands; back-to-back about fifty dates. It was exhilarating. The Specials had put out their second single, 'A Message to You Rudy', we had 'On My Radio', and Madness had 'The Prince': three chart bands touring together; it was an immense feeling. Within the first few days it was complete madness. Ridiculous stuff was going on. We filmed the video for 'Missing Words' on the first or second afternoon. We were challenging a lot of the way the music business worked because we had done it all ourselves. We'd created a label in a little provincial city and gained national success. We felt very empowered.

RICK ROGERS Coventry City Football Club had just got a new bus, so we got their old one and it actually had things like seats with tables in it. Several times the coach would have to stop while I made calls from a roadside phone box to find out what venue we were in, in case it had been put up a size. Initially, it was £2.50 for a ticket, the same price it would have been to see a single band. It was a bit less than half of what it would cost you to buy an album, rather than five times more which is what it's like now. And what kept us going was selling T-shirts and ties. As soon as the doors opened I had to jump across the table and start helping because just a swarm of people wanted to get this stuff.

NEOL DAVIES We desperately needed someone to manage us so I said to the band, 'Let's invite Juliet', which we did in the dressing room in Brighton

The Selecter on-set filming the video for 'Missing Words', November 1979.

on the first night of the tour. It was an obvious thing to do because she'd been involved right from the beginning. She was really clued-up, very young, very competent and a very attractive blonde girl who was really fired up managing a black band with a white guy in it. We didn't have a standard record company acceptably suited manager type, quite the opposite, and I'm proud of that. And Pauline was very comfortable that she had another woman on the road.

PAULINE BLACK Juliet was very important to us. She was fun and bubbly and seemed very capable. She was doing PR stuff and getting us interviews and it went from there. It was unusual to have a female manager. The tour was like a school outing. It was an old bus that as schoolkids you might have gone to the swimming baths in; you just had a bit more luggage with you and instead of getting in the pool you got on stage and did your thing.

FRANK MURRAY Pauline was the only women on the 2 Tone tour with a busload of testosterone-fuelled men. She used to read a bit and was into radical left-wing politics. She was a very strong presence and could handle herself.

NEVILLE STAPLE Me, Trevor and Rex were the black boys off the street and

I think we were a bit rough cut for the rest of 'em. Pauline, being a girl, we would have been a bit rough for her: 'Bloodclaat . . .'. We were in people's face.

PAULINE BLACK It was generally accepted that you didn't get in an argument with me because you were likely not to come off the best. I was good with words. Neville always used to say, 'Oh God, here comes Pauline. She's swallowed a dictionary again.' But I never ever felt I was any less on stage.

LYNVAL GOLDING Pauline wasn't make-up and all girly stuff. She was like one of the lads. It had to be tough on her. There were so many hooligan guys but she stood her ground.

RHODA DAKAR The first time I saw the Selecter was on *Top of the Pops* doing 'On My Radio'. Pauline dressed like a boy but sounded like a girl. It was like, 'Yeah, I can go with that.'

PAULINE BLACK A lot of people thought that I was a boy because I wore a pork-pie hat, jacket and trousers. The first time we were reviewed for *Sounds* Giovanni Dadomo likened me to Jimmy Clitheroe, a white northerner who wore school shorts. I would never deny that I was a woman but I would deny having to be trapped in a straitjacket of conventional dress for womanhood. Wearing dresses made me feel unpowerful. To go on stage I had to feel powerful. I wasn't the backing singer or one of Bob Marley's I Threes. I made a very conscious decision that I did not want to be like that. I still had full slap on. But a bit of androgyny never hurt. Look at Mick Jagger. But usually women are afraid that everyone's going to call them a dyke. It was the age of feminism and it was also the age of black politics coming into fruition. I thought naively, 'Hey, here I am fully formed.' Dave Wakeling thought I was a boy when he first saw me.

DAVE WAKELING I had gone to a Selecter concert with a friend of mine, and Pauline jumped on stage with a suit and a hat on, and he goes, 'That's the kind of bloke I like.' About two songs in she took her hat off and I go, 'Ha, ha.'

SHERYL GARRATT Here was this girl that had taken this whole Jamaican style and made it her own. She was androgynous but not in a male way. She looked bloody gorgeous. The clothes she wore and the way she moved. It was obvious she was a girl and she was very powerful-looking. I immediately went out and bought a suit.

JULIET DE VALERO WILLS Punk had produced some really strong front-women but it was still very much boys in bands. Pauline was analytical and outspoken about the politics of society and economics. And the music journalists liked that initially. But beyond that a lot of people in mainstream media were frightened off. For a long time, our relationship was important and we gave each other a huge amount of moral support. We were the only two women on the bus who weren't girlfriends or wives or one-night stands. It was very male and macho. 2 Tone was about black and white but there were contradictions throughout. It wasn't about sexism. You can espouse or truly believe in political ideals but everybody struggles to actually live them every day.

FRANK MURRAY I was the tour manager on the 2 Tone tour and I remember ringing Stiff Records and saying, 'Tell me about Madness.' Dave Robinson said, 'OK, there's six guys and a dancer.' I said, 'A what? What do you mean, a fucking dancer?' He says, 'You'll see it.' Cathal turned out to be the dancer – he explained that kids in Camden couldn't pronounce Cathal so they called him Carl. He gave Madness an excitement to their music. He used to start their set by shouting, *Hey you, don't watch that, watch this. This is the heavy, heavy monster sound . . . 'One Step Beyond'*.

PAULINE BLACK Madness were just out of school. We would probably have been their teachers because we were all a bit older than them. With age I've probably mellowed in what I thought about them then. There was this camaraderie and rivalry of being on tour with two other bands and this tremendously idealistic ethos: 'We're going to rotate the bill.' 'Oh wow!' 'We're all on *Top of the Pops* this week!' 'We'll do it and come back by car!' 'Ah, but we're coming back by helicopter!'

RICK ROGERS The only really annoying part of it was trying to get that many people on a coach in the morning. Sometimes we'd be sitting there for two hours before we got everyone on, but the atmosphere at the gigs was amazing. This was a plan coming together. It was new. It was happening.

FRANK MURRAY You give it a title, the '2 Tone tour', and it will become a movement. It was like an old-style revue with three chart-topping acts, so everybody came to see them. It was an event. All three bands seemed to have this unreal energy that went through them twenty-four hours a day, I mean really. The Specials used to start with 'Dawning Of A New Era'. I loved the excitement. It just seemed like constant motion. Lynval and

Neville were always moving, and Jerry pumping away at the keyboards. Terry was a solitary individual and wouldn't say a lot. He'd join in the banter and crack a few jokes but when you saw him walk on stage he just looked so fucking tense. Then he did that first jump and started to sing and the whole night you could see it coming out of him. He was very good at making sarky comments to the audience that would cut you in half.

RICK ROGERS It wasn't so much what individuals were offering. It was the collective energy and spirit and how that engaged an audience in a joyful way. It was a whirlwind. I'd never ever seen that before. You couldn't take your eyes off them, and with this grumpy, solitary character in the middle there was a huge juxtaposition going on that just made things work. The natural barrier between performer and audience wasn't there because there wasn't a single person controlling that. It felt more like you were having a party that was being led by these characters. Later on when people from the audience started coming on stage and joining in at the end; that's what it made you want to do. It was absolutely extraordinary. I had never been blown away like that.

NEOL DAVIES The Specials were mind-blowingly good and just hit it. It was very competitive. We were explosive on stage. Nobody had seen a black band play or behave like that before. It was way ahead of its time. People didn't quite know how to take us. If you ever saw the Selecter play live you'd never forget it as long as you lived.

NICKY SUMMERS I saw the tour at the Lyceum. I remember seeing Pauline and thinking she had a great voice. People were just dancing. I'd met Mark from Madness a few times and used to chat to him about getting my own band together. He was really supportive, so I was also quite analytical, 'What are they doing?' 'Oh, they use that amp.'

JUNE MILES-KINGSTON The Specials were gods. They were doing everything I'd ever wanted to do. They were amazing musicians and really worked as a band.

FRANK MURRAY And the Specials having Rico Rodriguez's imprimatur on it was like the icing on the cake. He had played trombone on so many original ska records: 'I've worked with all the legends and now I'm working with these guys.' That was so important.

CATHAL SMYTH Rico used to leave the tour and go and score grass and then sell it. I'd join him. It was exciting.

The Specials: (L–R) Roddy Byers, Neville Staple, Horace Panter, Terry Hall, John Bradbury, Lynval Golding , Jerry Dammers, Hammersmith Palais, 21 August 1979.

The Selecter: (L–R) Neol Davies, Compton Amanor, Pauline Black, Arthur 'Gaps' Hendrickson, Desmond Brown Tiffany's, Edinburgh, 12 November 1979.

TRACEY THORN 2 Tone was joyous musically. It was lighter than punk, with a political message of positivity and harmony coming off the stage. And yet they attracted this horrible violent contingent. I'd be at gigs where bottles would be thrown, fighting would break out, and the gig would be stopped. You came to almost expect that. I went to three or four gigs to see Madness, the Specials, the Selecter and it ended badly.

DOUG MORRIS I wasn't allowed to go to see the Specials because my mum had read in the *Daily Express* about stabbings. Going to see the Specials or Madness felt like you were taking your life in your hands.

RHODA DAKAR I was at the Hatfield Poly gig midway through the 2 Tone tour – I remember the Specials marching in, all carrying their suits like the Beatles getting into a cab in *A Hard Day's Night* – where it was invaded by a group of knife-wielding thugs and people got cut. There was a palpable sense of fear in the place.

NEOL DAVIES I remember walking around the town before the gig and being quite scared. There were lots of rumours and scuffles and some unpleasant-looking characters. It felt like something was going to happen.

JERRY DAMMERS The Hatfield gig quickly became the stuff of schoolyard myth and it's really hard to work out exactly what happened and the extent of it. The perception was out there that a section of people who turned up at Madness gigs at that time were National Front or British Movement supporters; hardly surprising when some of them insisted on doing Nazi salutes. A group burst in through the fire doors, presumably to try and teach whoever that Nazi behaviour was not acceptable.

TRACEY THORN The vast majority of the people in the crowd were just there at a gig not really wanting it to be World War III.

JERRY DAMMERS Some accounts claim the group had a banner saying 'Hatfield Mafia', which wasn't exactly a great name for an anti-fascist group. There were also rumours that some of the Cockney Reds were involved, who were London-based Man. United supporters, some of whom got involved in anti-fascism; but who knows? There didn't seem to be that much in the way of fighting back, although there was some, mainly in the bar, I think. A glass door got smashed and there may have been some injuries from broken glasses.

RHODA DAKAR It was stupid and unpleasant and violent and aggressive.

Whether it was bully boys from the right or left, it didn't legitimize the action. I can just as well understand it being the Trots: 'We'll sort it out after the revolution.' 'Yeah, course you will.'

JULIET DE VALERO WILLS It was reported eleven people were arrested, ten people were hospitalized and there was £1,000 worth of damage.

JERRY DAMMERS I think the anti-fascists were a slightly older generation and possibly still assumed all skinhead-looking kids were racists, which I don't think was true in the 2 Tone era at all. What is known is that the real NF and BM were extremely violent, inciting racist hatred, and a lot of people were actually getting killed in racist attacks on the street. The police and government seemed to be doing next to nothing to counteract these organizations, so some people were tempted to take the law into their own hands. If I'd have known they were coming, though, I wish I could have talked to them first and tried to explain that we were trying to achieve similar anti-racist and anti-fascist goals, but by using music – and that we seemed to be getting somewhere. Most of the kids in the audience were still quite young. It was a horrible and very sobering night that took some of the euphoria out of the 2 Tone tour.

PAULINE BLACK We had to be smuggled out of there. I remember being in a car park, freezing cold, and being very worried because it looked as though we were going to get a battering. The police were called and then of course it got in the papers. There was some confusion that we were right-wing bands that attracted this element. But the audience was mainly tribal: mods, punks, skinheads and people with longer hair who hadn't quite given up the Seventies. Far-right groups were targeting 2 Tone bands and often at gigs there would be a faction who would start Sieg-Heiling and it would kick off. As the frontperson you felt obliged to say something: 'Could you please stop doing that?' And then you'd start up again and if it persisted you'd say, 'Right, if all these people here are doing this and the rest of you are having fun, what's your feeling about that?' You'd try and shame them publicly. Sometimes it would be enough if they put the lights up; then perpetrators could be identified and the bouncers would throw out the ringleaders.

NEOL DAVIES It was isolated pockets that wanted to cause trouble. It was mainly the London racist skinheads that didn't like black people but liked reggae music. It was a very small minority but they had a large voice. Most skinheads weren't like that but there was a confused core that loved ska but hated the guys who made it.

FRANK MURRAY When you see somebody getting kicked your stomach tends to tighten up. At Hatfield I went backstage and the bands were despondent. Nobody wants to be tainted with violence. For some reason everybody seemed to come to the conclusion it was Madness's fans who might be responsible so they played a shorter than normal set to get the Specials on.

NEVILLE STAPLE Madness's fans were all skinheads.

RANKING ROGER You heard rumours about Madness because they were all-white but Jerry would never have had them on 2 Tone if he thought they were a racist band.

MYKAELL RILEY The complication around Madness was, 'Who is your audience? Are you supporting the fascist movement or not, because the majority of your audience does and you play to them?' Their political stance wasn't initially explained or resolved. It was just floating, so you only needed a few agitators on occasions to galvanize the audience in a particular way. Retrospectively, Madness were on the 'right side' but at the time it didn't feel like that. It was like, 'We don't want to take sides in this; it's better to say nothing.'

JERRY DAMMERS I hope any Madness fans that needed to learn something did learn something from being involved in the 2 Tone movement generally, and I know Madness themselves soon came to realize you can't just sit on the fence when it comes to racism.

DENNIS BOVELL Madness didn't want to jeopardize the paying crowd; they didn't care who came to listen as long as they paid.

RICK ROGERS Madness were the only all-white band in this multiracial line-up and as kids might have had some dodgy connections. It's context. In the areas they grew up, they would have been exposed to anti-black ideas and some of them had flirted or hung around with people like that. Once they saw what 2 Tone was about and were part of it they were 100 per cent signed up to the agenda. There's no question about that.

JULIET DE VALERO WILLS Suggs said, 'If we were fascists what would we be doing playing ska and bluebeat? If we'd wanted to talk about politics we'd have formed a debating society, not a fucking band.' But by the time

Madness realized what they had embraced it was too late. They were part of that Camden soft skinhead look: DMs, braces, cropped hair. That was what was so brilliant because they brought in that really important element. People think they didn't challenge it enough. I think they were too young to think it through. Any understanding of socio-economic politics, sexism or racism that existed was a blunt instrument at that time; there was nothing refined about any of it.

FRANK MURRAY I had big issues with skinheads because I'd been around at their first incarnation when I was a hippy and if they caught you they'd cut your hair. The look was quite brutal. The term 'aggro' came out of that: 'You want some aggro?' There was talk that a couple of the guys pre-Madness had had a brush with the National Front but had since disowned it. When the press were looking to point the finger they went at Madness because they were all-white, but it was like growing up in Belfast and saying you knew somebody in the IRA; of course you would. You do things by example: if I was a racist and I didn't like black people I wouldn't go on tour with them, d'you know what I mean?

CATHAL SMYTH The seventies had been a time of racist TV, of racist attitudes, of ignorance, of violence, of social deprivation, of fear; and this had a phenomenal and tangible effect on culture. There were a lot of conflicting energies. There were punks and skins and Teds and rockabillies, but then suddenly you get the agitators in the audience. It was frightening. Deanne Pearson wrote an article about Madness in *NME* called 'NICE BAND, SHAME ABOUT THE FANS' where I was quoted as saying, 'We don't care if the crowd are in the NF, or BM or whatever, so long as they're behaving themselves, having a good time, and not fighting. They're just kids.'

SHERYL GARRATT 2 Tone was never contrived to make a political statement with the multicultural bands, and as it was obvious to them they weren't racists, they felt it should be obvious to everyone else. But it clearly wasn't. It must have been bloody terrifying for Madness but we couldn't understand why they didn't speak out and make a statement.

CATHAL SMYTH I was young and not very eloquent and the *NME* misunderstood me. Our guitarist, Chris, thought I was a fucking idiot because his girlfriend was black; her family hated me and thought I was racist. I felt absolutely fucking insulted. I was trying to say, 'We didn't want to be in politics. You have to communicate with idiots to change their minds. You have to let them in.' I was trying to say, 'How can you have change through distance? You have to have proximity. It's a fucking disease. You can't cure a patient from 100 yards away; you've got to be in the room with him. You have to recognize the disease, locate it and lance it. Not shout at it. You can't help a person if they don't feel comfortable with you. You've got to be an agent of change, not punishment.' People were confused. Travelling abroad gave me the realization that every country seems to have a fuckin' scapegoat and it's usually an ethnic minority. For me the frightening people were the ones in the shadows. In the end we issued a statement:

> 1) Madness do not support any political group which has racial poli-
> tics. 2) The career of Madness has been inspired by many people.
> Their first-ever hit, 'The Prince', was dedicated to a Jamaican, Prince
> Buster, who is the godfather of ska and reggae. This record was
> released on a label belonging to the Specials who have both black and
> white members. It is consequently very upsetting to Madness that it
> could be assumed by anyone that Madness could support any racist
> group. 3) At the concerts at Hammersmith Odeon when the National
> Front and the British Movement were outside selling literature all
> possible efforts were made by Madness and the promoters of the
> concert to stop such literature being sold. 4) Finally, Madness will
> make it absolutely clear that they did not support any racist policies
> and hope that their fans of all ages and all nationalities do likewise.

TIM WELLS I'd listened to 'Embarrassment'; Madness spoke out in the music.

NEIL SPENCER A lot of the Nazis embraced 2 Tone. There was a huge contradiction. Why were all those skinheads dancing to black music? I don't know how to explain that away.

JULIET DE VALERO WILLS You hear a lot about the violence and the aggression and things kicking off in the crowd, and that happened too, but there was an incredible atmosphere with a lot of people who had come together just so excited by what was happening and to be part of this thing that had not quite been defined yet. It was only later when factions started to form behind the bands. It was always the odd thing between the songs – people sieg-heiling – and then the audience going nuts during the songs and skanking. We just couldn't fathom it. You'd try to look at it logically and say, 'The mods and skins are natural enemies and they instinctively want to fight,' yet they had an absolute shared love of black music. But

Cathal Smyth
(front left) and
Suggs of Madness,
Hammersmith
Odeon, London,
16 February 1980.

the skins felt they had some sort of proprietorial right over ska. When it bubbled over the skinheads were getting challenged heavily by the bands from the stage; actively naming and shaming all the time.

JERRY DAMMERS Despite all the hugely exaggerated stories I can only remember it happening to the Specials three or four times, involving a maximum of three or four people, and we would always stop playing immediately because those incidents really upset me. There was one guy in Brighton who I invited on stage and asked him to explain to the audience why he was doing it, and when he started speaking I pushed him off, to a huge cheer from the rest of the audience. And after an incident at Brunel University I led the band off the stage and we chased them out. Roddy was waving his guitar above his head and they fled in terror long before we reached them. Imagine that, *Top of the Pops* coming to life and running towards you!

LYNVAL GOLDING It was a fashion trend. There would be about ten racists who would Sieg-Heil amongst 2,000 people but they would get the front-page news. The Specials never looked at anyone and said, 'You can't come into our gig.' Everyone was welcome. I was in Portsmouth once after a gig talking to these people with a racist attitude. One said, 'You're the first black guy I've ever talked to. I get it now.' Skinheads began to see everyone merging together and say, 'I want to be everyone.'

BILLY BRAGG I'd just had my hair cut really short for a bet and they wouldn't let me in at the Hammersmith gig. There was this whole line of skinheads sat on a wall across the road and the guy said, 'Sorry, son, if I let you in I've got to let all that lot in too.' I eventually saw the tour in Lewisham. Apparently, promoters made certain skinheads remove the laces out of steel-capped boots so they couldn't be used as weapons.

JERRY DAMMERS Any violence was too much violence for me. I hated it. But it does have to be seen in the context of literally hundreds of gigs which were completely joyful celebrations with no trouble at all.

RICK ROGERS Gigs being disrupted and violence at gigs was a minor part of what happened. When it was recognized it was swiftly dealt with from the stage and not tolerated. If you're doing something powerful and you're putting a powerful political message out that is challenging a racist agenda, then the racists are going to try and infiltrate and protest. If you're extreme, then the extreme will try to screw you up. On top of that, some of the clothes were taken from what had originally been associated with right-wing culture, so it starts to reappropriate signs and symbols; so some people got confused.

HORACE PANTER Ejecting fascist skinheads from the auditorium wasn't what I'd signed up to do. I just wanted to jump around with the bass and impress girls. Most of the stage invasions were to do with alcohol and football: 'It's Saturday night, let's get really pissed.' It had nothing to do with the bands particularly. It's the British working-class predilection for drinking too much and fighting. You pay to come and see a pop group to disrupt the concert? I never got that. Lynval talking to that guy with the BM sign shaved into the back of his head. That would be the photo: conquering England one fan at a time.

•

JERRY DAMMERS The stage invasions at Specials gigs started in Liverpool at Eric's when some lads came up from Coventry. There were bad vibes from some of the Scousers and they came onstage partly to feel safer, I think. They said, 'This is our band. We've got as much right to be on the stage as you because you're representing us.' That then became a statement of solidarity between the band and audience. The previous punk statement had been gobbing on the band, which we caught the end of. It wasn't pleasant but it was stating that the band weren't superior to the audience by putting them in their place. To make it clear I put the line *Nobody is special* in the 'Skinhead Symphony' medley. For us it was saying, 'We're all in this together.' Having the audience on the stage with us was great and at first it was restricted to the end of the set or the encore, but then it got to be disruptive when kids wanted to get on stage in the third number.

RICK ROGERS It was very much Jerry's agenda of *nobody is special*. 'Just because we're pop stars and we're in a band, that doesn't make us any more special than you.' And in every little way that that could be addressed it was addressed. Getting on stage was a natural thing because it was completely inclusive. And it was a political statement. The fact there were black kids and white kids and that there was performer and audience and you were all made to feel the same. It was extraordinary. Never seen before and never seen again. But things progressed and as the band got bigger that inclusivity went to people being able to get on the coach, to coming back to the hotel, to being put up in people's rooms, and obviously, from a keeping-it-together point of view, that made my job more difficult at times.

HORACE PANTER Fans coming onto the stage started off as spontaneous joy but in the end it was like, 'Please be careful, you're going to fall over the drum kit.' We had these lighting towers at the back of the stage and how none of them tumbled onto people is an absolute miracle. That's why we had a second tier of risers, so we had something to go back to when the lip of the stage had 200 fans on it. The PA crews didn't like it because they invariably got stands bent and lost a few microphones. Jerry would express it to me politically: 'The music belongs to everybody; to be part of it.' I really struggled with it. But Jerry was, 'No, let them do it.' You'd have to stop the show for five minutes: 'Can you get off, please.'

FRANK MURRAY There was a lot of unruliness and the audience would be dancing up there and knocking over microphones. The bouncers were told to stay away and the fans were totally exhilarated, dancing their arses off.

The Specials at the Top Rank, Brighton, 10 October 1980.

Jerry loved all of that breaking down the barriers. I just saw it as fucking hassle, letting all these clowns on the stage. It was a nightmare for me because you can't control those kinds of kids. And if they start getting lippy some band member will always stand up and defend them when you're trying to keep a little bit of order in the chaos.

JERRY DAMMERS I was actually more worried about the safety aspect than people probably realized, but it seemed like once the stage invasions had become established, trying to stop them would have been even more dangerous than letting them carry on. And I was proved right. When we did have to try to stop one in Dublin for safety reasons, it caused a near riot.

JULIET DE VALERO WILLS One of the most important reasons why 2 Tone worked was because of the dancing. At the end of the Specials' set all the other bands would pile on. And then Jerry would invite the audience on as well. I would spend a lot of the time by the mixing desk skanking away and teaching kids and various record-label execs how to do it. It became like the dance hall thing where being able to dance well and being part of the audience was as important as being up there. You were contributing. Jerry said, 'It was the first time white males danced.' The atmosphere at those gigs was the most exciting thing you could ever experience. Three bands one after the other. It was non-stop. The crowd were going fucking nuts. The shows were like a steam train; they were almost impossible to stop because the crowd would become this one mass of energy.

JERRY DAMMERS The energy at the gigs was absolutely unbelievable: the steam rising off the crowd, and the whole place jumping up and down. You could feel the building shaking. In Hastings we were on the pier and it only had wooden slats and between the cracks you could see the waves crashing on the rocks beneath. I really thought the audience might go through. And in fact in Southend they did. The PA stack was swaying and from the stage you could see huge holes appearing in the dance floor and kids falling into the cellar ten feet below because they were stomping so much. It was bonkers. That was the injection of African rhythm in the music. Ska is very energetic and it really lifts off and is relentless.

LYNVAL GOLDING We'd get to a venue and jump on the stage to make sure it would hold. In Bristol the stage just collapsed. It was really important, the fans coming on the stage, because the audience was part of the band. And people travelled with us on the coach. In Belfast, I had to sleep on the floor because my bed was taken by other people. It was crazy. We'd give out our passes every night; backstage was full of people that weren't in the band. We broke down a lot of black and white barriers.

HORACE PANTER 'Horace, can you put up these five skinheads from Catford?' It was like, 'Can't I get some sleep?' It was taking it too far. I resented that imposition. 'Yeah, but I've got six skinheads staying on my floor.'

JERRY DAMMERS We weren't just a student band preaching to the converted; we took the message right out into the lion's den, so to speak, of the so called skinhead revival and I was always aware that strategy had risks and dangers and might not work 100 per cent, but I do think overall, along with other campaigns like Rock Against Racism, that 2 Tone did ultimately help make the kind of general racism I grew up with unacceptable in this country.

STAND DOWN MARGARET

The Beat. UB40

SHERYL GARRATT I was under the impression that you joined a band, played locally for six months, then got on *Top of the Pops* and were famous, because that's what happened to all of my friends in Birmingham. I had a real crush on Terry Hall so I was always pushing for us to book the Specials at the Birmingham RAR club, and UB40 and the Beat both played, so 2 Tone connected up with Rock Against Racism. And what was important politically was that it was pulling it back from the drift to the right. We were saying, 'Hey, there's another way.'

RANKING ROGER The RAR club used to have a couple of punk bands to start off with and then end with a reggae band to balance the evening and tone it down. And the DJs used to play tunes like 'The Model' by Kraftwerk, 'White Riot' by the Clash, 'Borstal Breakout' by Sham 69 and then 'MPLA' by Tapper Zukie which fits smack-a-dom in the middle, and the whole place would be dancing. It was like rebels together. But when the Clash played at Barbarella's the skinheads were chanting, '*Sieg Heil, Sieg Heil* . . . National Front' and all the punks were booing. I was by the DJ booth and they were saying, 'You've got to say something to 'em, Roge.' So I picked up the mic and started toasting at them: *Fuck-off / Fuck-off de Na-tion-al Front / Fuck-off / Fuck-off de Na-tion-al Front.* There was a riot. Music can turn you into a fool but it can also turn you into a hero. After that I decided that I was going to do everything within my power to put a stop to this racism.

DAVE WAKELING In the Beat our reaction to Rock *Against* Racism was, let's do something 'for' something and make a group that looks like Rock Against Racism. Don't get me wrong, I think Rock Against Racism turned history, but at the same time it was being very white about it. It was almost like inviting everybody round for bacon sandwiches in favour of religious tolerance. That said, I wore both my RAR and Anti-Nazi League badges with pride – I had a pink and black one – and I've often wondered if that influenced how the Beat colours turned out, which were pink, black and white.

The Beat at the Rock Garden, Covent Garden, London, circa November 1979. (L–R) Andy Cox, Saxa, Ranking Roger, Dave Wakeling, David Steele.

RANKING ROGER I was playing drums in a punk band called the Dum Dum Boys and we were due to play a place called the Matador in the Old Bull Ring. The Beat contacted us and said they wanted to open up for us. We said, 'Yes, but we've got to hear if you're good enough first.' They came to our rehearsal room upstairs in the Socialist Workers bookshop in Digbeth a couple of weeks before and played 'Mirror In The Bathroom', 'Twist And Crawl' and 'Jackpot'. I was like, 'Wow!'

DAVE WAKELING My first notion of the Beat was the industrial angst of the Velvet Underground with the *joie de vivre* and the survival message of Toots and the Maytals, and Petula Clarke and the Buzzcocks on top; and then I got to be Bryan Ferry and Van Morrison, and Tim Buckley if I could get the notes. At house parties, Andy Cox and I used to DJ and we noticed if we played all punk singles, the place would become frenetic and people burned out pretty quickly, but if we played all dub reggae 'slates', people would lean against the wall nodding their heads as if they were dancing. So we'd alternate between punk and reggae records and then the dance floor was packed all night. One night, Andy said to me, 'What if you could mix both elements into a three minute single, what would we have then,

Dave?' I went, 'Punky reggae party; that's what you'd have'. That was the big moment. We started up this residency at the Mercat Cross in the meat market. The area was dead at night and the owner was keen to get anybody in. We would notice Roger in the audience. He was only sixteen and well over six foot with short orange dreadlocks and a ripped-up Union Jack over army fatigues. It was like, 'Oh hello, who's that then?' And then before I'd spoken to him he jumped on the stage and started toasting. It was ironic because Roger was black and a big punk fan, and me and Andy Cox, the guitarist, were white and big reggae fans.

SHERYL GARRATT We all knew Roger. When he turned up with the Beat you were like, 'Yeah, of course.' They would sometimes just be playing to four of us. They'd stop between songs and say, 'Do you wanna a drink?' And if we wanted them to play at the club I'd just nab one of them afterwards and say, 'Do you want to play the Friday after next?'

RANKING ROGER The first time I went down to the Mercat it was empty. I said, 'I'll go and get some people.' I went up the Crown where all these punks were bored out of their minds. I said, 'Do you remember that band the Beat I told you about? They're playing down the road. Let's go!' We were walking down the road and there must have been about 150 of us and these police wagons were driving past slowly and then going round the block thinking, 'Is there going to be a riot here or something?' At the Mercat the place was heaving. I did a couple of numbers and the crowd pushed me back on. After, the band were thanking me and saying, 'You were really good. Shall we see you next week, then?' I could have joined UB40 because I used to get up on stage with them as well but I decided to go with the Beat because they were more versatile and aggressive. There was a lot happening in Birmingham.

LYNVAL GOLDING Charley Anderson had UB40's first demo cassette on the 2 Tone tour bus. We heard *I'm a British subject, not proud of it / While I carry the burden of shame* and got really confused. We didn't realize it was a white guy singing. It makes sense: a black British guy; a white guy, no, man! We wanted to sign them but Jerry said they weren't 2 Tone enough.

JERRY DAMMERS It was probably a mistake not signing UB40 but I thought 2 Tone should build on its slightly twisted retro ska identity and they were more like straightforward current reggae and might confuse the identity. Also, I was uneasy about the lyrics to 'King'. It was a beautiful tune, but *King where are your people now? / Chained and pacified / You tried to* *show them how and for that you died* could be taken as saying Martin Luther King's policy of non-violence might have been wrong. I didn't think it was, but I thought, 'Who the hell is 2 Tone to even imply that when he gave his life?'

NEIL SPENCER The arrival of UB40 confirmed the West Midlands as the epicentre of British reggae, though they took a different path musically to the Specials or the Beat. They had more of a stoner vibe and they had a sufferer's voice in Ali Campbell. Politically they stood for stubborn resistance rather than brazen defiance. There was no punk-style posturing, and they seemed wary of signing up to anyone else's agenda. Their hearts were clearly in the right place though, and 'King' and 'One In Ten' had a welcome international dimension. Initially, I thought *I am the one in ten* was about being gay until I listened harder.

JIMMY BROWN I wrote the words but not the melody. I have always been pissed off with the way politicians use statistics. They dehumanize the suffering their action, or lack of action, causes. The song really is just a list of statistics. Starting small, unemployment, but as we go through the song it takes in all kinds of stats: pill-popping housewives, middle-aged men with heart disease, etc., eventually going global with refugees, cancer and starvation, suggesting that it's pure luck, or accident of birth, that separates those that suffer and those that don't.[36]

TRACEY THORN Being called UB40 was quite a statement in itself. They took their name from the registration document issued by the Department of Employment known as the 'Unemployment Benefit Form 40'. Ali Campbell said, 'The title UB40 gave us three million card-carrying fans, instantly.' Their early stuff was incredibly powerful and quite hard-edged.

TOM WATSON I was in fifth form and we played 'One In Ten' all the time. We knew what it meant: 'You haven't got a fucking chance.'

ANGELA EAGLE My sister and I were the first people in our family to go to university but when I came out there were no jobs. I was unemployed for a year and had to come down to London to find work.

RHODA DAKAR I was offered a job as a civil servant in the dole office – 'So you're recruiting now? Yes, all right. I can do that.' I used to work on the personal issues counter and sign on the homeless people. I used to make it my business to try and remember their names before they handed in their cards: 'Good morning, Miss So-and-So. Here we are.' 'Don't you need my card?' 'No, I know who you are.' I thought, 'If I can just do that.' It was sad. You'd see kids coming down from the north and the first week, I'd say, 'What are you doing?' 'I'm looking for work.' 'There's nothing doing here.' And I'd try and persuade them to go back home. They'd gradually get dirtier and then one week they'd come in completely clean and you'd think, 'Shit.' You'd know that they'd gone on the game. It was tragic. I remember in winter walking home and one of my claimants, this old African lady, came up to me and said, 'Ooh, do your coat up. You'll catch a cold.' I was thinking, 'You're bloody homeless living on the street and you're worried about me.'

CATHAL SMYTH Dole was the only way for a lot of people. Signing on was a social stigma. I remember once being given the runaround from three fucking different branches to collect something like £6.90. All these things to bring some dignity back into one's right to a voice and welfare and one's right to a decent life.

ROBERT HOWARD Without the dole half the bands would never have existed. It was a social safety net. My parents had paid into the system all their lives in order to provide; that's how it works. And I've certainly paid my fair share of tax since. I got signed as a songwriter and that was the first time I ever saw any money.

PAULINE BLACK If you had a job you were only one pay cheque away from being unemployed, so the name UB40 was very resonant. We did a gig in Birmingham at an outdoor festival and it was the first time I heard 'Food For Thought': *Ivory Madonna dying in the dust / Waiting for the manna coming from the west.* I remember thinking, 'They're amazing.'

JULIET DE VALERO WILLS UB40 were more of a traditional reggae band and their stage show was more laconic. The Beat was more of a natural fit to 2 Tone. Also we all knew John Mostyn, who had been booking the Specials, and he was trusted and he then started managing the Beat. They were part of the same seed and the Specials seed blossomed first. They had that black–white thing and the look – it was a no-brainer – and Roger jumping around all over the place. He looked amazing and absolutely summed up the youthful energy of 2 Tone. He always had a smile on his face.

RANKING ROGER We had sent a demo to Jerry Dammers and he came with Lynval Golding to one of the dates the Beat gigged with the Selecter and they were dancing down the front with Neol and Pauline. Then at the last gig of the tour at the Electric Ballroom, Jerry came again with his briefcase and he had some papers: 'We really like you guys and want you to be the next 2 Tone band. Can you do a single within three days?' We were like, 'WHAT!' They wanted 'Mirror In The Bathroom' but we said, 'No. You can have "Tears Of A Clown".' Days before we went into the studio we found Saxa [Lionel Augustus Martin]. He was this old, loud Jamaican man that just got drunk all the time and was always aggressive and cussing and swearing. There must have been a good thirty-five years' difference between us but as soon as he blew that saxophone, baby, you'd shut up.

DAVE WAKELING Everett used to take us to the Crompton in Handsworth where Saxa played. He was the most mesmerizing saxophone player we'd ever heard. He played a couple of gigs with us and then said, 'I've been waiting all my life for you boys.' Everett was from St Kitts and had been working in a kettle spinning factory for twelve years. When he first came down to rehearsals he didn't immediately get our songs and said, 'What do you want a reggae drummer for?' The first few practices were a bit tenuous. Then he said, 'Why don't we try a song that we all know?' It took about ten minutes to hit on Smokey Robinson's 'Tears Of A Clown'. We would play 'Mirror In The Bathroom', then 'Tears Of A Clown', then 'Big Shot', then 'Tears Of A Clown', then 'Twist and Crawl', then 'Tears Of A Clown', so that became the best song in the set.

RANKING ROGER It's amazing how it all came together. 2 Tone put it out and it went to number six in the charts. Before I knew it we were massive in everyone's living room. The B-side was 'Ranking Full Stop', which gave me a chance to show my light within the Beat. Toasting is the same as MC'ing or rapping. It's just in a Jamaican accent. My parents are from St Lucia and I grew up around Jamaican music and picked up being able to speak patois off the street. It was hip but a lot of people couldn't understand the accent. I'd go, 'Wha'ppen?' and they'd go, 'What?' Apart from Rupie Edwards, me and Neville Staple were probably the first two MCs to come forward from West Indian origin and actually do something in the charts.

NEVILLE STAPLE With toasting you just go with the rhythm of the bass and drum or the keyboard. People didn't understand what I was doing at first. For example, in 'Nite Klub', *Nah bother dally down at the Nite Klub, come mek we'll boss it*. 'Nah bother' is 'Don't bother': 'Don't bother fuck about and hang around the nightclub, come on, let's go and enjoy ourselves.'

Patois is just broken English. I had to cut the Jamaican down to make it more English. In 'Too Much Too Young', *Oh no, nah give me no more pick-ney*, I'd have to cradle my arms on stage to illustrate the meaning.

DAVE WAKELING Once the Beat started touring outside of Birmingham people saw Roger and me dancing on stage together and it was the first time they'd ever seen black and white people do that. In London when we opened up for the Selecter a big contingent of skinheads came to talk to us. We were like, 'Take a deep breath here, then.' They said, 'We like black and white geezers on stage together.' 'Oh, yes, well if you like it we did it on purpose.' The black and white mix in the Midlands had been because of forced industrial integration on the factory line and in time people started to understand that they had more in common than perceived differences. There were plenty of pubs where white and black and Indian blokes drank together. Then when we went down south there seemed to be parallel societies and at the start we attracted right-wing elements. You'd see three people link up with one arm – like the Isle of Man flag – with a razor blade in the other and spin through the crowd slashing at people's faces and disappear out of the exit door. It was like a military operation. And we had spitting and stuff.

RANKING ROGER There was racism in the first year but it was always the minority. I was told to ignore them. But then I learnt how to use the crowd against them. As soon as there was a fight, 'Right, everyone stop. Spotlight on them two. What do you lot think of this lot?' And the rest of the audience would boo. 'OK, you want them out? Let me hear you say, "Out, out, out."' That was the power of the microphone. You'd get a big cheer and then go into the next number. Sometimes a little fight was better for the gig. It brought everybody out of their shells and loosened everybody up.

DAVE WAKELING One time, Roger caught a penny in his forehead. They were shouting, 'We hate spades,' and Roger shouted back, 'It's funny how much you like the music then.' And they shut up. You're in a strong position to ridicule the Front but then they razor someone in the toilets on the way out and you've accomplished nothing. But if you don't do anything you condone their behaviour. I said to the band, 'We should have a girl as our emblem because the 2 Tone man on the sleeve bags needs somebody to behave with and he'll behave much better if there's a skin-bird in the room.' At original skinhead dances, because of the girls, boys behaved and didn't have their fighting gear on; so instead of Levi's and Doc Martens you wore a Crombie, Sta-Prest, a Ben Sherman and too much Brut – so we got the Beat Girl. And we'd have loads of girls at the front dressed as her and within a month the fights started to diminish, and within three months they were a thing of the past.

RANKING ROGER There was a picture in *Melody Maker* of a girl dancing next to Prince Buster in the sixties, and Hunt Emerson, the cartoonist, took it and turned it into the Beat Girl. The Specials stole for it the advert on 'Too Much Too Young' and had the Beat Girl with a little baby. It was like a sign of respect. The Beat was definitely a political band but we had love songs and a commercial side too. It was a balance. It was politics at home: meaning politics with your woman, or whoever is governing your country, and world politics. And it was our experiences. We saw racism; we wrote about it. We saw unemployment; we wrote about it. We saw war; we wrote about it. We were singing about realities, like punk and the reggae acts from the past. We just updated it to what was happening to us. Like 'Doors Of Your Heart', *Stick him in a room and turn off the light / Bet you couldn't tell if he was black or white?* The philosophy behind Beat lyrics was throwing questions. Give them a story and let them decide for themselves. The spirit was promoting peace, love, and unity.

The Beat Girl holding an image of Prince Buster dancing with unknown female.

RICK ROGERS Everybody was like, 'The Beat are brilliant.' 2 Tone was the obvious place for them to be. They knew it and as soon as we knew them we knew it. I actually thought if there was anybody who was going to be a serious contender for the Specials' crown it would be the Beat. They had a uniqueness and something completely different. It was also great that they took the spirit of 2 Tone to go on and form Go Feet and have their own label.

DAVE WAKELING 2 Tone had more of a political ethos than a musical direction. That's why we just did 'Tears Of A Clown' and then moved on. It seemed as though the Specials had been set up to make a statement. We wanted to have a more organic musical ethos and let the politics follow along on the back of that.

RANKING ROGER 2 Tone carried us at first but we all would have made it in our own right. We did one single and then we got our own label and then for the next three years we spent all our time getting away from anything to do with it: 'You're with 2 Tone.' 'No. Go Feet.' We didn't dislike the Specials, we just didn't want to be carved into any particular style. They were more ska punk whereas the Beat did punk and reggae and merged it together, and we did soul and a bit of disco. We said, 'We're dance music.'

NEIL SPENCER I didn't think of 2 Tone as political except by example, like when the Beat did 'Stand Down Margaret': *I see only sorrow / I see no chance of your bright new tomorrow.*

DAVE WAKELING Let me tell you how 'Stand Down Margaret' came about. We were going to do a gig supporting the Au Pairs – I'd got a bit of a crush on Lesley – and we made a poster, like a Pirelli calendar, with a muscular-looking torso of a woman holding a whip, with a tattoo on her arm which said 'Au Pairs / The Beat'. We put them up all around Moseley Village and the next morning there was a knock at the door and Lesley and her manager threw them all at us shouting, 'Sexists!' Then we had to be interviewed about whether we were going to get to do this gig at all. Lesley said, 'Are there any women in the band?' I was stuck for words and they stormed off and everything was in limbo. I told the band what had happened and Everett said, 'You could have told her you'd got a darkie on drums; that's got to count for something?' Finally, we were allowed to do the gig and Everett said, 'Now it's all peaceful why don't we do a really dirty Prince Buster song?' So we learnt 'Whine And Grine' and everybody enjoyed the joke. And we kept it in the set because it was going down well. But then I started to feel it was a good joke in Moseley but as an international banner of what we stood for it wasn't quite adequate. I would often have tapes of Saxa from the gigs just going off on these beautiful solos, and listening to the instrumental of 'Whine And Grine' and perhaps making up for the sexist beginning of the song, I started singing this: *Stand down Margaret stand down please* about my fears and feelings about Margaret Thatcher.

RANKING ROGER We were recording 'Whine And Grine' for our first album *I Just Can't Stop It* and near the end we said, 'Let's turn it into a twelve-inch,' one song going into another. It looked like we were heading towards world war and Thatcher was the type who would press the button. It was very serious: the standard of living was going down, interest rates were going up, unemployment and crime rates were going right through the

The Beat 'Stand Down Margaret (Dub)' sleeve, August 1980.

roof. We put out a remix single of it with 'Best Friend' and the money from it went to the Anti-Nuclear Campaign and CND. We raised fourteen grand. It was about putting your money where your mouth was and the Beat's way of putting something back.

DAVE WAKELING The idea in the Beat was to be subversive; we decided it would be like the Monkees with John Lennon and we'd try and get ourselves on as many things as we could and then drop mind bombs if we got the chance. We got on *Cheggers Plays Pop* and Keith Chegwin said, 'Hey Dave, some of the blokes up in the production room are saying this song is about Margaret Thatcher. It's not, is it?' I said, 'Of course it's not. Are you kiddin' me?' I looked at Saxa and said, 'It's the name of a dance from Jamaica, isn't it?' and he started going into this backwards merengue. Cheggers said, 'I knew they bloody got it wrong.' We started the song and everybody took their jackets off and we'd all got a picture of Margaret Thatcher on our T-shirts.

SHERYL GARRATT It was obvious that Margaret should stand down and the Beat should write about it. Music was a way of communicating that there was an alternative. It was key in changing people's opinions. For someone like me, living in the suburbs of Birmingham, it was how you could communicate there was another world. My parents owned five books, and they were kept on display in a cabinet.

DAVE WAKELING Thatcher represented a class betrayal: that somebody from above a grocer's shop in Grantham who had gone to Oxford was now looking down their nose at everybody. It seemed a bit kippers and curtains to me. Then Andy Cox finished 'Stand Down Margaret' off with one of the best satirical lyrics in literature: *how can it work in this all white law*, which was Geoffrey Howe and William Whitelaw; both cabinet members in Thatcher's regime.

BILLY BRAGG The first time I heard 'Whine And Grine / Stand Down Margaret' was on *The Old Grey Whistle Test*, on the soundtrack to an unrelated abstract film clip. I thought, 'This is a nice reggae song.' Then all of a sudden it started talking about *white law* and that pricked my ears: 'Wait a minute, *stand down Margaret*. This is incredible.' It was one of the first anti-Thatcher songs I ever heard. I went straight out and bought it.

DAVE WAKELING There'd been a novel called *The Third World War* written by Sir John Winthrop Hackett [sic] where he postulated that the first nuclear bomb would go off above Winson Green Prison and destroy all of England's communication. It was not only right above the hospital I was born in, but also right above the pub where we started the Beat. We weren't very optimistic and were very much of the mind that it was apocalypso and the world was going to end. So we thought, 'There's a few things that need saying and a few dances that need to be had before we go.' Virginia Woolf said that, 'Everything with beauty is tinged with a certain sadness.' It seemed to me that when I danced my mind was freer somehow and I could understand lyrics better and my mind and my heart felt more open. I thought if you could get people dancing they'd perhaps feel a bit stronger to ruminate on some of the lyrics. So I sang about our worst fears. You saw the audience moving as one creature and you got this emotional connection between them, the band and the song.

LESLEY WOODS You can't knock 'Stand Down Margaret'. We used to sit round in the kitchen plotting how to kill Margaret Thatcher: 'Why doesn't somebody kill that woman?'

RANKING ROGER People stand more chance of listening to a musician than they do to a politician. That was proven with 'Stand Down Margaret'. I was watching the BBC news and I could hear the miners in Wales singing it. I knew I'd done what I needed to do.

DAVE WAKELING Years later, I met somebody from her government who was a big Beat fan and, just to show you think you're making an astute political point, he said, 'What did you have against Princess Margaret?' I didn't know if he was taking the piss.

CALLING RUDE GIRLS

Bodysnatchers

JULIET DE VALERO WILLS 2 Tone was a socialist idea, whereas the politics of Rock Against Racism and the Anti-Nazi League had been primarily motivated towards defeating the National Front at elections, but it was a platform to examine personal politics, not just within the audience, but also amongst the bands themselves. On the back of the first 2 Tone tour there was a sense of, 'What do we do now? How's it going to work?' Jerry had managed to pull off this amazing deal at Chrysalis where he had a label and a budget to record ten singles a year. Who were they going to sign and on what terms? It was going to take a small army of admin people to sustain and run it, but 2 Tone wasn't making that kind of money. None of it was cheap. But with everybody as directors; there's a recipe for disaster straight away. And you couldn't hope to get the fourteen people in the Specials and the Selecter physically around the same table ever because they were too busy.

RICK ROGERS When the Selecter said, after the double-sided release with the Specials, 'We would like to continue working on 2 Tone,' we said, 'OK, then you'll become part of the cooperative.' Everything was what was said to each other and a handshake. We didn't work under contracts.

JERRY DAMMERS 2 Tone was my concept but I can't remember ever saying, 'We'll have fourteen directors,' or even using the word 'cooperative'; it just happened how it happened. Everybody in the Specials and the Selecter had a say but 2 Tone had no real structure. It was never even a company. There was nothing as formal as that. It was just an idea and a label that put out records through a major label once we moved to Chrysalis from Rough Trade.

RICK ROGERS There's no question that Jerry was the leading force behind the whole thing: the ideas, the philosophy, everything that was there started somewhere in Jerry's soul. I was an equal partner in the Specials and treated like the eighth member of the band. There was no management percentage: if they got paid £50 one week, I got paid £50. When record royalties came through they were divided equally. The way the business ran was as close to equal as we could possibly deal with. It was the way that everything was done. The songwriting credits were generous to a fault, even to the point there was a percentage of the publishing put into the pot to share equally amongst the band, whoever wrote the stuff. The whole spirit was based on principles of fairness and equality. 2 Tone was a mini socialist republic in itself but it exploded so fast it was insane.

LYNVAL GOLDING Fourteen directors was a wonderful idea but for a co-operative to work everyone's got to be willing to work together. It was difficult to find the middle ground. Jerry was a very single-minded guy. He wanted things done *that way*. The Specials, from a business point of view, was a disaster. You can't run a label and not have money coming in. Chrysalis gave us £1,000 to record each single but you needed more than that to run a business. We ended up giving half our merchandising away. Rick should have controlled that better.

FRANK MURRAY Rick was too soft on the band but he had issues he was coming to terms with. I would have called the band in and said, 'Look, this is the way this thing works. I know you want it to work differently and we'll try and get that happening.' It's great Jerry had the vision, but in a way that should have been monitored. In order to achieve the dream sometimes you need guidance. If you see trouble up ahead you've got to be able to come to the dreamer and say, 'Look, wake up here for a moment, there's an obstacle ahead and I'm going to help you avoid it.' And that was never done.

RICK ROGERS I was only twenty-nine. I also hadn't 'come out' and I came from a strictly evangelical Christian family so there was all sorts of shit going on. It wasn't easy in a band gang-mentality culture; being gay in many ways was more difficult than being a woman. So I was partly to blame. But we are all to blame. Frank's probably right, I was too soft. But I don't think he's in any way innocent of some of the dissatisfaction that was caused within the band.

JERRY DAMMERS What started off very idealistically ended up being completely impracticable. It was fairly obvious which bands should go on 2 Tone at first but then we probably should have just concentrated on the Selecter and the Specials. There was always this incredible pressure to find more bands. And everybody was on my case day and night to put out their record. There was an Oi! band called Criminal Class who more or less demanded it because they were from Coventry. I was sent literally hundreds and hundreds of cassettes. It was just crazy. Prefab Sprout was the only one that I was aware might have been worth signing.

JULIET DE VALERO WILLS Straight after the 2 Tone tour the Specials went to America and the Selecter were in Europe. Communication was so limited; no mobiles, no internet, no faxes. You were relying on being able to get the odd phone call in to get a decision from Jerry. There were a lot of notes: so-and-so said this; they're on a tour bus; in hotels; doing gigs. Transatlantic calls weren't easy and then you had the time difference to deal with. Meanwhile, both of their careers were going nuts. The pressures on them were huge. 'On My Radio' was out and the Selecter needed to follow up with an album quickly and do their own tour. You can't just suddenly stop and wait. All the bands came up against the hard realities of being in a commercial industry and the pressure to work in a certain time frame because of the momentum. My concern was that the Selecter would be seen as the Specials' B-side.

NEVILLE STAPLE It was ridiculous and everybody thinks they're it. Jerry used to go to Chrysalis and say, 'I like this band.' That's how the Bodysnatchers came about. It wasn't all of us.

NICKY SUMMERS I had wanted to be involved with music since I was about thirteen. I had studied piano but had no idea how to go about playing in a group. Girls rarely played electric guitars. I liked the bass and thought it would be easier. I was also listening to dub reggae, where you'd hear a lot of bass riffs and repeated lines. The music scene in London was changing and I was looking to put an all-girl group together. All girls was a new thing. I wanted to make a statement. I was looking for some sort of musical hybrid but it was quite difficult to get together. I placed four or five adverts in the music press and the Bodysnatchers came together as the 2 Tone tour gathered momentum.

RUDE GIRL types (guitar(s) with noisy vocals, drums) sought by similar bassist (rudimentary but improving) Ska, rock, reggae, early punk ideas for fast, emotive, danceable stuff. Sharp Brains Around 20 years. 01-886 9775 (Nicola).

Advert placed by Nicky Summers in *NME*, 26 May 1979.

RHODA DAKAR I'd gone to see a band called Sta-Prest at the Greyhound in Fulham. I was chatting with Shane MacGowan and he said, 'My friend Nicky wants to have a word.' She said, 'Can you sing?' 'Yeah.' 'D'you want to be in a band?' 'Yeah, all right.' Oddly enough, I had seen the advert in the *NME* but by that time I'd answered so many dodgy ads I just thought, 'Oh yeah, another one. I won't bother.'

NICKY SUMMERS The band was in place as a six-piece when I met Rhoda. I was intrigued by her image and invited her to a rehearsal. I got on with her and found we had similar interests and outlook.

RHODA DAKAR I was doing a French class at Institut français in South Kensington and I had to rush from there to the rehearsal in a dank basement in Camden.

NICKY SUMMERS We were all largely beginners. Stella and Sarah Jane played a few chords. Penny had played piano as a child. The sax player, Miranda, hadn't played a note. Jane assured me she had a drum kit but I never saw it for six months. We rehearsed in this dive for two or three hours from six or seven for seven weeks, three nights a week, on Royal College Street. When we played it came out to be a modern take on rocksteady.

RHODA DAKAR We were nearly called Pussy Galore which now would be funny. Then, it was fucking stupid. It was SJ's idea: 'Well, my mum just thinks it's to do with James Bond.' I said, 'Yeah, I know. Where does your mum live, in a shed at the bottom of the garden? Fuck off. If you want to call this band Pussy Galore you do it without me.' Bodysnatchers was the name that everyone hated the least.

NICKY SUMMERS People said, 'You just need to do a gig.' A friend of mine managed Shane's band, the Nips, and said we could support them at the Windsor Castle on the Harrow Road as a try-out. Everyone turned up: the Selecter, Jerry Dammers, Richard Branson, Gaz Mayall, the Mo-dettes. We thought it was a laugh and were somewhat ramshackle. My hands froze for the first song. I was terrified and we kind of fell apart towards the end doing 'Time Is Tight'. Gaz loved it. We did two Saturdays running and practised a lot between the first and second gig and we played it perfectly the second time; Gaz was disappointed and said he preferred it before. And we had already been mentioned in the *Guardian* by Terry Hall: 'Seven-piece all-girl ska band.'

The Bodysnatchers: (L–R) Stella Barker, Nicky Summers, Rhoda Dakar, Miranda Joyce, Sarah Jane Owen, Penny Leyton, at the 101 Club, Clapham, London, 13 December 1979.

JULIET DE VALERO WILLS I saw the Bodysnatchers at the Windsor Castle with Pauline. Straight away it was Rhoda. She looked fantastic and had such a great presence and strength about her. She was doing a girlie Sixties thing but it was empowered. Rhoda always looked taller because of her big beehive. She was very statuesque and composed. They had some good songs. An all-girl band was so rare.

PAULINE BLACK Rhoda was very much younger. I was twenty-six. She'd been into the New York Dolls and was extraordinary. She had a very commanding presence, a whole style completely of her own, but whether the Bodysnatchers were any good or not is an entirely different question. They held their own. But it's hard to play instruments when it's mostly men standing around and you're thinking, 'Oh God, I can't play.'

RHODA DAKAR I'd done Shakespeare at the Old Vic, darling! So some crappy gig in Harrow Road didn't impress me that much. Being in a band was so much easier than acting but not as demeaning as modelling. I used to dress in old Sixties clothes from Kensington Market and wear a white ribbon in my hair. At Chelsea College of Art they had this thing where you had to dress up like the Sixties and I won. I remember Gaz saying to me, 'Oh, it looks like fashion's catching up with you.' His family had this big house on the Bayswater Road and loads of people would sit in the basement round this massive bed and he'd just play tunes. That's where I first heard ska. I'd grown up hearing rocksteady and early reggae. Gaz said, 'You've got to have an anthem,' so I wrote 'Ruder Than You' and he played it on his piano. It sounded brilliant. When the Bodysnatchers did it I remember thinking, 'It doesn't sound as good as when I did it with Gaz.'

NICKY SUMMERS Jerry was in America but the message was, 'It's a two-single deal.' So we recorded 'Ruder Than You' and 'Let's Do Rock Steady' with Roger Lomas, to sound good on the radio. We did twenty-six takes and he kept saying, 'Play faster.' It wasn't the point of punk to be a proficient musician. It was about getting your thoughts across or your attitude or energy or fury or whatever it was. That was a large feature of the Bodysnatchers.

JULIET DE VALERO WILLS We were suddenly going, 'Come on tour.' They'd barely played two gigs. They didn't have a clue about all that. And they needed an awful lot of help very quickly.

RHODA DAKAR The second 2 Tone tour was the Selecter, the Bodysnatchers and Holly and the Italians. And then they left, so it was the Swinging Cats. It was nine women and Juliet.

JULIET DE VALERO WILLS Women had a civilizing influence on the tour, for sure. Rhoda was really funny, very dry, and great to hang out with. She was self-assured with clarity of purpose and thought. It was women being supportive and having a great time, women with views, women who didn't have domestic ambitions, women with a strong work ethic. We weren't being strident feminists particularly, but we were slightly on a mission to show the boys we could do it too. It was like the women were answering back, in a way, and getting some momentum with the 2 Tone idea.

FRANK MURRAY I came back from the American tour with the Specials and Rick suggested I should be the Bodysnatchers' manager. I lasted two months. From the time you met them they were looking at you going, 'I hope you're not going to try and change us or tell us to do anything.' They were very defensive, like a locked shop. I don't know what they wanted from me. You can either help somebody or you can't. They were like, 'Come on, let's see what you've got.' And I was like, 'Well, you ain't getting what I've got.' It was a mismatch.

NICKY SUMMERS 'Let's Do Rock Steady' was going to come out to coincide with the second 2 Tone tour at the end of February 1980. It was all very fast. Within two weeks we had to make a decision who to sign with and find a lawyer. 'Shit, I'm out of my depth here.' We voted between EMI and 2 Tone. I didn't vote for 2 Tone because it was the safe option and predictable.

FRANK MURRAY Nicky was a tough nut and was going to let everybody know she had her own opinions. They had that attitude, 'It's always men telling us what to do.' I guess that was valid but I'm not sure whether it was clever. I never had a problem with taking instructions from a woman. But their physical sound was quite weak. They didn't seem to play with strength or a thud in their sound. Not their arrangements, but how they actually played. But the funny thing was, none of the girls were telling me they'd just learnt their instruments. They were walking around as if they were queens of the castle and they seemed to think they knew an awful lot more than they actually did. There was this sense of non-cooperation and they were suspicious of everything.

NICKY SUMMERS As a band, we would vote on things. We had dilemmas like who to sign to: hands up. We didn't really argue. We would talk and discuss stuff. The Bodysnatchers were a sum total of a few strong components.

RHODA DAKAR We were only a band for fourteen months. After Frank we never had a manager so that became a problem. If we had to go and see the lawyer we all went. If we had to go and see the record company we all went. And shouted until we got what we wanted. The Bodysnatchers' problem was we didn't have a leader. It was a democracy. If you get a group of boys together they fight until they know their pecking order but girls don't do that.

NICKY SUMMERS Richard Branson offered us this album deal but the rest of the band wouldn't meet him. There was a lady who represented him and she used to contact Rhoda. I went down to meet her in Notting Hill and she bought us pancakes in Asterix. Branson wanted to take us to Memphis where Aretha Franklin used to record. Fuck knows why we didn't do that. Five people refused to play ball. How can you let that go? We didn't need a manager for direction or content but we needed somebody who had links to business.

FRANK MURRAY I wasn't managing them by then but they deserved that chance. 2 Tone was a record company that didn't want to be seen as a record company because that would be seen as playing the man. You couldn't go to Jerry and say, 'Look, can I have an album contract for the girls so we can make a record and we can get an advance?' Chrysalis ran 2 Tone for Jerry. I had to twist his arm to get him to produce the second Bodysnatchers single and all the time the girls were going, 'When are we going in? Is Jerry doing it?' He wasn't a producer per se but he could get a sound in the same way Elvis Costello did on the Specials' first record.

NICKY SUMMERS 'Easy Life' was produced by Jerry and suddenly it came across as an anthem with this very slick production. We were taken aback. The riff came forward and it had this catch-line. Rhoda wrote the lyrics. It was about not taking the easy option and girls doing something more challenging, more creative than going for the safe norm. I did modern languages at school and was told the best I was going to be was a bilingual secretary.

RHODA DAKAR I was twenty. You don't know that much. *I could stay at home, play houses / There's a brain here.* The good thing about young people is that their ideas are pure and unfettered. It's like, 'Yeah, let's do it. Let's go to the moon.' There's no notion of having to build the rocket. *Is it our natural fate? / Do we just have to procreate?* The other misunderstanding is that I thought motherhood would drag you down but with the genius of hindsight I now know that it's an empowering role. Once you have physically invested in the future you're going to make damn sure there's going to be one. Whereas 'Too Much Too Young' was all about why you should take the pill and *try wearing a cap*; 'It's all your fault.' I don't know at what age those lyrics were written but Jerry was at least five years older than me and old enough to know better.

NICKY SUMMERS I questioned the Specials lyrically. They were a bit misogynistic in places with slightly spiteful lyrics. *Too much too young*, but *you should be having fun with me.*

JERRY DAMMERS Misogyny means hating all women: 'Too Much Too Young' was written about one woman and I didn't hate her at all – it was very rude, sarcastic and adolescent, punky and angry, 'cos those were the times. Politically it could be seen as a feminist anthem. It wasn't saying, 'It's all your fault.' It was saying, 'Young women shouldn't allow themselves to be used just for creating babies; they should take control of their own fertility and contraception. Don't let men dictate what happens with regard to contraception; don't let them decide when you should have children.' In the seventies there was still pressure on people to settle down, get a steady job and a family by the age of twenty; some people spent their lives in unhappy marriages. But it was unexpected getting *keep a generation gap – try wearing a cap* to number one, and that brought in what is still the biggest problem facing the world today, population growth: *Do you really want a programme of sterilization*, but just persuasion: *Take control of the population boom / It's in your living room.*

RHODA DAKAR The first song I wrote for the Bodysnatchers was 'The Boiler' – 'old boiler' was a phrase Nicky told me she'd hear men use to describe ugly women. They started playing the riff and I just started telling a story someone had told me about a rape. I'd been writing songs and plays since I was a kid so I was used to improvising. It was inexperience. When you don't really know how to do things you do stuff that you're not supposed to and break the rules.

NICKY SUMMERS 'The Boiler' was a Sixties' keyboard riff we used to jam on and gradually this piece of music grew. The manager of the Nips used to refer to women as 'boilers'. We used to play it quite fast towards the end of the set. Rhoda used to do it as a piece of method acting and there was generally stunned silence. The audience hardly even used to clap, but they were definitely transfixed. It was a powerful and challenging song.

RHODA DAKAR If you read Stanislavski there's a technique called the 'emotion memory' where you take something that has made you terrified and you reuse that feeling using the words you've got to speak. That's all it was. The rape recounted in the song didn't happen to me. I was used to acting so therefore I was used to having an effect on the audience. I would have been more horrified had it just gone over their heads and they didn't react to it.

PAULINE BLACK The audience were totally and utterly perplexed by 'The Boiler'. 'Mmm . . . yeah, well, she's stopped now.' And then it'd all be back to dancing. We're talking unreconstructed male personages who might have been able to take on board the black–white thing, but expecting them to do anything else? No. Rhoda has my undying admiration for the song.

FRANK MURRAY Rhoda was a very strong young black woman with a great sense of social justice. She didn't back away from tough subjects. To scream for the last minute on a song was revolutionary.

PHILL JUPITUS They did it when I saw the Bodysnatchers support Lene Lovich at the Lyceum. It was the most disturbing song I've ever heard. I think Peel played it on the radio once and there were complaints and he couldn't play it again. I just remember the screaming bit at the end, 'Oh my God, this is a rape.' It was fucking unbelievable. It's the most horrific and powerful record I own, without fucking question. Everything about it – the arrangement, the rhythm, the downbeat delivery of it in the first few verses: *I went out walking last Saturday*. And it got to number thirty-five in the charts!

LUCY WHITMAN Any female band was at risk of a lot of leering at best and aggression or patronization both in terms of audiences and music press. It was easy to be Bananarama but not easy to be writing songs about rape. It was very daring.

NEIL SPENCER The very fact that Rhoda was reclaiming the word 'boiler' was in itself a riposte to everyday sexism; never mind that she was talking about rape. It was terribly courageous and harrowing.

JUNE MILES-KINGSTON The Bodysnatchers was all so girly. Their stuff was quite fluffy and then you had this one song that really stuck out. It was on a par with Terry Hall's song 'Well Fancy That!' about being him abused by his teacher on a school trip to France. It was a real performance art piece. You couldn't dance to it and it wasn't easy to listen to. There were two bands there.

JULIET DE VALERO WILLS 'The Boiler' set the Bodysnatchers apart and sent out a signal: we are not just going to be 2 Tone fluff. It was challenging rock 'n' roll male attitudes towards girls. Rhoda had total balls to do that. Most of the 2 Tone audiences were too young to have strong political views. If they were experiencing the urban issues being played out on the stage, I don't think they were old enough to articulate it to each other, but they found common cause at those gigs. Politics was something that grey men in suits did. I think the fans thought they looked fantastic and the music made them want to dance. Once 2 Tone went beyond being just a great dance sound and a great image and tried to deliver on its mandate, the media started to pull back. They didn't want to engage with the difficult substance.

DOESN'T MAKE IT ALRIGHT

Specials

JERRY DAMMERS I had expected the Specials to be an underground band. It was a shock we were so commercially successful. I'd grown up listening to pop music so that was a big part of whatever I wrote into a song, but that wasn't the intention. It was just a happy accident that people liked it. 2 Tone became more popular than punk. It was a really huge phenomenon and that affected your life.

LYNVAL GOLDING We were in Norman, Oklahoma, and it was the middle of the night and Rick said, 'I just got a phone call from Chrysalis. "Too Much Too Young" is number one.' It was an amazing feeling. And from where I'm coming from, 'Jesus Christ! I can't believe it! We've got a number-one record. Whoa!' We could never see ourselves in the same league as the Stones or the Beatles. My father worked in a foundry and my upbringing was to work hard. 'You have to achieve more than I have achieved, son.'

RICK ROGERS I was sharing a room with Jerry and when I got the call I leapt around the room and woke him up; he was most annoyed. It was really exciting because that's what I wanted to see for them. That's where they deserved to be. Jerry was pleased really but I think they all would rather have been at home to celebrate it.

JERRY DAMMERS It was a little bit scary because it all happened so fast. It was like going from being an observer to being the observed. It was a lot to take in. I didn't particularly celebrate it but Rick was going absolutely bananas. I was going, 'I've got a hangover here, can you calm down a bit.'

PAULINE BLACK It was amazing. It really made you feel part of a movement and that was the reason why people were in 2 Tone; we all felt a responsibility.

RICK ROGERS 'Too Much Too Young' was clearly a live favourite. You could feel it by the reaction before the record came out, but I argued against it being lifted from the album as the third single because I didn't think radio would go for it. I was easily swayed from that when Jerry said, 'We do a whole live EP.' The Specials were at their best live. That's what it was all about. That's where you experienced the 360 degrees of the Specials. The record encapsulated everything about that first period.

JULIET DE VALERO WILLS It was a killer EP with all the old ska classics: 'Guns Of Navarone', 'Long Shot Kick De Bucket', 'Liquidator' and 'Skinhead Moonstomp'. And you'd got Rico!

JERRY DAMMERS Having Rico involved brought authenticity and a link to the original Jamaican ska; that mournful trombone was so central to the Specials sound. It was beyond our wildest dreams that he would actually come and play with us.

HORACE PANTER In the Specials everyone was the rhythm section. In African drumming each individual instrument combines to make a whole sound. That's how I saw reggae: the guitar and keyboards play conga rhythms, the bass drum and the hi-hat play a steady thing, and the snare improvises; so the whole thing is held together by the bass, which plays the melody. Everything is arse about face in terms of rock 'n' roll. The Specials were as much a punk band as we were like the Skatalites or Bob Marley and the Wailers. The live version of 'Too Much Too Young' is like fucking Motorhead. It's so fucking fast. The punk spirit was behind all the songs we did: 'Do The Dog', 'Dawning Of A New Era', 'It's Up To You', 'Concrete Jungle'. But sometimes we'd get laid back: *Court in session*, nice and slow. And 'Doesn't Make It Alright' is a regular reggae song. My heart swelled when we played it. It was the essence of what we were doing.

JERRY DAMMERS 'Doesn't Make It Alright' started as a song written by a school friend of mine called Mark Harrison and a friend of his called Dave Goldberg, called 'We Can Make It Alright'. I think it was a love song. I said, 'Would it be all right if I completely rewrote the lyrics?' and they agreed. A lot of bands were doing Rock Against Racism gigs at the time and that influenced me to put anti-racism into the lyrics. I wrote the bassline and changed it to reggae. Roddy's guitar solo was fantastic; that still gets me emotionally every time I hear it.

GORDON OGILVIE *It's the worst excuse in the world* was a fantastic line. I said to Jake, 'This exactly fits what we should be doing.'

JAKE BURNS The Specials were astonishingly powerful live and we were on the same label as them so we had all managed to snaffle pre-release copies of their album. But when I heard the recorded version of 'Doesn't Make It Alright' I was disappointed. Live, it had more power and menace and intent behind it. So we wanted to put the anger back into it. But it was a risk for Stiff Little Fingers to do another reggae cover, especially because the Specials were at the time flavour of the month.

LYNVAL GOLDING The very first time I heard James Brown's 'Say It Loud – I'm Black And I'm Proud', it kicked you. It was like a freedom. I can say, 'I'm black and I'm proud' because James Brown is telling everyone. Or when Bob Marley sang, *Get up, stand up, stand up for your rights*. It was so powerful. That's how I felt about 'Doesn't Make It Alright'. *Just because you're a black boy / Just because you're a white / It doesn't mean you've got*

Front cover of the Special AKA live EP, 'Too Much Too Young',
taken at the Lyceum, London, 2 December 1979.

to hate him / It doesn't mean you've got to fight. It was speaking out to the audience because the majority of the Specials' audience was white.

HORACE PANTER We would play to punk audiences and they were all white and generally working-class. Very few black people came to see the Specials unless they were mates of or related to people in the band.

JERRY DAMMERS 2 Tone's anti-racist message was aimed primarily at white people, but certainly in Birmingham and Leeds the Specials had a large black following, which was very pleasing; and in London too. Ideally, there would have been more because it would have helped create that atmosphere and solidified the idea. Some of the most loyal supporters of 2 Tone were mixed-race kids who really took it to their hearts as their music. That was really touching because those kids were being ostracized by both sides. On the front-cover photograph of 'Too Much Too Young' you can see the make-up of the audience. It was black and white: the majority men, but there were girls too.

LYNVAL GOLDING Early on in 1978 we opened for Sham 69 at the Locarno in Coventry. That's probably part of the reason why blacks didn't come to our gigs, because we had the leftover from the punk era. We would have loved to have seen more blacks. I remember when I went back to Gloucester and some of my friends would say, 'What's wrong with you, man? You play in a punk group. You're diluting the reggae music.' I was like, 'No, you don't get it.'

DAVE RUFFY 2 Tone was a reflection of how it had changed. It was mixed up. There was aggro but it weren't the same aggro. A lot of it had been dealt with because people were happy to embrace the whole thing. Two-tone: it's black and it's white, without saying anything. It was obvious because the music does it.

RICK ROGERS 2 Tone was trying to reach everybody. It was trying to reach humanity. It was trying to appeal to the better parts of people's human nature and celebrate them. But the audience was largely white and male. That's how pop music was. More non-white people came when we progressed. The Specials had started in the era of punk. And punk celebrated black music but there wasn't much of a black audience. But the generation under them that only heard the Specials on the radio and on the records, that's where the difference and effect was in bringing black and white kids together.

DENNIS BOVELL The 2 Tone audiences were a mix of people who were being converted and the nationalists were desperately trying to hold onto their following by saying, 'Don't mix with them. They must be kept apart.'

RICK ROGERS There was the infamous thing of some people referring to them as the Specials plus two. They couldn't even add up, because by that time there was nine people on stage, three of whom were black.

PAULINE BLACK I overheard a conversation in a pub and 'Specials plus two' and 'Selecter plus six' was used to distinguish between the white and black members of the bands. That hurt deeply.

NEOL DAVIES It came from uneducated types, mainly Londoners in right-wing circles, I'm afraid.

RHODA DAKAR I remember hearing about 'plus two' and 'plus six'. The only time we had any racist overtones was in Middlesbrough on the second 2 Tone tour. Our van got vandalized and we had to have a police escort out. We were chased to the hotel and we had to drive round the town to get away from these people. The band were talking to some of the audience after and they'd said, 'Yeah, Rhoda's black but she's all right.'

LUCY WHITMAN I was a little bit concerned that the black guys in the Specials seemed to exaggerate the way in which they performed. Not *Black and White Minstrels*, but going in that direction. It was the clowning around which made me uncomfortable because the white members didn't do it. They might well say they were sending it up.

MYKAELL RILEY Ranking Roger and Neville Staple played specific roles within those bands. They were very much caricatures. It wasn't deliberate. It was all just about having fun. You could see it when the Specials did 'Monkey Man'.

JERRY DAMMERS Toots Hibbert had written 'Monkey Man' about some bloke that had stolen his girlfriend and we used to dedicate it to the bouncers. It wasn't meant to be a statement.

HORACE PANTER 'Monkey Man' was so exciting: *This one's for all the bouncers, big, big monkey man*. I don't know whether Neville realized the cultural irony so he went *ooh ooh* like a monkey. I think he was just having a ball and entertaining people and going wild and having the most fun he'd ever had in his life. I was totally in awe of Neville. He was just this dynamo. He'd get into the van for the next day's gig and say, 'Me not sleep

Neville Staple at the
Montreux Jazz Festival,
Switzerland, 11 July 1980.

yet, y'know.' He was so wired up. His energy was incredible. If you could climb it he'd be up there. It made performing incredibly exciting, if not a little dangerous.

RICK ROGERS I go to 'Monkey Man' and see Neville on top of the speakers and playing to stereotypes of being a black man. It was part of the whole idea of challenge: do you get embarrassed? He's playing it but he's a big, strong major character in that front line. The message was really clear.

LYNVAL GOLDING We were called 'monkey' so Neville turned it back at the National Front in the audience: 'We're laughing at you because you've paid to see us make monkey noises.' No one could touch Neville. He was crazy, like an untamed wild animal; so much energy.

NEVILLE STAPLE I took on a persona. 'Fuckin' hell, look at him running across there, climbing up the speakers.' I didn't give a fuck if they wanted to abuse me or call me a monkey. I'm doing it. Remember how I grew up. I didn't take shit. At school somebody called me a wog once and I nearly

killed him. I grew up knowing not to let people get away with shit because
they'll keep doing it. Then people would come up to me and say, 'Nev, this
guy's fuckin' me around. Can you help me?' I was always that guy who
people came to for help. Even when I was in Borstal nobody fucked with
me. I got on with everybody.

JULIET DE VALERO WILLS The persona Neville developed was to be hugely
successful, own that stage and take no prisoners. And he was brilliant at it.
He was bursting with a visceral youth and ambition. He was king of the
rock 'n' roll life and he was going to make the most of it.

NEVILLE STAPLE In the Specials I was an entertainer bringing out whatever
the song was: *my name is Judge Roughneck and I will not tolerate any dis-
obedience in my courtroom.*

JERRY DAMMERS Judge Roughneck was a character that Neville developed
based on Prince Buster's Judge Dread and we incorporated it into 'Stupid
Marriage'. I had the idea for Neville to wear a wig and gown on stage to take
the mickey out of the legal system: *Rude Boy, I hereby sentence you to four
hundred years.*

PHILL JUPITUS I was at the Rainbow gig, which was a May Day Jobs for
Youth benefit for the *Morning Star*, and me and my mates were stood at
the back discussing tactics for getting down the front: 'Right through the
middle or sides and in?' Suddenly, the lights went out and the drums
started beating 'Concrete Jungle'. I went, 'Fuck, they're on.' I ran from the
back of the stalls down to the front like a fucking speedboat, casting
children either side of me. I thought, 'Oh God, the others won't be with
me.' I looked round and there was my mate – who's now an activist in the
Conservative Party. But I don't think the Specials were a political band as
such. It was kitchen-sink politics; the politics of pregnancy and unemployment and violence.

BILLY BRAGG The Specials didn't have to sing political songs. You could
just see. They were making a statement about Britain and what Britain
could be.

TINY FENNIMORE 2 Tone didn't seem political to me. The Specials were
addressing the social issues of youth. They weren't trying to drive any
agenda forward.

LYNVAL GOLDING At the beginning of 'Concrete Jungle' we'd chant, *you're* *gonna get your fuckin' head kicked in*, because kids would say that on the football terraces.

HORACE PANTER We used to have a mock theatrical fight during 'Concrete Jungle'. We got these stage bottles made of sugar that looked like glass and bashed them over each other's heads. Sometimes Neville would really hit Jerry and he would limp back to his keyboard, which was quite funny, but it didn't last very long and we ran out of bottles as well. There was so much going on that it was kind of unnecessary: Jerry was jumping up and down on his keyboard, Lynval was dancing around, Terry would be the foil and would dance a bit, Neville you couldn't keep still, I danced around a bit, and Roddy was throwing shapes. At the end of the set there was just this huge pile of guitar leads like spaghetti.

NEVILLE STAPLE Even though it looked like we were fighting on stage, we were just having fun. We were playing out what the song was saying. You'd hear skinheads walking along the street singing, *You're gonna get your fuckin' head kicked in.*

PAULINE BLACK The Selecter used to have a mock fight during 'Too Much Pressure'. Most people used to think we were actually doing it, and sometimes we were, depending on how much dissension was going on in the band between people at the time. It was a way to offset fights in the crowd and show that unbridled violence is pretty senseless. It was an interesting experiment: black folk of all kind of hues and a girl all lamping each other. It was quite a thing to behold. Subliminally it was saying, 'We're finding it really difficult to get along. Is this what you want?'

NEOL DAVIES I had nothing to do with that fight idea. The Specials had horseplay and mucked about a lot and jumped into each other. Ours was thought out. I was incredulous: 'Are you seriously going to have a fight?' It was Charley, Compton, Gappa and Desmond. My excuse was I had to keep the rhythm going. Pauline got involved in it a bit. It was staged, but the guys really went for it. Guitars would get bashed and needed repairing, and bruises were created. It was at the end of the show when we were building up to this crescendo of 'Too Much Pressure' and then 'On My Radio'. A lot of the audience were shocked but it was hugely entertaining and it became a big part of the set. It was naively thinking, 'If we're fighting they don't have to.'

JULIET DE VALERO WILLS It was designed to hold a mirror up to the various factions in the audience to make them question the violence. Violence only makes sense when you're in it and fuelled by the anger. Just watching, it becomes ludicrous and pointless. It looked real. Like one of them had totally fucking had enough. People were shocked. By the time they picked up their instruments again people would have forgotten where they were at. Well, that was the hope, it didn't always work out like that!

FRANK MURRAY It seemed to be a lot of pushing and shoving. I've never been a fan of violence or anything that might be encouraging it in any shape or form. If the statement was to hold a mirror to the audience it was very naive of them, because there wasn't fighting going on in the audience. There was this kind of a dance like a stomp, which was quite aggressive in itself, but the audience knew the self-imposed boundaries. There was a lot of elbows and knees going up and pushing guys out of the way but everybody knew what it meant.

RHODA DAKAR The audience didn't know that there were real feelings behind the play-acting. All the 2 Tone bands used to scrap and squabble. You have to remember you're cramped together in this goldfish-bowl space and you let off all your steam on stage and you come offstage and you're still up; inevitably people are going to argue, people are going to have a drink, and it's all going to go horribly wrong sometimes.

RANKING ROGER We did one tour with the Specials in Ireland. It was fucking absolutely brilliant. We didn't know the people wanted the music that much. They were so starved of music. We were the biggest thing since bloody Jimi Hendrix as far as they were concerned. We travelled on one big coach and they were going, 'The Beat are our heroes,' and we were going, 'The Specials are our heroes.'

DAVE WAKELING We were all terrified about going to Belfast and when we got to Ulster Hall one of the roadies said, 'There's a skinhead wants to speak with you and Jerry.' It turned out they were representing Protestant and Catholic skins and they were so grateful we'd come and that normally this would be the most wonderful opportunity for a ruck so out of respect for the bands they'd tossed a coin and decided that the Catholic skins would stay downstairs and the Protestant skins would stay upstairs. After, we were told that nobody in the balcony had used the bathroom and they just pissed over the top. It was the most wonderful tour and we alternated support and headline and then both bands came on for the encore which was either 'Enjoy Yourself' or 'Jackpot'. Then we went to Dublin and the worst fight that I'd ever seen broke out during the Specials' set.

JERRY DAMMERS The Stardust Ballroom in Dublin was by far the worst place we played. It was an absolute shithole, and dilapidated. The gig should have been cancelled. It had a crappy little stage which was completely unsuitable; it came up out of the floor on pneumatics and it was obviously dangerous for us and the PA, let alone allowing a stomping audience on stage. I explained this to the audience but some of them started accusing us that it was because they were Irish, and that we let the English kids on. Some of them stormed the stage and things went from bad to worse when the bouncers waded in wielding lead coshes. It turned from a shithole to a hellhole and was the worst night in 2 Tone.

RANKING ROGER The hall was overfilled and part of the PA fell down. It was during the Specials' 'Sock It To 'Em JB'. There were so many people just shoving forward. It was chaos. Fights were breaking out and I thought, 'I need to get out of here, man.' There was me and some roadie and we were kicking these back doors which were padlocked. I used to do martial arts and was kicking full force but we couldn't open them.

DAVE WAKELING Skinheads got on stage and broke all the gear up and drums were flying everywhere. The Specials and skinheads came running backstage and there were fights in the dressing room. We ended up barricading ourselves in a room with sofas. When we came out there was blood up the walls and broken glass everywhere. Two weeks later the whole place burnt down and forty-eight people died, when it was a third full.

JUNE MILES-KINGSTON Punk had allowed people to get up on stage and express themselves. It broke down that 'them' and 'us' thing. That was the whole reason I was up there. Yeah, a lot of young kids came to see us to look up your skirt but they understood that these girls were up there singing about them and they identified with the songs. It's weird because girls look to young boys to do that for them on stage and they all stand there adoringly; they're singing 'to you'; everything they say is 'for you'. The young lads in our audience got that from us, but we're not saying, 'Yeah, we're women and you don't count.' That was quite something.

RUTH GREGORY The achievement of 2 Tone was its combination of high-octane entertainment coupled with the political stance of the music. It was in the look of the bands, the fact there were prominent female voices, that the lyrics addressed the social issues of the day. By 1980 our dream in Rock Against Racism of a cultural black and white union had manifested into a 2 Tone Britain. Their music was dominating the charts and the fashion was everywhere on the high streets.

CELEBRATE THE BULLET

Politics. Class. Seaside tour

RICK ROGERS Addressing racism was never going to be as simple as resolving the obvious skin colour differences between black and white youth. The challenge was far greater. Class, gender, upbringing, all contributed to the social and political climate. And these divisions deeply affected not only how culture was received by 2 Tone audiences but created by the artists.

JULIET DE VALERO WILLS 2 Tone was a natural reflection of society: a microcosm of the black–white issue, working class mixing it up with art-school middle class. Authenticity about background mattered a lot. It's very easy to think that 2 Tone was a fully conceived idea that then got executed, but, to a degree, everyone was making it up and reacting to events as it went along: everyone was very young, and making their mistakes in public. What we were trying to do was really hard. And because of that it was very difficult and fraught with contradictions. There were going to be lots of failures and things going wrong and antagonism and misunderstanding. As everyone was going along they were learning about their own racism; things they hadn't even challenged in themselves before. And there was a good dose of white middle-class guilt in there as well. So you throw that into the mix, and it can become overcompensatory, and skew things out of whack as well.

JERRY DAMMERS 2 Tone was a very strong expression of unity and solidarity. But it was a struggle to keep it to the original political ideals. There was always a tension between the commercial side and trying to keep the creativity and the politics involved.

HORACE PANTER In the Specials, Brad, Jerry and I all had fine art degrees. Neville was 'from country' whereas Lynval's background was Jamaican middle class. The Goldings are one of the five families in Jamaica; the eighth prime minister was called Golding. Roddy's dad worked at the Jaguar plant. He did leather-finishing, which was one of the top working-class jobs you could do in Coventry. Terry's mum worked as a cleaner. Class had a big impact on the band when we started getting money. When you become famous what you were before becomes exaggerated, so if you were a bully you're going to be an even bigger bully; if you were a drunk you're going to be an even bigger drunk; if you were shy you're going to be even shyer. You change. Fame has an impact on you. You're not the person you were two and half years ago.

DAVE WAKELING In the Beat we were all educated differently but came up out of the same working-class system. Me, Andy, Everett and Roger had a very similar view of where we stood at this point in history. I was proud to be working-class and come from Balsall Heath and then I got to go to a posh school and talk a bit different from the other lads in the street. I liked the ambiguity of it.

NICKY SUMMERS 2 Tone was about people from different backgrounds making music together. I had what might be considered a working-class background: born in Hackney and grew up in Southgate. My mother was fairly bohemian and was into film, art, fashion and textiles. My father worked in Soho Market as a greengrocer and had been a singer in his youth. I helped out on the stall and remember it as a village where you met people from all walks of life; Paul McCartney and Lynne Franks were both customers.

RHODA DAKAR There was definitely a class split in the Bodysnatchers. It wasn't about education. It was about, 'Should we upset the neighbours or shouldn't we upset the neighbours?' For instance, there was talk of releasing 'The Boiler' as a single before Nicky and I recorded it with Jerry. The people that wanted to be a pop success were like, 'No, we can't. Oh, my God!' It was kind of a class thing but then there were people who were ambiguous and weren't worried because they had enough financially to not be worried. And then there was this class who didn't care what anybody thought. Maybe it was education. SJ and Penny had both got art degrees, so they designed the band logo and the writing of the name Bodysnatchers and knew how to talk to art directors. That was a practical difference – it was much the same in the Specials with Horace and Jerry: if you can actually draw that vision and say, 'It looks like this,' that makes a huge difference because you're not relying on someone else's interpretation. And in the Selecter, Pauline and Neol were both well educated so therefore their conversations were about different things. Yes,

Neol Davies (right) with Arthur 'Gaps' Hendrickson (centre) and Compton Amanor (left), backstage on North American tour, circa May 1980.

Pauline was adopted into a white family but she also had a degree and a profession.

NEOL DAVIES We saw ourselves in the Selecter as a political expression just in our existence. I was white. Pauline was female and of African heritage. Compton was from Ghana. And the others were either from Jamaica or St Kitts. The common experience for them as children was being told very quickly they were leaving Jamaica to go to England. From the Caribbean to Britain at that age of puberty, brought up by parents you don't know or by your grandparents who are a different generation and whose experience is the racism of the fifties: the Selecter was a prime expression of that cultural trauma, the anger that they felt and the racism they received day-to-day, walking down the street. It was everywhere. And there were seven of us, which was always difficult: seven strong opinions, seven really strong personalities. It was a very traumatic experience. We all treated each other badly.

JULIET DE VALERO WILLS The Caribbean islands are incredibly different culturally. St Kitts is softer. Barbados polite. Jamaica is in-your-face culture and Trinidadians are somewhere in the middle; party people with a long-held rivalry with Jamaica who traditionally were seen to look down on them. None of it was simple, and the hierarchical nuances of the inter-island cultural mentality came over with many of their parents. It was not even black and white, it was every shade in between. Most of these bands were the first generation UK-born. They were the transition generation and that was very hard for them as well.

NEOL DAVIES We were all so angry. That's why we started to think of ourselves as a political statement. We had something really strong to say about people and society and the way that functioned. 'Look, we're finding it difficult, but we're doing it and you can do it, too.' You can't just say, 'People should get on.' It's too easy. 'Black and white unite?' 'Yeah, how?'

PAULINE BLACK It's mainly white people who say, 'I thought you were all about being together and unity.' We were continually arguing. The mix of the Selecter was such that all our problems were like a microcosm of society. But I think that's cool. It's how you deal with those arguments. But it's no damn use if people are arguing and being destructive, which went on within the band.

JULIET DE VALERO WILLS The Selecter made all their mistakes in public and developed a reputation for being trouble. As individuals they were fine, but together they were hard work, invariably late and often arguing. They didn't take to being challenged or organized in any way at all. They were a band that had huge potential for self-sabotage. The whole black–white thing was there every day waiting to trip us up, despite our willingness to engage with it. The black members were finely tuned and understandably sensitized to any perceived white favouritism, given they had grown up with that as an every-day experience. And Neol was hard-wired to try and navigate this, which could lead to defensiveness on both sides. Different members had previous friendship bonds as well, so, once fault lines appeared, they tended to define the dynamic of sides taken.

PAULINE BLACK I'd always been interested in the 'black' question, for want of a better word. When I was fifteen, sixteen, seventeen, the best place to have a look at that was America. Then I came to Coventry and I met my husband, who worked at Rolls-Royce. The Socialist Labour League had just turned into the Workers Revolutionary Party and we formed a branch and used to go out selling the *Workers Press* outside the Potterton factory and around Coventry and Leamington. I was a Marxist and I wanted the overthrow of capitalism and for socialism to link up internationally with other countries in that fight. But I'm not sure my political views ever merged with culture and music. Music is a subjective art form. Politics is objective. I don't know of any revolution that's happened in the world that has been spearheaded by music, but hearts and minds may have been changed. It's the spirit within the sound which is rebellious and against the status quo. Even something as mundane as 'Bye-Bye Blackbird' was about runaway slaves. The spirit of rebellion has always been within black people because of the nature of how the African diaspora has been treated throughout the world for the past 400 years.

DAVE WAKELING We made the Beat a socialist cooperative where everybody was earning the same. Me and David Steele had written the lion's share of the songs at this point and we just said, 'Everybody should get the same,' but then we fell into freeloading socialism where if the wages were the same on a Thursday why would you bother going into the office on a Tuesday? And there's my dad in the corner: 'Ah, socialism, I tell you what, Dave, you ask them for a tenner if you're ever short and they won't bleedin' have it.' You can have too much cooperation and not enough competition.

NEOL DAVIES I'd written most of the songs in the Selecter and it was assumed that I was being greedy and running off with all the money. That perception grew and festered and was the source of many arguments, and I'm sure there were overtones of culture and colour. I was subjected to some serious verbal abuse but I believed in the band and carried on. But we had those issues to deal with and we dealt with them in public.

JULIET DE VALERO WILLS There was always a bit of resentment about whether it was Neol's band. The accusation, 'Yeah, it's his band because he's white,' would be used in the heat of arguments at times. Band clashes over ownership are as old as the industry itself, but they don't usually have to address it through the distorting prism of racism. It was difficult for Neol. And also he had this sparky, sparring relationship with Pauline, who always felt torn in the middle. She had been brought up in a white family in Essex, only later to find out she had an Anglo-Jewish mother and a Nigerian father. It seemed she had long wanted acceptance in the black community and suddenly she was being accepted into this black world but was then having to take sides in the arguments.

PAULINE BLACK Before the first 2 Tone tour I was working in a radiography department, having days off saying I was ill but really doing gigs. There was a music fan in the department who didn't know what I did but I thought he was going to see my adoptive name, Pauline Vickers, in the music papers, so I thought, 'Fuck it. I need another name.' Charley Anderson was saying, 'Pauline . . . Pauline . . . she's black . . .' And I shouted, 'Yeah, Pauline is black.' It was the one thing about me that was absolutely definitive. So I changed my name by deed poll. It was like someone who was always in me waiting to get out. You've always got this thing: black people want you to be black and women want you to be a woman. The glory of 2 Tone was that it was anti-racist but also anti-sexist. My main belief was, 'I'm a black woman so I'm going to stick up for any feminist thing that I can by just existing and wearing what I wear and having an attitude.'

MYKAELL RILEY Pauline had to deal with being female in a very male chauvinistic industry. She played that card really well.

PAULINE BLACK On tour I'd never seen the male animal in that close proximity. At work it was mainly women and I'd come directly out of that to this: 'Whoa!' That was quite an adjustment.

JULIET DE VALERO WILLS I may have been only twenty and appeared to be a 'fluffy bottle-blonde', but I had a very clear idea of what I wanted to do as a proper manager, but had to square that with all the youthful testosterone unleashed on tour for the first time, with inevitable results. That was a real dilemma. The young feminist in me could be quite appalled and be thinking, 'You can't treat young women like this'. And then the other part of me would be, 'But you're my friends and I really like you and I don't know what to do with this contradictory behaviour'. But it was hard to be assertive about it, not just because of being young and female, but primarily because this was the late seventies and deeply sexist attitudes were the acceptable norm; it was as if the female empowerment of the sixties had never happened. You're on this rollercoaster and you've got to live with these people and you're sharing profoundly formative experiences together. So it gets laughed off. Rock 'n' roll was, and is, a deeply macho culture and universally accepted as a lifestyle. There was no sense of accountability because there was no sense of accountability in wider society towards those attitudes. In the same way as there was casual and institutionalized racism everywhere, there was also casual and institutionalized sexism.

PAULINE BLACK Lots of girls would be asked back after the show. There's video evidence from one night of certainly more than two people present of both sexes and a bit of a free-for-all; apparently that did the rounds of the record companies. I don't really care what people do. But there's a difference between being a man in band and being a woman in a band and being on tour. If you're going back to a hotel, I mean, come on, it's not going to be just coffee, is it? Young women got disabused of that idea fairly quickly by Neville and his Rude Boy roadie friends Rex and Trevor, and occasionally were to be found occupying hotel corridors having a little cry. I would say, 'Come and crash and use the other bed in my room.' And of course the poor creatures would be seen in the lobby the following morning and then everybody thinks you're a dyke. But hey-ho, I saved a few souls along the way, I'm sure.

FRANK MURRAY We stayed mainly in guest houses and B & Bs on the first tour so I didn't see waifs and strays around. Most people went off and smoked. But two consenting adults going to a room, I didn't have a problem with that.

RHODA DAKAR I didn't have a lot of sympathy with groupies. 'You got yourself into this; you get yourself out of it.' It's not my problem because they didn't appreciate it. When the Bodysnatchers did the Seaside tour in the summer of 1980 with the Go-Go's and the Specials it was much better to have more females on tour. There was less bullshit and nonsense. We didn't have to wait ages for people to be woken up. Women could get up, get their breakfast, pack their suitcases and be on the coach at the time they're supposed to be. Female musicians are generally more together than male musicians; if they know where their passport is you're in luck.

NICKY SUMMERS We would have been twelve females on the Seaside tour. It was more relaxed. The Specials were outnumbered. Previously they used to room it with each other so they'd be two to a room and then they all chose a single room with a double bed. One of us did get off with someone. There were often groupies or girls turning up. They were going to get hurt. But it was nothing to do with me.

JULIET DE VALERO WILLS Pauline made a point of being approachable, so at least if anybody felt they needed any protection they had a friendly ear. I was also a single girl in the midst of all of that, so you're going to get knocks on your hotel door at one o'clock in the morning that you knew definitely not to answer. Loneliness is notoriously a big thing on the road, and Pauline and I were good company for each other, and mutually supportive as two young women in this intensely male environment – Pauline

**Pauline Black (front) and Juliet De Valero Wills on the 2 Tone tour bus,
circa February 1980.**

is quite male in her attitudes and approaches to life and I think she would be the first to agree with that. She was incredibly contained, very pragmatic, strong and focused, and with a withering wit. This tough persona also contained a softer, caring and empathetic person that was carefully guarded for much of the time – until the ill-fated relationship with our tour manager that wasn't approved of.

PAULINE BLACK Juliet was respected as much as a twenty-year-old young blonde woman can be respected within the industry. She held her own. It was good to have another female to bounce around with, until she hooked up with our tour manager, Malcolm Rigby.

JULIET DE VALERO WILLS The rest of the band were all finding companionship – Pauline had a one-night stand with one of them briefly, which she mentions in her autobiography – and I started what became a serious long-term relationship. That finished it. I was subjected to rules that a male manager wouldn't have been. I felt that for as long as I remained this unobtainable self-contained island with no discernable needs of my own, I was the manager. Being a woman in that role, the expectations were very different. I was always there for them and suddenly there was a competing demand on my time. But you're a human being and sooner or later you also get lonely and you need a relationship.

NICKY SUMMERS As a band you don't all necessarily hang out with each other; socially you're not always everyone's cup of tea. We used to split off and come back for soundchecks. It was natural. By the Seaside tour we were more accomplished as a band, but the Go-Go's suffered. They were on first and used to come offstage and say, 'They're waiting for you.' The audience saw it as rock music and they didn't want that. The Specials were more accomplished musicians than all of us. They had been playing their instruments ten years longer and were way ahead of the game. Initially, we played to predominantly male audiences, but towards the summer we had more young girls coming. It meant that we had reached out and inspired young women, in a way, to do something more with their lives; to take action for themselves. The few all-girl groups that had emerged, like the Slits and the Mo-dettes and Poly Styrene from X-Ray Spex and Pauline Murray from Penetration, had really inspired me and in turn I hoped the Bodysnatchers could inspire women also. But there was a point where motivation and intention changed.

RHODA DAKAR Five of the Bodysnatchers wanted to be pop tarts and Nicky and I wanted to keep going in the same tradition. They endured the politics but that wasn't their motivation. Life had been good to them; they didn't really need to change stuff. We played the Oxford Ball where Penny's dad was a professor. It was like, 'What do you need to change, particularly? Your life's OK.' There was no reason to swim against the tide.

NICKY SUMMERS We had gigged solidly for the best part of a year and it was tiring. I wanted us to take a break to regroup: to rehearse, practise, write new material, maybe look at what direction we were going in. And some members of the band were more interested that we'd achieved some public recognition and wanted to capitalize on that. 'Do you just want to be, "Have I got the right T-shirt?" and, "Do I look good in a photo-shoot?" or do you really want to say something and try and open up a new road?'

I was only twenty-one and wasn't skilled enough at handing seven different personalities pulling in different directions. I was caught in the middle. There was an argument between two people: whether you just wanted to be a fun girl band or whether you wanted to do something else. Recording 'The Boiler' was something else.

PAULINE BLACK They got rid of Rhoda, the person that made them good, and became the Belle Stars. There's never been anything like the Bodysnatchers since or before.

•

NEOL DAVIES The original line-up of the Selecter and the main thrust of success lasted less than a year – we'd had four chart singles and a top-five album – but we were all so angry and under pressure. We weren't very nice to each other. We left 2 Tone in the summer of 1980 issuing the statement: '2 Tone was intended to be an alternative to the music industry, a label that took risks and, we hope, injected some energy into what had become a stale music scene. The time has come when we want to take risks again.'

JULIET DE VALERO WILLS They drafted in these two new white lads and the music changed. Then we went on the 'Reasons To Be Fearful' European tour and that was the beginning of the end. Again, the black–white issues had been raging: who had to share with whom; if somebody had a better room in a hotel. It was minefields everywhere you went. What we were trying to do was hard. The black and white mix had come together for a reason: to try and shine a really strong light on this issue. It made for very uncomfortable experiences at times and we had to deal with a lot of anger and resentments. It got to the point where you thought, 'Anything we try to do gets sabotaged by finding racism in it; we trip up on it everywhere and can't seem to find the way around it no matter how much we try'. It would often be something small that would become big and could tip over into physical confrontation. I'll never forget having to peel Desmond off Pauline on the tour bus when he had her by the throat and was shouting, 'You t'ink you're the Queen.' In later years, it turned out this was also the early signs of mental illness. Everything had become fractious and confrontational. I had naively thought that what I lacked in 'male authority' I could make up for in being super organized and conscientious, but that just backfired. In the end, it was all about firefighting most of the time. I defy anybody to have successfully navigated the Selecter out the other side of all that. The irony was that it was the sheer intensity of their interpersonal beliefs and relationships that made the band such a powerfully authentic force on stage – but it was also their undoing.

PAULINE BLACK We bought into the ethos of 2 Tone: celebrating the things that unite you rather than the things that divide you. But we were subjective animals. It was hard to do on a 24/7 basis, particularly if you were all trying to be creative, trying to do music, trying to get everyone to do this and this; and some stupid bloody touring schedule, and people's pettiness going on, and the record industry are not necessarily on your side because they'd much rather have Madness's fun and frivolity than this moody bunch of bastards over here. It was all of this kind of nonsense. We were our own worst enemy.

JULIET DE VALERO WILLS We did three nights at the Michael Sobell Sports Centre supporting Ian Dury. It was a fuckin' nightmare. They felt they were being limited in every way: the lighting, the PA, the rider, you name it. 'We're not the "support band", we're the "special guests".' It was, 'We're not doing it. We're pulling out.' I had to have mediating sessions, to- and fro-ing between the dressing rooms. The band was exhausted and fractious and didn't want to be in each other's company, let alone play together. I was still negotiating with Dury's manager, Pete Jenner, while half of the Selecter were up the motorway going back to Coventry. It was shit, so I wrote the 'Alternative Ten Commandments (or) The Selecter

Peter Jenner (standing) with
Ian Dury, Hammersmith
Odeon, 27 December 1979.

Shake-Up Manifesto', based on Prince Buster's 'Ten Commandments Of Man', which I sent them all in the post in the hope that the humour of it might cut through some tension. Commandment Ten was: *If you care about THE SELECTER then you must care about each other.* The idea was to let everybody simmer down over the holiday, get some rest and hopefully be able to commit to each other and to the venture in general in the new year. It didn't fucking work.

NEOL DAVIES We were desperate, but I was determined to try and make it work. We put out the single 'Celebrate The Bullet' in February 1981 which had a staunch anti-violence, anti-war theme, but irony was its downfall and Mike Read at Radio 1 took it literally and wouldn't play it, presumably because John Lennon had been murdered three months before.

PAULINE BLACK Irony very rarely works in music because it can mean different things to different people. A month after the album was released there was an assassination attempt on Ronald Reagan.

JULIET DE VALERO WILLS 'Celebrate The Bullet' was a disastrous choice for the single. The Selecter had gone through a very destabilizing personnel change which had also started to dilute and confuse their audience. The atmosphere and the underlying tension in the studio was pretty bad. It felt as if the music wasn't really happening, but nobody wanted to admit it. My relationship with them had broken down, I wasn't being listened to at all and they decided they could manage themselves, so I left during the recording of the album. *Celebrate the Bullet* was released shortly after, but seemed to be out of step with a new prevailing mood in pop taste and culture. And that was the end of the Selecter.

ALL WI DOIN IS DEFENDIN

Linton Kwesi Johnson. 1981 riots. 2 Tone legacy

JULIET DE VALERO WILLS The 2 Tone bands had all formed under the fag end of an ailing Labour government. They were a generation coming of age into a Britain at war with itself, culminating in the Winter of Discontent of 1978–9. But it took the brittle policies of Margaret Thatcher's government to make the social message of their songs resonate so strongly with working-class youth. And black youth, in particular, not only suffered the crushing effects of ideological austerity, they were ruthlessly victimized by a police force that was 'institutionally racist' and largely unaccountable.

LINTON KWESI JOHNSON It was a period of intense class-struggle. Thatcher had arrived on the scene and the philosophy of the Tory Party was, 'We have to claw back the gains that the working class had made in the post-Second World War settlement: the welfare state and all of that, to gradually strengthen the hand of capital and weaken the hand of labour.'

ANGELA EAGLE The 2 Tone bands were very important because they were more politically developed than punk bands. They were anti-racist and by definition they commented on some of the segregation. I didn't dress in sharp suits and wear a pork-pie hat but I understood the political importance of being in that space. Those bands very much accorded with the anger and the hopelessness that people felt about what was happening in places like Coventry and Liverpool and the mass unemployment.

ROBERT ELMS If you want the voice of angry but beautiful black Britain, if you want to understand the riots of '81, Linton Kwesi Johnson is that.

LINTON KWESI JOHNSON I was writing poems of resistance articulating how the youth of my generation felt about what we were experiencing from the police and in the courts and in educational institutions, even in the place of work. I was expressing what I felt were the prevailing sentiments based on my own experiences as a part of the black communities. I was coming from a black power background. Our slogan was, Black Power People's Power. We weren't about setting up an independent black nation but we knew that the question of race was of paramount importance and couldn't be covered up under the carpet of class. We weren't anti white people. We were anti the white ruling class. Black people were on the margins of British society. We didn't have a middle class. We didn't have Members of Parliament. We didn't have councillors.

KATE WEBB There was a sixteenth birthday party on 17 January 1981 at a house in New Cross and a fire swept through and killed thirteen young black kids. It was believed to be arson but much to the community's outrage the police inquiry concluded that the fire had started in the house. Two months after, there was a largely peaceful march from Deptford to Hyde Park. The *Sun* headline the next day was, 'DAY THE BLACKS RAN RIOT IN LONDON'.

LINTON KWESI JOHNSON The Black People's Day of Action was the first significant watershed in those struggles because it made the state cognizant of the fact that we had some power; that we could put 20,000 people on the street; that we could shut down the centre of London. The New Cross fire had happened in London but the mobilization was national: Manchester, Birmingham, Leeds, Liverpool, Bristol, Derby, Leicester. And culture and music played a part because a lot of the mobilization was done through sound systems and local radio stations. The march culminated in Hyde Park and then we sent a delegation to No. 10 Downing Street. I was one of the stewards trying to keep the youth from running too many shops. It was a turning point.

PAULINE BLACK There was a benefit at the Hammersmith Palais for the National Council for One Parent Families with the Selecter, the Specials and Linton. The way he used words and the authority that he had on stage, he was like a young Malcolm X. That was quite a potent image when everyone was going round being a dread at the time.

BRINSLEY FORDE Linton took the political mantle and spoke like a politician. He was a life politician. Listening to his albums would be like listening to *News at Ten* but the proper version, particularly 'Sonny's Lettah'.

RANKING ROGER Sonny got caught up in an accident trying to save his brother and killed a police officer. It was a fantastic story. Linton got through to a lot of people, raising their knowledge and awareness.

LINTON KWESI JOHNSON 'Sonny's Lettah' was written as a contribution to a campaign that was being waged in our communities against the infamous sus law – a Vagrancy Act from 1824 which had been dormant for many years and was reinvoked – in which a significant number of black youth were criminalized by racist police officers. A policeman could just simply say that he had reasonable suspicion that you were thinking about putting your hand into somebody's handbag or pocket. It was as vague as that. The black communities were up in arms about it. Even parents who believed very much in law and order began to side with the youth because they realized that it was almost like a systematic process of criminalization. I had been arrested by the police and brutalized and assaulted and charged with assault and GBH, so 'Sonny's Lettah' drew on that experience plus the experience of many other people I knew who had been unjustly persecuted by the police.

LORNA GAYLE I used to listen to 'Sonny's Lettah' over and over again. Linton was my voice and world. He was a man coming from where I was coming from. I was an inner-city kid and got myself in trouble with the establishment for stupid, petty crime. I was quite unruly. I knew a lot of people who had that kind of lifestyle and ended up in prison. The sus laws were like an excuse to arrest us and keep us down. It didn't make much sense. I saw a lot of innocent people wrongly accused and beaten by the police and a lot of retaliating because it made you angry. Like when you were stopped: 'What are you doin'?' And you're like, 'What? What?' 'Say one more word.' 'What?' 'Get in the van. Shut your mouth.' If someone's talking to you like that your back's just gonna get up and it starts something. The police had a way. They knew how to click you off, especially if you had a bad temper anyway. And it would always turn into a disaster unless you were strong enough to say, 'Sorry, officer. I'm just walking minding my own business. Thank you, officer. Have a nice day, officer.' I didn't have that in me.

JUNIOR GISCOMBE There were curfews on the street, and if there were more than two people together you'd get stopped or you'd have the white van guys who would jump out and beat you up. The emphasis was on 'Colour, coming to ruin the country.'

JOHN NEWBEGIN There was rampant racism in the Metropolitan Police and Brixton was on the front line of that. The sus law gave the police enormous power to stop and search people without apparent reasonable cause and they targeted young black people. The SPG were very macho and brutal in the way they treated people in the community. We had transit vans racing up and down the street with the back doors open and police hanging out waving their truncheons and shouting, 'Come out and fight, you fucking monkeys.' It was pretty extraordinary.

PAULINE BLACK We'd been to America during the riots in Miami in May 1980 triggered by a black Marine Corps veteran being viciously beaten to death by the police – it was only a month after the St Pauls riot in Bristol triggered by a police raid on the Black and White Café. The sense of unease and continued lack of black people's empowerment in society was inter-national. Racism was rife. You'd got all these things that were decimating working-class people. Thatcher was in power. The country was in turmoil and recession. It was racism on two different continents. And you coupled that with what was going on in South Africa; pretty much wherever there was a black person there was some degree of turmoil.

JOHN NEWBEGIN Tension was rising and in April 1981 it just blew and there was a huge riot; a lot of property was destroyed and vehicles burnt. The police were completely taken by surprise at the intensity and ferocity of what happened and it took them a long time to regroup. I had a friend who was a community copper in Brixton and there was this joke in the station, 'Why are the SPG like bananas? Because they're bent, they're yellow, and they go about in bunches.' Thatcher was attempting to turn the police into a nationally organized force for class oppression and chief constables resisted that very forcibly, as we now know from the evidence that has come out.

DENNIS BOVELL The SPG went around unscrupulously stopping and searching black people going about their business to clean up Brixton. It was a move to agitate communities and crack down on whatever they thought was wrong within the community. Admittedly, there was ganja on sale quite openly and gambling was quite commonplace, but one street in Brixton hardly deserved the attention of the whole of the British police force. Brixton was a mixed community – like Ladbroke Grove, like Toxteth, like Handsworth – so when ordinary working-class people were beginning to feel the same pressure as the minorities, they suddenly realized there was a common thread. Then all you need is a few people to go, 'Per-haps they need to hear our voice? Yeah, let's have some disorder.' Linton captured it in 'Di Great Insohreckshan': *It woz in April nineteen eighty wan / Doun inna di ghetto af Brixtan / Dat di babylan dem cauz such a*

Northern Carnival Against Racism poster, 4 July 1981.

frickshan / Dat it bring about a great insohreckshan / An it spread all owevah di naeshan / It woz truly an histarical occayshan.

LINTON KWESI JOHNSON It was after the Black People's Day of Action and then the summer riots that government racial-equality policies slowly began to emerge. This idea of parliamentary democracy was not relevant. The reason why we had so many people at the march was the groundswell of anger and bitterness, combined with horror.

CLARE SHORT I had been the director of AFFOR [All Faiths For One Race] in the late seventies and we had published a report called *Talking Blues* which was a collection of verbatim commentaries of young black people from Handsworth talking about how the police behaved. All sorts of stories came out about kids getting messed up by the police. It was outrageous. It had been there for a long time. I went down on the streets of Handsworth the day after the riots in July '81 and it was desolate and cars were turned over. The spark was a big rise in unemployment which had shot up very fast and then it was young black youth angry with the police. But it spread beyond the inner city and others joined. It was an explosion of justified anger that was speaking about social conditions.

LYNVAL GOLDING The Specials did a Peaceful Protest Against Racism at the Butts Athletic Stadium in Coventry after the teenager Satnam Singh Gill had been murdered in a racial attack in the city centre in broad daylight. It clouded over everything. It was a horrible experience. I was playing and I couldn't feel anything.

JERRY DAMMERS The concert was to show solidarity and to take a stand against racism in general. You had to do something. It was a really terrible time in Coventry. Dr Amal Dharri was stabbed to death by racists in the chip shop twenty yards away from where I lived, apparently for a £10 bet. It was absolutely horrific. In the lead-up to the concert there had been rumours of a National Front march so a lot of people were scared to come – but that never materialized beyond about twenty people. A white guy had been beaten up by some Asian kids in a low-level retaliation and he came on stage and made a little speech saying how he completely understood why they'd done it, which was really touching.

HORACE PANTER Three other Asians were attacked with knives and bottles in the same week. It was like, 'We need to do something here.' We lost an absolute fortune and it was quite overcast but the atmosphere was great.

I was thrilled we'd been able to do it. And then on 4 July we did the final Rock Against Racism gig in Potternewton Park in Leeds.

JERRY DAMMERS As we drove into Leeds we saw this big National Front march which looked like a giant red, white and blue slug creeping through the town. It was very sinister with lots of Union Jacks. The impression I got was it was mostly older normal-looking blokes. There was really quite a strong atmosphere in the town.

RHODA DAKAR We were driving in Neville's car through the march and there were hundreds of people and flags. We were low down so people seemed taller. It was all a bit scary. We ended up at this field in Chapeltown and I sat down by this woman in the audience and said, 'Are you listening to the tennis?' She said, 'I know it's a bourgeois construct but I can't help it.'

JOOLZ DENBY There were Rude Boys and skins and proto-punk goths. You just felt, 'This is what revolution is like.'

DOUG MORRIS I went to the Carnival wearing my Harrington, Fred Perry and a pair of jeans. And it was interesting the Au Pairs were on. They were quite confrontational in their attitude: a strong, confident band. It was a new era of gender and social politics.

LESLEY WOODS I remember being in the dressing room with members of Misty and they were passing round the spliff and they wouldn't pass it to the women. They passed it to me because I transcended being a woman because I was a musician. I passed it to the other women. They didn't object. I objected.

RHODA DAKAR Misty went off on one about how Rico shouldn't work with the Specials. 'They're not Rastas. You shouldn't be working with them.' It was a load of bollocks. They were all, 'Nah, dread.' They never spoke to us at all. I thought, 'What's that all about? We're here trying to get everyone together and you're busy trying to split them up.' That really pissed me off. Rico refused to play the solo on 'Ghost Town' because they got to him.

CHRIS BOLTON That's bollocks. How ridiculous with the history of Misty and the bands we've helped out. We never put down another band at a Rock Against Racism show. No fucking way. We were always very respectful to Rico for the contribution he made to music, way before we arrived. Rico had never been intimidated in his life not to play. He would have decided himself. He was his own man.

Lesley Woods of the Au Pairs at the Northern Carnival Against Racism,
Leeds, 4 July 1981.

RICK ROGERS I wasn't party to the conversation but one of the band came into the dressing room and said, 'Misty are accusing of us of stealing their music.' It was really hurtful and horrible. I was having to deal with the difficulty of keeping it all together; maybe I got myself so drunk because it was difficult.

HORACE PANTER Misty were very down on Rico because he was 'playing with Babylon'. But the gig was shit. Our sound engineer didn't know it was in the afternoon and he didn't arrive until after we'd finished. It was one of our last ever gigs in England. We hated one another. We went on stage and didn't care. There was no cohesion. It wasn't a band at all. We just went through the motions.

JERRY DAMMERS I think the crowd thought it was a fantastic gig, apart from one fight which was a mystery what that was about. The atmosphere was amazing and the message came across loud and clear. I don't think anyone in the crowd would have known there were any serious problems in the band. I didn't even know myself at that stage. 'Ghost Town' was racing up the charts and we played it as the big climax to this massive concert. It came to the solo and Rico didn't play. He said, 'Jerry, me nah feel fe play.'

I thought it was funny. I don't know if anyone from Misty, or possibly with one of the other reggae bands, had said anything to him. It wouldn't have been right but I could sort of understand, I mean, a lot of them were better singers and players than us and struggling, while we were having chart hits. I think Rico had just been having a few spliffs with whoever and he was just a bit moody and missing playing with the brethren in a real reggae band. To me, Misty were fantastic singers and massive supporters of RAR from the start to the finish.

DOUG MORRIS There was lots of fighting down the front towards the end of the Specials' set and their singer, Terry, shouted at them.

SYD SHELTON There was a hell of a lot of Rude Boys and Rhoda did that incredible rape song 'The Boiler' with the Specials where she's screaming. It was daunting: just silence.

JOOLZ DENBY I was thinking, 'Good on you. Do it. Go on, tell 'em.' Rhoda was brave, because there were people around me going, 'For fuck's sake.'

Rico Rodriguez backstage
with the Specials, Spa Centre,
Leamington, 15 April 1981.

LYNVAL GOLDING 'The Boiler' tackled such an emotional subject in a direct way; and seeing the expression on people's faces, 'This is heavy shit.' But the day was like a big party. The audience and the togetherness; you could feel it. In Leeds we always had more blacks at our gigs than we ever had anywhere else. Neville said, 'It's like a zebra crossing, black and white, black and white as far as you can see.'

HORACE PANTER Everybody came offstage and went off into their own little worlds. The band was falling apart and I felt really ashamed. I went back to Coventry and watched the riots in Toxteth on television. But in Thatcher's Britain I was a pop star. I was aware of people having a hard time, yes, but personally I had a blast. I toured America. I went to Europe. I actually had disposable income and I owned a car for the first time. I wasn't affected by what government was in power. Jerry was a lot more politically savvy. I remember him saying that when we played in Glasgow he saw all these people selling their crockery and cutlery in the street.

RICK ROGERS Jerry was able to see things that not all of us were able to see and was able to respond and write about it. I feel quite ashamed of myself but I was completely sheltered from it all. I do remember having this wonderful conversation with Jerry while driving him to a mixing session where we were talking about the state of the country, and after I thought, 'I've got to bring myself back down to earth a bit.' That's quite a painful thing to say. I wasn't aware of some of the things I should have been aware of and the Specials' bubble protected me from really knowing what else was going on in the country under Thatcher. You don't notice a recession when every six months you get more royalties than you got six months previously. I was thinking about the moment.

LYNVAL GOLDING We saw the cutbacks and how working-class people were affected. We were all feeling it. Jerry had the idea to do 'Maggie's Farm' which was a Bob Dylan song.

HORACE PANTER *I ain't gonna work on Maggie's farm no more*: that was, if you like, the anti-Thatcher tune. And then Jerry wrote 'Ghost Town', which became the soundtrack to the riots. It was the only time that social realism got to the top of the charts, while Toxteth and Brixton and Handsworth all kicked off. Poor old Peter Powell on *Top of the Pops*, 'Now, it's good-time music from Coventry.'

ROBERT HOWARD 'Ghost Town' made perfect sense, with that spooky clarinet line and Terry Hall's delivery without vibrato. It was the sound of what was really going on. I remember walking down Acre Lane in Brixton and I got chased into a basement just near the crypt and a policeman came right up to my face with his baton and shield and went, 'Aaarrggghh' and then ran off. I'd only been back in the UK for about three weeks. I was thinking, 'What the fuck is this, man?'

RANKING ROGER 'Ghost Town' was profound. We were on tour in Manchester and Toxteth had gone up. I thought, 'That's amazing, the answer is at the top of the charts.'

TOM WATSON Every kid in the Midlands lived in a ghost town. There were kids I knew who literally didn't get work for five years. It was a direct result of the 1981 budget which Peter Tapsell, the Tory grandee, said was 'the most illiterate budget in history'. It wiped out a third of the West Midlands manufacturing base in two or three years. We hated the government and we hated Thatcher. It added to our sense of powerlessness as teenagers, but songs brought people together. When you've listened to the music and you've danced to the music and the posters are on your wall and you've read everything about the band, then you start to think about the lyrics and the politics start to develop.

KEITH HARRIS I took 'One In Ten' and 'Ghost Town' back to America and played them to Stevie Wonder to explain what was going on.

MYKAELL RILEY 'Ghost Town' is really important because the Specials mastered reggae as oppose to ska. It was one of their most experimental records in terms of a production.

JERRY DAMMERS I got the title 'Ghost Town' from a Nips song which was Shane McGowan's band before the Pogues. And the wailing *ay ay ays* in my mind conjured up the idea of the Third World rising up. I was trying to link my personal feelings to the political situation and I wanted an atmosphere of decay. I had been overwhelmed on tour seeing how unemployment had hit in places like Liverpool, where all the shops had cast-iron shutters, and Glasgow, where there were old ladies on the street selling household goods and cups and saucers. The *boom town* was Coventry.

NEVILLE STAPLE I didn't find any problems with Thatcher. I wasn't really a political guy. I knew it was doom and gloom but what could I do about it? I didn't go out and preach. I could sing about it. *This town is comin' like a* *ghost town / All the clubs have been closed down.* And then *people getting angry.*

JERRY DAMMERS At first I felt guilty writing in patois because I don't think many white people had ever done that at the time. But it's a very strong poetic and rebellious language and I was writing for Neville to sing, so why not.

RICK ROGERS 'Ghost Town' is the best track the Specials ever recorded. It's an absolute masterpiece; a most beautiful piece of music. I said at the time it was going to be their 'Vienna'; terribly embarrassing.

LYNVAL GOLDING We had the biggest record; three weeks at number one. And then me, Neville and Terry walked away from the band. By that time we were so out of touch with each other. When we did 'Ghost Town' on *Top of the Pops* we knew this was it. It was a relief. The weight and negativity was too heavy. And Roddy was always pissed off. Anybody in authority he hates. And he had all these gripes with Jerry and would disagree just for the sake of disagreeing.

RICK ROGERS It was the Specials' second number one but it wasn't celebrated in terms of everybody being together, no. Everybody lived in different places and the mentality that was there at the beginning had dissipated.

JULIET DE VALERO WILLS By the time 'Ghost Town' became the soundtrack of the riots and everything was going up in flames, 2 Tone was crumbling.

LYNVAL GOLDING The Specials broke up because we couldn't work together, but on stage we were preaching harmony and unity. Recording the second album had been painful. It wasn't like a band together.

RICK ROGERS People definitely turned against Jerry because of outside influences who wanted to control the band and saw it as a huge money-making machine. The agenda was challenged when it had always been driven by Jerry. It was people not understanding his complete push to move forward and push boundaries. It's the difference between *Specials* and *More Specials.* But some of them hated doing the second album. The Specials would never have got to 'Ghost Town' without that creative push and that never being satisfied and always taking risks and never mind the consequences. I remember Jerry saying, 'Why don't we just put out singles for the next year?' I'd love that idea now but I argued against it.

And there was talk about bringing in Rhoda as a permanent part of the line-up.

RHODA DAKAR The decision to include me in their touring band was not the Specials' decision; it was Jerry's. I think that was a problem. I was possibly the buffer, so in the end it meant that everything could be my fault. I don't know if it was intentional. But the audience didn't want the music to change. I admired Jerry because he wanted to move it forward.

JERRY DAMMERS I thought it would be good having a woman involved and Rhoda's backing vocals added another element to the second album, but I don't think I ever expected her to fully join the band. If it had been a majority decision Rhoda would probably have been sent away. I stuck up for her mainly because I thought 'The Boiler' was important and we could play it to people because the Bodysnatchers had split up. It did get a bit silly at times: she was on *Top of the Pops* for 'Ghost Town' and didn't even sing on the record.

RANKING ROGER *More Specials* was one of the first ever ambient albums but lots of fans were disappointed. You had to be chameleon. It's why the Clash survived so long because they were willing to experiment.

NEVILLE STAPLE The reason why *More Specials* wasn't like the first album was because Jerry was thinking further ahead than everyone else. He was the one with the brains and told them what to play. While we were getting together and tighter we were crumbling away. That's fame. Because everybody thinks they're better than one person. 'I need to say something now.' 'I need to do this.' 'I need to do that.'

JERRY DAMMERS Certain people were either not seeing or not interested in the big picture, which was that the Specials and 2 Tone was an amazing thing: the gigs had an incredible energy, solidarity and unity; plus we were protesting against Thatcher, who was closing down huge swathes of British manufacturing industry despite literally millions of workers making a living and good stuff being produced.

FRANK MURRAY What I saw as the main problem around the Specials was they became successful quite quickly and all of a sudden crowds were going mad for them every night. Jerry tried to keep things in hand but he didn't seem to like the fame and the popularity. He was an anti-star. But in the music business you have to go for broke. You can't be going on a scale of one to ten, 'Just let me be popular number three.'

The Specials: (L–R) Terry Hall, Lynval Golding , Rhoda Dakar,
Peaceful Protest Against Racism, Coventry, 20 June 1981.

JERRY DAMMERS I came up through the era of Rod Stewart. It was a big deal when he appeared on TV with Britt Ekland buying ludicrous art deco lamps and being really flash; a lot of us fans were very disappointed. And then with punk we all thought, 'At last, this is going to be something different.' But when we supported the Clash, they were staying in what seemed to me like really overly flash hotels. I was really disappointed. I loved the Clash but I didn't want to put more kids through that sort of disillusionment I had felt.

RICK ROGERS As soon as we got to America the PR person would feed cocaine to those that wanted it. And you didn't need to have money in your pocket to buy drinks, they were bought for you, so we drank more. All these weird pressures started attacking the little bubble we were in and causing internal problems. And people very close to the core circle started talking in ears and jealousies started to arise: 'Why d'you do everything Jerry tells you to do?' And although, like me, Jerry was a drinker at the time, he started recognizing that things were going off kilter. I didn't. With my relative inexperience and naivety I did not recognize the rot that was setting in.

FRANK MURRAY When we were in America a limousine was sent to pick us up but Jerry had an issue with that. Why not travel in comfort? I'd travelled in limousines lots of times and I never mistook them for personal wealth; people would look at you and go, 'Wow!' but I wouldn't have a penny in my pocket. It doesn't change you as a person. Fans have never given a shit about how an artist travels around. Just because you're a middle-class kid it doesn't mean you don't know what a working-class kid is about, or they won't like your music.

JERRY DAMMERS I love Frank, he used to make me laugh: 'Don't fight fame, Jerry!' He'd spent too long with Thin Lizzy. He missed the point, I didn't want to repeat the mistakes of the Sixties' bands: I knew promoters and record companies would send bands a limo, stick them in a flash hotel, make sure they got a ton of drugs and hope they wouldn't notice the company were keeping most of their profits. And if the artist died so much the better; sell more records. I'm not saying our record company were that bad, of course, but I was generally hoping not to fall for all that old rock 'n'roll nonsense. Limos have one purpose, which is to say, 'Look at me. I'm rich. I'm powerful. I'm more important than you.' The whole thing was bullshit. I worked that out at a very early age.

RHODA DAKAR It appeared from the outside that the Specials were a democracy. The Specials were not a democracy. I got who Jerry was. I'd met his sister and his brother and I'd gone to church schools. I was in a class with this one girl and I used to go to her house and saw the value system of an Anglican vicar's family. And that's where Jerry came from. It makes for conflicted people: 'We don't care about money because money's not important.' But actually we don't have any.

JERRY DAMMERS I've always known money is very important, which is why I didn't like wasting it on the road. It's just that money is not the reason I do things creatively. You can always tell if music has been made for that purpose. That was part of the original mod thing, 'Why would you want to listen to the sound of someone relieving you of your money?' To me, music is supposed to be inspirational more than aspirational; or if there is aspiration it is hopefully part of some kind of collective aspiration, not just for the band but for the audience and society in general.

CATHAL SMYTH Jerry's dad was a libertarian theologist. I read his book *Lifestyle: A Parable of Sharing* and suddenly understood why Jerry wouldn't go in the five-star hotels in America or why he gave his seat up for a fan on the coach even when he was tired. Small is beautiful because of its effect.

HORACE PANTER I wasn't aware of Jerry's dad until I saw the obituary in the *Telegraph* in 2004. It was like, 'Now I understand where Jerry was coming from.' He hated the fact that money would be spent on champagne or expensive hotels. That's why he encouraged us to buy second-hand suits.

JERRY DAMMERS I think of myself as a socialist; leftist politics in general, anti-racism, and some ideas from the non-superstitious side of Christianity, Marxism, liberalism and environmentalism were all in the background somewhere. And my general ideas of justice and fairness and not wasting resources must have been influenced by my upbringing to some extent, but most of it was just common sense and hopefully some sort of intelligence of my own. But at that time it was mostly anarchy, hell-raising, partying and being contrary in general. Most of all, I was influenced by music through the sixties, through black music and rock music which had a lot of political counterculture messages. There was also a very sound financial reason for being reasonably sensible, which was ultimately the band have to pay for everything because it's taken out of your royalties. I was just trying to make sure we kept as much of our earnings as possible.

LYNVAL GOLDING Me, Neville and Terry went to see Jerry and said, 'We can't cope with this anymore. We're done with it.' Obviously he was upset but then he said, 'You're not allowed to leave. You have to stay.' We said, 'There you go, Jerry, that's why we're leaving. You're not listening to us.' It was like you were never allowed to express an idea or be yourself. You've got to be what Jerry wants you to be. It worked up to a certain stage but after that individuals are going to want to just throw some ideas in.

JERRY DAMMERS I don't think I would have said, 'You're not allowed to leave,' except possibly as a joke, which might have been over Lynval's head. He had missed the point so completely by that time, that even me wanting them in the band would have been seen as evidence of me telling them what to do. It was crazy. I encouraged everyone to go off after the American tour and write songs and put their ideas in, and then we would reconvene for the next album. Terry, Neville and Lynval thought the first thing they came up with, 'The Lunatics (Have Taken Over the Asylum)', was so fantastic that they didn't need the rest of us anymore and they probably thought they could make more money without us. It's as simple as that.

RHODA DAKAR I didn't know Terry, Neville, and Lynval were leaving but when I look at it now it's completely obvious. I went on the Specials' last American tour and in the airport Terry played me 'The Lunatics' on a Walkman. I was like, 'This is absolutely brilliant.'

JERRY DAMMERS I couldn't believe that they could be so destructive and disloyal as to leave when we were doing such great stuff. We were at the top of our game: universal critical acclaim; commercial success; one of the top bands in the country on the verge of really establishing ourselves internationally.

LYNVAL GOLDING The last three Specials songs were 'Ghost Town', 'Why?' and 'Friday Night, Saturday Morning'; from those songs you can see the faces of the Specials; two blacks and one white. I was thinking, 'Wow! We've broken down barriers there.' 'The Lunatics' was a natural follow-up, *I see a clinic full of cynics who want to twist the people's wrist.* Ronald Reagan and Margaret Thatcher were the lunatics: *Go nuclear, the cowboy told us.* The world was becoming very dangerous.

NEVILLE STAPLE I was stupid leaving to do the Fun Boy Three with Lynval and Terry.

RICK ROGERS I don't think any of the colour, class or education differences caused the problems that happened internally within the Specials. It was fame, pressure and money. Jerry saw that and wanted to bring it back down to earth a little bit. When anybody becomes hugely famous in a very short period of time you get surrounded by people telling you what is the right thing to do.

CATHAL SMYTH Madness was a very democratic process and that's why we lasted and the Specials only lasted two years; because they weren't friendly. They had no mutual respect. There was jealousy, anger, frustration, a lack of fucking gratitude for each other's existence. We went into a room with them to record a piece of music and the fuckers couldn't stop arguing. We were like, 'Oh my God!' It was sad.

JERRY DAMMERS I started the Specials initially to do my songs and everyone knew I was bandleader, but later I was trying to share the load and responsibility and it's actually that which only lasted about five minutes. Of course we discussed things in the Specials and I always tried to incorporate the best of everyone's ideas. It's often actually the idea that bands should be completely democratic which has probably destroyed more bands. There are no rules in music and everyone is not equally good at it or has equally good ideas; democracy and music are not necessarily related concepts. Democracy requires commitment, responsibility and loyalty. But sadly, it's true: there was very little loyalty in the Specials compared with Madness.

DAVE WAKELING Socialism assumes that everybody is going to do their best, and sadly as human beings the only thing we've got in common is that we fuck up and we often do our worst and don't even know why until it's too late. We set up all these great plans with altruism and deep conviction, but then, put in a corner, everybody would eat their mother's face. That sums up a lot of the differences between my dad, Eric Clapton and Enoch Powell, and Jerry Dammers, me and Red Saunders. Everybody starts off with the best of intentions, but we're terrified creatures and we're very reactive so we often do rotten things. So I understand why the French say that 'If you're not a socialist under the age of forty you have no heart and if you remain a socialist past the age of forty you have no brain.'

•

HORACE PANTER 2 Tone was Jerry's. But if you ask the seven people in the Specials any one same question you will invariably get seven different answers. History is written by the people that write the books.

TINY FENNIMORE 2 Tone had a really important part to play in the early years of the Thatcher government. Just because all those bands existed was political. It was white and black coming together. It's to do with the social and the political and the musical all coming together at the same time to make a special moment.

JERRY DAMMERS It's very hard to quantify what 2 Tone achieved. It helped alongside Rock Against Racism and a whole lot of other campaigns in making everyday racism unacceptable. Before that it was really common to use language like 'nigger' and 'wogs'. I hope 2 Tone contributed to making that situation better. It was part of an ongoing struggle; racism didn't go away.

DOTUN ADEBAYO That whole period of multicultural music is Rock Against Racism's lasting legacy. Would there have been 2 Tone without it? My friends who grew up in Coventry always say there was a mixture of black and white and the reggae gigs had as many whites as blacks, but that's not the same thing. The Beat were two-thirds white; the Selecter were mostly black, one white; and the Specials mostly white with two black guys: pretty multiracial. Are they black or are they white?

RICK ROGERS 2 Tone spoke directly to a young, disaffected generation. It was massively political. The power of the message in the songs, in the artwork, visually; just the fact that there were young black and white kids together in a band making music: that the audience could relate to and understand and share. It had an enormous effect.

DAVE WAKELING Political music has a negligible effect at the time because you're mostly speaking to the choir. But if it resonates it puts a mark in history that affects things generationally, but for a certain generation marks were made to do with diversity and compassion. I have two black American children now and it's fascinating watching them grow up with kids from Iran and India and Russia and not describe each other by their skin colour. My parents' generation only spoke about people of different colour in order to give you a warning to stay away from them.

ROBERT ELMS 2 Tone in its very existence was important. It didn't have to be explicit. It was just there on stage: it's black and white guys singing on stage together; it's Pauline Black singing with a band of black guys. That was more important than anything Rock Against Racism did with slogans.

NICKY SUMMERS 2 Tone did a lot for racial integration but I think it largely appealed to a white audience. Right at the end we had some young black girls come to our gigs and they were talking to us. I thought we'd really done something there. I knew I couldn't replicate black music. I don't think anyone can replicate music, but you can do your contemporary take with your input and your life added into it. 2 Tone bands had this tremendous lift of energy and everybody worked very hard onstage. And the audience danced. Its most basic reduction was that it was dance music.

PAULINE BLACK It was a two-year blip that occupied that space between punk and those hideous New Romantics that turned up in '81 and '82. 2 Tone let the genie out of the bottle. It would be another twenty years before anybody came up with the concept of institutional racism and certainly that long again before anyone came up with the word multicultural.

JULIET DE VALERO WILLS There was a lot of walking wounded at the end. Then suddenly we were competing for attention at Chrysalis with bands like Spandau Ballet and Ultravox. These were the people we were being measured against. You thought, 'What happened? Was 2 Tone just a

2 Tone single and album front covers 1979–1984.

fashion?' That same generation who were actively supporting quite overtly radical influences and music, to move to superficial clothes and hair-styles? Politics was so unfashionable immediately. 2 Tone came out of nowhere, burnt unbelievably bright, and burnt itself out just as quickly. The bands were trying so hard to wrestle with what it was going to be and what it could achieve, it killed it. What did it achieve? We don't really know because we were in the eye of the storm. It was such a force of nature. Musically and culturally we would be a lot poorer if 2 Tone hadn't happened. It may not have changed attitudes but it started something. There was no way of going back.

BOOK THREE
RED WEDGE

1. SHOUT TO THE TOP

LIFE IN THE EUROPEAN THEATRE

Thatcherism. CND. Paul Weller

JUNE MILES-KINGSTON All of this is about class. The whole of England works on a class system. Rock 'n' roll is a working-class thing but in the eighties it completely changed. Suddenly everybody wanted to be a pop star. The period totally promoted being middle-class and being upwardly mobile. That was a very dangerous situation because it takes away the yearning for the right reasons for doing it. It distils and homogenizes everything. But you also had all this great diverse music about and it gave you that feeling that you had the power. It wasn't a power of money and it wasn't a power of fame. It was a power of voice and representing yourself.

BILLY BRAGG I didn't vote in '79 because I couldn't see any difference between Margaret Thatcher and Jim Callaghan. Even I, as somebody who ended up as political as I am, couldn't work out the difference between Conservative and Labour.

RICHARD SWALES We would do gigs for petrol and chips and they were very cheap to get in. You got treated really well by the audience and the organizers and the people would put lots of energy into it. But at a certain point in the eighties it all changed and if you did gigs for free you got treated like shit. The new way was to charge as much money as you could possibly screw out of people and then people treated you nicely. It was a change in attitude which was to do with the Seventies hangover philosophy of 'money is evil and creativity is freedom', to the Eighties' attitude of 'you get what you pay for; if you don't charge anything it ain't worth anything.'

BRINSLEY FORDE By 1983, suddenly you had three million people out of work. People were getting hit with the themes that the ethnic communities had been going through for years.

JUNIOR GISCOMBE Black people were more politically aware than people could ever imagine. We had my generation, born and bred in Britain, seeing what was going on and understanding Thatcherism was all about the individual. I started to think, 'You're the guy with the fast car', 'You're the guy with the big house on the hill', I want to do like you. But I'm being told I should live within my means so you've got me like a fool. The Conservatives gave people false hope of being able to move forward and get on the ladder: you've got to think about you now; if you could screw the man next door, screw him. But I'd been brought up with more of a community spirit: bob-a-job.

GORDON OGILVIE I disliked Thatcherism intensely. It's the easiest thing in the world to motivate people by saying, 'You're only badly off because the guy over the road's got something you haven't. Hate him.'

STEVE WHITE I couldn't stand Thatcher. She homed in on that aspiration and turned it on its head. But it would be hypocritical to say as a family we didn't benefit from those policies. I remember the Winter of Discontent. There needed to be a correction of dialogue and curtailing of the power of the unions, because eating dinner in candlelight wasn't much fun. But Thatcher took it too far and came in with an agenda to smash what was the decent working class by denigrating pillars of the community. She realized that if you can politicize the education system then you've got a certain degree of control. You don't want five million thinkers; you want five million people addicted to bullshit aspirational politics of one-upmanship, and it started with the ownership of council homes, unfortunately.

CATHAL SMYTH It was the beginning of the dismantling of the welfare state, the destruction of culture, riots, poverty on the streets. Thatcher was putting more air in the ice cream and taking out the cream. There was nothing left in there but a load of fluff and bad fucking shit. Where's all the goodness that was in the ice cream?

STEVE WHITE It was the politicization of the police force, the denigration of the education system, the belittlement of the role of teachers, the first assaults on the National Health Service, being an aircraft carrier for America, closing the pits, smashing manufacturing. She had no sympathy with what it was like to live under her policies. She closed it all down and left those people with nothing. I got to tour in places like Newcastle and Liverpool and Manchester and saw the deprivation, and it felt like, having a voice from the south, people would look at you as if to say, 'You must be one of them.' London was apart from the rest but we were all from the same background. My grandparents survived the Blitz in London. My wife's grandparents survived the Blitz in Manchester. I could see the injustice but essentially we were all working-class kids.

SHERYL GARRATT '79 was the first election I ever voted in and then for the next two decades I never voted for a government to be in power because the Conservatives won again and again and again. Barbara Castle and Betty Boothroyd were politicians I felt could be my Nana but Margaret Thatcher was not like any women I had ever met. She was like some starched woman on the telly that you'd seen in sitcoms. I cannot articulate how much we hated her. I had discovered this exciting new world where women could be something different, other than wives and mums and shop girls, and she was crushing that world and dismantling everything that was important to me. It was a class war. And there was so much about being working class that I hated, like casual prejudice or the roles women were assigned to. But I could criticize that, not Thatcher or the Conservatives.

ALEX DALLAS People would say, 'You've got yourself a woman prime minister,' as though, therefore, feminism had been sorted: 'You've got equality now.' The famous *Spitting Image* sketch where she's dressed in a man's suit peeing at a urinal was exactly what I thought of her. She was so abhorrent. It reinforced your feminism.

FRANCES SOKOLOV All the generation who would have been in love with John Lennon songs, who wanted a better world, who wanted some freedoms and who wanted some representation, didn't want to be tied up by Thatcher. We had been riding on hope for a long time. We blamed Thatcher. I didn't like her tone of voice. I didn't like the way she looked. We'd had female headmistresses. We'd had female magistrates doing the dirty. It's not enough just to be a woman. To be a woman is something you have to work with.

LESLEY WOODS Thatcher wasn't a woman to me. She was a caricature. And her claim to fame that she came from a working-class background: fascists and racists come from working-class roots. Nazi youth was made up of working-class, disaffected, bored kids. There was nothing romantic or mysterious in the fact that she was a greengrocer's daughter. What would have been romantic was if she had been a revolutionary, and a greengrocer's daughter.

KAREN WALTER The first job I got after school was working in the features department as junior secretary on *Woman's Own*, which at the time was the bestselling women's magazine, and I met Maggie at the Children of Courage Awards which they sponsored for nominated children who have shown tremendous courage. By then I thought she had horns and was the devil. I couldn't even understand why she'd agreed to go. It was at Westminster Abbey, so it was a huge occasion. This particular day was absolutely foul and everyone was walking in with their winter shoes so the floor was filthy. We went into the Jerusalem Chamber and there was a little boy who had been nominated and had some kind of brittle bone disease and was normally in a wheelchair, but he insisted on walking. He had the smallest pair of crutches and was only five or six but he was like a two-year-old because he was so small. He was standing talking to Maggie Thatcher and all of a sudden his legs gave way and he collapsed. Everyone rushed over to pick him up and she said, 'No, I'll go down to him,' and she knelt on the floor and started chatting to him. It just threw me completely. I thought, 'I wouldn't kneel on that floor. It's absolutely filthy.' The mother in her just took over and she didn't worry about her lovely blue suit or her tights. It was a maternal instinct and it showed me you can't paint everybody so black and white.

TRACEY THORN I grew up in a house that was pro-Conservative but I couldn't override what she seemed to represent politically with any positive feelings about it was good that a woman was in charge. I probably disagreed with everything she ever stood for. But ironically, in Everything But The Girl, Ben and I were successful young people during the era she was in power: economically we thrived; she lowered our taxes. It's that awkward thing of being a successful Labour voter; you're always voting against your best interests. But I come back to the great Ben Elton joke about being wealthy under a Tory government when he said, 'I don't want to have to wade through an inner-city riot on my way to the squash court sipping my Pimm's.' However successful and well off you are, it doesn't benefit you to live in a broken society. Yes, I wasn't personally suffering under this but you're a thinking, sensitive, feeling human being; you don't like looking around and seeing your society vulnerable and people in it suffering. You don't have to be the one on the end of this punching fist not to like it.

BILLY BRAGG One of the more troubling features of Margaret Thatcher's first term in office was the ramping-up of the Cold War. We were getting leaflets through the door explaining what to do in the event of an attack: basically, it was hide under the table and don't come out for fourteen days.

Annajoy David, CND office, London, 1981.

I remember an education minister being asked on TV if the defence spending on cruise missiles would be better used to provide free school meals. He said, 'What good are free school dinners if they are being fed to our children by Russian paratroopers?' I was like, 'Fucking hell!'

<u>ANNAJOY DAVID</u> I became the vice-chair of the Youth Campaign for Nuclear Disarmament. It was bonkers that we were all pointing cruise missiles at each other that could kill us all. There were events all around us and so many different young people and groups doing things on the ground, and that helped to frame a lot of my thinking that we could develop alternative models to do things. I went to a peace conference with E. P. Thompson and Petra Kelly, who started the Green Party, organized by the Eastern Bloc states to show that they really did believe in peace. We secretly met with Charter 77 and the underground that was connected to the arts movement, who were preparing for a revolution; that we saw come to fruition at the end of the eighties. The meeting was broken up by the

special police and I was arrested. It had a huge impact on me and helped to define my political DNA about outside movements who were well organized for change and working with people in parliamentary movements. I definitely got that.

PAUL HEATON The Campaign for Nuclear Disarmament was seen as outside of politics. My girlfriend was vegetarian and wore a CND badge and she said, 'You against nuclear weapons?' I thought, 'Yeah. If Joe Strummer's against them, I must be.' The Clash used to perform with all these Spitfires on their backdrop but Strummer knew where he stood. So we went on this long march in London to Hyde Park. There were at least a quarter of a million people. That was the first time I'd taken part in anything. I'd been cynical about those types of people. It was a crossing point and an affirmation of goodness.

ANNAJOY DAVID I was asked to speak at this rally. I must have been about sixteen or seventeen. And I had no idea that about 250,000 people would be there. I turned up in this tartan Vivienne Westwood-type suit and started by quoting some lyrics from Stiff Little Fingers: *They never ask us if we want a war . . . we're saying, 'We want no more of that.'* Paul Weller heard the speech on LBC radio and rang CND. He said, 'My name's Paul Weller and I want to support what you're doing.' I said, 'Who are you?' And he said, 'I'm in a group called the Jam.' I didn't know who he was, which I think he found rather endearing. I was reliably informed that he was in the biggest group in the country. We met and he said, 'I want to help you. I think you're great. Let's do something.' So the Jam got on the back of a big truck and played for CND. That's how it kind of started. It was the making of me. And Paul and I formed this great alliance and political relationship that endured for the next fifteen years.

DAVE WAKELING In 1981, CND put together the album *Life in the European Theatre* with many of the 2 Tone bands: the Specials, the Beat, Madness and also the Jam, XTC, Ian Dury, the Stranglers, the Au Pairs, Peter Gabriel, the Clash, and the royalties were split between CND, Friends of the Earth and local anti-nuclear arms projects.

ANNAJOY DAVID I helped put together the album, and Paul wrote, 'Until we achieve nuclear disarmament, we are living on borrowed time. While you're listening, dancing and enjoying this music, please don't lose sight of why it was put together.'

DAVE WAKELING I wanted the record to be called *Live in the European Theatre*, but Warner Brothers said everybody would think it was a live album so they suggested '*Life*' instead.

CATHAL SMYTH Madness contributed 'Grey Day'. But then I realized after a CND march shouting 'Maggie, Maggie, Maggie. Out, Out, Out,' it was a waste of fucking time because on the news coverage the camera angle was intent on just showing a couple of fucking punks, whereas if you pulled back there was all these people from Hampstead in their duffle coats, ordinary good human beings. But on television they made it look like it was a subversive and aggressive protest. We walked past a war exhibition off Leicester Square and when I saw the fuckin' blue-rinse people looking out of the windows I realized we should have been singing 'God Save The Queen'.

STEVE WHITE I was on a CND march with a Spitfire pilot veteran and a Franciscan monk who was a pacifist. They were very elderly and I was thinking, 'If I'm standing here with a bloody war hero and he's telling me that nuclear weapons are wrong I will hold this belief forever.' That was about the time that Thatcher started to use the term 'the enemy within'. I thought, 'No, that pilot and that monk are not the enemy within, even if I am.'

ANNAJOY DAVID A year or so later I organized a 'Festival for Peace' in Brockwell Park with Madness and the Style Council. It was only six months since Paul had split up the Jam – and it was absolutely packed. The festival was a turning point and it took it all up to a different level. The Style Council recorded 'Money Go Round' for Youth CND and donated its profits to us. He contributed a piece to our magazine *Second Generation* to explain the meaning behind the song:

> I get times when I 'think' I see things clearly but those thoughts once written down on paper can sound banal or clichéd. This is the reason why I have never written an actual 'anti-nuclear song' as such. To do it you have to forget any such criticisms and my only justification is that it is truly what I feel, which is obviously more important than just being clever. The lyrics are not only about the nuclear arms race and madness but about capitalism as a whole in which I hope I captured both the desperation of my feelings and also my cynicism. Optimism is an elusive thread of light. I catch it now and again before it darts away again behind some ugly, sinister cloud.

TOM WATSON 'Money Go Round' was a totally different feel and sound for Weller after the Jam. It was amazingly risky for him. But there's not a day goes by when the words *too much money in too few places only puts a smile on particular faces* don't bubble up in my mind.

STEVE WHITE The lyrics were absolutely fantastic. Who puts that on a record? Paul and I went to the RAF Greenham Common airbase, the proposed site for ninety American cruise missiles, and I remember walking up to the perimeter fence on a beautiful misty morning and a transporter had just landed. A lady who was with us said, 'They're nukes.' It was the scariest thing that I had ever seen. I just thought, 'Wow! That could destroy the planet.' There were tens of thousands of women there who had a formed a peace camp in protest against the nuclear site, and they told us the base was experimenting with sonic pulses that were disrupting their fertility cycle and they were having irregular periods, and that sonic booms were being directed at their camp to keep them awake. There was a teenage lad by the perimeter fence and he said, 'What the fucking hell are you doing here with those cunts?' Then he gobbed on the ground and walked off.

PAUL WELLER We'd been down to Greenham to deliver some food and clothes to the women; a fucking scary place to be.[37] I went through a period of political awakening, a realization of how the system worked.[38]

TOM WATSON Weller was on a journey politically. I started to genuinely believe in him when I saw him at the CND gigs. You could tell he believed it in his songwriting. That was at a time when he would have seen his fans losing jobs. He was getting so angry with the way the country was going and people respected him for that. It felt like a class was under attack by Thatcher: *The public enemies, number t-t-t-ten.*

SYD SHELTON Back in 1977, Paul Weller had told *NME*, 'We'll be voting Conservative at the next election.'

NEIL SPENCER Paul Weller was a patriot. He loved his country. There was a thing then about running down the country and slagging off Britain. I was always looking for an alternative patriotism and was very influenced by George Orwell's *Lion and the Unicorn*, where he was trying to square being a patriot with his socialist beliefs.

PAUL WELLER That fucking *NME* interview we did. I wasn't right-wing. I was just an ignorant, green kid from a little suburban town, and I really didn't have any views.[39] I was eighteen. It was our first big interview. I really wanted the trendies to hate us and I succeeded in that. It was a mistake.[40]

TRACEY THORN Paul had a lot of unpicking to do to make clear who he was and perhaps it took him until Red Wedge to really make it clear where he was coming from.

ROGER HUDDLE The Jam had done the odd RAR gig towards the end but it wasn't until much later that you realized Weller's songs in terms of consciousness of young people fighting back, that expression of stand up and fight. That's why on the back of the Jam's album *Sound Affects* there's the quote from Shelley's 'The Masque Of Anarchy': *Ye are many – they are few . . .*

DOUG MORRIS Reading Shelley on the back of *Sound Affects* was a big thing for me. It sounds trite, but it was those introductions to literature. Weller articulated that voice of working-class frustration. 'When You're Young' was particularly resonant when I was seventeen: *The world is your oyster but your future's a clam.* And 'The Eton Rifles' which I remember seeing on *Top of the Pops* in my mum's front room, with the smell of Embassys and fried food. I had just got back from school covered in mud from playing football, and seeing *our* band on the telly in the top ten singing *What a catalyst you turned out to be / Loaded the guns then you run off home for your tea* was quite something. The Jam weren't trendy and that was incredibly important.

ROBERT HOWARD I loved the conversational nature of *Sup up your beer and collect your fags.* It's a great opening line. 'The Eton Rifles' was about class: boys with public-school ties and badges. It had a profound effect on me. I'd failed the eleven-plus and been sent to this low-rent boarding school, and that year was my awakening to the realization that there was a class divide. My parents were typical in the sense that that they were working-class and wanted better for their kids and they thought that meant to be middle-class. Paul's education was music, people like Ray Davies and John Lennon and the poetry that came from that. That's what set the Jam apart; the sheer power of the songwriting.

TRACEY THORN 'The Eton Rifles' is a really complicated lyric. It's one thing to be able to write political songs and have ten people buy your record, but to couch it in such a way that you make it catchy and inclusive and you

Tracey Thorn at the ICA, London, performing with Paul Weller, 5 January 1983.

make people feel welcomed rather than alienated – it's really difficult to do. And things like 'Going Underground' or 'Down In The Tube Station At Midnight' which aren't necessarily political but are realist. There's that thing about describing gritty events in real people's lives, recognizable things, that people might go, 'That's happened to me.'

ROBERT ELMS 'The Eton Rifles' was about knowing which side you were on. Are you from a private school or a state school? You can't put it in class-war terms because quite a lot of people on the 'right' side were middle-class. It was a war of progressive versus reactionary.

BERNIE WILCOX Weller wrote 'The Eton Rifles' after a Right to Work march had a bit of a scuffle with the lads from Eton College. I was just gob-smacked how the Jam, who we all thought were Tories, had written the best lyrics of the lot.

PAUL WELLER The unemployment march started out in Liverpool and passed Eton College. All the young chaps came out to jeer and take the piss. It was a mini class war being played out. 'The Eton Rifles' is supposed to be a funny song, but there's also a real sense of resignation to it: *What chance have you got against a tie and a crest?*[41] Eton was just a symbol for the song. It's an imaginary setting, the two classes clashing, with the trendy revolutionary saying to the man in the pub, 'Come on, sup up your beer, there's a row on up the road.' It's like, 'The revolution will start after I've finished my pint.' It's not a political song in the sense of 10 Downing Street politics, but of everyday politics. It's not that I'm bitter about my own education; it was pretty good, in fact. But I think that everyone has a right to a good education. It's the same old story, isn't it? Every man is equal but some are more equal than others.[42] When you're confronted by headlines every day about mass unemployment, when you're seeing devastation of industry and public services, it's going to find its way into your lyrics. 'Going Underground' was a frustrated response to the old saying that the people get the government that it deserves – *the public gets what the public wants*. That anger fuelled a lot of my material at the time.[43]

KAREN WALTER From *NME* letters I knew the fans wanted Paul to be with the Jam forever and he'd let them down in some way by splitting the band up. But that was a younger, angry kid. Paul was changing, growing older and settling down. He was still really passionate but he just packaged his views in a different way. 'Walls Come Tumbling Down!' was such a powerful song. It was in your face. It was like the passion from the Jam.

DOUG MORRIS To get into the top ten a lyric that says, *Are you gonna get to realise / The class war's real and not mythologised / And like Jericho – You see walls can come tumbling down . . .* takes some doing.

STEVE WHITE 'Walls Come Tumbling Down!' had that unashamed message of optimism: *Unity is powerful.* I thought, 'Yes!' When we did the demo Paul said, 'It's got to be a balls-out soul tune. I want it to be very on-beat like a Motown thing. When you do the drum fills, think of Keith Moon.'

PHILL JUPITUS It was those first three lines: *You don't have to take this crap / You don't have to sit back and Relax / You can actually try changing it.* It was the inertia of people wound up. As a pop artist you're seeing the power of your audience every night. You're seeing enthusiasm and surely there's more to it than them dancing and singing along to your songs.

PAUL WELLER *You don't have to take this crap* was about Frankie Goes To Hollywood, and all those crappy fuckin' bands who were like the pop aristocracy, with their suits and pearls.[44] People shouldn't take it too literally. I wouldn't like it to be taken as our final statement as it tends to oversimplify everything we said before. There's a brilliant quote on the album sleeve from Tony Benn which says, 'But, as history teaches us, time and time again, it is not enough to speak or write, or compose songs or poems, about freedom if there are not enough people who are ready to devote their lives to make it all come true.'[45]

TIM WELLS There were a lot of pop bands who were working-class but they weren't singing about it. It was cocktails and girls' music. I wanted to find working-class politics in a band.

PAUL WELLER [Thatcher] and the Tories were trying to dismantle the communities of the working classes: attacks on the trade unions, small businesses disappearing, and so many aspects of English life being closed down to people. There was a phoney pretence that we could suddenly all be middle-class because we were allowed to buy our own houses, get a mortgage, and be in debt for the rest of our lives.[46] If you've got any kind of compassion at all and you see other people suffering, unless you're a complete nonce then I can't see how you can feel, not exactly how these people feel, but you must be able to see that it's wrong and this whole situation is wrong.[47] If you forget the lyrical side I think there was a real optimism in our music.[48]

ROBERT ELMS The Style Council were by far and away my favourite incarnation of anything Paul Weller ever did. Much of the middle-class left had an anti-style, anti-materialistic thing. Well, it's very hard to find working-class people who were anti-materialistic because you've got to have quite a lot to be anti-materialistic; less is only more if you've got loads. I don't see any contradiction between wanting to look good and being left-wing. Lots of people from middle-class backgrounds thought you had to wear a donkey jacket to be authentic. That was bollocks. So I loved it when Weller while being at his most political became his most overtly stylish. I also thought that his message was internationalist and that was important; embracing Europe-ness was very anti-Thatcher. She hated Europe and all it stood for whereas the Style Council were calling records 'The Paris Match'.

BILLY BRAGG Weller was an example to all of us to smarten up and not reject anything stylish out of hand. That's why Weller is the key. You put out a record like 'Shout To The Top' with a B-side called 'Ghosts Of Dachau'. Who else was doing that? And then the cover of 'Walls Come Tumbling Down!' is a picture of Mick Talbot looking lush in eye make-up. It was a parody of a Smiths' cover. It was such a great song. And 'Blood Sports' with the credit on the sleeve: 'The writing royalties to this track go to the Bristol Defence Fund for John Curtin and Terry Helsby, currently in Bristol Prison for anti-bloodsport activities.' If anybody thinks that Weller was sitting at home twiddling his thumbs after the Jam, wearing eye make-up and drinking cappuccino with Mick Talbot . . .

JERRY DAMMERS 'Walls Come Tumbling Down!' was a biblical reference to when they blew the trumpets and the walls of Jericho came tumbling down. Archaeologists now believe that the walls were undermined first; so it wasn't the music. But that is a good point: music on its own isn't going to work. You have to work with non-musical people and political movements that are connected.

DOUG MORRIS I attribute my involvement with political activism to Paul Weller. It was a fan thing at first and it snowballed from there. There's no hiding from it. It's what you pick up on the way.

STEVE WHITE The front cover of the 'Shout To The Top' record sleeve was a model called Stacey Smith – she was Paul Young's girlfriend at the time – wearing a pom-pom-type skirt, orange T-shirt and cardi combo. Girls dressed like that were everywhere at the time. And then on the reverse you get:

> No! To abolition of the GLC & the local councils
> Yes! To the thrill of the romp
> Yes! To the Bengali Workers Association
> Yes! To a nuclear-free world
> Yes! To all involved in animal rights
> Yes! To fanzines
> Yes! To Belief

It was such a positive message.

ROBERT ELMS The cover says you can be young and that being left-wing and being anti-Thatcherite doesn't have to be grim.

TRACEY THORN Having slogans but with really glamorous imagery showed that we'd gone somewhere new. That it was not 1978 any longer. There's no home-made Letraset or things being stuck on with Sellotape or handwriting. It's actually quite mainstream and major record in all its imagery and yet you've got these slogans. Paul was adamant that he wanted to move forward.

ROBERT ELMS These were much more divided times and much more passionate times. In geopolitical terms there was a notion that whilst there was a socialist block there was still an alternative to capitalism. And therefore that was worth fighting for. It was something to shout for, to parade for, to sloganize for. It was something to write songs for.

STEVE WHITE Paul got approached by the Polish Tourist Authority so we made the video of 'Walls Come Tumbling Down!' in Poland and saw the other side of the socialist dream. Warsaw was depressing. The alcoholism was staggering. They'd drink anything. And there was nothing in the shops. You'd come down for breakfast and they might have cornflakes and milk but no sugar. Then the next morning there'd be milk and sugar but no cornflakes. Something was missing all the time. I was never a drinker and the second night I was like, 'I've got to have a drink.' It was so penetrating. That wasn't socialism. That was a brutal dictatorship. There were troops on the street. We only had that in Northern Ireland. Thatcher had aspirations of a one-party state but would never have got that far. Poland was like taking an idea like religion and ruining it with the force of man. That was never going to work in this country. We're too arsey for a start.

PAUL WELLER I didn't know what to make of Poland; I came away totally confused by it. I couldn't tell whether it was that drab and boring because of the supposed Russian presence or oppressive state, or that's how they are as a nation.[49] People always hold up the Eastern bloc as examples that socialism doesn't work, but it [wasn't] socialism, so that argument was redundant. Socialism doesn't mean everyone should have nothing, it means everyone should have something.[50]

PERVERTS SUPPORT THE PITS!

Billy Bragg. Miners' Strike

BILLY BRAGG For many of us, our first experience of mainstream politics was the Miners' Strike of 1984–5. Suddenly, we were involved on the front line, side by side, playing on the picket lines. I was pretty politicized by punk and Rock Against Racism but the Miners' Strike was how I got my degree in politics. When the National Coal Board announced the decision to shut down twenty uneconomic coal mines with a loss of 20,000 jobs in March 1984, the leader of the National Union of Mineworkers, Arthur Scargill, claimed there was a long-term strategy to close over seventy pits. As a result, more than half the country's 187,000 mineworkers were soon out on strike. This was exactly what the Tories planned, their revenge for when the miners went on strike and knocked Ted Heath out of office a decade before. It was ideological and personal. Thatcher was going to cash in on the kudos that she'd gained from the Falklands War and use it to smash the vanguard of the Labour movement. This was class war.

TINY FENNIMORE Thatcher had changed a law prior to the strike to stop miners' families getting any benefits if the main breadwinner went on strike. She was enormously vindictive. Closing the mines was political and not just economic. It had been on the right's agenda for a long time. I had moved to London at about the same time Thatcher arrived. I didn't fit in, in Buckinghamshire where it was very affluent: sit back and relax because we are already very rich. I was political but it wasn't personal at that point. But in London I met lots of people whose lives were really being affected by Thatcher and who were really angry about it. She politicized us all. And then the Miners' Strike made us think about our politics a bit more seriously. It wasn't single-issue groups any more. It was about changing the political status quo. There was a benefit gig at the Wag Club in Soho and I met Pete Jenner who was really gobby. He was telling it like it was and then I noticed this really quiet person next to him. And that was Billy. I thought, 'I want to work with them.'

PETER JENNER Billy ended up with me as his manager through a series of connections. He knew someone in Barking who used to paint the back-drops for the Clash who said, 'You should go and see Pete Jenner.' Billy pulled a stroke, posing as a TV repairman to get past the receptionist, and managed to get in and see me. I remember to this day listening to his tape, and the lyric of 'The Busy Girl Buys Beauty' got me. The company was broke so I persuaded the publishers to pay for two demo sessions. We were all in desperate straits. I was skint. Billy was skint. It was all just done on tap. We had to find a way of making money for something which was against the standard drift of the pop market. Billy's first album, *Life's A Riot*, was political with a small 'p'. It was all very Spandau Ballet and Duran Duran and people in silly glamour clothes and on yachts. Billy was the opposite of that. He wasn't fashionable. He sang songs about real people. It was quite clearly an anti thing in the spirit of the Clash and punk and folk music. It was about the people's music.

TINY FENNIMORE The first time I saw Billy was at the Dominion on Totten-ham Court Road when he was supporting the Style Council. I remember thinking, 'My God, this is a whole room full of people who think exactly like me.' It was like my community and a natural home. And Billy was so powerful on stage; just one man and his guitar. That was the first time I thought anything might be achievable. That pop and politics had com-bined with somebody that was popular; and quite hot, actually. It was the force of his personality. He was very charismatic and sugared the pill of politics with wit. People wanted to listen and the entertainment value was driving the politics forward.

BILLY BRAGG The electric guitar was an ideological statement against both the synthesizer and the folk club. I still felt the burning fire of punk rock. It had left the front of the *NME* but it hadn't left me. At the Rock Against Racism Carnival in Victoria Park when Patrik Fitzgerald came out and played with an acoustic guitar and they bottled him off, I remember think-ing, 'You fucking idiot. All that solo singer-songwriter stuff is dumb.' If he had come out with a Telecaster and cranked it out he would have gone down a storm, whereas it was the Clash who sealed their fate as rock's greatest rebels that day. It was their greatest moment and I naively believed the Clash were going to change the world. Later, I realized you don't change the world by simply just singing songs and doing gigs.

PETER JENNER The key difference between Billy and the Clash was that he walked it as he talked it. There was coherence with Billy and he was writing socially aware songs. I wasn't pushing the agenda of his songwriting but I was pushing the agenda of the environment in which he performed. I certainly had a conscious view that in some senses he was Bob Dylan for his times. I always thought with the Clash there was an element of bullshit. I had taken them on as they were recording *London Calling* and I never felt that Joe Strummer had an articulated position. He was unbelievably inconsistent. There was no political coherence and a contradiction between what the Clash said and what they did. The Clash didn't talk it like they walked it. And they were really hurt by the fact that they were dependent on CBS Records. They wanted to do the people's show but on the other hand they wanted to be rock stars and do the big show and stay in big hotels. I remember having a discussion with them and saying, 'Really all the punters want is to see you; everything else is not what they're paying for.'

ROBERT HOWARD Pete Jenner was my manager for many years. He used to say, 'Joe Strummer was all over the place, and just used to write slogans.' What were the Clash meant to deliver, politically? Were they meant to ascend to Parliament and become our representatives? No. What they delivered was Billy Bragg. But what is politics if it's not sloganeering? You have to chuck these things out there in order to capture people's attention and stimulate their imagination and hopefully lead them into some form of self-knowledge. The Clash were fucking brilliant in terms of dropping little pieces in the ointment that would expand and lead you to amazing places. I hadn't heard of Sandinistas before the Clash and I went searching and that led me on to all sorts of stuff. Joe Strummer is going to be a far more pivotal, inspirational figure to you as a teenager than some politician. But in the end it has to come from within. You can't create with the weight of responsibility. You write it and you put it out in the universe and let it take care of itself. And if it's true, it transmits. You can't manufacture that.

DAVE WAKELING It was worrying for me with Joe Strummer – and Jerry Dammers – coming not just from a higher class than me, but from the political *nomenklatura*. If you're born in an embassy and you've got a family seat in Hertfordshire, is it all right to want *a riot of your own*? I knew from the riots in Handsworth that the next thing is there's no buses and you have to walk two miles to get a bottle of milk and the shops don't come back. I couldn't agree with Kevin Rowland that *the only way to change things is to shoot men who arrange things*. I said to Jerry and Joe that we should be very careful [about] abusing the goodwill and the big hearts of the working class and we shouldn't say, 'We're doing it in their name.' Jerry got it but Joe didn't talk to me for a bit.

NEIL SPENCER It wasn't Joe Strummer's job to have a coherent political credo. His job was to be a creator. We ask too much of musicians. It's not their job. But Billy did it. He modelled himself as Woody Guthrie plus electricity.

TINY FENNIMORE Billy definitely walked it like he talked it. There are always going to be people that are going to have a pop at you when you try and do good things. Billy was a prime target. Touring with him opened my eyes and I went to a lot of places where people were poor and disenfranchised: a lot of love but awful poverty, no money. He was just cutting his political teeth and I was writing about politics in *Jamming* and other magazines, but he caught up very quickly. I'm not saying I wasn't influential but Peter is key to Billy's politics. He was a Cambridge graduate of politics, philosophy and economics and a teacher at the London School of Economics at twenty-one. If you went on tour with Peter you went to all the political landmarks: Martin Luther King's church; Trotsky's house. He was always pushing books Billy's way.

PETER JENNER I had a lot to do with tuning Billy's mindset. He hadn't been particularly political or even voted in '79, but there was a strong Labour Party tradition where he came from. Barking was trade union territory. I came from an academic background so in a sense he was the pupil and I was the professor.

•

PETER JENNER Then there was the Miners' Strike: Billy would have his guitar and amp and would do any gig anywhere if they would pay his fare, put him up and give him a meal. It gave him this incredible personal link with the various unions and miners and support groups. A lot of people said, 'No, no, don't do that, it will be really bad for you. You'll never get on radio.' But I was saying, 'No, go for it.' I'd been through the Sixties and I realized if you do something which is anti that is moving with a social movement, it's a good move. Billy's music was providing a place for people to meet and express their solidarity and have a bit of fun. It was a demonstration of political solidarity and he was always very good at never laying down the party line. What the solution was and where do we go and how do we politically organize wasn't our job. My father was a vicar in working-class parishes. They were always doing things to raise money for the church – whist drives, socials – and in some sense it was going back to that. It was the process of having money raised that was as important as the money that you raised.

BILLY BRAGG Tiny and Peter played their part. But they didn't come and sleep on the sofas in miners' houses, which made me start to think and write and talk ideologically. I could travel lightly with a little amp, guitar, and bag on my back and I would think nothing of jumping on a train with my punk sensibility and Clash covers to tell them how it was. The first one I got to there was some really old geezer called Jock Purdon singing a cappella. He'd got his hand over his ear, and his songs are so much more radical than mine. I'm thinking, 'Shit. I'm going to have rethink how I'm going to do this. It's not quite how I expected it.' I talked to them and they said, 'This is not something that just happened this week. Jock represents a tradition of political radical songs and by coming up here and standing with the miners you're joining that tradition, son.' I thought, 'Flippin' heck. You're right.' I knew enough about Bob Dylan to know some of the old English folk songs that had inspired him and which I had borrowed from Barking Library as a teenager, so I wrote 'Between The Wars'; a hymn to socialism and Thatcher dragging us towards a 1984 situation.

'Between The Wars' meant between the last war and the next one. It was me saying, 'I am not *of* the tradition but I am *part* of it now.' It's almost like a broadside ballad; when an event would happen and somebody would write a song and they'd sell them for a penny on the street.

ANNAJOY DAVID 'Between The Wars' was such a beautiful song. It was a call to Britain to say, 'Don't forget who you are.'

ROBERT ELMS *Sweet moderation, heart of this nation* is one of the great lines of any piece of British political pop music. What Billy so cleverly did was turn the tables by portraying the right as the aggressors and the war-mongers. And the left as those that like peace and are the moderates and don't want to divide people by class or race.

TRACEY THORN I remember Billy doing it live on *Top of the Pops* and being introduced by Steve Wright, 'This really is an evocative song . . .' Billy is someone who's very positive about political action and a believer in people; *sweet moderation, heart of this nation* is his politics in a nutshell. Political songwriters are often characterized as negative and constantly slagging things off and criticizing, but I do think of Billy as one of life's great positive thinkers. He is the standard-bearer for it all.

TINY FENNIMORE It felt like victory when we got 'Between The Wars' on *Top of the Pops*. Billy's father had been in the tank regiment and at the Go! Discs office I had a letter stuck on the wall from a soldier who had heard the record and had bought himself out of the army and was now a political activist. Whenever I made tea the letter would galvanize me. I would say to Billy, 'We're changing hearts and minds one by one.'

BILLY BRAGG The gigs during the strike were incredibly powerful. I had been on the cover of *NME* so to the audiences I was quite well known, but for the miners and their families who tended to be a little bit older they weren't really listening to this kind of stuff. Their response was more, 'Why

Between The Wars EP front cover, March 1985.

is a pop star from London coming to do this?' It was in trying to explain to them why that I learnt to speak the ideological language of Marxism. And I was defining myself politically as a socialist, which I hadn't done before. There was a gig at the Sunderland Bunker that really stands out because it was the first time I saw the Miners' Support Groups in action. These would be working-class women who had never spoken in public before, and that really impressed me. I dedicated the *Between The Wars* EP to them. Being there wasn't just a show of solidarity: it was a means by which you allowed other people to show their solidarity. In political terms it allowed you to feel that you were not alone. It was exactly the same experience I had at Rock Against Racism.

•

STEVE WHITE From the Style Council's point of view the Miners' Strike was pivotal. The industrial strike was dividing Britain north and south and we were doing a lot of benefits for the miners' families, raising money for kids' toys for Christmas. Those families were being treated appallingly. The miners' wives galvanized themselves amazingly and held themselves with real dignity. They were very gracious and were very happy to accept the help in the spirit of what we were giving.

PAUL WELLER If you travelled up north you could see how hard the Thatcher Gang's economics had hit it. By the end of her tenure, there weren't any vital industries left. And all this was done whilst still flying the flag. Incredibly, she got away with it for eighteen years.[51]

JUNIOR GISCOMBE I'd go up with Paul and you'd see areas where there was nothing, just weeds; people still living but nobody working. The clothes were dowdy. We talked to miners' wives who'd bring their little kids and you'd hear how they'd been treated. They told us that the police would come and knock on their doors and take their husbands and beat them outside their house. We went to a school where families lived in the main hall and had no food and they were scared to go back to their houses. This was England. This wasn't political, this was now about food. You were seeing injustices and talking with people who were completely different to you and hearing how they saw things and how they lived. I was angry.

PAUL HEATON I had first-hand experience of the strike on the picket line, at Hatfield Main and Thorn, and Armthorpe. Nobody had heard of the Housemartins, so I'd just say I was from the Hull Musicians' Collective,

Paul Heaton (far left) with the Housemartins, circa 1985.

which was me just making it up but it was another name they could read out on the list. We tried to get to Orgreave but we got turned back on the road out of Hull. The policing was outrageous but the coverage of the strike was unbelievably biased against the miners. Arthur Scargill was on the BBC News one time. It was supposed to be impartial but the venom towards him was unbelievable and totally reactionary.

KEITH HARRIS I was president of Dundee Students' Union during the miners' strike of 1974, but I don't think I'd ever seen the forces of the establishment so totally aligned before as they were a decade later. It was the first time that I was seeing the police force being used as a tool of the government; almost as a quasi-paramilitary organization. The role of the police is to keep peace and order, not to take sides in a political dispute. And what bothered me more was, the media seemed to reinforce that position. There didn't seem to be any balance.

STEVE WHITE I had a friend who was a police officer and he'd wind me up: 'You all right, Trotsky?' And I'd say, 'How you enjoying being one of Thatcher's bootboys?' 'Bloody overtime, yeah, I'm lovin' it. I'm off to South Yorkshire, gonna give a few a crack.' Years later, I said to him, 'What did you think about all that?' And he said, 'We were being used, weren't we?'

He said, 'It was the politicization of the police. The job has never been the same since.' During the strike, they would move a police force around; a tactic employed to ensure that police had minimal sympathy or commonality with the protestors, so you'd get the Met going to South Yorkshire or the Cumbrians going to the fields in Kent. It was very clever, very decisive, very calculated and very disheartening.

CATHAL SMYTH I felt the police had been duped by the machine. They'd lost sight of their purpose to protect and defend society.

NEIL SPENCER It all started to get very sinister. The BBC reversed the clip of the Battle of Orgreave, showing the miners throwing stones at the police on horseback first. Everything was being manipulated. Thatcher had an iron grip on the police and the media. It was scary. It wasn't politics as anybody in post-war Britain had experienced it.

KAREN WALTER I remember seeing Orgreave on television and just not believing it. It was so atrocious: police and miners in pitched battles. *NME* was involved and we had miners coming down to the office. We had a benefit at the Wag Club with the Redskins and Julian Clary, who performed with Fanny the Wonder Dog. At one point he got really angry with the dog because it wouldn't do as it was told, and, as animal lovers, we were disgusted.

COLIN BYRNE I was walking down the Holloway Road with a member of the National Union of Students executive and saying, 'Isn't it cool that Wham! are on *Top of the Pops* and also backing the miners?' Now, that would be like One Direction suddenly backing Labour in the next election. It was pretty momentous stuff.

STEVE WHITE Wham! played with the Style Council at a miners' benefit at the Royal Festival Hall and somebody had a go at George Michael because he was miming. I remember biting their head off: 'At least they're fucking here.'

PAUL HEATON The strike began to motivate my lyrics and we started doing political gigs in favour of the miners. I had a point to prove and I had a lot of anger in me. On *Wide Awake Club* Tommy Boyd asked me, 'Who's your hero?' and I said, 'Arthur Scargill.' There was a stony silence. My dad was a believer that people on the far left are important to stretch the Labour Party. Ask for Utopia and you might get a decent lifestyle, which is why bands like the Redskins were important even though they didn't sell the records. Chris Dean made my position look more plausible for a start, as my position made Billy Bragg look good; everybody out there on the left made it easier for one another. Alone, you were very open to attack.

RICHARD COLES The Miners' Strike got very brutal, especially after David Wilkie got killed when two miners dropped a concrete block on his taxi in South Wales which was carrying a strike-breaker. I remember Paul [Weller] condemned the action, but as a class warrior – I'm ashamed to say it now – I thought it was collateral damage of a just war. Paul quite rightly said, 'This is not acceptable.' He had a broader conscience.

PAUL WELLER It seemed whenever you turned on the news there was a policeman smashing someone on the head with a stick somewhere in the world. And then it was happening in Britain as well. One minute the miners were the nation's heroes, bravely digging our coal, the backbone of the nation; the next they were the filthy red scum.[52]

I always regarded the class division as the real rot in our society, especially growing up in Woking, where affluence and financial struggle were very apparent.[53]

ANNAJOY DAVID The Miners' Strike was very brutal, not just physically but emotionally on families. You're telling people that everything that they stand for is valueless. That was wrong. They needed a voice. How Thatcher did it was not just inhumane but inexcusable. The whole Jam / Style Council scene became really politicized through the strike. It was a big stand for that generation of working-class kids. There was a lot at stake: the impact of this huge moment of de-industrialization of Britain. It was incredibly important to stand up collectively. That's why you got the 'Soul Deep' record; the notion of the collective, the responsible, coming together to change things. It was a way of saying Britain is a collective society; it does have other voices. We're going to stand by those.

JUNIOR GISCOMBE I got a phone call from Paul saying, 'I've got this track but the whole thing is not to make a Style Council record. I've got Dee C. Lee, Jimmy Ruffin, Leonardo Chignoli, Vaughn Toulouse and Dizzy Hites'. I went down to the studio and did my vocal on the same day as Jimmy Ruffin.

PAUL WELLER We put 'Soul Deep' out as the Council Collective because there was equal involvement from everybody, and also as a way of putting the song first. We didn't want who it was by to matter; we wanted people to listen to what it was saying. I think it was important to have records in the charts which [showed] a more realistic side of life. There [were] all these bands making videos in exotic places and singing about what a great time they were having and how marvellous the world [was]. But everything isn't marvellous for everyone.[54] We raised £10,000, which we sent to Women Against Pit Closures just before Christmas: that was one of the main objectives of the record. The other one – which was a bit naive – was that maybe we could get across the miners' point of view and why people should have supported them.[55]

JUNIOR GISCOMBE After we finished recording the record I went on tour in America and then came back to find London Records had tried to take my voice off it; one of the promotions guys in a drunken stupor started telling me what was going on. I'd go into a meeting with three white guys in a record company and they were amazed. They'd sit back and say, 'Junior, you're the first black guy I've ever met who's articulate.' You'd sit there and think, 'You stupid bastard. I'm sitting in front of three hood rats and you're dealing with a street rat that knows how to manoeuvre.'

KEITH HARRIS I was managing Junior at the time and the record company saw him as a lightweight, lovable pop artist. And they were probably rightly aware that being involved with 'Soul Deep' would damage his chances of going on to be a much-loved pop artist, given that he was black. Lots of British black performers would have one hit and then disappear. In order to have more than one hit you needed to get support from radio and press, but there was a one-at-a-time policy. I'd been aware of the issues when I had been head of promotions at Motown Records. I remember taking a Commodores record to Radio 1 and being told, 'Well, we're already playing Earth, Wind and Fire: that's enough of that kind of music.' So the record company were not supportive of Junior being involved in such an overtly political record. It was OK for Paul Weller, because that was hip, but for Junior it was, 'Know your place; you're not meant to have that insight.' A black pop performer wasn't perceived as being capable of talking on these issues; where would he get the intelligence from? I could write a book on why black artists never got airplay.

JUNIOR GISCOMBE The B-side of 'Soul Deep' was an idea Paul and myself had spoken about. We said, 'Kids should be able to turn the record over and listen to the miners' plight.'

PHILL JUPITUS 'A Miners' Point' was a conversation between two striking miners and was tangible evidence of what Thatcherism was doing to the country. This was an age when you could look at a group of MPs and physically tell them apart: 'Labour, Labour, Tory, Labour, Tory, Labour'; just literally quality of clothes.

NEIL SPENCER In a speech to the 1922 Committee at the House of Commons, the Prime Minister compared mining communities with the Argentinian dictator General Galtieri and talked of her own citizens as 'the enemy within'. That could have come from a talk by Adolf.

RICHARD COLES I remember the iron in my soul when she described the striking miners as 'the enemy within'. I thought, 'They're the people you were elected to serve, actually.' I remember vowing one day I would dance on her grave and, irony of ironies, years later, I walked into my church and there was Margaret Thatcher at the back. She was a frail old lady who wasn't sure what was going on. There she was, a real person, confused and frail and vulnerable. I said, 'Hello.' It told me something about the distance I'd travelled. In retrospect, there was always a vicar in me trying to get out; back then pop music was my hymns.

BILLY BRAGG I woke up on tour in Salford on 12 October 1984 to discover the IRA had bombed the Grand Hotel in Brighton – killing five people and injuring thirty-five – in an attempt to assassinate the Prime Minister. Everything But The Girl were staying above me in the hotel and they had complained about us staying up all night making a noise; Ben and Tracey were like your mum and dad on tour. I remember saying to them when none of the cabinet had been killed, 'Well, thank fuck for that, because in the middle of the Miners' Strike if the IRA had killed the government, who do you think would have been in charge tomorrow morning?' It would have been someone with a peaked cap and a uniform; martial law would have been declared, and the miners' leaders would have been rounded up.

TINY FENNIMORE Margaret Thatcher's personal papers reveal that at the Conservative Party conference the day after her assassination attempt she had intended to talk of 'an insurrection' and declare that 'our country is not to be torn apart by an extension of the calculated chaos planned for the mining industry by a handful of trained Marxists and their fellow travellers'. But most incredibly, having previously called supporters of the Miners' Strike 'the enemy within', she intended to accuse them now of being 'enemies of freedom and democracy itself'.

•

ANGELA EAGLE During the Miners' Strike the *Sun* headline was 'PER-VERTS SUPPORT THE PITS!'

TOM ROBINSON Working on Gay Switchboard in the early seventies we'd had calls from miners saying they'd dared not come out and how terrifyingly macho that whole culture was. A group formed called Lesbian and Gays Support the Miners and they went with collecting tins, putting on gigs and marching in solidarity with the miners to raise money for their families. Then at Gay Pride, a Welsh miner's wife from the valleys came on to thank all the lesbians and gays for their fantastic support and how deeply it was appreciated. She said, 'I would be proud for any child of mine to be gay.'

CLARE SHORT I did lots of meetings and collecting tins of beans. The miners and the miners' wives were heroic. But the National Union of Mineworkers not having a ballot and allowing the division; Arthur Scargill led that really badly. He would have won it. The miners would have been completely united instead of divided. Scargill's ego was out of control so the strike-break back to work on 3 March 1985 was a tragedy. But again, you knew whose side you were on. And political resistance had to go on to not allow forces of reaction to be victorious. You might have lost the battle but not lost the war.

TINY FENNIMORE Arthur Scargill said, 'We face not an employer but a government aided and abetted by the judiciary, the police and you people in the media.' He later accused Neil Kinnock of 'betraying the miners' for not fully supporting the miners' strike action.

JOHN BAINE Kinnock betrayed the miners and yet I thought, 'We're trying to get this fucker elected.'

NEIL SPENCER Neil would have hit the roof at being accused of selling out the miners. He was quite inflammable. It was also completely untrue. Thatcher played her hand well. They starved the miners into submission and there was the tactic of Spencerism where you bribe people to go back and be scabs. That was articulated in *Billy Elliot* when his old man goes back to work and he's on the coach and all the rocks are coming down.

ANDY MCSMITH It was unfair to say Neil Kinnock wasn't backing the miners. He was saying that the miners should have called a ballot.

LARRY WHITTY Neil was not sufficiently supportive but his supposed lack of empathy with Scargill may have been right. Neil was right to be suspicious. But the Labour Party weren't there, and that was a deficiency and a disaster for all sorts of reasons. If you went to a concert or you were walking down the high street and there were people collecting for the miners, 'Why is the Labour Party not behind it?' It was a real disillusionment factor, but life is more complicated than that.

NEIL KINNOCK The miners saw what I did. They saw what I was. They knew where I came from. But the strike was bloody devastating. It inflicted serious damage on the Labour movement because of our association – of which I was very proud – with the coal miners, and with Arthur Scargill and his leadership, which I despised. There was a difference between coal-mining communities, the case for coal – of which I made forty speeches at the time – and Scargill. The miners' defeat in my view was an avoidable defeat or one that could have been substantially mitigated. The strike inflicted appalling misery on the coal-mining communities, of which one, Islwyn, I represented. But besides all that was an amazing solidarity. There was a common struggle and all kinds of barriers of distance, class, taste and custom just came bloody crashing down as people helped each other; and part of that was music.

SARAH JANE MORRIS I did over 150 benefits for the miners with the Happy End, a twenty-one-piece political band. We recorded 'Coal Not Dole' and the lyrics were written by a Kent miner's wife called Kay Sutcliffe. It was an anthem of the strike and we performed the song at the Bush Theatre knowing the miners had basically lost. All of us were crying. It was a terrible feeling. All the way through the strike we had felt so much we were part of something.

PAUL HEATON On the last day of the strike there were hundreds and hundreds of miners in tears singing 'You'll Never Walk Alone'. It was incredibly moving and their strength gave me strength and inspired the way I work to this day.

BILLY BRAGG I was at RAF Molesworth being chained to a fence at an anti-nuclear demo when word came through on the radio that the miners had decided to go back. For those of us who had been active it was like, 'Well, is that it? Do we all go back to our stupid fucking jobs, turning up in *Smash Hits*?' I spoke to a few people and said, 'The next viable opportunity we're going to get rid of the Tories is the next election.'

ANNAJOY DAVID The turning point to move into a party political sphere definitely came during the strike. My lasting memory was when I saw a bunch of women in Wales in a mining community literally fighting for their families' future and their whole social identity. I thought that was criminal. It wasn't only about jobs: it was about a way of life, about people's cultural references, about who they were and where they'd come from and what Britain was. I felt it was time for us to take our cultural politics into that world and stand beside it and say, 'This is wrong.'

THE MILKMAN OF HUMAN KINDNESS

Live Aid. GLC. Jobs For Youth. Solid Bond

PHILL JUPITUS The most political record of the era was Band Aid's 'Do They Know It's Christmas?' in December 1984. Bob Geldof and Midge Ure got their black books out; got everybody they knew, got studio time, and then got record companies to turn it round quickly so it shot straight to number one. And then that mania that Geldof had on the day of Live Aid, 'Just send us your fuckin' money.' Direct action. It was getting something done. Charity and politics is tugging at the heartstrings.

STEVE WHITE There was 'before Live Aid' and there was 'after Live Aid.' It's really easy to sneer about that kind of thing but musicians and creative people are always the first to be in the queue; they're giving people.

COLIN BYRNE Live Aid was something different: to campaign against terrible poverty in Africa. It reached out across a whole giving generation but it wasn't political with a big 'P.'

ALEX DALLAS Live Aid was another big step in terms of musicians having an opinion and actually doing something and not just being rock stars.

JUNIOR GISCOMBE I was seeing people on the street in England who weren't eating and here we were asking people at home to give to Africa. I've got nothing against giving to Africa but I figured this was more important because this was home.

TOM ROBINSON Live Aid was able to change the world in an immeasurable way through music in a way we hadn't before. It reached a global mass audience. And you could say that thanks to Bob Geldof's efforts literally hundreds and thousands of people did not die. I don't care what his motivations were. Who gives a fuck? Who knows what anybody's motives were for anything that any of us did: Joe Strummer, me or Rock Against Racism? The only thing that you can measure is the result: was there was a measurable change for the better?

PETER JENNER Did Live Aid do any good? A remarkably small amount of money actually got through, to people getting food. The important thing about Live Aid was raising the issue and making people aware. That's what political music can do; make people aware of issues.

JERRY DAMMERS 'Do They Know It's Christmas?' showed pop stars still had power to try and do good things even if they weren't specifically political in their lyrics. And I like to think '(Free) Nelson Mandela', nine months before, was in the back of Bob Geldof's mind somewhere when he thought of Band Aid, and it had at least showed that you could bring artists together on a record, and pop music could still be used for some sort of good purposes. In the seventies there was a Philly record called 'Let's Clean Up The Ghetto' by MFSB (Mother Father Sister Brother) which had a lot of artists singing on one record for the cause of clearing the rubbish from the streets. I think it was the first time that had been done. I thought it would be good to revive that idea.

And then shortly after, a fan walked into Madness's office in North London and suggested they do a version of the Pioneers track 'Starvation' in aid of the Ethiopian appeal. I was brought in to produce and arrange the record and many of the artists in and around 2 Tone got involved – members of UB40, the Beat and the Specials. We just wanted to do our bit and show solidarity with the Band Aid record.

NEIL SPENCER The terrain of British popular music in the early to middle eighties meant that you did have mainstream charity records like 'Soul Deep' and 'Starvation' and Band Aid next to people like Crass and the Redskins but you also had the club crowd and DJs. It was a very radical force in youth culture. That was where black and white youth encountered each other, and suddenly we've got British soul. There was a real disconnect between the world of Boy George and Spandau Ballet, and Billy Bragg; they represented something unspeakable to a lot of *NME* readers.

ROBERT ELMS It divided into different musical camps. Working at the *Face*, I was seen as being in the Spandau, trendies camp. There was a lot of that but we all knew we were on the same side. Many people perceived the whole Blitz Club scene as right-wing and benefiting from the wealth and individualism that Thatcher was promoting. Believe me, it wasn't. I knew lots of people, artists or musicians or fashion designers or photographers or DJs, who were intrinsically left-wing and had a lot to offer to a vague anti-Thatcherite cause. Spandau Ballet were all out of council estates in Islington. Sade was the daughter of a nurse in Clacton. They had genuine left-wing conviction but it wasn't of that solid, northern, collectivist kind like Glenn Gregory and Heaven 17. It wasn't Little England. The clubs were a place for cross-dressers and people of all different colours, and that was a radical thing to be in favour of in the late seventies and early eighties. It was dangerous. You'd regularly get beaten up or chased up the road for having a gay or black mate alongside you. I hated small-minded little England which manifested itself, like Thatcher, in this vehement distaste for everything that was different. But at the same time I respected that working-class trade union tradition that my family came from, but which I knew was dying on its feet. It was a generational battle between an old England and a new England: the old England represented by Thatcher, and the other England is what we've become: open, tolerant, multicultural, and less homophobic. That's what all those songs were about. I'm sure that the Billy Bragg contingent treated us with huge wariness: 'Who are these fancily dressed people in all their expensive clothes?' Even though my mum worked in Woolworths, my dad was a trade unionist.

•

NEIL SPENCER The two great engines of national regeneration are creativity and education, and whether the Tories liked it or not the identity of the country had much more to do with the Beatles than World War II or the Falklands. I remember talking to Ken Livingstone, the leader of the Greater London Council, and he said this amazing thing: 'If you invest in the arts you end up employing a lot of people because a lot of people work part-time so you actually create far more jobs than you think you're going to.' You fund a theatre company, you were employing all kinds of misfits who hang around the edges and get a little bit of money here and there; people who were never going to work for the Royal Shakespeare Company.

PETER JENNER The GLC was very important. It was political and they were very aware of the need to utilize public spaces. It solidified the whole Labour London thing and it was back to the Sixties' free concerts, in a sense: we could play free concerts and therefore get access to large numbers of people.

TOM SAWYER The GLC was a cultural beacon. Ken Livingstone helped a lot of gigs in London get off the ground. You didn't have to be rich to see these artists out on a stage in a park in London. It was part of an anti-Thatcher movement.

TINY FENNIMORE All those free concerts were a fantastic focus of opposition and a platform to get across to huge audiences. But they were also a huge promotional tool for the GLC. Ken Livingstone was seeing it as a way of inspiring young people to vote Labour.

TOM WATSON There was an amazing guy called Peter Wells-Thorpe who ran the Youth Trade Union Rights Campaign. He put on a gig in Jubilee Gardens with the Style Council and The Men They Couldn't Hang. It was a great day. I used to brag when I went back to Kidderminster that I had roadied for Paul Weller but what I actually did was run a few errands for Peter and he let me hang around backstage.

SARAH JANE MORRIS We were fascinated by Ken Livingstone. He had such energy and conviction and we liked what he stood for. Nearly every weekend there was some kind of multicultural festival going on. Just generally living in London in the eighties was very exciting when you were an artist: fringe theatre, fringe music, fringe film, the Shaw Theatre, the Bush Theatre, Roland Muldoon's CAST New Variety project. It was touring socialism with music and poetry and stand-up comedians. It's where I started out. Thatcherism was taking hold and nearly all the material was against her. It was about knowing the enemy, and we made politics swing.

JULIET DE VALERO WILLS The GLC always had good generous budgets; even if you were quite low on the bill you would get paid a proper fee. They approached it from a union perspective: 'You've got to pay people properly.'

JOOLZ DENBY There's a hilarious photograph of me and Ken Livingstone that was in the *NME* where we appear to be discussing deep and serious matters – the meeting between goth and politics – and we were actually talking about newts. He liked newts and I had a pond.

RICHARD COLES Ken was one of the reasons we were in existence and was a hero of mine. It was the first time I had ever voted for somebody who made an improvement to my life. He put money into September in the Pink, the first London festival of lesbian and gay arts. Bronski Beat got together to play that gig.

JOHN NEWBEGIN 1985 was United Nations International Youth Year and the GLC and the Inner London Education Authority wanted a director of the London Youth Festival, and I got the job. One of the first events that I organized was in Jubilee Gardens. Hip hop was just coming into style

and I got Tim Westwood, who was then an unknown DJ, and lots of break-
dance crews and graffiti artists from all over the country. And tens of
thousands of black kids turned up. The police got very edgy and closed
Waterloo Station; then they closed Embankment Station; and then finally
they pulled the plug on the whole event and said, 'We're concerned that
this is going to get completely out of hand.' Subsequently, the GLC was
very much criticized for a bread and circuses approach, but those big free
events were hugely significant. It was probably the only time in the history
of local governments when the institutions of local government were
regarded as cool by young people and by young black people. Everybody
thought that the GLC was cool. Thatcher was immensely frustrated by the
fact that the Tories were unable to get control of the GLC and the ILEA.
They represented everything she hated. It was a manifestation of the
public benefits of state spending. Thatcher's answer was to abolish it.

ANNAJOY DAVID Paul Weller became president of the British Youth Council's International Youth Year in 1985 with the actress Julie Walters. There
was a lot of regional work supporting particular kinds of arts-based projects and learning projects in schools, leisure and sports, and on housing
estates. I would help to set those up and Paul and Julie would come in and
be supportive. It was perfect for Paul to move on beyond CND to a wider
youth audience on a broader scale. And a lot of people in the arts in the
eighties were working-class. That was really significant because it brought
a culture and a language of understanding of where you'd come from to
where you were going.

JERRY DAMMERS Annajoy got us to do something for International Youth
Year and on the wall they had the United Nations logo with the laurel
leaves on it. Paul said, 'I recognize that. Where's that from?' I said, 'Fred
Perry shirt.' He said, 'Oh, yeah!'

PAUL WELLER I spoke at the first national conference in Sheffield, which
was interesting. There [were] several different aims to it, [depending on]
who you talked to. There [were] lots of hiking clubs and Brownie groups,
which [was] fine, but there was also the people whose interest [was] more
political – that was more the side I [wanted] to be involved in; to create a
circulation of information among young people through all these groups,
then use it in a political way.[56]

ANGELA EAGLE The Tories were describing what Ken Livingstone was
doing in London as 'loony lefties'. We were all being labelled as vegetarian,

lesbian, black-loving, whatever, and that was all true but it was an exaggeration of what was going on. There was a broadening and an understanding of what we needed to do to properly represent the whole of our country.

JOHN NEWBEGIN Ken always positioned himself as an outsider. He was a tricky politician but personified the GLC. The relationship between Ken Livingstone's and Neil Kinnock's office was very poor. There was a lot of personal animus.

LARRY WHITTY It was part of my mission as general secretary of the Labour Party and one of the people around Neil to pick up on what the GLC had done despite Ken Livingstone and Neil being at daggers drawn. The GLC had mobilized all sorts of people artistically and politically in London, which included the women's movement and to some extent the gay movement, which the Labour Party were a bit iffy about but the GLC weren't. The original term 'New Labour' was about Ken Livingstone's approach and the rainbow coalition of feminism, ethnic minorities and gay liberation; all of these things were pejoratively thought of as new Labour with a small 'n'. And that was spilling over into the Labour Party having to address these issues more positively.

PETER JENNER Labour had lost in '83 and then lost the Miners' Strike. I thought, 'Right, what are we going to do about winning the next election?' My political background is such that I had no fear in just phoning up the Labour Party and saying, 'I want to come and see you.' My grandfather, Edward Frank Wise, was an important member of the Independent Labour Party in the thirties. He died of a heart attack just after he'd run off with Jennie Lee, who would later marry Nye Bevan and become the first Minister for the Arts in 1964 under Harold Wilson's Labour government. Politics was in the family. In '68 and '69 I did the Hyde Park free concerts with Pink Floyd and the Rolling Stones, and that put me in touch with the possibility you could just do things. It was linking my political background with an awareness of being underground and that coincided with Billy Bragg's less well articulated sense of where he was and what he was doing.

BILLY BRAGG If you'd seen Jenner's passport photograph in 1984: he looked like he was in the *OZ* trial. He had hair down to here. We were in the van driving to a gig and he chucks Tony Palmer's book *All You Need is Love: The Story of Popular Music* over to me and says, 'See if I'm in there?' I go to his very first entry and he's managing Pink Floyd and driving them

Neil Kinnock at the Free Trade Hall, Manchester, 20 May 1984.

to Felixstowe to catch a ferry. And here he is all these years later driving me to a gig. The point is, I had a manager who was as hands-on as that and who wanted to get involved. We went to the Euro Election campaign at the Free Trade Hall in Manchester and if I tell you who else was on the bill you'll see what a problem Labour had with the arts: the harmonica player Larry Adler; Bill Owen, who was Compo in *Last of the Summer Wine*; and Clive Dunn, who was [Charlie 'Grandad' Quick in] *Grandad*. I was standing in the stalls helping to tie up balloons and Neil Kinnock walked onto the stage, picked up a guitar and started playing 'Help Me Make It Through The Night'. I thought, 'That's fucking incredible.' I was really impressed.

NEIL KINNOCK It was not a very good rendition and I was too embarrassed to play in front of Billy again after that: me and my five chords. I went home and said to my kids, Stephen and Rachel – and what they didn't know about music wasn't worth knowing – 'Tell me about Billy Bragg?'

ANDY MCSMITH There was a very energetic researcher called Tony Manwaring and he got a call out of the blue from Pete Jenner, who said, 'We've got a singer by the name of Billy Bragg who is going to be big and is keen to get involved in the Labour Party.' Peter came in with Billy and they were clearly the real deal.

TONY MANWARING I was head of the general secretary's office and running the Party organization on behalf of Larry Whitty. I had a licence to operate which said 'to do good and impressive things'. This was from a party that was a long way from power and needed to go through a lot of soul-searching and reflection. Larry and Neil understood the scale of the task and the very profound gap between where Labour was and winning an election. There was a sense of a new socialism about building values and principles in the community, and we were hugely motivated and committed to making Britain a better place in the context of what clearly was not happening under Margaret Thatcher.

ANDY MCSMITH Tony Manwaring and I had the task of convincing John Smith who was shadow Trade and Industry that Billy would be an asset to the party. There was a blank reaction. John went back to Edinburgh for the weekend and he came back on Monday morning full of enthusiasm. Apparently he'd asked his daughters who Billy Bragg was and they had excitedly endorsed him. That paved the ground for the Jobs and Industry tour.

TONY MANWARING The context of the Jobs and Industry campaign was Thatcherism, rising youth unemployment, and youth training. There was a key meeting at the House of Commons with Neil, Billy and Pete, and that provided the bridge of permission, daring to hope that this might be something real.

CLARE SHORT The purpose of the Jobs and Industry tour was to mobilize young people to not just be fed up and angry about unemployment but to use their political power to demand change. In the '83 general election over half the young employed did not vote. The link between radical music and Labour was because of the mood of Thatcher: unemployment, riots, young people angry, 'We need to do something about this.' From the Party's organizational point of view it was a chance to reach young people, get some leaflets, go round universities and so on. That was normal. What was unusual was the music linking directly in support of Labour to convey that message. A lot of disgruntled youth just don't vote. Take no action. It was getting them to think it was not hopeless: 'You're entitled to be angry but a better life is possible. If everyone gives up then nothing will ever change.' People have to get together and say, 'This isn't right and something can be done about it.' Tony Benn always used to say, 'You start off and everyone says, "This is a mad lunatic idea," and then more and more people say, "This is interesting," and then you get to a point where every-one says, "Well, I always thought . . .".'

LARRY WHITTY We probably didn't appreciate what a departure the Jobs for Youth tour was for the pop world at the time, but the media woke up to the fact that the Labour Party was adopting a different approach. Billy had great enthusiasm although I didn't know much about his music. Pete Jenner was the key operator in all of this. He was the networker and the person who knew what needed to be done.

TOM SAWYER Mrs Thatcher was introducing all these Youth Training Schemes for sixteen- and seventeen-year-olds and there was an outcry, particularly in inner-city areas like London, Newcastle, Birmingham and Glasgow. In effect, it was a programme of national industrial conscription, because if you refused a place you had your benefits cut. The youth had never had such a difficult time. Billy and Pete were angry about that.

PETER JENNER Youth unemployment was going through the roof and I was very aware about trying to get that link between politics and young people and social movements. Also it was a calculated professional move, 'How can I do something which is a bit more than just another Billy Bragg tour?' 'How do we keep feeding the story?' So it seemed like a good idea to have MPs in the auditorium at every gig. It was a good political press story. You know that if you're going to Brighton and the local MP turns up the local paper will do an extra story about you. It was mutually beneficial. Clearly, Billy wasn't going to get a lot of Radio 1 play. He was the old foghorn; he just sang and played an out-of-tune guitar.

BILLY BRAGG I never claimed to be a great singer. My claim to fame was to write incisive lyrics and then come up with the actions which matched them. On the first album there was politics: *Just because you're better than me doesn't mean I'm lazy*, but I'm not articulating it in the same way as I did in 'Power In A Union' or 'Between The Wars'. By *Talking With The Taxman* I had an ideological perspective that was lacking on the first two albums.

TOM WATSON I came down to London at the age of seventeen and applied for a job as a trainee library assistant in the Labour Party HQ at 150 Walworth Road. I was a Young Socialist. I'd been on many marches with CND, and I'd come out of 2 Tone and loved music, and thought London was it, and couldn't believe I was working for the Labour Party. There was a launch for the Jobs for Youth tour at eleven o'clock in the morning and they thought they were being really trendy having it at Ronnie Scott's, but it was a bit early for some of the guys. The accounts department organized a coach trip down to Guildford Town Hall to see the first gig.

CLARE SHORT I remember this journey down the motorway with Billy and Pete. That was our big meeting and sharing of life stories and views of the world, which weren't very different. We were on the same kind of wavelength. Billy had this sort of dream that music and songs could contribute to changing the country. He didn't make speeches but it was there on the tip of how he talked about everything. I liked him. And he gave me a few records. Historically, the Labour Party always had big links to folk music and political music and political songs. It was normal. But people were surprised to see me in the foyer. I was asked questions about disarmament and unemployment and Northern Ireland. It was hard and tough and honest talking. People were critical. They weren't going to be conned by anyone.

RHODA DAKAR When people used to sing, from time immemorial they sang about their situation, which is political, if not party political. You only have to listen to blues or folk so it's not anything new, it's just that pop was the new mode of popular music, as it were.

NEIL KINNOCK We were very proud to be involved in the Jobs and Industry tour but there were people who said, 'Bloody Bragg.' They got very short shrift from me.

TINY FENNIMORE It was the first time MPs had been taken out on a rock tour. We felt we were getting them out of their smoked-filled corridors and onto the turf of young people to speak to them about issues that were important to them. I do remember some very suited MPs looking very uncomfortable in the foyer.

BILLY BRAGG Before the first date we went to Kinnock's office and Robin Cook was saying, 'What exactly do you want us to do?' I said, 'I don't want you making speeches. Be available for people to speak in the foyer.' I remember when we left the Birmingham Powerhouse, Clare Short was still standing there smoking a cigarillo with her back against a pillar arguing with a couple of guys with Mohawk spikes. It impressed the shit out of me.

PHILL JUPITUS Backstage in Southend, Robin Cook said, 'Is it all right if we have a drink at the bar?' Billy said, 'Only if you don't fuckin' spill it down

Billy Bragg on the Jobs For Youth tour, Guildford, 19 March 1985.

your shirt fronts.' I had first met Billy at the University of Sussex where four months earlier, as Porky the Poet, I was bottom of the bill and was paid £20. I was watching Billy every night and listening to what he was saying between the songs. He used to do a set list with 'raps' in between. That's what he called them: 'the raps' – the fith-fath between the songs. He was as funny as any stand-up I'd seen. And with him being a solo performer there was a lot of interacting directly with the audience. I was ceaselessly impressed by him.

ANGELA EAGLE I went to the date at the Royal Court in Liverpool. The tour was trying to reach out in a way that hadn't ever been tried before and reconnect to young people who had been left on the scrapheap and didn't vote, but paradoxically were the most affected by the policies that the Tories were pursuing. There was a complete loss of industrial jobs and the kinds of apprenticeships where unions traditionally picked younger people up from – when my dad went to his first-ever print union branch meeting as a young apprentice he was given a copy of *The Ragged-Trousered Philanthropists* and taught all about the capitalist money trick – so we were reaching out in the absence of an industrial structure in which young people could be educated in politics.

PHILL JUPITUS There was a quite active student political movement, mostly connected with CND, and you'd do the marches. Initially, you don't know why, other than it seems a bit of a laugh and it seems wrong. And the role that Billy filled in many people's lives was giving definition to a general malaise with the way things were: *There's only a future for the chosen few*. You were singing that at gigs and it was worming its way into you. Have you ever met a Tory Bragg fan? There are loads. They switch off during the politics, but when he does 'The Milkman Of Human Kindness' they're back in. He met a bloke once who said, 'I really don't care for your politics but you write some of the best love songs I've ever heard.' Billy spoke to your heart on both levels.

HILARY CROSS Love and relationships are part of life and politics. You underestimate Billy's personal songs at your peril. He sang overtly political stuff but also about the difficulties of relationships. It's all part of the debate about politics. Later, I wrote in *Well Red*, 'According to the *NME*, Billy Bragg is the thinking schoolgirl's crumpet, so we butter him up and give him a grilling.'

•

ANNAJOY DAVID I wasn't so involved with Billy's set-up, whereas I was very much part of the Weller family's. I went on tour with the band a couple of times and Paul would introduce me in the middle of the set. I became quite well known to the hard-core fans and they'd sing, 'Come on Anna. Come on Anna.' I'd speak for about three minutes about CND and then later the Tories. I'd be in the foyer afterwards giving out leaflets to young people having a go or having a chat. And then I'd jump on the tour bus and watch them all lose at cards to John Weller.

ROBERT HOWARD Annajoy would stand up at Jam gigs and shout them all down; this little girl. She had amazing power and energy. She never stopped talking. She was what you might call 'on point'. She was an inspiration and a force of nature.

STEVE WHITE Annajoy used to come on mid-set and do a couple of minutes. She would hammer home the message and talk about empowerment and voting. It wasn't a massive political rant. It was, 'Look, the reason why we're all here is because we think you should think about politics and what you can do with your vote. And obviously have a great time.'

COLIN BYRNE I remember going to see the Style Council with Annajoy at the Royal Albert Hall and thinking, 'They're cool and politically subversive and we're in this pillar of the establishment.'

ANNAJOY DAVID Paul's studio, Solid Bond, was a place for him to think about what he wanted to do after this enormous thing called the Jam. It became the hive for lots of young people doing creative things on the margins of politics who had something to say. We would have postbags from really great people starting up theatre groups, music venues, cooperative youth projects, and being inspired by what Paul was saying. I remember his dad, John Weller, laughing and saying, 'Blimey, there's sacks of post . . . we've made you a little office, Anna,' and then tutting, 'More money I've got to find!' I would sift through stuff with Paul once a week and he would answer everything. He would be incredibly generous. I don't just mean financially, but with his time and his thinking and putting people on to other people to help. The studio became a cornerstone for the whole fanzine movement. It was like the foot soldier of the cultural protest movement, in a lot of ways. I don't think people should underestimate just how significant that was in promoting a counterculture to the government. A lot of writers were big fans of Paul Weller and he really encouraged creative writing and fanzine production and helped with their funding. He was like a one-person networking organization.

ROBERT HOWARD Paul would get a lot of people turning up at Solid Bond or sending in poetry and being encouraged to express themselves through his publishing company, Riot Stories, and the record label, Respond. It was a buzzy, central thing going on. Paul was stepping out of himself.

KAREN WALTER It was like a social club and a focal point for people coming together and talking and discussing ideas, and often parties at weekends. Paul was a magnet to young, talented people. It was Annajoy's second home.

PAUL WELLER It wasn't a time to be non-partisan. It was too serious a time, too extreme. I wasn't waving the Labour Party flag but the socialist red flag, that's for sure. In the Jam, I didn't want to be a part of any movement. But this was different. Thatcher got into power and from the Falklands War onwards, that was her wielding her power; the trade unions were being worn down, we had the Miners' Strike, there was mass unemployment, there were all these issues. You had to care and if you didn't you had your head in the sand or didn't give a fuck about anyone but yourself. You couldn't sit on the fence. It was very black and white. Thatcher was a tyrant, a dictator.[57] I think she should have been lined up against a wall and shot.[58] We were trying to stir up a revolution of some kind, which I know sounds a bit pretentious now, but that's what I felt at the time.[59]

DON'T GET MAD. GET ORGANIZED

Red Wedge

PETER JENNER Red Wedge was an independent broad left alliance set up by young artists and like-minded people involved in the media. Politically, we wanted Thatcher out and Labour in. That was absolutely clear. You've got to realize the hatred we had for Thatcher. She was a class warrior. She went out to smash the unions. She was out to destroy the post-war social economic agreement. What the Tories were doing was absolutely catastrophic.

BILLY BRAGG If Red Wedge could be defined as anything it was a collection of artists that opposed Margaret Thatcher. The Jobs and Industry campaign was absolutely crucial in convincing everybody that it was a viable thing to do. It was a dry run for Red Wedge: the turnout had been good, the press was good, the commitment from the Party was good. Red Wedge was sort of recharging our batteries after the shocking defeat of the National Union of Mineworkers and giving us something positive to believe in and take forward. We were showing that the country still had a commitment to a compassionate society.

PAUL WELLER Red Wedge was the direct result of the wonderful Jobs and Industry tour which proved such a success that it had to be followed up. [We made] no bones of its intentions: we wanted the Tories out and a socialist government in. We were not saying that the Labour Party had all the answers, not by a long chalk, but if it was a choice between them and Thatcher's gang, or the SDP [Social Democratic Party], then there was no contest. It was worth a try and better than sitting around moaning about the state of the nation.[60] We [hoped] that if the whole thing took off and became strong enough, that we [would] act as a kind of pressure group within the Labour Party, where maybe we could push to change certain policies. Some people will say that was totally unrealistic, but it was worth trying.[61]

ANNAJOY DAVID Margaret Thatcher was taking 300 years of Britain's industrial history and tearing it up and that would have serious implications for where Britain would go in the future. People had to stand up and be counted. It was a call to arms. It was a huge injustice to say to people that suddenly they had no value. To say, 'It's this way or no way.' The real question was: do you decimate and de-industrialize a country in ten years driven by an ideological belief that the market can fix everything? Where is the social compact and the rights of our own humanity to make a decent living and to have a good way of life? I felt it was really important that she was held to account. That a young generation of people said, 'No, this is wrong.' It was about the social compact of what a society is worth and what it values. They basically turned to the dollar and said, 'You rule. You are God.'

BILLY BRAGG We had grown up listening to songwriters with a social conscience and bands like the Clash who were going to change the world through music, and all of a sudden there was an opportunity to break some new ground and find out if music can really make a difference. Pop music was a predominant medium of discourse for young people. We talked to one another through our music. It was a Sixties' idea that you were going to change the world through the music. Those ideas were still valid in the 1980s. Music was a counterculture, particularly for those of us who had come out of Rock Against Racism, and 2 Tone. We were the alternative.

JULIET DE VALERO WILLS Billy watched 2 Tone happen. It spoke to him. Later on there was a chance to be part of that lineage.

ANNAJOY DAVID I talked to Paul way into the night about it many times and said, 'We've got to help to get rid of this government; we can't just sit on the sidelines.' And then Billy came into our lives. We argued quite a lot politically but it was a great triangular working relationship that endured and took us into Red Wedge.

PAUL WELLER There [were] only two alternatives as far as I see it. One [was] armed revolution and the other one [was] the ballot box. An armed revolution isn't that easy to organize, is it? Not in this country, anyway. So I guess you have to try it the other way: the supposedly democratic way.[62]

NEIL SPENCER I came to be involved through Billy. He was the dynamo of it all. I'd had enough of editing *NME* and my resignation and the start of Red Wedge coincided. It was open house. You wanted the debate. There was a terrible element of despair in large sections of Britain and especially the young because the post-war consensus had been torn up and trashed by the Thatcher regime. Young people bore the brunt of unemployment. And the Tories were in a triumphalist mode. We were coming off the back of the dreadful rancour of the Miners' Strike and a rising tide of militarism. Reagan was fighting the Sandinistas in Nicaragua and once he started talking about a war in northern Germany being winnable and putting Pershing missiles there a lot of us felt we couldn't be passive. It was fucking madness. Even someone like the fashion designer Katharine Hamnett felt animated enough to wear her '58% DON'T WANT PERSHING' T-shirt when she met Margaret Thatcher at Downing Street.

BILLY BRAGG Neil Spencer was absolutely crucial. He had given me a platform and put me on the front cover of the *NME*. He was a child of '68 and still believed that music should say something and that as a musician you should be able to express an alternative lifestyle to the mainstream.

**Billy Bragg (left),
Neil Spencer and
Paul Weller,
November 1985.**

NEIL SPENCER There were lots of writers who didn't like my politics: 'Neil's a fucking stupid old hippy,' because I always championed things like the CND Glastonbury Festival. I always knew that it was a really important event. There were a lot of strands of dissent and it was about getting the Labour Party to address them, not necessarily endorse them, but simply to think about them. Rock Against Racism fed into Red Wedge. If the Trots could do it why couldn't we? The fact that musicians would get involved with parliamentarians showed how angry everybody was about what was going on. And Billy and Annajoy would stir you up and get you going and animate you.

TRACEY THORN Anyone who'd done a benefit gig was rounded up. You knew who the likely candidates were. It was about, instead of everybody just doing individual political benefit gigs, thinking, 'Well, look, these causes have all got something in common, haven't they? So maybe we could harness all that energy and rally the youth vote and get people to see that a lot of these ideals are represented by a political party.' I thought that was quite sensible. It was a way to feel that you were not absolutely powerless. We were all so frustrated and alienated by Thatcherism. This wasn't the time to be too sensitive about your own personal conscience or worrying if this party is going to 100 per cent represent everything you feel. You just thought, 'You've got to do something. We can't just sit and watch these people be this powerful and go around dismantling the country.' It was a black-and-white political time. I didn't have any grey-area feelings about the Tory government; everything they did just seemed to be vile. I felt quite optimistic and positive about Red Wedge.

RICHARD COLES Inevitably, Bronski Beat had found themselves on the same bills as Billy and Paul, Everything But The Girl and the Style Council, and it was very obvious we were all part of the same thing. With Margaret Thatcher there was a great foreshortening of the imaginative horizons for what you could do. And very soon after that you had a sense that people didn't think that you could really opt out of the capitalist model. It was about making money and carrying a gold card. There was a swing in the pendulum to the right after the disappointment of the Callaghan administration and I thought that pendulum would swing back to Labour as it always had. I wanted to galvanize young people to vote and see off the Tories and be a vehicle of revolution leading to the overthrow of the forces of capital and the institution of a communist world order. Although, there's a difference between what you think taking the dog for a walk in the morning and what you actually think when you're pouring the tea.

PAUL WELLER You get to a point in time where you think, 'Where's it all leading to?' Benefits and raising money are obviously good things but you're still only dealing with the symptoms; you're not getting to the core. It was potentially a culmination of all those things and actually to get somewhere. There was that constant dialectic thing: Marxism, Leninism and Trotsky. That was irrelevant. It was a different era. You had to stop talking in those funny antiquated ways and bring the whole thing up to date and make it more stylized and streamlined. I wanted to see us put over socialist ideas and ideals in a very accessible way to young people. I just think of my experience: it took me years to ever get any kind of bearing on my own political train of thought, with a lot of unnecessary confusion. So it was a very positive thing to do. The media was constantly bombarded by right-wing ideas so there'd got to be something to redress the balance.[63]

BILLY BRAGG There's a big difference between a single-issue campaign and trying to change a government. Paul wanted to carry on the fight and not surrender. He was already quite active of his own volition. Red Wedge didn't wake him up.

ANNAJOY DAVID Billy was the link and it took us beyond our comfort zones into something we didn't know where it was going to go. We met Neil Kinnock in his offices at the House of Commons to find out if he was an all-right bloke and to see if we could come in on something. And to say that we would broadly create a cultural platform for Labour to be able to speak to young people through and they would have to accept criticism. We were very clear that we would have to do it our own way. We were not going to be told what to say or do. Billy was a great reference for Neil and really felt that Neil wanted to welcome us to encourage young people to think about politics through music and the broader arts. Neil was a good guy and the Labour Party needed him. He was really forward-thinking and helped to put the Labour Party on a really important path to finding itself again, to help and define it, and to help rebuild its confidence.

ANDY MCSMITH The 1983 general election was the worst defeat the Labour Party had suffered since the Second World War. The usual explanation is to blame Tony Benn, who wrote the manifesto, *The New Hope for Britain*. It was just too wild: too many commitments to nationalize industries, to pull out of Europe without a referendum, to abolish nuclear weapons. Gerald Kaufman called it 'the longest suicide note in history'. The dispute was bitter and the Party was deeply split, mainly between Benn and his supporters and Neil Kinnock. Labour was really on the ropes. In the seventies, inflation was running at 26 per cent and the Thatcher government had succeeded in getting it below 5 per cent by 1983, which meant for most people the panic was over so they were prepared to put their faith in the Tories.

LARRY WHITTY '83 was a terrible defeat for Labour and so much of the political party and the commentators blamed the manifesto. We had to find new ways of communicating.

CLARE SHORT If you looked back at the polling after Mrs Thatcher took over, she became deeply unpopular and then the Falklands changed the atmosphere. It was a dilemma, because you can't let a fascist dictator succeed in military force, but it seemed to me most people thought the Falkland Islands were somewhere off Scotland. The country went mad and I saw especially men getting very excited. It was a lesson from history when they used wars to keep the working class happy when things were miserable.

ROBERT ELMS Economically, the tide was beginning to turn: people were starting to be better off, and that was always going to win an argument. The Conservatives were doomed to win a second term in office.

ANNA HEALY You could draw a line across England somewhere around Birmingham and there wasn't a single seat south of that line where Labour came second in the '83 election. We were nearly the third party because of the Social Democratic Party split. It was a tremendous and long and painful process to rebuild.

NEIL KINNOCK The outlook for the Labour movement in Britain looked pretty bad. Margaret Thatcher was transcendent, especially in the wake of the Falklands. They were slashing and burning the economy. Unemployment was going up through the bloody roof and naturally the kids were getting hit the hardest. There was widespread poverty amongst old-age pensioners. In 1972, the moment unemployment hit a million, Ted Heath changed all his policies. This lot simply intensified the policies. And here was Labour divided left and right. We were getting absolutely bloody battered.

BILLY BRAGG All you needed to know about Neil Kinnock was he was the honorary president of the Gene Vincent Appreciation Society. Neil was passionate about his music. He was the first leader of any political party who had been born after the Second World War. Margaret Thatcher was twenty-two when the welfare state was founded. She had a concept of politics that had been formed before pop music, whereas Kinnock's politics had been formed through pop music. He understood the importance of how music could be a vehicle with which to motivate and engage people. I've happy memories of him late at night in the bar with us singing 'Bandiera Rossa'. He was a committed European, a committed socialist; someone who you felt like you could have a conversation with.

NEIL KINNOCK I know sod-all about rock 'n' roll from about 1968 on but I'm encyclopaedic from 1955. I wept on the way to school the morning that the Big Bopper and Buddy Holly were killed. I remember when I was in office somebody called and said, 'Would Neil Kinnock like to meet Little Richard?' 'Shit, is Christmas on 25 December?' In he comes. He was a little guy. He didn't have as much fuzzy hair but he was unmistakably Little Richard. We had a good long chat and when he found out that I knew Pete Seeger and Tom Paxton it was just bloody great. He gave me two LPs and autographed one, 'To a great man in the cause of liberty', and like a bloody idiot I auctioned them for Labour Party funds a few years later for £2,000. Being the leader of the Labour Party was pretty shitty but it did have its moments.

LARRY WHITTY Neil loved music and he liked talking to artistic people. He had a lot of enthusiasm for creativity and was genuinely committed in terms of popular culture and its effects on the quality of life, and indirectly on politics. He felt it was the compensation for a lot of the misery of life and that it needed to be encouraged, developed and if necessary resourced. He was an inspiring person and the artists saw him as someone you could trust carrying forward issues they believed in.

PAUL BOWER He was in his forties and from South Wales, where culture is a fundamental part of being a socialist: singing, and waving banners.

PETER JENNER Kinnock coming in as the youngest leader of the Labour Party and being thirty years younger and much more interesting than the Party's previous leader Michael Foot had something which you could relate to. It was an age thing and an awareness of music.

TOM WATSON Frankly, Michael Foot, good guy that he was, wasn't speaking to the nation's youth. Walworth Road was stuffed with men in brown suits and whatever the skirts were at the time. And then Billy came in, in his Levi 501s.

NEIL KINNOCK The stuffed shirts who will one moment tell you sport and politics don't mix, and then music and politics don't mix and this and that don't mix, then you have to say to them, 'What the bloody hell does mix with politics, then?' There was a bit of, 'Music's got a place in politics, obviously . . .' but it was very 'Kumbayah My Lord'. So there were reservations in the Party but I didn't give them any choice. That sounds terribly anti-democratic but the forces of resistance, such as they were, were just so bloody antediluvian.

ANGELA EAGLE '83 had been so damaging and driven us back into our redoubts. Partly, that was about Michael Foot not being a very good leader in terms of the discontent between more modern methods of communication rather than the old ways of doing things, which was to have huge rallies and orate. Neil understood that you had to modernize. And that you had to change the Party. We had to be more professional and updated and have a more nuanced message that was shaped for the country as a whole, not just the activists.

NEIL SPENCER Neil was quite a breath of fresh air. He was open-minded and very realistic. He was good at tempering expectations. Left-wing purism and ideological nonsense drove me potty. It's very easy to be an anarchist or Trotskyist because nothing's ever good enough, so you never have to compromise; you never have to do real politics; you never have to do a deal because you're always above it.

RICHARD COLES We were constantly going to conferences with various revolutionary groups and you'd meet them on demos: our little tribes waving banners. You'd see faces there that later became very familiar, like Peter Mandelson or David Aaronovitch. One of my close friends was in the Revolutionary Communist Party. They had an annual conference with the rather ambitious title 'Preparing for Power'.

•

KAREN WALTER The Labour Party invited us to hold a meeting at Walworth Road in July 1985 because they had a huge room. There were about twenty-five people there, maybe more: Jerry Dammers, Neil Spencer, Paul

Weller, Rhoda Dakar, Keith Harris, Robert Elms. They'd chosen quite wisely so there was a really strong core spectrum of left-wing-thinking artists and media people who were broadly in favour of a Labour government. We had to introduce ourselves and then Billy said what he thought the group should do to appeal to young people, because almost half of under-twenty-sixes hadn't voted in the 1983 election. And he voiced doubts whether Labour could do any better in government than the Tories, but we had to do something. And then we were asked if we had any ideas of other people who should get involved, and that's how it rippled through.

ANDY MCSMITH We decided to have the meeting in the boardroom upstairs and it was absolutely packed out. It was the prerogative of Gwyneth Dunwoody, of the National Executive Committee, to be the chair, but fortunately she decided she didn't want to meet a load of kids so Tom Sawyer presided over the meeting. I can't help but think that if Gwyneth had been chairing it the whole thing would have died at the first meeting. Tom said, 'We understand you're all here to help the Labour Party,' and a voice piped up: 'Kinnock didn't do much for the miners.' Instead of telling this person to grow up, which is certainly what Gwyneth would have done, Tom was very conciliatory and said, 'It was a very difficult time for all of us.' I noticed the voice was Paul Weller. Gwyneth wouldn't have known who he was and would have told him to shut his gob, and Red Wedge might have been stillborn.

PAUL BOWER The Labour Party had a network of clubs across the north where they put dodgy comedians in so I wrote to the Party suggesting that they wake up to alternative comedy. The letter got passed on to Andy Bevan who was a leading light in the Young Socialists and Militant Tendency, and he invited me down to a meeting which turned out to be the inaugural meeting of what was called, at that point, Youth Arts for Labour. I was looking round the table: 'Oh, that's interesting, that's Paul Weller. Oh, and Billy Bragg. And that's Nigel Stanley who represents Robin Cook.' Even somebody from Motown Records was there!

BILLY BRAGG The initial meetings were huge. There'd be sixty or seventy people, with people coming from all over with crazy ideas. There wasn't a lefty pop star club. We didn't all hang out at the Groucho. We had all met on benefits before and during the Miners' Strike. You'd have guys from the union asking, 'Who do you represent, then?' I'd say, 'Paul Weller!'

PETER JENNER We didn't want to be exclusive. Bananarama signed up, which was good. Ray Davies of the Kinks, Stephen Duffy, Ben Elton, Dawn French, Everything But The Girl, Prefab Sprout, John Peel, the actor Tim Roth, Dave Stewart from the Eurythmics, Strawberry Switchblade, Wet Wet Wet, Robert Wyatt; it was all about numbers. We wanted everyone in.

MIRANDA PITCHER We put all the desks round the edge of this room and sat round. It was a bit like a classroom.

ANDY MCSMITH Jerry turned up and we thought, 'Great, we've got Jerry Dammers.'

KAREN WALTER Jerry was very opinionated and involved. I remember going out for dinner with him a few times after meetings and mulling over it. He doesn't suffer fools gladly and he questioned some people's involvement. There was a time when people were coming in because they wanted to meet people or they had their own agenda.

STEVE WHITE I remember thinking, 'I wonder if we could get Sade involved,' because Robert Elms was going out with her at the time. And it was really refreshing that there were black faces involved. Junior was eloquent. It was important to be inclusive when people were still watching *Love Thy Neighbour*, and Jim Davidson doing impressions of black people was considered funny. I remember Billy saying to me, 'It's not necessarily about voting for Labour, it's about thinking about politics.'

TINY FENNIMORE Billy came up with the name 'Red Wedge' and Lynne Franks, the PR entrepreneur, questioned the wisdom of using the word 'red' in the title.

BILLY BRAGG She said, 'You can't use "red", people will think you're socialists.' What the fuck did we need Lynne Franks for? There was a bit of that. Are you going to tell Paul Weller how to shape taste? The name came from a fabulous, angular piece of constructivist Soviet art by El Lissitzky called 'Beat the Whites with the Red Wedge'; the whites being the counter-revolutionary forces in the Russian Civil War after the 1917 Revolution.

ROBERT ELMS I thought it was a very good name. I knew about Russian constructivism and it had been very trendy in the whole Blitz scene and the design of the *Face*. 'Red' could mean you were a Trot, a Labour Party member or an ordinary socialist. It was all-encompassing and I liked the mannequinism of 'red' versus 'blue'. It was football and tribal. Our tribe is 'red' and her tribe is 'blue'.

KAREN WALTER I liked the idea of flirting with the red flag. Also it was the 'thin end of the wedge' and that was the whole idea. It said everything about what we were. A lot of people thought it was a little bit pretentious.

ALEX DALLAS I remember feeling a little bit intimidated because I was sitting there with these types that you read about in the *NME*. I was definitely star-struck by Paul Weller. He was desperately shy and not a talker. Annajoy was young and very strident with a very powerful personality that overtook the room.

RHODA DAKAR Annajoy used to keep everyone in order. And you'd see unlikely people sitting in the corner: 'Is that Robert Elms?' And then the next time there'd be another unlikely person in the corner. It was funny because there'd be some musicians sitting there desperate to get to the pub: 'Is it still that time?'

ALEX DALLAS 'Red Steady Go', 'More to the Point', 'Moving Hearts and Minds' were other potential names before 'Red Wedge'.

BILLY BRAGG I rang up some artists who thought it was wrong to align themselves with the Labour Party. Elvis Costello was heartbreaking. He more or less said that it would be better if Thatcher took her toll and the whole shithouse went up in flames and people were out on the streets. Joe Strummer wasn't sympathetic either.

LUCY HOOBERMAN There was a generation of people who had grown up with new models for political activity taken from single-issue movements like CND, anti-apartheid, the women's movement and the spirit and practice of the GLC, coupled with a profound sense of mistrust of all political institutions. Red Wedge believed in a movement for change to motivate young people to get active in politics, by registering to vote; connecting them with existing organizations; and by initiating projects locally, regionally and nationally. The catchphrase was 'Don't Get Mad. Get Organized.'

ANNAJOY DAVID We said, 'We need to inject people with a new enthusiasm for socialism and the Labour Party must be seen to present real alternatives and accept direct input into youth policies.' To do that, we needed to grasp the imagination of young people and show them that they could effect change and demand a say in the future, using all the art mediums.

PETER JENNER When Annajoy came in she took a lot off my shoulders. Billy would talk with Paul, and Annajoy was key in that link. But there was always a bit of strain between us because she knew all the answers and I knew all the answers. Paul's involvement was very important in terms of he was a bigger act and he had resources. He didn't talk politics much. He left it to Annajoy, but you knew if Paul did or didn't approve. He was enormously important but in a way quite difficult to deal with because he was distant. He was more linked up to the traditional music business: hits and chart places.

TONY MANWARING There was a natural and totally understandable suspicion from people like Paul Weller: Can I trust it? Is there integrity to it? Am I being used? You could respect that. The irony of it was, that just wasn't where we were coming from.

PAUL BOWER The Labour Party was flattered and delighted that Paul was attaching his good name.

ASHTAR ALKHIRSAN I'd met Paul before at gigs because I used to follow the Jam on tour everywhere. He was smart and articulate but quite non-conformist. He was always an outsider and never seemed a great one for joining in mainstream thinking. I remember him saying that it could be the downfall of Red Wedge if they aligned themselves with the Labour Party so closely.

BILLY BRAGG Paul was as committed as all of us but he was voicing the possibility 'we've got to be careful about this'. He was suspicious of politicians but whatever scepticism he had was kept in check by the possibility of getting rid of Thatcher.

PHILL JUPITUS The reason I got involved was 20 per cent ideological, 30 per cent because I loved Billy Bragg and 50 per cent the chance to meet Paul Weller. Weller is always the difficult one. Politics is boring and Paul doesn't like boring things. He didn't like admin. He was about passion. He liked music, good food, wine, ladies and schmutter. He got politicized by CND and he was just at that point. I think we caught him at a weak moment.

RICHARD COLES I remember Paul saying he wouldn't mind if young people voted Tory, which was a deeply shocking concept to me. He wasn't concerned that they connected with his politics, which I thought was quite circumspect and had a maturity about it.

PAUL WELLER The Labour Party [was] the only viable alternative to the Tories, but there [were] just so many things that [were]frustrating about them. There was a lot of mouthing off but there [didn't] seem to be any kind of real physical support for young people. They were never gonna win them over with mere words. One minute they [announced] their youth drive to try and win over more votes and the next Kinnock was condemning the school strikes.[64]

ANNAJOY DAVID It's very hard for artists to manage their expectations about what politicians can and can't do. We were saying, 'Don't vote Labour and expect them to clean the mess up for you. Vote with them and get involved in cleaning that mess up together.'

NEIL SPENCER Red Wedge was conditional: 'We'll support you but you've got to give us something back. You've got to take our ideas on and incorporate them into what you're offering young people.' This business of engaging directly with the Labour Party wasn't antipathetic to me personally. I didn't have that widespread cynicism about the democratic parliamentary process. As Richard Neville once remarked, 'There may be only an inch of difference between Wilson and Heath but it's in that inch that we live.' The Labour Party was never going to articulate everything I believed and stood for, but parts of it did. It's compromise. It's Britain. It's always a fudge.

TINY FENNIMORE The Labour leadership didn't support the Miners' Strike because they said that there should have been a ballot. And they were funny about nuclear disarmament. There were lots of the politics that young people were interested in that they didn't seem to be pursuing. But the idea was, if you got involved you could influence policy, and that's what we were trying to do. We all knew it was a dangerous step, and Neil Kinnock was such a suit. We knew that we were rolling our sleeves up and we were going to get our hands dirty. My view was that unless there was a Labour government nothing would ever change. We had to get that by all means necessary and if Billy thought it was a good idea then I was coming too.

PAUL BOWER I was volunteered to answer the phones and 'run' the office because I'd a loud mouth and was the only person that spoke pop music and Labour. And I was the key contact person with Larry Whitty, the general secretary of the Labour Party, who kept us at arm's length.

LARRY WHITTY Red Wedge were linked into the structure at Walworth Road but they weren't part of the structure. It was part of the upping of the image of the Labour Party to make it reach out to a younger generation and get people interested in politics. My view was, let them get on with it and keep them at arm's length because it seemed the only way we could do it without the central party wanting to control it. Putting it through the machine would have been counterproductive. Red Wedge told us what they were doing and we were giving a nod of approval: 'We can get people together to endorse you', 'We're not going to go on the normal campaign trail', 'We can do concerts'. They gradually recruited more and more names, most of which I'd never heard of – I wasn't exactly in touch with the scene – but Neil and his people around the leadership were enthusiastic. Generally speaking, political parties are fusty organizations, so culturally it wasn't that easy a fit. But clearly for Labour to be voted in again we needed a big youth vote that was fairly pissed off with Thatcher and a higher electoral turnout. We gave Red Wedge carte blanche to get out there and organize it.

PHILL JUPITUS I worked in the office as a volunteer. You'd go in the front door and there was an atrium, then you'd turn left, go through a corridor and down to a front office with a window. I was in there answering the phone and helping Paul Bower, who would occasionally give us money for buses. There was a lot of optimism and good intention and 'we can do this', but it became quite apparent that we were seen as a frivolity by the Labour staff. There was a lot of, 'Who are they?' But once they'd given us the office and the photocopier key and helped us to print leaflets it was like, 'Right, OK, well, they're doing their thing now.'

LUCY HOOBERMAN Early on, Pete Jenner was proposing a five- or six- date tour culminating with the Style Council at the Wembley Arena which was already booked for the beginning of December. Neil Spencer circulated a draft charter.

PAUL BOWER I used to hear Neil Spencer on the phone persuading Prefab Sprout or Morrissey to get involved. He introduced the concept of 'soul-calism.'

TOM WATSON I used to help them out and chat with them over the tea urn: 'Oh, do you need some paper?' So they invited me to the meetings. I remember Paul Bower, who was this Spanish-speaking, deeply interesting, incredibly charismatic character who had come out of the Sheffield music scene and used to dress in a 1950s suit and kipper tie. He was doing a report back but none of these people had ever organized meetings. They thought because it was the Labour Party they had to do the minutes of the last meeting: 'I'd like to thank Porky the Poet for helping us with the office. He's found us all pencils.' It stuck in my head as quite bizarre. But the idea that the Party would work with iconic bands to achieve political aims started to be discussed and Red Wedge began to emerge, and I was aware of this idea that we'd create this energetic appeal to first-time voters who were being done in by Thatcher.

RICHARD COLES I remember having a meeting after hours and some fierce Labour dame shouted at me outside, thinking I was trying to break in. There was an old guard and they would look at us and think, 'Who are these whippersnappers coming in?' We had to persuade the Labour Party we had something to offer. When we went to see Neil Kinnock at the House of Commons they led us through the chamber and I remember thinking, 'You're doing this on purpose to impress upon us that we are at the very mother of parliaments here.' There was a kind of getting-to-know-you: what could they offer; what could we offer.

TOM SAWYER I didn't particularly want to meet any rock 'n' roll stars because I thought that was inappropriate. My right-hand man at the National Union of Public Employees [NUPE] was Bill Gilby so I said to him, 'These young people are knocking on the door and they want to do something.' Bill met Annajoy and as a consequence NUPE got involved. The trade union movement had grass roots across the country but felt they'd lost touch with the young – the average age of a union member was forty-six; that tells you something – so the excitement of working with a group of socially committed musicians was very appealing. If you said to young people, 'Will you come to something the Labour Party is doing?' they'd probably say, 'No.' But if you said, 'Will you come to a Red Wedge gig where they'll talk about politics and play some interesting, socially committed music?' they'd say, 'Yes.'

BILL GILBY I saw my role as trying to get them to focus a bit more instead of firing off in twenty different directions. Weller was quite combative and pretty anarchic and almost as hostile to the Labour Party as he was to the Tories, but was absolutely influential. His vote was equal to a union block vote, and Billy was nothing like I thought he was going to be from just having seen his posters on walls. A lot of the artists saw NUPE as an opportunity to get financial support but I did feel at times you were playing the role of supposedly wise old fogey, even though I was in my twenties myself. Neil Spencer was generally a positive guy but a bit quirky like they all were, and Jerry Dammers would be hard to forget because his front teeth were missing. He was sporadic with his attendance and contributions. Time is generally a problem with creative people; they're almost in a different world to those of us who are planners. It was seat-of-the-pants stuff. A lot of these meetings would be brainstorming and ideas would get thrown out. I was somebody who got things done.

ASHTAR ALKHIRSAN If there was any disagreement about carrying a motion Bill Gilby would always produce a card and pronounce that he had a block vote that overrode what anybody else had to say: NUPE had 125,000 members!

BILLY BRAGG The unions had money to put on events and they had young people who were members who they weren't afraid of, unlike the Labour Party, who were scared of their young people.

ANNAJOY DAVID For people in popular culture, from music to comedy to film-making to fanzines, to come together with the trade union movement brought a completely different dimension of young people into broad left politics which we hadn't seen before. NUPE and the Transport and General Workers' Union [TGWU] helped with funding and events and venues on the ground but the national team and the infrastructure was all paid for by the artists. The Labour Party gave us an office and they helped fund a few bits and pieces and got us started but essentially it was a self-funding organization. That was really important to the artists. We begged, stole and borrowed but once we got going there was money around.

TOM WATSON The Labour Party was terribly disorganized and near-bankrupt. They were living on overdraft. There were times when staff didn't get paid for a day or two because bank payments didn't go through.

COLIN BYRNE Labour headquarters was an absolute shambles. I was like a young, trendy firebrand suddenly thrown into the middle of this bunch of people who were actually quite happy in opposition, in some ways. I remember doing a photo with Neil and some members of the cabinet under the Red Wedge banner. Weller would wander off one way and Billy the other. I thought, 'This is cool,' but it was like herding cats. It was symbolic that these people were not to be controlled and politicians naturally like to control things. It was a very interesting meeting of two different cultures.

ASHTAR ALKHIRSAN The office was a bit like a youth club in a grown-up establishment. I called us the Ragged-Trousered Regional Organizers. We'd always get calls like, 'I know it's short notice but could you get us the Style Council for our dinner dance on Saturday?' I was quizzical about it all: 'I'm not sure how effective this is, really?' There was thinking that young people had a predisposition to vote Labour and I used to think, 'Am I just being negative?' We were all quite heady and excitable.

ANNAJOY DAVID We were bringing together a group of artists from all different walks of life and sometimes they agreed and other times they didn't. I don't think that there was one doctrine. We had lots of steering committees, people from film, from art, journalists, all coming together to see how we could impact using their skills. It was a very important dynamic to have these very creative people working together behind the scenes to get the message out there in our language and through culture.

KAREN WALTER The driving force for Red Wedge was when it evolved into smaller satellite groups. And then we would relay everything back to the full meetings.

RHODA DAKAR We all came from our little corners and said, 'I'm fighting this bit.' In a way it made it more effective because we weren't all saying, 'Let's agree on this.' Annajoy defined her politics and probably Billy did and the rest of us were a little more ambiguous. We had musicians' meetings in the canteen at Solid Bond and I remember tearing someone off a strip because they said, 'We're not socialist if we don't believe in a united Ireland.'

PHILL JUPITUS With Rhoda there was a pragmatism and practicality to the whole thing. She could see broader and further ahead, and for someone who was a musician I admired that.

TINY FENNIMORE I ended up at the Labour Party headquarters working as a press officer. The first day I went there I was in a big black hat with a really wide brim and a long black coat to the floor and pearls and Dr Martens. It was like a space alien had walked in, because there were lots of people in corduroy trousers. One guy came in every day and put his slippers on. The first thing I did was buy a load of mugs and a teapot, because no one made each other tea. I thought, 'We're socialists. We're supposed to be nice to each other.' Everyone was dog-eat-dog. And there wasn't a good-looking man in the building.

ANNAJOY DAVID Walworth Road was a very happy place. We moved up to the third floor, where there was a glass panel between us and the press office. It wasn't that big. There were lots of telephones and we made lots of noise. Peter Mandelson was opposite and he had just come into the building. He didn't know what to make of us and smiled and waved and occasionally asked us to turn the music down. His staff thought we were great – Anna Healy, Colin Byrne, Andy McSmith – and would often come to meetings and work with us on campaigns and set up interviews with the political press lobby. Labour had never done anything like this before so there was a lot of new territory for them too. I got quite involved with the policy groups, and Larry Whitty kept the dogs off so we were able to run amok in the building. He was our protector in a way because you had these outsiders inside the political establishment. It was the most bizarre thing.

COLIN BYRNE I was hired by Peter Mandelson from the National Union of Students where I'd been the press and campaigns officer, to make sure that Red Wedge didn't run amok and say things which were going to embarrass us or knock the shine off Neil's carefully crafted modernizing image. Red Wedge was like the radical outriders who gave us a cool façade, but a lot of the bureaucrats were worried that they were uncontrollable. Early on Annajoy was very hostile and suspicious and saw me as Mandelson's spy, and to a certain extent I was. You had to be invited by Annajoy to go to a meeting and pass the Annajoy smell test. They didn't want to be the trendy, shiny pawns of these dull politicians.

KAREN WALTER Most of the meetings at Walworth Road were closed because often we were talking about something that we didn't want them to hear.

TINY FENNIMORE They just had no idea what the hell we were or what we were doing. I remember a woman ringing me up and saying, 'Do you think we could gather some of your musician friends together to have a cheese and wine party and introduce them to some of the members?' It was a real collision of worlds, but they knew they had to be nice to us. There was an article in the *Sunday Times* about me which was all about the new face of Labour and how socialists these days didn't wear dungarees. They wore make-up; so I was cool. Peter Mandelson said, 'I want more of those, please!'

PAUL BOWER Mandelson was this new guy in his early thirties. There was a big fanfare because he was an ex-TV producer from London Weekend Television who was going to modernize the Party. He was ambivalent towards Red Wedge. But we understood that the Labour Party needed people like him. He said they'd done these posters. One was of a quite attractive young blonde woman with her child looking up at a tower block. I said, 'They're quite well designed, Peter, but they're a bit *Triumph of the Will* . . . a bit . . . Nazi.' 'Oh . . . well . . . oh . . . that was not the intention.'

TINY FENNIMORE Peter understood the value of Red Wedge. He knew that Labour wasn't very cool or appealing to young people and could see we could deliver them votes. It was a gift. They didn't have to do anything other than nod. But they did more than nod: they came to gigs and listened to what people had to say. That was a step forward.

PETER JENNER It became difficult with Mandelson because he felt he knew and we felt we knew so there was a certain amount of conflict about how far we could go on things. We were always much more radical. He had some sort of poll man that came in to talk to us and I remember taking him to pieces because it was just really third-rate thinking. There were all sorts of things I just wasn't buying. Mandelson was always very suspicious of us because we weren't under control. We were unstructured. Political parties don't like unstructured things.

TOM WATSON Red Wedge was a movement. It wasn't an organization. It was uncontrollable. When Mandelson got there he inherited Red Wedge and immediately began the journey of command and control communications which reached its apex a decade later with New Labour. What attracted Red Wedge to this great movement was 100 years of history, which is precisely what Mandelson was trying to ditch. He wanted the energy but he didn't want what came with it. He walked in the door and there were people setting up fashion cooperatives and doing fanzines with no editorial control and some of them wanted to renationalize this and others wanted to sign the Peace Pledge. He knew Neil Kinnock wanted it, so there was lots of tension behind the scenes. It became increasingly troublesome and unruly for him as people started to challenge what the Labour Party stood for and did. There were resource issues and of course the artists started to make more and more demands.

NEIL KINNOCK We had to make ourselves more mainstream respectable. My reputation for being a sports-crazy rock 'n' roller who liked a pint had to be subdued. And if you're short and ginger you learn very early that you're a target unless you hit back. The only time I've ever hit anybody is when they've hit me first but I'm not saying that's part of my temperament or any bullshit like that. Peter wanted to make the image more hygienic – he would rather go to the Royal Opera House, especially on a black-tie night – so any distancing that might have happened might have come from his political reading of where I was and where the Party was and was entirely benign, not contemptuous of Red Wedge. In the South Wales valleys high-quality music was as normal as books on the shelf and rock 'n' roll hit us like a bloody storm, so it was no good trying to shake me out of that. But Peter was trying to create a more prime ministerial image for the Labour Party.

ANNA HEALY For a political party, Red Wedge was quite a big risk and quite an adventurous spirit, on our side, to engage. I was amazed that artists were coming in because punks wouldn't have had anything to do with a political party. We were the establishment. The fact that they were prepared to work with Her Majesty's opposition was quite a big step forward. We were trying to rebuild the Party structure so that you could get us all saying roughly the same thing on policies. We had to respect that they were independent of us. We acknowledged them and welcomed them but we didn't try to control them. They were talented and young and attractive to young people's votes, who we desperately wanted, and if Red Wedge was the means of making it, at least young people might think that we might be OK to consider voting for because we were getting their endorsement.

PAUL BOWER I was taken round the Labour Party offices and shown all these files: 'If they call a snap election we've got our battle plan.' 'Yeah, but you were virtually wiped out in '83. Don't you think you might kind of change something?' The Labour Party had about 160,000 members. It was in a shocking state. Someone had created a map of the United Kingdom with all the constituencies and they said, 'We do not print this map to discourage you but these are the constituencies where Labour is now third and have to win a majority of one at the next election.' Labour was broke and on its arse and in the middle of a civil war. They knew they'd failed completely to reach out to young people and a lot of people had voted Thatcher because they'd said, 'She's for people like me that want to get on: entrepreneurs.' It was so bloody disorganized. They were fighting to stand still. For a large period they were on 23 to 26 per cent in polls and the SDP–Liberal Alliance was running ahead. It was an enormous risk to have a load of free-thinking musicians in their building. Say if there'd been a huge drugs bust? There were clearly worries, but people like Tom Sawyer and Larry Whitty made a decision and said, 'We've got to shake things up and do something.'

NEIL KINNOCK Red Wedge was a real bloody uplift. Billy was an ex-soldier and gave the appearance of a rough diamond even though he was very refined, actually. He said, 'Let's get out in the street, not just the halls.' It was a massive encouragement. I used to make the argument all the time that the early struggles of the late nineteenth- and early twentieth-century organized Labour movement had very strong links with culture and music. Just like the Civil Rights Movement in the USA always had a musical background. Just like most of the transformational Labour/socialist efforts of the last 150 years have always had evocative, poetic songs; marching tunes; the people's music. Red Wedge was absolutely bloody natural for us. That's why I put such emphasis on it. We had a conversation in the Shadow Cabinet Office and I said, 'The triumph of ideals must be organized.' Billy said, 'That's bloody it, isn't it?' It was a very old socialist phrase I'd been using since I was fourteen or fifteen. It does mean joining up. It does mean getting finance. It does mean having bloody auditors and committees – all those really boring things.

JOHN NEWBEGIN It has often not played well for politicians to have pop stars up on a platform with them – William Hague wearing his baseball cap backwards at Notting Hill Carnival being the classic example. Politicians usually fuck it up and get it wrong. Red Wedge was perfect for Neil. A balding Welsh miner with red hair is not everybody's idea of cool, so for him it was quite a risk. But it was a risk that Neil thought was worth taking. This was a real attempt to say, 'Labour's agenda is a cultural agenda.' But Neil had a real struggle inside the Party with changing the relationship with the unions and breaking the power of Militant, because the Party tended to think and work in very conservative ways. Suddenly, 'What's all this stuff with pop music and a new, funky, gay communications director?' People were suspicious.

TOM SAWYER John Newbegin was quite exceptional in that he was in the centre of parliamentary power but he wasn't an archetypal special advisor. A lot of what Neil did was at the encouragement of John.

BILLY BRAGG The whole point of Red Wedge was to stimulate debate amongst young people about whether or not it was worth voting for

Labour at the next election. It was incredibly radical. We were using the Labour Party as a vehicle to connect young people to mainstream politics and to encourage them to engage in the political process. We were putting information about socialism into the *NME* and *Melody Maker* and *Sounds*; places it never went. The relationship was, 'We are *for* the Labour Party, not *of* the Labour Party.' It involved a lot of trust. And Kinnock's office were as intrigued by what the possibilities were as we were. It had never been done before. But we weren't there just to make things look pretty. We wanted some input. If we'd been seen to be controlled by the Labour Party we would have sunk like shit. We wanted them to aspire to better things and on some issues they did listen: gay rights, AIDS, youth policy.

RHODA DAKAR The Labour Party didn't know how to talk to young people. It was just fat men in ties. We had our agenda and they had theirs. It's when you've had your first couple of photos with Neil Kinnock you think, 'Fair enough. It's a game. We're not idiots. We know what you're doing.' I thought, 'Fair enough, you don't get anything for nothing.' Yes, we were getting influence on their policy, but they were using us to tart up their public face. It was a symbiotic relationship.

JULIET DE VALERO WILLS Red Wedge was trying to mix some very disparate elements that were very uncomfortable with each other. The politicos had never dealt with rock 'n' roll before and vice versa. They were worlds apart. It was being forced through by the sheer willpower of Billy and Annajoy.

NEIL SPENCER It was two things: drumming up support for the Labour Party in an attempt to reach out to the younger generation who we thought were dangerously politically disenfranchised or disinterested, and putting pressure on the Labour Party to have an arts policy that would engage young people. The support wasn't unqualified. There was a kind of, 'We'll support the Labour Party, but only if you've got policies which we think are worthwhile promoting.'

PETER JENNER It was about a mass movement: if you could mobilize the people who are being fucked by the government to rise up, then you can get a different government. Young people hadn't voted and they were being shafted by the system. We wanted Labour to be a lot more liberal about issues: drugs, entertainment, cultural policy, facilities for making music. It was about trying to getting them to focus and make decisions: 'You're being fucked,' 'Build a better world,' 'Do something about it,' 'Get organized.'

2. NOW THAT'S WHAT I CALL SOCIALISM!

IT'S THE PARTY I LOVE

Launch. First tour

PAUL BOWER The official launch of Red Wedge was held at 11.30 a.m., 21 November 1985 on the terrace of the House of Commons. Anna Healy had been delightful and said, 'If we have it in Parliament and Robin Cook books it you'll get it for free. Also we'll be able to get Neil [Kinnock]' On the day, he was the first to speak and said, 'Can I first of all disabuse anyone of the idea that Red Wedge is the name of my hairstyle. Red Wedge is a call. It's an invitation and we hope that young people in their hundreds of thousands will respond and come and find out what we've got to say to them.' I also remember the line, 'The system promises young people paradise but gives them hell.' Then Billy said a few words, 'Rock 'n' roll loves a party, and thank God it's the party I love. We are not asking people to vote Labour. We are asking them to look at what it has to offer, and if it's not what they expected, to join to try to change it.' There was also a telegram read out from Sade, who was on tour in America, directed at the Prime Minister: 'If we shed a tear for all the sorrow she's caused, we'd drown.' The next day the *Sun* did this half-page which slagged off Sade for supporting the miners and claimed we were a Bolshevik organization.

Red Wedge launch invitation.

What do PAUL WELLER, JUNIOR GISCOMBE, GARY KEMP, TIM ROTH, HELEN TERRY, BILLY BRAGG, JIMMY SOMERVILLE, DC LEE, ROBERT ELMS, JERRY DAMMERS, LLOYD COLE, HEAVEN 17, NEIL SPENCER, LORNA GEE know about?

Find out for yourself at ▷

ROBIN COOK MP

AS SPONSOR OF THE LAUNCH PARTY FOR

R E D   W E D G E

REQUESTS THE PLEASURE OF YOUR COMPANY
AT THE MARQUEE ON THE TERRACE, HOUSE OF COMMONS,
LONDON SW1.

ON THURSDAY, NOVEMBER 21ST 1985

FROM 11.30 AM.

ENTRANCE: St. STEPHENS

SORRY, NO PARKING FACILITIES

ADMITTANCE BY THIS INVITATION ONLY

RSVP: PAUL BOWER, RED WEDGE, 01 708 1400

Launch of Red Wedge Houses of Commons Parliament, 21 November 1985.
(L–R) Kirsty MacColl, Tom Robinson, Ken Livingstone, Neil Kinnock, Jill Bryson
(Strawberry Switchblade), Billy Bragg, Paul Weller

ANDY MCSMITH I don't think the mainstream journalists thought it was very important. They thought it was amusing. I addressed a meeting of MPs and read out something that described Billy Bragg as 'a big-nosed bastard from Barking'. They roared with laughter. It had never occurred to them this might be how you express yourself. What Pete Jenner found funny was watching rock journalists who would spend a day with Boy George and be totally blasé about it but if they got near Neil Kinnock they were quite overawed.

PAUL BOWER I heard a couple of reporters talking about how they'd been doing a load of charlie the night before. There were loads of photographers shouting over to him, trying to wind him up. It was like the caricature in *Spitting Image* of the paparazzi being like rodents. I thought, 'Is this what you have to put up with?' How he didn't go mad or turn to drink.

PHILL JUPITUS I took a picture of Billy in his usual Billy-looking camouflage with Peter Saville who was in this unbelievable houndstooth jacket, elegant trousers and pumps. There was a lot of plummy-voiced, 'Tell me about this Red Wedge thing. What is it? I don't understand. What is it you are doing?' I grew up in Barking – I lived round the corner from Billy but we never knew each other – I was lower middle-class and my mum was like Ian Dury used to say: 'arts and craft; working class'. Mercifully, Red Wedge seemed class free.

TOM SAWYER If you look at the photographs I was slightly embarrassed about being there. I've got a suit and tie on. It was a normal working day for me.

SARAH JANE MORRIS Most people turned up in the same clothes that I'd seen them in at the meetings. It felt very exciting and I was a little bit in awe of famous politicians and people like Robbie Coltrane and Emma Thompson and Kirsty MacColl. I was very impressed by Neil Kinnock.

NEIL KINNOCK It was a great morning and a real lift. Red Wedge was meeting the soul of socialism; be creative, have some bloody fun. It isn't all about marching up and down and waving bloody banners or going on picket lines or going on strike. Engage with the parts of society conventionally neglected by democratic politics: young people, music. The best way to encapsulate it is a quotation from Professor R. H. Tawney, 'At no time should socialism be too austere. Human beings need to enjoy themselves, otherwise life is impoverished.'

PAUL BOWER The amount of ego in that room, you could have powered a nuclear power station with it. But it was positive ego.

BILLY BRAGG There was a band called Blue Rondo à la Turk there – can you imagine Spandau Ballet pretentiously: bowler hats and recherché moustaches. I was like, 'Elms! Did you invite this lot?' He said, 'If you can bring the Frank Chickens I can bring them.'

ANNA HEALY Billy was very excited and he introduced me to somebody and the only word I heard was something like 'commotions'. I thought it was a PR guy who was very big in the industry and I noticed later some teenagers were getting terribly excited about this PR man. I was then informed that he was Lloyd Cole.

JOHN BAINE I was offered a drink by my punk hero Patrik Fitzgerald. He was wearing a bow tie and was serving canapés and champagne to the assorted pop stars and windbags on the terrace. I hadn't seen him for years. I said, 'What the fuck are you doing here?' He thought it was really funny and when he got off we pissed off down to the pub. It summed up something about the nature of organized politics.

PETER JENNER I'd had a lot to do with setting up Red Wedge, but if it was at all seen as a Billy Bragg promotion campaign there would be suspicion and I didn't want it to become a punch-up between, as it were, the Bragg management division and the Weller, Solid Bond division. So after the launch when we announced the first Red Wedge tour I consciously took a back seat.

PHILL JUPITUS The January '86 tour was the statement of intent: the curtain raiser; the scale of what we could do. Here we are. We are Red Wedge.' Weller was very, 'These gigs have to be big and proper.' And then we would spread out and do other smaller things.

RHODA DAKAR Paul financed the first tour. If it hadn't been for him it wouldn't have happened. It was his road crew, his tour manager, his PA, his lights, his bus. Solid Bond organized everything. Billy didn't have that kind of financial muscle. Paul was making money. No one else was.

PETER JENNER Paul was very generous. It was like a Style Council tour with a different badge on the top. And it was necessary to have people like Neil Spencer and Annajoy in there so that it was seen as a general manifestation of youth view.

PAUL BOWER Up until two weeks before the tour kicked off we'd not sold all the tickets and John Weller was seriously considering pulling out. Part of the problem was people didn't actually believe we'd pull it off. 'Oh yeah, we're going to have Billy Bragg and the Communards and the Smiths and Paul Weller and Junior Giscombe and Glenn Gregory and, oh yeah, Madness, but without the drummer because he finds it 'distasteful'. And then we got the front cover of *Melody Maker* and *NME* and all the tickets sold out. BANG!

STEVE WHITE Pick-up was at the Hilton in Kensington on a Len Wright Travel bus. The core touring party was Billy, the Style Council, Lorna Gee, Junior and the Communards. And then other people would join for a couple of shows. Madness, Jerry Dammers, Rhoda.

NEIL SPENCER I'd been on rock 'n' roll tours before but always as a journalist, so it was a very different vibe for me. Jerry Dammers had this big fuck-off beat box. I remember talking to him about house music, which had just come out and I didn't quite get it. He was going, 'This tune. That tune.' Madness were hilarious but quite cruel in some ways. They'd take the piss out of people something wicked. Richard Coles was so droll. He

Red Wedge tour ensemble: (L–R) Jerry Dammers, Joolz Denby, Glenn Gregory, Junior Giscombe, Paul Weller, Billy Bragg, Tom Robinson, Richard Coles, Steve White, Billy Chapman (Style Council); (back row, L–R) Jimmy Somerville, Lorna Gee, Mick Talbot (Style Council), Camille Hinds (Style Council); (front row, L–R) Helen Turner (Style Council), Steve Sidelnyk (Style Council).

came from the same part of the world as me and we talked on the bus about that and even then his Christian faith. There was great conversation to be had. Tom Robinson was a fantastic conversationalist, as were Billy and Pete.

KAREN WALTER Pete was the soul of Red Wedge and pulled everything together. He was a very quiet presence and very much like a father figure. Billy was like Bob Geldof and Pete was like Midge Ure; the one behind answering the questions and getting all the bits and pieces done.

NEIL SPENCER Paul was proud and wary. It was very brave of him to sign up because he had a lot to lose. It was Paul leaving his rigidly controlled comfort zone. He'd got his team and he'd got his credo. It was fantastic he was there. He was very passionate, a man of conviction, but I don't think his father was ever a natural-born Labour supporter.

STEVE WHITE John Weller didn't want a lot to do with Red Wedge. And Paul said to us, 'If you don't agree with this you don't have to do it. It's not obligatory because you're working with me. You do it because you want to do it.'

BILLY BRAGG Paul had a great vision. Without him, Red Wedge would have just been a bunch of noisy lefties doing little gigs. His status at the time was so huge. He was a number-one artist. He was absolutely crucial.

His dad didn't share it. But it was clear he was making what Paul wanted happen. It was like being on the Stax Volt tour – Booker T. and the MGs and Otis Redding – all these bands together on an old-style Magical Mystery Tour bus going from city to city. The atmosphere was really positive.

LORNA GAYLE I had been to a meeting and had a picture taken with Neil Kinnock and they'd explained what this whole thing was going to be about and how they wanted to get young people involved in voting and use music as a tool to make that happen. I was the kind of person they were trying to reach out to. I was like, 'Really! And going to all these places with all *these* people?' The only coach I'd been on was a church trip to Great Yarmouth. It was just like a family. Everybody looked out for each other. At first I was a little bit intimidated, I can't lie, but these people were so just down to earth.

JUNIOR GISCOMBE We carried on like kids. Paul and Dee were this young love in full bloom. And we'd all sing together and mess about on acoustic guitars making things up and rip one another: *Billy's a this, that and the other*. And he would come back in his English accent. It was wicked.

LORNA GAYLE The biggest star for me was bloody Jimmy Somerville, with his potato head, and Richard Coles with his glasses. There was something very honest and genuine about them. Billy was another passionate one. When he talked he didn't use to take a breath. He was like, 'We've got to vote and this is what's going on and that's going on and this is and that is and then we're going to go down theeeere!' I was like, 'This guy's good, man!' He was so popular everywhere he went. I was like, 'How come I've never heard of this guy?' But he speaks the people's language. That's why he was so popular. Paul and Dee C. Lee were having a little thing and were always snogging. And Jerry was a right one. He was cool, man, so unassuming. And listening to Suggs! This is someone I'd seen on *Top of the Pops* every week. And he cared about people. That really touched me.

PAUL BOWER Paul, when he was in the right mood, was very funny. And

Jerry was on great form, for all his intensity and seriousness. I remember them all walking around with boxes on their heads.

ANGELA BARTON I had been singing gospel in a church and Paul Johnson rang me and said, 'Junior's working on an album and needs some backing vocals. Are you interested?' 'Yeah.' Then it was, 'Can you get a week off work? You're going on tour.' I didn't know anything about Red Wedge. I was twenty-four, twenty-five and I didn't know who was going to be on it. I turned up with my bag and there was Billy Bragg and Jimmy Somerville and Dee C. Lee and I'm like, 'Oh my God!' I recognized them from *Top of the Pops*. It was such a buzz. The Style Council had their own van because there was so many of them in the band and they tended to stick together. You'd sit with whomever and have a gossip and a giggle and a laugh. It was like when schoolkids get together: banter and chatting. If there was a spare seat I'd sit next to Jimmy. He was really sweet and cute. I remember him having a crush on Billy.

JIMMY SOMERVILLE One of the best things for me was duetting with Billy on 'Tracks Of My Tears' because I had a bit of a crush on him at the time. I think he knew it too. I mean, you can't help it, can you? He was pretty irresistible. [Richard and I] were very out and proud then, and it was great to be two very loud gay blokes in this bus full of straight men.[65]

RICHARD COLES We all had a crush on Billy. And Paul was a heart-throb. I was a Jam fan so he was a hero. It was like meeting the Queen, so I was a bit scared of him too. He's an exceptionally gifted person and really exciting to be around: original and tough.

TOM ROBINSON Whenever we pulled into motorway services fourteen-year-old girls in pink mohair jumpers with notebooks would materialize from nowhere and hassle Paul for his autograph, and he'd sign them and shake their hands.

NEIL SPENCER Jimmy was a handful. He was always last onto the coach because he'd copped off with someone the night before. There would be a ragged jeer when he was eventually located and brought to heel.

TINY FENNIMORE I remember Jimmy skipping around a lot. He had a lot of energy. Richard was more the calm intellectual.

BILLY BRAGG Jimmy was a very straightforward working-class Glaswegian, really funny, really camp and really angry about what was happening to his community. His energy was intense but the wee man had a wicked sense of humour. Richard had a long view of it and would think things; Jimmy would say them. You need someone like that.

RICHARD COLES Jimmy used to surf on the bus by standing on one leg with his arms out to the side and drive Kenny [Wheeler], the tour manager, mad. I used to entertain everybody with card tricks that always went wrong or sit with the crew and play brag. I remember Lorna's brother had the first mobile phone I had ever seen. It had the handset and a separate battery unit.

STEVE WHITE It was like a brick. Somebody asked him if they could use it: 'Yeah, no problem.' Then it was like, 'Who did you phone? 'Ah, it was just my friend. Syd.' 'Sid?' 'Yeah, Syd. Sydney. Sydney Australia.' That would have cost about £400 in those days.

PETER JENNER Traditionally in the music business it's, 'Who's top of the bill? How big a hit have you had? Who's had the most gold records?' Quite clearly that was Paul. He was the key draw. But Billy had the advantage of not being competitive. He wasn't after your spot on *Top of the Pops*. It was amazing how it worked in that respect.

BILLY BRAGG I had toured with the Style Council before and Weller did a great thing. He went on first, did three songs, got everybody into the hall, and then put me on. So that was a structure for Red Wedge. I went out at 7.30 and got to kick the whole thing off and set the tone.

TOM ROBINSON Billy used to warm the audience up even though he was one of the biggest names. He would be side-splittingly funny, judging the moment just right and knowing just what to say.

SARAH JANE MORRIS He talked to the audience more than anyone. We were all in awe that he could do that. Billy's never been an amazing singer but it's what he sings about. It's a bit like Dylan. The power is in the balance: if you can seduce someone with a beautiful melody and get them to go away singing it.

BILLY BRAGG In the legend of Billy Bragg, the motivation to do what I do was seeing Spandau Ballet on *Top of the Pops* singing 'Chant No. 1 (I Don't Need This Pressure On)' – they were an utter betrayal of everything that I believed in: a bunch of young herberts wearing their mum's living-room curtains. It was a reversal of the content over style – sitting in front of the

Paul Weller on the Red
Wedge tour, January 1986.

TV watching them I suddenly realized nobody was going to write the music I wanted to hear, so I said to myself, 'It's going to have to be me.' I stormed upstairs, picked up my guitar, and everything's been a blur until you walked in this morning. I was rude about Spandau Ballet everywhere. Then suddenly, 'Gary Kemp is coming to Manchester.'

RICHARD COLES I thought, 'Spandau, mmm, should you be here?' Gary's family had all been in the National Graphical Association dispute so he was the genuine article, but I remember thinking, 'Ideologically doubtful.'

BILLY BRAGG Everyone was like, 'Don't let Billy anywhere near him.' Jenner was saying, 'Keep him away for his own good . . . poor lad . . . coming to do something for the cause.' Half an hour before the whole thing there's a knock on the dressing-room door. It's Gary! He's got his guitar. 'Billy, can I have a word?' 'Yeah . . . ?' 'To be honest with you I've never played solo before and I was wondering if there's any tips to doing it.' I thought, 'Fuck me. And he's come all this way to do this.' I said, 'The trick is the little red sign at the back of the hall that says "Exit". If you sing at that,

Gary Kemp at the
Manchester Apollo,
25 January 1986.

generally everyone gets a bit. That's what I do.' He said, 'That makes sense.' He went out and played 'Through The Barricades' for the first time and it was really powerful. I had to respect him for doing it and it changed my view.

KAREN WALTER Gary and Martin Kemp used to be post boys when I started at *NME*. I wasn't precious about him coming on board. You're not going to turn somebody down just because you don't like their music or that they're quite flash and travel the world and have got lots of money. I liked Gary Numan, who came out on the side of the Tories, so it works both ways. Live Aid got lots of artists who shared a common cause and that was basically what Red Wedge was about. If you felt passionately, that's where you needed to be. And the audience responded to that.

PAUL BOWER Gary was charming and articulate. I met him at the airport and he told me about his background and said, 'We were comfortably off working-class and glad to be here.' So, hats off to Steve Dagger because some managers would have desperately tried to talk him out of it.

TINY FENNIMORE It was always, 'Who's going to come today?' It was exciting that we were creating a groundswell and people were joining in. Every time somebody did it you thought, 'Fantastic, you've made the leap.'

BILLY BRAGG Johnny Marr turned up in Manchester and that meant a lot to me. He understood it 100 per cent. We worked on a couple of songs together: 'Back To The Old House', the Stones' 'The Last Time', and on 'A Lover Sings' he put the intro from 'This Charming Man' on the front.

JOHNNY MARR It was a good opportunity for me to finally get off my butt and try and wield some of this so-called influence that popular musicians are supposed to have over their audience. Not to get involved in any preaching, patronizing political stance, but just to show that I was as disenchanted as the next person with the government. And the Labour Party, who I always thought were about people from my class, maybe try to motivate them to change their ideas and listen to what the Red Wedge audience want and share in this general disillusionment and do something about it.[66]

RICHARD COLES By the end of the first evening it had become plain that something big and beautiful had just been born. Then, Lloyd Cole and the Commotions joined us in Birmingham.

Johnny Marr at the Manchester Apollo, 25 January 1986.

LLOYD COLE Billy asked me to do some dates and it was a way to make our political stance public.[67] When I arrived Weller came up to me and demanded to know why I had slagged off his single 'Walls Come Tumbling Down!' I told him it was because I thought it was crap and he said: 'Well, "Forest Fire" ain't changing nothing,' to which I had to agree. Then he said: 'So you really slagged my song off?' I said, 'Yes' again and he looked at me for a minute then said, 'That's all right, then. Everybody else tries to deny it.'[68]

ANNAJOY DAVID Porky, and Cathal and Suggs from Madness, kept everybody laughing. There were a lot of cards being played, a lot of jokes, drinking and some good political discussions. It was a great thing to see. They'd tease me for being quite serious but they worked their craft.

SARAH JANE MORRIS I loved it when Madness were part of the tour. Talk about party animals. Cathal and Suggs were naughty boys and very flirtatious. My friend Claire didn't shave her legs and they were *so* rude to her. She was angry and really went for them. I remember thinking, 'I'm glad I shaved my legs.'

PHILL JUPITUS I desperately wanted to be Suggs, but Madness had already got one. What was interesting about them was that their politics were

Cathal Smyth at the Birmingham Odeon, January 1986.

much more on the down-low. It was really subtly done. You let 'Michael Caine' get into the charts and do its magic and then you tell people it's about IRA informants. 'Blue Skinned Beast' was about the Falklands and there was stuff about domestic violence. Madness were getting really interesting and dark and I was enamoured with that. They were doing some of the most interesting stuff on the tour.

CATHAL SMYTH I was a Labour Party member but I was really only involved under the Greenpeace banner. They were the first thing I'd joined since the Tufty Club. I'd stood on the Archway Road collecting money for them in a fucking jam jar. They were a majority feeling in Madness and we'd recently donated 'Wings Of A Dove (A Celebratory Song)' to a Greenpeace album. But Madness was like being in the fucking Liberal Party. The rallying cry was compromise. Our politics were hidden. We wrote songs with a sprightly melody which brought in the message to the subconscious. It was writing music about the everyman and that was who Red Wedge was trying to reach.

NEIL SPENCER The kids were there to see the stars and then suddenly we were confronting them with Lorna Gee, a rapper. 'Three Weeks Gone Mi Giro' was fantastic.

LORNA GAYLE I was shocked that all of these places were sold out: 'OK, you guys did some serious promotion then.' I thought it would be just a little tour with a couple of hundred people and some of it might be a bit boring because it was politics. I hadn't even voted before because I didn't feel that my voice was important. I was completely blown away: just the energy of the audience. It was a big thing to me, man. I was still on the dole living in Brixton.

ANNAJOY DAVID Lorna brought a completely different cultural emphasis to Red Wedge. She could hold her own.

PETER JENNER The atmosphere at the gigs was great. I remember scurrying around backstage and making sure everything was all right and yet not being in the way and meeting and greeting politicians with Annajoy.

RICHARD COLES In Leicester, we made Ken Livingstone play on 'Don't Leave Me This Way' and he very embarrassingly shuffled on stage in a safari jacket. He ended up signing more autographs than the rest of us put together. I clearly remember Madness trying to get a GLC grant out of him.

SARAH JANE MORRIS Ken Livingstone played tambourine very out of time with us. He was one of the few politicians allowed on the musicians' coach.

LUCY HOOBERMAN I'd never heard the Communards before. They were amazing. Jimmy was tiny but had a huge presence.

SARAH JANE MORRIS There was no rehearsal. We were learning as we went along. I did a lot of dancing and bending down to Jimmy because I'm five foot eight and he's five foot.

PAUL BOWER The Communards with Sarah Jane always went down a storm. But we were fairly strict and keen to keep politicians off the stage. Michael Foot turned up at a reception and was cheered to the rafters.

RICHARD COLES My parents came and my dad was mistaken for Dennis Healey, the shadow foreign secretary, and they were asking him questions. In the bar after, two really leery lads came over and I remember thinking, 'I'm going to get my head kicked in here.' So rather than get huffy and walk off I talked to them. They said they'd come to see the Style Council but because of the whole atmosphere they'd started thinking about things in a different way.

PAUL BOWER Suggs was on the phone to his wife and I heard this, 'Yeah, yeah, of course I know. See you tonight.' He put the phone down and said, 'Oh fuck, I completely forgot it's my mother-in-law's birthday. I'm sorry, guys, I've got to go back to London tonight.' And we all cheered. During their set everyone came on and did the Madness nutty conga dance with Weller at the front and Suggs was laughing his head off. The next night in Bradford we made an announcement: 'Due to unseen circumstances Madness won't be playing tonight but we do have Glenn Gregory from Heaven 17.'

RHODA DAKAR Heaven 17 just went in with both feet. It was so refreshing to hear the same thing 2 Tone had been saying put through different music. It was almost like passing the baton.

PAUL BOWER Glenn was going to do something live over backing tapes but on the night he couldn't find them. Weller said, 'I know the song,' so he played guitar and they did a version of '(We Don't Need This) Fascist Groove Thang.'

JERRY DAMMERS The words to 'Fascist Groove' were fantastic. It was a semi-ironic black American thing and great to have coming from Sheffield.

Suggs at the
Birmingham Odeon,
27 January 1986.

ROBERT ELMS 'Fascist Groove Thang' showed that you could make a dance record that was politically overt. There would have been people in the seventies who would have told you that going out to have a good time and dance was a bourgeois distraction from the class struggle. This music was a rejection of that kind of left thinking.

PAUL BOWER Glenn was always clear that he supported Labour, which shocked a lot of the tabloid press because they saw Heaven 17 in smart suits doing well. Glenn said, 'The reason that we're doing well is because we got support from all the things that the Tories are trying to take away from people.'

JOOLZ DENBY In the soundcheck, Jimmy Somerville sang 'Summertime' a cappella in the empty hall. It was riveting. This cleaner stopped and was leaning with her hands on the back of a seat. It was this most beautiful moment of perfect artistry. Later, I bummed a fag off Paul and he chatted to me. I've never forgotten it. Not because it was Paul Weller but the fact that he deigned to pay attention to you in a matey, casual kind of way. It was so unusual. It's difficult to explain the lowly position that women inhabit in the sausage fest that is rock 'n' roll unless you're pretty and you're a singer or do the catering. I thought, 'Good lad.' And somebody sent me a bouquet of flowers, which was very unusual for me. I was thrilled because this was a big thing and not my normal scene, but I'd been a socialist all my life and I thought if it brings socialism to even one person of sixteen then it's a good idea.

PETER JENNER Bradford was a difficult show. The racial issues were tense there. And the venue was ropy. We didn't do the business. Sales were difficult. It was a difficult local party. We couldn't find the gig and the weather was foul. It was all a bit uphill.

JOOLZ DENBY Bradford was notoriously corrupt and badly managed. I went out on stage and the Lord Mayor was in the audience. The first thing I said was, 'How in the name of Christ can you justify spending £60 on ashtrays when there's kids off school with dysentery?' There was a deadly hush followed by massive standing applause. I got proper ticked-off afterwards.

PHILL JUPITUS Joolz commanded such respect and silence. It was the fact there was room for poets. I always liked the direct communication. It was

Phill Jupitus (front) at St David's Hall, Cardiff, 26 January 1986.

very immediate. I'd do 'Scheme Of Things', about the Youth Training Scheme and then 'Noddy', an anti-nuclear poem. And Joe Norris would stand behind me with a little handheld Casio keyboard. We were in suits waiting to go on and Mick Talbot wandered over and said, 'What you got there? Let me have a go.' Then Richard Coles comes over and starts poking at it: 'What's that? I've seen these.' At which point, Jerry Dammers comes round the corner: 'What the fuck are you lot doing?' So we've got the keyboard player from the Specials, the keyboard from the Communards and the keyboard from the Style Council all tapping away at our Casio. Talbot and Richard wander off and Dammers is poking away on a single note and goes, 'I fucking hate music,' and walked off too. We were gobsmacked.

JERRY DAMMERS I was DJ'ing in between the acts and the best record I put on was by mistake, 'Keep The Pressure On' by Winston and George. It was the power of randomness. Then I would come on for one song with the Style Council to play a version of Jimmy Smith's 'Back At The Chicken Shack'. It was the first time I'd been on stage since the Specials so it was strange and subdued by comparison: fun, but it wasn't the same energy.

ANGELA BARTON I was interviewed for Channel 4 and I was asked, 'Why do you think you've been picked?' I said quite innocently, 'Oh, to add a bit of colour.' I meant a bit of razzmatazz but when I repeated it to Junior and Paul they both went, 'Oh, no.' Then the penny dropped.

LUCY HOOBERMAN We filmed the tour using local film and television workshops in Cardiff, Edinburgh, Birmingham and Newcastle, and a main crew followed the tour bus. Video was like the cheaper, indie version of film. It was innovative and experimental and exciting and slightly under the radar.

I would often be on the stage and around the set-up and interviewing the artists in dressing rooms with mirrors and bad lighting. We filmed Porky in front of a loo and put some plants around it and he did a poem.

PHILL JUPITUS It was guerrilla film-making: 'Porky, come and do a poem.' We'd go down the corridor and Don Coutts, the director, would go, 'Right, you come out the door and we'll film it.' BAM! Done.

RICHARD COLES At each venue there appeared two enormous flight cases with the Style Council logo on. At first, I thought they were Steve White's drum-kit; then I saw Paul open up one to reveal a vast portable wardrobe – it looked like half a street in Milan – and thus the mystery of the Style Council's sartorial elegance was solved. I remember leaving my favourite pair of brown DMs in the Novotel in Bradford. And the hotel: instead of numbers, all the rooms had women's names. Billy was staying in 'Margaret', which struck me as incongruous. I was in 'Doreen'.

PAUL BOWER I shared a room with Neil Spencer through the whole tour – he snored. He was really passionate and enormously influential. Although we were always puzzled that he was into astrology. Jerry got him to guess what his star sign was and I think it took seven attempts. Jerry was going, 'Neil, that's worse than half!'

JUNIOR GISCOMBE I shared with Billy on tour. I'd never met anybody like him before.

BILLY BRAGG Junior was the king because he really was a soul singer. He took it outside of the post-punk ethic. He had a mainstream career that was not known for its politics so for him to come and join us was a big risk for him.

JUNIOR GISCOMBE I wrote 'Come On Over' for the tour, trying to show from a musical standpoint that I didn't just have to do 'Mama Used To Say'. And I felt it was right for what we were doing: *Come on over to my place / There's a solution to the problem.*

KAREN WALTER I had so much admiration for Junior. His music was very different from anybody else involved in Red Wedge. He was articulate and reasonable. I was used to people not being so reasonable at the *NME*.

KEITH HARRIS The atmosphere in the dressing rooms before the shows was really good. I particularly remember Tom Robinson playing a lot of acoustic guitar and being impressed by how good he was.

SARAH JANE MORRIS One of the highlights of the tour was Tom doing 'War Baby'. That was such an emotional song.

TOM ROBINSON 'War Baby' was my comeback. I wrote it whilst I was in tax exile in Germany after the Tom Robinson Band collapsed. Peter Jenner had called me up and said, 'Come on, get out of the studio and come out and rock.' So I was going on with just an acoustic guitar; strolling on between bands.

TINY FENNIMORE Tom Robinson was important to Red Wedge. He was older than all of us, but one of us, singing about gay people. It was a connection to Rock Against Racism.

Junior Giscombe on the Red Wedge tour, January 1986.

LORNA GAYLE When we went to Edinburgh we stayed in this beautiful castle and I remember the bed sheets and the curtains. It was just this amazing print. I was like, 'I've never been in anywhere like this before!'

RICHARD COLES Dalhousie Castle was over 700 years old. It was like staying in someone's stately home. We were followed back from the gig by some of the fans with whom we'd been expressing our solidarity and they were kept back and left outside while we were inside sipping champagne and having fun. There was a Scots baronial library and Steve White walked in and went, 'Blimey, what a load of videos!'

STEVE WHITE Richard's much dined-out-on quote! But I don't think many of the people on the tour were particularly wealthy. Obviously Paul, but he wasn't ostentatious about his wealth. Clothes and records is Paul. Billy was starting out. Junior had had one hit. I was on a wage. We had jobs, but nobody was swimming in money. Somebody had a go at Kenny because he liked to drink champagne. He said, 'Fuck you. The French drink it and they've had a revolution.'

PAUL BOWER In Edinburgh, Jimmy said, 'My mam is coming tonight so no bad language.' Mrs Somerville was obviously very proud of her son. She had a very heavy Scots accent and was smaller than Jimmy!

BILLY BRAGG I'd been awfully foul-mouthed on stage and Jimmy introduced us to his mum and dad and I thought, 'Oh fuck, I've said all that
effing and blinding in front of his parents,' and unfortunately the 'Oh
fuck . . .' bit came out as I shook hands with them.

The last night in Newcastle was absolutely fucking incredible. Morrissey turned up. Nobody knew. Johnny had said to him, 'Come on. Let's
show this Style Council what's what.' I've subsequently read there was
some rivalry between them about who was the best band in the UK. It
was the high point of the tour.

STEVE WHITE Newcastle was insane. We had eleven bands on and Kenny
said no one in the crowd knew when to go for a piss because they thought
they'd miss something.

TOM ROBINSON There was a big excitement backstage about the Smiths
turning up. Then, 'Oh my God!' There they all were. After the interval,
without any pre-announcement, they went out and did four numbers –
'Shakespeare's Sister', 'I Want The One I Can't Have', 'The Boy With The
Thorn In His Side', and 'Bigmouth Strikes Again' – and tore the fucking
place up. Within thirty seconds Morrissey's shirt had come off. It was
un-fucking-believable: the power, the energy, the passion. It was just so
intense.

JOHNNY MARR The gig at Newcastle City
Hall was one of the best things we ever
did. Andy and I had done a couple of gigs
already in Manchester and Birmingham
the week before. I was telling Morrissey
about it and he was fairly up for just
doing an impromptu show. So we
drove up to Newcastle, without telling
anyone. We had no instruments, so we
borrowed the Style Council's equipment and just tore the roof off the
place. The place went bananas. I was
so proud of the band. It was like my
mates showed up and shut everybody up. It was great.

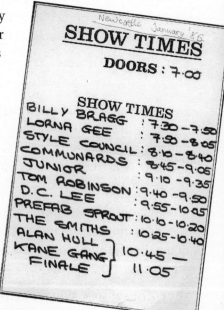

Show times for Newcastle City Hall, 31 January 1986.

Morrissey at Newcastle City Hall, 31 January 1986.

<u>MORRISSEY</u> We made a very brief, but stormy appearance. When we took to the stage the audience reeled back in horror. They took their Walkmans off and threw down their cardigans. Suddenly the place was alight, aflame with passion![69]

<u>NEIL SPENCER</u> I'd never encountered them before. They were unbelievable; full-on. You don't think of the Smiths as 'they rocked' but they did.

<u>PAUL WELLER</u> The Smiths were fucking brilliant. When they came on, it was just this BANG! – this wall of energy. Morrissey just exploded; the audience did. I haven't really seen that level of energy since the Jam, for that kind of hysteria, in a great, positive, electric way. I just thought, 'Fucking hell, that's really what's it about.[70]

<u>RICHARD COLES</u> I remember thinking, 'We're unstoppable now.' Morrissey was unapproachable and frightening. I wasn't really sure what he was doing there. It was too explicit for him; too much a statement of who you are.

<u>LUCY HOOBERMAN</u> What I remember most is when they all jammed together at the end. They looked so happy. They were motivating songs.

Encore: (L–R) Paul Weller, Jimmy Somerville, Sarah Jane Morris, Billy Bragg, Junior Giscombe, Birmingham Odeon, 27 January 1986

ANGELA BARTON Everybody would pile on at the end for the encore, dancing about and singing.

STEVE WHITE It was very powerful getting a band for twenty minutes and getting all the hits, and then we'd all come on at the end and do Dennis Edwards' tune, 'Don't Look Any Further'. The audiences were incredibly up for it. There was a real buzz.

BILLY BRAGG Whatever people say about the politics, the gigs were just amazing. We all would sing 'Move On Up' and Lorna would sing 'Many Rivers To Cross' beautifully. I got to do a verse in 'People Get Ready' and the Style Council christened me 'Curtis Mullard', they said I was like a cross between Curtis Mayfield and Arthur Mullard.

TINY FENNIMORE Junior and Paul singing 'Move On Up' every night was very special and uplifting. They had so much fun when they were working out the soul songs.

LORNA GAYLE They got me to sing 'Many Rivers To Cross' and everyone came on and sang it with me. That was the biggest accolade they could

Encore: (L–R) Paul Weller, Cathal Smyth, Billy Bragg, Junior, Sarah-Jane Morris, Jimmy Somerville, Leicester de Montfort Hall, 28 January 1986

have given me. I felt like that song was my story. It spoke volumes to my heart and I could sing it with truth.

PAUL BOWER Everyone just went crazy. They also did *It's been a long time coming but I know a change is gonna come.* Weller was like the musical director and his band was used by the other acts.

BILLY BRAGG We were basically a bunch of soul boy wannabes. We should have been selling white socks at the gigs. I'd just written 'Levi Stubbs' Tears' and when I played it in the soundcheck Weller came over and said, 'Is that about Levi Stubbs from the Four Tops?' I said, 'Yeah.' He looked at me and said, 'I thought you were supposed to be a folk singer?' I said, 'I am, Paul. It's soul-folk.'

RHODA DAKAR On the final night in Newcastle, we stayed in Lumley Castle in the middle of nowhere and ended up telling ghost stories and playing Murder in the Dark. Jerry was put into a large box and didn't get out until the morning.

RICHARD COLES Murder in the Dark was naughty. It started at midnight and ended at six in the morning. Coventry City Football Club were also staying at the hotel and Jimmy took advantage of the circumstances to give the footballers a night they'd never forget. I think everybody got a bit of a grope. And our tour coordinator was found asleep in the coal chest.

PAUL BOWER I was fairly shambolic. I was up in the bar drinking with everybody until about half past four so I rarely got more than three hours' sleep. Richard said to me, 'Paul, you like to burn the candle at both ends. Stick it up your arse and give it a good twist.'

Before the gig, some people had been demanding tickets and shouting, 'You're all wankers.' Kenny went out to remonstrate with them. He said, 'I think Neil Kinnock's all right but Tony Benn's a wanker.'

RICHARD COLES Kenny put the 'edge' in Red Wedge. It was only his iron discipline that kept the tour on its feet. He fined me £10 for losing my pass.

TINY FENNIMORE He was organizing us all. It was like a little crocodile line of getting on and off the coach. We were terrified the bus would go without us.

PHILL JUPITUS And then he left Mick Talbot on the way back to London. It was proof that he wasn't fucking about because Mick was one of the Council. Fearsome. I was impressed.

BILLY BRAGG We stopped at the services for a pee and left Mick behind. 'Where's Mick!'

RHODA DAKAR I was driving the minibus and I found him at Leicester Forest East service station. At Solid Bond there was a big picture: 'Have You Seen This Man?'

STEVE WHITE Apparently, Mick had come running after the bus and Kenny was horrified because it was the first time that he had ever left somebody behind.

RICHARD COLES At the end of the tour it was very important to keep our momentum and not let our commitment tail off so we added two extra dates.

BILLY BRAGG We had to do London and Liverpool. The GLC and Liverpool Council made us do it. We had made a conscious decision not to go to those places and then it was, 'Oh God, if we must.' Derek Hatton and Ken Livingstone didn't need us.

RICHARD COLES We did a TV show with Derek Hatton who was the deputy leader of Liverpool Council. I sat down and he gave me a big conspiratorial wink. I thought, 'I'm not playing. Whatever you think you're doing, I'm not doing it.'

ROBERT HOWARD Hatton turned up and was more of a diva than any one of the rock stars.

STEVE WHITE There was always somebody turning up saying, 'Can you do this? Can you do that?' I could see that Paul was getting pulled from pillar to post. There was the initial peripheral, 'Yeah, yeah, yeah,' and once it got talked about and the gigs were selling out, that's when the career politicians started turning up. There was a constant demand for photo opportunities. We were not a political party, we were a band.

ANGELA BARTON We came on with Junior and the audience was being racially abusive: shouting and jeering. At one point I dropped my head and thought, 'Oh my God, this is awful.' I was like, 'Why is this happening? I'm here to sing and entertain. You're being disrespectful.' Junior was very calm about it. I came offstage so angry and Julia Roberts, from Working Week, said, 'Don't you ever drop your head again. You hold your head high.'

JUNIOR GISCOMBE People in the audience were shouting out, 'You black cunt.' I couldn't believe it. I stopped the show and shouted out, 'Whoever it is come out and say it here. Let everybody see the racists.' I was about to jump offstage and Tom and Billy ran on and grabbed me and whispered, 'Don't do it. Play it off. Talk it out.'

TOM ROBINSON Billy went out like a head teacher and sorted them out.

NEIL SPENCER I was absolutely appalled. It just showed how backward Britain still was.

JUNIOR GISCOMBE The tour made me understand that there was no way that the message of young black people being involved in politics was going to get across because it was tarnished by the white media. I may not have achieved what I wanted but it was still hugely important that we did what we did. It was the last stand. We spoke out. We talked. We acted.

ROBERT HOWARD The Blow Monkeys didn't do the first part of the tour and then 'Digging Your Scene' was a hit in March '86 which changed everything for us, so we said, 'Yeah, we'll come and do some gigs.' Cathal introduced us and said, 'Here we go, ladies and gentlemen. Here's a new band straight from *Top of the Pops* – the Blow Monkeys.' I thought, 'Oh fuck. Cheers, mate.' My feeling was, the band was going to have to prove itself here. There was going to be people thinking we'd just jumped on the bandwagon and who weren't aware of us being political – although 'Digging Your Scene' was specifically inspired by a quote by Donna Summer about AIDS being 'God's revenge', which she later denied. But the initial impression was pretty boy singer, pop group, so I was giving it a large one politically.

STEVE WHITE In Liverpool we did a version of 'Liquidator' and Jerry started it off so slow I was going, 'Come on, come on.' And then they said, 'Do you know "Madness" by Prince Buster?' I was like, 'Yeah!' Jerry Dammers and Madness and me playing drums. I was like a 2 Tone pig in poo.

ROBERT HOWARD At the end, I got on stage with my guitar to play 'Move On Up' and Billy said, 'Plug it in but don't turn it up, just let Paul play it.' I was thinking, 'I know this song.' Then Paul goes, 'You do the solo.' I thought, 'I'm fucking having it. I'll show you,' because no one knew me as a guitarist. After, Paul said, 'You played that well.' I think I'd impressed him by playing the riff to the Jam song 'A Place I Love' in the soundcheck. It was a buzz, all doing something together. It was like a throwback to things like George Harrison's Concert for Bangladesh where musicians were doing something for a better cause rather than their own betterment.

PETER JENNER: It was a super-heroic and amazing thing. We got it together.

PAUL BOWER If it had been shambolic it would have been, 'Socialists couldn't organize a piss-up in a brewery.'

ANNAJOY DAVID At the end of the tour Neil Kinnock wrote each of us a letter of thanks:

> The first tour has been a spectacular success. Everyone – MPs, young people and the Party workers – who attended the concerts has told me that the people they talked to were inspired both by the evening's event and the day's activities which went before.
>
> I'm sure you've had many ideas on how the Party should respond to Red Wedge. Naturally we should do everything possible to build on your experience.

NOW THAT'S WHAT I CALL SOCIALISM, VOLUME 3

Day Events

ANNAJOY DAVID I absolutely insisted that Red Wedge would not just be about the concerts and the music. There had to be interaction between the musicians, politicians and disenfranchised young people. So I organized all the Day Events with a whole team of brilliant unsung heroes who helped to get local people on the ground active. This is the really interesting bit of the Red Wedge model because it set up a parallel network around the country.

ASHTAR ALKHIRSAN The Day Events gave expression to the frustration and desire for a Labour government and an emergence of socialist principles and it gave young people more of a profile and an opportunity to have their voice taken seriously and make a contribution to the development of ideas.

BILLY BRAGG Annajoy knew the tour had to offer a programme rather than just a load of gigs. She had a vision and understood how all the bits fitted together. She was crucial in pulling focus and taking charge of the Day Events.

ANNAJOY DAVID They took months of planning. I'd get on the phone and ask unions to help find people, and get in touch with Labour councils and say, 'Who leads on youth services in your area? I want to talk to them.' And then I'd go to somewhere like Wolverhampton and find youth organizations and record shops and theatre groups and local rehearsal studios and pirate radio stations and we'd talk about what was important to them. Then on the day of the gig we'd have local bands and theatre groups and anti-apartheid organizations and people against the Youth Training Scheme and local clubs that needed money or people trying to raise money for rehearsal space or selling fanzines or T-shirts. Then round about teatime or during the soundcheck I would grab some artists to come down together with some local or national politicians and there'd be this

Red Wedge press conference, Leicester, 28 January 1986:(L–R) Paul Weller, Richard Coles, Billy Bragg, Mick Talbot, Rhoda Dakar, Steve White, Junior Giscombe.

great big Q&A. They were packed. I mean, can you imagine getting 1,000 young people just turning up at a hall to hear politicians and artists and local bands now?

PAUL WELLER It wasn't just a few pop stars going out on the road.[71] One of the best things was getting out and talking to youth about political issues. Young people [were] generally beginning to realize that it [was] in [our] hands to do something. It was very positive.[72]

ANNAJOY DAVID They were hugely successful. It was all part of the Red Wedge Regional Development programme supporting and resourcing youth initiatives. And if Paul [Weller] had specific projects he and I would go off and have meetings with them and give them a really big push, like the Cultural Club in Liverpool with young people from working-class estates doing theatre, or the Leigh Cooperative, which was a resource centre to help young unemployed people with skills and training, and other similar youth organizations across the country in places like Gateshead and Stirling.

PHILL JUPITUS Annajoy was a real powerhouse and getting out to the people who wouldn't normally do things. They'd see where a local council wasn't addressing a real need for a youth cultural base and help in practical terms. I did a day of gigs reading poetry for the Norwich Venue Campaign, and Weller and Dee C. Lee did a little acoustic set. Then in the evening we DJ'ed at Henry's Night Club. The apoliticals came to see Weller, and the Red Wedge politicos would be trying to give leaflets out to all these ageing mods. We were lighting fires.

NEIL SPENCER Annajoy was very big on helping young people build their lives. We had a propaganda brochure called *Fact Not Fiction* about housing, youth training, unemployment, allowances for the low-paid, gay rights. Annajoy was a fantastic bridge between the parliamentary people and us.

RHODA DAKAR The music was to get them in and chuck them a few leaflets but the Day Events is where the political discussions took place and for people to discover who we were. It was them saying, 'You've all landed here from *Top of the Pops*: what difference are you going to make to my life?'

Red Wedge
Fact Not Fiction No.1
pamphlet, 1986.

SARAH JANE MORRIS We were doing a lot of defending and being bombarded by right-wing views but we believed that popular music had a power; that things could change because of music.

LUCY HOOBERMAN Red Wedge was obviously a Labour Party-blessed entity but when asked direct political questions the artists would answer the questions according to their own points of view. Paul was quite often attacked for being famous and wealthy. Somebody shouted out, 'What are you going to do for me?' And Paul said, 'What am I going to do for you? I ain't gonna do nothing for you. What are you going to do for yourself?'

ANNAJOY DAVID It's a really important question if the attraction of the Day Events was Paul Weller and Billy Bragg or the politics. The answer is, it was people realizing that they could be part of something as a collective voice. That's what took over in the end. Jerry was very outspoken. I remember him saying, 'The worst possible Labour Party is better than the best Tory government.'

BILLY BRAGG There was undoubtedly an element of people wanting to meet Paul or me or Jerry. We were all aware of the contradictions. None of us believed that electing a Labour government would solve everybody's problems, far from it, but we were committed to doing whatever we could do.

PAUL WELLER The grass-roots work was the real meat for me: working with drug rehabilitation centres and other local groups. But the real struggle was less campaigning to young people than campaigning to the Labour Party. We felt they were totally out of touch. We wanted to find a way of closing the gap between youth and the Party, but there were so many factions within the Wedge, and so much red tape to go through within the Party – it took ages to change anything.[73]

RHODA DAKAR I don't think Paul's political nous was the same as Billy's but he had very definite ideas. He said, 'The main thing is to politicize young people. If they don't know why they're in Shit Street we'll give them facts and figures.' He was small 'p' political. It was perfectly reasonable.

NEIL KINNOCK Paul never had Billy's political sophistication, and I don't mean that in a cerebral intellectual sense. They were different individuals who had in common their desire and willingness to use their fame on behalf of a very good cause and try to get a fair deal for youngsters. And they did it in a slightly different spirit from one another. Billy in his gut understood the nitty-gritty of politics. Paul knew right from wrong and had come to politics through discontent, which is perfectly reasonable. Bloody hell, if I'd been contented as a kid with what was going on around me I'd probably have never joined the Labour Party. We were delighted that he was around but he would only do what he wanted to do. I wouldn't have it any other way. But there was an edge about Paul: a taste for the absolutism, or, if you like, the Militant Tendency.

CLARE SHORT I saw the Day Events as attempting political mobilization and inclusion. Using music and culture is normal when you're trying to do that.

RICHARD COLES In Wales, these Labour people came and I got in a fight with one of them in a rare moment of anger. They basically said, 'Make sure you tell people to vote for us.' I said, 'That's not how it works.' It was a moment of realization that we were not there simply to whip in the Labour vote.

JUNIOR GISCOMBE A lot of the people came not because we were pop stars but because they were genuinely concerned. We would sit in a line and ask people what they were going through.

CATHAL SMYTH A woman said, 'Why do you have to be intellectual to be in politics?' and Bedders, Madness's bass player, said, 'You don't have to be. It's just a gut feeling. You can start with, my granny's ill and she can't get a bed in hospital. Surely, there's something wrong in that?' It was as much a journey and a new adventure for us as for everyone who we were seeing. It was born of hope. As Bernard Schumacher says, 'You've got to be part of the cure rather than part of the disease.'

BILLY BRAGG In Leicester there were two Day Events simultaneously: me and the Communards went to the Phoenix Arts Centre and Weller and Junior went to Highfield's Workshop Centre behind the British Rail station.

ANNAJOY DAVID Paul got a huge cheer when he said, 'People have become pessimistic because the media, big business and corporate power are all on the side of the right. Socialism must confront these things, but it must also remember that it is about movements, people coming together to bring about change. No matter how much the right increase the powers of the police or implement social order acts, that basic demand of people to organize themselves to effect change is quite simply unstoppable.'

Day Event: (L–R) Jerry Dammers, Billy Bragg, Richard Coles, Paul Weller,
Birmingham, 27 January 1986.

NEIL SPENCER One of the ideas behind Red Wedge was of a rainbow coalition – a phrase the American congressman Jesse Jackson came up with
– so you would have people whose principal interest was gay rights alongside CND or whatever. There was this sort of hysteria about gay people
because of AIDS, the 'Gay Plague' as they called it, and because you had
Jimmy Somerville and Richard Coles and Tom Robinson these young kids
would come along specifically and say, 'Thanks for sticking up for us.'

RICHARD COLES We met the excellent Keith Vaz, the local prospective
candidate – who said, 'I will take on board the issues raised and pass on
your comments to Neil Kinnock' – and spent the afternoon answering
questions to an audience of about 300. I talked to some people from the
Left Out Collective, an organization of socialist lesbians and gays. It was
the first time they'd ever done something in tandem with the local Young
Socialists and consequently the first time they'd had the opportunity to
meet and talk to young people from all over Leicester. That, for me, was
what Red Wedge was all about.

PAUL BOWER In '83, Labour had lost Leicester West by about 1,700 votes,
Leicester East by just over 900 and Leicester South by just seven votes;
so they were keen to get young people registered. I remember Keith Vaz

saying if he was elected he wouldn't take his £18,000 MP's salary but instead take a 'worker's wage'. Then he said, 'Young people really don't like Neil Kinnock.' I said, 'No, Keith, they don't like politicians.'

CATHAL SMYTH A woman said: 'I don't know how to be political.' So the concept of boycott was explained to her: simple, hit them in the fuckin' pocket; direct action; stop shopping there; find out who owns it; go elsewhere. The reaction was hopeful. But then a bloke who was ex-British Telecom went, 'You're not bloody politicians.' I said, 'Hold on, mate. It's a democracy. We have the right to express our voice.' Some people were offended but they were the people who did nothing but moan. I was putting myself on view as taking a stance. If you can connect a good idea with the right group of people then you've got a chance to make a significant change.

PAUL BOWER As well as the Day Events, the other side of the Red Wedge story is the by-elections. In Newcastle-under-Lyme Llin Golding was elected by a few hundred votes. And somebody from the Labour Party said, 'Red Wedge absolutely helped. It might have even won us the seat because they were registering people to vote and getting people to fill forms in. It was the first time anybody had thought about reaching out to young people.'

Day Event audience, Birmingham, 27 January 1986.

ANDY MCSMITH Red Wedge also got involved during the Fulham by-election campaign in April 1986. The Faith Brothers agreed to play in support of the Labour candidate, Nick Raynsford, and their main song was 'Fulham Court'. Nick went on the stage and their fans were all shouting *Fulham Court, Fulham Court*. Nick thought they were talking about the council estate and said, 'Fulham Court is disgraceful.'

NEIL SPENCER A letter was sent to out to all first-time voters in the Fulham constituency signed by Neil Kinnock and all the Red Wedge musicians. It was an astonishing document: seeing pop stars directly backing a party political candidate. There was also an afternoon event at the Brunswick Boys' Club with Heaven 17 and Ken Livingstone but Rhoda described it as a 'miserable failure' after there was a problem with attendance due to a lack of leaflet distribution.

RHODA DAKAR I was dubious about us having a part in the event. The idea of famous faces, both political and musical, being bussed in to do some rather unwholesome baby-kissing and backslapping and to say, 'Vote Labour,' despite having no knowledge of either the local politics or the candidate, was unpleasant in the extreme. And we were not welcomed by the by-election office; they were interested in being 'respectable' and appealing to the middle classes. We were spitting in the wind.

RICHARD COLES MPs would come over all, 'Lovely music, my daughter's got all your records, what a splendid show,' and patting us on the head; but we were more often than not surrounded by local young people wanting to know why they didn't have jobs and houses and chances.

PAUL BOWER We took the politicians to places to listen to people they otherwise wouldn't have met. For some it was a welcome break from leafleting in the pissing rain but often the debates could be quite tense: 'You're all sell-outs,' 'You're all bastards,' 'You've come up from London, you don't realize our struggles here.' We'd listen to people patiently but unfortunately it got a bit like the Monty Python 'Four Yorkshiremen' sketch, 'Aye, you were lucky . . .'

STEVE WHITE MPs wore tweed jackets with patches on the arm, one up from a geography teacher. They were always in awe of Paul.

PAUL WELLER There was a great camaraderie amongst the musicians. But meeting the politicians reinforced what I already believed; that they were just out for themselves.[74] There were so many careerists among them.

Once we started meeting these MPs it was just like, 'Oh God, we don't want to be part of this.'[75] They were more showbiz than the groups. It was an eye-opener, it brought me full circle in how I feel about organized politics. It's a game.[76] It's not what we were about. It got to the stage where every interview was politics, politics. You think, 'Whatever happened to the music?'[77] If I was an author I wouldn't get questioned so much about, 'Is this the right thing to do; should politics be in music?'[78]

TINY FENNIMORE The MPs looked very uncomfortable but I admired them for coming. They were out of their comfort zones, and people were angry. There was a lot of pointing of fingers and shouting in frustration that they couldn't get jobs, and a lack of trust in politicians that anything could change. There was shock at how Red Wedge had tapped into the strength of feeling amongst young people. The main thrust of the Day Events was getting young people to register to vote, but they didn't feel like anybody was talking to them. There were very few places to read about politics and about why we didn't like Mrs Thatcher.

KAREN WALTER It seemed like the Tories had been in for so long that people had become apathetic.

NEIL SPENCER It was very much about making the MPs accountable to the people whose votes they were counting on. Of course they were very often anxious and uncomfortable with that because they'd never met local youth, and then to be confronted in that very raw way. MPs were felt to be remote and part of a Westminster club and not accountable to the ordinary citizens. Keith Vaz was a box of tricks. I was very impressed by him but then his subsequent career made me question how authentic he was being. And Anne Clwyd, in Mid Glamorgan, was very composed. She thought it was all wonderful.

ANDY MCSMITH In Newcastle, a local councillor said to me, 'This is the best thing the Labour Party has ever done.'

STEVE WHITE In Birmingham we were in this room fielding questions from the nationals and the *Guardian* asked Dee, 'What are your thoughts about the government's policy in Northern Ireland?' She didn't really know what to say. We were out of our depth. We were not politicians but we were being spoken to as if we were. It was a mark of the impact that Red Wedge had had in a very short amount of time. That's when people's individual agendas started to fractionalize a little bit: 'Are we musicians or are we a political party?'

Red Wedge press conference, Leicester, 28 January 1986: (L–R) Mick Talbot, Rhoda Dakar, Steve White.

CATHAL SMYTH We were asked to comment on the news and we picked up on the train drivers' strike, but they didn't want us talking about that. They thought, 'Madness: funny.' They wanted wackiness: 'Fred Bartham's married his milkman; first man to marry his milkman,' and comfortable stuff like that.

PAUL BOWER Birmingham was the same day that the Westland debate took place in the House of Commons over the future of the British helicopter industry. Two ministers had already resigned and there was speculation Thatcher might go – and the artists were so disappointed with Kinnock because he dropped the ball and didn't score; open goal, Thatcher. He could have really devastated the government and he just wasn't strong or sharp enough. The artists were looking for professionalism. They were saying, 'I'm a shit-hot musician. I'm putting myself on the line for you. I'm expecting you to do that as well. If you let me down that makes me wobble.'

KEITH HARRIS Birmingham had some real aggression and hostility from the local youth towards the artists' support for Arthur Scargill during the Miners' Strike. But the success of the events was that it made it clear that they weren't mindless pop stars doing something for publicity. They actually had ideas about society and how it should be, and they were extremely articulate and had some good points to make.

LORNA GAYLE A lot of the events I zoned out. It just wasn't my world. I remember thinking, 'I've never seen so many white people in one place. I didn't know there were so many in the country.' That is so rank and stupid but I was like, 'Where are they all coming from?' I was just a black girl growing up in Brixton, where there was so much negativity, and just MC'ing on sound systems and doing odd jobs in Pizzaland or as a chambermaid. But we were under a Tory government and we were falling under. Labour was for good people, poor people, working-class people, black people, people that felt like the underdog. I was more like, 'If you want a better life get up and do something for yourself.' I saw a lot of people fronting and I just couldn't do that and take the chance of looking stupid. Junior was like, 'Look around you. You need to have a voice. Your voice is as important as anyone else's. We need to be heard. You've got as much right to be here as Paul Weller or Madness.'

JUNIOR GISCOMBE Lorna was very fresh. It was like, 'Stick with me. I've got an angle on this.' Politicians want votes: I was saying, 'Let's bargain those votes. You want us? You do what we want for a change.' SDP, Labour, Conservative, it didn't matter to me as long as you were getting the chance to say, 'Well, actually, I don't like that, but I do like this.' I was saying, 'If we don't vote they don't have a mandate. If they have no mandate they need us more than we need them.' I'd never had that before. Billy and Paul thought I was too radical.

KEITH HARRIS Junior was from a working-class family from Jamaica. He was aware of the gap between the establishment and the workers. In some respects, I was surprised at how formed his opinions were.

JUNIOR GISCOMBE I never claimed to be part of the Labour Party but for once people had come together within the pop world to say things were wrong in our society. Politics was another world to these young people but what was going on in their areas was political. We were in a multiracial society but the Tories were playing working-class white against working-class black. I was showing through music you didn't have to be white to have a radical view; you didn't have to be white to say you disagreed with the Falklands War. I live here too. Tom Robinson said, 'You can live in hope but don't live in politicians' hope.'

KEITH HARRIS We were both alarmed about what was going on in society. I moved to LA in 1978, the year before Thatcher came to power, and when I came back in 1982 the contrast was dramatic. It's a small thing but it's illustrative of the way things had changed: in LA, I was astonished how everybody was so security-conscious; everybody had a burglar alarm and bars on their windows. I thought, 'This society is crazy.' I was back in the UK less than three weeks before I got burgled. All the messaging coming out socially had changed from being a moral message that you shouldn't steal from people, to 'If you don't have a burglar alarm and get burgled it's your own fault; if you leave things on display in your car expect them to be stolen.' Crime rates rose dramatically because of the rise of unemployment but it was also aligned to the central message of the Conservative govern-ment which was, we are a collective of individuals who are responsible for ourselves, not everybody. Community was a thing of the past. If you think of films like *Wall Street* and Alan Bleasdale's *Boys from the Blackstuff*, that was the mood of the times. I hoped Red Wedge would change the attitude of a lot of younger people who in their formative years had been fed this message and at least make them question whether there wasn't another way for society. The artists were extremely brave because they were putting themselves up to be shot at and ridiculed because it was such an unfash-ionable thing to do.

TOM SAWYER This was a musical movement that was connecting with young people in a way that the Labour Party hadn't been able to. But it wasn't a new cultural phenomenon as such. Go back to Bertolt Brecht. Go back to the 1930s. Go back to Joan Littlewood's Theatre Workshop. But Red Wedge was the first generation of rock 'n' rollers who were directly political.

PETER JENNER A lot of artists don't want to be political. It was a balancing trick, 'My art may reflect the world in which I live but I'm not going to be a hack for some bunch of political crooks.' Politicians are like door-to-door salesmen; you may not want to buy double glazing from them; you might not want to buy their political message. So the official line was that it was cross-party. We would always invite the Tories and the Lib Dems but nobody responded because they knew it was a Labour Party fix. They weren't stupid either.

ANGELA BARTON Ultimately, you wanted young people to vote Labour, so it was a form of propaganda. It was difficult for people to understand what was occurring within Parliament. When you looked at the make-up of government it was predominantly male and from a higher echelon of society. So the Day Events were a fantastic way, more on our level, to show people you can have an influence: 'This is the Labour Party and this is what they want to do for you. Is that what you want?' They gave the youth a mirror to say, 'You can make a difference. Don't just leave it to people who are in power.' It was groundbreaking.

LARRY WHITTY It was quite a liberating way of getting more people to talk to the Labour Party. There is a cultural problem between most politicians and dealing with problems of youth.

TONY MANWARING When you talked to people within the Labour Party they knew they'd taken young people for granted. They genuinely understood that they had to talk about politics in a language that people understand. I was pleasantly surprised when I got off the National Express coach and went to a Day Event at how open-minded people were. These artists rolling up in town energized and inspired a lot of local organizers who had just come out of an absolutely gut-wrenching election defeat. But there was a tradition of Labour that just didn't get it. It wasn't hostile. It was more like *Men are from Mars, Women are from Venus*. But in many ways, the Day Events were pockets of invisible experience. That's awful and tragic and really sad.

TOM SAWYER The Day Events weren't understood properly or valued enough. Annajoy was a pioneer. She fought against the grain in a good way. She'd be very angry and she'd swear a lot but she knew she was up against a party that was out of touch.

COLIN BYRNE I remember talking to Labour backbenchers who'd been to some of the Red Wedge events and they'd come away (a) enthused because they were hanging out with the cool guys, but (b) it opened their eyes that there was more to politics than the smoke-filled rooms. They recognized that these were events that young people actually wanted to go to. It gave Labour a terrific shot in the arm.

NEIL KINNOCK The Day Events were really effective communicators with youth and the politicians. MPs would seriously try to answer the kids' questions and show in very direct and sincere terms that they were listening and they were trying to respond. The feedback of the kids was repetitive: they wanted decent jobs, places to live that they could afford.

Paul Bower interview for *Music Box*, Leicester, 28 January 1986.

The greatest challenge we had was convincing youngsters that their desire to extend education and to get better training or get a job was entirely feasible, and it was within the realms of political power and the right government to be able to do it. We put the whole political argument to them and when it worked it really was utterly bloody brilliant and when it didn't, well, at least we were making the effort.

PAUL BOWER At a press conference I announced that we'd made a massive impact on the Labour Party's communications because they would not be releasing a written manifesto at the next election. Instead, they were just going to do a cassette called *Now That's What I Call Socialism, Volume 3*. Journalists were taking it down. I remember Neil Spencer snorting.

IT'S JUST A RUMOUR THAT WAS SPREAD AROUND TOWN

Militant Tendency. Newcastle

TONY MANWARING Militant Tendency was a secret entryist organization within the Labour Party who had had control of the Labour Party Young Socialists. By the mid-eighties they claimed to have over 4,000 members. It was deceptive and brutal and seen as ugly and evil. It was about intimidation and beating people up. It was wrong and the energy and the focus around it was Derek Hatton in Liverpool.

ANDY MCSMITH The big drama in 1985 was the moment when Neil Kinnock got up at the Party conference in Bournemouth and talked about 'the grotesque chaos of a Labour council – a Labour council – hiring taxis to scuttle round a city handing out redundancy notices to its own workers'. Derek Hatton stood up and jeered. I had asked Billy Bragg and Pete Jenner to come and listen. And then the Labour backbencher for Liverpool Walton, Eric Heffer, stormed off the stage. He went past us and Billy applauded him. I was quite surprised but Billy said, 'The guy stood up and said what he thought.'

PAUL BOWER I remember being tipped off that Kinnock was going to say something really explosive: 'Make sure you're watching on TV.'

ANGELA EAGLE I was up in the balcony in the big sweeping hall at the International Conference Centre and I could see Derek Hatton sat on the end shouting, 'Liar, liar.' We were all on our feet. It was an extremely electrifying moment and the turning point in our fight back to be able to be electable again. I had joined the Labour Party in Crosby as a teenager when it was being infiltrated by Militant. We knew what they were like: it was nose-to-tail follow you home and threaten your dog time. I knew what had to be done.

NEIL KINNOCK Even though we'd inflicted a serious defeat on them, the Militant Tendency had been running a campaign against the Youth

Training Scheme which I agreed with because it was a bloody appalling system. But they were manipulating people in the same way the ultra-left always does. The advantage of embracing a doctrine is you've only got to make up your mind once in your life. I could never accept that because life is not like that. There was a concern of Militant infiltration into Red Wedge.

PETER JENNER There was a war between the Labour Party and Militant and they tried to fuck us up. If you were keeping out of that you were almost keeping out of politics. It was very tricky not being aligned with either and keeping communications open. There was a lot of suspicion from both sides. Our perception of us all being lefties together – 'We're all fighting for a better Britain' – was being denied by the political structure, which was much more traditional rigid party line. The Young Socialists didn't want anything to do with anything that wasn't the party line.

JOHN NEWBEGIN The youth vote has always been a difficult one for parties to engage with because young people think of mainstream political parties as boring. And when people thought of Labour Youth they thought about Militant and a bunch of deranged nutters running around.

LARRY WHITTY There were those that felt Red Wedge was letting in the Trojan horse; that they were a threat or a front for some other organization. We were all worried about that. Paul Weller expressed views on occasion which people raised eyebrows at.

TOM WATSON Labour was a party in transition and split from top to bottom ideologically around personalities. That was physically personified on the second floor of Labour HQ, where you had the Young Socialists at one end of the room run by Andy Bevan, a revolutionary socialist, and then the other end you'd got the Students' Office. There was a deadly struggle for who speaks to youth and all of a sudden here are these overwhelming creative people coming into the building suggesting new ways of doing things. Red Wedge didn't do political nuance or political sectarianism. I remember saying to Paul Bower at Christmas, just before the first tour, 'This sounds a bit daft but I just overheard Militant in the toilet talking about packing the next meeting to demand we support Liverpool Council.'

PAUL BOWER Tom was very upset and he confided their plan to me. I told him I would sort it out and then we packed the meeting with even more people than them. My fear was people like Gary Kemp would pull out if they thought Militant had anything to do with Red Wedge, and the Labour Party would understandably see the whole thing as too much of a risk.

ANNAJOY DAVID Militant might have occasionally turned up but they never had a hold because Red Wedge was operating outside of those organizing traditions. It was really successful at actually keeping the central message and the power and the control in young people's hands that were doing creative things.

TOM SAWYER When Militant started to say 'Comrade Bragg, if we don't nationalize the top hundred companies,' young people just switched off.

PAUL BOWER One of the joys of Red Wedge was there wasn't any real structure, which used to drive Militant mad. You couldn't take it over because it was too anarchic. Pete Jenner would say, 'Don't worry about it, Paul. Just tell 'em to fuck off.' I offered some mild criticism at a meeting once of Ted Grant, who was the leader and ideologue of Militant, and one of their members was screaming at me. It was as if you had criticized the Pope to a fanatical Catholic. Andy Bevan said, 'Paul, what you've got to realize is some of these people are basically Conservatives.'

BILL GILBY NUPE helped to bring about Militant's expulsion from the Party. They were almost like a religious organization. We started to take them on and were seen as organizing a witch-hunt.

ANNAJOY DAVID Red Wedge and the musicians were masterful at walking a tightrope to push all that out; it was like the parting of bloody Moses' waves, so young people could come in and sound us and the politicians out. That was best displayed when Paul [Weller], Billy and I met Derek Hatton. There was a quite a rebarbative conversation about Liverpool and racism and we felt there was a sense of denial. My view of Derek was best revealed when he said, 'We build council houses for *our* people.' It was this very paternalistic view. Across Liverpool every single door was the same colour; any individuality or creativity was non-existent. It was important that Liverpool Council was defying the Thatcher government, but on their own failures to address issues of care, equality and race, Derek was silent. We found that troubling. It was about Derek Hatton. He loved the glamour and the glitz and was a bit flash. That troubled Paul. As far as he was concerned he was involved in an independent organization that was there to get young people involved in politics, to think about politics, and to be part of a wider counterculture against the government. On the other hand, the work that they were doing to shore up the council against the backdrop of huge government cuts was admirable and what was really important was that there was a collective voice against the government of the day. We felt that the Labour Party needed to understand some of the new and important cultural dimensions that express themselves first in culture and then permeate into civil society: gay rights, and what was happening to black people.

•

KAREN JOHNSON Ten of us had set Riverside up as a collective with the purpose of providing a venue and facilities for local musicians and youth. After the riots in 1981, and again in 1985, the government wanted to be seen supporting young entrepreneurs – as Labour supporters, it was quite an eye-opener – and we got letters of support from Margaret Thatcher and were granted £150,000 for three years. Michael Heseltine pushed it though. It was quite a strange feeling. There we were very anti-Tory because of the Miners' Strike and being young, but it was actually an old-school Labour council blocking us from creating a new project. It didn't seem right, somehow.

BILLY BRAGG Very often, through the Young Socialists, Militant were using everything they could to exploit what we were doing for their own ends. In Derby the Labour Party said, 'We don't want Red Wedge coming here. We don't have any young people!'

PAUL BOWER In Edinburgh, during the first tour, a journalist asked about the after-show gig with a new local band called Wet Wet Wet, and somebody piped up at the back, 'It's been cancelled.' I said, 'It's not been cancelled.' He said, 'It's definitely been cancelled.' I said, 'That's a lie.' I was really angry. I went down to the gig and they said the Young Socialists had been going round giving leaflets out saying it'd been cancelled. And then in Newcastle all hell broke loose.

KAREN JOHNSON I was the publicist and marketing person at the Riverside in Newcastle and the venue was booked on the Red Wedge afternoon for seminars and workshops by Paul Bower. It quickly became apparent that the local Young Socialists had hijacked the event and put the rumour out there was going to be live music.

We had been told that Day Events didn't have live music, but the rumour mill had gone mad and the venue was absolutely rammed. There were at least 500 or 600 there and it was a very heavy, scary, intimidating atmosphere. Half the crowd were Militant Young Socialists, winding up the whole atmosphere of aggression and confrontation, and a few trouble-makers all baying for a live band. Me and a colleague had been on the phone to Peter Jenner to say, 'Can Billy help us?' But then Red Wedge got offered the live music programme *The Tube* so they said, 'We can't do it.' We said, 'Oh God. There's going to be a riot here if something doesn't happen.' *The Tube* was a two-minute walk down the road, so we were like, 'Well, can't you do both?' We were really panicking.

TOM ROBINSON *The Tube* had said, 'Can you send a couple of people along from the tour to talk about Red Wedge,' and me and Sarah Jane Morris were both desperate to be on telly so we said, 'We'll do it.'

SARAH JANE MORRIS Obviously, nobody wanted to miss out on *The Tube* exposure. It was my first time on TV and we did a version of 'Tracks Of My Tears'. Jerry played keyboard. Jimmy and Billy did a verse each and I shared a microphone with Tom.

Red Wedge performing 'Tracks Of My Tears' on *The Tube*, 31 January 1986: (L–R) Steve Sidelnyk (percussion), Billy Bragg, Jimmy Somerville, Jerry Dammers, (keyboards), Sarah Jane Morris, Tom Robinson.

KAREN JOHNSON By this time it was about three, four o'clock in the afternoon, so we sent our head barman down to the Tyne Tees studios to see if he could nab somebody, and he found Elvis Costello, who had been booked to perform 'Don't Let Me Be Misunderstood.' He begged him to come down to the Riverside and Elvis said yes. When he arrived he asked for a pint of lager, a pint of orange juice and a guitar. And then he went on stage and said to the audience, 'I don't know where the fuck the others are,' and started playing a wonderful rendition of 'Shipbuilding'.

RICHARD COLES 'Shipbuilding' sent a shiver down my spine: *It's just a rumour that was spread around town.*

JAKE BURNS The beauty of 'Shipbuilding''s subversion was this gorgeous tune allied to this really heartbreaking and hugely political unpleasant lyric. It's that great Tom Waits quote: 'What I love is beautiful melodies telling me unspeakable things.' It was a perfect indictment of Thatcher's bravado in going into the Falklands War.

ANGELA EAGLE Elvis's lyrics eloquently captured the inchoate rage that a lot of people who were disempowered by Mrs Thatcher felt about her: that powerlessness and disgust at what you couldn't change. It was cathartic. It was about reviving the economy by having a war and was seen as a criticism of the jingoistic and political response and the way that Mrs Thatcher exploited the outcome of the Falklands to her own ends: 'Just rejoice,' and all that.

ELVIS COSTELLO The things that she visited on society as a whole we'll never ever recover from; the dismantling of this society, that she said was 'invisible', was truly wicked and evil. It was beyond politics and into morality.[79]

KAREN JOHNSON Elvis played for about forty minutes and then Billy Bragg and Jimmy Somerville and Sarah Jane Morris and Jerry Dammers arrived. There were a lot of questions from the audience. It started off quite aggressive but everybody was cheering and happy at the end – and they did four or five songs themselves and got an amazing reaction.

TOM ROBINSON I'd just done a live interview on *The Tube* and the presenter Muriel Gray gave me a hard time about 'patronizing and preaching to the converted in Scotland' and, 'Shouldn't you be playing the Home Counties, because they're the Tory voters?' I had no answer. What could I say? I said, 'Give us time. This has been a really good strong start.'

BILLY BRAGG People like Muriel Gray misunderstood what we were trying to do. The way we went into the Conservative south was through the *NME* and *Melody Maker* and *Sounds* and the *Face*. Part of our job was to go in to the heartlands where we could rally the troops after the Miners' Strike and try and connect with the next generation. These were the Billy Braggs of 1979 who couldn't tell the difference between Jim Callaghan and Margaret Thatcher. I was that soldier.

PHILL JUPITUS The greatest level of criticism levelled at Red Wedge was that we were preaching to the converted. That came home to roost massively in '87.

PAUL BOWER There will always be people on the left that aren't satisfied. 'You've got Elvis Costello, but where's Bruce Springsteen, you bastards?'

KAREN JOHNSON It was called *Red* Wedge. It wasn't *Blue* Wedge. In Newcastle you felt disengaged, and actually having artists who came to do something and to connect with a younger audience using politics was great.

•

PHILL JUPITUS There were people who wanted to fuck Bower and Red Wedge over. Before we arrived in Newcastle somebody rang the university and said Weller was going to do the after-show party. Why would that happen? We were quite a tight ship and very well organized. One possible explanation is an event promoter thought, 'If I bill it they'll have to come.'

JONA COX I was the social secretary at Newcastle University and I also got a call from Paul Bower two weeks before, saying, 'We're organizing a special end-of-tour party for Red Wedge after the evening show as a benefit for Miners' Solidarity. And we want to bring 500 miners down from Ashington NUM and some of the bands are going to come across and play.' I said, 'Paul, OK, but we sell out every Friday night so you cannot announce this.' I was having a bit of hoo-ha with the police so I was being very careful with my licence. I said, 'Who's going to be coming?' It was just, 'Yeah, yeah, yeah. Just get a PA in and we'll be there.' Three days before, I saw an advert in *NME* saying all the tour regulars including Madness and Tom Robinson would be attending and possibly Sade. I phoned Bower and went mental: 'What the fuck are you doing?'

NEIL SPENCER Weller found his name being advertised on these flyers and he was expected to show up. That was blackmail. I received a letter from

Ken Smith, Militant's press officer after the tour had finished, but dated the same day as Newcastle, which said, 'We believe that Red Wedge has a vital role to play, along with the Labour Party Young Socialists, the Youth Trade Union rights campaign and NUS, in winning the support of young people for the much-needed Labour victory at the next election.' The Trots played dirty and were always trying to sabotage what we did.

PAUL BOWER I remember Weller stony-faced saying on the bus, 'What's all this about, Paul?' I said, 'I've got no idea, but I think I know who might be responsible for it.' Militant were on a recruiting mission and telling people we'd let them down. They wanted to make Newcastle the next Liverpool.

NEIL SPENCER I went down to the university after the main City Hall show and there was a lot of fucking people there.

PHILL JUPITUS There's footage of Bower onstage in front of this baying crowd who were expecting the Style Council.

PAUL BOWER People were heckling: 'Where's Weller?' And some wanker called me a 'class traitor'.

JONA COX It was due to kick off at eleven. Junior turned up and was heckled off. Nick Brown, our local MP, was there, and Peter Mandelson with his beard. I was going absolutely ballistic. Outside the union a mob had come up from the concert and was trying to climb over the wrought-iron gates. Cowboy fights were breaking out. I'm in this corridor and I said to Bower, 'Where is everybody?' He goes, 'Sorry, mate, everybody's a bit tired and gone back to the hotel.' I lost it then and started punching these metal lockers: 'Tired! You're jeopardizing my fucking licence. You can't do this.' I held him out with one arm and handed him to one of my Ents crew and then turned to Mandelson and Brown as the colour was draining from their faces: 'He's going to be locked in my office and if you're not back in an hour with some artists I'm going to feed him to the crowd.' Suddenly, one of my mates runs up and says, 'Jona, Billy Bragg's just walked through the back door.' I said, 'Fucking hell.' I threw my house keys at him and said, 'Go and get my guitar. Now. Run.' I went down to see Billy and explained the situation. He said, 'Get me a cup of tea. I'll be ready in fifteen.' I walked back through the dressing room and came onto the side of the stage to watch and this little scouse Militant bloke said, 'Fuckin' sell-out.' I was absolutely flying on adrenalin and had the power of ten men and launched him with one arm over the barrier.

RICHARD COLES Two thousand angry people were on the verge of rioting. Cue the courageous Billy Bragg who managed to not only pacify them but send them home happy with an impromptu performance.

JONA COX He played for two hours. It was half one when he finished and all these miners were leaning over the barrier and pinning their NUM strike badges on him. After, I wrote Billy a letter with a big marker on student union paper and it just said, 'Thanks for saving my bollocks, Big Nose.' He said he pinned it above his desk in his house.

AIN'T NO STOPPIN' US NOW

Women's tour. *Well Red*. Gay Rights. Black Sections

<u>TINY FENNIMORE</u> Following the success of the first national music tour we announced the Reds Laugh Louder comedy tour: seventeen dates with four of the country's best young acts – Mark Miwurdz, Sensible Footwear, Skint Video and Craig Charles – plus an array of special guests. Comedy was another vehicle to get your ideas across.

<u>ALEX DALLAS</u> The message was always very political and we were very strong, unified, loud, hilarious and assertive. We were deliberately putting ourselves into places where the context would be really challenging. We did shows about rape and stereotyping gender and sexism, but we tried to present them in palatable comedic sketches. We ended every set singing a parody of 'Que Sera, Sera': *You're a girl, you can't,* and people thought we

Red Wedge comedy tour, including Skint Video, Craig Charles (top left), Sensible Footwear (Alex Dallas, centre), and Mark Miwurdz, February 1986.

were singing *You're a girl you cunt*. We were creating what we considered to be a new cabaret, so for us Red Wedge was a natural extension. Every time I went to a Billy Bragg gig I felt better because someone on the stage was saying all the things I thought. Where else would I get that?

TINY FENNIMORE I was the press officer and it was much more anarchic than the music tour. The comedians weren't quite as committed to the cause and they were doing a lot more nodding than they wanted to. The tour was a great success. We combined comedy and politics and we were reaching out to new audiences.

HILARY CROSS It was vital that we expanded Red Wedge because it was fronted by male pop stars. But the people that ran the office were all women.

BILLY BRAGG There were a lot of women at the heart of Red Wedge and the office became important because they were the poor bastards after every-one went home who were left answering the phones. People like Tiny and Annajoy and Juliet and Belinda Braggins and Sally Johnson and Annie Weekes were all doing the day-to-day and getting it together. In the front row it was a bunch of lads but behind the scenes they were driving us to make decisions and articulating what we were singing about.

ANNAJOY DAVID I was very gender-conscious. Belinda and Annie were both university graduates who came and helped on the political side of things and Karen Walter from the *NME* was absolutely amazing doing loads of back-up stuff. It didn't feel like a blokey culture until you went on a tour bus.

NEIL KINNOCK You come across people in politics occasionally who are like benign nuclear reactors: there's very little noise, there's no smell, but the energy they're pumping out could light up a town. Annajoy was one of those people. The way in which she grabbed the role of organizing was a real bloody blessing. You can have any number of creative people around who turn up for the gigs and are committed but then when it came to organizing committees or fixing the Day Events or resolving problems; that was Annajoy. It couldn't have been done without her.

JULIET DE VALERO WILLS She just burnt through it. She'd get really passion-ate and angry but she never let anything get personal. She didn't fall out with people in that way. Problems were something to blast through with an avalanche of words, and if that didn't work, with hugs and smiles. It was all about the politics, and the music was just a means to an end. She had to remind herself sometimes that without the music she didn't have that leverage. She was a total force of nature.

ASHTAR ALKHIRSAN Annajoy really defined the philosophy and the purpose of Red Wedge. She was driven by an ideology and a real passion and she knew where she wanted to go. I was more amorphous and probably more typical of young people at the time. I didn't have a fucking clue; most of us didn't.

TOM WATSON You could hear Annajoy at the end of the corridor. 'No' wasn't a word she understood. She would face anyone down no matter what their status and have a cogent argument for everything. People either withered on the vine or just lay down like puppies and gave her what she wanted. I really admired her. I don't think she quite knows what part she played in changing the Labour Party.

TOM SAWYER Annajoy established herself as a mover and shaker. She was trying to hold a musical and a political side together and, as nature has it, people drift in different directions. No one stays focused for long and time moves on.

BILLY BRAGG It was quite frustrating working with the Labour Party on a day-to-day basis so she'd run up against Mandelson and the forces of resistance within the Party. Annajoy was in that invidious position that women often find themselves in, in the music industry, of people not taking them seriously. Without Weller's or my authority it was difficult for her. That was my sense of it.

RHODA DAKAR We had a fringe meeting at the Labour Party conference at Blackpool and later that night we went to the Imperial Hotel, where we were staying, for drinks, and the Tory press were on us like flies – they thought we would let something slip – and buying us drinks. It was hilarious. I thought, 'You're gonna buy musicians drinks and hope they're going to say something stupid. It's going to cost you a fortune, mate.' I got absolutely arseholed. The guy who'd decided to go for me used to write a column for the *Daily Express*. He said, 'I'll introduce you to people,' and took me round. You could see the horror on their faces: 'Oh my God, they've got one of those musicians.' His opening gambit was, 'I'm going to introduce you to the first sitting member of Parliament who's going to die of AIDS.' I thought, 'You bastard.'

ALEX DALLAS When the boys' tour happened I remember thinking, 'Why is everybody male and white?' So Annajoy and I got together and said, 'We've got to do a women's tour.' It was a big deal because women never got space in music and comedy; they just got left out. At the beginning it was hard to find women to commit who were political. The question was, did women want to affiliate themselves and risk alienating their male fan-base and be accused of being feminists?

ANGELA BARTON There weren't many female big names in the music industry. Off the top of my head, it was Bananarama and Sade.

KAREN WALTER We had a wish list of people that included Kate Bush, Liz Fraser, Alison Moyet and Cait O'Riordan from the Pogues.

ALEX DALLAS It was about promoting women to the point where they would think women's votes counted. When you canvassed doorsteps you'd say, 'I'm from the Labour Party. Would you consider voting for our candidate?' And the answer would be, 'I don't know, I'll ask my husband.'

JOOLZ DENBY You have to examine the place of women in the music industry. It's very disheartening. You get immune to having to prove over and over that you're not a groupie. If you start a project and some guy gets involved he will take it over. It's to do with male privilege and natural assumption.

ALEX DALLAS If you play in a working-men's club in Worksop the first instinct is to shout, 'Get your knickers off. Show us your tits.' Gender politics are not easy because it requires one gender to pull back a bit and do a bit of self-analysis. Men always used to say to us, 'Where's your woman Picasso?' 'Where's your woman Beethoven?' 'Where's your woman Dickens?' It was to prove that we were therefore inferior because we were not the most famous artist or writer or playwright. 'Where's your woman Shakespeare? See, women are no good. You've never produced a Shakespeare, have you?' We used to wear these horrible masks and tell mother-in-law jokes like, 'What does a woman put behind her ears to make her more attractive to men? Her legs.'

JOOLZ DENBY I used to be in the *NME* as a style icon, a bit of an 'It Girl', partly because in the ranting poetry scene there weren't any girls. I was the only one that had the neck to stand up in a venue full of drunken arseholes who would chuck lighted cigarettes at me. I stood on stage, a lone woman, and said the things that nobody wanted to talk about, dealing

Red Wedge Womens' Tour handbill, February 1987.

with subjects like violence against women and grooming. It was like having a hypodermic stuck in your neck instead of gently in your arm. I've been bricked in the head, beaten, threatened with rape, ostracized and had abuse screamed at me. If people bottled me my stock response was, 'I was only booked for fifteen minutes and I'm going to do half an hour now, you bastards.' So the Red Wedge Women's Tour was a chance to say, 'Can we just be free to do this?'

ASHTAR ALKHIRSAN We called it Cooking Up Trouble and it started in the Shaw Theatre in London during International Women's Week in March 1987. It was a big event and I was producing the film shoot. It was the biggest thing I'd ever done, with four or five cameras and an all-woman crew.

ALEX DALLAS About four days before our opening show Sandie Shaw phoned up and said, 'I'm pulling out,' saying she didn't want to be branded as 'the man-hating Sandie Shaw'. I can remember sitting on the floor for two hours persuading her not to. She said something like, 'I've been to my Buddhist women's group and they don't think it's a good idea. It's too affiliated to the Labour Party.' I was trying to explain to her that it wasn't a Labour Party thing and she wasn't telling women to do anything apart from have a voice. I knew she had a daughter and I was saying things like, 'What would you say to your daughter if she had to face this issue?' It was like talking her down from the edge. On the day of the gig, I wasn't sure if she would turn up. And then she arrived with Johnny Marr. He was the only man allowed on stage. There was an immediate standing ovation and I stood in the wings and cried because we'd done it.

RHODA DAKAR Sandie Shaw didn't talk to anyone. I said 'hello' she said 'hello'.

SARAH JANE MORRIS Somebody backstage made a sexist comment and Sandie walked off and slammed the door.

ALEX DALLAS And then Sarah Jane led the finale, 'Ain't No Stopping Us Now'.

JOOLZ DENBY They had this dreadful thing where they wanted everybody to get up at the end and sing *W-O-M-A-N, I'll say it again*. The idea was mortifying. I'm ashamed to confess that I ran and hid in the ladies' toilets. Being a notorious school absconder, you crouch on the toilet so they can't look under and see your feet, and I was sitting there thinking, 'Fuck, what shall I do? You've fucked it now. They'll think you're a complete weirdo.' I was sat there sweating and I suddenly became aware there was somebody in the next cubicle. I got down and looked under the gap but couldn't see any feet. I thought, 'Fuck, they're doing what I'm doing.' So I said, 'Are you crouched on the toilet seat to avoid the song?' And this voice went, 'I am.' I said, 'Who are you?' And she went, 'I'm Sandi Toksvig, the short one.' I'm very tall, so it was funny – Sandi did a skit about the Virgin Mary and Shake 'n' Vac – but for some reason we didn't come out of the cubicles and just had this conversation about the Frank Chickens who were on the tour. Sandi and I were just, 'I don't know what to say to them. They don't listen.' The tour was quite bitchy. You get a load of women together and they jostle for hierarchy. I went to an all-girls school and it was a bit like, who wants to be head girl?

ALEX DALLAS Joolz was this amazing person with flaming red hair and piercings and tattoos everywhere. She was a raconteur and told brilliant stories. And Sandi was the MC. She loved it. I shared a room with her and she told me lots of naughty lesbian stories from her boarding school days. I was shocked and excited and it was very illuminating because I didn't really know any lesbians. Frank Chickens were absolutely hilarious and did Japanese pop music: *I'm a Fujiyama mamma / I'm just about to blow my top.* They were managed by Pete Jenner and he said to me as we drove off, 'You know what happens when you're a tour manager, Alex? You tell them that the minibus arrives at ten o'clock and if nobody's there you get in that bus and you drive to the gig and if anybody's late they will find their own way and they will never be late again.' I was like, 'OK, in that case I will stick to it.' And we did. Hope Augustus was late and then she went to the wrong place. She totally cocked it up and was never late again.

ASHTAR ALKHIRSAN Hope was from Birmingham and was the big smash find. She sang 'A Nightingale Sang In Berkeley Square' and the slave song 'Peaches' a cappella. It was amazing. She had such a powerful voice.

ALEX DALLAS I was thrilled Rhoda did it. And Tracey Thorn came, without Ben, from Everything But The Girl, which we thought was amazing.

JOOLZ DENBY There was a feeling amongst us that we were under the shadow of the boys. Simply because we stood on the stage and did it we actually changed the perceptions of a lot of young women. It showed a lot of young girls that they don't have to just concentrate on hair and nails.

ALEX DALLAS Coming Up Roses came, who were a fabulous punky, feisty band, with Deborah and Hester from Dolly Mixture. And We've Got a Fuzzbox And We're Gonna Use It!! were special guests in Birmingham. On the tour poster I remember we had to put 'funny' because feminists can't be funny. I had lots of meetings with Bill Gilby, and NUPE paid for all the printing and the food for the rider.

BILL GILBY The Women's Tour seemed an obvious thing for NUPE to sponsor because 60 per cent of our members were women. We were always looking for ways to promote the rights of women, and the cover image for the programme was one of Caroline della Porta's.

TOM WATSON You'd look at some of Caroline's illustrations and think, 'Fuck me. Is this something political?' Mixing fonts like that and using woodcuts to present imagery. It was amazing and quite sophisticated. I'd never seen anything like it before. Labour had one guy doing graphic design, called Jack Stallard, and he used to tell me stories of parties at Downing Street with Harold Wilson and long conversations he used to have with Clement Attlee. He was that old. The Labour Party still did political documents with Letraset.

NEIL SPENCER Red Wedge had some great illustrators, painters and designers who got involved and formed the Visual Arts Group. And then we had *Well Red*. You had to have a magazine. That was important. It was an outlet for a lot of talent.

TINY FENNIMORE I wrote articles in *Well Red* about politics in popular culture like nuclear disarmament and South Africa. I would have great fun reading Peregrine Worsthorne and Woodrow Wyatt's columns in the Sunday papers because they were both so right-wing. You could reprint it in our world and everybody would go, 'Oh, how terrible.' Things like '. . . expect changes in apartheid but don't expect one man one vote: after all, if you were a white South African would you like that?'

RHODA DAKAR *Well Red* was selling a different idea to anything else. We had journalists and designers, people who could make the magazine and people who could be in the magazine. It was like, 'Are we good at writing political policy?' 'Nah.' 'How about doing a magazine?' 'Oh yeah, we can do that.' Music glossies were on the rise. It was a good call.

HILARY CROSS Neil Spencer was our guru. He was a proper journalist and the rest of us were a bit amateur who had done fanzines. There was a discussion at one of the editorial meetings where we'd done South Africa and the Sandinistas and Ireland and he said, 'Enough of this foreign stuff. We need to do one about Britain and money.' So we had interviews with the comedian Harry Enfield and the Labour backbencher Dennis Skinner and articles on the privatization of the welfare state.

ASHTAR ALKHIRSAN There was a series of campaign posters that came out, and one with Margaret Thatcher on a TV screen and next to it, it said, 'THERE IS ONLY ONE LOONY LEFT!' and the word 'loony' caused the most controversy. It was a brilliant double-page poster.

ANGELA EAGLE The gigs started you thinking and the work that *Well Red* did was enormously important for developing new ways. It got ideas across to people who might not have been able to read between the lines of the bile that was coming out of the *Daily Mail*.

TOM WATSON Red Wedge was curious and newsworthy but then it became powerful and a threat, so they started this narrative about mixing pop and politics and trendy lefties and mouthy Ben Elton. The media did not want a mass movement of youth moving to Labour. We were at war with the *Sun*. They were trying to traduce Neil Kinnock as a character and devalue his politics. But if you've got the designer Neville Brody or Robert Elms or Capital Radio DJs or gigging artists who are talking to their audience by the thousand every night . . . and then the football terraces started getting involved with Red Wedge stuff in the programmes. Robert Elms went on *The Tube* holding up a Red Wedge T-shirt, saying, 'This is what cool is.' I used to wear mine like it was a uniform.

NEIL SPENCER We had some right shits at the press calls. The *Mail* and the *Express* and all that would be there to have a pop. I worked for the Labour Party press office and then I found out just how toxic the tabloid press can be; absolutely unbelievable. When someone rings you up and says, 'I hear such-and-such a council have banned black bin bags because they're not politically correct,' you go, 'You've invented this story and now whatever I say is going to be part of your story.' Peter Mandelson was unbelievably effective with dealing with the media. He understood completely what Red Wedge was trying to do, but would have thought it was a bit of a sideshow, especially once the election was over.

COLIN BYRNE There was in the press office paranoia principally about the *Sun* but largely about every newspaper bar the *Daily Mirror*. Everything would be scrutinized by, 'What is the *Sun*, the *Mail*, the *Express* going to say about this? Is this going to be turned into an anti-Labour story?' The regime that Peter ran was 'project': project the modern image of Labour beyond our traditional core vote. And at the same time 'protect', because we were literally at war with the tabloid media. It was a constant tension.

NEIL KINNOCK The media attacks were bloody awful and incessant. OK, you're a politician, you understand the terrain in which you're fighting: if you kowtow they're going to kick you in the face, or you say, 'Fuck you,' and carry on being normal. Occasionally, grudgingly, they had to say what I'd done with Militant or the economic policy, or the speech he made last week was incomparable. The rest of the time – in diaries, in little bits of columns, in any embarrassing photograph, eating a sandwich: Jesus Christ, the last time I ate in public was in 1984 – anything they could use, they would use it. There was a telling example at the Eurofest in Manchester. I was outside with Clive Dunn and Bill Owen and it started to rain. There was a guy with a top hat on so I said, 'Can I borrow that for a second?' I put it on and started to sing *I'm singing in the rain* on the pavement with my arms round Clive and Bill, and all the old-age pensioners around thought it was bloody terrific and joined in. That was just me being bloody natural. The *Daily Mail* and the *Telegraph* cut me to bloody shreds. Jesus! It was much worse than appearing in a Tracey Ullman video. This was evidence of me lacking gravitas: 'Can you envisage this man as prime minister?'

NEIL SPENCER Neil appearing in the Tracey Ullman video doing a Madness song was funny but probably ill-advised. It's hard to be around pop stars. It's hard to do pop music. There's a skill to it. You're never going to come out of it looking funky.

ANGELA EAGLE Most people in the Labour Party were fazed by Neil appearing in the 'My Guy' video. He was trying to go to places that politicians hadn't been. It was mass appeal that didn't quite work.

NEIL KINNOCK The record got to number five in the charts. But on reflection, Tracey and I would agree that it was probably not a good idea. Tracey was a very strong Labour Party supporter but she said after, 'It was fun, but as the leader of the Labour Party you're not supposed to have fun.' I should have realized what take the enemy would have on it.

ROBERT HOWARD Hats off to Kinnock! He was an inspiring, passionate, eloquent public speaker. He was also a human being with humour and if that takes doing a Tracey Ullman video . . . But the Murdoch press was massacring them. The *Sun* could crucify you. The power they had was beyond words.

•

JUNE MILES-KINGSTON AIDS was a taboo subject and we lost friends because nobody wanted to do anything about it. The gay situation was where politics had to move on more than anywhere. People in government were gay, people in royalty were gay, people in industry were gay yet there were still laws against it. You didn't talk about it.

RICHARD COLES As the Communards, Jimmy and I had a clear brief to fight for gay rights with Red Wedge. If you were gay growing up in the 1970s it was a pretty brutal experience. It was a time of constant discrimination, constant prejudice and violence. I remember coming back from Gay Pride one year and walking down Upper Street in Islington at ten o'clock at night and two guys were holding hands and got attacked and then at the Tube station these skinheads pushed us onto the tracks. It was a different world.

JUNE MILES-KINGSTON I had to save Jimmy once when were in Dijon. We'd gone out to find something to eat and this car full of boys stopped – they

June Miles-Kingston during Fun Boy Three's 'Our Lips Are Sealed' video shoot, April 1983.

obviously knew who Jimmy was – and they all got out. I thought they were fans but they started pushing him about, going, 'You're gay, la, la, la,' in French. I thought, 'Fuck,' so I piled in and jumped on this guy's back and held onto him. He twisted round and turned me off and punched me on the chin. I was knocked out. Jimmy said they sped off in the car. It was a big thing to 'come out'.

ANNAJOY DAVID Jimmy and Richard sent us some great volunteers from an emerging gay community which was beginning to get itself really organized for the first time with the onslaught of the AIDS virus.

ASHTAR ALKHIRSAN One of my first jobs at Walworth Road was to pick up a gay rights leaflet that Red Wedge was going to produce. I was sent down to the lobby to meet a friend of Jimmy's called Mark Ashton. He was wearing cut-off denims and pink ankle socks and open-toed sandals. I was completely naive and thinking he wouldn't want everyone to know that he was gay so I just whispered, 'I'm here for the gay leaflets.' He just laughed at me and we ended up becoming really good friends.

RICHARD COLES Mark was the first of our friends to die of AIDS. We had been to Paris with him to Père Lachaise and saw Mur des Fédérés [The Communards' Wall] where they were all shot in 1871, and Mark told us the story of the Paris Commune and we were full of romance for that. We liked the idea of the first experiment in communist living so that's how we became the Communards.

ASHTAR ALKHIRSAN Mark was an amazing person. He came to work as a volunteer. He had been a founder member of Lesbians and Gays Support the Miners and was the general secretary of the Communist Party, but he was more about socialism in action: how do you practise your political philosophy on a day-to-day level?

KAREN WALTER Everyone loved him. He was one of those people who knew everyone and everyone just warmed to. And then he was ill and it was all very quick. It was the only awful thing that ever happened at Red Wedge because most of it was upbeat.

ROBERT HOWARD There was underlying ignorance about the causes and effects of AIDS, and pointing the finger at the gay community. The government's TV broadcast was like a horror movie. Although I wasn't gay I was going to a lot of gay clubs – in London they were the only places open after hours and you'd meet people like Mark E. Smith and Boy George there –

and then the fundamentalist Christians got on board and used AIDS as a weapon with which to attack homosexuality. It was all part of the right-wing agenda.

TOM ROBINSON Remember Thatcher's response to AIDS? There wasn't one. People were dying. The government didn't start a health warning campaign until the 'Don't Die of Ignorance' campaign in 1987. And then their response was to bring in Section 28 which stated that a local authority shall not 'promote the teaching in any maintained school of the acceptability of homosexuality'. My entire position was summed up in 1978 on the back of *Power In The Darkness*: 'I got no illusions about the political left any more than the right: just a shrewd idea which of the two sides' gonna stomp on us first. All of us – you, me, rock 'n' rollers, punks, longhairs, dope smokers, squatters, students, unmarried mothers, prisoners, gays, the jobless, immigrants, gipsies . . . to stand aside is to take sides.'

RICHARD COLES When AIDS came along I stopped fearing the bomb and started fearing the virus. I remember we had a meeting at Red Wedge about the general election and somebody said to me, 'But AIDS isn't really a political issue.' The first senior politician who did get it was the Health Secretary, Norman Fowler.

RHODA DAKAR The Labour Party would not come out in support of gay policies and there was a point at which they needed to sign with or against, and they sat on the fence. We were at a meeting at Solid Bond and the Communards left. They said, 'We can't support the Labour Party because they're not supporting us.'

RICHARD COLES The Labour Party had passed a resolution at conference in 1985 committing them to supporting lesbian and gay rights. But they'd passed a lot of resolutions; it didn't really mean anything.

JOHN NEWBEGIN Thatcher was very deliberately parading Victorian values. She was presenting such an extreme picture of a backward-looking, xeno-phobic, uptight Britain rather than celebrating all the progressive things that were going on. Neil Kinnock was saying, 'We are going to be relevant to the realities of Britain in the future and particularly young people. We've got to listen to voices that are coming from outside and have an international outward-looking confidence.' By encouraging dialogue with musicians like the Communards it helped to shift thinking within the Party and the way that lesbian and gay rights were dealt with by the Labour Party.

COLIN BYRNE Gay politics wasn't really talked about because Labour was still a very male macho party. We were starting to pay more attention to the sexual politics of gender, although most of the trade unionists thought it was some whingeing lefty crap so there was a lot of questioning about, 'OK, we have to pay lip service to this but how much do we actually have to . . .'

ANGELA EAGLE You could never fault Mrs Thatcher for not having an opinion. There was a big switch in attitudes to gay people but she was not sympathetic and the public moved far ahead of where the government was. The Conservatives used prejudice to entrench themselves in power. It was a very effective stick to beat us with. If you look at what they said in the newspapers about 'loony lefties' and 'the blacks' and 'the queers', they were scapegoating. But it's quite hard to scapegoat somebody who's at the top of the charts.

JUNIOR GISCOMBE Labour could see that we could bring in young votes: the black vote because of me; the gay vote because of Jimmy and Richard and Tom. But we were explaining to Kinnock that you can't put the two together; that black people and homosexuals were not exactly the same. There was no way that any black guy was going to turn around and say that he was the same as a homosexual.

CLARE SHORT There were some left thinkers who were saying that the way to defeat Thatcher was to unite all the minorities and you've got a majority. Neil's instinct would be to be inclusive and draw together black people and gay people and young people. He wasn't seeing Red Wedge as a magical solution. It was part of a mobilization of all elements that would sweep Labour to power and enable us to change the country to a better place.

NEIL KINNOCK We weren't doing enough for gay rights. It was a civil rights issue as far as I was concerned but I wanted to ensure that we were in a position to actually change the bloody law, and in order to get that position we had to be careful with our coverage. That was all. I said to the gay rights charity organization, Stonewall, 'Listen, do you want to wave a flag or do you want the law of the land changed? I'm the leader of the Labour Party, simply permit me the discretion to give an absolute solemn undertaking to you to find a language that isn't going to frighten bloody people

off. You help us become elected and we'll do it.' And, five years later than
it should have been, we did. We also had a hell of a row over the Black
Section, who were a group of black and Asian members within the Party
arguing for greater minority representation. I saw it, like a lot of my black
comrades, as an absolutely unacceptable way of defining people in the
Labour movement. It was totally unacceptable for people who had been
fighting apartheid for decades. This wasn't just a spontaneous movement
that would bring on young black people who lacked confidence. It was an
effort by a few to get a new affiliated organization that could manipulate
and dominate. To say the only way to ensure fair representation is to have
a Black Section was not true. Then we found a third way, which was to
establish an ethnic minorities office.

RHODA DAKAR Milton Dillon organized a Black Arts and Entertainment
Working Group meeting at Liberty Hall in Hackney with Diane Abbott,
who was the prospective parliamentary candidate for Hackney North, and
Paul Boateng, the candidate for Brent. Paul dressed down but he should
have worn his suit because he was completely uncomfortable. Stuart Cos-
grove turned up. I was like, 'Why is he here?' 'He writes for *Blues and Soul*.'
'OK, that makes as much sense as anything else now.' The proposed motto
for the group was, 'Until the colour of a person's skin is of no more significance than the colour of their eyes then there shall always be war,'
which had been adapted from a Haile Selassie speech and Bob Marley's
'War'. I thought Diane was a bit of an idiot. She made a presentation which
began, 'It seems that the Labour Party likes black people, the further away
they are.' I had a complete wobbler with Marc Wadsworth from the Labour
Party and absolutely lost it. He was saying, 'Yeah, but you can't be this, if
you think this.' It was like, 'Where do you get off?' The Black Section had
a very specific way of looking at the world. It was nonsense and very difficult.

ANGELA BARTON I'm not comfortable with separatism: 'Right, let's do our
own thing because you're not doing it for us.' But equally, I can understand
why people want that because they're thinking, 'You're not representing
me. I'm going to have to do it on my own.' Historically, Gandhi springs to
mind, and Martin Luther King. They did it so well, so things did change – is
that what Diane Abbott and Paul Boateng were trying to say?

RHODA DAKAR Generally, in meetings, it was who had the most currency.
My currency was I had some political nous – musically, I had been and

gone – but I understood how it worked and how it operated and how to manipulate situations. Being black and a woman meant I could shout and unless someone had a really well-constructed argument I was right, because I had been wrong for centuries. I didn't do it that often. One time a gauntlet had been laid down to say that I wouldn't go to an Outrage meeting at the Lesbian and Gay Centre, so obviously I went. At the meeting this girl pulled out a letter from a guy who was part of a paedophile exchange and the motion was: should paedophiles be included in the room? I was already going, 'What?' And then the girl read out the letter from this guy talking about his eight-year-old lover. I went absolutely ballistic and totally demolished them. 'Do you really not understand the basis of a relationship and power?' I may well have been the only black woman in the room, in which case I had even more currency than usual. Peter Tatchell supported me and the motion was denied.

BILLY BRAGG Rhoda was a force because of what she'd done with 2 Tone. She was incredibly powerful and wouldn't take any bullshit. When the Black Sections came to talk to us we listened to them politely and then Rhoda stood up and ripped them to shreds. We all stood up and clapped. Rhoda has an ability to see through a lot of the bullshit around politics and rock 'n' roll. Chairing the Red Wedge steering committees is a credit to her commitment to trying to make music that says something and does something. It takes a lot of organization to continue to come up with ideas and move forward.

NEIL SPENCER Rhoda was a voice of sanity, very down-to-earth, very pragmatic: 'This is what we can do.' No ideological axe to grind but very sharp about cultural politics.

ANNAJOY DAVID We did a lot of work to get black and Asian MPs into the Commons, and talking about black British music and racism in the music industry. If you look at some of the positive aspects of the culture of the Labour Party – women, black people, gay rights – a lot of it started culturally in the Red Wedge base. Everybody was saying, 'You're mad. You can't do this.' And I said, 'Of course we can. This is who we are.'

THE OSCAR WILDE SCHOOL OF SOCIALISM

Italy. Redskins. Move On Up tour. 1987 election

BILLY BRAGG The Labour Party represented a form of democratic social-ism so anybody who wanted to abolish capitalism wasn't going to be involved in Red Wedge. And as a consequence people saw me as a sell-out. It's very hard to get in the mud with the politicians and not get some of it on you. We used to have anarchists leafleting the gigs and revolutionary socialists handing out little bits of paper attacking Red Wedge. There was an anarchist initiative called Black Wedge which Joe Strummer did a gig for. Joe said, 'I would play for Red Wedge but I'd rather play for Green Wedge.' He didn't care if it was Thatcher or Kinnock who implemented it.

NEIL KINNOCK The only thing I'd give Maggie Thatcher credit for is that either through arrogance or through dogma or through stupidity she used to frequently announce that she was there to crush out socialism.

PHILL JUPITUS Socialism is about passion whereas I think Conservatism is about pragmatism and duty and doing as you're told and not questioning things. That's what always appealed to me about Red Wedge: at its best it questioned the status quo, the way youth were treated, the way wealth was apportioned throughout the country.

PAUL WELLER I [was] a socialist not only by my thoughts, but by my actions as well, and what I [did] with my money and how I rechannelled it. I can see there are contradictions, but we [had] to start somewhere.[80] I don't believe that a human being's responsibility is to keep up his payments on his television, or that he cleans his car once a week. I'm sure there's got to be more to it than that. I'm not saying that everybody should come to a concert and attend it like it was a political rally. But there's no reason why you can't do both things at the same time. I can't see the dichotomy between entertainment and serious messages. Look at Billy, probably 80 per cent of his material [was] love songs. But he [led] by his actions and his example.[81]

CATHAL SMYTH Once one's privileged one has a responsibility of privilege to do the right thing. You have to be giving something back, even if it's respect for someone's opinion or their space.

NEIL SPENCER Thatcher had defined Britishness. She flew the Union Jack. So people who didn't want to be part of Thatcher didn't want to be part of the flag. Suddenly nobody was English. Everybody said, 'Actually, my cultural identity is more complicated than that; my parents were Jewish immigrants . . .', 'Well, I'm not really English because I'm black . . .', 'I'm not really English because I'm Irish . . .' But some of us had nowhere to go. I was the last Englishman standing. 'We're English. Sorry.' Belonging to this nation had to be redefined so one wasn't 'the enemy within.' I thought there was a way to make socialism sexy again but the historical weight of the USSR and the Socialist Workers Party and all those ABC alphabet soup factions rendered socialism toxic. For me, socialism was about going to a great club and meeting different kinds of people and not being tribal. Not saying, 'We don't have anything to do with gay people or black people,' which was Thatcher's attitude.

PAUL WELLER I'd read *The Ragged-Trousered Philanthropists* early on and coming from a reactionary working-class background it opened up my mind to politics.[82] There was a blinkered view of socialism that [came] from the right wing that says that socialism is going to drag everyone down to the sewer level. But the idea of socialism to me is to raise people up to a comfortable level, where the necessities are provided for. If we sat around debating whether people will vote Labour, and whether Neil Kinnock [would] just sell us short, nothing would ever get done. I [wanted] to do something about it.[83]

CATHAL SMYTH *The Ragged-Trousered Philanthropists* made me see the value of unions. Pre-unions, if you fell off the ladder and broke your ankle the whole family was destitute and in the poorhouse. There was no back-up system. Nothing. The unions gave the average man a voice, without which he was lost; out there in a vast ocean of vested interest that couldn't give a frigging monkey's about him. If the focus of society is to generate growth and if everybody is not sharing in that growth, then why are we all involved in it? If profit isn't giving something to everyone then something is inherently wrong. When the Athenians came of age they had to take an oath that they would leave Athens better than they found it. We all know when we're taking the piss and taking what we shouldn't and more than we should. It was not a question of politics. It was becoming aware of one's right to life and one's right to be treated with dignity and respect. It was as simple as that.

DAVE WAKELING *The Ragged-Trousered Philanthropists* confirmed every-thing I believed in. I was somebody who was young enough to believe that everybody else is going to act with their best intentions at all times.

ANNAJOY DAVID William Blake was a massive influence on the spiritual politics of the time and the sort of Robert Owen utopian socialist collec-tive, using all the skills of all the people. It was the emotional side of socialism, about how creative people could be if they had the opportunity to develop to their full potential through culture. I was sending Paul books on Blake. And Billy and Neil were both big fans.

PAUL BOWER Generally, left-wing equals humourless and wearing shit clothes. When people said, 'Oh, you're all fancy in designer clothes', I would say, 'Do you think my father's generation left the factory and hung around in jeans? No, they wore sharp suits.'

KAREN WALTER Chris Dean, who was the lead singer of the Redskins and wrote for *NME* as X. Moore, came in one day and he'd just bought a pair of new Lonsdale boots round the corner from Carnaby Street, and I said, 'You're a member of the Socialist Workers Party: how do you justify that amount on a pair of boots?' He said, 'Karen, we're not against people buying Chanel coats; we just think everybody should be able to afford to buy Chanel coats.'

ANNAJOY DAVID I was always interested in fashion: in fact, more than music because my father was really into clothes. He did all the stalls at Petticoat Lane Market and took me around a lot of the buyers. I got my first pair of Levi's when I was eleven, just before he died.

PAUL WELLER We were made to feel guilty for talking about each other's shoes. It was like, 'How dare you? Clothes are a bourgeois trapping.' I love clothes.[84]

ANNAJOY DAVID Paul is a very humble, private guy and one of the most decent and thoughtful people I've ever met. And I think he quite liked the way I looked. I was very slender and my hair was quite long and I dressed very Jackie Onassis in style. Paul would get me some of the most fantastic clothes, like little late-Sixties Miss Levi trousers and tops. I loved scooters and got a Lambretta and Paul and his mate Paolo Hewitt would tease me about music because I wasn't really into it. Later, I certainly had one of the best record collections in the country, thanks to them.

ROBERT HOWARD When I joined Red Wedge the artists used to take the piss out of me and say, 'You think Red Wedge is about a haircut.' I was very skinny, dyed hair. I was like a cross between a mod and a goth with make-up. I said, 'I represent the Oscar Wilde School of Socialism.' Paul was of a similar mind: flamboyance and being extrovert; there was no clash between that and your beliefs. You didn't have to wear the clothes of rebellion or dress down to be a rebel. My belief in socialism was giving everybody the same opportunity to express themselves and be whatever they were. *The Soul of Man Under Socialism* was one of the greatest essays on socialism that you're ever going to read. Are you going to slag off Oscar Wilde because of the way he presented himself? He was an aesthetic genius.

RHODA DAKAR Robert was really interesting. He was going places other people weren't going. I was clearly from the same Oscar Wilde School of

Robert Howard aka Dr Robert
of the Blow Monkeys, Red
Wedge tour, March 1986.

Socialism because the Blow Monkeys I got, but I wouldn't play Billy Bragg. 'Digging Your Scene' was blue-eyed soul. 'Days Like These' was folk music.

TOM WATSON I would sing 'Days Like These' at the end of political events: *Peace, bread, work and freedom is the best we can achieve / And wearing badges is not enough in days like these.* There are a lot of blokes in the Labour Party in their forties now who could tell you that song word for word.

BILLY BRAGG 'Days Like These' was my key song on the Red Wedge tour. We were in a time when songs still had a crucial role to play in communicating ideas. And another key text I wrote was 'I Don't Need This Pressure Ron': *Neither in the name of conscience nor the name of charity / Money is put where mouths are in the name of solidarity.* I was trying to articulate the contradictions and complexities of being on stage and talking down to the audience. *We sing of freedom / We speak of liberation / But such chances come but once a generation.* You can't just put out a fucking record and do a gig and expect the world to change. *So I'll ignore what I am sure are the best of your intentions.* Good intentions are positive but it's actions that make a difference.

ROBERT HOWARD We can't all be Billy Bragg but we're all on the same side with the same message. I loved Eddie Cochrane as much as I loved Woody Guthrie. Music is about the heart as much as it is about the head. One of the most emotional concerts I've been to was Fela Kuti where there were no lyrics for half an hour. It was just the feeling. It's about the intention behind the song, not specifically the lyrics, and transmitting a joyous message about humanity and human nature. That's the job of a musician.

BILLY BRAGG All through 1979 when I was being a punk rocker in Oundle in East Northamptonshire I had a badge that said, 'I am an enemy of the state.' What the fuck did that mean? I was an enemy of the state getting £25 a week from the state to be an enemy of the state. I was a true believer in the Clash and I thought by buying their records and cutting my hair and wearing drainpipe trousers I was going to change the world. The Clash were naive to suggest it but I was naive to believe it. During Red Wedge I was trying to move beyond the consumerist end of the pop culture experience and get into the real activist end of it. And having been at the sharp end of the deal I now realized that wasn't how the whole thing worked, but there was something going on because I'd felt it at Rock Against Racism.

And if I could engender that feeling in the audience then that was a much better thing than just trying to get records in the charts.

ANNAJOY DAVID I went out to Italy to speak at a conference and really for the first time I saw the cross-pollination between clothes and fashion and music and socialism, and out of that they invited Red Wedge in the summer of 1986 to take part in a benefit concert for Southern African movements.

NEIL SPENCER Italian socialism clearly meant something rather nice and going to Naples, and then Reggio Emilia – 'Red Reggio' as it was called – was amazing because it was loads of people with really nice BMWs and fantastic food and very middle-class. As far as the Italians were concerned the tradition of socialism was not austerity and antithetical to people wearing nice clothes; everything was *la dolce vita*.

BILLY BRAGG Reggio Emilia was a fucking great trip. The Italians do these wonderful celebrations of socialism called Festa de l'Unità which are put on by the Communist Party to extend political ideas through culture. They were simpatico with what we were doing and the same kind of vibe as what the GLC had been doing on the South Bank. We stayed in a castle. Heaton was knocking around and he was most dismissive, and Junior wouldn't stay in the top of the turret because he said it was haunted so they made me stay there.

LUCY HOOBERMAN We went with Working Week, the Communards, Madness and the Style Council, and there were all sorts of Italian journalists who were very dishy. Paolo Hewitt, Neil Spencer and I ran a workshop and we showed the Artists Against Apartheid [AAA] film of the Clapham Common concert.

JERRY DAMMERS The Communist Party leaders pulled up in these big flash cars with screeching brakes, all the bodyguards jumped out, and they were all wearing shades and immaculate suits. It was brilliant. The Party's two official songs were 'Imagine' by John Lennon and the Special AKA '(Free) Nelson Mandela' which they played over the tannoy. They were all clapping along on every beat!

NEIL SPENCER Napoli was fascinating but also shocking because it was so poverty-stricken and criminal. We'd done the gig on Saturday night and then there was a fantastic meal at this wonderful old-school restaurant. People stayed up to the small hours and then Sunday morning, get on the

Annajoy David (left) and Lucy Hooberman on the Red Wedge tour bus, January 1986.

fucking coach; get to the fucking airport or else. And then someone realizes Paolo's not out of bed. We go back into the hotel and he's completely gone to the world; one of Working Week's roadies went WHOOSH and pulled everything into the bag. The room was cleared in sixty seconds and Paolo was dragooned onto the coach. We were a whisker away from missing the flight.

PAUL BOWER I was floating around somewhere in the middle by the summer of 1986, drinking too much and increasingly feeling it was all getting on top of me. I went away for a few weeks to Spain where there was an attempt by some socialist musicians to get something similar going to Red Wedge called 'Dinero Rojo' which means 'Red Money'. They understood 'wedge' not through El Lissitzky but 'wedge' as in the cockney for cash. It lasted for three months and then everybody fell out.

PAUL HEATON It's really important for people to know that if there ever was 'our system' we'd have a laugh. It's not going to be Stalinist. I was from a working-class background where you're supposed to go on stage and be an entertainer and make people laugh, smile, and grin. The Housemartins, lyrically, were in your face, but the songs were very melodic and it fitted in with getting the message across because I thought, 'Who's going to listen to me if I'm just droning along?' But with bands like the Redskins there was a lot of shouting and not much smiling to be done.

KAREN WALTER I was very close to Chris Dean and he was always telling me about his band, the Redskins. I remember going to see them for the first time and I thought they were amazing. We all loved Chris but he was quite suspicious of Red Wedge and suspicious of the Labour Party and their motives.

NEIL SPENCER Chris was a really good subeditor at *NME*. He understood language. He was a good bloke but obsessed with an absolute position. The moment he started doing the Redskins you weren't having a discussion any more. The Trots were like a sect. They were never going to sign up for Red Wedge. They always hated the Labour Party more than the Conservatives.

JOHN BAINE The Redskins were a logical extension of Dexys Midnight Runners, only with great politics. They took the skinhead thing and it was focused and direct. Chris was strange and awkward but he wrote great songs. 'Keep On Keeping On' about the Miners' Strike and 'The Power Is Yours', a love song to the working class. I've never known anybody more totally, obsessively political. He couldn't switch off at all. *Take no heroes only inspiration.*

TINY FENNIMORE The Redskins dressed in Doc Martins, Harrington jackets and had shaved heads. It reflected back to the hard working-class original skinhead look and, thanks to bands on 2 Tone, had never really gone away. I was a fan but then they did a Redder Wedge night at the Mean Fiddler in Harlesden. It was disappointing – Chris and Billy had grown up together on stages during the Miners' Strike and they had a fondness and respect for one another. Chris began to criticize Billy's political position when I felt we should be working together. He would say things like, 'Billy's acting as Neil Kinnock's publicity agent.'

BILLY BRAGG The Redskins were kicking us in the shins all the time. There was 'The Great Debate' in *Melody Maker* in the week of the first tour with Paul Weller, Jerry Dammers, Clare Short and me versus the Tory MP for Derby North, Greg Knight, Stewart Copeland of the Police, and Chris Dean who was sat on the same side of the table as the Tories. I was yelling at him, 'Chris, look who you're sitting with. Can you not see what you're doing?'

He wasn't having any of it. I said, 'If Red Wedge was as controlled by the Labour Party as you are by the SWP I wouldn't even join it. Where's your independence? It's the party line, party line.' The SWP had a tight rein on the Redskins.

JOHN BAINE The tragedy was when Chris's mentor, Tony Cliff from the Socialist Workers Party, told them that it was time to stop playing music and start selling newspapers outside factories because what they were doing wasn't as important as directly contacting the organized working class.

BILLY BRAGG When they split up they had to write a *mea culpa* in the *Socialist Worker*. It was like a Stalinist show trial. The media were always trying to find people against Red Wedge. Poor old Gary Numan was always being put up against me to argue on the telly. I used to feel sorry for him. His idea to vote Tory was based on the idea of being a small business. It wasn't ideological. If they threw all the Tory voters out of the charts back in those days there wouldn't be many of us left.

PAUL HEATON I was asked to a Red Wedge meeting by Andy MacDonald and Juliet at Walworth Road. The room was set out with a series of tables going round in a square so everybody was facing the middle. But right

Red Wedge debate: Clare Short (right) gesticulating at Chris Dean.

from the start I wasn't sure. There were people without any shoes or socks on and a lot of musicians I didn't recognize. And there were a lot of very posh people, which was a real surprise coming off the back of the Miners' Strike. I said, 'Could I ask one question? Are we including nationalizing the record industry?' And all the faces dropped: 'Well, I'm not sure we can have that.' I was told that was not something we were here to discuss, but was I interested in getting involved? 'No,' was the answer. I sat around for a bit and as soon as I could I got out. They weren't going to accommodate my opinions on the country.

KAREN WALTER There were a few people who came and thought it was people messing around not quite knowing what they were doing. Unless you'd been to a few meetings and been to the smaller steering committees, groups as well and seen how things filtered through then you might feel like we weren't actually getting anywhere.

ROBERT ELMS The minute you got sucked into it: people taking minutes and talking in this terminology, it was antithetical to musicians and writers and nightclub people. These are people who would have been very happy standing on picket lines or singing protest songs but you could just feel the will to live seeping into the walls of this rather old-fashioned committee-bound Labour Party with people nodding off in the corner of the room. There is an uneasy alliance always between the visceral politics of pop music and the perhaps inevitably organized rather stultifying politics of political parties.

PAUL HEATON I should have asked for the abolition of the monarchy but as soon as they said no to nationalization I realized I wasn't in the right room, so to speak. There was something suspicious about it. I'm not saying they were, but I might have seen it as 'worthy southerners'. But mainly I didn't want to pin our flag to the mast. It was the same with Militant. You just wanted to tickle them under the chin and say, 'Look, stop being so bloody serious and have a laugh.' I've discussed nationalizing the record industry many times since: 'Here are our songs. Take them if you want. They're worth quite a bit of money to this country.' It would be simply putting the state in charge and it would mean the income would go to us rather than private companies. And instead of us going over to places like Belgium alone and having some drugged-up record company idiot working for us, we'd be representing the country and be exported like you would British coal or British oil; the government would be trying to get people to buy its music.

CATHAL SMYTH Bollocks! Madness set Zarjazz up as a socialist label. All the artists were in a sense misfits and came from awkward, troublesome origins and we tried to give them a leg up. We gave out free demo time but were naive about contracts, naive about people doing the right thing, naive about what makes a good record. It didn't work. We thought people were human and would follow the goodness for others. They didn't. We were not record men. We were artists and we made mistakes. Principles are hard to enforce.

ANNAJOY DAVID Paul's idea to nationalize the music industry was an interesting argument but what did I know about the music industry? That was for the artists to talk about. Three million unemployed was quite enough to be concerned about; and nuclear weapons; and the anti-apartheid movement.

BILLY BRAGG The Soviet Union had *one* record label called Melodiya. It wasn't a good model. A nationalized industry would mean having a committee who decided who made records. Suppose it was a Tory government? Red Wedge had to meet the Labour Party halfway. Politics is all about the art of compromise.

JUNIOR GISCOMBE There was a *TV Eye* debate between Billy and Miles Copeland, who was Sting's manager, and Miles was saying, 'When you listen to these artists, when you listen to a Paul Weller song and he talks about the class conflict, he perpetuates the myth that people are divided according to class. They perpetuate the evils of the British system and create a climate that is negative.'

BILLY BRAGG I said to Miles, 'These ideas are not compatible with sitting back, becoming rich and going on *Top of the Pops* every other week. If they're going to have any meaning I've got to match the songs with action, and that's what Red Wedge gives the opportunity to do.'

•

PHILL JUPITUS The general election was announced for 11 June 1987 so the Move On Up comedy and music tours felt they were towards a purpose because they were part of an actual campaign.

BILLY BRAGG The first tour is what defined us. It was our big splash. Who are we? We're Red Wedge. BANG! And then 'Move On Up – Go! For Labour', the marginal constituencies tour in late spring 1987, represented

Move On Up comedy tour at Ronnie Scott's, London, May 1987:(L–R) Robbie Coltrane, Steve Gribbin, Harry Enfield, Andy Smart, Jenny LeCoat, Brian Mulligan, Billy Bragg, Captain Sensible, (front row) Ben Elton, Angel Abela.

our attempt to take that out to as many people and different places as possible. It was to get away from the idea that Red Wedge was just rock stars for Labour. We took in twenty-eight dates and over fifty parliamentary seats trying to bolster the youth vote in places like Bristol, Oxford, Wrexham, Merthyr Tydfil, Newport, Shepton Mallet and Southampton. We were trying to live up to Muriel Gray's criticisms on *The Tube*.

PHILL JUPITUS I was DJ'ing and MC'ing. One of the first dates was at Bay 63 in West London. It was a really big deal because it was the first time that Matt Johnson from The The had gigged in London in an age. He played three or four songs and was off really quickly; people were like, 'Fuck!' Lorna Gee did a set and her manager said to me, 'You've got to play this

track for her and then she will dub along, like a selector for a reggae singer.'
I played the wrong track and all the irate The The fans were going, 'What
are you doing?' I remember looking across to Lorna's crew and going, 'Jah
Porky play again?' and they pissed themselves. All night her entire guest
list was calling me Jah Porky.

PAUL HEATON Billy said to me, 'Leeds is looking incredibly narrow. Any
chance you'll do the gig? It's just about getting people out and voting
against the Tories.' I said, 'Yeah, fair enough. We'll do it.' I went with Colin
Burgon, the candidate for Elmet, to the Whinmoor Estate near where I was
born, and walked around. I remember Billy was holding a baby. I realized
then I better not do any more of this because I'd got too much of a big
mouth. They didn't want to destroy the monarchy and I did. They didn't
want revolution and I did. Red Wedge had good intentions but I thought,
'Who on earth would want to listen to me telling them what to do?'

Lorna Gayle aka Lorna Gee,
circa 1986.

TOM ROBINSON There was a homophobic smear campaign against Chris Smith who was the first openly gay MP. He had a majority of 363 in Islington South and Finsbury, so we went to the town hall specifically with Lloyd Cole, Matt Johnson, the Communards and Glenda Jackson. If we had any effect on Chris's election victory that would be worth the whole campaign for me: that we came together to support a beleaguered gay Labour MP; fantastic.

PHILL JUPITUS At Wolverhampton Civic Hall, I remember Captain Sensible from the Damned walking around with a brown-paper bag just eating sugar snap pods and then ending up shirtless lying on his back being groped by a woman. Annajoy wanted me to play 'Move On Up' but I didn't have it. She was going, 'Porky, we've got to play that. You've got to get a copy.' Then when the house lights came up I put on '(Free) Nelson Mandela' and nobody left the room. The whole crowd stood there and sang *Free Nelson Mandela* and danced to it. All the techies and the crew were shrugging at me. It's the only time I've ever seen that at a gig. It was magical.

TRACEY THORN Everything But The Girl did Nottingham Royal Court with the Style Council, the Blow Monkeys, Billy Bragg, Junior, Lorna, Black Britain and Dave Wakeling. Glenys Kinnock was backstage and she gave me her little red rose badge to wear on stage. I had been admiring it on her and as I went on she said, 'Go on. Wear it.' I tried to keep it after but she wanted it back.

BILLY BRAGG They put on the poster at Nottingham 'surprise guest'. Who the fucking hell could the surprise guest be? Prince!

DAVE WAKELING I was honoured beyond belief that Paul Weller invited me to play the show. When I asked Roger he said, 'When people have got money they ought to vote Conservative,' so Junior Giscombe played Ranking Roger. We did a roasting version of 'Stand Down Margaret': Billy was on my right, Glenys played the tambourine and Paul was smiling at me all night. On the train home the local Labour MP was absolutely hammered and was gargling political rhetoric and staggering around the train. We were like, 'Oh my God, we thought pop groups were bad enough. What are we getting into bed with here?'

TRACEY THORN I'd absorbed a lot of slogans and ideals that I couldn't always back up with actual facts and knowledge and I do remember worrying at the Day Event that we were all making ourselves very prominent, making a big fuss about politics and that I'd get caught out. I was sensitive to accusations that pop musicians shouldn't be dabbling in stuff they don't know; sometimes I'll have an opinion and then I'll read something and go, 'Oh God, actually, no.' So there are gaps in your knowledge or weaknesses in your argument and it's unsettling to have that pointed out to you. And there were objections on grounds like, 'How is pop music going to change anything?' or, 'You shouldn't vote for a party just because Paul Weller tells you to,' or, 'Should young people be listening to people just because they like their records; should they not be finding out their political information through more reliable sources?'

RHODA DAKAR I had moved to Leicester so when the tour came to the university I hung out with the Blow Monkeys. We went to an Asian Neighbourhood Centre with Keith Vaz, where there was a problem with the guitarist, Brian Bethell. They were saying to him, 'You're NF.' 'Me? What makes you say that?' 'You've got red laces in your boots.' We were trying to stifle our laughter: 'What? Red laces in your boots mean you're NF? Really? Well, not where we come from.' They were finally convinced that he just wore red laces in his boots to be a little outré. And then Keith leaned over to me and behind his hand he said, 'It's all right, when we get elected we're closing this place down anyway.' I thought, 'You bastard.'

ROBERT HOWARD Keith Vaz seemed to be doing it through gritted teeth and there was some hostility from the audience. These were kids probably living on council estates looking at you going, 'You're just a pop star living in a nice house in London. What do you know about it?' You'd have to justify it and say, 'Three years ago I was on the dole. It doesn't change what you believe in and what you think's going on.' The question was always, 'How can you support a political movement like this, directly?' And the answer was always, 'Things are so bad that the first thing we need to do is get Thatcher out.' I was a believer in first getting your hands on the levers of power and change from within. They were desperate times. I felt that Conservatism was contrary to human nature and at its core was this equation of the survival of the fittest: 'There's no such thing as society,' just individuals; winners and losers. You don't inspire people through fear. I didn't see that humanity could evolve that way. You do it through hope. I self-financed a four-page leaflet called Register to Vote which said on the front cover, 'How can you complain about the state of the nation; your vote cast is your only salvation.'

Register To Vote pamphlet
financed by Robert Howard,
1987.

TINY FENNIMORE There were some very angry young people out there and a lot of despair. We really did tap into the fact that people felt they were not being heard and they were losing their opportunity for a life.

BILLY BRAGG In Wrexham someone stood up and said, 'We don't need the Labour Party here, Billy. We need guns.' I thought, 'Fuckin' hell.' It was pretty rough in places where the de-industrialization had already started.

ANNAJOY DAVID I kept a diary of the tour: 'Bristol – group of twenty on Youth Training Schemes with visibly crushed self-confidence. Forest of Dean – first large gig in three years . . . Labour coaches provided to bring people from the other villages and local Tories demanding we take the Red Wedge banner down! Leeds – parts of Whinmoor Estate really run down and inadequate community centre. Hackney – Africa Organization with Billy, Lorna and Diane Abbott – 250 people of all ages, predominantly black, crucifying Tory candidate on dealing with a racist police force, the housing crisis. Worcester – distrust of all politicians. Visit to Crypt Youth Club in Wolverhampton cancelled because management decided Red

Wedge was too political. Students in Coventry really disappointed not to meet Billy since Labour Party had publicized the event using his name. Coalville – young people initially hostile and suspicious of a potential royal visit by right-on pop stars. Atmosphere altered when candidate Sue Waddington seen to be more interested in listening.'

PETER JENNER The tour was something radically different but it was really hard to make it work. There wasn't a continuity of artists. It was all sorts of odds and ends and different people and the local parties didn't know how to promote it or have connections with the young people. You'd go to Lydney Town Hall and there wouldn't be many people because no one knew it was on. Trying to get into a local audience from the London music industry, it's very hard to get some traction.

BILLY BRAGG As a thirteen-year-old white working-class schoolboy from Essex I listened to Marvin Gaye singing 'Abraham, Martin And John' and connected in some way with the civil rights struggle. So if Marvin Gaye had come to my town and said, 'We're having a meeting about the assassination of Martin Luther King,' would I have gone? You're sure as fuck I would have done. They were extraordinary events and some of the MPs got it and others were a little bit baffled. You got some real, great, local passion from people and local activists and we'd have to referee a debate between them and the local MPs.

NEIL KINNOCK If you'd just had a panel of three or four political speakers there would have been an audience of no more than ten. You'd be bloody daft to even try. But with Billy and Porky the Poet and Attila the Stockbroker it was full. 'Bloody hell! They're coming to our area. It's free. Let's go and see what they have to say.' That defined it, really. A piece of music can say more in ten lines than a speech can in 1,000 words.

•

ANNAJOY DAVID Out of all of our ideas over two years – the tours, the Day Events, the alliances abroad, the meetings, all the subgroups – a twelve-page pamphlet, *Move On Up: A Socialist Vision of the Future* was written in the lead-up to the general election. It spelt out the consequences to young people of a third term of Tory government and described our ideas for a socialist vision for the twenty-first century.

BILLY BRAGG The Red Wedge manifesto was the final victory of us and our own ideas. And it was endorsed by Kinnock.

Red Wedge Move On Up manifesto, 1987.

NEIL KINNOCK I wrote the introduction: 'To be young should be very heaven. Too often for too many it's very hell . . .' The manifesto gave us a chance to emphasize this point about Red Wedge being very much two-way. We didn't want them to hang party cards round their necks. If we were going to create a more liberal, tolerant, opportunity-filled, product-ive, efficient society and economy, it's not going to be done because we've got five million members of the Labour Party. It was going to be done because twelve million people understood what we were doing and agreed enough to vote for us. I finished by saying, 'I'm certain that when there's a Labour government elected Red Wedge will go on pressing for the voice of young people to be heard loud and clear in the planning and policymaking of that government. And we'll be listening and putting ideas to work.'

ANNAJOY DAVID Neil Spencer wrote up most of the manifesto and I wrote a lot of the policies – with the help of young writers like Paolo Hewitt and Marek Khan – about employment and jobs, housing, education, defence and human rights, and 'getting fresh – fight for your right to party'. There wasn't just one line. It was a group of artists all coming together so our policy emerged organically. I hadn't been to university. My skills were very particular and I tried to pull that together and develop a political narrative. I could see what was happening in Britain and that we needed a counterculture that stood up and held a mirror for a generation. The artists would have long political discussions around popular culture, about CND, about the anti-apartheid movement, the riots, the Falklands War, youth unemployment and about what Labour should do when it came into government. We were asking, what country did we want to live in? What was Britain going to look like in the future?

NEIL SPENCER It was time a few fundamental questions were raised about fairness and justice. It wasn't a bunch of slogans or glib phrases. It was down to political and moral ethics. We wanted Red Wedge to introduce long-term socialist ideals – not this partisan, greedy society that Mrs Thatcher and the rest of the Tories had introduced – and build something from the disgrace we found ourselves in. It was proper politics. There was a launch at Ronnie Scott's. I was quite nervous because you're being held accountable and held up to scrutiny. When you're the editor of *NME*, it's armour because it's a successful music paper, but being a press officer for Red Wedge and mixing it up with the big boys like the *Daily Mail* and the *Daily Express* was a different game. I certainly had pre-match nerves. There was some hostile questioning but the document wasn't challenged.

TINY FENNIMORE As press officers, we would think we were doing brilliant things and every day we would look at the Murdoch press who would be saying something completely different. Neil Kinnock was a really nice guy but I thought it would be uphill to get a Labour government with him as leader; he was too working-class and most *Mail* readers in the south wouldn't vote for him.

TOM ROBINSON I remember Kinnock being more physically impressive in the flesh than he appeared to be on television, but it was difficult to envisage him as prime minister. Thatcher had too much of a grip on the country. She was still in the post-Falklands invulnerability. She had changed the nature of what the country was and ground down those who opposed her so relentlessly that there wasn't the stomach for risking a protest vote, for the majority of the population. It was only eight years on from the Callaghan government and that was nothing to think back on.

TOM SAWYER The Tories hated Neil. There was no way that the ruling class was ever going to have a Welsh working-class man with an accent as well. They were out to get him. And although he was a really clever man it did get to him. Neil knew what it was like to be poor and he wanted to help people from his class background.

BILL GILBY Neil provided a bridge between the old failed regime and a stable ground for the next leader, John Smith. He played a critical role in making Labour electable again. It was only four years after '83 and there was so much work to do. I had a long-term view.

COLIN BYRNE In '83 Thatcher had trotted out Kenny Everett at a Young Conservatives rally shouting, 'Let's bomb Russia', and some other god-awful comedians – Bob Monkhouse and Jimmy Tarbuck – and you just thought, 'If that's what they're doing we've got to do something a lot cooler.' So '87 was the first time Labour actually campaigned with a bit of style. Red Wedge was focusing us on what gave us credibility with young people, like Neil Kinnock on the front page of *NME*. And the Party election broadcast was filmed by Hugh Hudson who had directed *Chariots of Fire*.

JOHN NEWBEGIN The election broadcast was all about Neil and his personal vision for the future of Britain. Everybody called it 'Kinnock the Movie'. It was mocked by the Tory press but it was a complete game-changer: Neil and Glenys walking hand in hand along the cliffs of the Gower Peninsula with 'Jerusalem' pumping in the background. It was not some politician in an oak-panelled office sitting behind his desk telling you what his party was going to do. The whole campaign had a different energy and style about it. The image in the press was of a really dynamic, energetic organization full of ideas. The rallies were fantastic. We had good advance teams. We had a really good press operation. And Red Wedge was all part of that.

PHILL JUPITUS I was so sure we were going to win because I had spent six months with nobody but Labour activists. I read the *Guardian* and I had been completely and utterly sequestered away from the wider world. I was doing the gigs and living a fake sort of reality. This is how fired up I was: on the day before the election I went to the local Labour branch office in

'A Tale of Two Punters', written and drawn by Porky, 1985.

Shadwell in East London where I was living, and said, 'Do you need any help? Is there anything I can do today?' It was like the 'who the fuck are you?' face we got in Walworth Road when Red Wedge first arrived. They said, 'You can go out door-knocking.' So I went round to the mainly Bengali community saying, 'Have you voted today?'

ASHTAR ALKHIRSAN I was living on Walworth Road on the Heygate Estate, just a bit further up from the Labour Party HQ, and campaigning and knocking on people's doors trying to get them out to vote.

ANGELA EAGLE I was going round in Battersea and being told that Labour was 'only for the blacks and the queers'.

TOM WATSON I was the youngest member of staff by about twenty years so they used me on Labour's first-time voter leaflets, called 'It's your first vote. The Conservatives would rather you didn't use it.' Four million young people had the vote for the first time in the '87 general election.

JOHN NEWBEGIN There was a fantastic buzz. If you're on the inside of a campaign you're surrounded by all the energy and you're meeting people who are voting for you: 'Yeah, we're going to win.' Nobody goes into an election without a partial belief that it's winnable. And of course, there were many moments during that campaign of looking at the polls every day and thinking, 'Maybe we will do it.' But heart of hearts, most people recognized it would be a two-stage process to get a Labour government; that '87 would repair the damage of '83 and present a radical new image of the Labour Party but it would take a second election to win a majority.

Tom Watson (left) first time voter pamphlet, published by the Labour Party, 1987.

RHODA DAKAR On the evening of the election we all went out to the Mean Fiddler in Harlesden. It was organized by Annajoy and Billy and we watched the results in horror.

NEIL SPENCER People were crying into their drinks as the results came through. A 3.2 per cent swing to Labour, but the Tories were still left with a 102-seat majority.

BILLY BRAGG The momentum had been with us. We believed we could beat the Tories. It was a real disappointment. I was walking home to my flat in Acton in the early hours looking at people in the streets and thinking, 'How could you have done that?'

KAREN WALTER I was with friends at a flat in Westbourne Grove. We sat up all night watching it and just couldn't believe it. I've never felt so completely gutted. It was demoralizing; and the next day just thinking, 'What do you do now?'

TINY FENNIMORE I remember waking up the following morning and we had subsidence in our flat in Camden. The assessor was coming round and he was going to tell us whether we were going to get the insurance money or not. He saw how depressed we were and said, 'What's the matter?' We were saying, 'We lost the election. We're heartbroken.' I think he felt so sorry for us that he signed off the insurance.

STEVE WHITE We'd done a song called 'Right To Go' which I'd written some of the lyrics to: *You know a third term's going to cost the earth*, but Thatcher had it sewn up at that point. The tide against Kinnock was so massive and Labour was still suffering massive divisions. Although we spurred a lot of youngsters to think about it, the election was being fought in the heartlands of *Daily Mail* readers. We reached out to our demographic but the outcome of the election was in the hands of people who probably didn't even know what Red Wedge was.

CLARE SHORT It was always the minority who voted for Thatcher but that's the British system. People didn't believe that we knew what to do. So although people increasingly thought there was something wrong in the country, they couldn't quite trust Labour. People say, 'It's governments who lose elections, not oppositions who win them.' I think that's broadly true.

TOM SAWYER At the end of the day the voters didn't think Neil was a credible prime minister. The electorate did like the fact that he sorted Militant out and he was a tough leader, but we still had a non-nuclear defence policy and the Tories played that really hard: 'Vote Labour and lose your defences.' We were also anti Common Market. Those things went against us.

NEIL KINNOCK I was supposed to be a raging lefty from the valleys who went round smacking people in the gob. I got elected in October 1983 and the miners' work-to-rule started in November. The strike came in March of 1984 and lasted for twelve months. It finished almost exactly two years before the 1987 election. It was such an understandable distraction for the whole movement and we got virtually no policy momentum going in that time. In those circumstances victory was out of sight. I had said to my team after '83, 'This is going to be a two-innings match.' Wounding Thatcher's majority was a possibility and in my view we did about half of what we needed to do. I said, 'If we can gain forty-two seats it's a bloody miracle.' We actually gained twenty seats and then the next twenty-two Tory seats the total majority of votes was 4,000; that's how bloody close we came. But never in my wildest dreams did I think we could win the election. The size of the task was too big and the Labour movement took so bloody long to get used to the idea that we had to change. It took another defeat for people to start really waking up to that.

LARRY WHITTY I don't think there was any way we could have won the election, frankly. In the first election poll the SDP–Liberal Alliance was ahead of Labour. The commentators were infatuated by them. Three years earlier the future of politics was being written about as David Owen and Shirley Williams. The fact that the Labour Party were in with a shot in the election was a bit of a surprise.

ANNAJOY DAVID It's a really hard question to answer why Labour lost the election. A lot of the people who were particularly badly affected by Thatcherism were not registered or didn't vote. They were still completely disenfranchised and disconnected. There's not just one answer. The country's mindset was not ready enough to move on to something new. There was also a really hostile media. But the youth vote of Labour did go up drastically. That is a fact.

TINY FENNIMORE It was a bitter moment for us all but more young people voted, which was the main thing Annajoy and I were banging on about. And there was a 7 per cent swing amongst eighteen- to twenty-four-year-olds to Labour which people like the press office and Larry Whitty credited to Red Wedge. We were getting closer to our goal. But even if Labour had got a 7 per cent swing everywhere we still wouldn't have won the election. And after '87 there was an incremental swing in the youth vote until Blair got in.

NEIL KINNOCK It may be true that more kids voted Tory but people who are made to feel insecure do not naturally or necessarily swing to the left. The whole of history will show you that those people cling onto Nurse and are naturally more Conservative for fear of something worse, unless they get really bloody angry. What appears to be the appealing stability of having people in charge who are 'born to rule', they learn, is a fallacy. The other factor is, whilst the youth element was very high it never affected the majority, so those who were in occupations felt that they had a vested interest in maintaining the existing order.

ANGELA EAGLE Labour had a good campaign and people thought we ought to have done better but the Party had been split by the SDP and our collective nervous breakdown at the beginning of the decade. We didn't reform the Party enough and we were up against a very slick, very well-funded, sophisticated PR machine with huge propaganda outlets. The Conservatives got another huge working majority and after the election had carte blanche to indulge in all of their bigotries. And that's what happened.

WAITING FOR THE GREAT LEAP FORWARD

Labour listens. 1987–90. Legacy

BILLY BRAGG The night after the general election I was on *After Dark* on Channel 4 and as it went to the adverts Teresa Gorman, who had just won the Conservative seat in Billericay, leaned across the table and said, *sotto voce*, 'You and your kind are finished. We are the future.' She was so smug. And because she was Essex I took it personally. Then she accused me of being a fine example of Thatcherism. I said: 'I am a fine example of Thatcherism but I still chose to vote Labour because I realize I have a responsibility to other people in society and to take some of my wealth and redistribute it. I believe that individualism is essential to socialism but from a collective base. I had the opportunity to be an individual because I was educated collectively, not because my parents had privilege and sent me to be educated. And that individualism came out because of the opportunities I got from the welfare state; because my health care was free; because I got free meals at school. I believe that most people in this country will not have the opportunity to express the individualism I believe is central to socialism.'

KAREN WALTER I don't know how Billy managed to do it. The wind had been knocked out of our sails.

HILARY CROSS '87 was a massive disappointment for Red Wedge because the election had been such a focus. But despite the feeling of abject misery there was still so much anti-Thatcher feeling and there were still so many battles to be fought on so many fronts. And we were young. We still wanted to defeat this feeling that Britain was all about Thatcherism. All those issues in the sixties: CND, women's rights, gay rights, abortion rights, were still relevant twenty years later. Some of those battles had been won but they were being undermined again and eroded as part of Thatcher's right-wing agenda. It was a continual battle about civil rights and justice and equality and the voice of the common people.

RHODA DAKAR Just because you don't achieve what you're after immediately it doesn't mean you stop trying: 'Oh, I pushed the door, but it won't open.' You have to keep at it. We didn't lose the election. They lost it. Kinnock was out of ideas. We got Keith Vaz elected. And Diane Abbott, Paul Boateng and Bernie Grant all got in. It was a significant move forward. So it was like, 'What are you going to do?'

HILARY CROSS So a lot of the post-election momentum went into *Well Red*. I became the editor but felt it was important that it was not just seen as Red Wedge's mouthpiece – in fact, more people read a copy than ever went to a Red Wedge concert. *Well Red* had to be a popular youth magazine that was thought-provoking and encouraged debate. There was no point preaching to the converted because the converted were such a small group. We said, 'We've got to broaden this culturally to talk about a wider diversity of issues – music, art, fashion, sport, film, history, internationalism – which might not be on Labour's agenda.' We made sure the politics was always there above the surface but not overbearingly. But the Labour Party was still really important because it was the only possible chance of getting rid of Thatcherism.

RHODA DAKAR They invested in us more after that. Before, it was all big meetings at Labour Party headquarters, and after there were a lot of smaller meetings, more focus groups, and side meetings. People like Giles Radice, who was writing policy, would be presented to us, or the shadow ministers of Trade and Industry and Youth and Culture. And that's when we started going into the Shadow Cabinet Office. That was quite significant. Our status was being elevated. Although you couldn't sit in Neil Kinnock's chair, the one with two arms. 'I'm sorry, that's Neil's chair.' 'Oh, OK. Shall I sit on one of these, then?' 'Yes, please.' I sat opposite and Neil talked about football: 'Did you see the match last night, lads?' And then Dr Robert, who was the biggest fan of all of us, said, 'We haven't come here to talk about football.' It was so funny.

NEIL KINNOCK We were able to illustrate our policy commitment by reference to these youngsters, but accusations I never got. I expected it. I would make a presentation and then say, 'What do you make of that? If you've got particular questions I'm more than happy to respond?' Nobody said anything like, 'If only you'd stuck with the miners,' or, 'You used to be a unilateralist and now you're not.'

PAUL BOWER The day after the defeat Kinnock went straight back on the campaign trail, which was very smart of him: 'We edge forward. Now is not the time to be downhearted.'

JOHN NEWBEGIN For Neil, the engagement with Red Wedge was because it said something about our politics. It said something about our values. It said something about what we believed. We worked with them before the election and we continued to work with them after the election. It wasn't window-dressing.

NEIL SPENCER There was a 'Red Wedge / Kinnock Meeting' three months after the election in the Shadow Cabinet Office, and looking now at the agenda it reflects very well on Kinnock: 'Regions and local government', 'The appointment of a parliamentary spokesperson on youth affairs', 'The reorganization of the youth service', 'Arts policy: the blank tape levy, community radio'. Kinnock knew who his friends were and realized that he was being offered a chance to get through to young people and the possibility of building a new consensus against Thatcherism. Thatcher won the election but she was beginning to lose her gloss. She was a victim of her own hubris and thought she was untouchable.

Red Wedge
Labour Listens
launch invite.

ANNAJOY DAVID I met Margaret Thatcher once, in the House of Commons. I sat in the Strangers' Gallery during Prime Minister's Question Time. I knew she represented everything that I disagreed with. What she believed to be important she absolutely believed with exactly the same conviction as me; that was the one thing we had in common apart from being Librans, as Neil Spencer kept reminding me, rather embarrassingly. There was a tuck shop that sold cigarettes and Bernie Grant, who was by then the MP for Tottenham, said, 'I'll take you to get some.' Mrs Thatcher was coming out with a bag of alcohol and Bernie made some sort of joke to her about it and she replied something quite shrill to him. We came face to face – I remember her handbag folded very neatly over her arm – and she said, 'Do I know you?' And I said, 'No, but I know exactly who you are.' She looked at me and then walked off with her bodyguards and her husband, Dennis. It was just a little silent second: two different generations of people both believing totally in what we believed in, but opposite. It was a quite a moment.

RHODA DAKAR We were always trying to refresh Red Wedge with new blood and initiatives because inevitably it ends up being the same old same old. We had artist meetings at Solid Bond with people like Paul and Billy and Tracey still, but also newer artists like The Men They Couldn't Hang and Attacco Decente.

ANNAJOY DAVID It was quite difficult to keep the momentum. Movements have to evolve. Everybody had other lives. They were musicians and comedians making albums and going on tours and writing shows. You've got to be clear about what you expect from other people.

BILLY BRAGG Winning the election was the focus, and would have been a vindication, but it wasn't the whole purpose. But after, I was out on the road a lot in China, Mexico, Australia, Japan, everywhere, so a lot passed me by without me realizing it.

PETER JENNER Politicians are control freaks, and a bunch of crazy musicians running around was dangerous. The artists were not in the system. You couldn't discipline them and that was why in the end Red Wedge collapsed. It wasn't two-way. Pop music people like winners. You had to be number one and we didn't win. Pop music is all about fashion. It's all this year's thing. In '86, '87 Red Wedge was groovy; '88, '89, '90 it wasn't groovy.

TRACEY THORN Pop music tries to regenerate itself all the time and stay fresh, and things do start to sound stale. Music goes in cycles. There is a sense that you're constantly reacting to what was done just a few years before. The Red Wedge generation were a very forward-looking group of people. Paul Weller had said, 'I don't just want to be in the Jam forever,' and that sat quite happily with his political outlook which was looking forward: 'How can we change things? How can we progress?'

RICHARD COLES Once you get geared into pop music you become part of the thing you decried. Red Wedge was a career-enhancing thing for us in a funny kind of a way and gave us more of a profile. And of course people were buying our records and coming to our gigs and before long that changes who you are and what you do. We were in New York and we had to go to Paris to do an SOS Racisme gig with Bruce Springsteen in the Château de Vincennes. We did a political discussion programme on the same evening and I was asked why we were there. I did this rousing reply about how important it was to express our solidarity with the oppressed people and the working class and the French immigrant population. There was a right-wing commentator there and he said, 'Richard, I sat behind you on Concorde yesterday from New York. What the hell are you doing talking about your solidarity with the working class?' Pop stars have to be inaccessible because it's unmanageable, the degree of interest, and that goes against the grain of solidarity.

STEVE WHITE Most career arcs in the music business are very short. I measure everything by the fact the Beatles had seven years. So from the time that Red Wedge exploded onto the scene and the trail that it blazed, it did very well. It was like a punk band that put out a couple of great singles and then they're gone. It would have cost Paul money to do that first tour, but once that went you're not going to be able to sell out Birmingham Odeon. Paul and Billy were a massive energy. Billy had the vision and Paul had the name, and when they stopped seeing a way forward that's when it lost its impetus. I remember Paul saying, 'It's like "rent-a-politic".' We could have been doing political events every night of the year.

PHILL JUPITUS Fuck it: off the back of Red Wedge the Style Council took me on the road. I was doing political stuff still and there was still that sense that Paul had his heart in the right place. But that said, within two years Paul found himself without a record deal for the first time since he was seventeen and didn't make records again until the nineties.

TINY FENNIMORE Paul came away with a bitter taste in his mouth. He was always very hostile and suspicious of the MPs and the whole political world. I don't think Red Wedge was exploited. We knew what we were doing. We all went in with our eyes wide open.

ANNAJOY DAVID My understanding was, Paul was peed off with the politicians, not with the Red Wedge model. There is a distinction there. Paul had a lot of doubts. He questioned a lot of things. He didn't ask to be the spokesperson of a generation. He's very modest. He'll always praise somebody else before himself, which is the mark of a great human being. He had a skill of pulling people behind him to produce interesting things around his music: creating a platform for other people to do things. It's not a skill that's easy. You wanted to get behind him but he didn't want to be used by anyone. They were valid doubts. But at the end of the day Red Wedge was bigger than that.

PAUL WELLER I would like to do something like Red Wedge again, but not for the Labour Party. I became disheartened with it all. I still have the same views, but how do you go about it?[85] Whatever misgivings I had about being involved in the Labour Party or becoming that partisan were overshadowed by the fact we should get people out thinking about politics and maybe change the way we were going in the country; naive or not.[86] But I think we were used and it put me off politics. I'm not really one for joining clubs.[87] I was doing a lot more before that, benefits and different projects we were involved in. And that kind of soured it all for me getting involved in the Wedge. Billy was a very amiable and very persuasive person and he kind of talked me round to that so I blame him.[88]

BILLY BRAGG 'Waiting For The Great Leap Forward' was my post-election Red Wedge song to let people know that I've not got all the answers and I now realize that music can't change the world. It was a direct reference to Maoism, as a metaphor rather than an endorsement: *Here comes the future you can't run from it / If you've got a blacklist I want to be on it.* I'd been talking about mixing pop and politics by that point for five years and what was the outcome? I was still waiting for the Great Leap Forward. Remember, I was still just a bloke doing gigs: *Jumble sales are organized and pamphlets have been posted,* it's what we'd been doing. *Even after closing time there's still parties to be hosted*: political parties but also piss-ups and the escape from it all. *You can be active with the activists or sleep in with the sleepers*: I'm not the guy that says, 'It's all shit. It doesn't work. Politics is pointless.' Our biggest enemy is cynicism. It's cancer to the soul. Cynicism is what people turn to when they've given up. And I'm not talking about doubt. Never trust anybody that doesn't have doubts because they'll probably try and sell you a copy of *Socialist Worker*.

LARRY WHITTY They all felt used to some extent and they all were, to some extent. They volunteered to do something in support of Labour so the Party used it. Paul Weller was naturally suspicious of formal politics. He was one of the bigger names involved and one of the ones that people who didn't know about the music scene would have mentioned. They were part of a cultural friendship much of which they dreamt up themselves.

COLIN BYRNE: If you're Paul Weller or Billy Bragg you already had an artistic platform but they also wanted an impact on Britain. Politics was a useful platform for them to talk about more than just whatever they were singing about. They both gained. Paul puts too grim a face on it.

RHODA DAKAR Paul was disaffected with where the Party was going. It's fair enough if he thought they were just pulling his chain. He admired Annajoy and she kept him on board if anyone did. And he was still coming to meetings a year after the election.

KAREN WALTER Red Wedge didn't let anyone down. Labour did. It was frustrating that we weren't being listened to and then new people were coming in that I didn't trust. It was almost like the time had passed and we were treading water.

JOHN NEWBEGIN History is littered with politicians demonstrating they are totally out of touch with popular culture. Red Wedge was not just seen as a series of gigs but was actually having a real sustainable input into the development of party politics.

ANNAJOY DAVID You can start to see some really detailed political policy thinking by Red Wedge after the election. We started doing a lot more work on the ground at a local level. I pinpointed fifty-two constituencies where projects could be established, encouraged and supported. In April 1988 we launched the initiative 'Red Wedge and the Labour Party Get Busy' which was an attempt by Labour to find out what young people thought before policy was decided.

RHODA DAKAR 'Labour Listens: Red Wedge and the Labour Party Get Busy' was a joint campaign initiative to listen to and learn from young people. It was about opening up the Labour movement at a local level. We were polishing their dodgy old ideas and making it shiny and new.

ROBERT HOWARD I ended up doing press conferences with David Blunkett, who was spokesman for local government, and Neil Kinnock. We had a photo shoot and Mandelson was circling in the background in his Machiavellian way. Kinnock said, 'Don't worry, they always make me look like a cunt.' I was like, 'Oh right. Yeah.' Often I felt out of my depth, but I was learning and I had this anger that I was able to channel through politics and identify an enemy. I wasn't a textbook lefty. I couldn't have quoted Keir Hardie or *The Ragged-Trousered Philanthropists*.

COLIN BYRNE There was major-league depression. 'Fuck, we've just run the most professional campaign ever and we still lose against Thatcher.' People were having a go at Neil. The knives were out. So from the Luddite tendency it was, 'You've had your chance; all you did was change the style and not the substance and we still lost.' So Labour Listens was an attempt to come out fighting and say we must learn from this defeat. And the lesson is, 'We don't go back to 1983. We go forward and engage people who should vote Labour but still don't trust us.' I remember Peter Mandelson waxing lyrical, 'We're going to go out . . . we're going to listen . . . we're going to invite ordinary people . . .' It was certainly based on the Red Wedge Day Events model. We wanted to be seen by the media, who were invited along, as fearless. We would listen to people who might actually say, 'You're crap.'

ROBERT HOWARD I knew I would get asked some serious questions and I knew that I had to answer those, otherwise it was bullshit. I did a press conference and the *Independent* guy thought he was going to talk to Dr Robert Runcie, the Archbishop of Canterbury, and I, Dr Robert from the Blow Monkeys, turned up. But you'd be playing these gigs then doing Day Events, and you'd think, 'My world and your world are very different.' I was living in a little flat above a record shop in Brixton and the record company would send round a posh car for *Top of the Pops* and I'd say, 'Send it away, for God's sake. I don't want this shit.'

RICHARD COLES We did *Top of the Pops* once and there was a strike by technicians and we crossed the picket line outside Television Centre. I huddled down in the back of the limousine embarrassed and thinking, 'There's some anomalies in this that perhaps need to be looked at,' but you couldn't turn down *Top of the Pops*.

COLIN BYRNE At the Manchester Opera House there was a woman sat in the front row with a Tesco bag on her head and we thought, 'Whose fucking idea was this to go and listen to lunatics?' The Day Events with the politicians were mostly god-awful and we were all grateful to get the hell out of there and back on the train to London.

ANNAJOY DAVID Red Wedge's end of Labour Listens was significantly successful. There was real communication between the Labour movement and groups of young people who were active locally in their communities. We wanted to make sure young people had that access to get involved in that process of change. We linked up with over thirty new project initiatives, from theatre to housing to anti-racist to music. The reality was, a lot of Labour local authorities were without the imagination and the vision, the dynamism, to develop new socialist policies on the ground. That's why we had to develop policy ideas to give the Labour Party a push. We stumbled across a political will and acted as a catalyst to bring it to the fore.

HILARY CROSS We were invited by both Catholic and Protestant community groups to go to Ireland, where the Belfast Musicians Collective was working across the divide. It was really important to us all that we didn't go out there and represent a Republican view and that we met kids from both sides of the divide. It was very much about what role can culture and music play to engage young people in political issues, which is why the gigs in the evening were a key part because it wasn't just sitting down and talking about politics; it was also about enjoying yourself. And after, Billy would always come back out and sit on the stage talking to people. There was always interaction.

BILLY BRAGG I learnt more about Ireland talking to two Republican women in Derry than I'd learnt watching telly in the last twenty years. Going to Ireland was Red Wedge taking the initiative, because the Labour Party was not organized there. It was exciting but also tough trying to find bands that didn't somewhere deep down have some element of sectarianism.

ANNAJOY DAVID I met Gerry Adams. He put his hand out to mine and I said, 'I'll decide if I want to shake that at the end of the meeting.' But I understood that Sinn Féin had a lot of respect on the ground in shared communities and represented an important body of people that would later form part of the peace process. The trip was very successful and showed the importance of popular culture going into really complicated political environments and talking to musicians and theatre groups and young people's communities and church groups on both sides to make an intervention and say, 'We support you in your efforts to try and break down this sectarian environment.'

TOM SAWYER I was one of the architects of Labour Listens but ultimately it was a failure because the Labour Party didn't believe in it and it just collapsed. The Party just wasn't very good at engaging with people. The idea might have been OK in my or Neil's mind but for most MPs it was, 'What am I doing going to Basingstoke tonight?' It needed a proper programme of real listening but nobody knew how to do it. I talked a lot with Pete Jenner during 1988–9. The question was, what we could both do together? I had links in the unions and he had links in the music industry. 'How can I learn more about your world and how can you learn more about mine?' 'Would it be good to try this?'

ANNAJOY DAVID I prepared a paper on youth provision and Pete prepared the document 'A Policy for Youth Arts' with Annie Weekes. It focused on the music industry and a National Arts Service which, it stated, 'could do almost as much to enhance people's pleasure in their lives as a National Health Service.'

JOHN NEWBEGIN Pete was a big guy in the music business: hugely respected and a radical left progressive Labour supporter to his core. We politically saw eye to eye and Neil spent a lot of time speaking to him. But Pete is a very impatient guy: 'Why can't we be more outspoken?' And the answer was, if a party was going to come from a long way behind and win an election, it had to present itself with a measured agenda which would appeal to a broad cross-section of people, not just radical young people. 'We've got four years to the next election. Let's take the whole machine apart, have a look at it, stick it back together again, and make sure we've really got something that does what we want it to do.' Red Wedge was very keen that there should be a coherent youth policy and a spokesperson for youth on the front bench. We had a series of exchanges and the pressure and desire for change began to filter through into a coherent set of policies.

NEIL KINNOCK I remember the argument and that was why John was emphasizing it so bloody strongly to Peter in their exchange of letters:

> Neil is anxious, as you know, that an appointment is not just a tokenistic gesture which has no real relationship to the necessary

realities of parliamentary life. What he is very willing to do is to find ways in which the Red Wedge agenda for highlighting youth concerns within the Party and in public politics, which as you know he welcomes, is adequately met.

We were never in dispute about ends. Politics is often about an argument over means. I could get a queue of politicians coming through my office for three hours. Pete and Annajoy were bringing more ideas in ten minutes. My office people were under terrible diary pressure. They used to say, 'You've got to prioritize.' And I'd say, 'I am. Get me Pete Jenner.' The point that I'm making is that Annajoy and Pete were policy feeders.

PETER JENNER The influence on policymaking was a problem because Labour didn't want a bunch of drug-takers and poofs and rock 'n' rollers coming in and telling them what policy should be: 'You stick to playing your music.' 'What do you know about politics?' Trying to breach that was always very difficult.

TOM WATSON You couldn't have Red Wedge without the silver-haired Pete Jenner. His brain was the size of a planet. Any man that organized the free Rolling Stones concert in Hyde Park has got Access All Areas. He was so unbelievably cool but also he had been up against it and knew how the world worked. He seemed like the wise old man of the industry. He understood systems and how you get change and start seeding arguments early. Annajoy would have just rung up and said, 'Look, Neil, if you fuck this up, right . . . you've got to do these three things, otherwise no young person will ever vote Labour again,' whereas Pete would have written a twenty-page document and given it to ten people to submit in parts to the policy process and Annajoy's three points would have been addressed eighteen months later. You needed both those kinds of people.

JOHN NEWBEGIN MPs have a tendency to overpromise and artists ask too much. It's always difficult for people outside the political machine to understand the constraints within which politicians have to work. So the fact that Red Wedge had an agenda and demands that were more radical than the mainstream agenda was no surprise. There was a balance to be struck. But there were lots of people that were suspicious and would say, 'Who are all these pop stars? This is frivolous stuff; this is American-style politics; we don't want it.'

LARRY WHITTY Some of the things that the Labour Party was saying, certainly on cultural issues, were very influenced by the people that Red

Wedge brought forward. It was the high point of Labour being the outsiders, and after, we had to get more respectful. And that certainly cut across what the Red Wedge input was pushing us towards. Post-election, the image became more important than the respectability and the policies.

COLIN BYRNE We were starting to put the architecture in of what became New Labour.

ANDY MCSMITH Kinnock and Mandelson and the rest were focused on the ratings, not the youth vote, and the artists felt disillusioned.

PETER JENNER As the nineties loomed, Red Wedge got killed. They put Tony Blair in to be our man. I had one meeting with him and didn't like him. There was something about him which was suspicious. He just seemed like a phoney. And he could see that we were not controllable. He was a bad guitar player and he never got it. Blair and Mandelson realized that people like me and Annajoy were not reliable, and in some sense we were tarred with all the reasons why Kinnock lost the election. Red Wedge was meant to win it. It didn't. Therefore, let's go on to a new agenda. It all became focus groups and polls.

CLARE SHORT Blair wouldn't have liked it because it was dangerous. Pop music: people might swear or say something deeply radical; you've got to keep everything tidy and manicured.

JOHN NEWBEGIN As attention focused on the next election, Labour was beginning to develop serious thinking about the music and film and fashion industry. The new generation of MPs like Gordon Brown and Tony Blair recognized that culture had not only a social but an economic significance, and that was one of the things the Wedgies were keen to promote. Gordon issued a statement, 'Music: Our Cultural Future' in 1990. In the first paragraph it said,

> . . . it represents the first time a major political party in Britain has published a serious, comprehensive policy for the music industry . . . there is still a widespread assumption that this is a marginal activity . . . treated by the Conservatives either as a hobby or simply a minority activity rather than as a major industry and employer . . . our document shows why that is wrong.

It was significant that it came from the Trade and Industry spokesman, not the shadow arts minister.

NEIL KINNOCK Gordon Brown's 'music paper' position was a vindication in some ways of my belief in what began with Billy's Jobs and Industry tour five years earlier. It was trying to install the idea that entertainment – creative industries, cultural industries, arts, music – were all significant contributors to the Gross Domestic Product. The idea that as a political party we should have a policy on housing or farming and not the creative industries was bloody lunatic. It was plain as a bloody pikestaff. The creative industries were employing five times as many people as the steel industry. It was daft. In 1992, four weeks before the general election, when we were in a relatively strong position in the polls, the civil service drew up papers in preparation for a Labour government, and a Minister for Youth was there, alongside revenue for the development of a youth arts. It was a vindication of Red Wedge.

NEIL SPENCER We weren't civil servants or bureaucrats or elected councillors or elected MPs, but the very fact that Neil Kinnock thought that some of those ideas ended up in a Labour Party manifesto is vindication.

JOHN NEWBEGIN And in 1997, we set up a creative industries task force so Red Wedge was early strands of what eventually came together as a coherent policy for the creative industries.

PETER JENNER Red Wedge had an enormous amount to do with Tony Blair becoming prime minister three times running. We made that generation Labour supporters. The whole '97 thing comes back to '86. And a lot of the younger people who came into the Labour Party came in because of Red Wedge; people like Tom Watson and Andy Burnham. You could not be a Tory and be groovy for five or six years. Red Wedge made having a political view and being a lefty acceptable. It made people aware of how awful Thatcherism was and how we needed an alternative agenda. It shifted the whole youth thing so you couldn't be anti-Labour.

ANGELA EAGLE The influence that Red Wedge and this cultural activity had during people's formative years resonated through subsequent elections. There is no doubt about that.

ANNAJOY DAVID Red Wedge was an experiment. Some of it worked really well and some of it didn't. That's life. Artists are not politicians. They respond emotionally to listening to their fans, to have a sense of duty, a call to arms when something is failing. Anybody says to you that Red Wedge was just about a bunch of pop stars that came out for Labour, you can tell them to bugger off. The artist bit was the cherry on top of a very dense cake of important stuff. It was a platform and a funnel for a counterculture that was fundamentally against a really vicious government that essentially didn't like people who weren't like them.

ROBERT HOWARD What I do know is, the people that came along to those gigs, for them they were magic nights. And a few of them might have been inspired by that in the way I was inspired by Rock Against Racism.

PHILL JUPITUS It was almost like punk went that way and Red Wedge came back this way with a, 'You need to engage with the wider world.' That, for me, was the appeal. Labour was giving us such a visible platform. They were up for it. It was reassuring. And they were sending MPs to the gigs and seemed to be taking it seriously, but then as things went on you realized that you were becoming a cosmetic campaigning tool. It was upsetting, but the importance of what we were doing was never diminished. We had our own agenda.

ANNAJOY DAVID The central core of Red Wedge was all about young people taking a stand and saying something about how they felt about the government through culture. They had a forum to tell the Labour Party what they thought. And we helped to facilitate that. And people should not underestimate the powerful good that did. And for a while it refocused Labour and gave the Party its confidence back after the battering it had taken in '83. It gave it a narrative and a voice again. We weren't politicians; we were all pretty young and emotionally led, which was good. From doing the first CND Brockwell Park gig, to bands playing on the back of lorries, to DJs and having club nights, right through Red Wedge and the Miners' Strike and the anti-apartheid concerts, there was a cultural community emerging that was very well organized and very united in purpose. If you only measure success by the result, i.e. that the left lost, then you will always be quite cynical about it.

TINY FENNIMORE When you go back to Rock Against Racism and 2 Tone, we were carrying on a tradition. We were getting our ideas into the smoke-filled corridors and they were using us to get votes. Labour culture policy changed. We influenced their green policy. There was conversation about their nuclear policy. We had managed to get onto Neil's agenda. When I first got involved I thought we were going to change the world. We were impatient and ambitious. Now I realize that our role was to resist: the Tories push us and we push back and sometimes you manage to find a little way through and things change. It's all influence. And even if we were just another view bringing pressure to bear on the Labour Party, that was part of the process.

ANNAJOY DAVID Red Wedge represented the counterculture conscience of a generation, and a whole generation was switched on to a view of life through a language and a culture that carries on to this day. Its impact on the Labour Party helped the Department for Culture, Media and Sport come into being in 1997, and we had helped to get Chris Smith elected, who became its first minister.

TINY FENNIMORE My husband was a special advisor at the Culture, Media and Sport Ministry during the Blair government, and his proudest moment was getting free museum entry through. Red Wedge raised that question.

LUCY HOOBERMAN The transaction of culture, of means, of knowledge is unquantifiable. I have always worked in that belief that there's something in the live encounter that can change you as a person.

BILLY BRAGG Our highest aspiration as songwriters is to offer the audience a different perspective on politics, on relationships, on their environment, and Red Wedge was the apex of my attempts to try and see how far that could go into completely uncharted territory. We were right to try and do it and I'd definitely do it again.

PAUL BOWER Red Wedge raised morale in the Labour Party and it turned them outwards at a time of almost catatonic depression and internal warfare. But let's not overestimate our influence. We were part of a longer story.

BILLY BRAGG You have to see Red Wedge as part of the end of the Sixties. It was the last time music took it upon itself to really try and make a difference on a big scale and change a government. Music doesn't have that vanguard role in our culture anymore. But I'm not sure that you can look at how culture influences politics and see a scientifically measurable effect. I was at the wrong end. I was already politicized. I was driving the bus. You've got to ask the passengers what effect it had on them.

STEVE WHITE I still meet people that say, 'I got into politics because I saw you at Birmingham Odeon or Newcastle City Hall. I didn't agree with everything but it made me think.' From that point of view it achieved quite a lot: more than some politicians did.

RICHARD COLES Pop music connects people. Songs touch people and articulate a pathos that others feel. Music performs a soundtrack of their lives at moments of intensity and meaning. The politics comes and goes but that feeling of being touched outlasts the political dynamics. Red Wedge meant more to me than having a number-one record because it was real. It was about touching people's heart and mind and soul, and that's what I was interested in music for.

CATHAL SMYTH Red Wedge was very healing and dignified and intelligent. I mean, fuck me, that's amazing.

HILARY CROSS You can't divide life from politics. It's entwined. Life is about politics is about music is about culture is about work. The big political issues don't just get debated in Parliament. They get debated in pubs and schools and at gigs. When you have compassion for the everyday, that journey takes you to politics. And Red Wedge recognized that the dry politics of Westminster – 'There's no such thing as society,' and all the other stuff that Thatcher said – had an impact on every single thing that we did within our personal lives and brought it together in one place.

TOM WATSON For two or three years this amazing creativity gloriously exploded. Nobody quite knew where it was going to go but it was a cauldron of arts and ideas and politics. It reached people that would never have been touched by politics or culture. It was of its time but it's a period that should be revered.

ALEX DALLAS It's part of history: a political history, a women's history, and an arts and culture history.

RICHARD COLES I honestly thought pop music and Red Wedge would bring down Margaret Thatcher. What I didn't understand or see was that there was a far more profound restricting happening as a result of Thatcherism and Reaganism and neo-liberal economics. I was a middle-class boy but not exactly a pond skater on the meniscus of political ideology. I didn't have that personal investment in class politics that Jimmy or Paul Weller did, who, to his credit, put his money back into things, and that began to be really challenging for me.

TOM SAWYER: Red Wedge lasted longer than I thought it would do. Musicians are not people who say, 'I'll join the Labour Party,' and, 'I'll be with you for the next twenty years.' They move on. When John Smith, and then

Tony Blair, took over as leaders they didn't have much to do with policy. It was all done.

LARRY WHITTY It's fair comment to say Labour had learnt from what Red Wedge were doing; that you could mobilize people and use music to get people interested in politics: that's the way you talk to the workers, that's the way you talk to the churches, and this is the way you talk to the youth.

ANNA HEALY Politics and governing is a really hard and boring business in some ways and you can't always deliver. Red Wedge opened us up to more creative influences and brought energy to our campaigning, together with the commitment to try and work with the local parties and engage with young people. We probably didn't offer enough support but we recognized they were an asset.

COLIN BYRNE Red Wedge set a new precedent but it also had the birth pains of more open political engagement. It was an uneasy alliance between the cool rebellious kids and the Party establishment and exposed the natural tensions between creative forces and politics which want to control the message. Red Wedge made Labour politicians and policy-makers aware that previous policies had been done in a vacuum and there had to be a way of listening and incorporating the views of young voters and getting them a real voice within the Party. They were doing pioneering work which was outside of the traditional party silo. No political party had done anything like it before. Music, where it had been political, was deemed as protest music; this was mainstream. It was bands who you could see on *Top of the Pops*.

TONY MANWARING There was a moment of crystallization of a new form of politics. It was brilliant and beautiful to see, and Red Wedge was reconfiguring the DNA. But I don't think the Labour Party had the reflective learning capability to draw and learn and honour what was being done. The Party was bound to let it down in some way because there wasn't a clear enough expectation and conversation about what 'good' would look like. It was much more fragmented, intuitive, responsive and reactive. That was the paradox but also the strength in the Labour movement. The answer isn't what Red Wedge brought to the Labour Party, it's what kind of politics we could have created together. If it had developed for another few years it would have been extraordinary.

3. FREE NELSON MANDELA

HATS OFF TO JERRY DAMMERS!

Artists Against Apartheid. 1992. Political pop

ASHTAR ALKHIRSAN The 2 Tone concept was born out of Rock Against Racism and it radicalized a youth movement to address the evils of racism. But where Red Wedge looked to the ballot box, Artists Against Apartheid, with many of the same artists involved, ran a parallel campaign and almost single-handedly proved pop's ability to provoke political change.

LUCY HOOBERMAN Can pop change politics or offer political solutions? '(Free) Nelson Mandela' energized a campaign and galvanized a lot of people into thinking, but the solution was a political solution.

PAULINE BLACK I'd been aware of apartheid all through the seventies. It just seemed like an insoluble situation and then in the wake of '(Free) Nelson Mandela' so much happened that you never thought was possible. The record is the perfect embodiment of pop music achieving extraordinary things. I always remember seeing a stadium full of people at a rally in South Africa before Mandela came out, singing *Free Nelson Mandela*. I thought, 'Hats off to Jerry Dammers! He's done what no one else has been able to do.'

JERRY DAMMERS Being anti-racist isn't political. It's just normal. Racism is a difficult truth that people don't want to face. I had a very good friend who just persisted with these racist views and there came a point where I had to say enough is enough. That's why I wrote 'Racist Friend' and then '(Free) Nelson Mandela'. It was painful. Obviously you try and persuade them first, but some people just refuse to change. Being friendly with a racist is supporting racism. I know it's really tough but how is anything going to change if you don't take a stand? 'Racist Friend' wasn't supposed to be an easy listen. It was supposed to be disturbing, to make the listener think.

ROBERT HOWARD *If you have a racist friend, now is the time for your friendship to end.* A lot of people were really inspired by that song.

RHODA DAKAR In theory, I would say, 'Absolutely. I don't want to hang around with a person who hangs around with racists.' But what if that's your mum or your dad? What are you supposed to say? A hard-line ideology is all very well but it doesn't necessarily allow for real life or things that you have to accommodate.

JERRY DAMMERS Racism always upset me. I remember when I was a kid and my parents had this Chinese man come to stay with us. We were walking down the street and these kids started racially abusing him. I was disgusted. I came to realize that racism and fascism are built on networks of family loyalties; that's how they survive. So what do you do?

TRACEY THORN 'Racist Friend' was politically dogmatic. It's not unproblematic having family members who you really don't agree with. And I'm not sure what the answer is – really, you don't ever speak with them again? Seriously, *your mother*? We're talking about people who are of a different generation from you. They've got old-fashioned views. So what else: homophobic friend, sexist friend? Well, that's my family out. The questioning it starts is good, but would you really stand by that forever? It'd be interesting to ask Jerry.

JERRY DAMMERS To be fair, the part in the song relating to your mother and father was put in the form of a question: *Is it your husband or your father or your mother?* If your family members are racists then maybe you should play the song to them, and show them the impossible position they are putting you in, and explain that if they really care about you, they should change. The point was to confront racism whoever it is.

DAVE WAKELING I disagreed with it entirely because if you have a racist friend you have to cling close to them and try and open their heart. The last thing you want to do is baptize another convinced racist by telling them you hate them. But as a public statement it was quite effective.

PETER HAIN The eighties was a period of great change: inside South Africa you had internal resistance building up to explosive, massive unrest in the townships, strikes and the economy starting to go sour. It's hard to imagine now, but Mandela was a very isolated figure on Robben Island for a long time, and deliberately so. The South African government had deliberately put him there to make the world and South Africa forget about him.

JERRY DAMMERS I had got involved in Peter Hain's anti-apartheid campaign against the South Africa rugby Springbok tour when I was about fifteen and put stickers all around school trying to persuade people to go and demonstrate against them. It was probably the first demo I ever went on. Then years later I bumped into an old school friend and he told me about an African Sounds festival concert at Alexandra Palace in July 1983 for Nelson Mandela's sixty-fifth birthday, which was being organized by a South African exiled musician called Julian Bahula. I'd never heard of Nelson Mandela but Julian sang a song about him. I picked up lots of leaflets and started learning about Mandela. He'd been imprisoned for twenty-one years at that point and one leaflet said, 'The shoes he had in jail were too small for his feet.' At the same time, I was working on an instrumental tune so I had the idea to put lyrics about Mandela to it.

PETER HAIN '(Free) Nelson Mandela' was absolutely crucial in Mandela's breakthrough and in him becoming a global figure. It brought his brand

Special AKA's '(Free) Nelson Mandela' front cover, March 1984.

Jerry Dammers (above) and Rhoda Dakar (below, left) on the video shoot of the
Special AKA single '(Free) Nelson Mandela', circa Spring 1984.

and his identity from the political world into people's living rooms; kids suddenly started wondering who it was and how to find out about the story. It was transformative. Jerry Dammers was a very important figure in this.

ANNAJOY DAVID Jerry was innately political. He stood up. His world view of justice and inequality was clearly framed and defined. And he had a clear perspective on race and class. '(Free) Nelson Mandela' helped to bring the whole anti-apartheid agenda really mainstream into the arts and cultural broad left of the day. That record shifted the consciousness of a generation.

ASHTAR ALKHIRSAN When the song was on *Top of The Pops* it was incredible. Everybody got to hear that name. Youngsters, seven- or eight-year-olds, were suddenly exposed to who Nelson Mandela was and people were going round singing that really catchy tune.

PAUL HEATON Because it was a nagging chorus it became almost like a catchphrase. You could sing '(Free) Nelson Mandela' at anybody who was dodgy. It became difficult to come out with racism because of that record.

TRACEY THORN The amount of information on the sleeve about Mandela and South Africa. And the lyrics. It was a political record as education: *Shoes too small to fit his feet.* It's on details like that political lyric-writing turns. It humanizes a story and makes you go, 'Really!' It was so tiny set against years of imprisonment, but it's what makes it vivid and brings it down to a little detail of human cruelty within what's otherwise just a big political thing.

ROBERT HOWARD It is the greatest political pop song of all time. It's got everything you would want: a fantastic lyric that says it in very simple terms, it's righteous, and you can dance to it.

MYKAELL RILEY '(Free) Nelson Mandela' was a brilliant track. It's where British ska grows up and takes ownership of its cultural identity.

LINTON KWESI JOHNSON '(Free) Nelson Mandela' made an incalculable cultural contribution to the anti-apartheid struggle. It should never be underestimated the impact it had, not only on the consciousness of people in this country but all over Europe.

ANGELA EAGLE It asked you to bloody well do something about it and helped to bring to the attention of people who weren't political that this battle was raging and that it was a moral battle. It was an enormous megaphone which helped to get things going globally.

RANKING ROGER It might be one song in half a million that has that kind of impact on people. After that everybody started looking at South Africa.

JERRY DAMMERS At the request of Dali Tambo, the son of the president of the African National Congress [ANC], I set up Artists Against Apartheid. It was around the same time Little Steven did Artists United Against Apartheid in America and 'Sun City' to support the boycott. We were also campaigning for artists not to go to South Africa and not to sell records there as part of the cultural boycott. We had a clause that we distributed to artists to put into their recording contracts to stop their records being sold in South Africa.

ASHTAR ALKHIRSAN People of my parents' generation thought Nelson Mandela was a terrorist. It's incredible now but I remember having huge arguments with my parents about apartheid. It just seemed like the most grotesque injustice to see people being clubbed by white policemen.

PETER HAIN On a larger scale the song is about Mandela breaking through from a freedom fighter supported by politically knowledgeable people around the world to his poster starting to adorn anti-apartheid meetings. He started to become the symbol. You have to remember Thatcher had denounced Mandela as a terrorist. She was an ally of South Africa. I'm not saying she was racist or actually supported apartheid but she opposed all sanctions; she opposed all boycotts.

JERRY DAMMERS Dali also introduced me to Chandra Sekar and together we organized our first concert with the Potato 5 at the Brixton Fridge. Then we did bigger and bigger concerts under the AAA banner which included Lloyd Cole, Working Week, UB40, the Blow Monkeys supporting Rod Stewart at Wembley, the Smiths with Pete Shelley in Brixton, Madness and Gil Scott-Heron, Billy Bragg and New Order in Sheffield, the Pogues and Elvis Costello in Paris, the Communards, Terence Trent D'Arby and Smiley Culture at the Albert Hall, the Bhundu Boys and Salif Keïta, even Curtis Mayfield and Michelle Shocked in Edinburgh. I then put together the bill for a free concert on Clapham Common in June 1986. It was the biggest anti-apartheid demonstration in the world and the proudest day of my life.

ASHTAR ALKHIRSAN One of the most powerful events for sheer scale was the Clapham Common concert. It was fucking amazing. I'd been on loads of demos but nothing as big as that. It was colossal – something like a quarter of a million people came. The day felt very different and very grown-up because of the presence of people like Sting and Peter Gabriel. It wasn't the normal ragtag bunch. It was heavyweight.

KEITH HARRIS Many of the artists involved in the Clapham concert were from Red Wedge – Bob Geldof had proved that if artists get together they can grab world attention – so it also came off the back of Live Aid.

ASHTAR ALKHIRSAN It was the hottest day of the year and the atmosphere was amazing. We were all saying, 'This is unbelievable.' You thought, 'How can the situation in South Africa go on when it's clearly the moral imperative to impose sanctions?' I went on the march first and then when I got to the common I was roped in as a runner on the film that was being made. The director, Don Coutts, said to me, 'Can you take these beers to the crew?' There was a tower in the middle of the crowd and I had to wade through this vast crowd with an armful of beers and hand them to the cameramen. Then I went back and Don was in this covered area with a bank of screens and he said, 'Now can you take these beers to so-and-so . . .' I had to walk across the stage: I saw the crowd and my heart literally pounded in my chest. It was the most incredible experience. What it must have been like for the musicians, I don't know.

LORNA GAYLE It was unreal. I was like, 'Look at me!' And all these thousands of people who want to get backstage and I've got a pass. I was so honoured to be a part of that. I was able to sing 'Got To Find A Way' and the audience were going crazy. It was really something.

JERRY DAMMERS That year the fashion, especially amongst the black community, was bright-green and pink and orange shirts and I remember looking out at the crowd and thinking of Poly Styrene's song 'The Day The World Turned Day-Glo'. It was as if she had prophesied the day.

PAUL HEATON: We turned up uninvited when we were at number three with 'Happy Hour'. We said, 'Can we play a few songs?' 'No, you're not allowed to.' 'We can do a cappella.' 'No.' 'OK, fair enough.' Later, our guitarist Stan said, 'Look, Sting's over there,' because he was a massive fan. I said, 'Go and say hello.' Sting was with what my mum would describe as 'a dolly bird' on one arm and round his neck he had a big live snake. Stan said, 'Excuse me,' and Sting gave him the hand, 'Go away.' He was close to tears. So we knocked on Elvis Costello's Winnebago and he invited us in and was dead nice to us. It was a real one–nil.

ANGELA BARTON Backstage, Peter Gabriel said, 'Does anyone know the

Festival for Freedom, Clapham Common, London, 28 June 1986.

song "Biko"?' I said 'Yeah.' He said, 'Do you mind doing a few vocals on it?' I went, 'Yeah, no problem.' Of course, you then got on stage: 'Oh my God!'

LUCY HOOBERMAN I was standing on the side of the stage when Peter Gabriel did 'Biko'. The sun was going down and everybody did that thing with their lighters like little candles which I'd never seen before. And Gil Scott-Heron, who was sort of the godfather of anti-apartheid music in the west, sang his anthem 'Johannesburg'.

JERRY DAMMERS I had made a concerted effort to involve the black community in the concert because the anti-apartheid movement had been accused of being a white middle-class organization. So we also had Hugh Masekela, Maxi Priest, David Grant, Sir Coxsone's sound system, and also Elvis Costello, Boy George, Roddy Frame, Billy Bragg, and Gary Kemp, who funnily enough had been given his first guitar by Trevor Huddleston, the leader of the anti-apartheid movement. I had been working full-time unpaid in a very small office coordinating and approaching people and

Elvis Costello, Festival
for Freedom, Clapham
Common, London,
28 June 1986.

taking all this flak and abuse from the press for supporting the cultural boycott. So when everybody came together towards the end to perform '(Free) Nelson Mandela' it was amazing.

KAREN WALTER When they all came and sang '(Free) Nelson Mandela' it sounded like this huge cry. I remember just thinking, 'He's got to be freed now.'

JERRY DAMMERS Big Audio Dynamite were playing and the police came and told us to turn off the generator because we'd run over time, so we went through this ridiculous ritual: 'Oh, the door to the power's locked. Who's got the key?' We were running round pretending to find it and managed to buy about twenty minutes. After Clapham Common there were discussions with the anti-apartheid movement about what to do next. Because it had been a free gig production costs had run to something like £30,000, so the movement had lost a lot of funds. So it was decided the next one had to be a paid gig; Wembley Stadium was suggested and that was pencilled in for the following year. The biggest band in the world at the time was Dire Straits and I wrote to them to ask if they would do it. They responded positively but said they weren't in touring mode that year. Then at the last minute Simple Minds said they were willing but by then it was too late. I asked Elephant House to produce the event and then got back to Dire Straits saying, 'How about the following year [1988]?' which also happened to be Nelson Mandela's seventieth birthday. They talked to Simple Minds and all agreed to do it. It all tied in beautifully and the whole thing took off. Once it was up and running I handed over to the producers because it was getting much too big for our tiny little office, but it was still under the banner of Artists Against Apartheid.

NEIL KINNOCK I saved the first Wembley concert by getting Ron Todd who was the general secretary of the Transport and General Workers' Union to write me a cheque for £25,000. The organizers had come to me on the Friday and said, 'We're going to have to cancel the concert because Wembley Stadium won't allow us to perform unless we pay this insurance.' There was a misunderstanding and they had thought the insurance was something like £12,000 – I'm not certain of the precise figure. I said, 'Give me an hour.' It took me two. But I did it.

JERRY DAMMERS Clapham Common had been the hard-core event where the music was in tune with the message, but Wembley was aimed at taking it to as wide an audience as possible. It turned out to be watched on TV by hundreds of millions around the world. It was an amazing experience. I kept pressurizing that they must have a major black artist to balance Dire Straits and give the event credibility, and for hip hop and reggae acts to be involved. When Whitney Houston came on board everybody could breathe a sigh of relief.

TINY FENNIMORE I was minding the VIP section at Wembley with all the dignitaries. Whitney Houston came on stage and said, 'Happy Birthday, Nelson,' and we were all thinking, 'Has she got it?' She was contracted to make advertisements for Coca-Cola and had a backdrop behind her instead of a picture of Nelson Mandela. She got a lot of stick for that. There was a lot of conflict about whether they were trying to make the concert anodyne for the Americans and in the process completely wipe out the fact that Nelson Mandela was still in prison.

BILLY BRAGG There was a direct link between Rock Against Racism and the Nelson Mandela concerts because Jerry had been inspired by the Victoria Park Carnival.

JERRY DAMMERS Eric Clapton played, I think mainly as a friend of Dire Straits. I asked him on the day if he would apologize from the stage for the comments which gave birth to Rock Against Racism. I thought it would be a fantastic opportunity for him given the occasion, but he just said, 'Don't believe everything you read in the papers.'

•

RANKING ROGER When Mandela was freed on 11 February 1990 I thought, 'That's what they do to people when they leave prison: they walk out and then they nab you and give you another six months. It's on world camera; if that happens South Africa's going to go up in flames.'

PETER HAIN The reason that South Africa negotiated Mandela's freedom was to save the country and save them because the country was becoming ungovernable. The economy was about to topple over.

BRINSLEY FORDE We were in Jamaica recording our album and we pleaded and pleaded when they announced a second Wembley show in April 1990 under the title An International Tribute for a Free South Africa. We said, 'We'll pay our own fare.' It meant so much to us. They gave us a slot before the actual gig started but luckily for us when the news coverage came on they had nothing to show and they ended up showing our little bit. We

**Jerry Dammers, International Tribute for a Free South Africa,
Wembley Stadium, 14 April 1990.**

took on Sly and Robbie and Maxi Priest and lots of different acts who
weren't billed to play. After, Nelson Mandela said, 'It was the music that
seeped through from the West that we heard that made us know that
people were listening to our plea.' That was the moment that you went,
'Oh, wow!'

JERRY DAMMERS Nelson Mandela used the second concert as the stage to
address a global TV audience. I went down into the audience and he got
the most amazing standing ovation. It lasted over ten minutes. I met him
briefly with about 600 other people and I think somebody told him who I
was. He said, 'Ah, yes, very good.' It was incredible. But, even then, apartheid wasn't over and we still needed to campaign. The fact is, according to
his memoirs, and completely unbeknown to any of us, by the time of the
first Wembley concert Mandela was already in secret negotiations with
P. W. Botha and F. W. de Klerk. But I think the concert helped keep the
pressure on the regime and solidify worldwide knowledge and support,
and when he did come out he was probably the most famous and popular
man in the world; so all that hopefully helped back up making sure he
could finally get rid of apartheid and become president.

**Nelson Mandela, International Tribute for a Free South Africa,
Wembley Stadium, 14 April 1990.**

TINY FENNIMORE I saw Mandela in the street in Camden two days after he arrived in London. He was going into a trade union building and had lots of his African supporters with him. They were all doing that ululating thing that they do. I stopped and cried because he was free and I felt I'd done my little bit to get him out of prison.

JERRY DAMMERS Many years later I was at Abbey Road and Paul McCartney came in a bit cross and said, 'Why wasn't I invited to play at Wembley?' I said, 'I'm really sorry. I don't know why.' He said, 'You know the Beatles supported Mandela.' I said, 'Really?' But I didn't really know whether to believe him or not. And then at an event at South Africa House I told the story to this old sort of church lady who was one of the founders of the anti-apartheid movement and she said, 'Oh yes, the Beatles did offer to do a benefit during the Rivonia Trial in 1963 but I'd never heard of them.'

•

JOHN NEWBEGIN Nine months after Mandela was released Margaret Thatcher resigned on 23 November 1990. A year previously the Berlin Wall had fallen. But the real disappointment was when Labour didn't win in 1992.

SARAH JANE MORRIS I got heavily involved in the '92 campaign and I was booked to sing at the Labour Party Sheffield rally a week before the election.

LUCY HOOBERMAN Ironically, it was April Fool's Day. And it was a disaster. You could tell straight away it was a no-no. Kinnock was so triumphalist for no reason: like a celebration rally. It was the wrong tone and it gave the media a lot of ammunition in the final week before the election. Here we are, the Labour Party, and this is what it's all about.

TINY FENNIMORE Neil was introduced on stage as 'the next prime minister' and went, 'We're all right!' Three times. It was really embarrassing. It was like he was a pop star. The *Sun* headline on election day was 'If Kinnock wins today will the last person to leave Britain please turn out the lights.'

CATHAL SMYTH Kinnock stood up and repeatedly shouted, 'Aw' right.' You look like a fucking geezer down the pub, you twerp.

RICHARD SWALES Tony Hancock said, 'You've got the Conservatives there in your sights and then the bloody Labour Party gets up in the way.'

BILLY BRAGG It was a real body blow. And lots of people thought, 'Now she's gone at last we're going to see the fruition of this,' and then for John Major of all people to win with a twenty-one-seat majority.

NEIL KINNOCK The month after I lost the election I did the British Comedy Awards. Jonathan Ross introduced me. And when everybody cheered he leaned into the microphone and said, 'I hope all you bastards voted for him a month ago.' It was a sweet moment.

DOTUN ADEBAYO If somebody said to come to a dance run by the Labour Party or the Conservative Party I wouldn't have gone. Music refuses to be captured in that way. Music is free: that ultimately leads to the demise of all these movements, whether it be Rock Against Racism, 2 Tone or Red Wedge; they catch a time and period precisely and either the audience moves on or the theme can't sustain longevity.

CHRIS BOLTON You're talking about moments in history when there's a certain energy level, and that comes in waves. There's not a French Revolution every week. There's not an October Revolution every October. It only happens in certain very special moments.

TOM ROBINSON Bob Geldof said *a tonic for the troops*; preaching to the converted, which is the most common accusation made against political pop. But political change is affected by the individual members of those audiences. It's individuals who went out after a Rock Against Racism or 2 Tone concert who picked up their dad or their classmate or their work-mate or the bloke in the pub who made a racist remark because the night before they'd been in a room with 2,000 other people all singing the same songs. You could feel the energy of an audience singing along and we were empowering them to go out with a message.

NICKY SUMMERS Music can motivate a whole generation. Punk changed a generation. It opened a door for the future with music, with fashion, with art, with film. 2 Tone also did to a certain extent, in that we now take it for granted music of black origin is played and enjoyed by all sorts of people. A three-minute song can inspire people to put their hand into their pockets and say, 'OK, we're going to do this.' Music can feed Africa.

COLIN BYRNE Whether political pop ultimately works in party politics, i.e. vote for this lot, as opposed to a consciousness-raising movement like Rock Against Racism or Live Aid . . . it can engage people in an issue. 'I'll think about voting because I like this band.'

RED SAUNDERS It's all about music. The power of music in your life is extraordinary. Without music I wouldn't have done any of these things. It was sex, drugs, rock 'n' roll and peace.

JAKE BURNS As a songwriter you can't change the world but you can change a listener's individual perception of the world. If I had solutions I'd be a politician. My job was to rabble-rouse and turn up and be Stiff Little Fingers for the night.

TIM WELLS I'm not going to look to any singer, whether it's Paul Weller, Billy Bragg or Jerry Dammers, for political solutions. I'm going to look to them for some good music, and hopefully some of it tells me something I recognize and think about. The music papers and gigs were the forums where ideas were discussed. Music offers a culture where it's OK to talk about things. It offers a medium where ideas can flow. Songs can be good rallying points for people but if I want a political answer I'm going to read a book.

PAULINE BLACK All you can do is put a song out there. It's not what *you* do with it. It's not what anyone *does* with it. It has a life of its own and that's something that's unquantifiable. It's exactly the same when you perform: something intangible happens between you and an audience. People talk about metaphysical energy between people and I do believe that. You get energized by an audience and there's a feeding off.

PETER JENNER Pop music can be an excuse for people to get together and make a difference to the atmosphere. But if pop music is all about just having fun and getting fucked and getting stoned then that will affect the society one way, but if popular people are about changing and improving the world then that will have an effect another way.

TOM WATSON I didn't disaggregate music from politics. Robert Plant was born in my constituency and used to call my mate Trotsky. He said, 'When you've got £50 million in your current account you tend not to think about politics very much.'

ANGELA EAGLE Pop music can reflect things that are going on and amplify them. It can help to organize. It can bring together people of like minds. Music gathers tribes and there is a symbiotic relationship between the tribes who gather and artists. You weren't going to buy 'Stand Down Margaret' or 'Tramp The Dirt Down' if you were a Tory. You were going to buy it and sing along with it if you were fed up with what was going on in the eighties and Mrs Thatcher. Elvis Costello was writing about the sheer impudent hatred of what she was doing to the country. It was almost the sort of person at bay like King Lear on the blasted heath, raging but powerless: *Blow, winds, and crack your cheeks! rage! blow!* We had our own ways and with the media being so controlled by the Tory narratives it was in between the spaces where you could actually communicate. Music was an outlet for alternative narratives. You could see resistance growing and portrayals of the UK as it really was, rather than Mrs Thatcher's ideological intolerant and simplistic view of life. She was never shy of having bare-knuckle fights and using the state to prevent resistance and crush opponents. She wanted to destroy as many communities as possible; to destroy anything that might be a public good. She read Frederick Forsyth novels and hooked in poor old Cilla Black and Kenny Everett for conferences. And we had all the exciting, interesting, vibrant stuff that was creative and socially concerned. Music was a way of getting energy and political reaction.

ROBERT ELMS It was a brutal time. It was a time when you knew what side you were on. And to know that you were on the side of the angels, on the side of all the best bands, the best clothes and the best songs: you felt right. Thatcher might have won elections, but culturally we won. Look at Britain now: it's a society where racism is absolutely frowned on; where gay marriage is accepted. It's totally different from that Little England that Thatcher tried to hold on to. This period from the mid-seventies to the early nineties was the last time that pop and politics sat together and where pop music meant anything politically. I'm not sure we'll ever see again such a combination of brilliant songwriting selling lots and lots of records and yet politically articulate, intelligent and meant. It didn't win an election but it won hearts and minds as part of a wave of a new notion of what being young and British meant.

ANNAJOY DAVID This whole period put culture at the centre of politics and helped to define the language of politics in a way that the country hadn't seen happen before. You had thousands of young people out on the streets with something to say who had taken politics into their lives. It helped to define a generation who brought together culture and politics to stand up and say something about the government of the day. Was it better to do nothing and let the fascists go unchallenged? Was it better to do nothing and let Margaret Thatcher go unchallenged? Should we have stayed silent? Of course we shouldn't. We had a duty to stand up and call people to account. That's what democracy is about. Walls did come tumbling down.

Timeline

(Records listed by release date)

1968

20 April: Enoch Powell 'Rivers of Blood' speech given to Conservative Association meeting in Birmingham

1972

9 January–25 February: Miners' Strike

1974

1 January–7 March: Three-day week

4 February–6 March: Miners' Strike

20 July: Eric Clapton 'I Shot The Sheriff'

1975

12 February: Margaret Thatcher elected leader of the Conservative Party

1976

5 August: Birmingham Odeon, Eric Clapton concert

30 August: Notting Hill Carnival riot

October: Aswad *Aswad*

October: The Princess Alice, with Carol Grimes

8 October: Aswad 'Three Babylon'

10 December: RAR Royal College of Art, with Carol Grimes, Limousine
and Matumbi

1977

January: Buzzcocks *Spiral Scratch* EP

26 March: Clash 'White Riot'

23 April: Wood Green National Front march

1 May: May Day Carnival at the Roundhouse, with Aswad, Carol Grimes
and Limousine

5 May: Greater London elections, National Front vote 119,000

28 May: Sex Pistols 'God Save The Queen'

August: Anti-Nazi League formed

13 August: Battle of Lewisham

21 August: Hackney Town Hall, with the Cimarons and Generation X

September: Nazis Are No Fun at the Royal College of Art, with John
Cooper Clarke, the Members, Misty In Roots, and 999

5 November: Sex Pistols *Never Mind The Bollocks, Here's The Sex Pistols*

1978

30 January: Margaret Thatcher speaking on *World in Action*: 'People
are rather afraid that their country might be rather swamped
by people with a different culture.'

11 February: Tom Robinson Band *Rising Free* EP

24 February: Central London Poly, with Misty In Roots and Sham 69

March: Steel Pulse 'Ku Klux Klan'

30 April: Victoria Park Carnival, with the Clash, Patrik Fitzgerald, Tom
Robinson Band, Steel Pulse and Poly Styrene

27 May: Tom Robinson Band *Power In The Darkness*

Summer: 'Labour Isn't Working' poster

17 June: The Clash '(White Man) In Hammersmith Palais'

28 June–27 July: Clash Out On Parole tour with the Coventry Automatics (name changed to the Specials during the tour)

13 July: Acklam Hall and Albany Empire firebombed

15 July: Northern Carnival, Manchester, with Buzzcocks, China Street, Exodus and Steel Pulse

August: Steel Pulse *Handsworth Revolution*

24 September: Carnival 2, Brockwell Park, with Aswad, Elvis Costello and the Attractions, Misty In Roots and Stiff Little Fingers

9 December: Eric Clapton in *Melody Maker*: 'Enoch is a prophet.'

16–17 December: Central London Poly, RAR conference

1979

February: Stiff Little Fingers *Inflammable Material*

17 March–14 April : Militant Entertainment tour

31 March–1 April: Misty In Roots *Live At The Counter Eurovision '79* recorded

April: The Specials and the Selecter 'Gangsters' / 'The Selecter'

23 April: Southall Riot. Death of Blair Peach

May: Linton Kwesi Johnson *Forces Of Victory*

3 May: General election. Conservative majority

8–12 June: Rock Against Repression Ireland tour

16 June: Ruts 'Babylon's Burning'

July: Steel Pulse *Tribute To The Martyrs*

13–14 July: Southall Kids are Innocent, Rainbow, with Aswad, the Clash, the Enchanters, the Members, Misty In Roots, the Pop Group, Pete Townshend and friends, and the Ruts

21–22 July: RAR 'Dub' conference in Birmingham

25 August: Madness 'The Prince'

14 September–18 October: Dance and Defend tour including
      Gang of Four, Delta 5, the Mekons, the Enchanters and
      the Leyton Buzzards

22 September: Slits *Cut*

October: Gang of Four *Entertainment!*, the Jam 'The Eton Rifles',
      the Specials *Specials*

19 October–3 December: 2 Tone tour, Madness, the Selecter and
      the Specials (Hatfield Poly, 27 October)

24 November: Bodysnatchers' debut at the Windsor Castle.
      RAR conference, Central London Poly

1 December: The Beat 'Tears Of A Clown'

1980

19 January: Special AKA 'Too Much Too Young'

14 February–20 March: 2 Tone second tour, with the Bodysnatchers,
      Holly and the Italians and the Selecter

16 February: Selecter *Too Much Pressure*

8 March: Bodysnatchers 'Let's Do Rock Steady'

April: 160 missiles to be deployed at RAF Greenham and Molesworth

25 April–24 May: Rock Against Thatcher including the Au Pairs and
      UB40

4–19 June: Seaside tour with the Bodysnatchers, the Go-Go's and the
      Specials

July: Selecter leave 2 Tone

12 July: Bodysnatchers 'Easy Life'

27 July: RAR election conference

8 August: Rock the Block festival in Belfast with the Au Pairs and
      Oxy and the Morons

9 August: The Beat 'Stand Down Margaret'

5 September: Rock Against Racism *RAR's Greatest Hits*

27 September: The Specials *More Specials*

1981

Life in the European Theatre LP

14–17 January: Ireland tour with the Beat and the Specials

17 January: New Cross fire

2 March: Black People Day of Action

11 April: Brixton riots

13 June: The Specials 'Ghost Town'

20 June: Peaceful Protest Against Racism, with the Specials

4 July: RAR Northern Carnival Against Racism, with the Au Pairs, Joolz the Poet, Misty In Roots and the Specials

10 July: UK riots

1 November: Fun Boy Three 'The Lunatics (Have Taken Over The Asylum)'

1982

16 January: Rhoda and the Special AKA 'The Boiler'

1983

7 May: Youth CND Festival For Peace with Madness and the Style Council

21 May: The Style Council 'Money Go Round (Part 1)'

9 June: General election, Conservative Party returned to office

27 August: Special AKA 'Racist Friend'

2 October: Neil Kinnock elected leader of the Labour Party

1984

21 January: Billy Bragg *Life's A Riot With Spy Vs Spy*

10 March: Special AKA '(Free) Nelson Mandela'

12 March: Miners' Strike begins

6 October: The Style Council 'Shout To The Top'

1985

3 March: Miners' Strike ends

9 March: Billy Bragg *Between The Wars* EP

12–21 March: Jobs for Youth tour, with Billy Bragg

4 May: The Style Council 'Walls Come Tumbling Down!'

13 July: Live Aid

23 July: Red Wedge inaugural meeting

21 November: Red Wedge launch

21 December: Billy Bragg 'Days Like These' / 'I Don't Need This
        Pressure Ron'

1986

25–31 January: First Red Wedge tour

15 February: Blow Monkeys 'Digging Your Scene'

28 February–16 March: Reds Laugh Louder tour

10 April: Fulham by-election, Nick Raynsford gains seat from
        Conservatives with a 9 per cent swing to Labour

13 April: Artists Against Apartheid launched

28 June: AAA Clapham Common concert, with Billy Bragg, the
        Communards, Elvis Costello, Jerry Dammers, Junior, Lorna Gee,
        Sade, the Style Council

August: Red Wedge in Italy

1987

26 January–3 February: Red Wedge regional political tour

28 February–6 March: Women's tour, Cooking Up Trouble

28 May–June 10: Red Wedge Move On Up manifesto launch and tour

4–10 June: Red Wedge comedy tour

11 June: General election. Conservative Party returned to office

1988

12 April: Labour Listens launch at Walworth Road

8 June: Nelson Mandela seventieth Birthday Tribute, Wembley

22–24 June: Red Wedge in Ireland

3 September: Billy Bragg 'Waiting For The Great Leap Forward'

1990

11 February: Nelson Mandela released from prison after twenty-seven years in captivity

14 April: International Tribute for a Free South Africa, Wembley

23 November: Margaret Thatcher resigns as leader of the Conservative Party

1991

September: Tenth and final issue of *Well Red*. Re-launched as *Back to Basics* the following year and published as a fanzine

1992

9 April: General election. Conservative Party returned to office

References

BOOK ONE: ROCK AGAINST RACISM

1. WHO SHOT THE SHERIFF?

1. David Widgery, *Beating Time*, Chatto and Windus 1986, p. 41.
2. *Playboy*, September 1976.
3. Allan Jones, *Melody Maker*, 29 October 1977.
4. *Beating Time*, pp. 42–3.
5. *Paul Weller: Into Tomorrow*, produced by Stuart Watts, 2006
6. Paolo Hewitt, *The Jam: A Beat Concerto – The Authorised Biography*, Omnibus Press 1983, p. 33.
7. *Punky Reggae Party*, BBC Radio 6 Music, 2011
8. Brian Harrigan, 'Spreading the Jam', *Melody Maker*, 23 April 1977.
9. *Sniffin' Glue*, No.8., March 1977.
10. *Beating Time*, p. 40.
11. *Beating Time*, p. 61.
12. *Beating Time*, p. 36.
13. *Beating Time*, p. 43.
14. *RAR's Greatest Hits*, sleeve notes.

2. INGLAN IS A BITCH

15. *Reggae Britannia*, BBC4, directed by Jeremy Marre, 2011.
16. *Beating Time*, p. 39.
17. *Beating Time*, p. 43.
18. *Beating Time*, p. 45.
19. *Beating Time*, p. 47.
20. *Beating Time*, p. 48.

3. OH BONDAGE! UP YOURS

21. *Beating Time*, p. 52.
22. *Beating Time*, p. 83.
23. Strummer, Jones, Simonon, Headon, *The Clash*, Atlantic Books 2008.

24. *Rude Boy*, directed by Jack Hazan and David Mingay, 1980, Special Edition, 2003.
25. *Radical America*, Vol. 12, No. 5, September–October 1978, pp. 75–7.
26. *Beating Time*, p. 94.
27. *Beating Time*, p. 93.
28. *RAR's Greatest Hits*, sleeve notes.
29. *RAR's Greatest Hits*, sleeve notes.
30. *Beating Time*, p. 38.
31. *RAR's Greatest Hits*, sleeve notes.
32. *Beating Time*, p. 8.
33. *Beating Time*, p. 9.

BOOK TWO: 2 TONE

34. *Beating Time*, p. 56.
35. Dave Thompson, *Wheels Out of Gear*, Helter Skelter 2004
36. http://www.ub40.co.uk/forum/general-anarchy/599563-one-ten-jb.html, 6 September 2010.

BOOK THREE: RED WEDGE

1. SHOUT TO THE TOP

37. Paul Weller, *Suburban 100*, Century 2007, p. 121.
38. *Suburban 100*, p. 83.
39. *NME*, 7 May 1977, interview with Steve Clarke.
40. *Sounds*, 16 June 1979.
41. *Suburban 100*, p. 55.
42. *Eton College Chronicle*, 16 November 1979; interview with Tim de Lisle.
43. *NME*, 7 May 1977, interview with Steve Clarke.
44. *NME*, 7 May 1977, interview with Steve Clarke.
45. *Internationalists* tour programme.
46. *Suburban 100*, p. 67.
47. 'Pop into Politics', *TV Eye*, ITV, 30 January 1986.
48. Paolo Hewitt, *NME*, 1 June 1985.
49. Paolo Hewitt, *NME*, 1 June 1985.
50. *Internationalists* tour programme.
51. *Suburban 100*, p. 68.
52. *Suburban 100*, p. 92.
53. *Suburban 100*, p. 31.

54. *Internationalists* tour programme.
55. Paolo Hewitt, *NME*, 1 June 1985.
56. John Reed, *Paul Weller: My Ever-Changing Moods*, Omnibus Press 1996.
57. 'Redemption Songs', *MOJO*, issue 150, May 2006, interview with Lois Wilson.
58. *NME*, 7 May 1977, interview with Steve Clarke.
59. *Shout to the Top, The Style Council Story*, BBC Radio 2, 2003.
60. *NME*, 18 January 1986.
61. 'Pop into Politics', *TV Eye*, ITV, 30 January 1986.
62. 'Pop into Politics', *TV Eye*, ITV, 30 January 1986.
63. *Days Like These*, produced by Red Wedge Video / Tall Pictures, 1986.
64. *Internationalists* tour programme.

2. NOW THAT'S WHAT I CALL SOCIALISM!

65. Johnny Black, *Q* magazine, March 1996.
66. *Days Like These.*
67. *Days Like These.*
68. Johnny Black, *Q* magazine, March 1996.
69. *NME*, June 1986.
70. *NME*, 7 May 1977, interview with Steve Clarke.
71. *Days Like These.*
72. Colin Bartie, 'Rebels with a Cause', *Wester Hailes Sentinel*, February 1986.
73. Simon Garfield, *Independent on Sunday*, 1990.
74. *Into Tomorrow.*
75. *Internationalists* tour programme.
76. *Q Magazine*, June 1995, interview with Paul Du Noyer.
77. *Shout to the Top: The Style Council Story*, BBC Radio 2, 2003.
78. 'Pop into Politics', *TV Eye*, ITV, 30 January 1986.
79. *Sign of the Times*, BBC Radio 1, April 1994.
80. *Melody Maker*, 1 September 1986.
81. Paolo Hewitt, *NME*, 1 June 1985.
82. 'Redemption Songs', *MOJO*, issue 150, May 2006, interview with Lois Wilson.
83. *Well Red*, No. 3.
84. Andrew Collins, *Billy Bragg: Still Suitable for Miners – The Official Biography*, Virgin Books 2002.
85. Matteo Sedazzari, 1990, http://www.zani.co.uk/archive/music-archive/item/331-paul-weller-rare-peom
86. *Paul Weller: Highlights and Hang-Ups*, directed by Pedro Romhanyi, Oil Factory, 1994.
87. *Sign of the Times*, BBC Radio 1, April 1994.
88. *Shout to the Top: The Style Council Story*, BBC Radio 2, 2003.

Publishing Credits

Alien Kulture 'Culture Crossover' Abbas, Ausaf Akhtar; Bilgrami, Pervez Ali; Jones, Huw; Rana, Azhar Mushtaq

Au Pairs 'Armagh' Munro, Jane; Foad, Paul; Woods, Lesley; Hammond, Peter

Au Pairs 'Come Again' Munro, Jane; Foad, Paul; Woods, Lesley; Hammond, Peter

The Beat 'Doors Of Your Heart' Wakeling, Dave; Cox, Andrew; Charlery, Roger; Morton, Everett; Steele, David: Beat-Brothers-Ltd Emi Music Publishing Ltd

The Beat 'Stand Down Margaret' Wakeling, Dave; Cox, Andrew; Charlery, Roger; Morton, Everett; Steele, David: Beat-Brothers-Ltd Emi Music Publishing Ltd

The Beat 'Two Swords' Wakeling, Dave; Cox, Andrew; Charlery, Roger; Morton, Everett; Steele, David: Beat-Brothers-Ltd Emi Music Publishing Ltd

Billy Bragg 'Days Like These' Bragg, Billy: Sony/ATV Music Publishing (UK) Limited

Billy Bragg 'I Don't Need This Pressure Ron' Bragg, Billy: Sony/ATV Music Publishing (UK) Limited

Billy Bragg 'Waiting For the Great Leap Forwards' Bragg, Billy: Sony/ATV Music Publishing (UK) Limited

Bob Marley 'I Shot The Sherriff' Marley, Bob: Blackwell Fuller Music Publishing Llc Blue Mountain Music Ltd

Bob Marley 'Small Axe' Anansi Music Cayman Music Inc Cayman Music Ltd Peermusic (UK) Ltd

The Bodysnatchers 'Easy Life' Summers, Nicola Rose; Joyce, Miranda Ann; Leyton, Penny Elizabeth; Owen, Sarah-Jane Mclaren: Chrysalis-Music-Ltd

Buzzcocks 'Sixteen' Shelley, Peter: Complete Music

The Clash '(White Man) In Hammersmith Palais' Jones, Mick; Strummer, Joe; Simonon, Paul Gustave; Headon, Topper: Nineden Ltd Universal Music Publishing Limited

Dexys Midnight Runners 'There, There My Dear' Rowland, Kevin Antony; Archer, Kevin Wayne John: Emi Music Publishing Ltd

Fun Boy Three 'The Lunatics (Have Taken Over the Asylum)' Golding, Lynval; Hall, Terry; Staples, Neville Egunton: Plangent Visions Music Ltd

The Jam 'The Eton Rifles' Weller, Paul John: Stylist Music Limited. Universal Music Publishing MGB Limited

Junior Giscombe 'Come On Over' Giscombe, Junior; Smith, Robin Albert: Junior Music Ltd Warner Chappell Music Ltd

Quotes from all Linton Kwesi Johnson poems are reproduced by kind permission of the author and LKJ Music Publishers: 'All We Doin Is Defendin', 'Want Fi Goh Rave', 'Five Nights Of Bleedin', 'Di Great Insohreckshan'

The Ramones 'Now I Wanna Sniff Some Glue' Colvin, Douglas; Cummings, John; Erdelyi, Thomas; Hyman (Jeffrey), Jeff: Bleu-Disque-Music Co Inc Warner Bros Inc Warner/Chappell North America Limited

The Ruts 'Babylon's Burning' Fox, Paul Richard; Jennings, John; Owen, Malcolm Geoffrey; Ruffy, Glen David: BMG VM Music Limited

Sex Pistols 'Pretty Vacant' Matlock, Glen; Jones, Stephen Philip; Rotten, Johnny; Cook, Paul Thomas: Rotten Music Ltd, Warner Chappell Music Ltd, A Thousand Miles Long Inc

Sex Pistols 'Whatcha Gonna Do It About It' Potter, Brian August; Samwell, Ian Ralph: Chrysalis-Music-Ltd

Special AKA 'Racist Friend' Bradbury, John Edward; Dammers, Jerry; Cuthell, Richard David: Plangent Visions Music Ltd

The Specials 'A Message To You Rudy' Thompson, Robert Livingstone: Sparta-Florida Music Group Ltd Tee Pee Music Co Inc Carlin Music Corp

The Specials 'Do The Dog' Dammers, Jerry: Plangent Visions Music Ltd

The Specials 'Doesn't Make it Alright' Goldberg, David John; Dammers, Jeremy David Hounsel: Plangent Visions Music Ltd

The Specials 'Ghost Town' Dammers, Jerry: Plangent Visions Music Ltd

The Specials 'Too Much Too Young' Dammers, Jerry: Plangent Visions Music Ltd

Stiff Little Fingers 'Alternative Ulster' Burns, John; Ogilvie, Gordon Archer: Union Square Music Songs Limited

The Stranglers 'Sometimes' Cornwell, Hugh Alan; Duffy, Brian John; Greenfield, David Paul; Burnel, Jean Jacques: Albion Music Ltd Complete Music Ltd

The Style Council 'Money Go Round' Weller, Paul John: Stylist Music Limited. Universal Music Publishing MGB Limited

The Style Council 'Walls Come Tumbling Down!' Words & Music by Paul Weller © Copyright 1985 Stylist Music Limited. Universal Music Publishing MGB Limited. All Rights Reserved. International Copyright Secured. Used by permission of Music Sales Limited

UB40 'Burden Of Shame' Brown, Jim; Campbell, Ali; Campbell, Robin Burns; Falconer, Earl: Acto Graduate Music Ltd Kassner Associated Publishers Limited Dep International Limited (PRS) Universal SRG Music Publishing Ltd

UB40 'Food For Thought' Brown, James Stephen; Campbell, Ali; Campbell, Robin; Falconer, Earl: Graduate Music Ltd Kassner Associated Publishers Limited Dep International Limited (PRS) Universal SRG Music Publishing Ltd

UB40 'King' Campbell, Ali Brown, Jim; Campbell, Robin; Falconer, Earl: Graduate Music Ltd Kassner Associated Publishers Limited Universal SRG Music Publishing Ltd

X-Ray Spex 'Oh Bondage! Up Yours!' Poly-Styrene: Westminster Music Ltd

Index

'A' Train (club) 232
Abbott, Diane 470, 498
Acklam Hall, firebombing of by National Front 112–13
Adams, Gerry 505
Adebayo, Dotun 12, 22, 25, 27–8, 61–2, 64, 70, 76, 77, 102, 104, 105, 141, 225, 234, 332–3, 532
AFFOR (All Faiths For One Race) 320
Africa 370 *see also* South Africa
African National Congress (ANC) xxv
AIDS 466, 467–8
Albany, firebombing of by National Front 112–13
Alexandra Palace gig 186–9
Alien Kulture 193
Alkhirsan, Ashtar 394, 398, 399, 433, 458, 461, 462, 464, 467, 493, 517, 521, 522–3
Allen, Jim 119
Amin, Idi 191
Anderson, Viv 120
Anderton, James 119
Angelic Upstarts 185, 210
'The Murder Of Liddle Towers' 185
anti-apartheid campaign:
    Clapham Common concert (1986) xvii, 522–7
    and '(Free) Nelson Mandela' 517–21, 527
    Wembley Stadium concerts (1988/90) 527–31
    see also Artists Against Apartheid
Anti-Nazi League (ANL) xx, xxi, 110, 114–26, 161, 282
    activities 119
    Clough's support of 120
    and demise of National Front 214
    difficulties in establishing and opposition to 118
    dislike of the Conservative Party 123–4
    donations 118–19
    and Jewish community 117–18
    and Labour Party 115–17
    logo 120, 121

and National Front 114–26
    'No Platform for Nazis' policy 122
    policy of confronting 122
    press stunts 116–17
    purpose of 122
    and Rock Against Racism xx, 124–5, 126, 129, 149, 161
    setting up of and launch 114–15, 116–17
    subgroups 118
    and Victoria Park Carnival (1978) 129
    visuals and graphics used 121
Artists Against Apartheid (AAA) xxi, xxv, 477, 517
    Clapham Common concert (1986) 522–7
    concerts 522
    Wembley Concert (1988) 527–8
    Wembley Concert (1990) 528–9
Artists United Against Apartheid 522
Ashton, Mark 467
Asian community 191–3
    and Rock Against Racism 192–3
    targeting of 191–2
Aswad 11, 41, 42, 58–9, 60, 67, 76
    and Brockwell Park Carnival 176
    'Three Babylon' 104
Au Pairs 52, 93–5, 157, 208, 209, 210, 211, 278, 321
    'Armagh' 157–8
    'Come Again' 94
    'Diet' 207
    'It's Obvious' 95
Augustus, Hope 462

Bahula, Julian 519
Baine, John 16, 52, 107, 187–8, 193, 205, 367, 409, 479, 480
Baker, Clarence 194, 195–6, 197
Band Aid 370, 371
    'Do They Know It's Christmas?' 370, 371
Barker, Colin 105, 115, 116, 117, 119, 120, 122, 123–4, 132, 134, 136, 138, 139,140, 142, 146–7, 149, 163, 164, 167, 168, 169, 196, 223–4